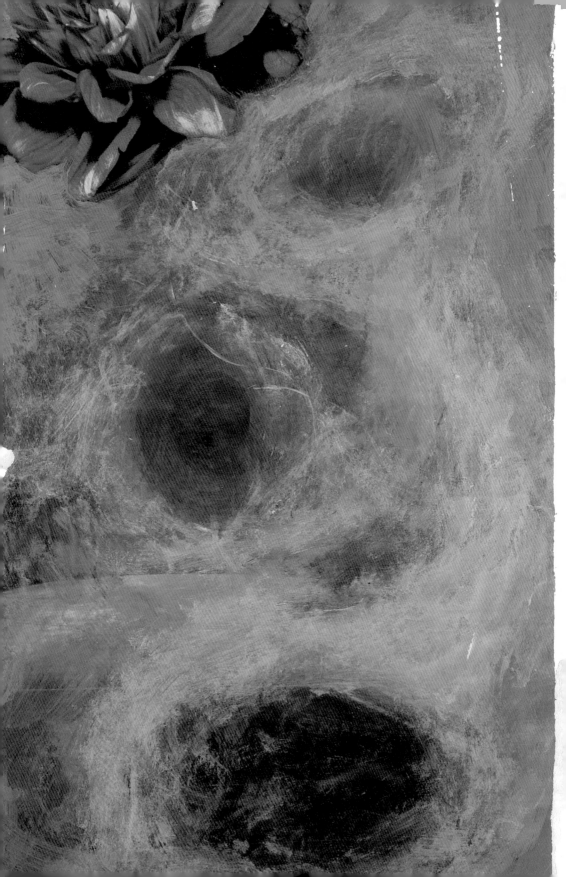

ADI PARVA
CHURNING OF THE OCEAN

via AMRUTA PATIL

HarperCollins *Publishers* India

TAT SAVITUR VARENYAM

SUTRADHAAR

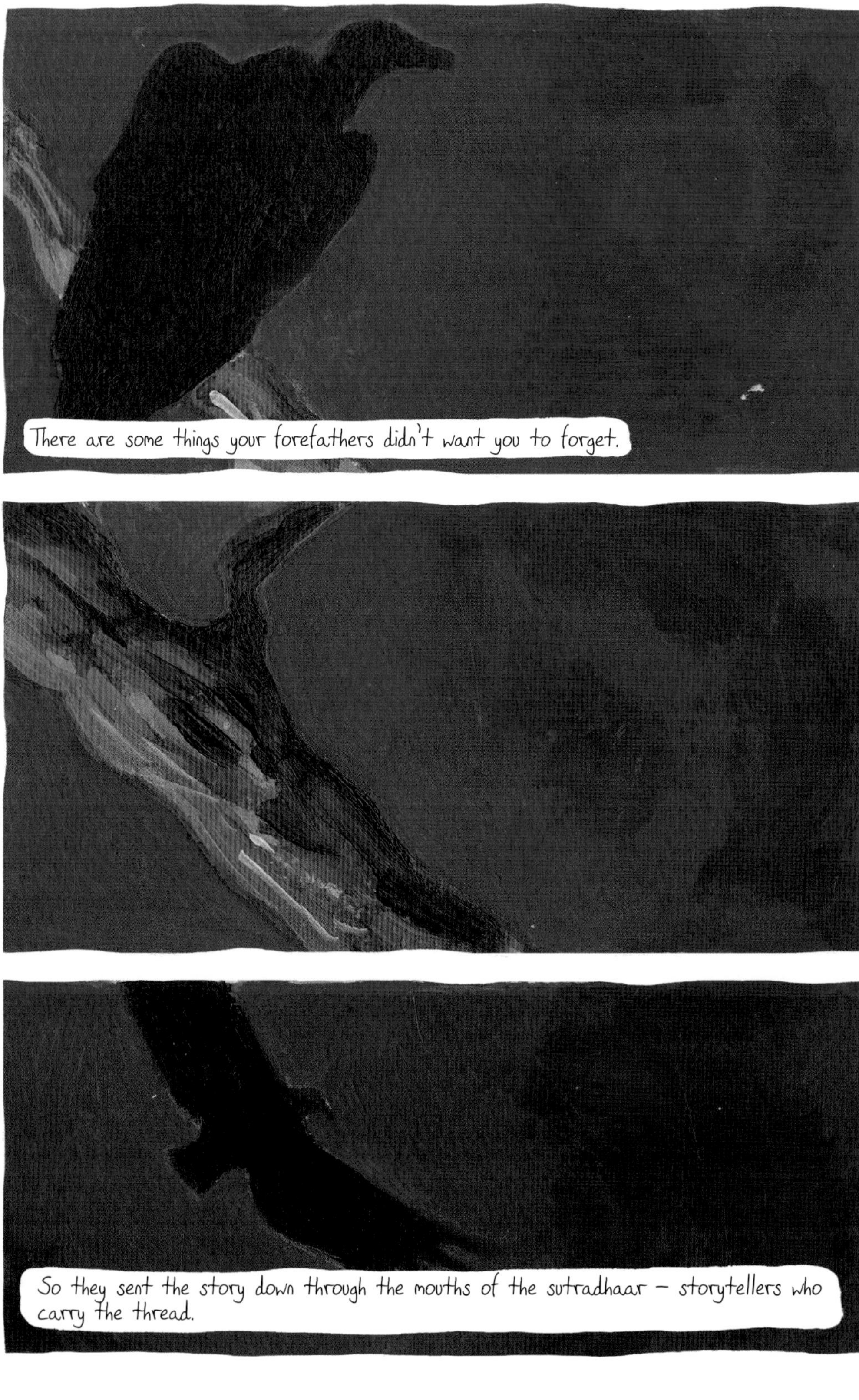
There are some things your forefathers didn't want you to forget.
So they sent the story down through the mouths of the sutradhaar – storytellers who carry the thread.

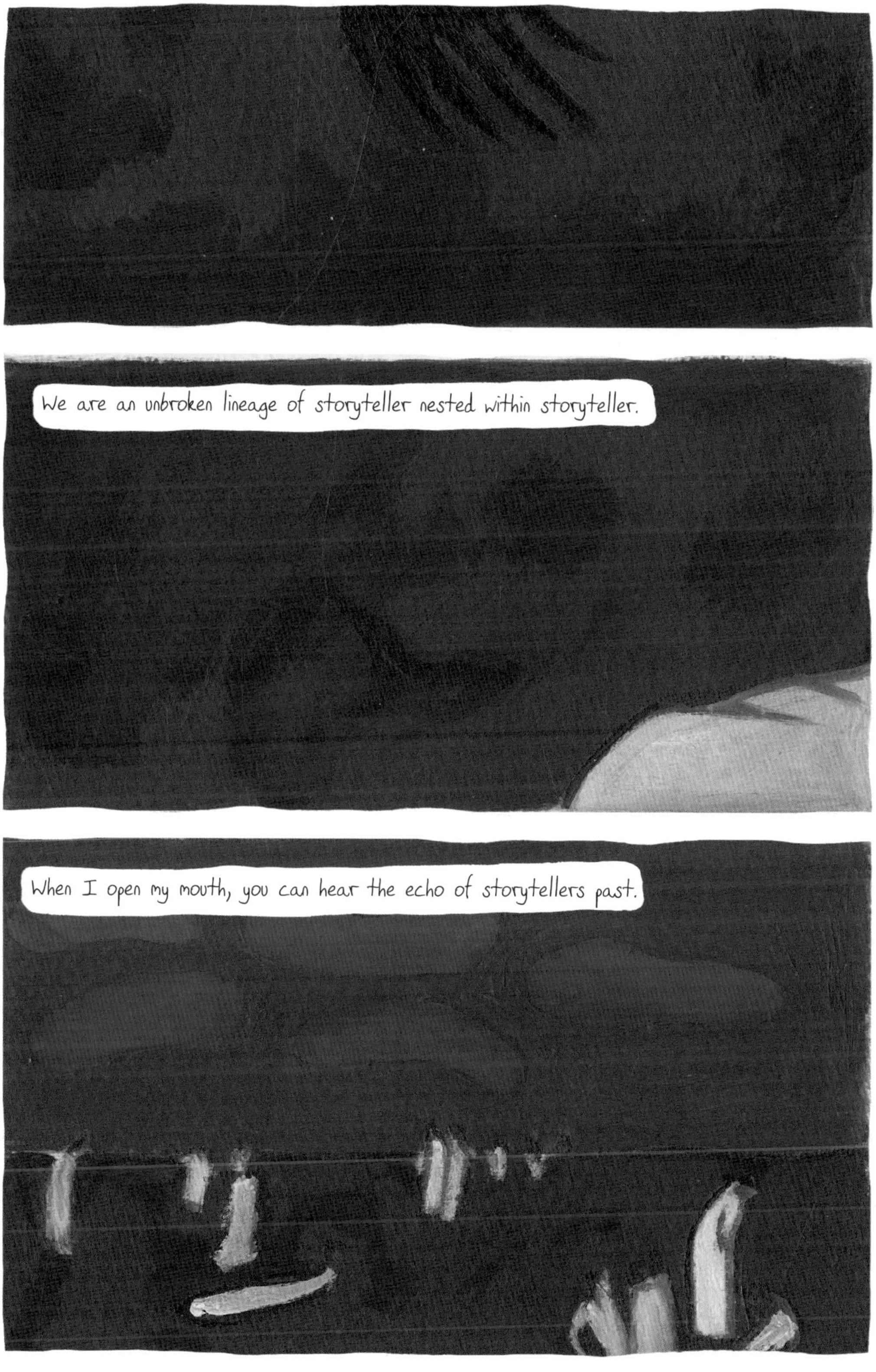
We are an unbroken lineage of storyteller nested within storyteller.
When I open my mouth, you can hear the echo of storytellers past.

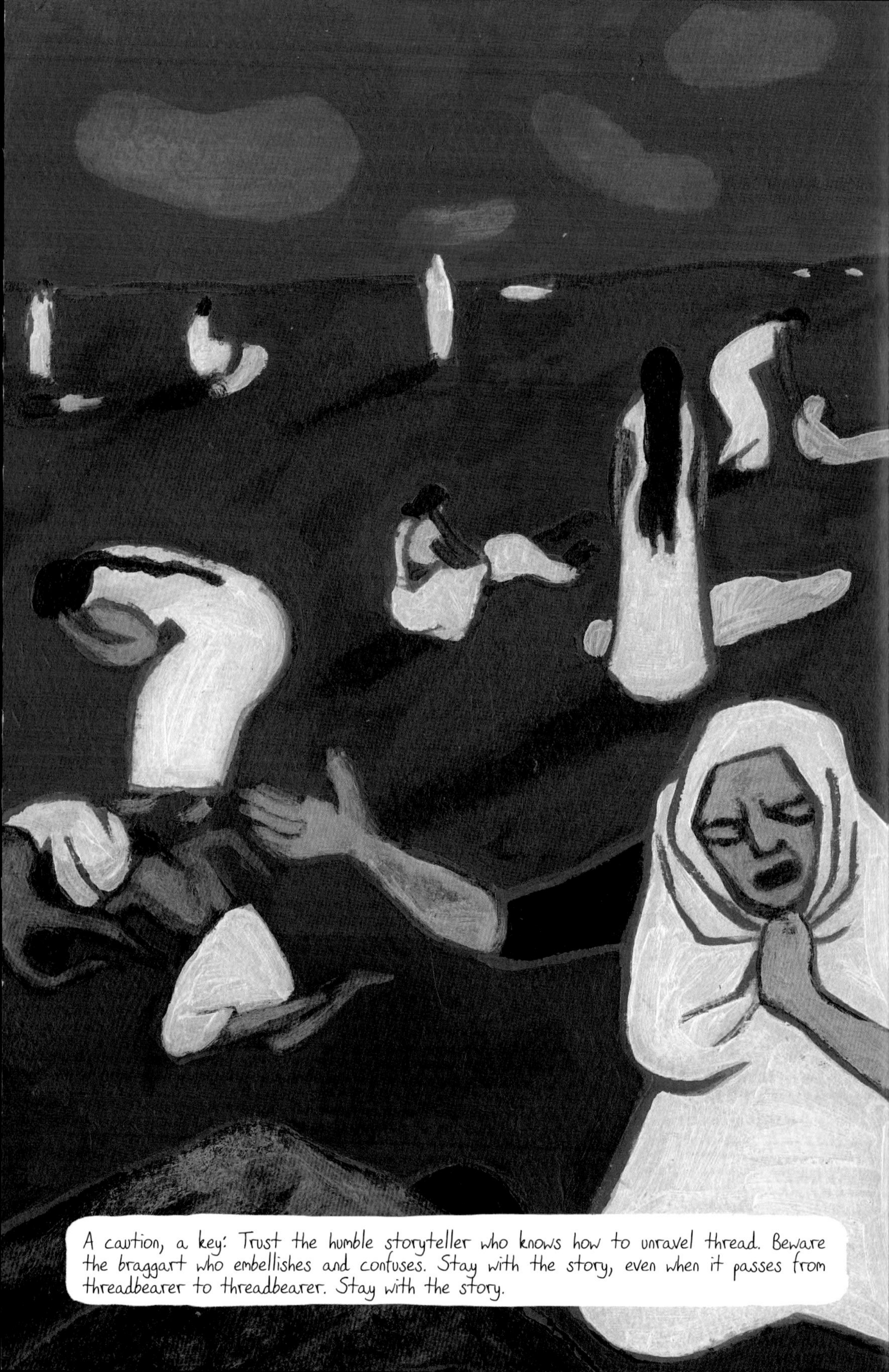
A caution, a key: Trust the humble storyteller who knows how to unravel thread. Beware the braggart who embellishes and confuses. Stay with the story, even when it passes from threadbearer to threadbearer. Stay with the story.

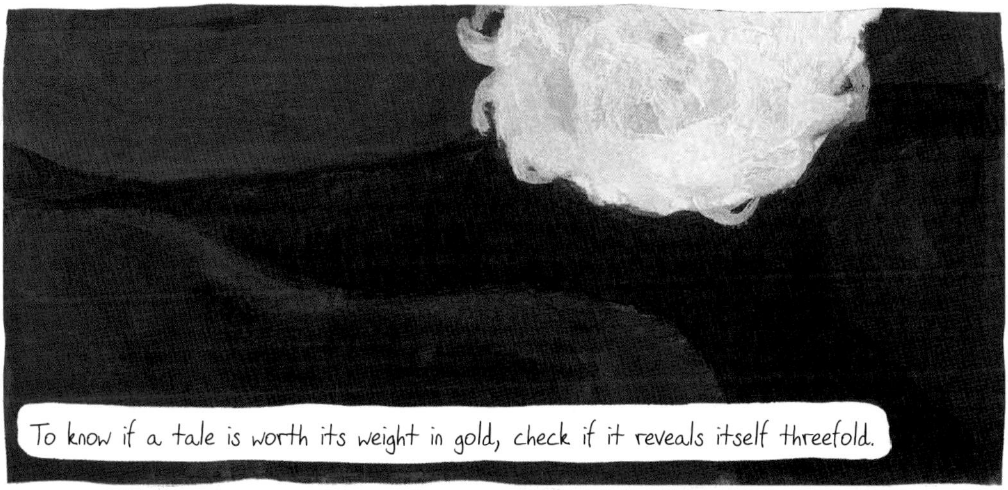
To know if a tale is worth its weight in gold, check if it reveals itself threefold.

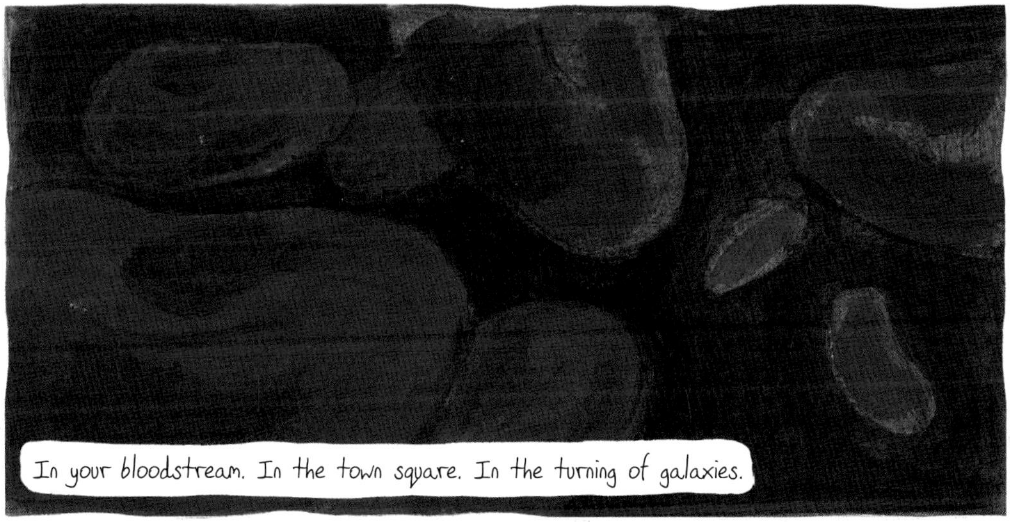
In your bloodstream. In the town square. In the turning of galaxies.

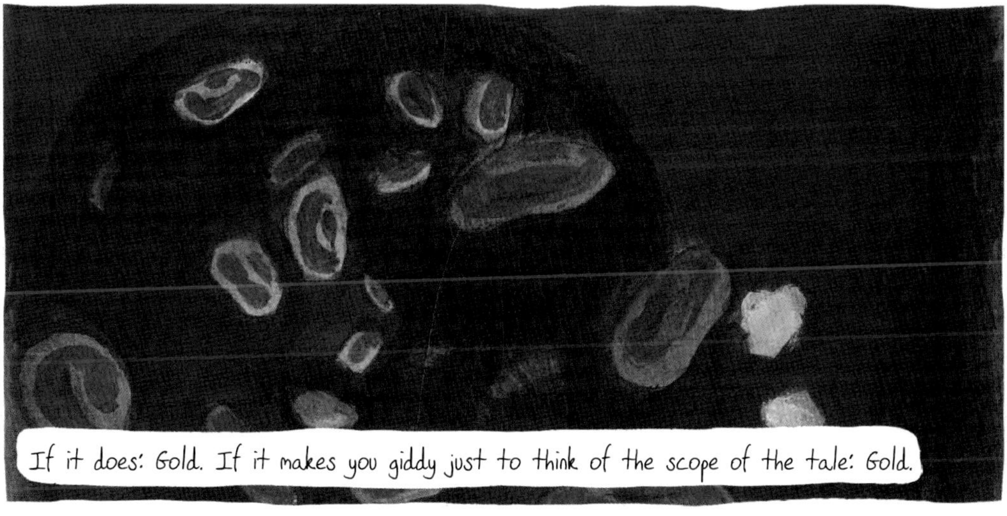
If it does: Gold. If it makes you giddy just to think of the scope of the tale: Gold.

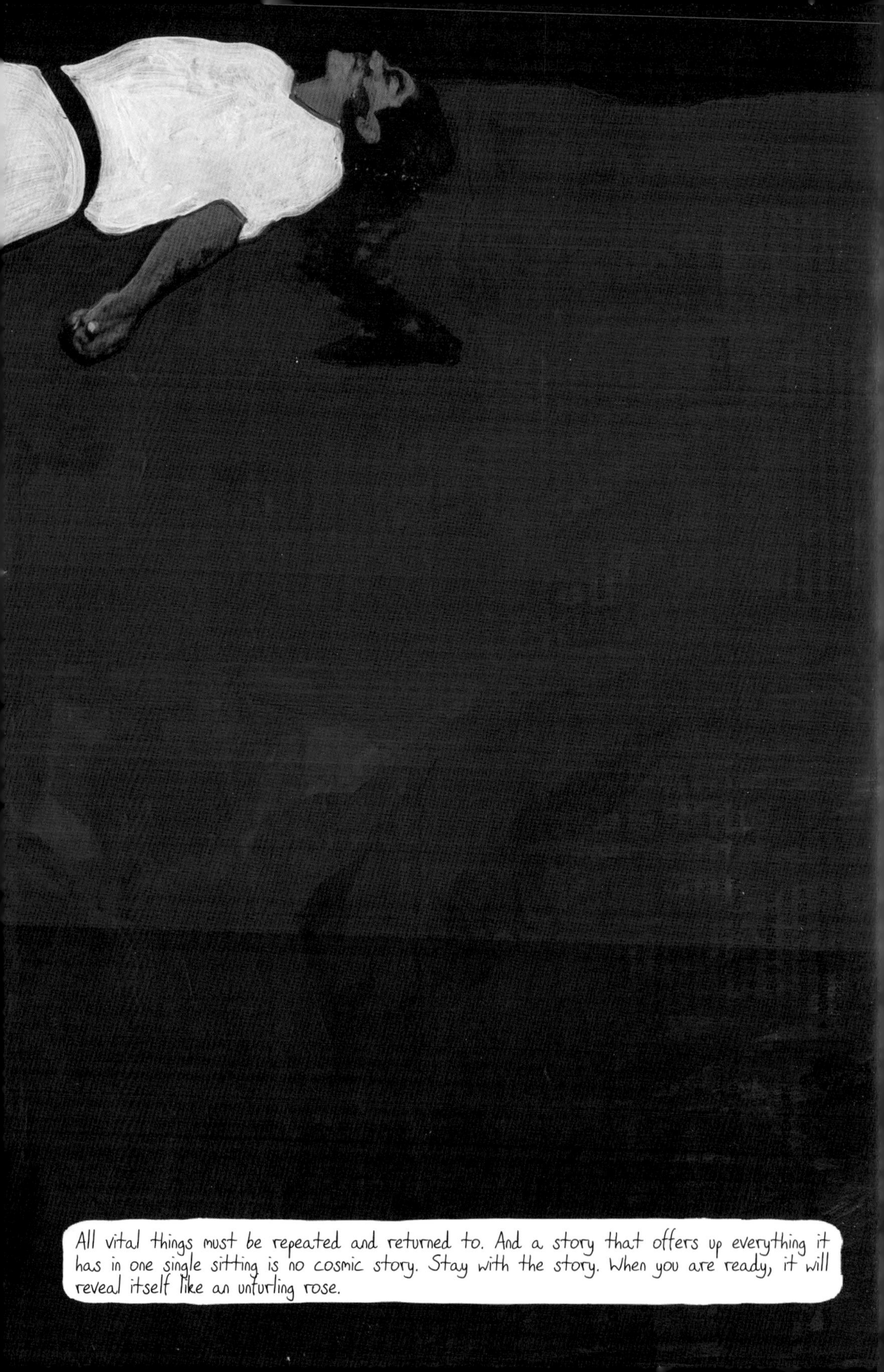
All vital things must be repeated and returned to. And a story that offers up everything it has in one single sitting is no cosmic story. Stay with the story. When you are ready, it will reveal itself like an unfurling rose.

FERRY-POINT

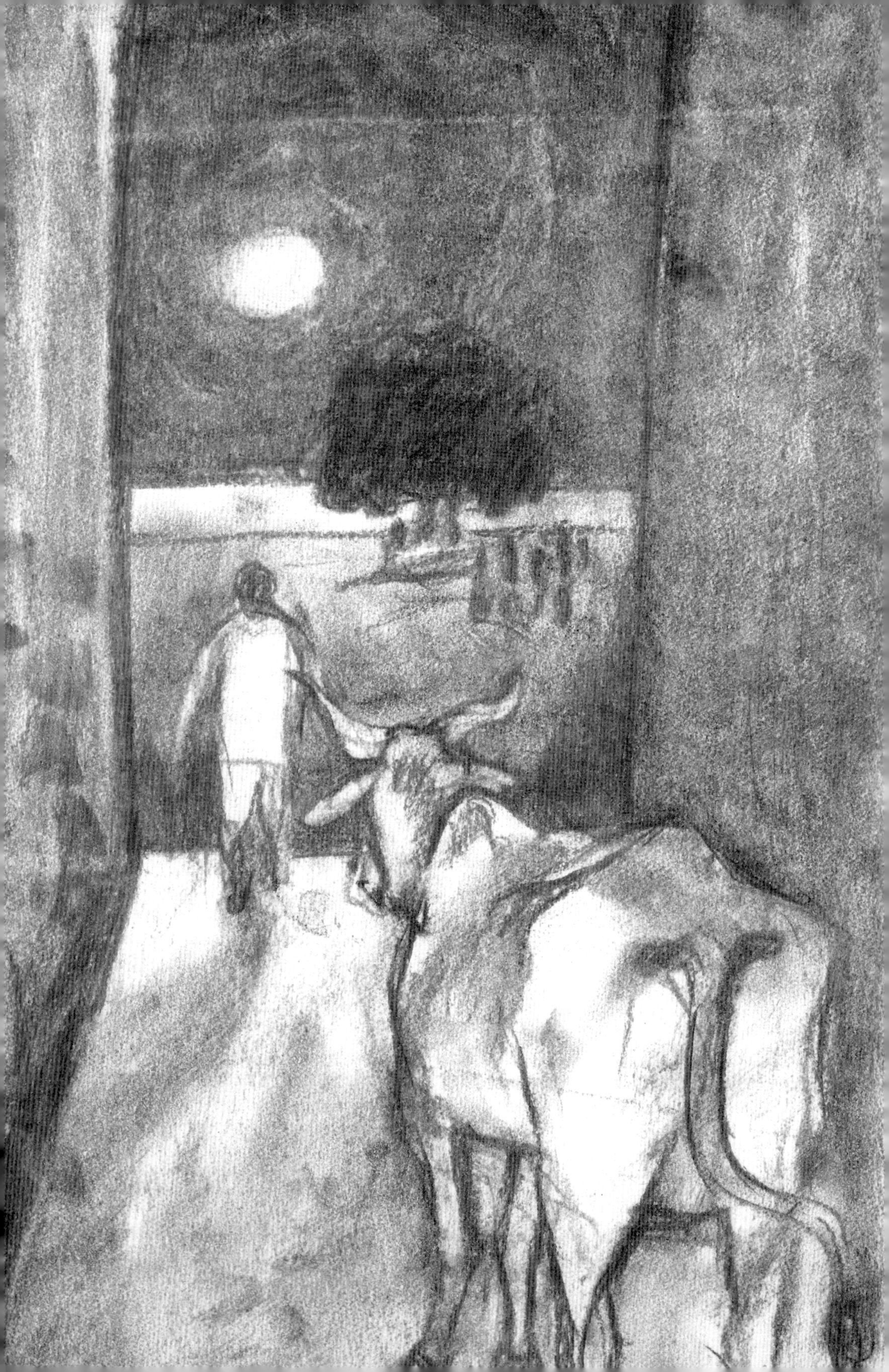

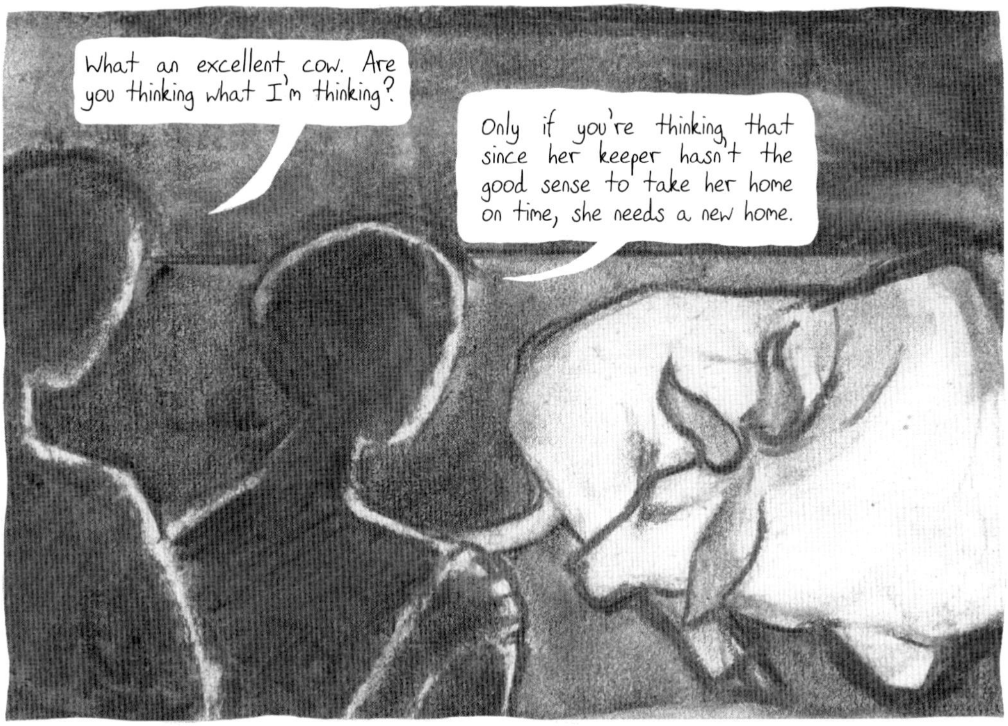
What an excellent cow. Are you thinking what I'm thinking?
Only if you're thinking that since her keeper hasn't the good sense to take her home on time, she needs a new home.

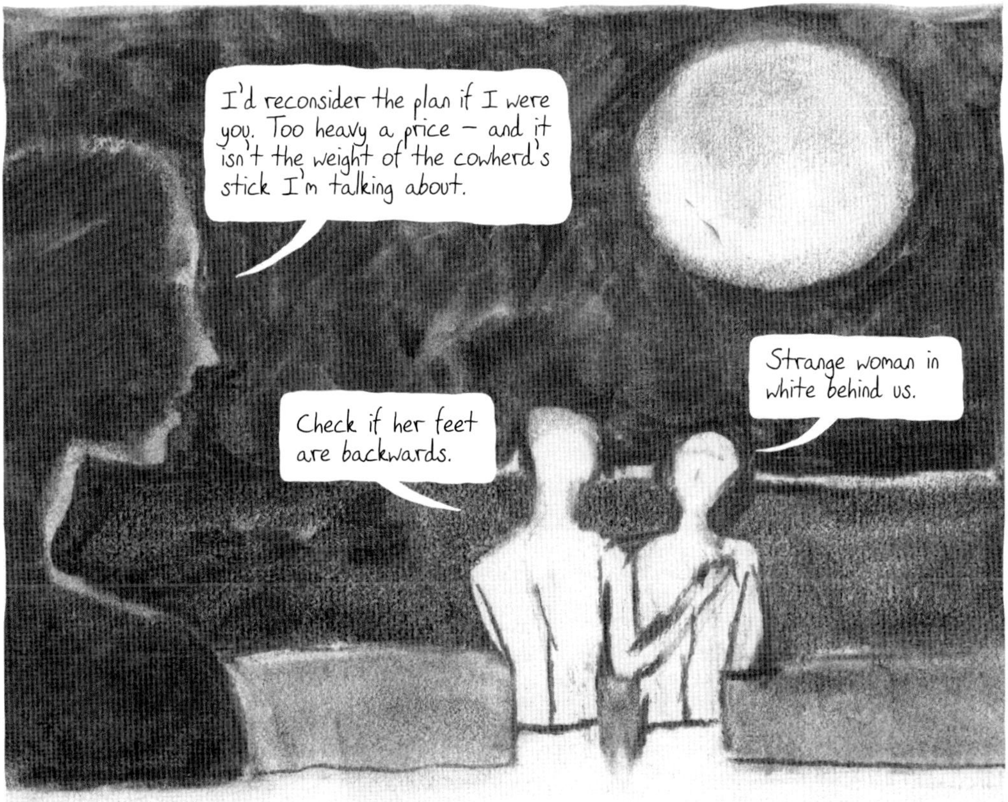
I'd reconsider the plan if I were you. Too heavy a price – and it isn't the weight of the cowherd's stick I'm talking about.
Strange woman in white behind us.
Check if her feet are backwards.

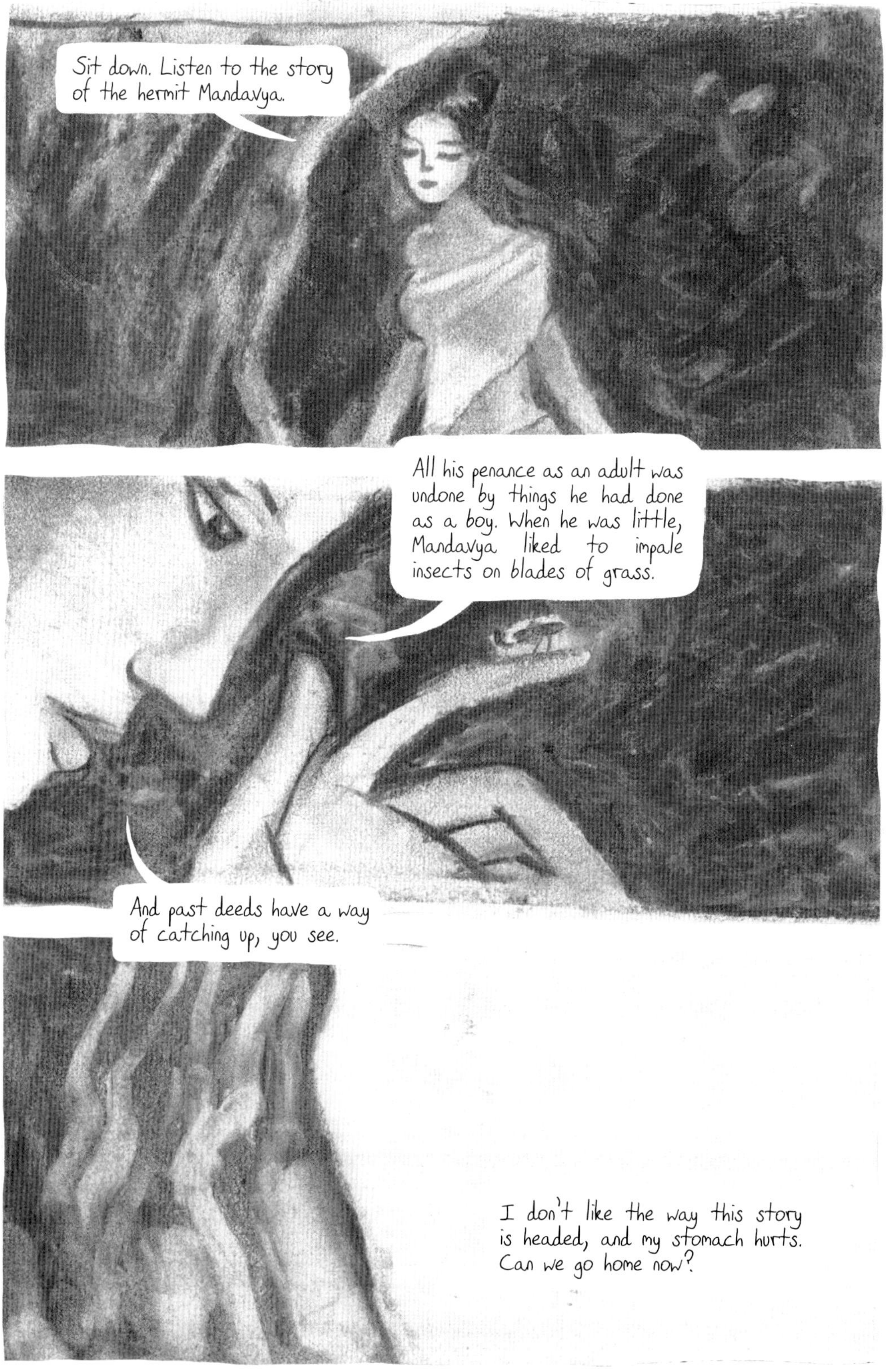
Sit down. Listen to the story of the hermit Mandavya.
All his penance as an adult was undone by things he had done as a boy. When he was little, Mandavya liked to impale insects on blades of grass.
And past deeds have a way of catching up, you see.
I don't like the way this story is headed, and my stomach hurts. Can we go home now?

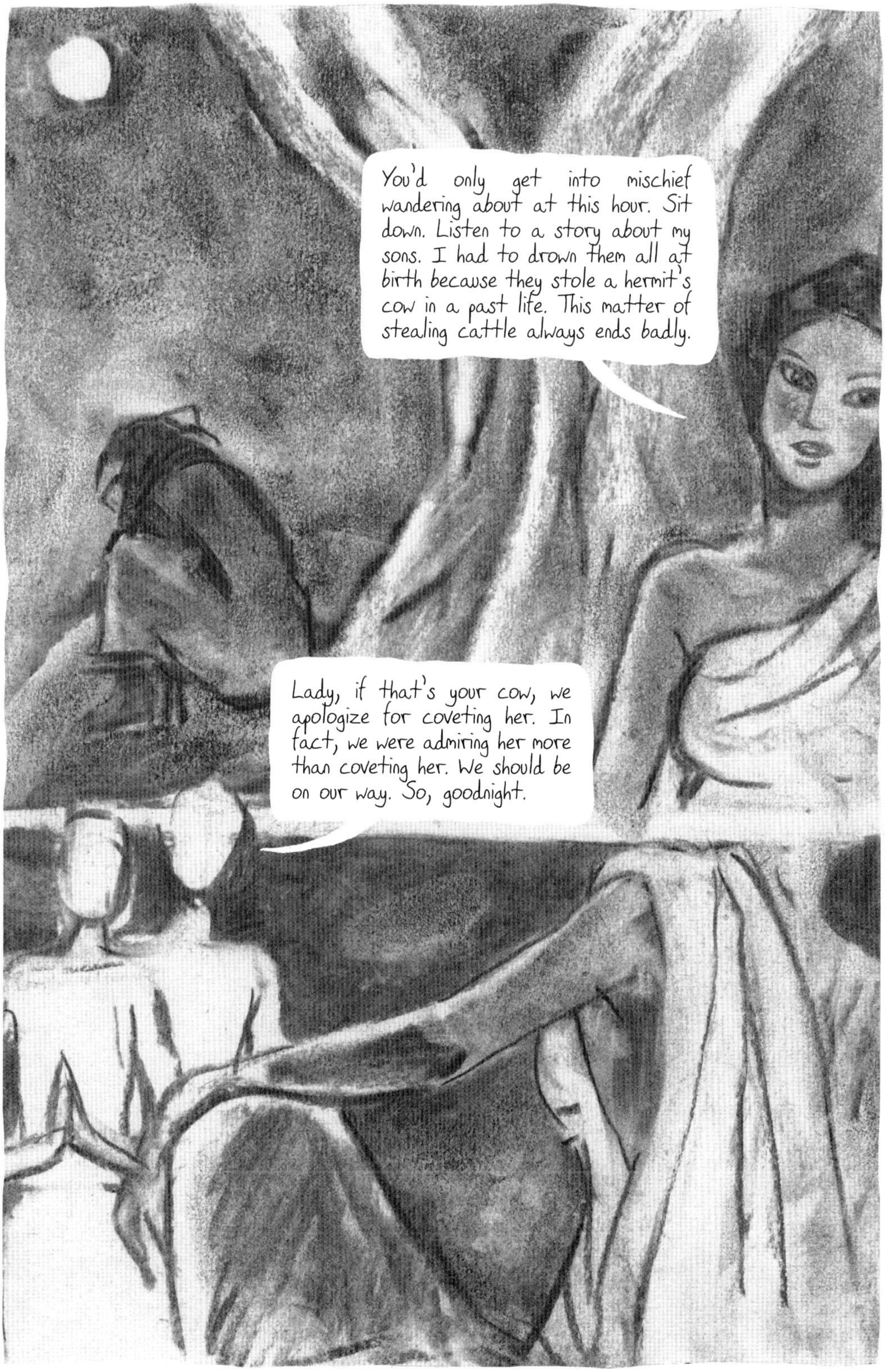
You'd only get into mischief wandering about at this hour. Sit down. Listen to a story about my sons. I had to drown them all at birth because they stole a hermit's cow in a past life. This matter of stealing cattle always ends badly.
Lady, if that's your cow, we apologize for coveting her. In fact, we were admiring her more than coveting her. We should be on our way. So, goodnight.

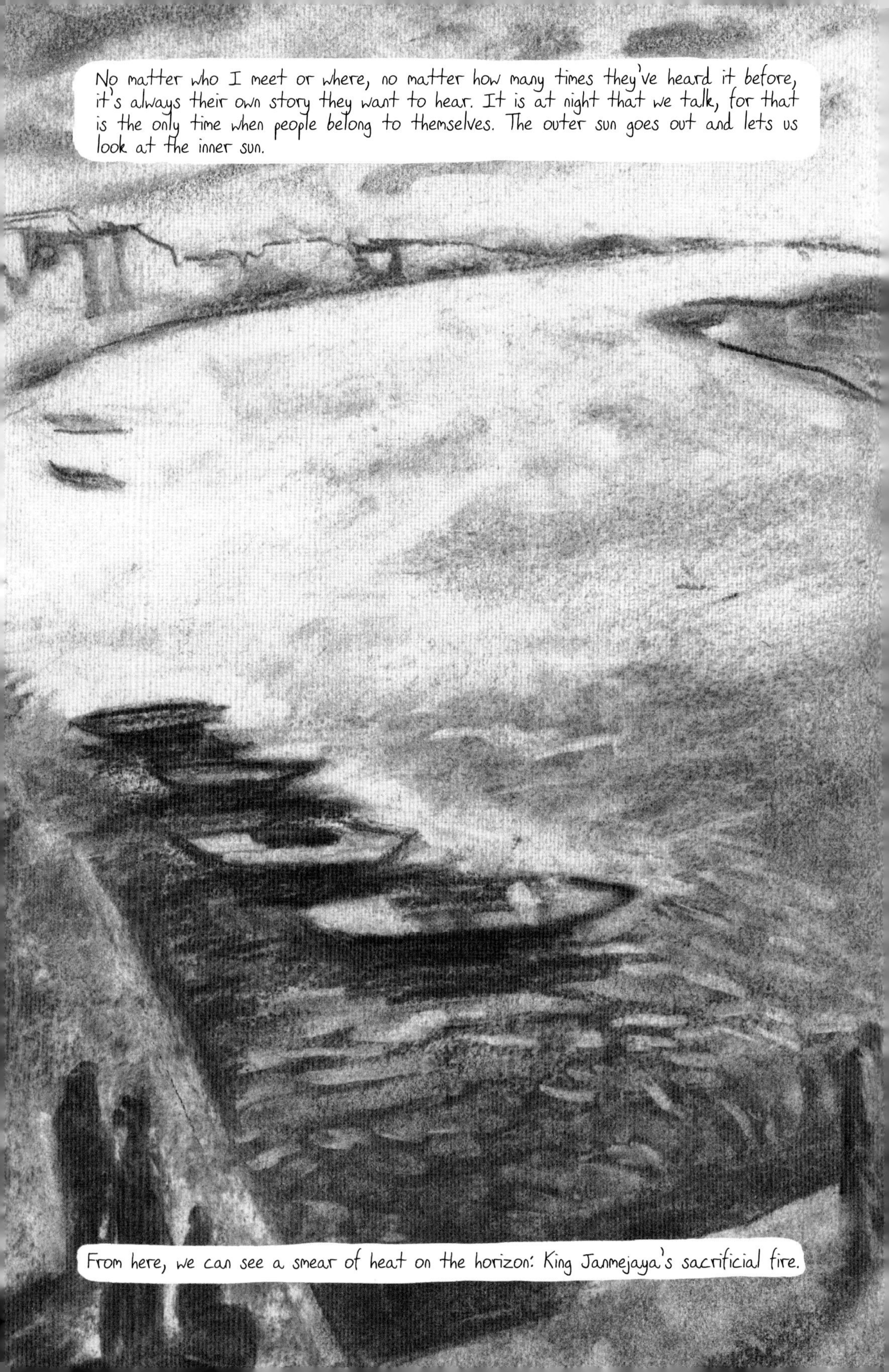
No matter who I meet or where, no matter how many times they've heard it before, it's always their own story they want to hear. It is at night that we talk, for that is the only time when people belong to themselves. The outer sun goes out and lets us look at the inner sun.
From here, we can see a smear of heat on the horizon: King Janmejaya's sacrificial fire.

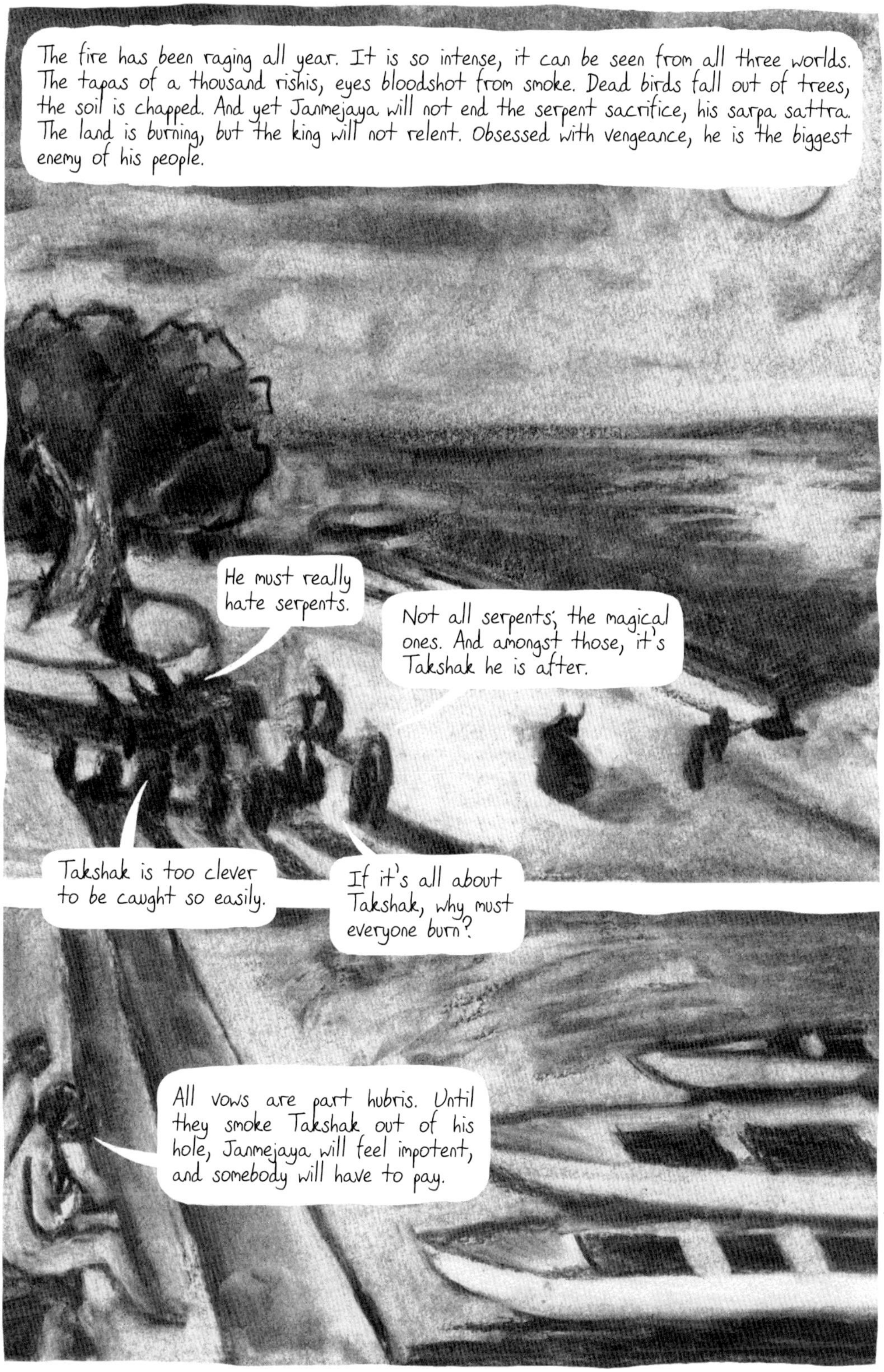
The fire has been raging all year. It is so intense, it can be seen from all three worlds. The tapas of a thousand rishis, eyes bloodshot from smoke. Dead birds fall out of trees, the soil is chapped. And yet Janmejaya will not end the serpent sacrifice, his sarpa sattra. The land is burning, but the king will not relent. Obsessed with vengeance, he is the biggest enemy of his people.
He must really hate serpents.
Not all serpents; the magical ones. And amongst those, it's Takshak he is after.
Takshak is too clever to be caught so easily.
If it's all about Takshak, why must everyone burn?
All vows are part hubris. Until they smoke Takshak out of his hole, Janmejaya will feel impotent, and somebody will have to pay.

BEGINNING

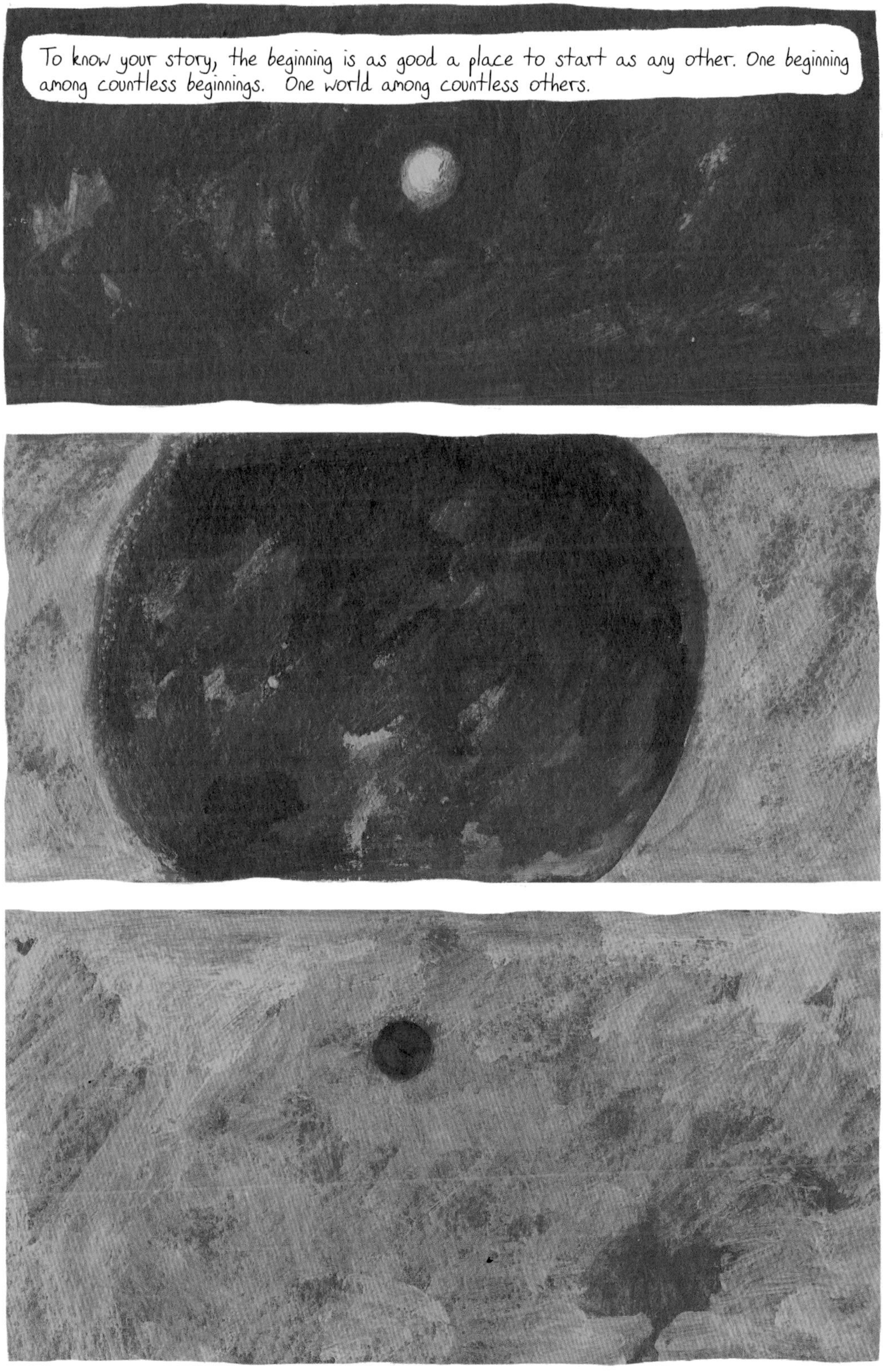
To know your story, the beginning is as good a place to start as any other. One beginning among countless beginnings. One world among countless others.

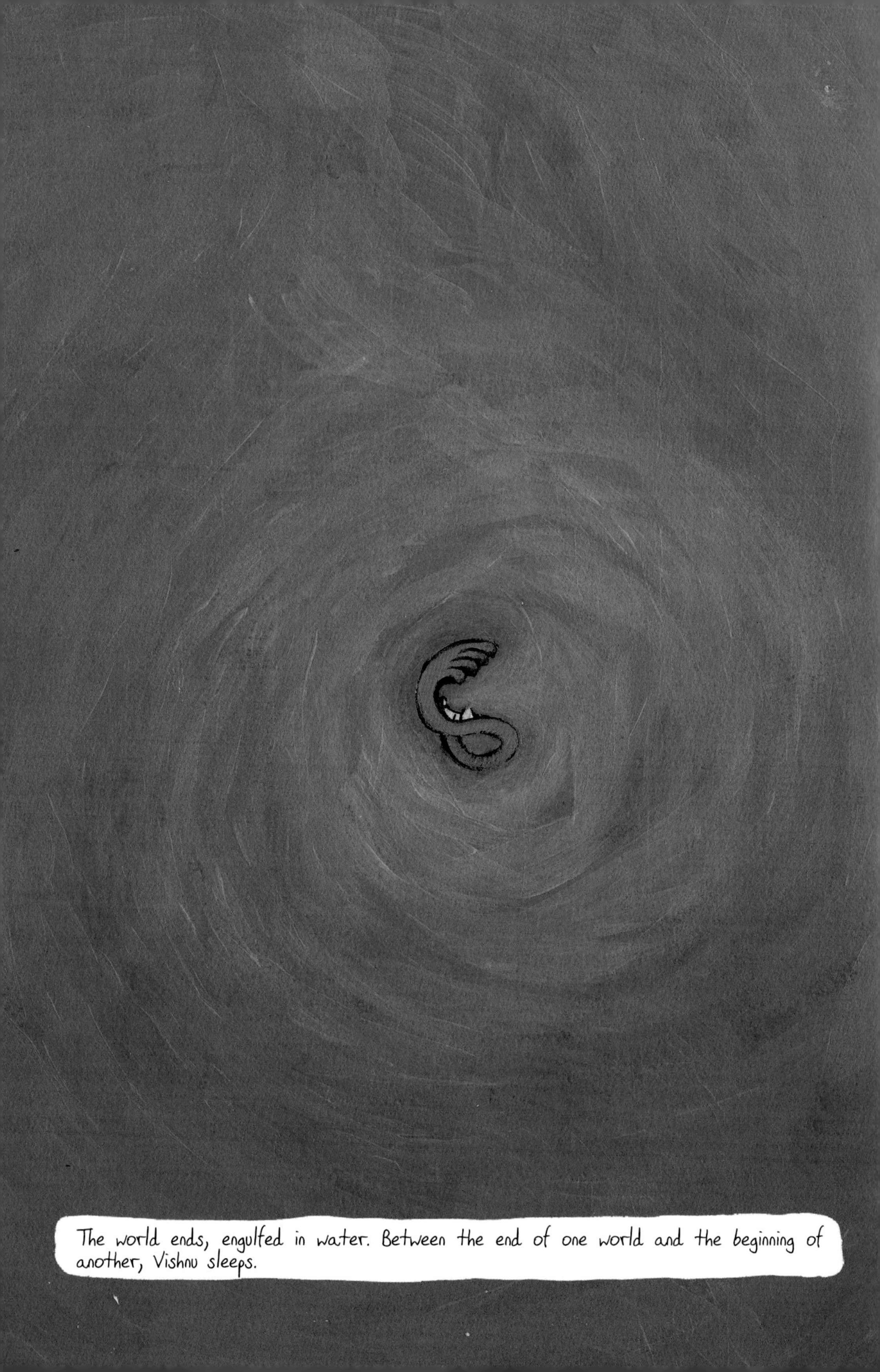
The world ends, engulfed in water. Between the end of one world and the beginning of another, Vishnu sleeps.

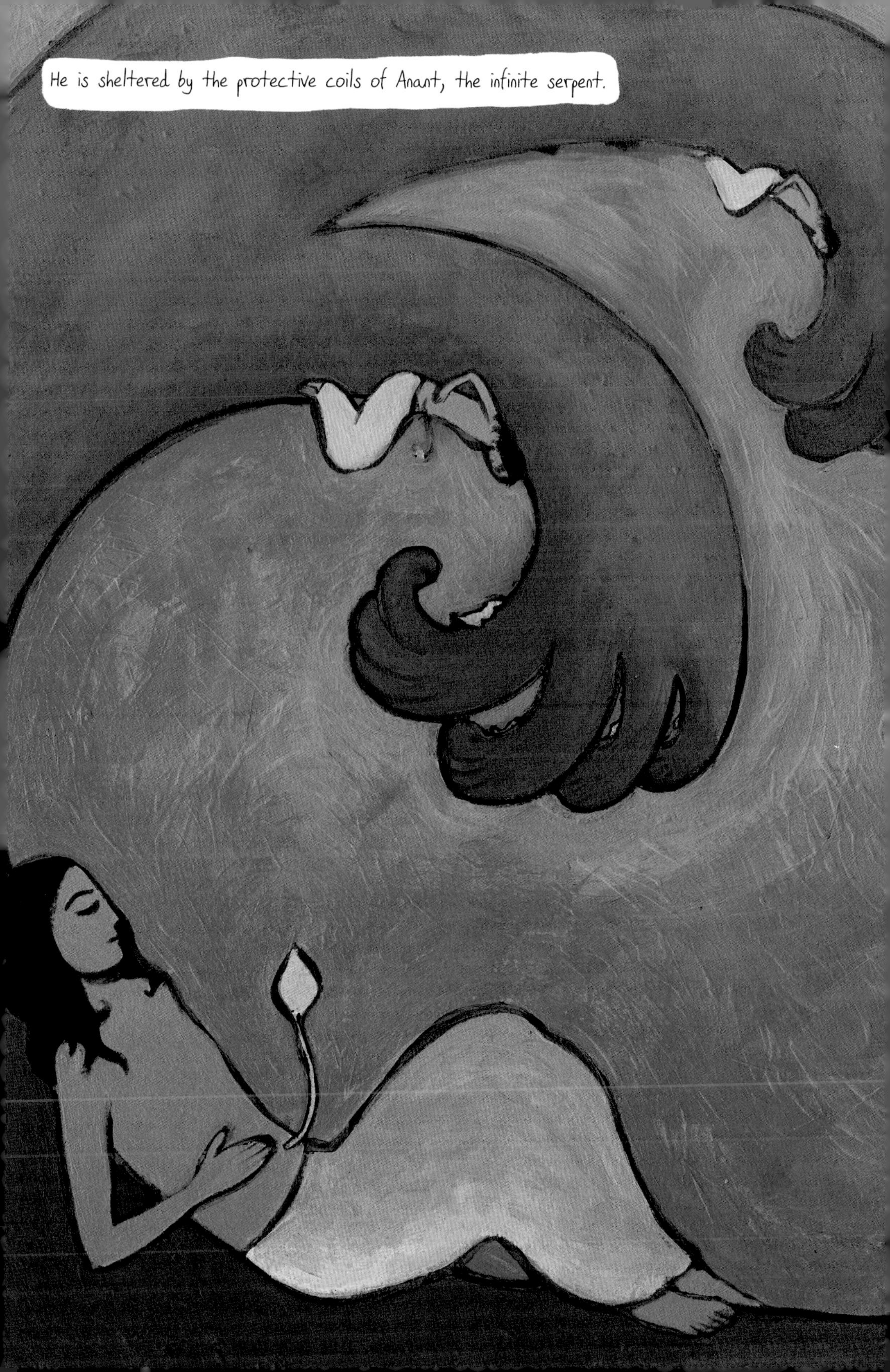
He is sheltered by the protective coils of Anant, the infinite serpent.

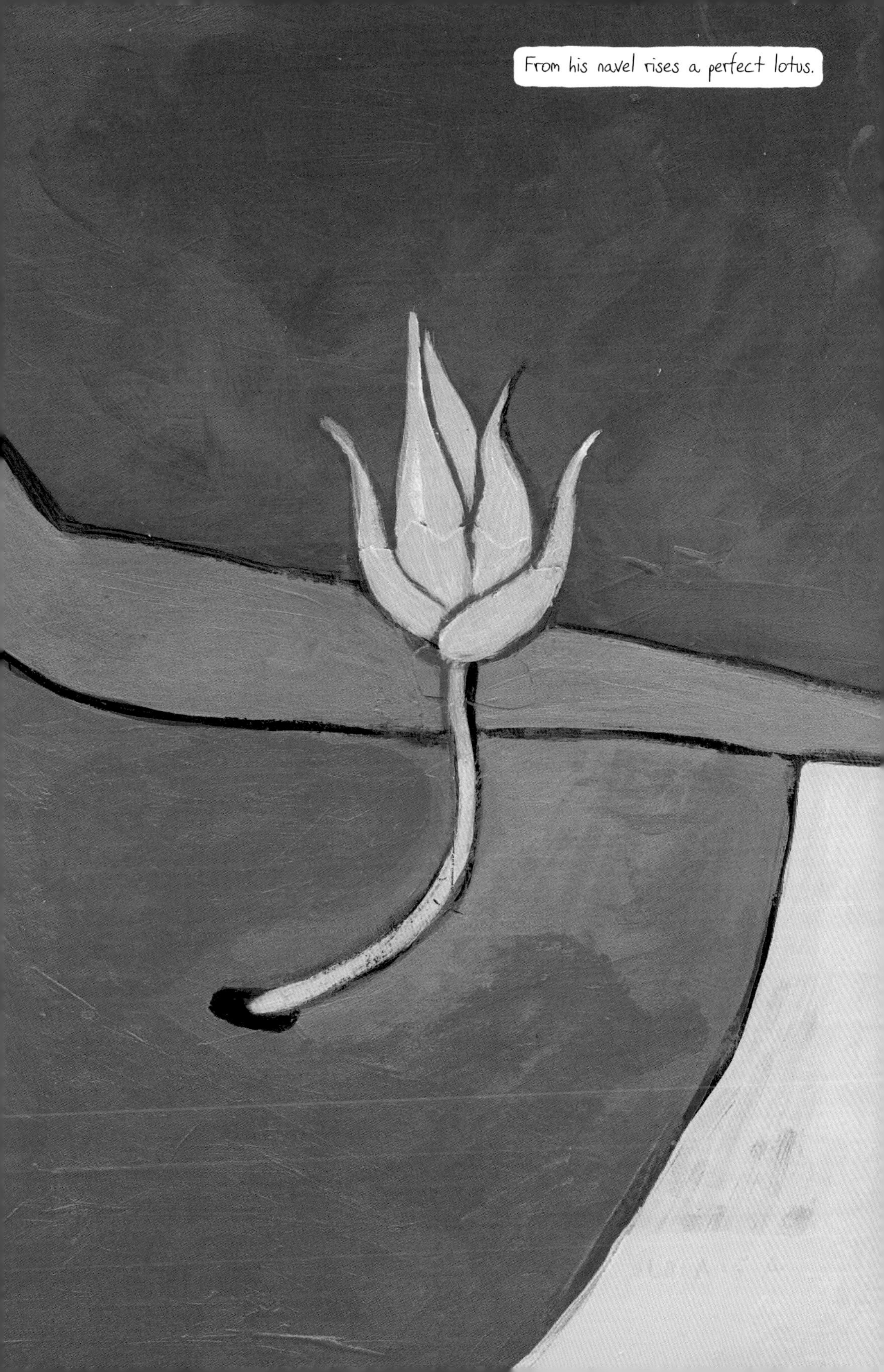
From his navel rises a perfect lotus.

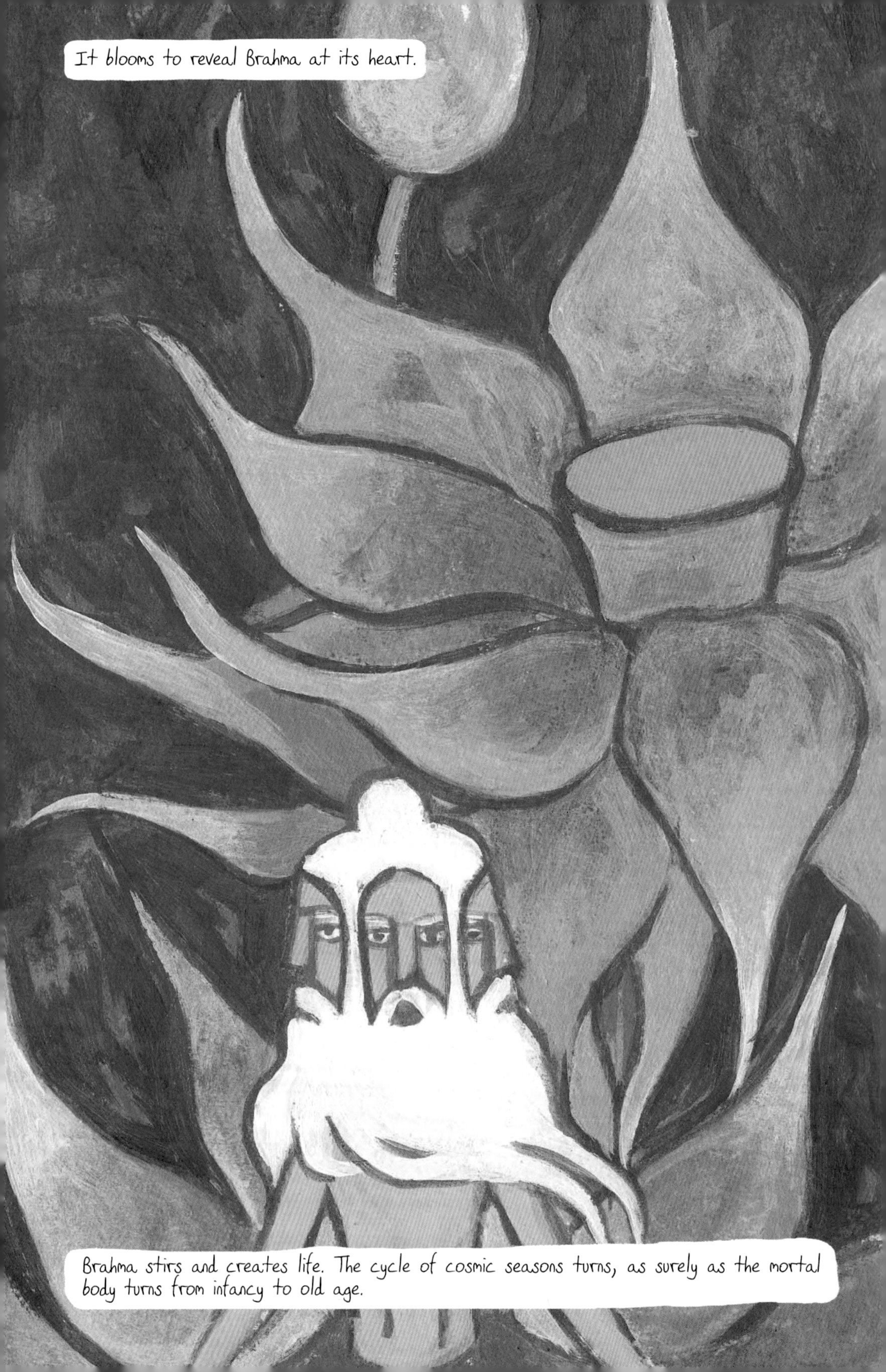
It blooms to reveal Brahma at its heart.
Brahma stirs and creates life. The cycle of cosmic seasons turns, as surely as the mortal body turns from infancy to old age.

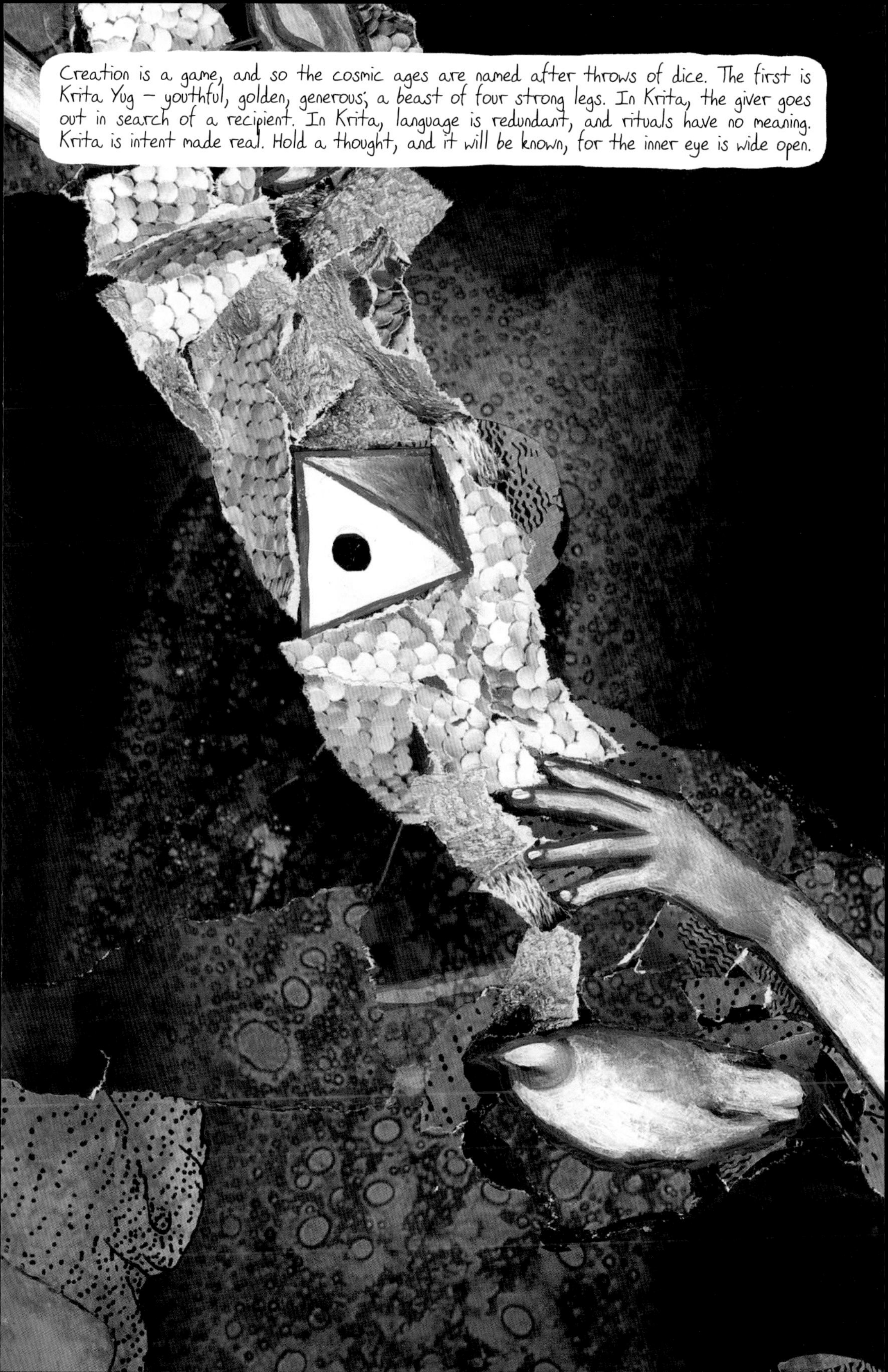
Creation is a game, and so the cosmic ages are named after throws of dice. The first is Krita Yug – youthful, golden, generous; a beast of four strong legs. In Krita, the giver goes out in search of a recipient. In Krita, language is redundant, and rituals have no meaning. Krita is intent made real. Hold a thought, and it will be known, for the inner eye is wide open.

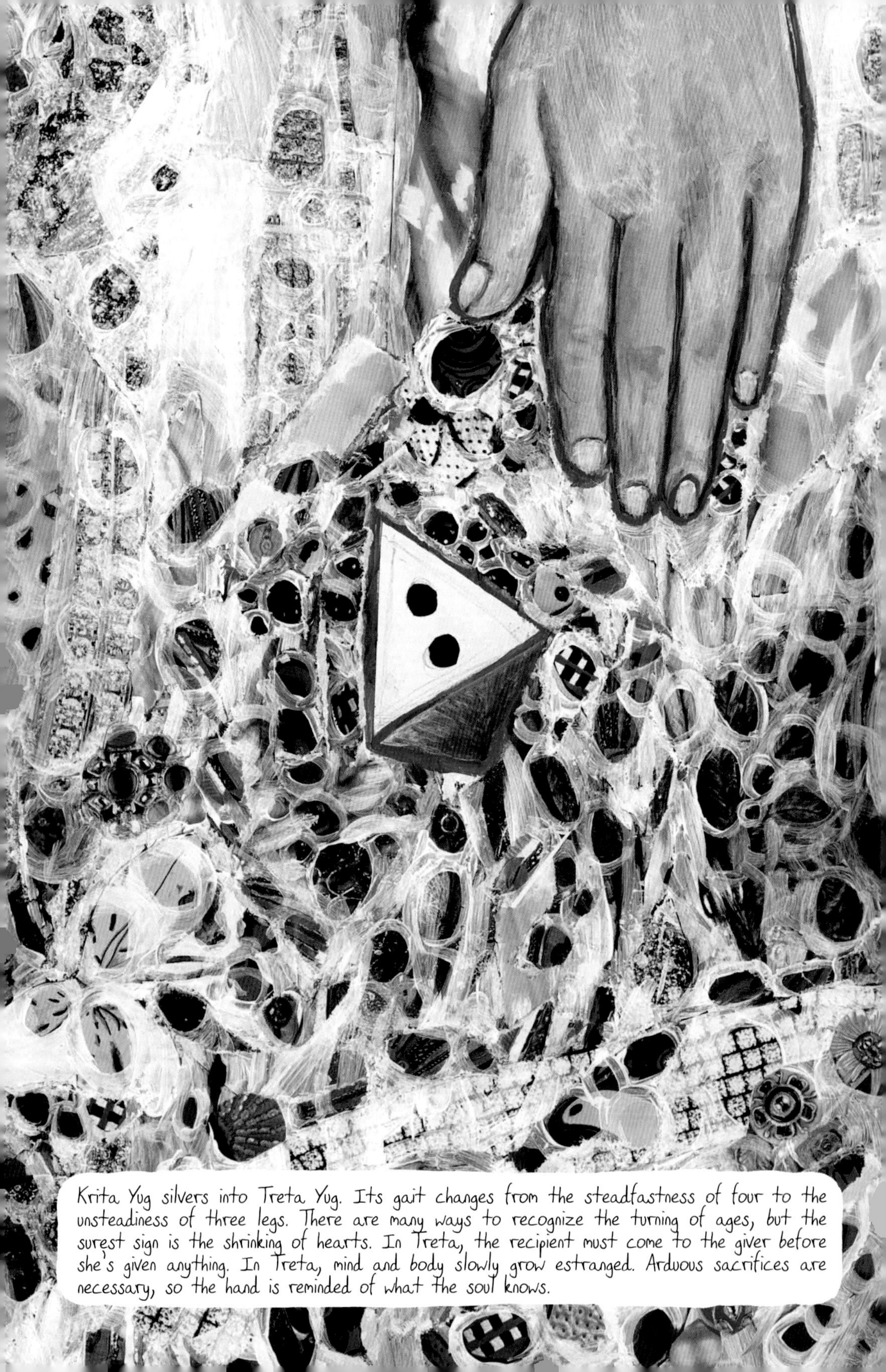
Krita Yug silvers into Treta Yug. Its gait changes from the steadfastness of four to the unsteadiness of three legs. There are many ways to recognize the turning of ages, but the surest sign is the shrinking of hearts. In Treta, the recipient must come to the giver before she's given anything. In Treta, mind and body slowly grow estranged. Arduous sacrifices are necessary, so the hand is reminded of what the soul knows.

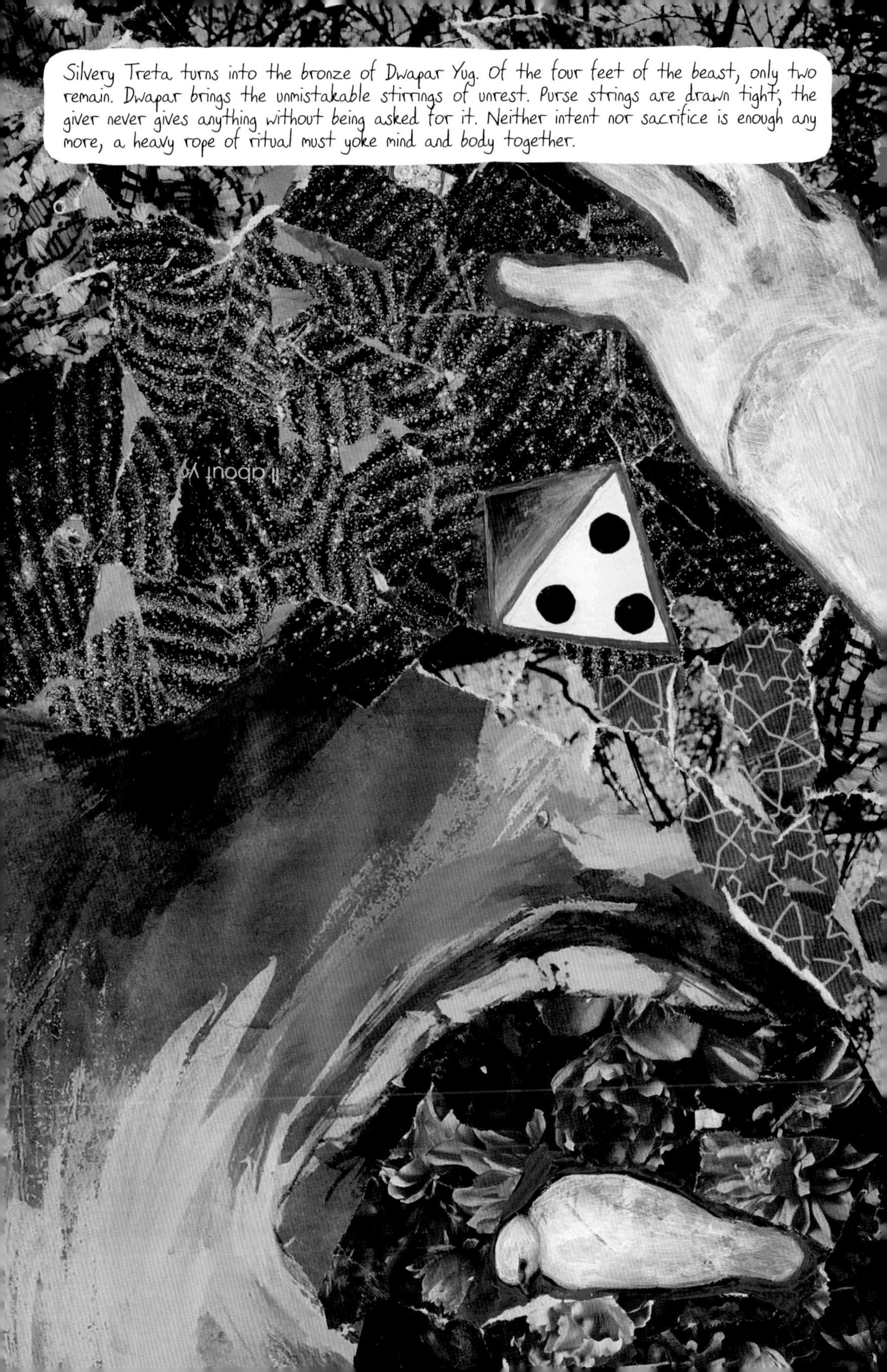
Silvery Treta turns into the bronze of Dwapar Yug. Of the four feet of the beast, only two remain. Dwapar brings the unmistakable stirrings of unrest. Purse strings are drawn tight; the giver never gives anything without being asked for it. Neither intent nor sacrifice is enough any more, a heavy rope of ritual must yoke mind and body together.

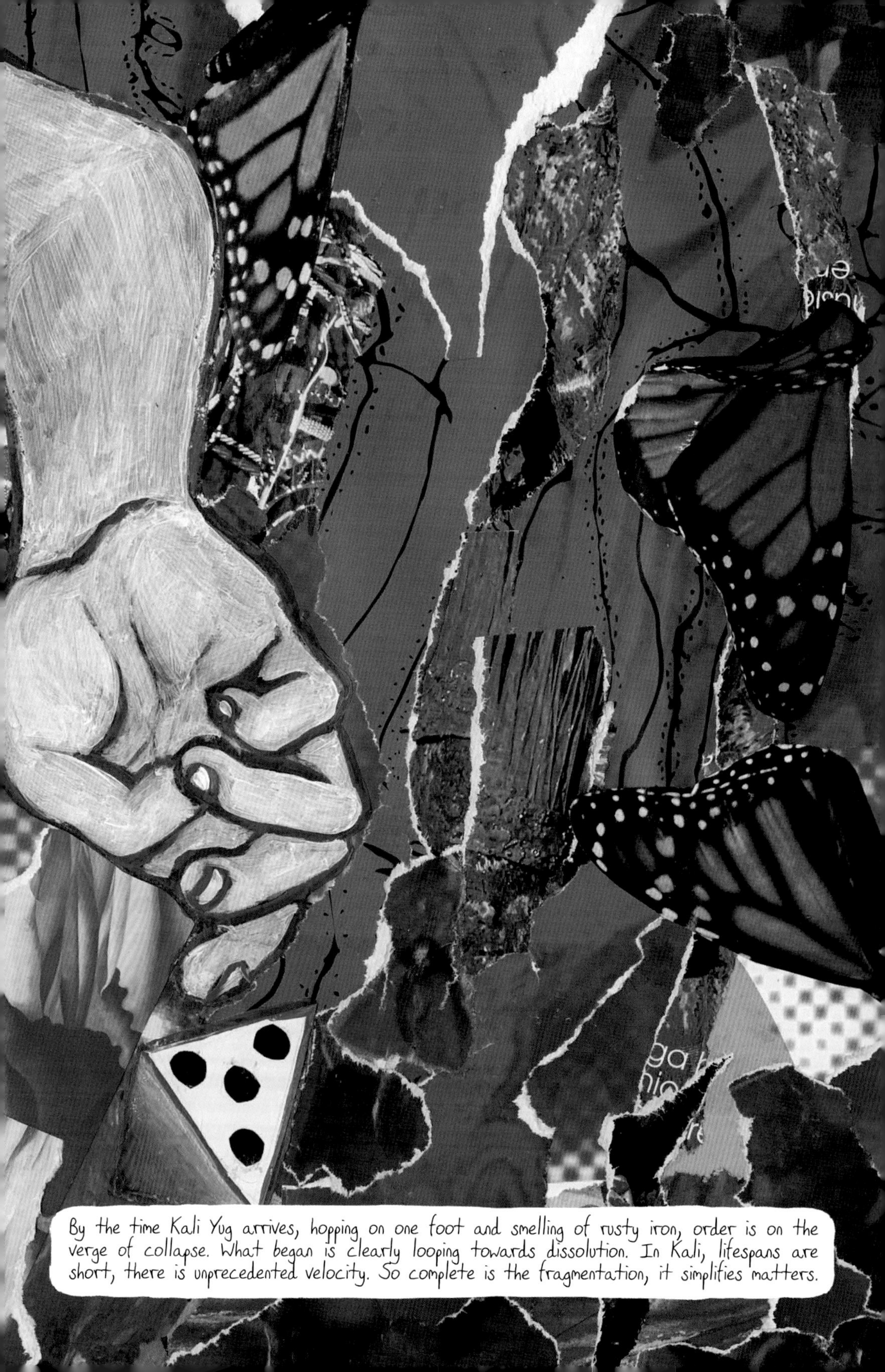
By the time Kali Yug arrives, hopping on one foot and smelling of rusty iron, order is on the verge of collapse. What began is clearly looping towards dissolution. In Kali, lifespans are short, there is unprecedented velocity. So complete is the fragmentation, it simplifies matters.

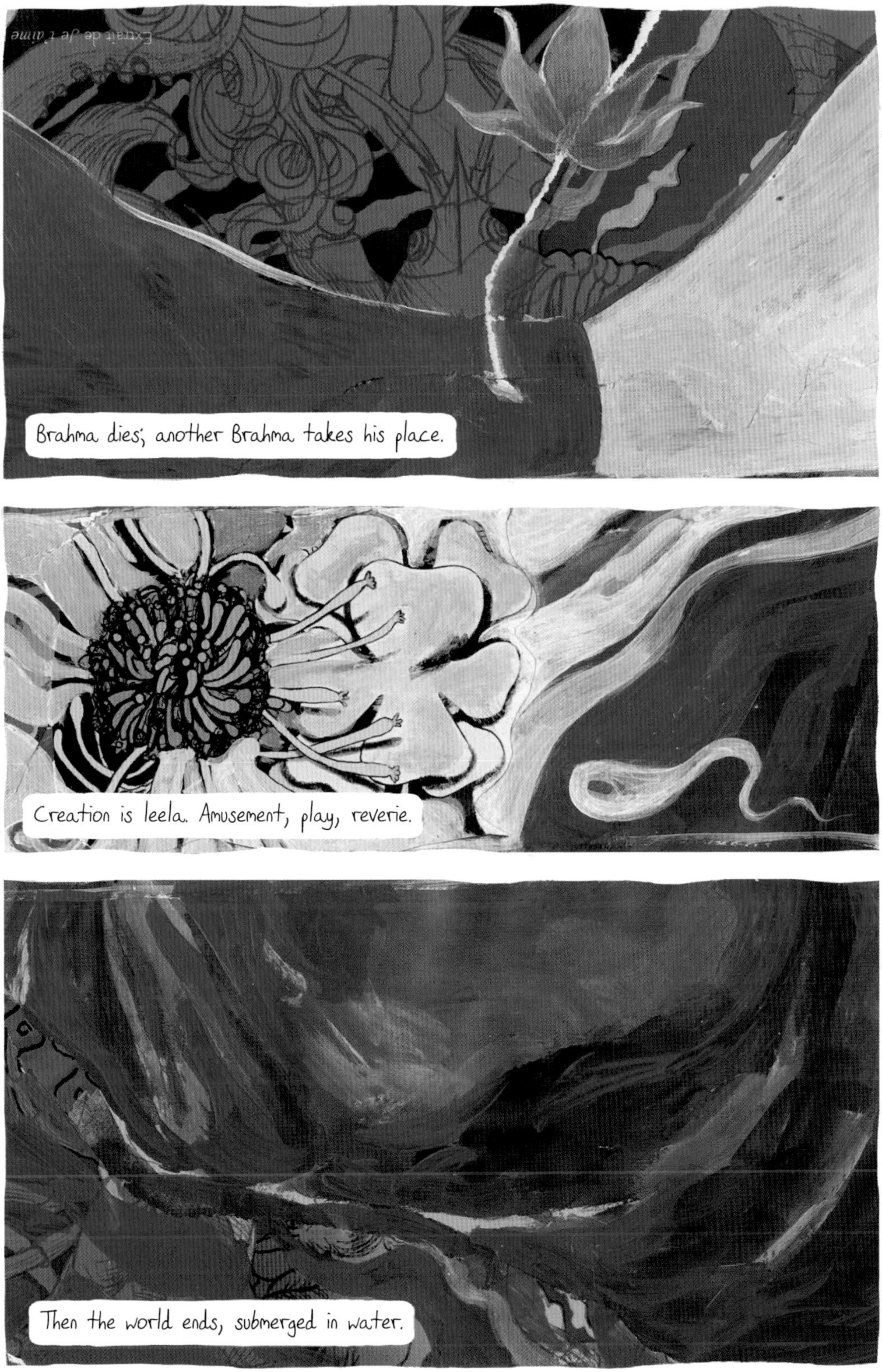
Brahma dies; another Brahma takes his place.
Creation is leela. Amusement, play, reverie.
Then the world ends, submerged in water.

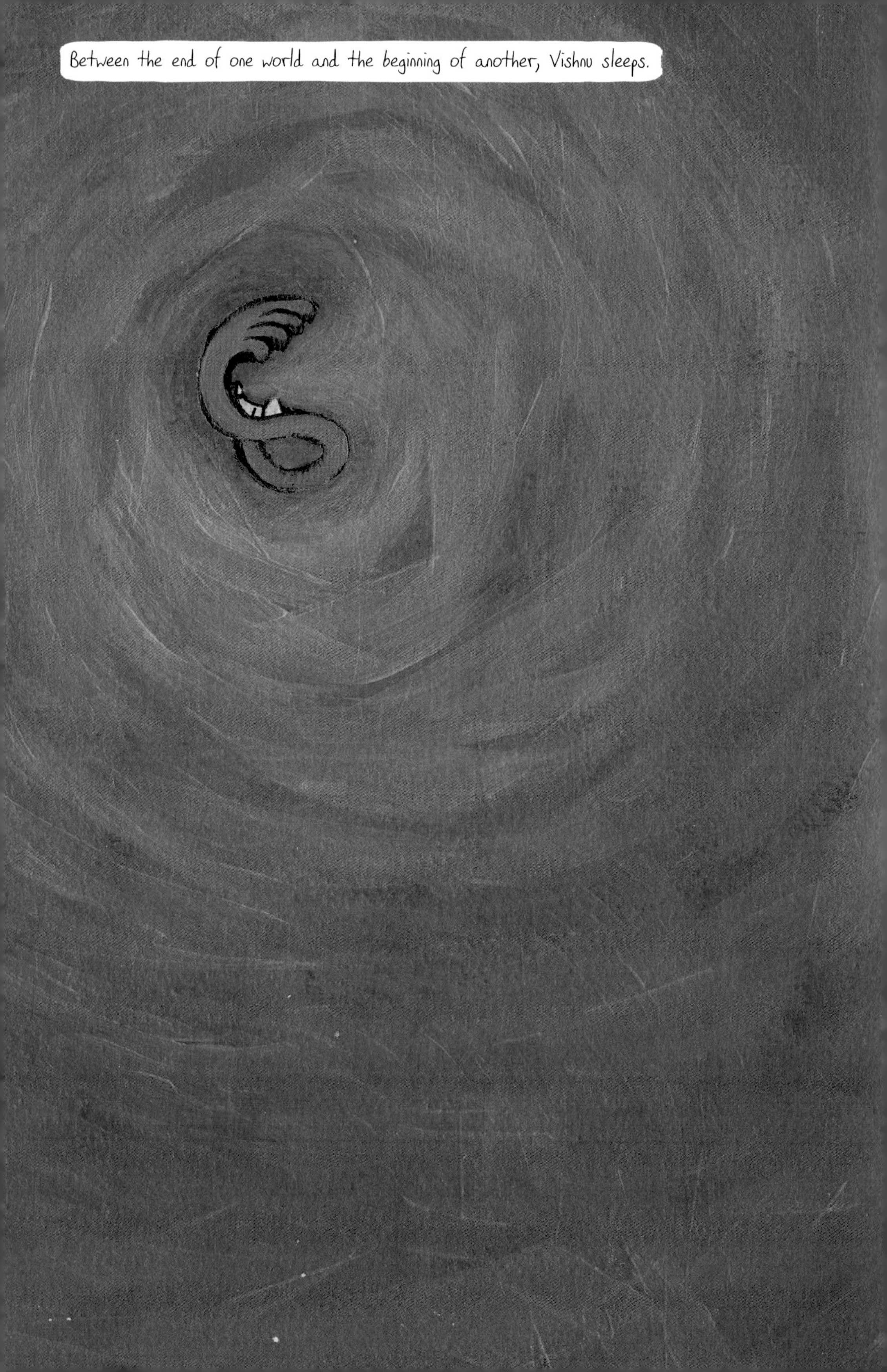
Between the end of one world and the beginning of another, Vishnu sleeps.

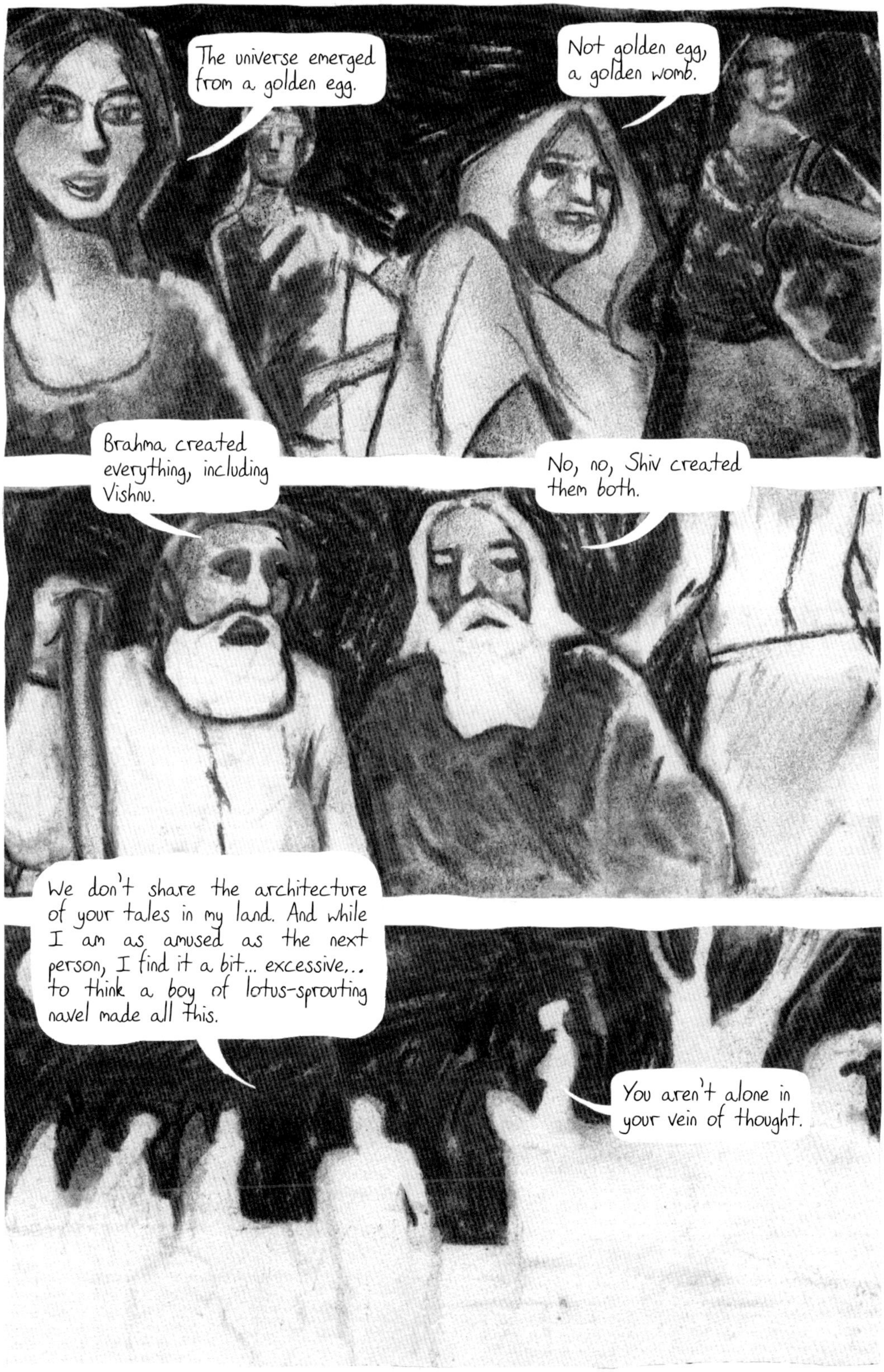
The universe emerged from a golden egg.
Not golden egg, a golden womb.
Brahma created everything, including Vishnu.
No, no, Shiv created them both.
We don't share the architecture of your tales in my land. And while I am as amused as the next person, I find it a bit... excessive... to think a boy of lotus-sprouting navel made all this.
You aren't alone in your vein of thought.

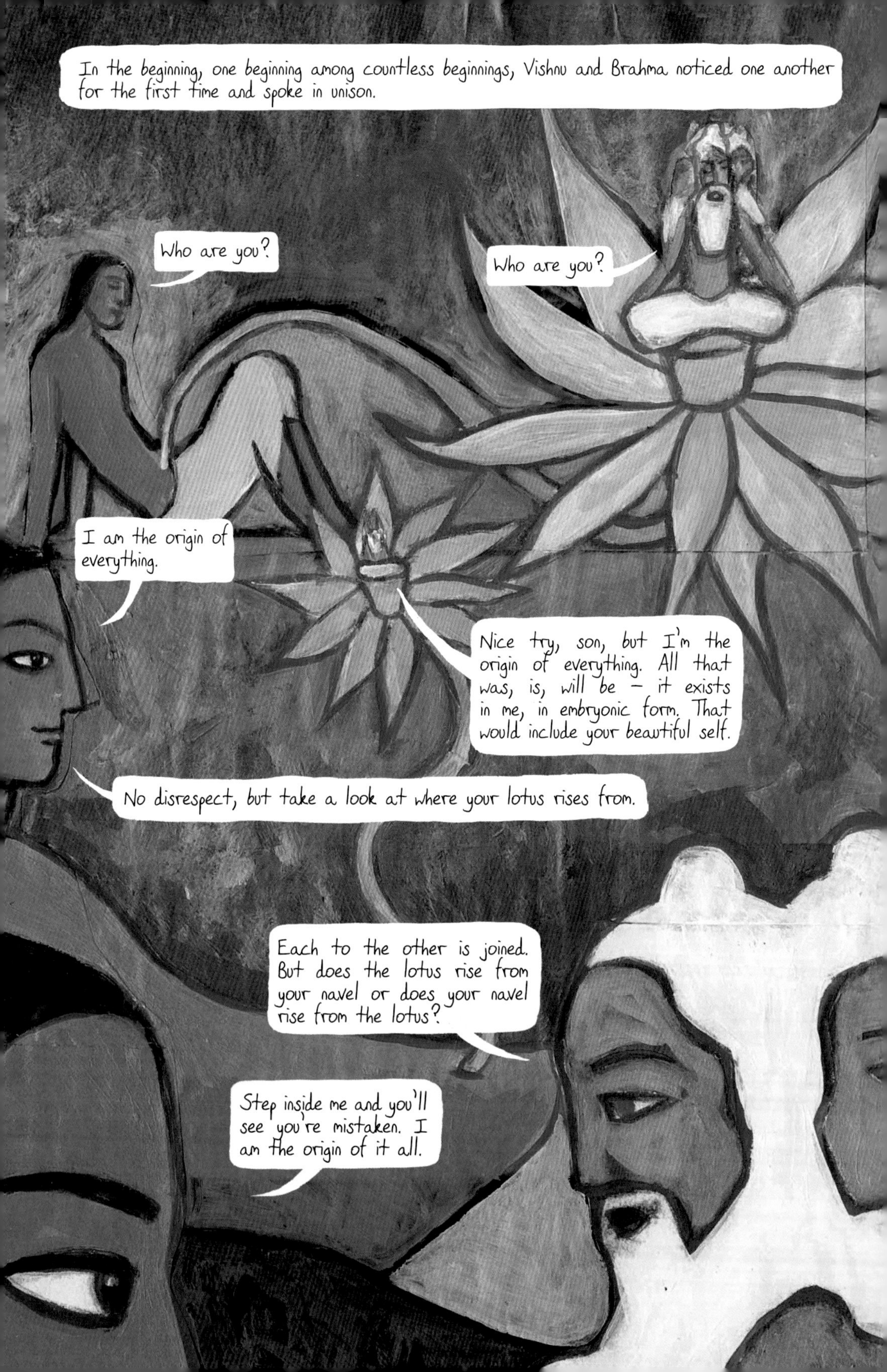
In the beginning, one beginning among countless beginnings, Vishnu and Brahma noticed one another for the first time and spoke in unison.
Who are you?
Who are you?
I am the origin of everything.
Nice try, son, but I'm the origin of everything. All that was, is, will be – it exists in me, in embryonic form. That would include your beautiful self.
No disrespect, but take a look at where your lotus rises from.
Each to the other is joined. But does the lotus rise from your navel or does your navel rise from the lotus?
Step inside me and you'll see you're mistaken. I am the origin of it all.

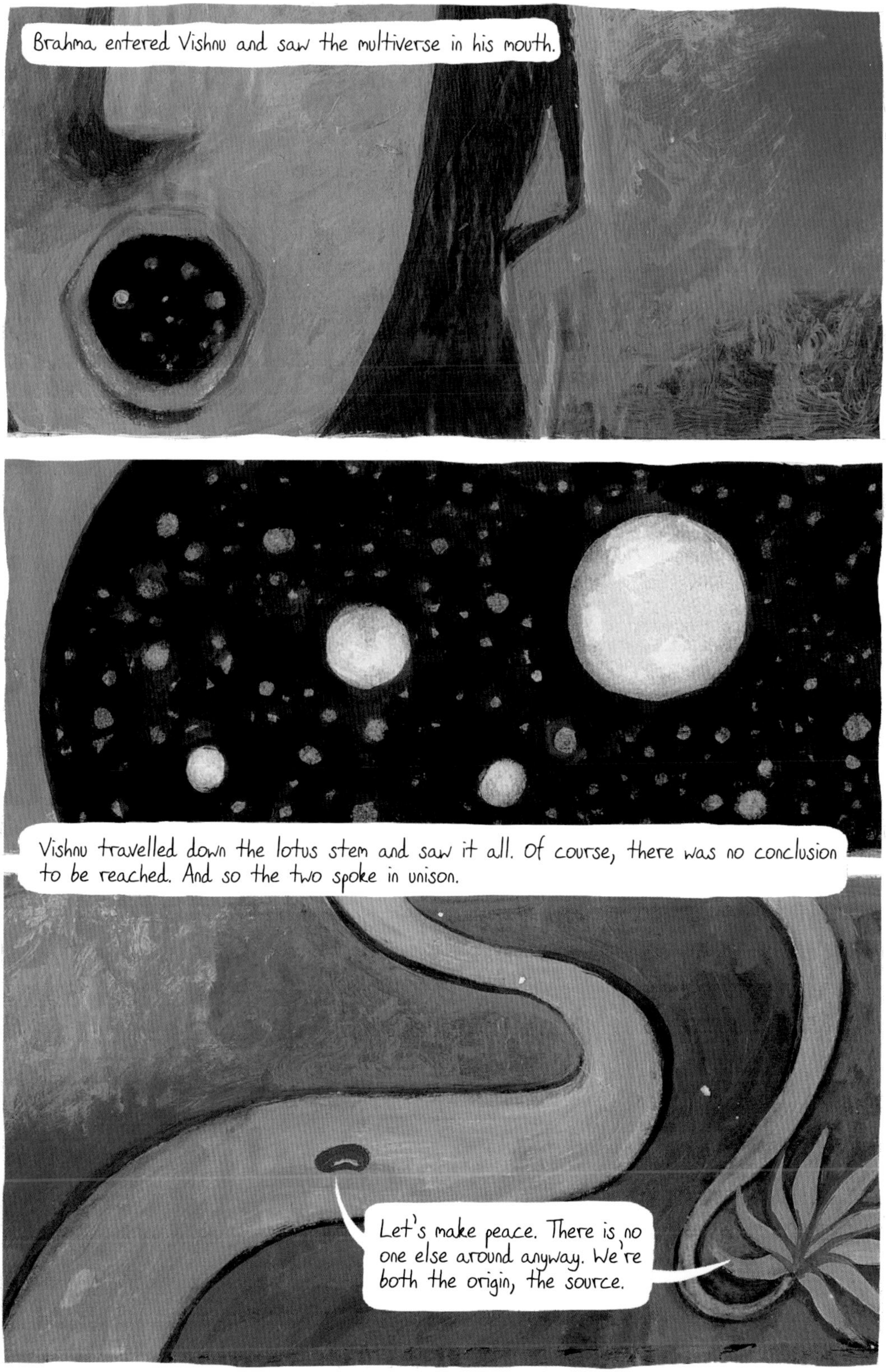
Brahma entered Vishnu and saw the multiverse in his mouth.
Vishnu travelled down the lotus stem and saw it all. Of course, there was no conclusion to be reached. And so the two spoke in unison.
Let's make peace. There is no one else around anyway. We're both the origin, the source.

Except that there was someone — something — else around. A vivid beam of colours, a form that was at once dancing and immutable. Brahma and Vishnu spoke in unison.

Who are you?

Who are you?

I am Shiv — the beginning and the end.

Travel along my light, you'll see I am infinite. I am the origin of it all.

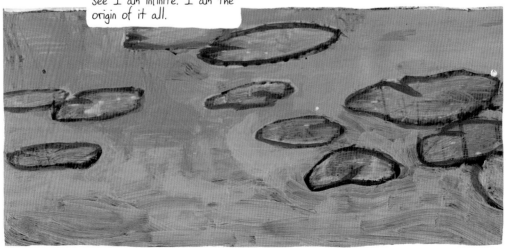

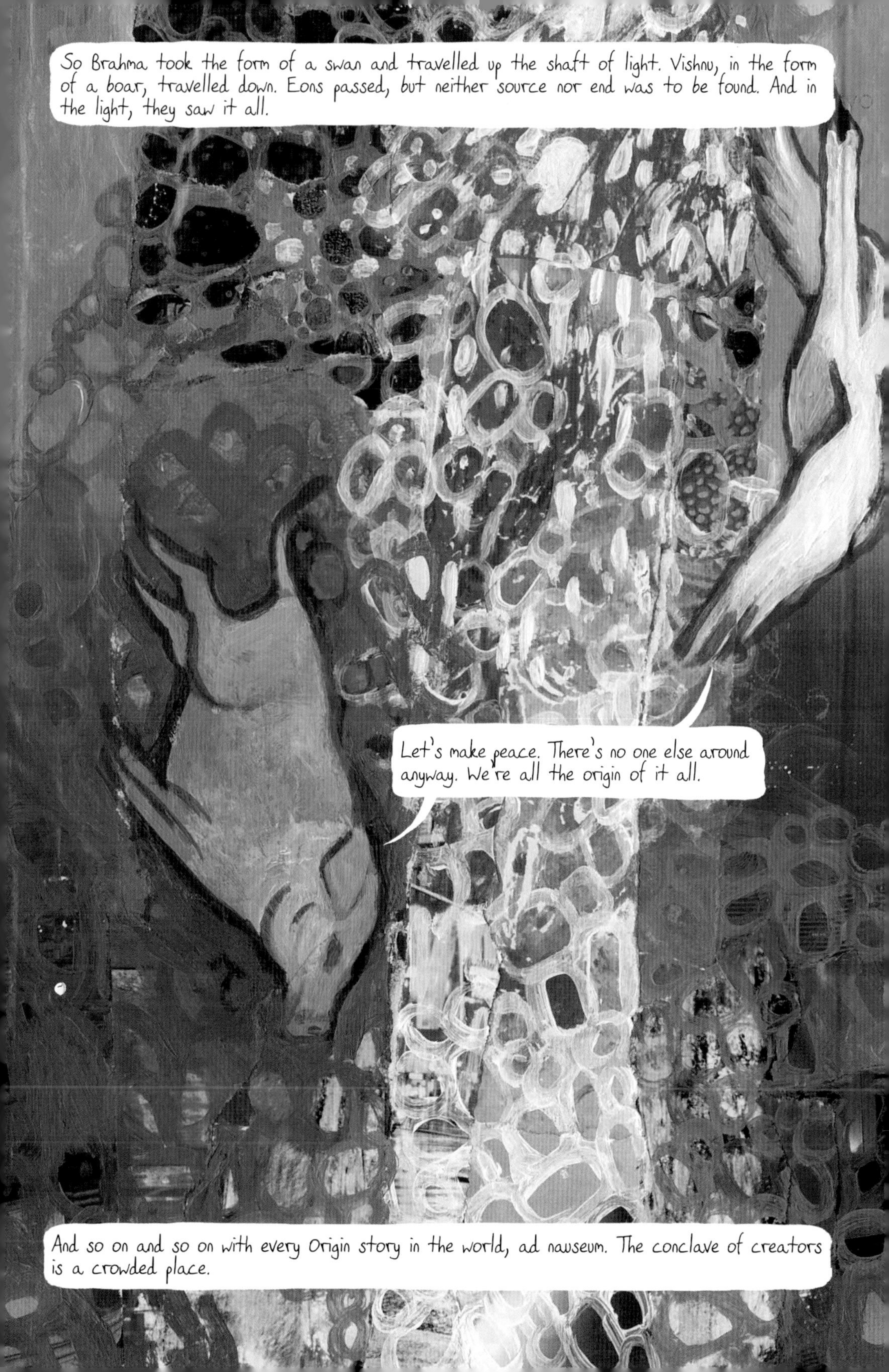
So Brahma took the form of a swan and travelled up the shaft of light. Vishnu, in the form of a boar, travelled down. Eons passed, but neither source nor end was to be found. And in the light, they saw it all.
Let's make peace. There's no one else around anyway. We're all the origin of it all.
And so on and so on with every Origin story in the world, ad nauseum. The conclave of creators is a crowded place.

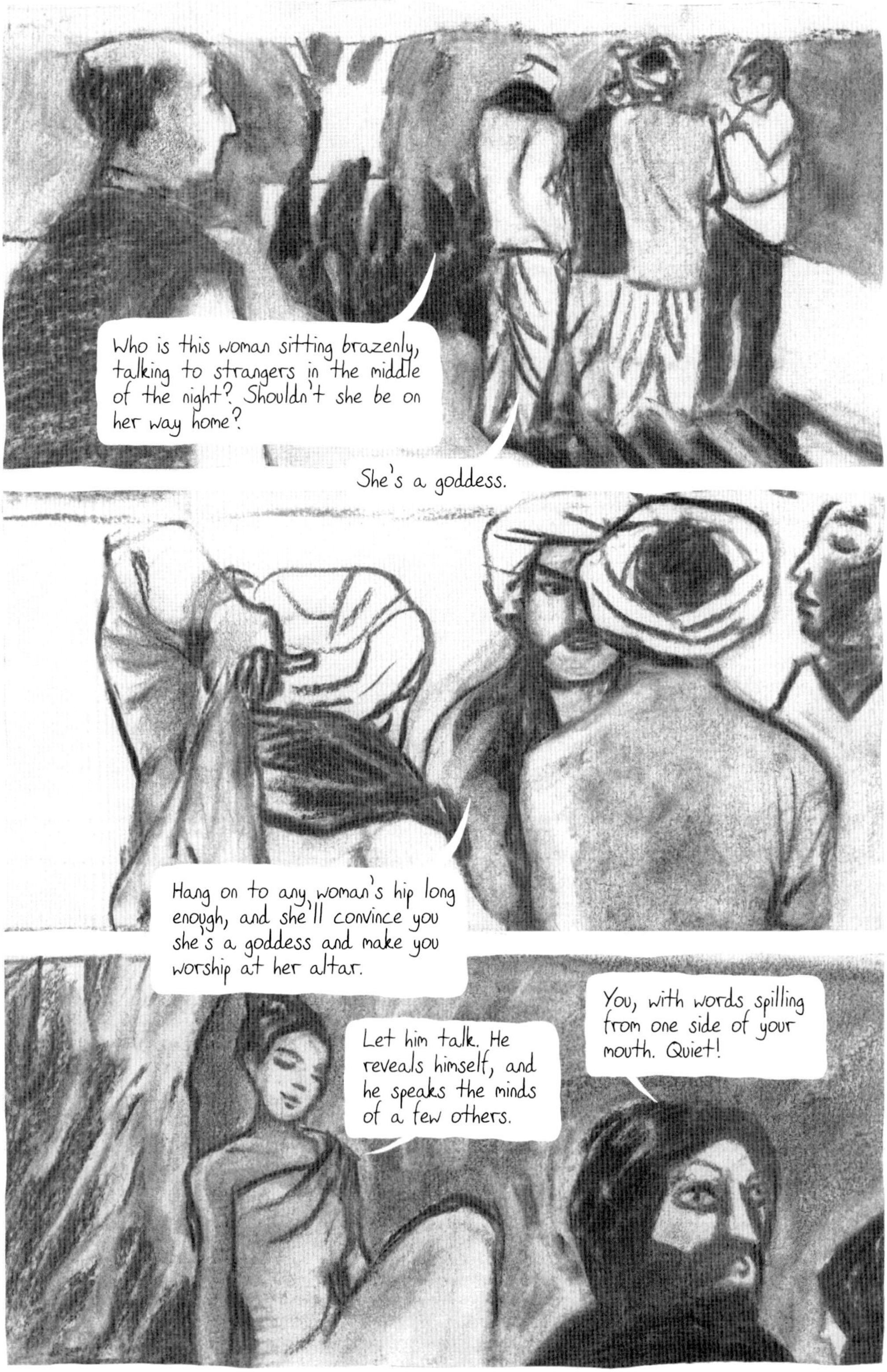
Who is this woman sitting brazenly, talking to strangers in the middle of the night? Shouldn't she be on her way home?
She's a goddess.
Hang on to any woman's hip long enough, and she'll convince you she's a goddess and make you worship at her altar.
Let him talk. He reveals himself, and he speaks the minds of a few others.
You, with words spilling from one side of your mouth. Quiet!

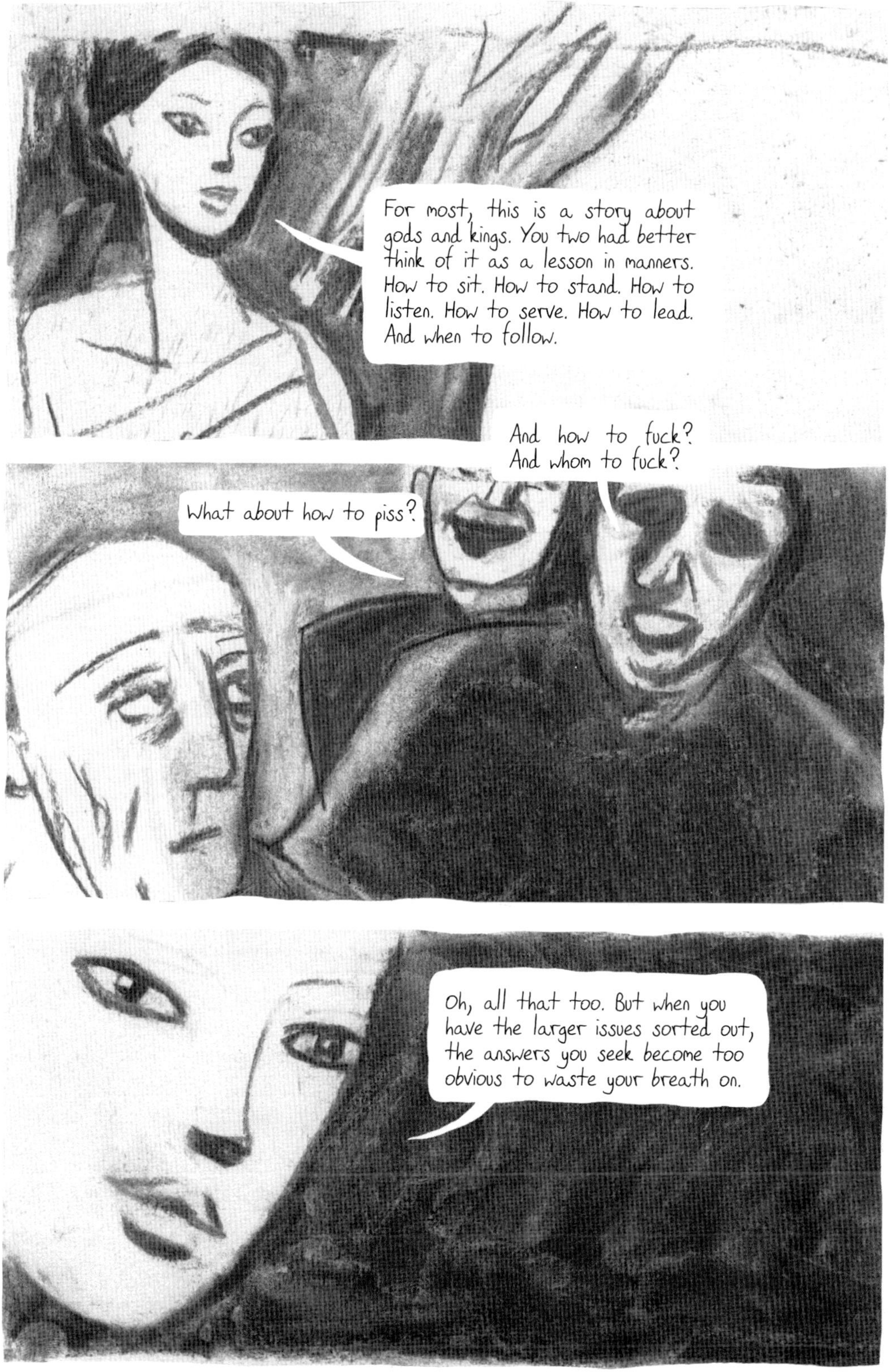
For most, this is a story about gods and kings. You two had better think of it as a lesson in manners. How to sit. How to stand. How to listen. How to serve. How to lead. And when to follow.
What about how to piss?
And how to fuck? And whom to fuck?
Oh, all that too. But when you have the larger issues sorted out, the answers you seek become too obvious to waste your breath on.

GANGA

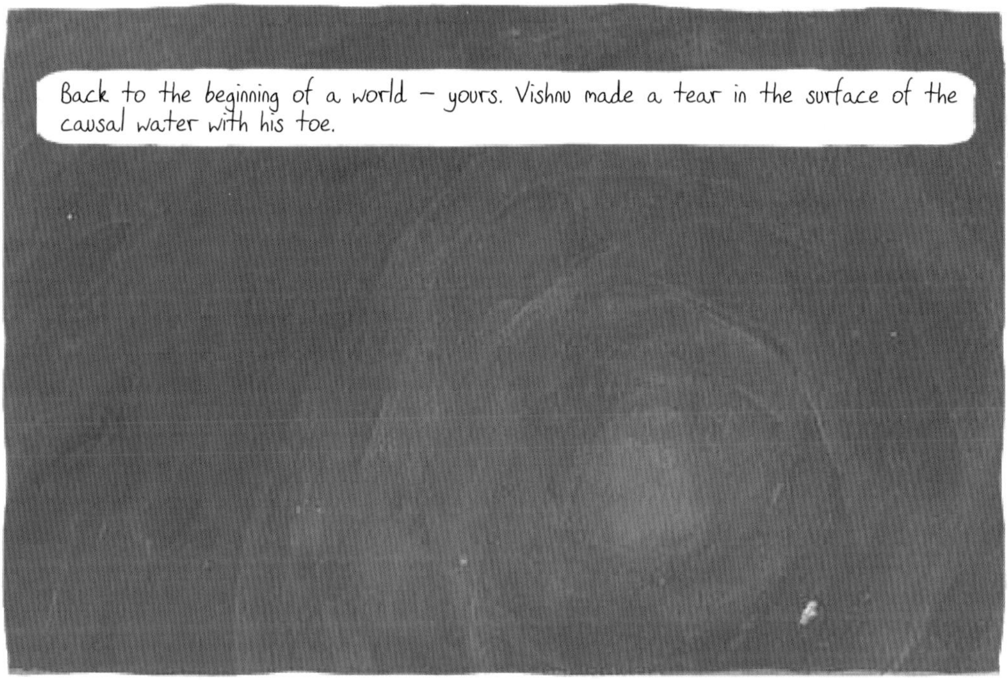
Back to the beginning of a world – yours. Vishnu made a tear in the surface of the causal water with his toe.

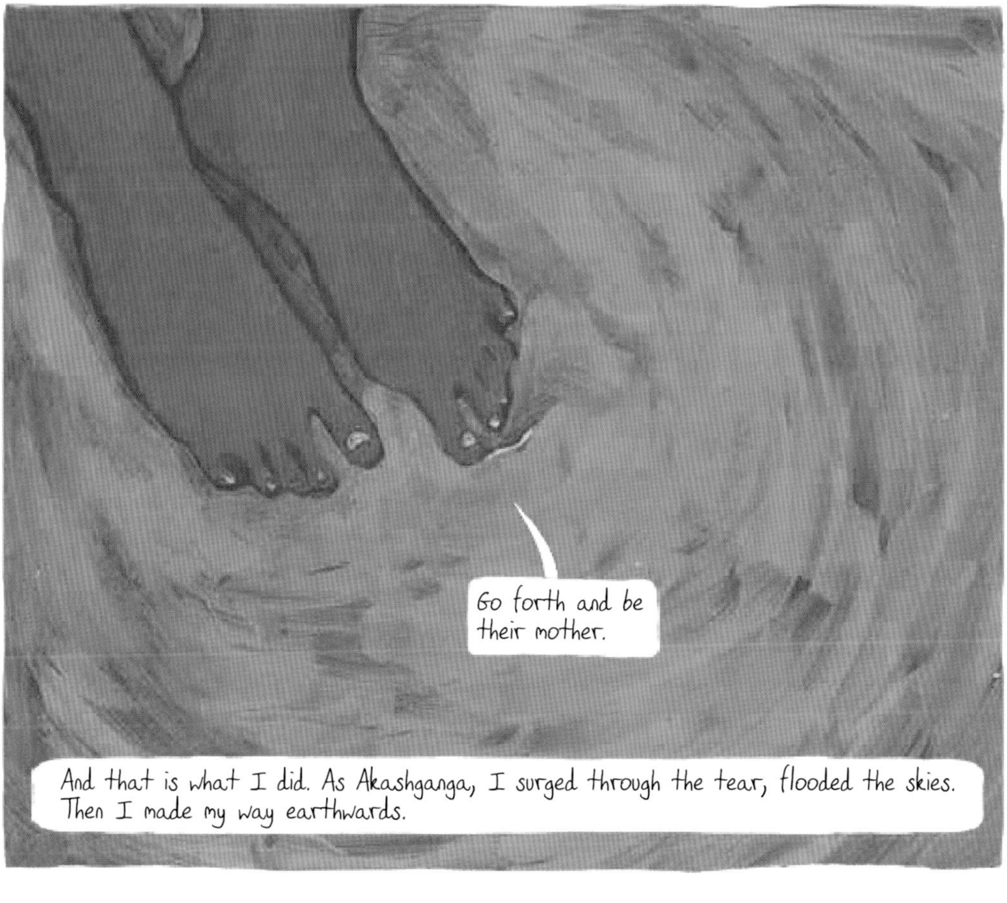
Go forth and be their mother.
And that is what I did. As Akashganga, I surged through the tear, flooded the skies. Then I made my way earthwards.

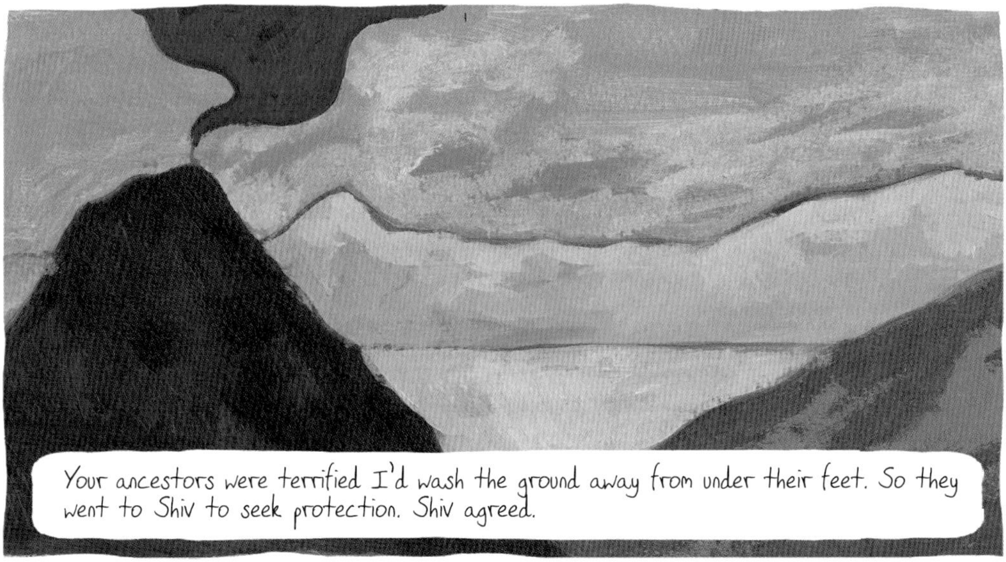
Your ancestors were terrified I'd wash the ground away from under their feet. So they went to Shiv to seek protection. Shiv agreed.

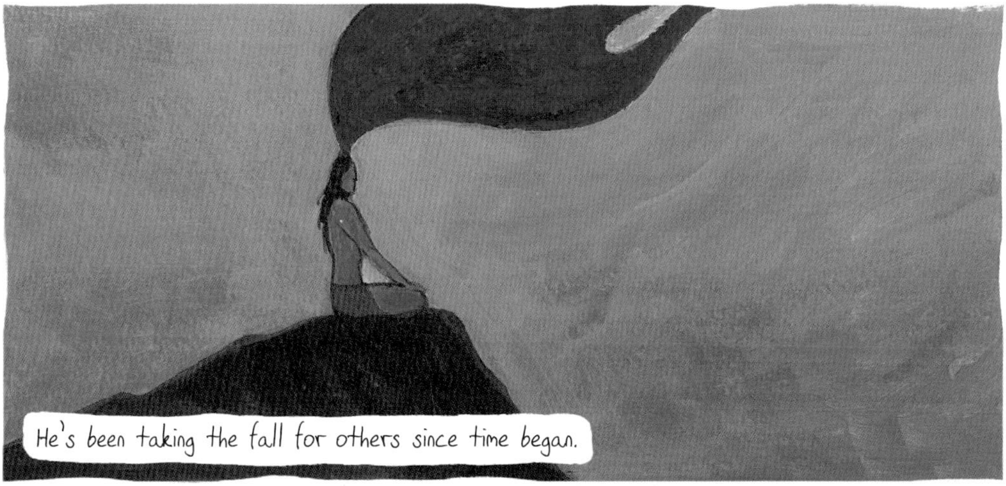
He's been taking the fall for others since time began.

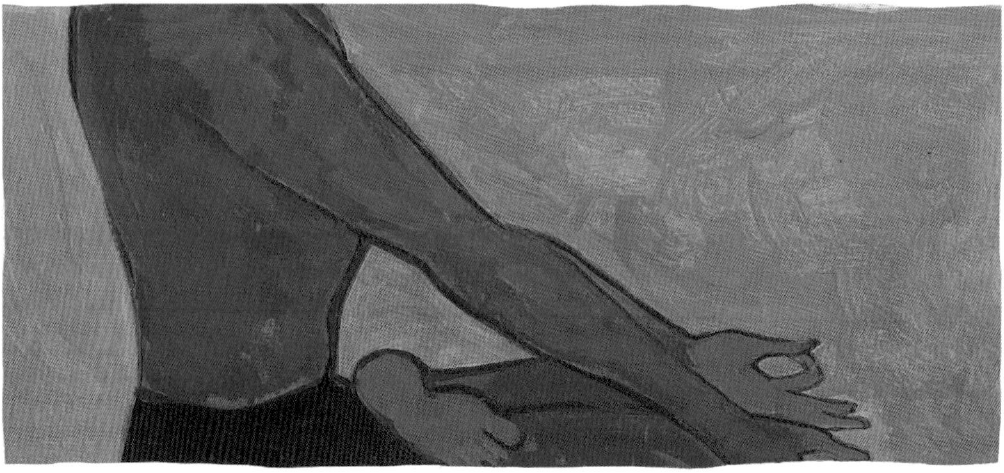

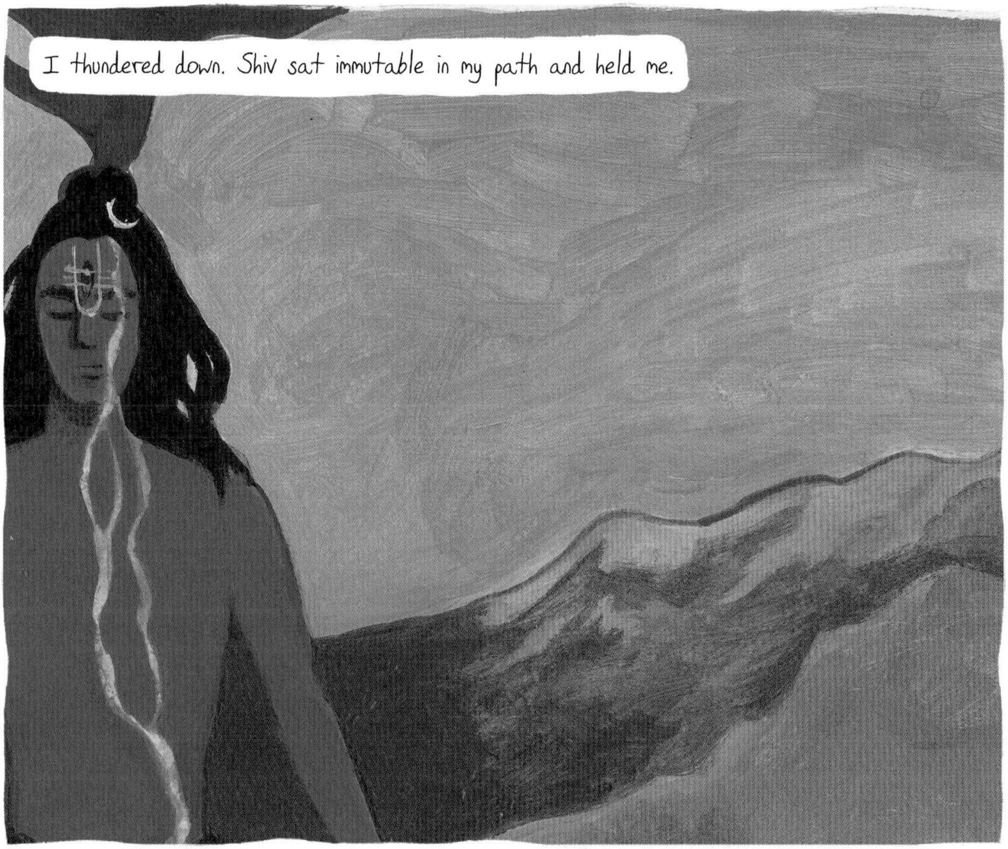
I thundered down. Shiv sat immutable in my path and held me.

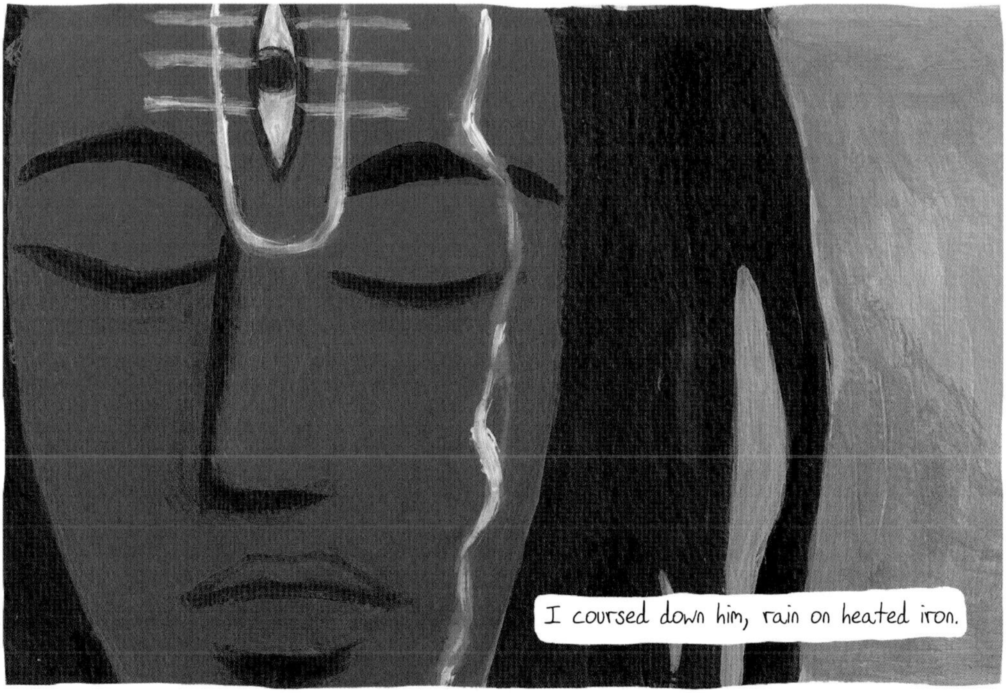
I coursed down him, rain on heated iron.

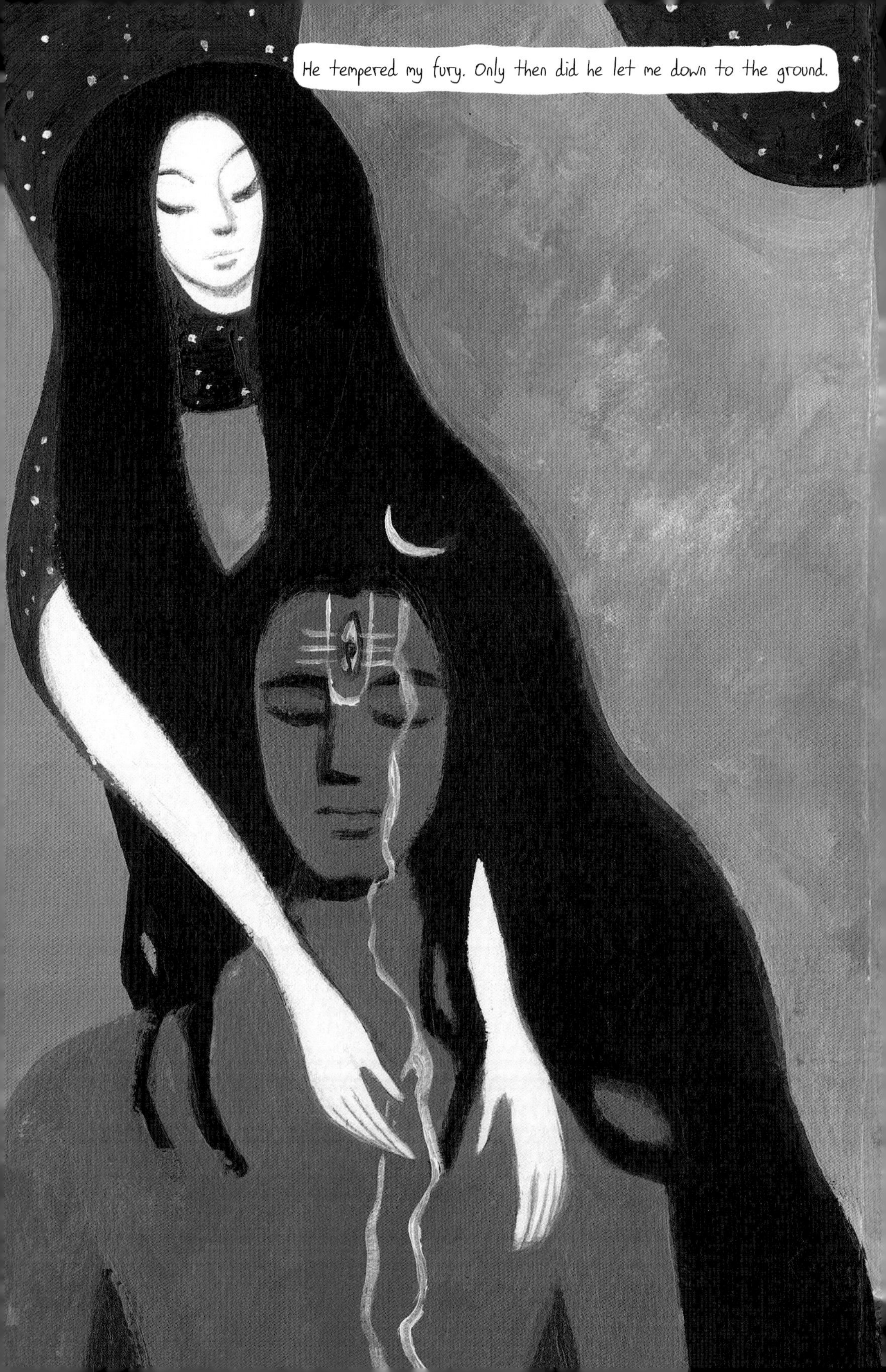
He tempered my fury. Only then did he let me down to the ground.

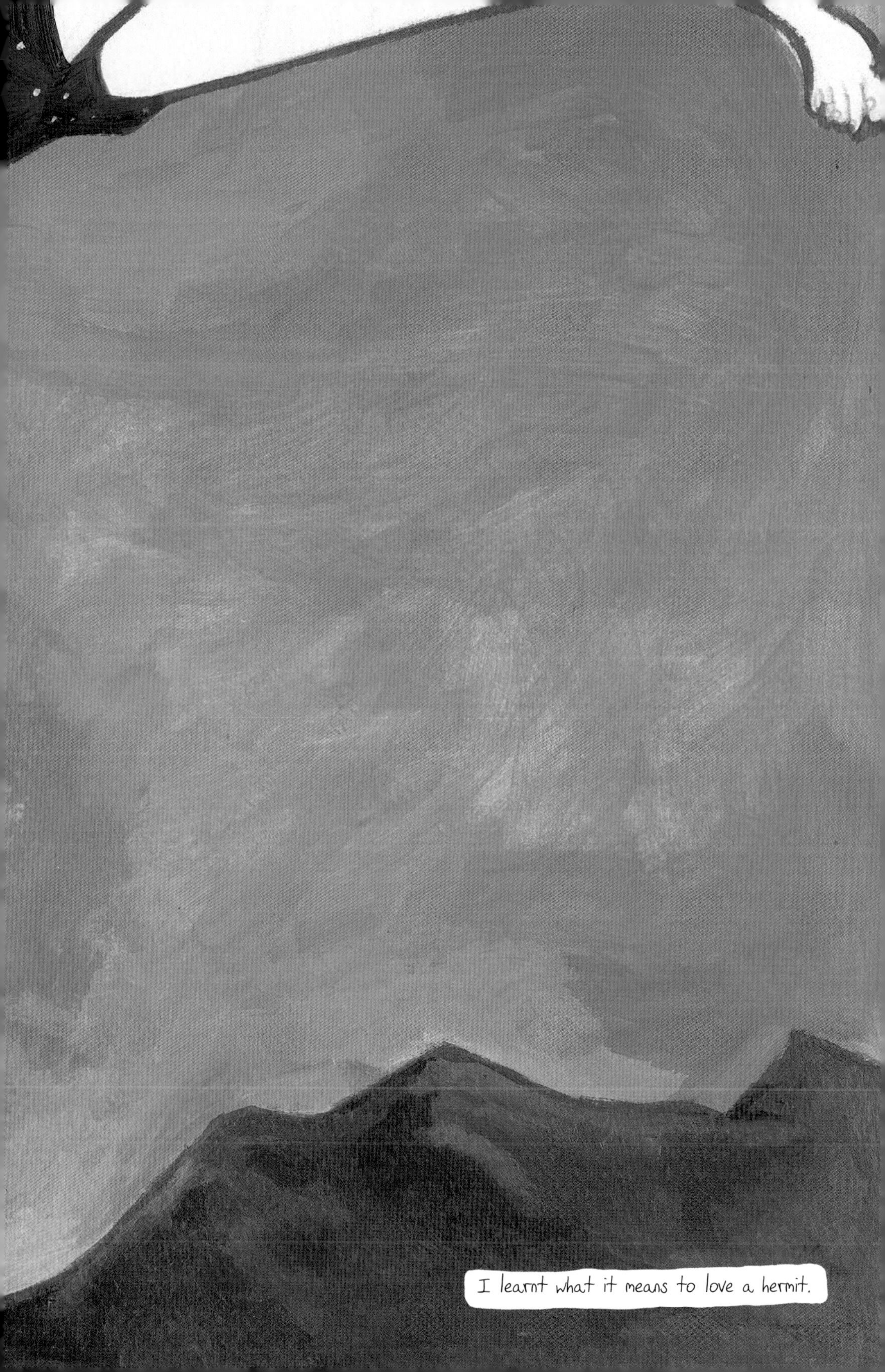
I learnt what it means to love a hermit.

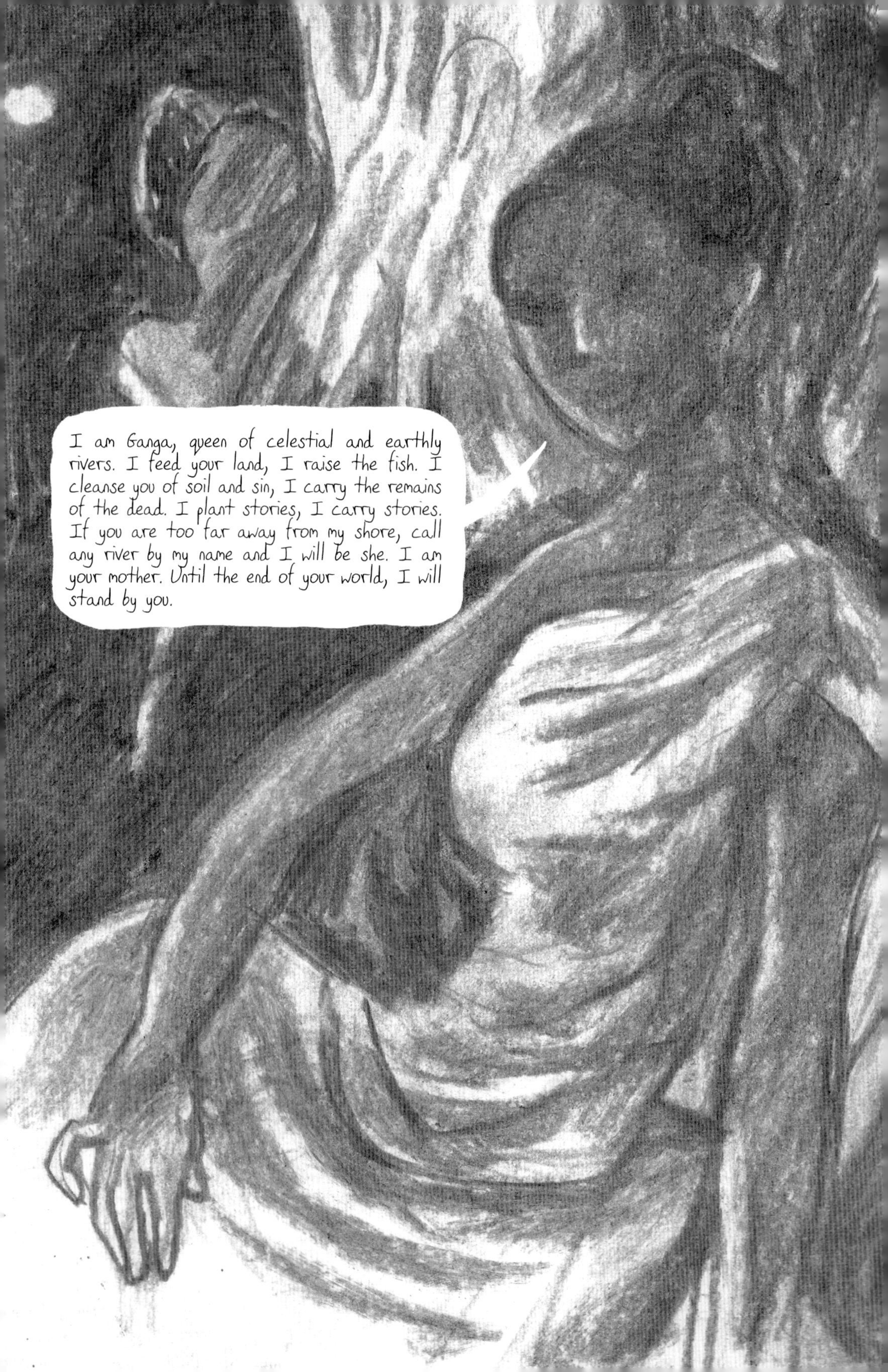
I am Ganga, queen of celestial and earthly rivers. I feed your land, I raise the fish. I cleanse you of soil and sin, I carry the remains of the dead. I plant stories, I carry stories. If you are too far away from my shore, call any river by my name and I will be she. I am your mother. Until the end of your world, I will stand by you.

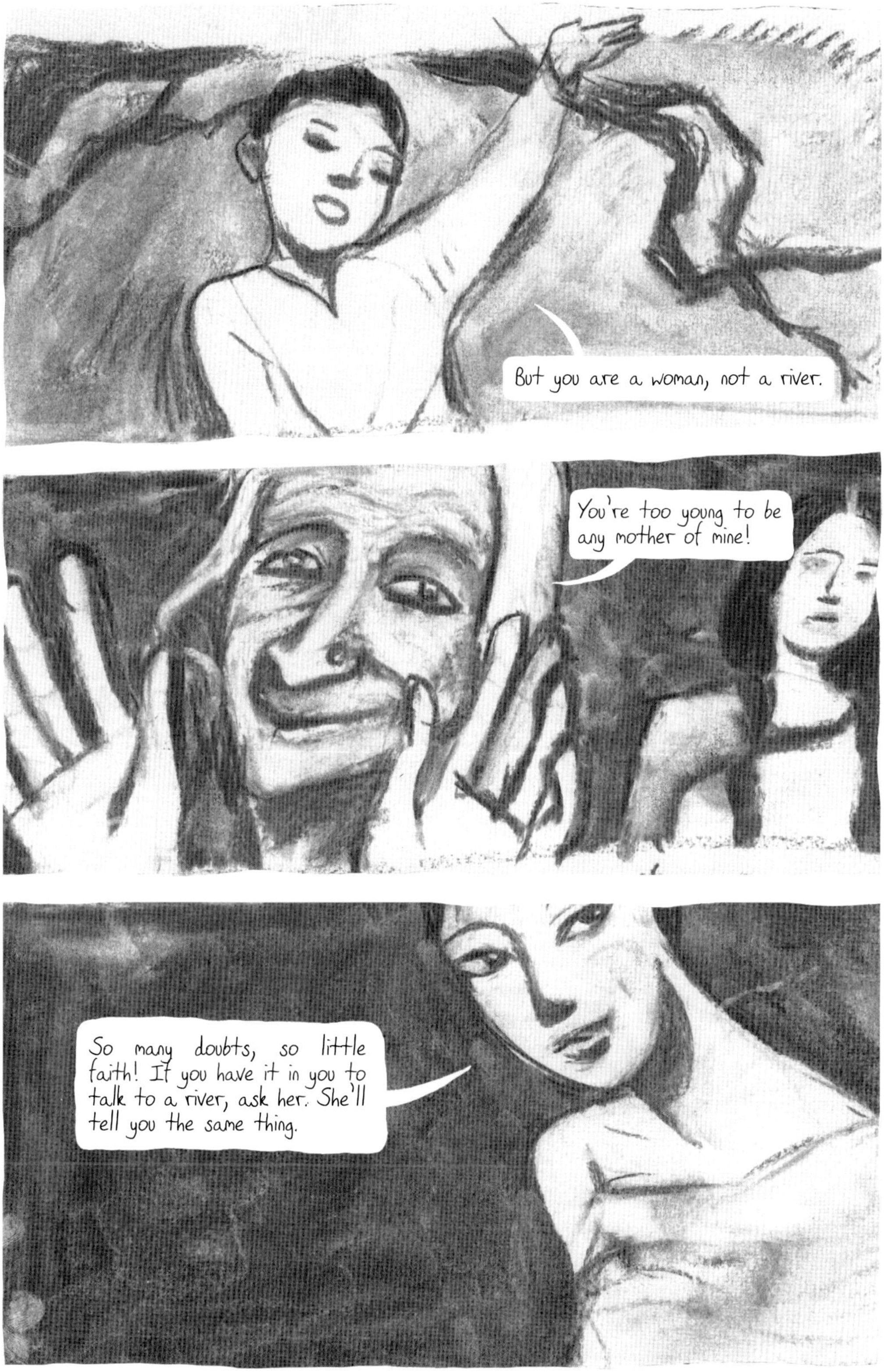
But you are a woman, not a river.
You're too young to be any mother of mine!
So many doubts, so little faith! If you have it in you to talk to a river, ask her. She'll tell you the same thing.

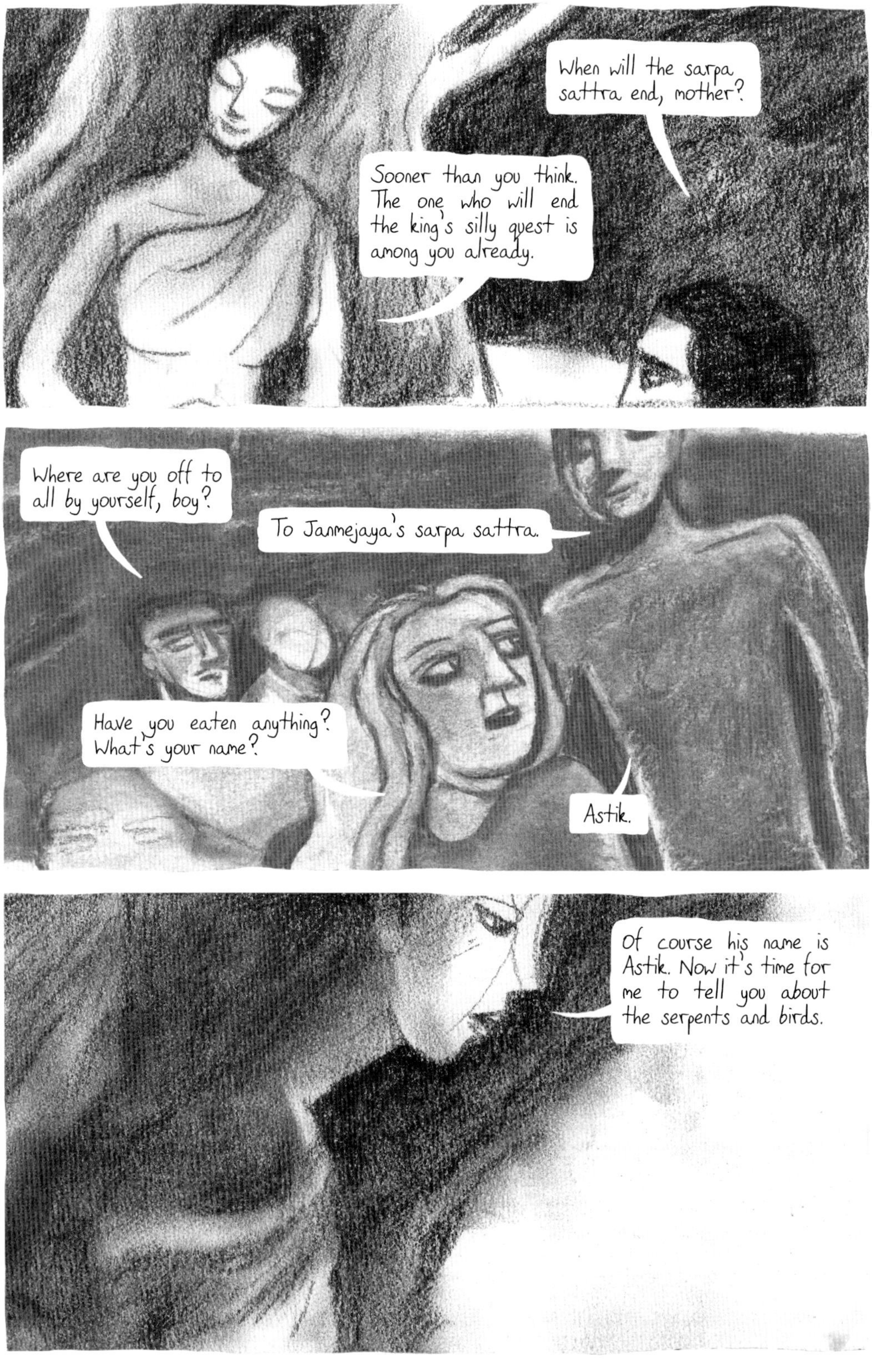
When will the sarpa sattra end, mother?
Sooner than you think. The one who will end the king's silly quest is among you already.
Where are you off to all by yourself, boy?
To Janmejaya's sarpa sattra.
Have you eaten anything? What's your name?
Astik.
Of course his name is Astik. Now it's time for me to tell you about the serpents and birds.

REPTILIAN MOTHER
AVIAN MOTHER

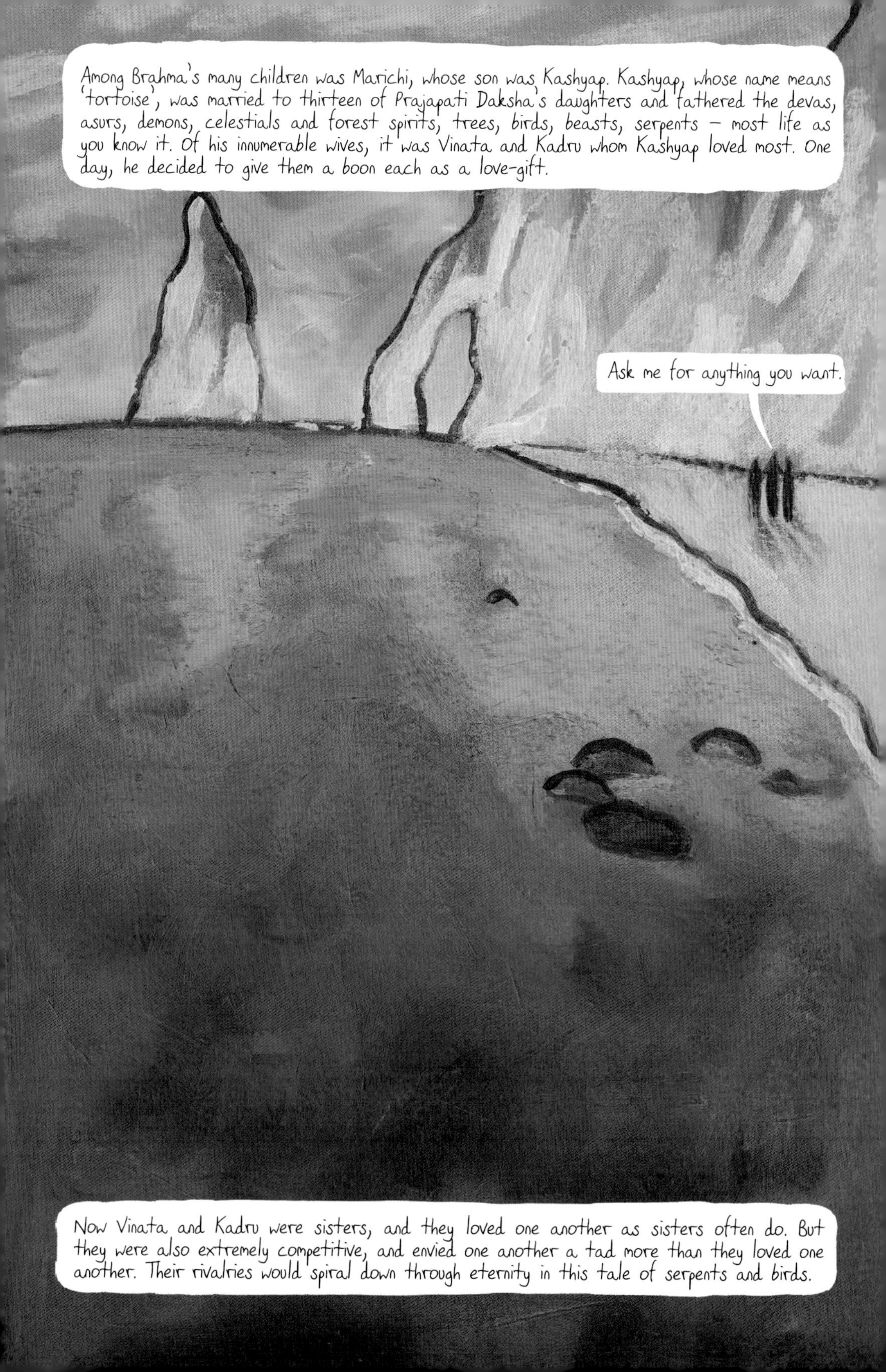
Among Brahma's many children was Marichi, whose son was Kashyap. Kashyap, whose name means 'tortoise', was married to thirteen of Prajapati Daksha's daughters and fathered the devas, asurs, demons, celestials and forest spirits, trees, birds, beasts, serpents – most life as you know it. Of his innumerable wives, it was Vinata and Kadru whom Kashyap loved most. One day, he decided to give them a boon each as a love-gift.
Ask me for anything you want.
Now Vinata and Kadru were sisters, and they loved one another as sisters often do. But they were also extremely competitive, and envied one another a tad more than they loved one another. Their rivalries would spiral down through eternity in this tale of serpents and birds.

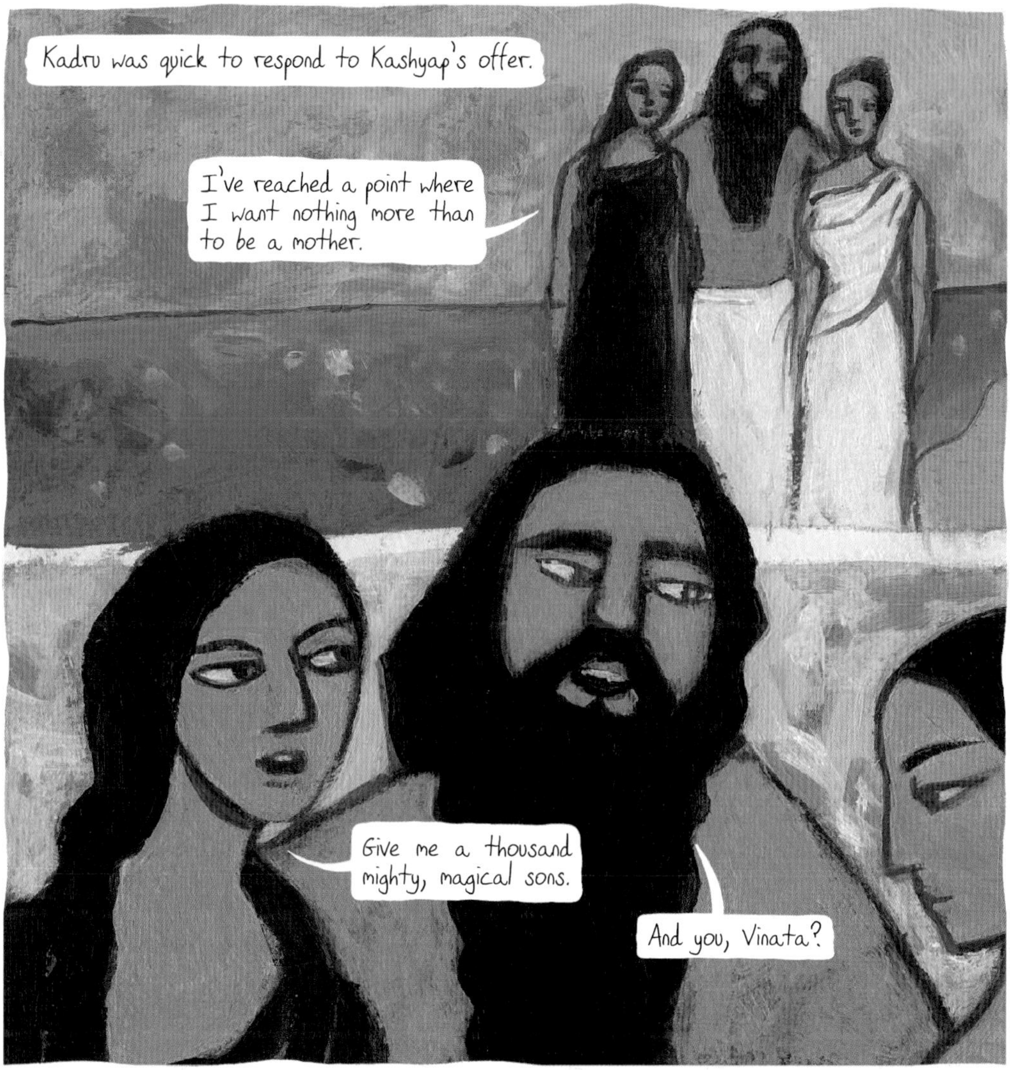
Kadru was quick to respond to Kashyap's offer.
I've reached a point where I want nothing more than to be a mother.
Give me a thousand mighty, magical sons.
And you, Vinata?

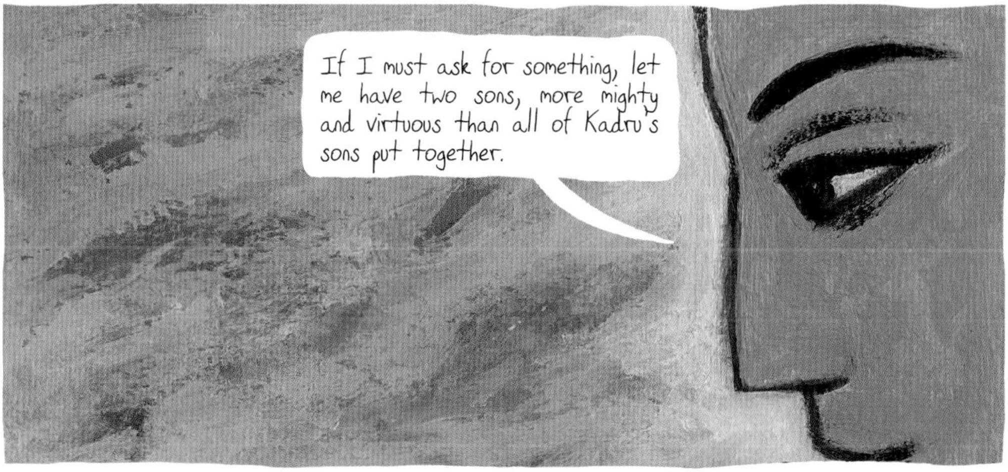
If I must ask for something, let me have two sons, more mighty and virtuous than all of Kadru's sons put together.

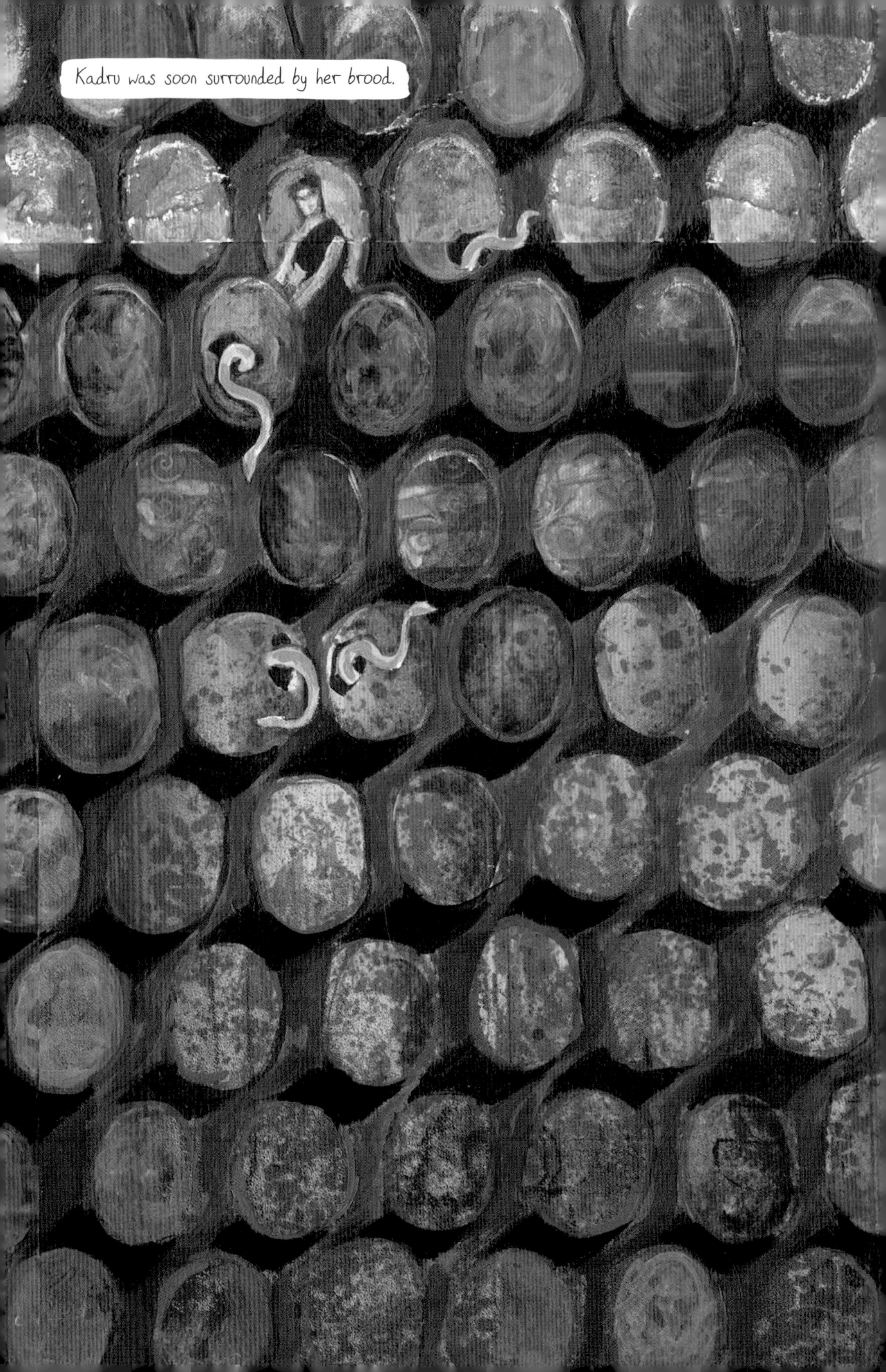
Kadru was soon surrounded by her brood.

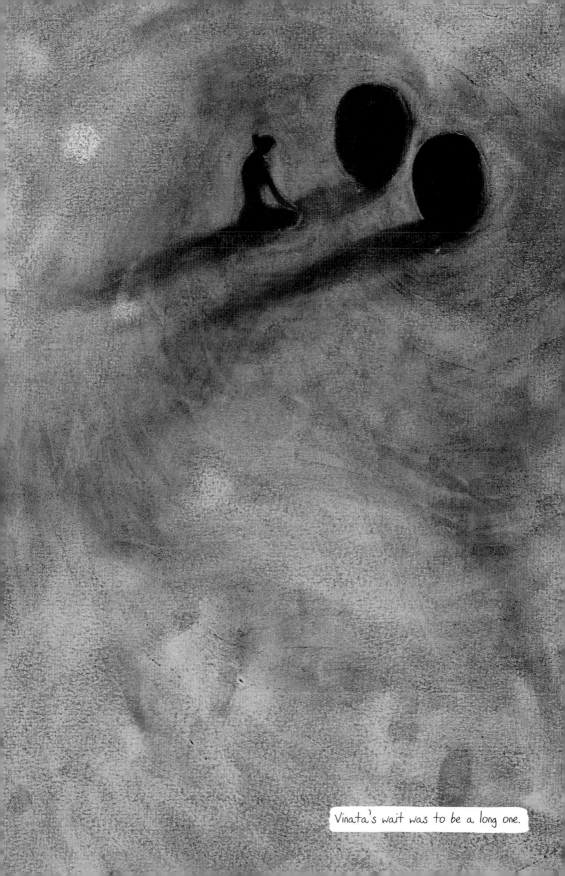

Vinata's wait was to be a long one.

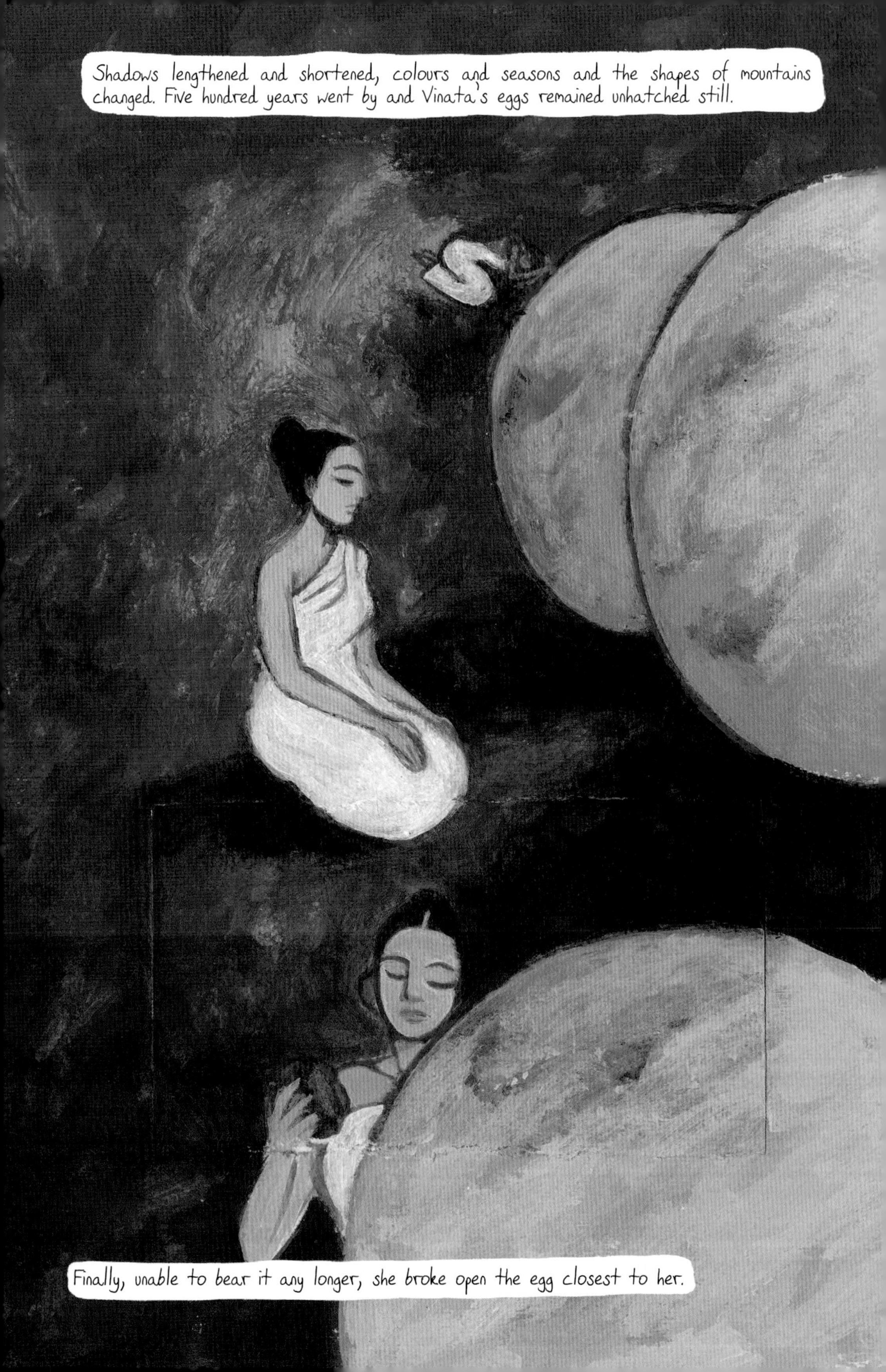
Shadows lengthened and shortened, colours and seasons and the shapes of mountains changed. Five hundred years went by and Vinata's eggs remained unhatched still.
Finally, unable to bear it any longer, she broke open the egg closest to her.

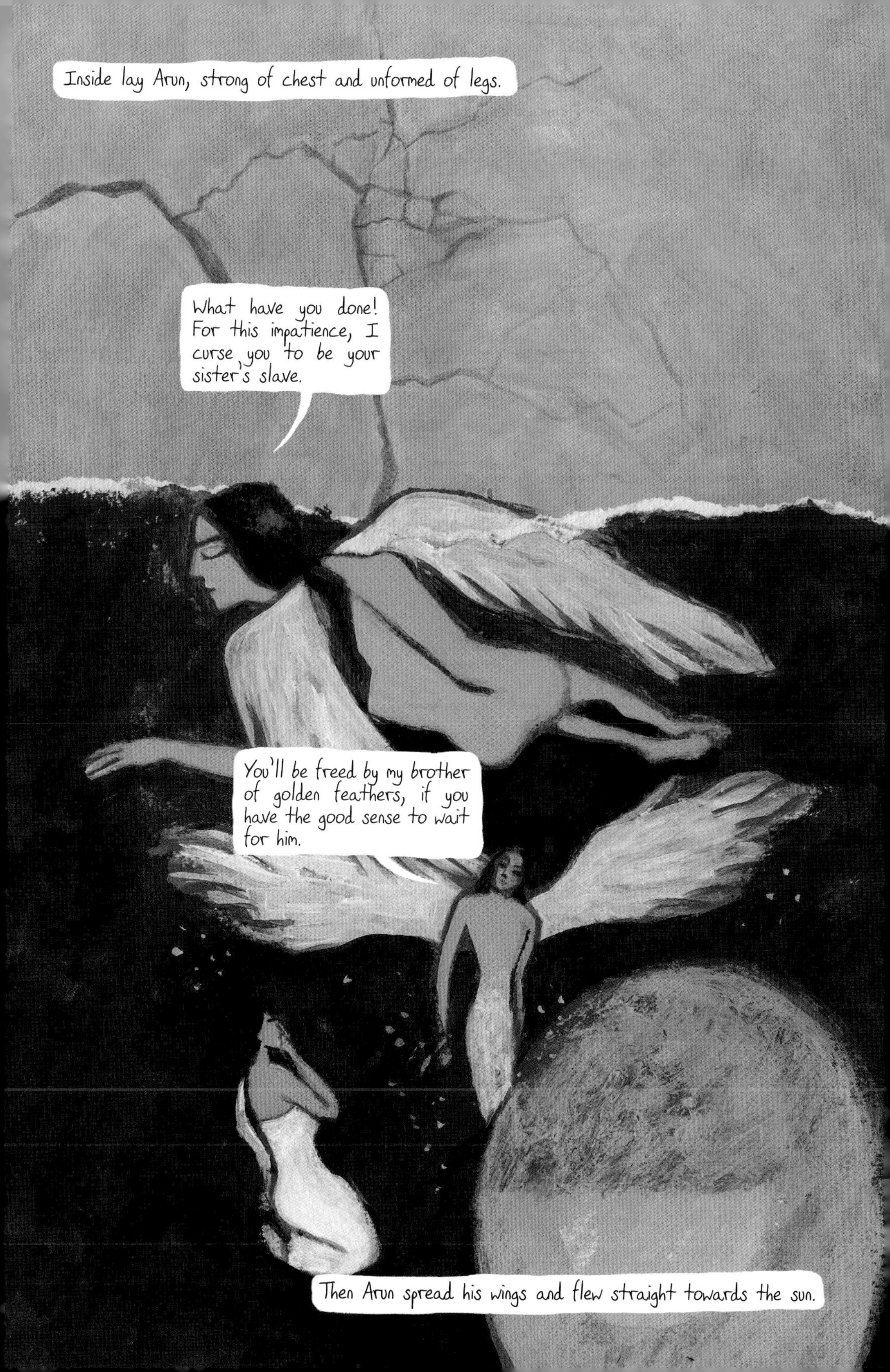
Inside lay Arun, strong of chest and unformed of legs.
What have you done! For this impatience, I curse you to be your sister's slave.
You'll be freed by my brother of golden feathers, if you have the good sense to wait for him.
Then Arun spread his wings and flew straight towards the sun.

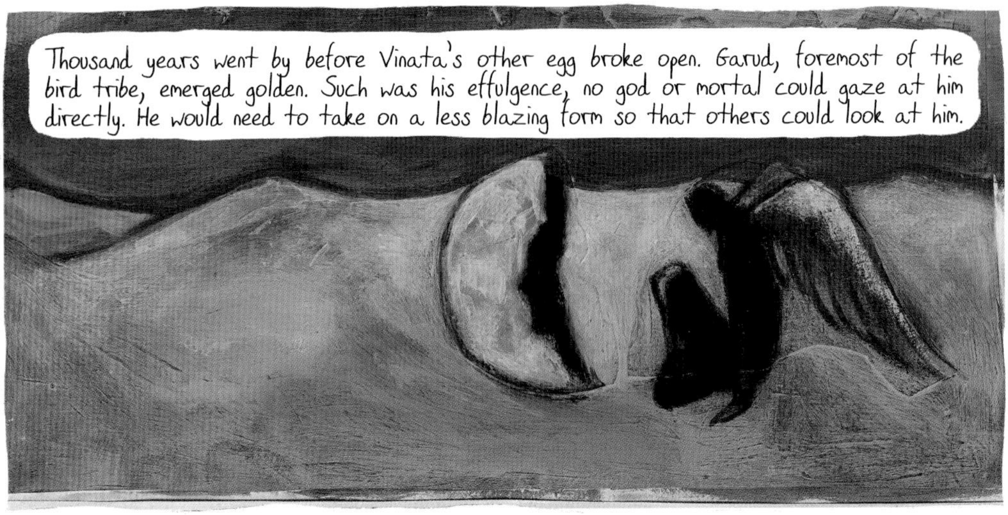
Thousand years went by before Vinata's other egg broke open. Garud, foremost of the bird tribe, emerged golden. Such was his effulgence, no god or mortal could gaze at him directly. He would need to take on a less blazing form so that others could look at him.

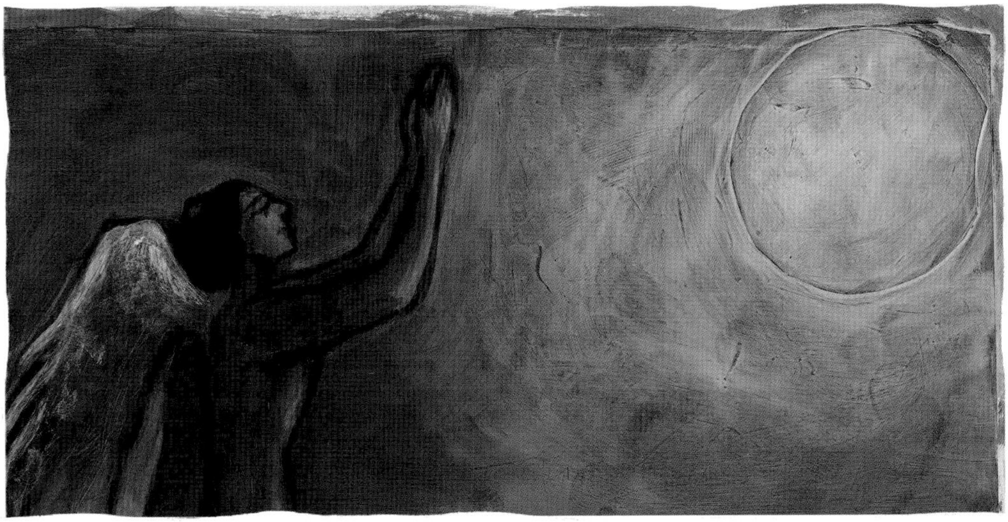

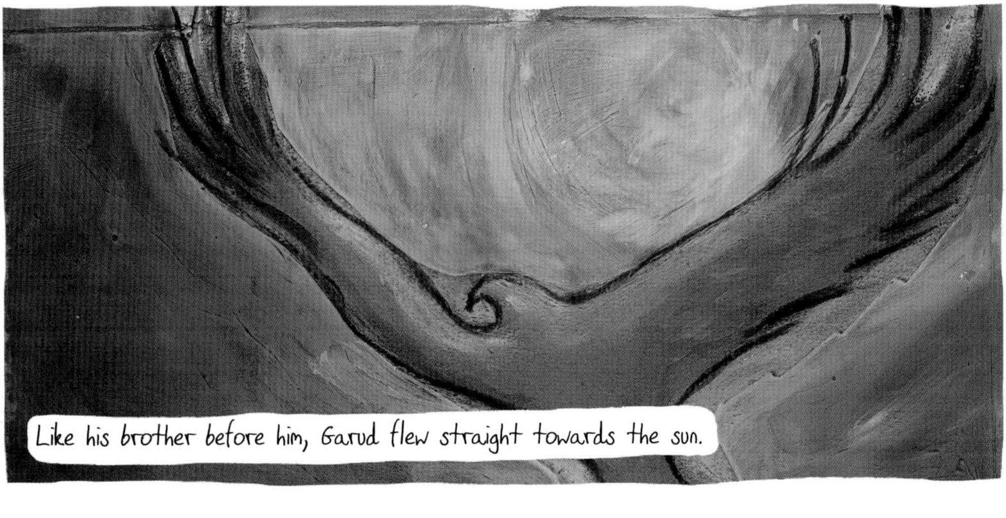
Like his brother before him, Garud flew straight towards the sun.

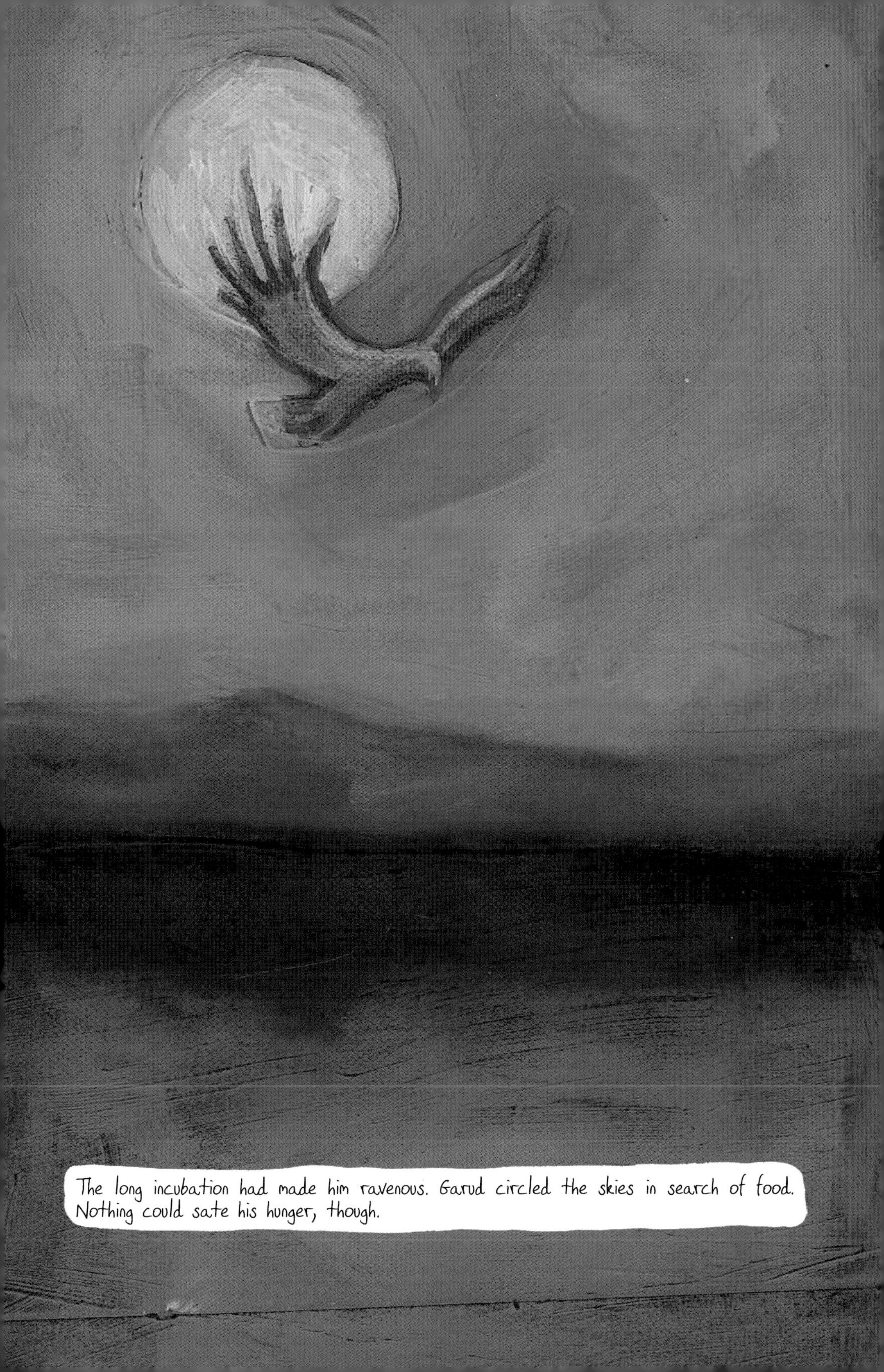
The long incubation had made him ravenous. Garud circled the skies in search of food. Nothing could sate his hunger, though.

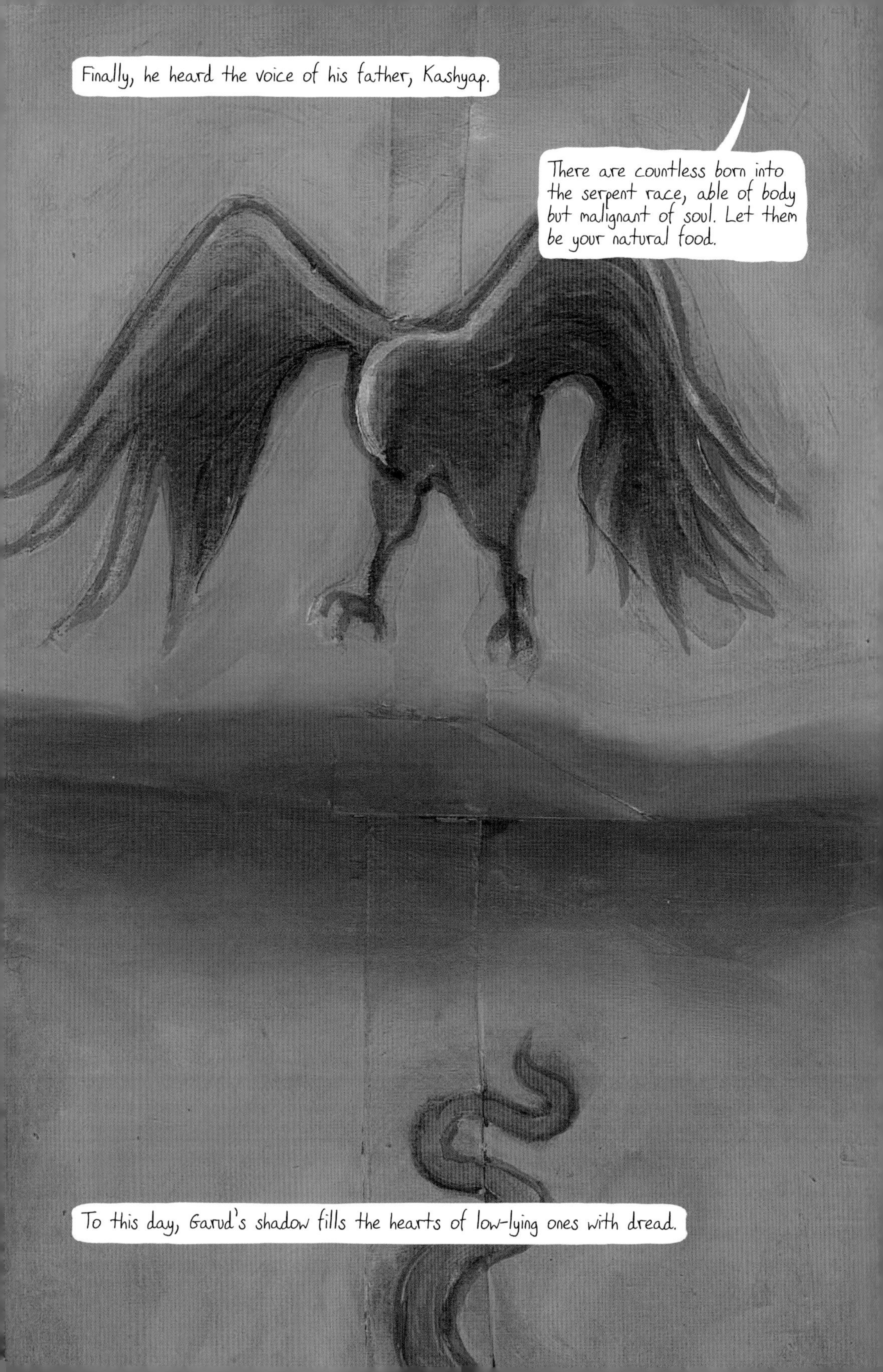
Finally, he heard the voice of his father, Kashyap.
There are countless born into the serpent race, able of body but malignant of soul. Let them be your natural food.
To this day, Garud's shadow fills the hearts of low-lying ones with dread.

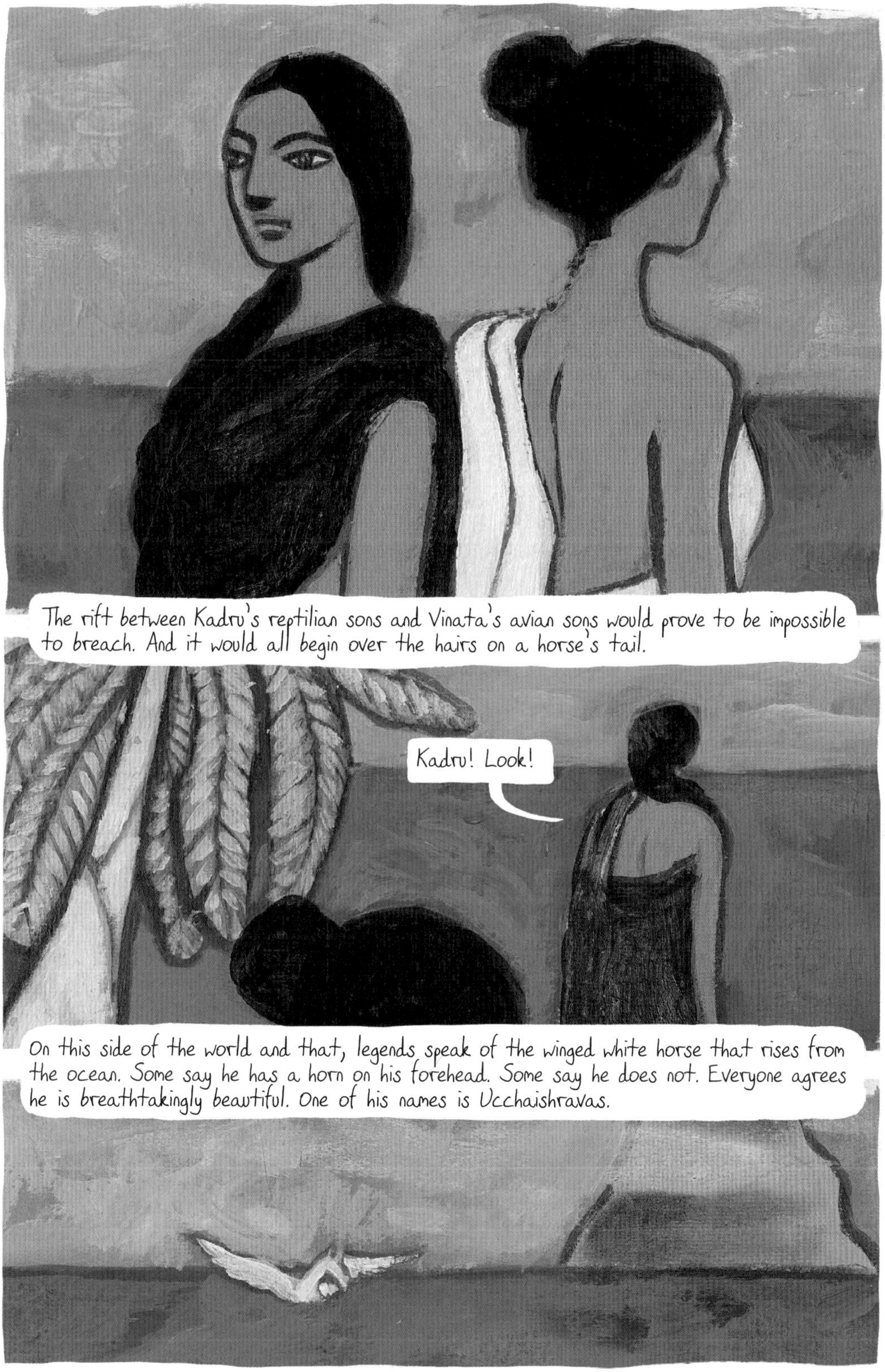
The rift between Kadru's reptilian sons and Vinata's avian sons would prove to be impossible to breach. And it would all begin over the hairs on a horse's tail.
Kadru! Look!
On this side of the world and that, legends speak of the winged white horse that rises from the ocean. Some say he has a horn on his forehead. Some say he does not. Everyone agrees he is breathtakingly beautiful. One of his names is Ucchaishravas.

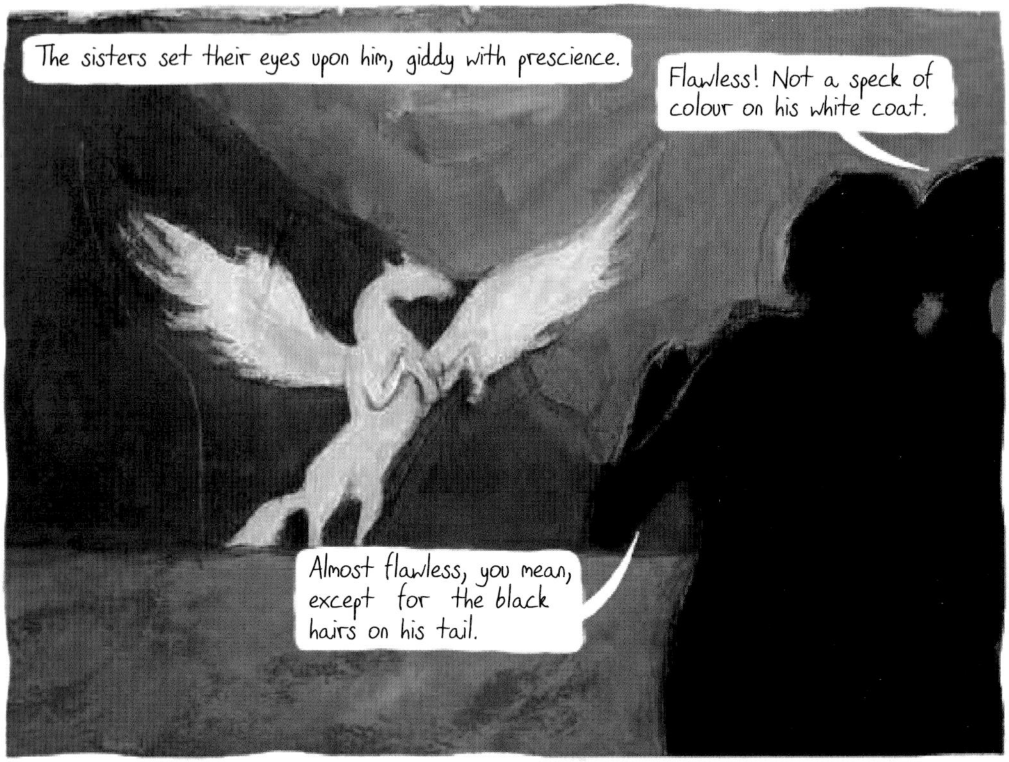
The sisters set their eyes upon him, giddy with prescience.
Flawless! Not a speck of colour on his white coat.
Almost flawless, you mean, except for the black hairs on his tail.

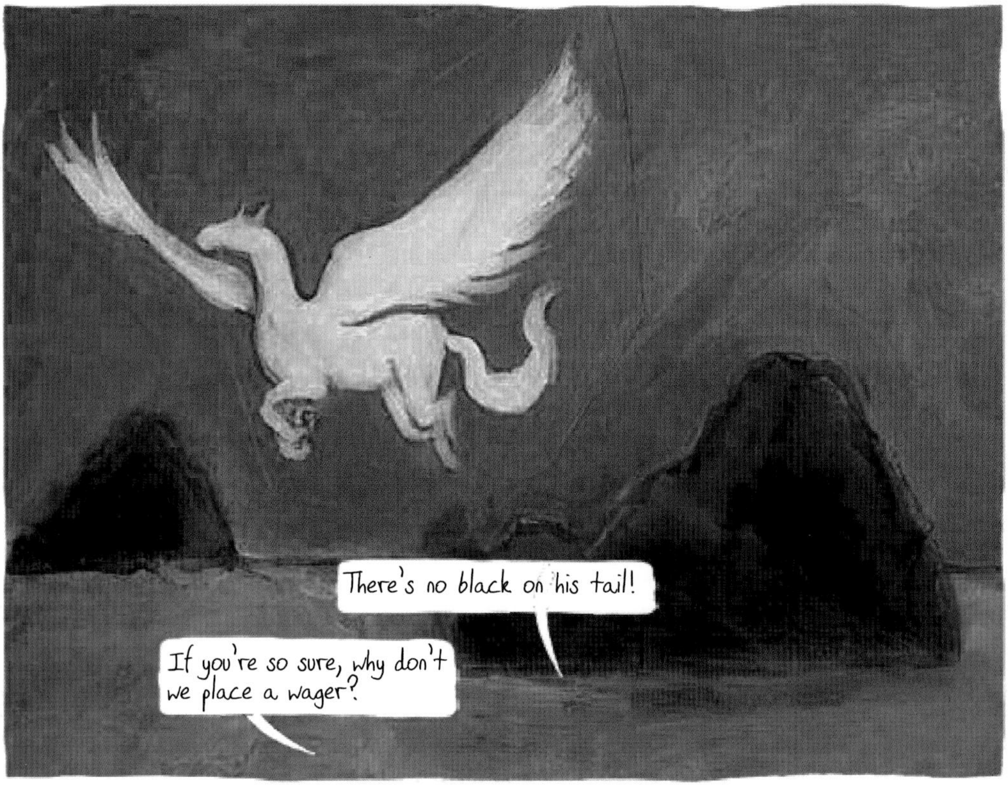
There's no black on his tail!
If you're so sure, why don't we place a wager?

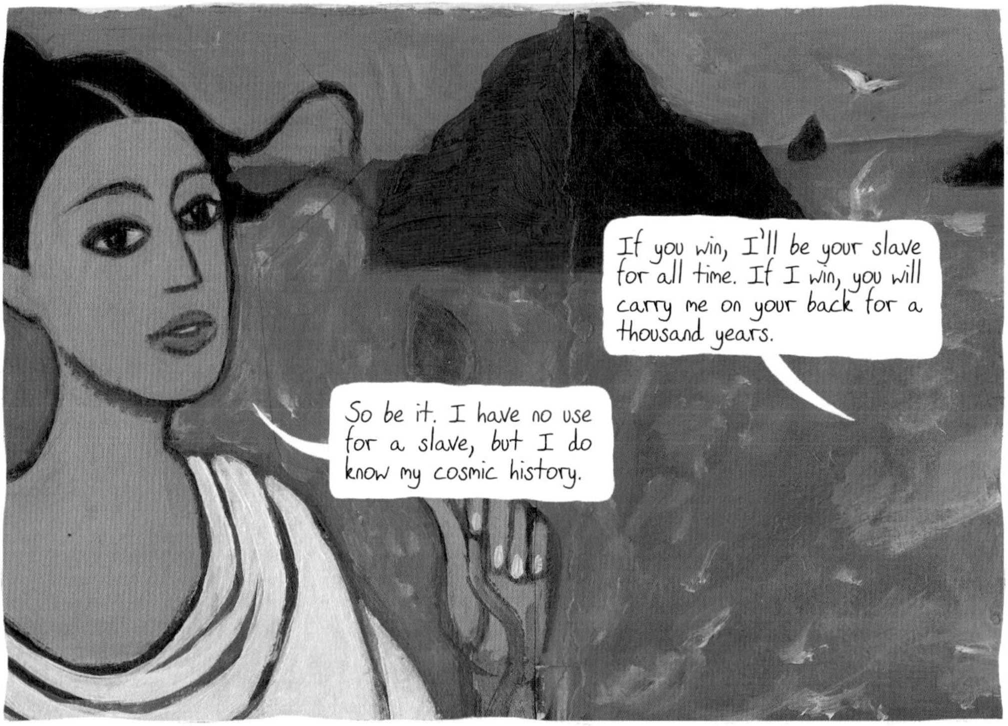
If you win, I'll be your slave for all time. If I win, you will carry me on your back for a thousand years.
So be it. I have no use for a slave, but I do know my cosmic history.

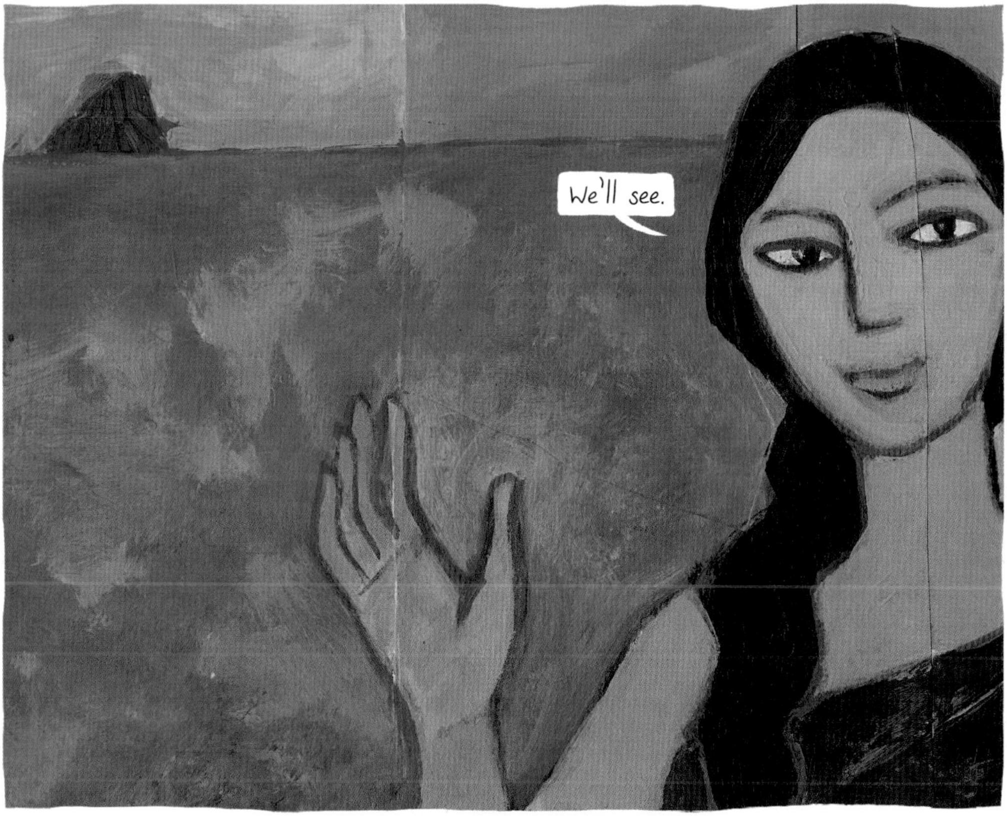
We'll see.

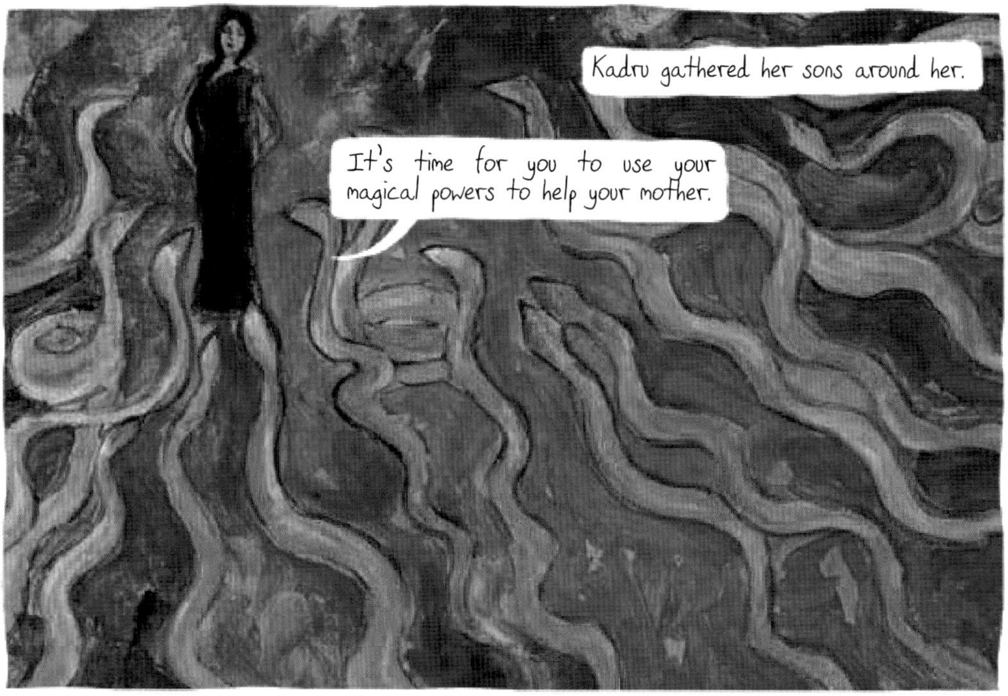
Kadru gathered her sons around her.
It's time for you to use your magical powers to help your mother.

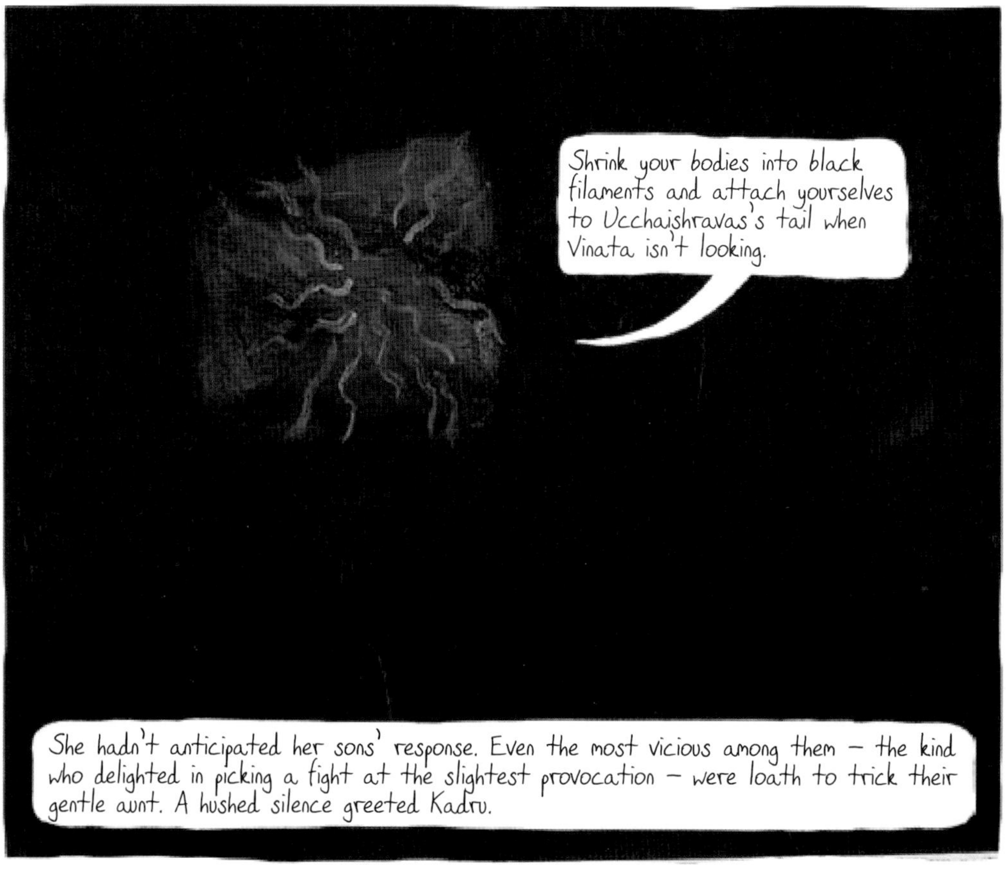
Shrink your bodies into black filaments and attach yourselves to Ucchaishravas's tail when Vinata isn't looking.
She hadn't anticipated her sons' response. Even the most vicious among them – the kind who delighted in picking a fight at the slightest provocation – were loath to trick their gentle aunt. A hushed silence greeted Kadru.

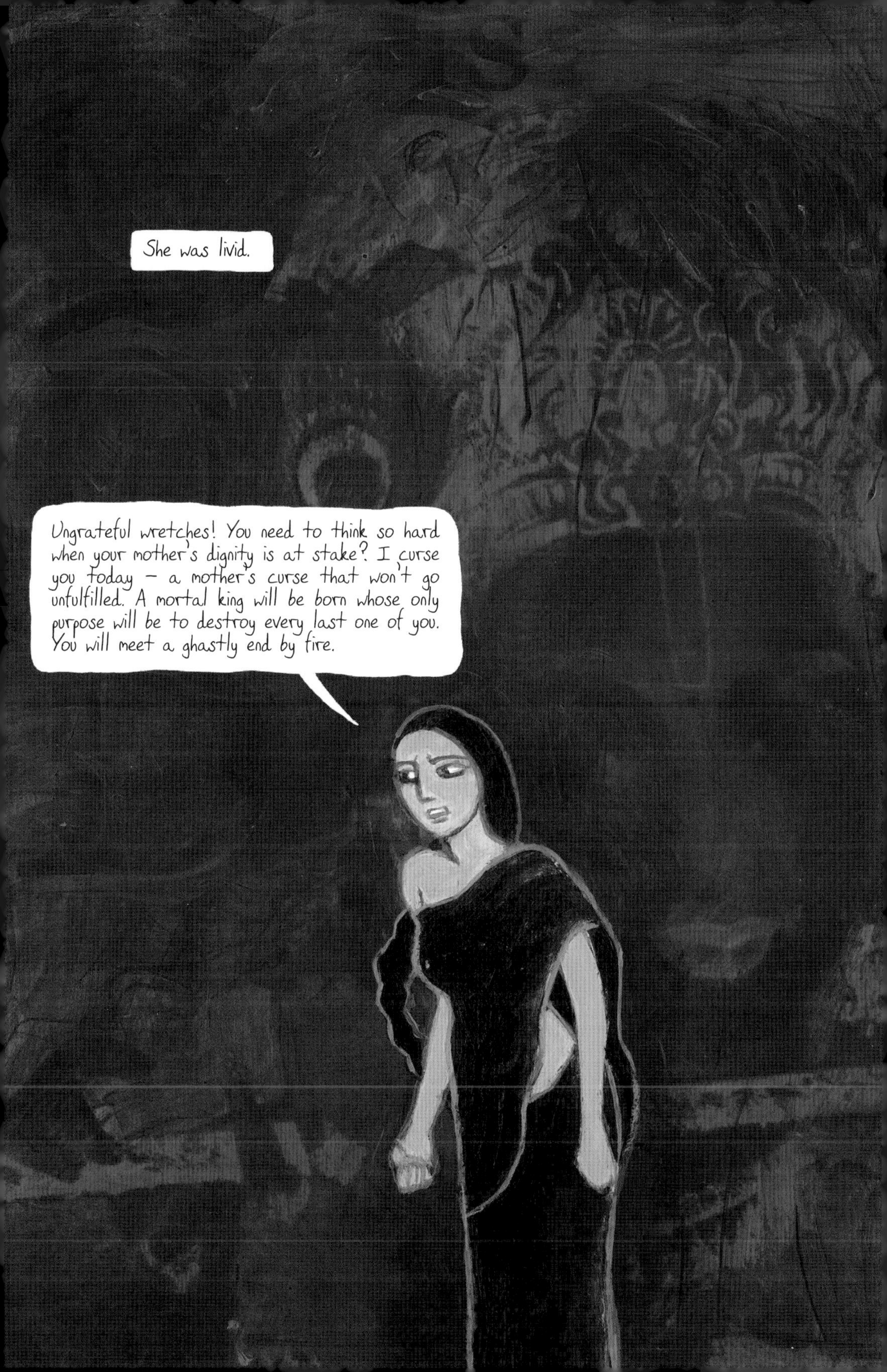
She was livid.
Ungrateful wretches! You need to think so hard when your mother's dignity is at stake? I curse you today – a mother's curse that won't go unfulfilled. A mortal king will be born whose only purpose will be to destroy every last one of you. You will meet a ghastly end by fire.

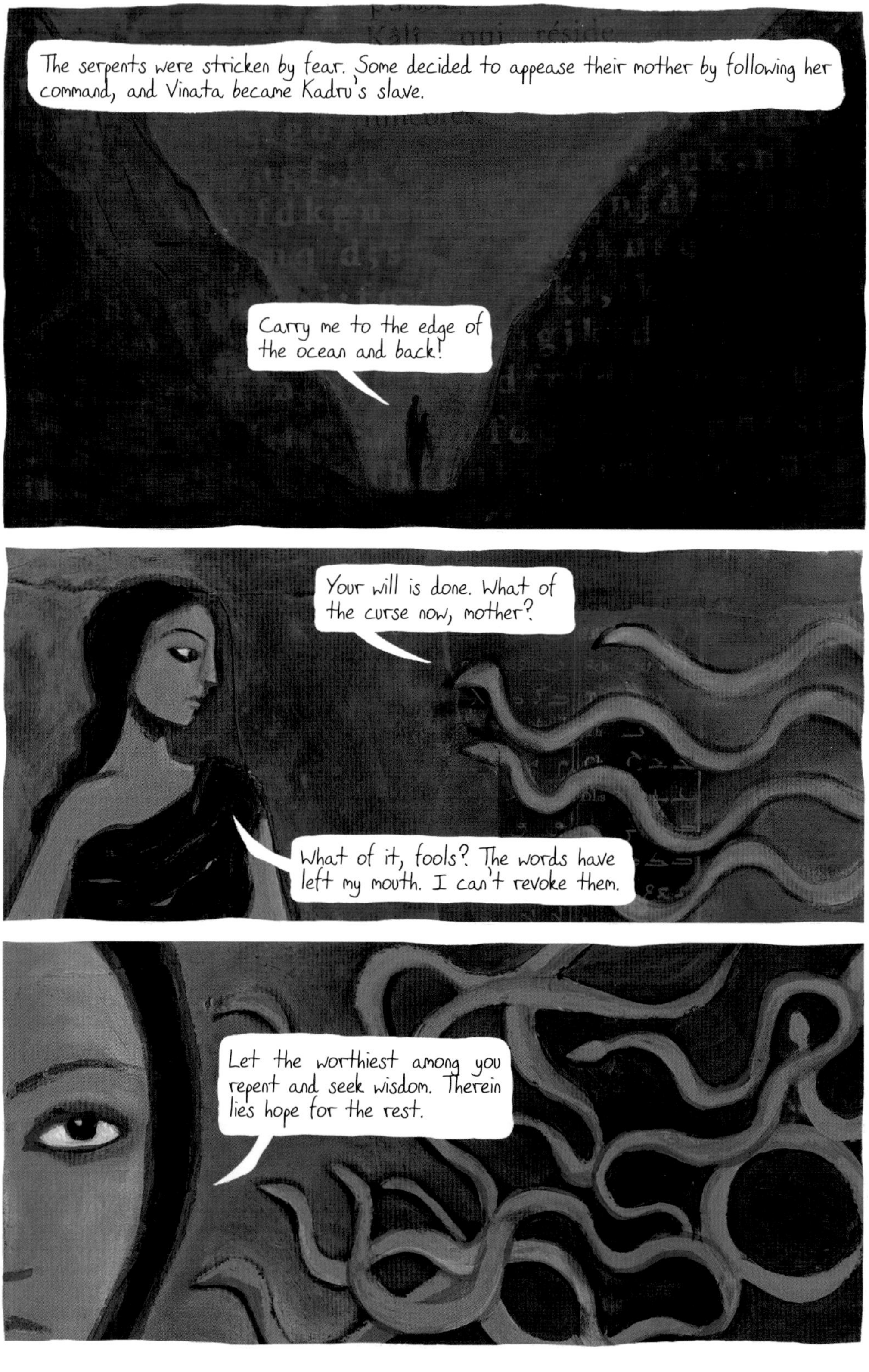
The serpents were stricken by fear. Some decided to appease their mother by following her command, and Vinata became Kadru's slave.
Carry me to the edge of the ocean and back!
Your will is done. What of the curse now, mother?
What of it, fools? The words have left my mouth. I can't revoke them.
Let the worthiest among you repent and seek wisdom. Therein lies hope for the rest.

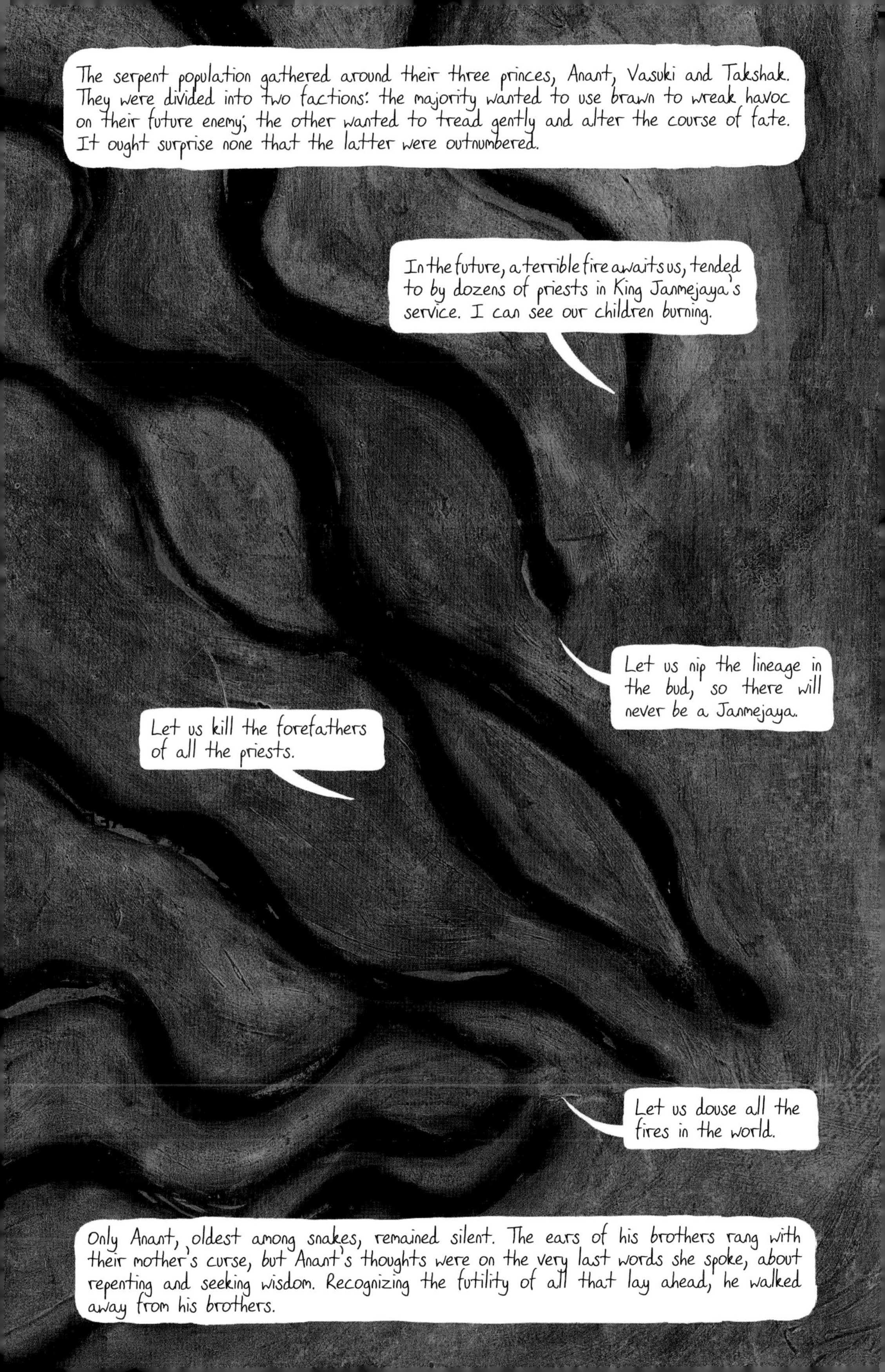
The serpent population gathered around their three princes, Anant, Vasuki and Takshak. They were divided into two factions: the majority wanted to use brawn to wreak havoc on their future enemy; the other wanted to tread gently and alter the course of fate. It ought surprise none that the latter were outnumbered.
In the future, a terrible fire awaits us, tended to by dozens of priests in King Janmejaya's service. I can see our children burning.
Let us nip the lineage in the bud, so there will never be a Janmejaya.
Let us kill the forefathers of all the priests.
Let us douse all the fires in the world.
Only Anant, oldest among snakes, remained silent. The ears of his brothers rang with their mother's curse, but Anant's thoughts were on the very last words she spoke, about repenting and seeking wisdom. Recognizing the futility of all that lay ahead, he walked away from his brothers.

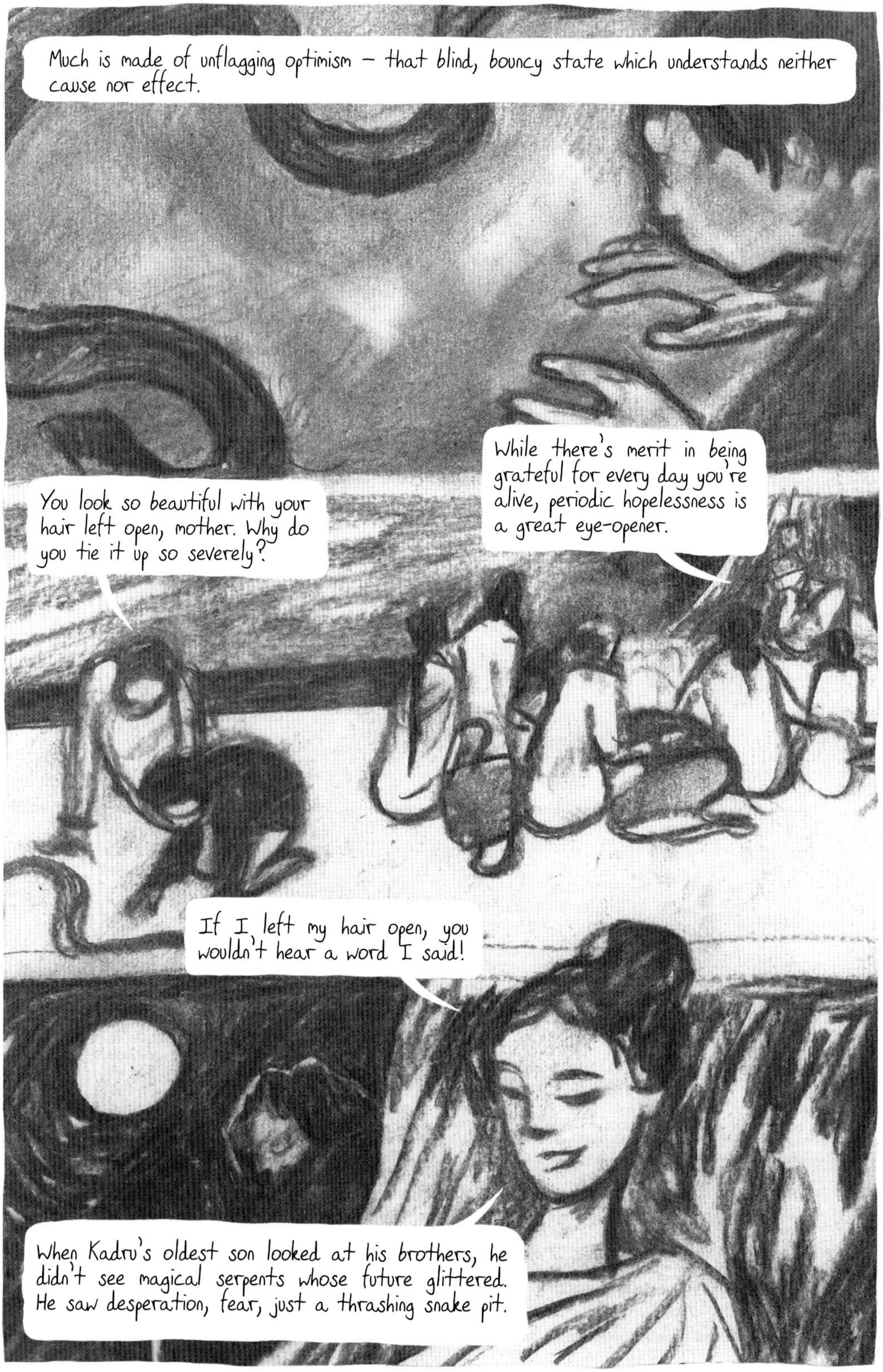
Much is made of unflagging optimism – that blind, bouncy state which understands neither cause nor effect.
You look so beautiful with your hair left open, mother. Why do you tie it up so severely?
While there's merit in being grateful for every day you're alive, periodic hopelessness is a great eye-opener.
If I left my hair open, you wouldn't hear a word I said!
When Kadru's oldest son looked at his brothers, he didn't see magical serpents whose future glittered. He saw desperation, fear, just a thrashing snake pit.

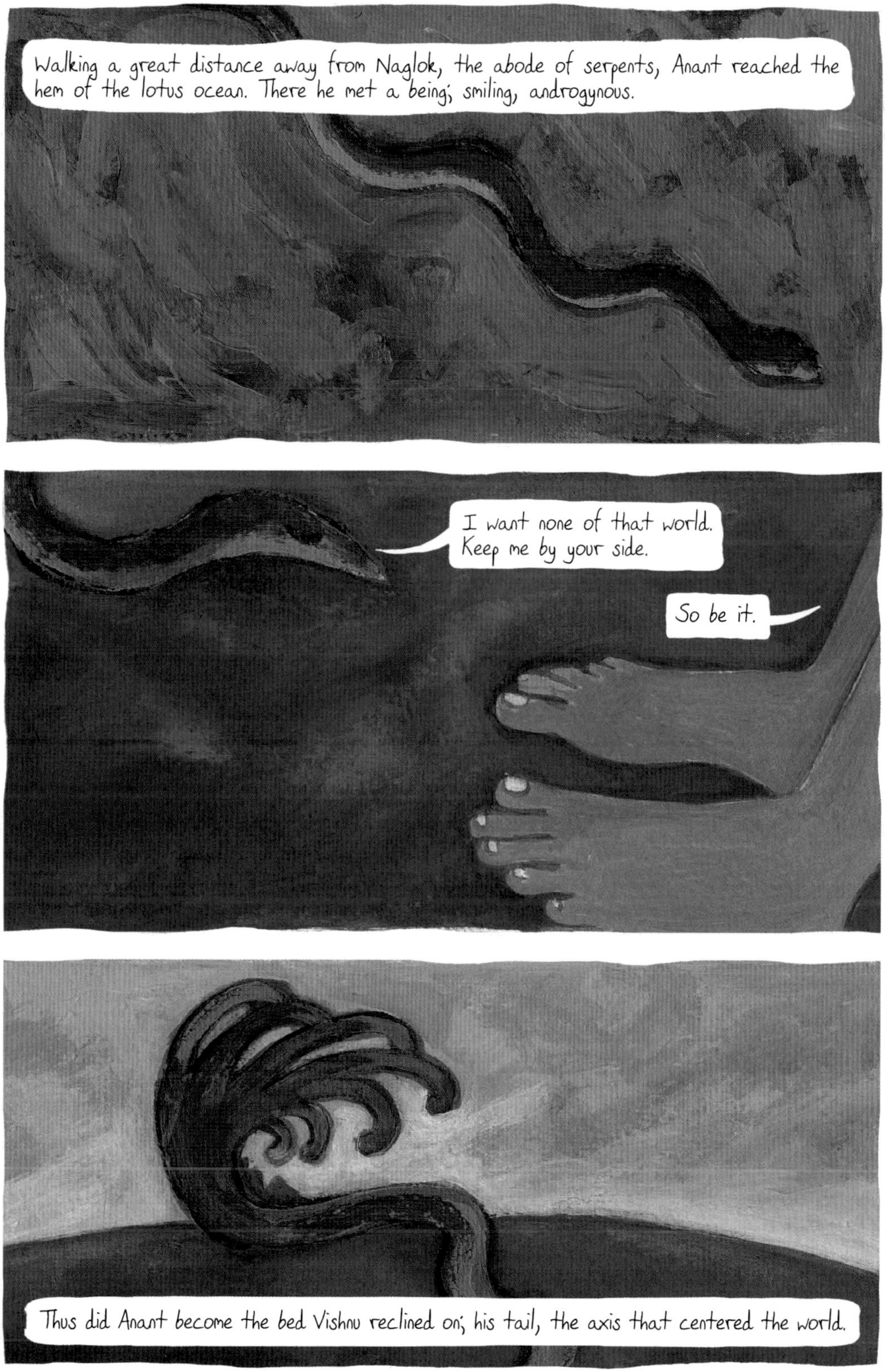
Walking a great distance away from Naglok, the abode of serpents, Anant reached the hem of the lotus ocean. There he met a being; smiling, androgynous.
I want none of that world. Keep me by your side.
So be it.
Thus did Anant become the bed Vishnu reclined on; his tail, the axis that centered the world.

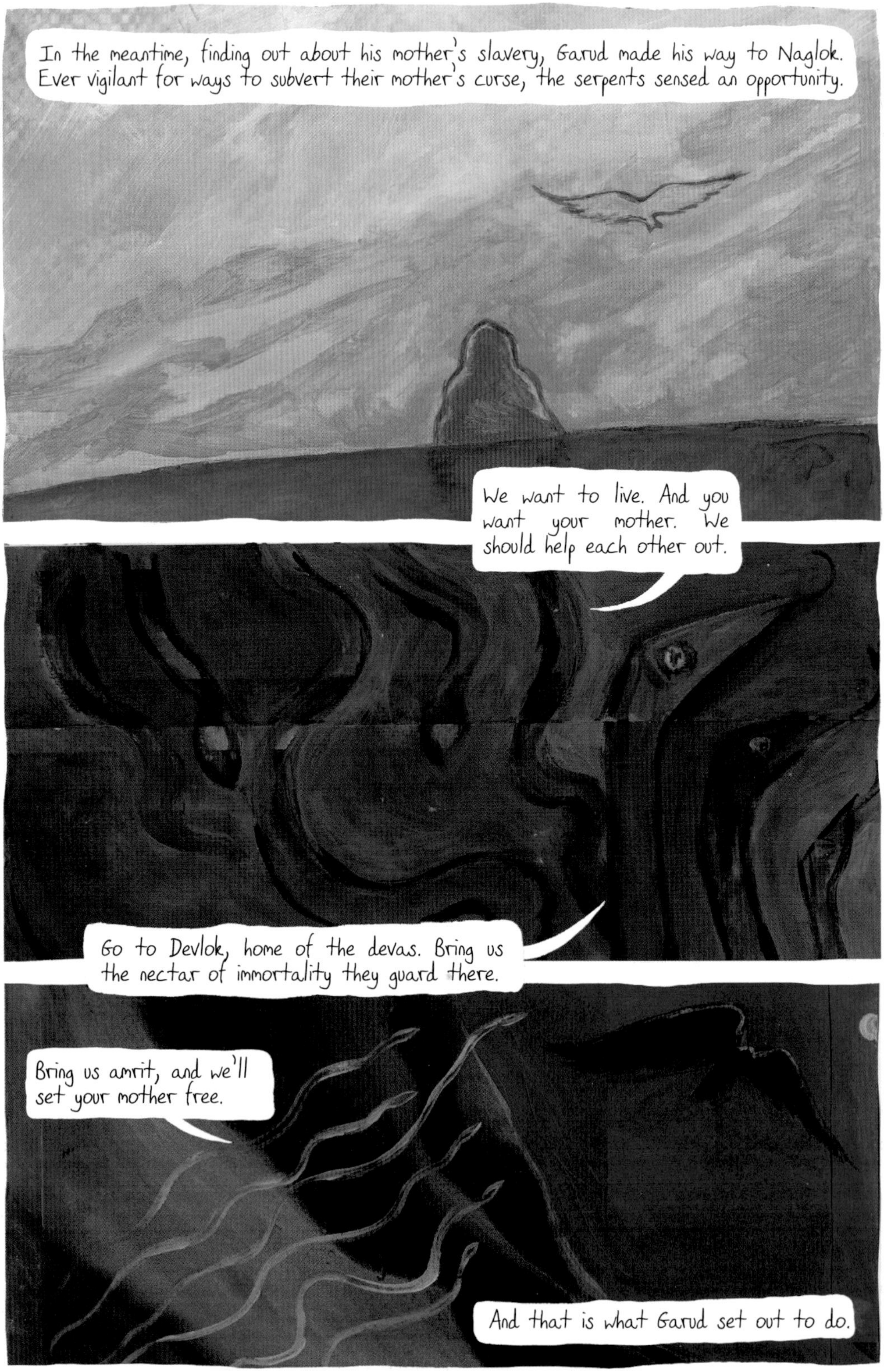
In the meantime, finding out about his mother's slavery, Garud made his way to Naglok. Ever vigilant for ways to subvert their mother's curse, the serpents sensed an opportunity.
We want to live. And you want your mother. We should help each other out.
Go to Devlok, home of the devas. Bring us the nectar of immortality they guard there.
Bring us amrit, and we'll set your mother free.
And that is what Garud set out to do.

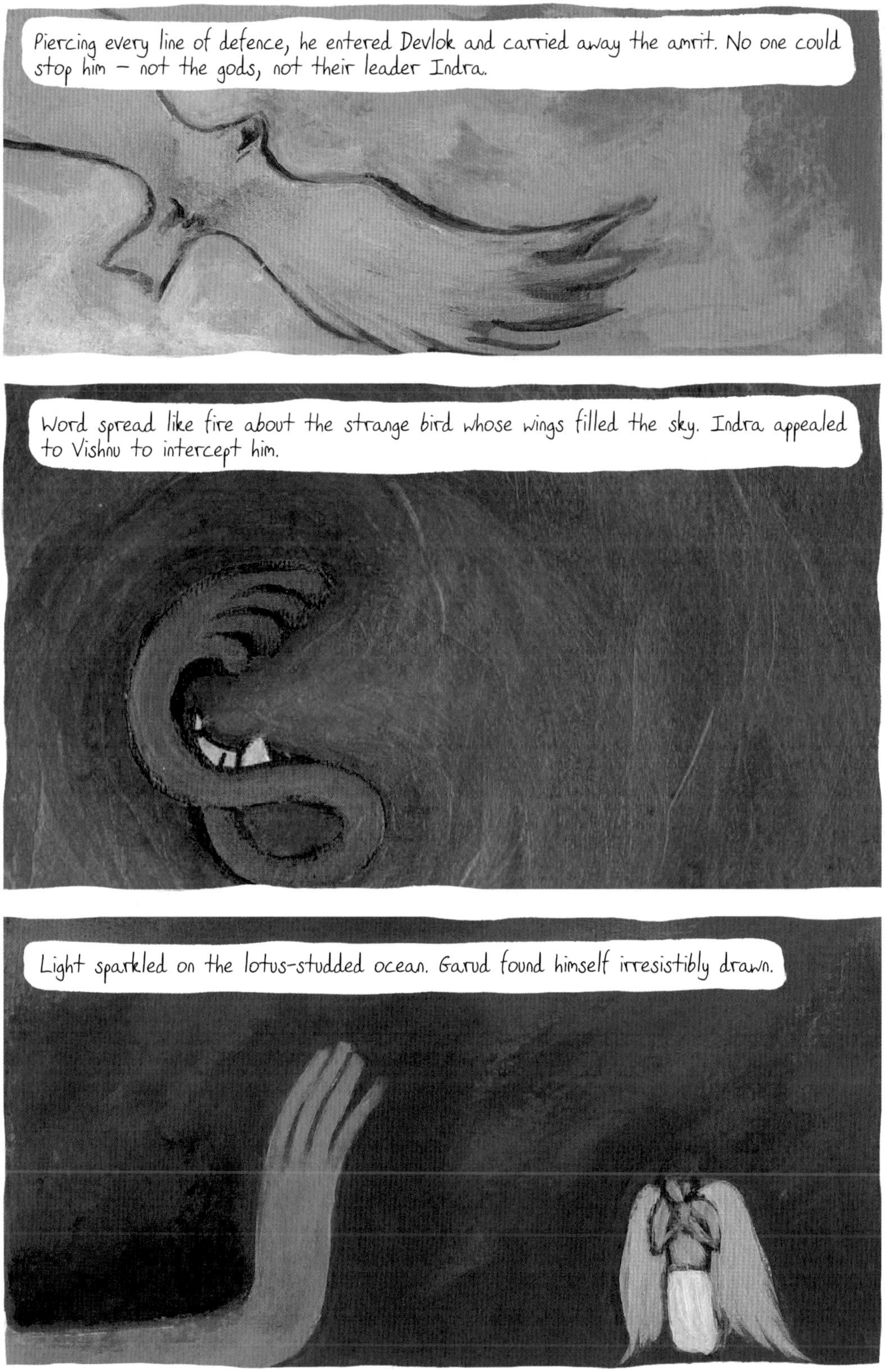
Piercing every line of defence, he entered Devlok and carried away the amrit. No one could stop him – not the gods, not their leader Indra.
Word spread like fire about the strange bird whose wings filled the sky. Indra appealed to Vishnu to intercept him.
Light sparkled on the lotus-studded ocean. Garud found himself irresistibly drawn.

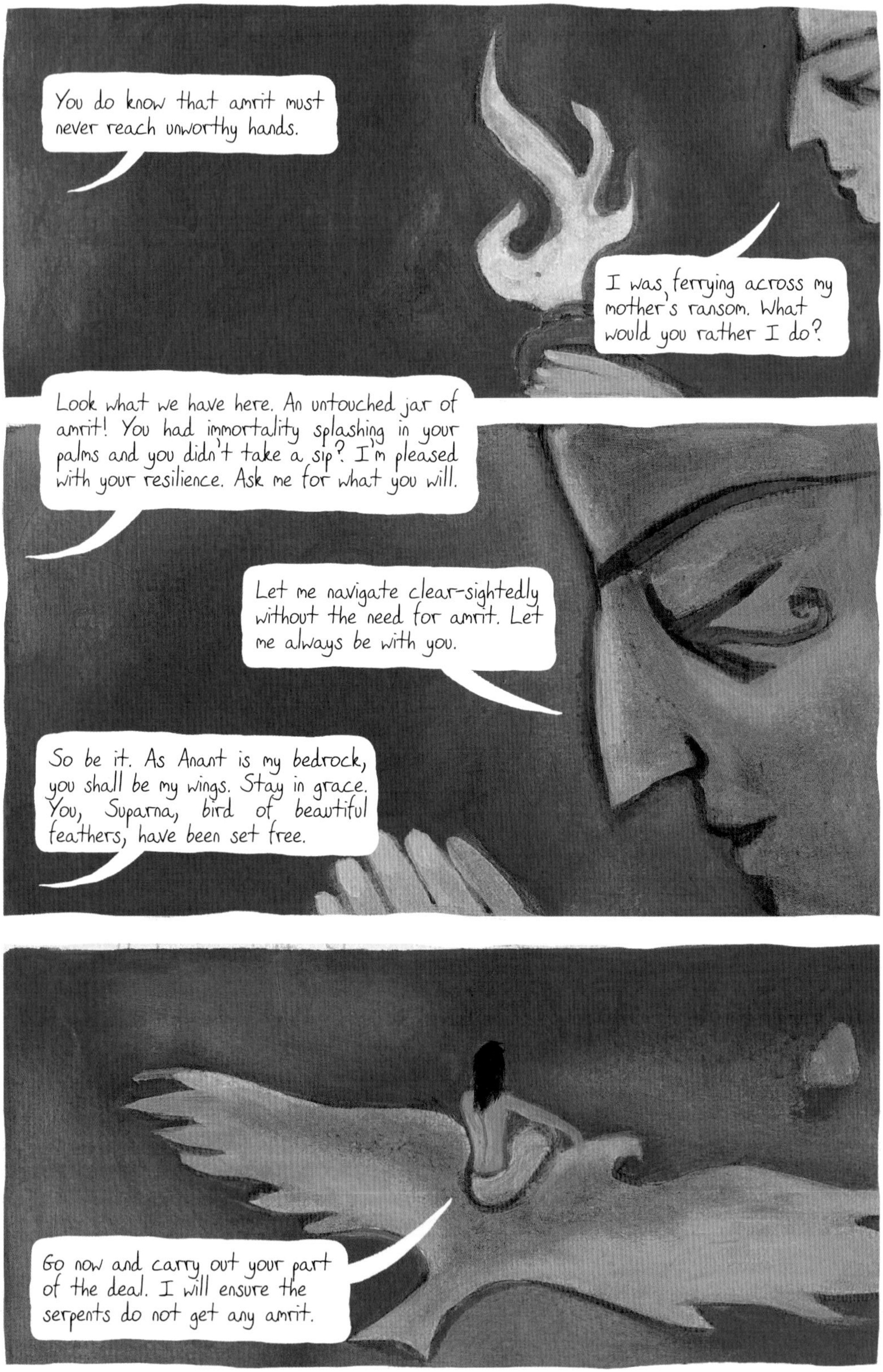
You do know that amrit must never reach unworthy hands.
I was ferrying across my mother's ransom. What would you rather I do?
Look what we have here. An untouched jar of amrit! You had immortality splashing in your palms and you didn't take a sip? I'm pleased with your resilience. Ask me for what you will.
Let me navigate clear-sightedly without the need for amrit. Let me always be with you.
So be it. As Anant is my bedrock, you shall be my wings. Stay in grace. You, Suparna, bird of beautiful feathers, have been set free.
Go now and carry out your part of the deal. I will ensure the serpents do not get any amrit.

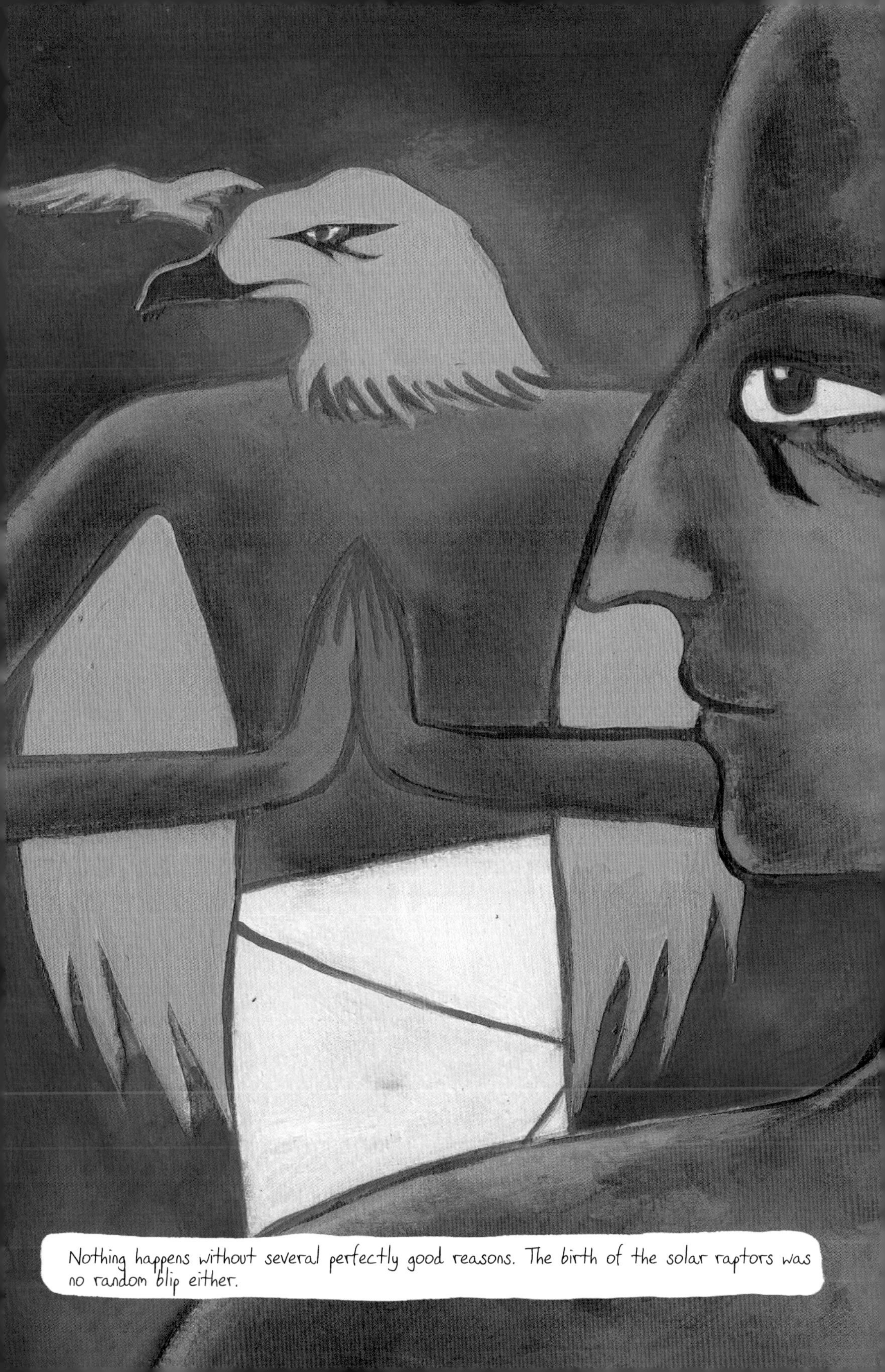
Nothing happens without several perfectly good reasons. The birth of the solar raptors was no random blip either.

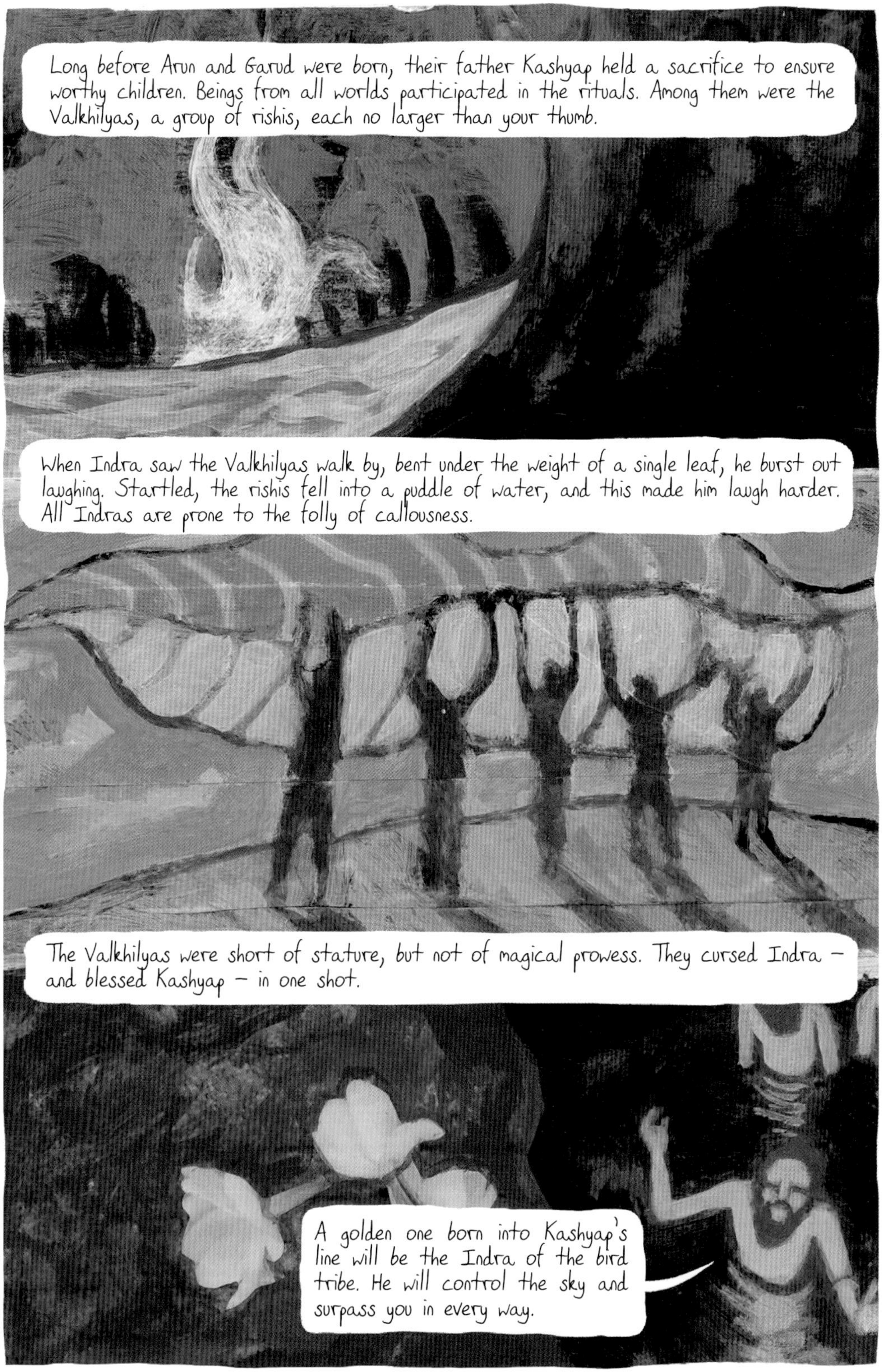
Long before Arun and Garud were born, their father Kashyap held a sacrifice to ensure worthy children. Beings from all worlds participated in the rituals. Among them were the Valkhilyas, a group of rishis, each no larger than your thumb.
When Indra saw the Valkhilyas walk by, bent under the weight of a single leaf, he burst out laughing. Startled, the rishis fell into a puddle of water, and this made him laugh harder. All Indras are prone to the folly of callousness.
The Valkhilyas were short of stature, but not of magical prowess. They cursed Indra – and blessed Kashyap – in one shot.
A golden one born into Kashyap's line will be the Indra of the bird tribe. He will control the sky and surpass you in every way.

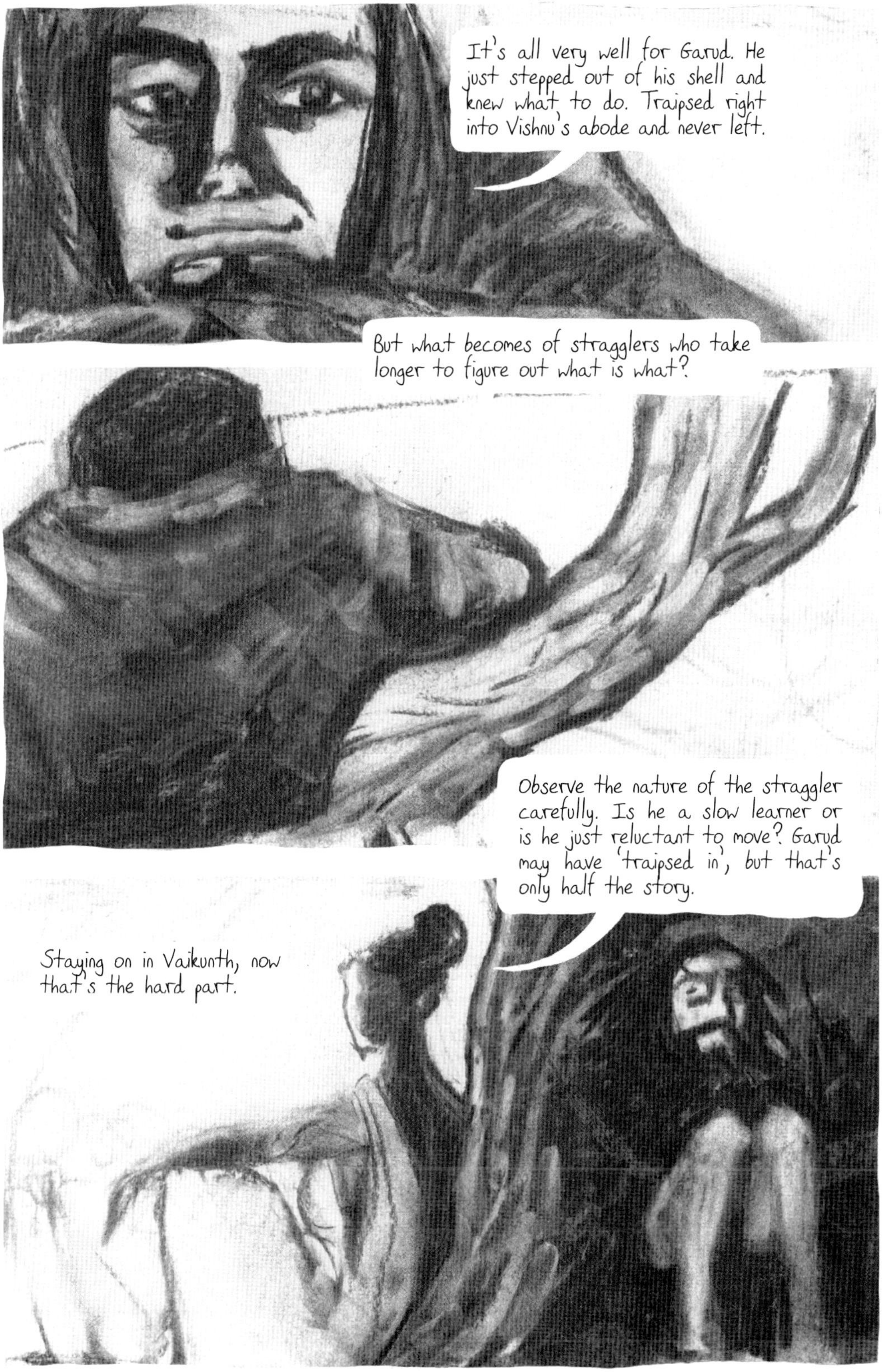
It's all very well for Garud. He just stepped out of his shell and knew what to do. Traipsed right into Vishnu's abode and never left.
But what becomes of stragglers who take longer to figure out what is what?
Observe the nature of the straggler carefully. Is he a slow learner or is he just reluctant to move? Garud may have 'traipsed in', but that's only half the story.
Staying on in Vaikunth, now that's the hard part.

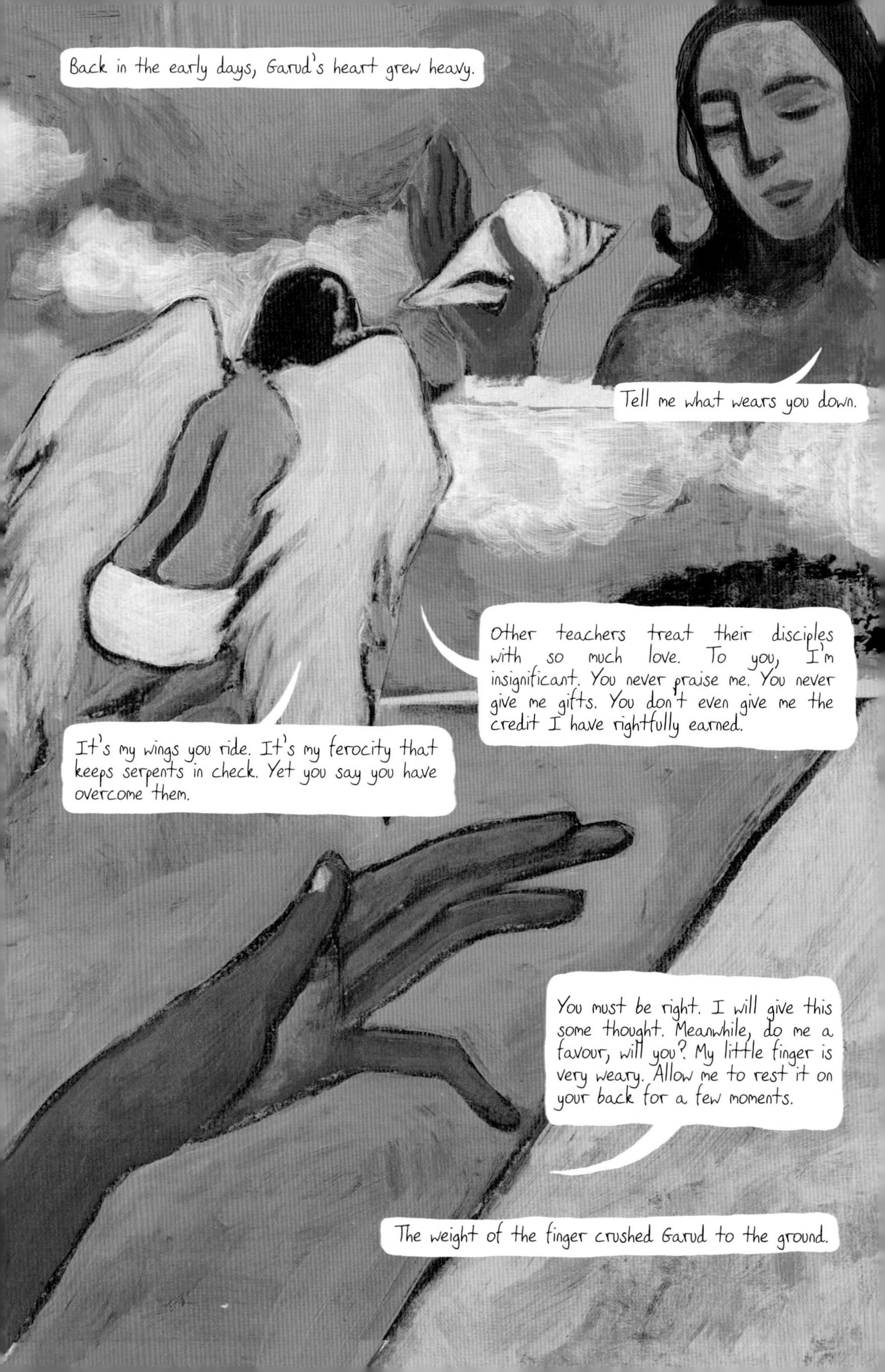

Back in the early days, Garud's heart grew heavy.
Tell me what wears you down.
Other teachers treat their disciples with so much love. To you, I'm insignificant. You never praise me. You never give me gifts. You don't even give me the credit I have rightfully earned.
It's my wings you ride. It's my ferocity that keeps serpents in check. Yet you say you have overcome them.
You must be right. I will give this some thought. Meanwhile, do me a favour, will you? My little finger is very weary. Allow me to rest it on your back for a few moments.
The weight of the finger crushed Garud to the ground.

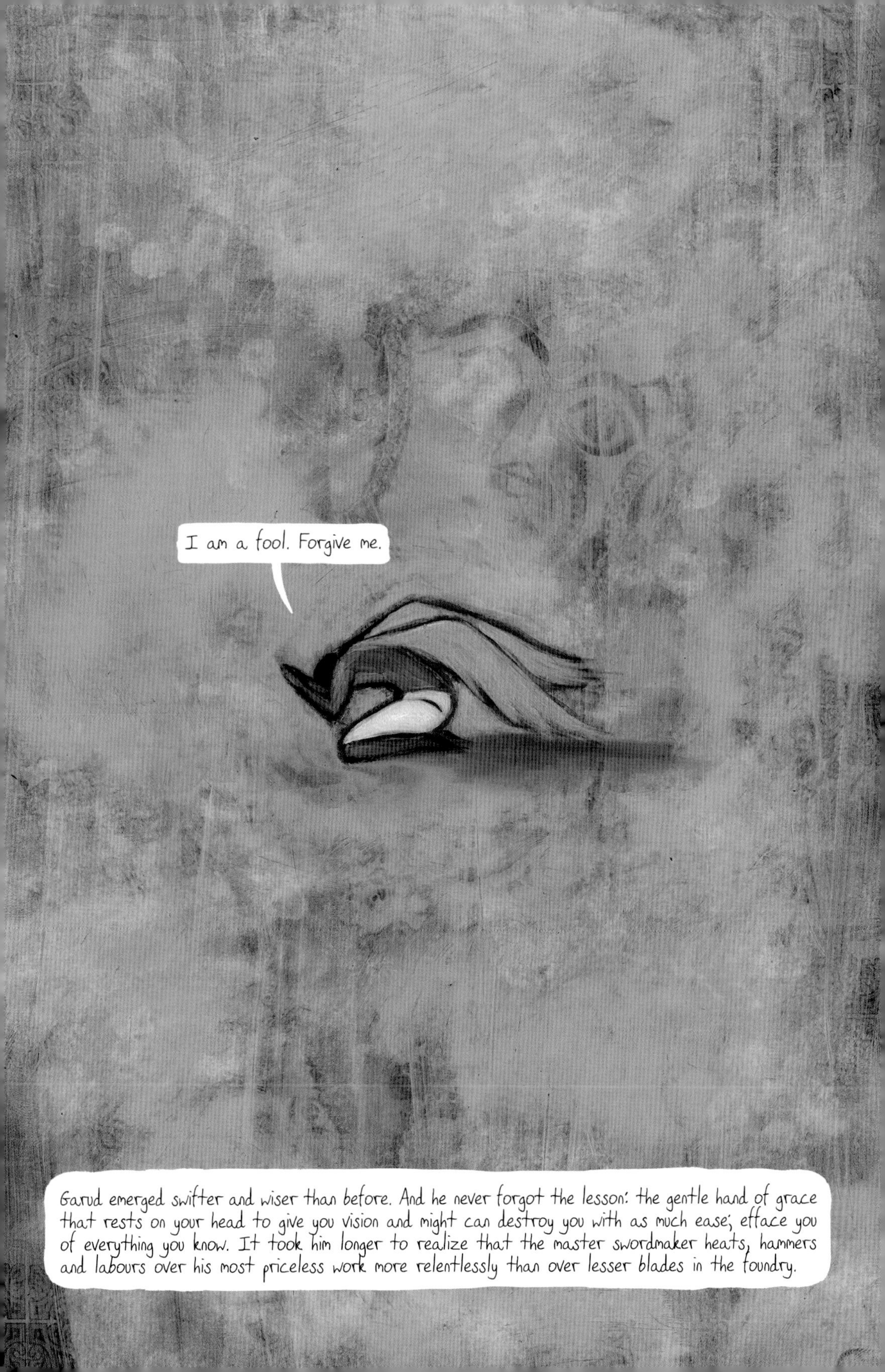
I am a fool. Forgive me.
Garud emerged swifter and wiser than before. And he never forgot the lesson: the gentle hand of grace that rests on your head to give you vision and might can destroy you with as much ease; efface you of everything you know. It took him longer to realize that the master swordmaker heats, hammers and labours over his most priceless work more relentlessly than over lesser blades in the foundry.

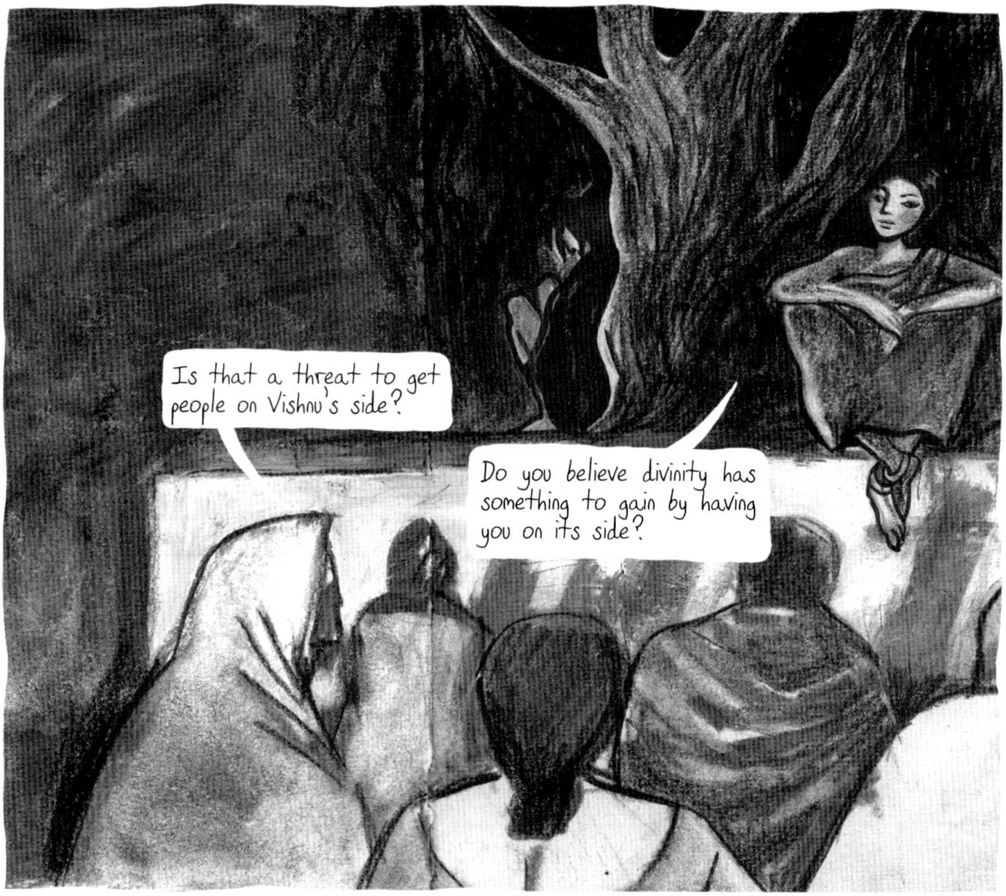
Is that a threat to get people on Vishnu's side?
Do you believe divinity has something to gain by having you on its side?

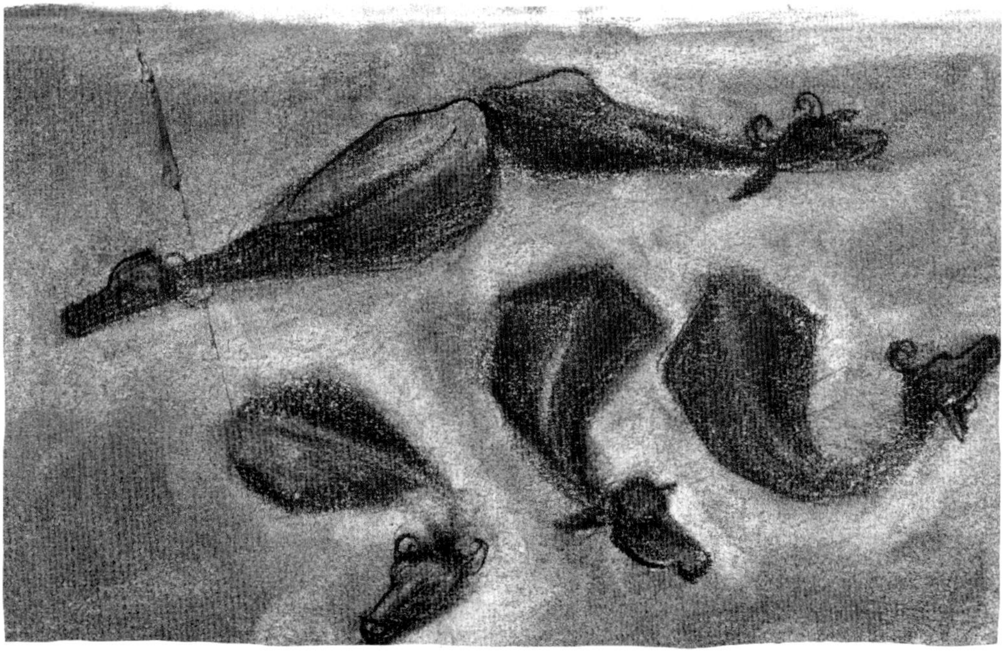

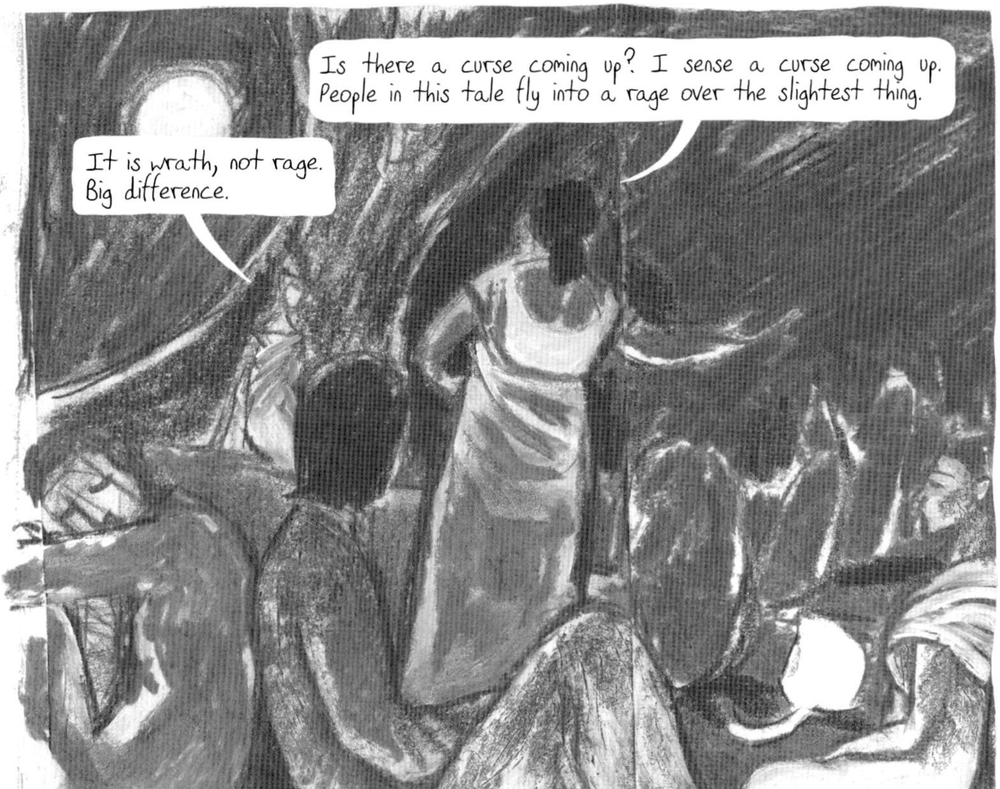
Is there a curse coming up? I sense a curse coming up. People in this tale fly into a rage over the slightest thing.
It is wrath, not rage. Big difference.

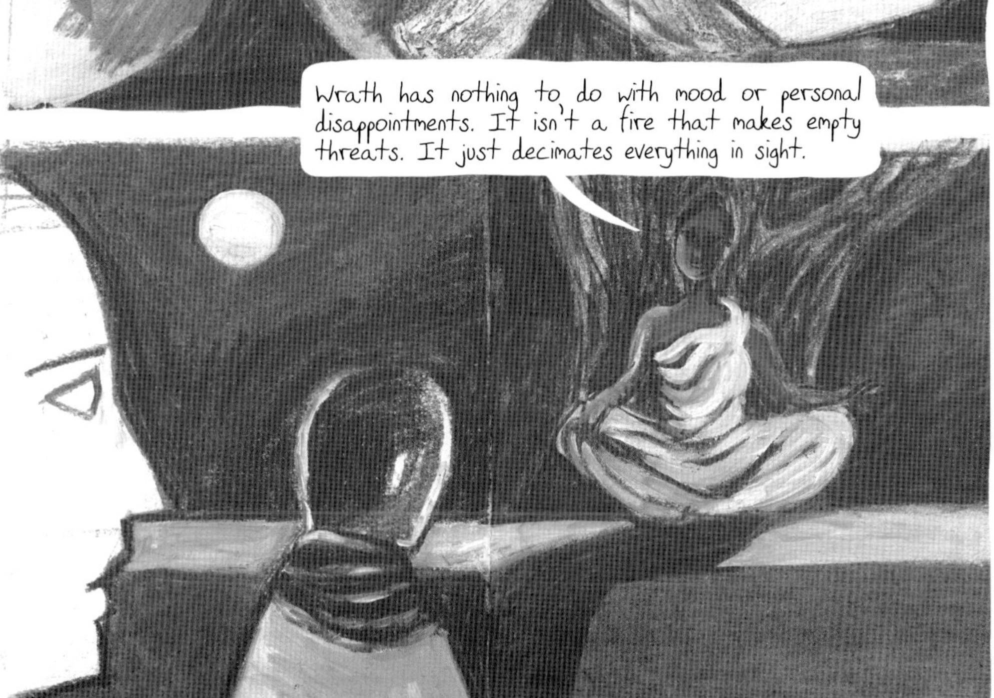
Wrath has nothing to do with mood or personal disappointments. It isn't a fire that makes empty threats. It just decimates everything in sight.

NAVIGATORS OF THE MULTIVERSE

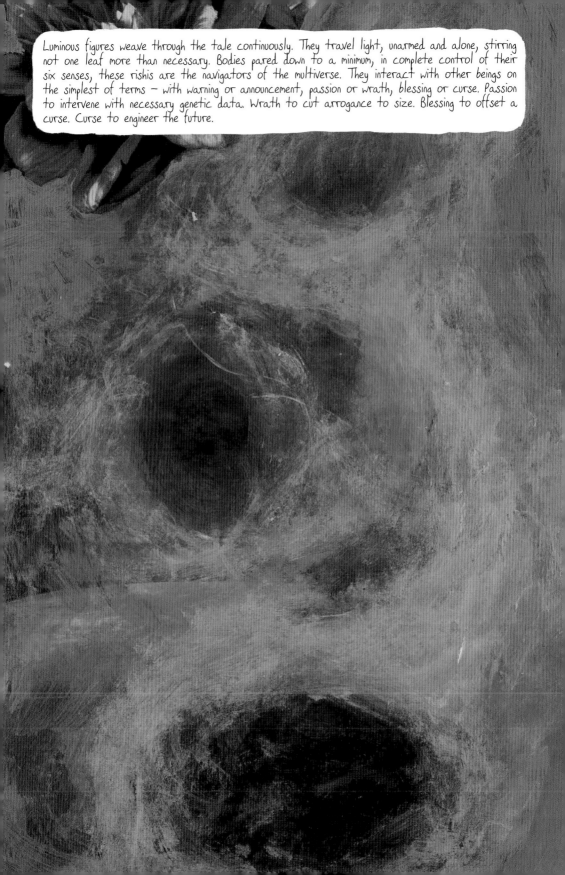

Luminous figures weave through the tale continuously. They travel light, unarmed and alone, stirring not one leaf more than necessary. Bodies pared down to a minimum, in complete control of their six senses, these rishis are the navigators of the multiverse. They interact with other beings on the simplest of terms — with warning or announcement, passion or wrath, blessing or curse. Passion to intervene with necessary genetic data. Wrath to cut arrogance to size. Blessing to offset a curse. Curse to engineer the future.

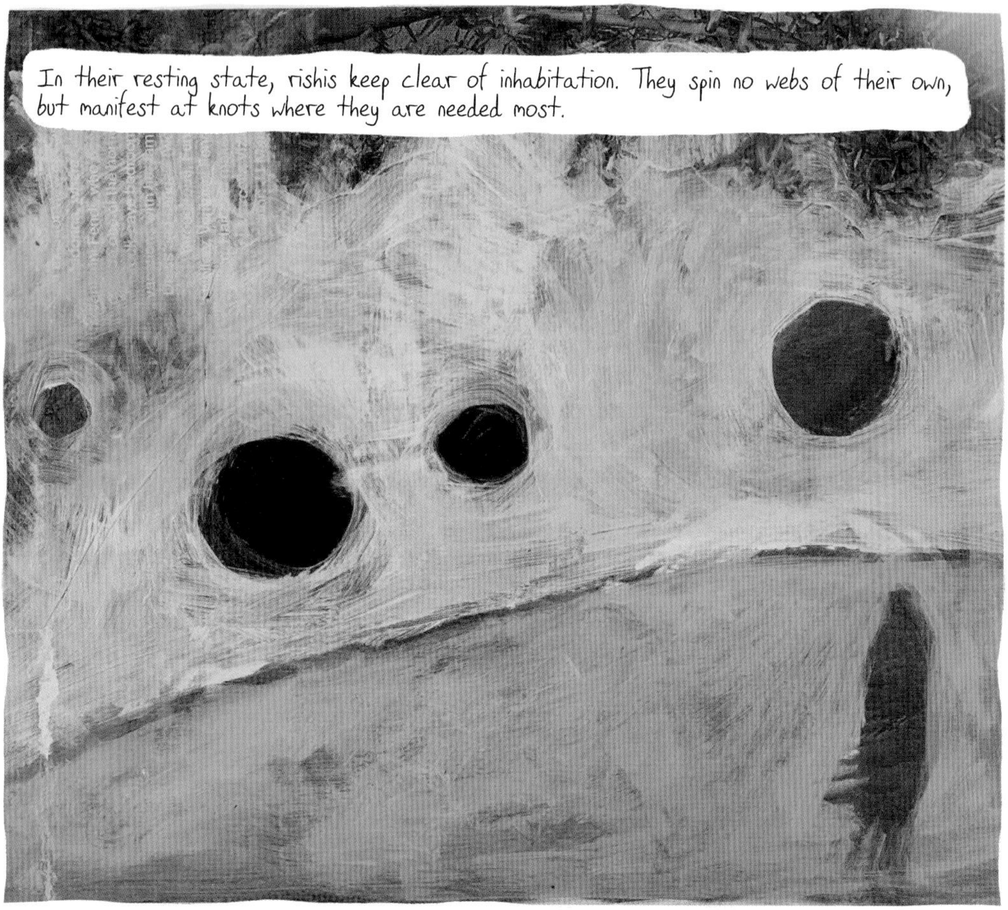
In their resting state, rishis keep clear of inhabitation. They spin no webs of their own, but manifest at knots where they are needed most.

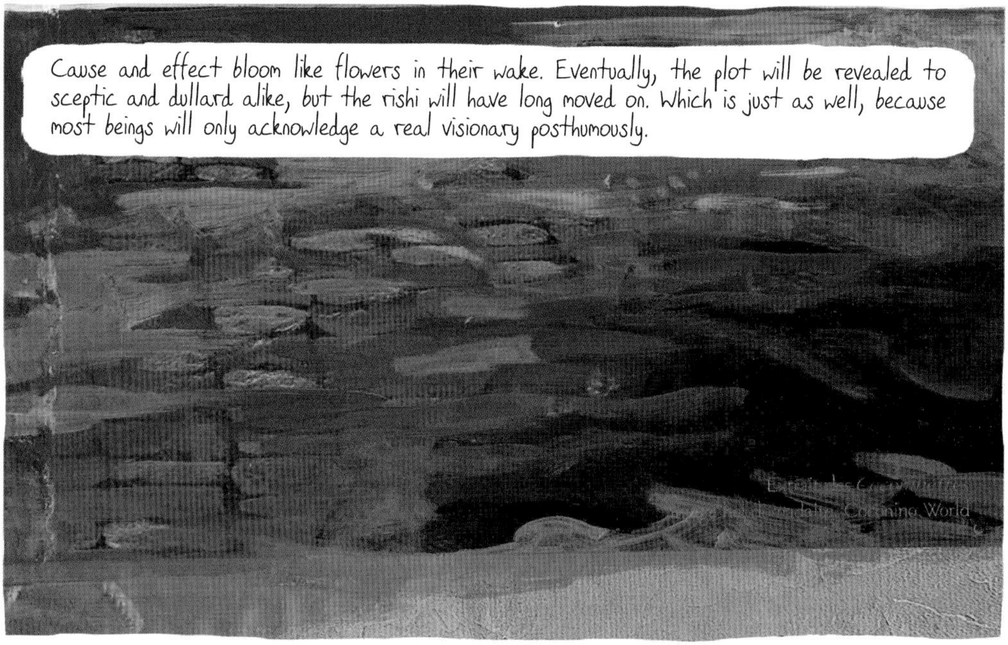
Cause and effect bloom like flowers in their wake. Eventually, the plot will be revealed to sceptic and dullard alike, but the rishi will have long moved on. Which is just as well, because most beings will only acknowledge a real visionary posthumously.

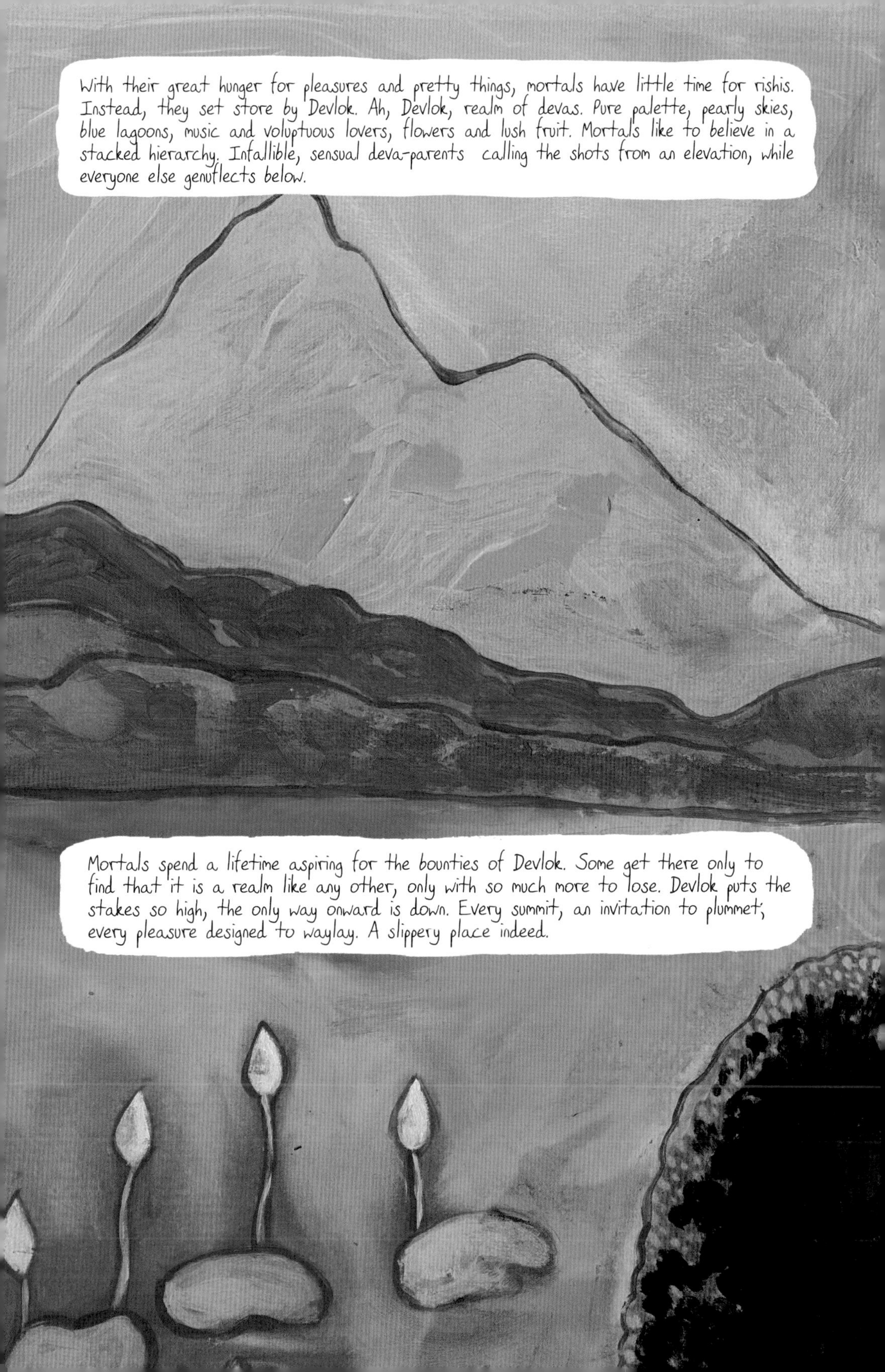
With their great hunger for pleasures and pretty things, mortals have little time for rishis. Instead, they set store by Devlok. Ah, Devlok, realm of devas. Pure palette, pearly skies, blue lagoons, music and voluptuous lovers, flowers and lush fruit. Mortals like to believe in a stacked hierarchy. Infallible, sensual deva-parents calling the shots from an elevation, while everyone else genuflects below.
Mortals spend a lifetime aspiring for the bounties of Devlok. Some get there only to find that it is a realm like any other, only with so much more to lose. Devlok puts the stakes so high, the only way onward is down. Every summit, an invitation to plummet; every pleasure designed to waylay. A slippery place indeed.

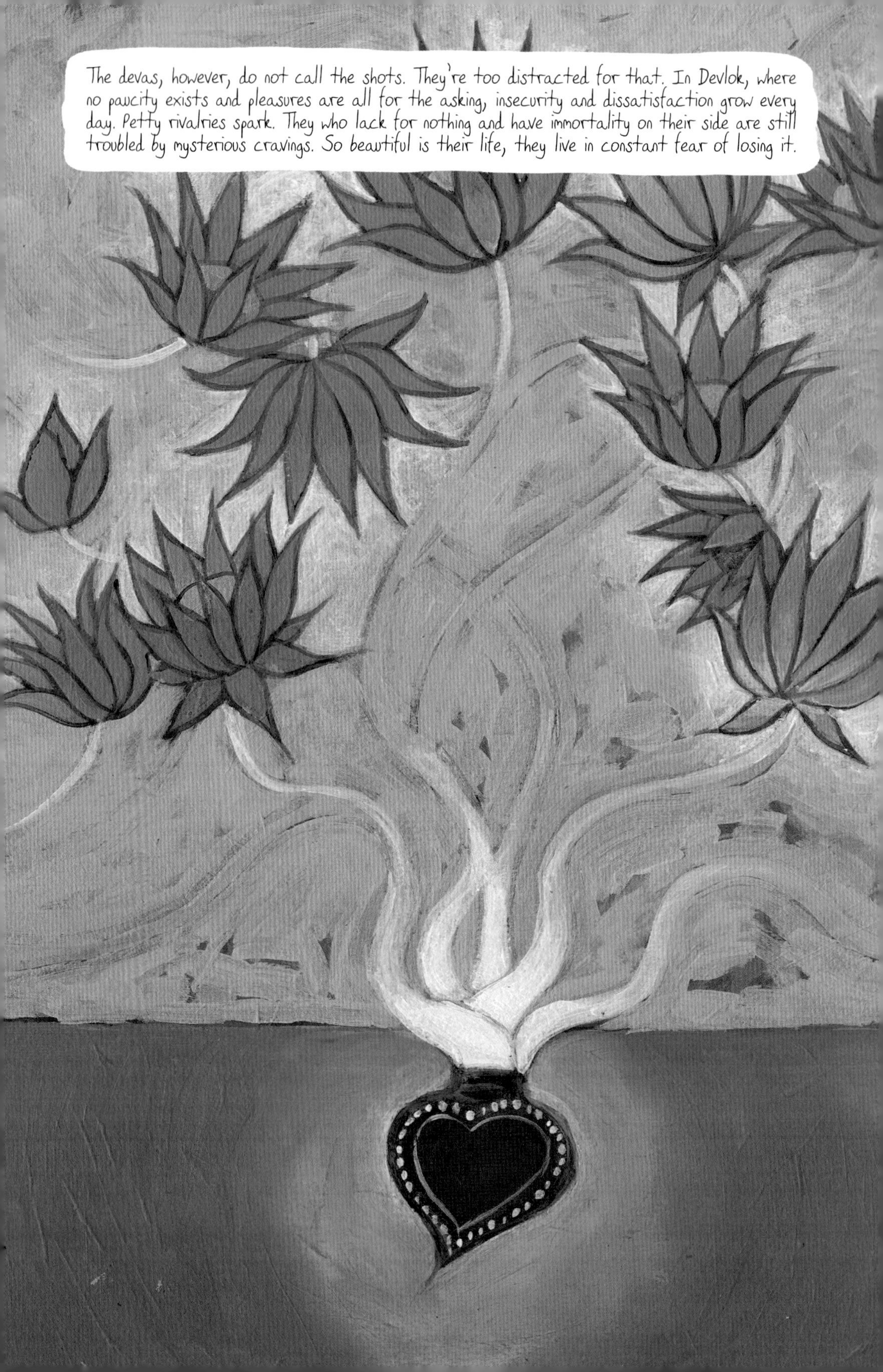
The devas, however, do not call the shots. They're too distracted for that. In Devlok, where no paucity exists and pleasures are all for the asking, insecurity and dissatisfaction grow every day. Petty rivalries spark. They who lack for nothing and have immortality on their side are still troubled by mysterious cravings. So beautiful is their life, they live in constant fear of losing it.

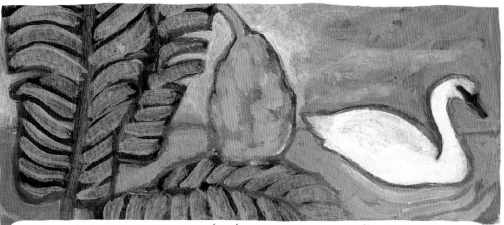

To be a deva is to be given the gift of amrit. Let me say it like it is — they are addicted to the stuff. They are addicted to a substance they cannot replace. Or produce.

Amrit is the nectar that makes their shields impregnable, their vision telescopic. It is the spice that lets them navigate the multiverse.

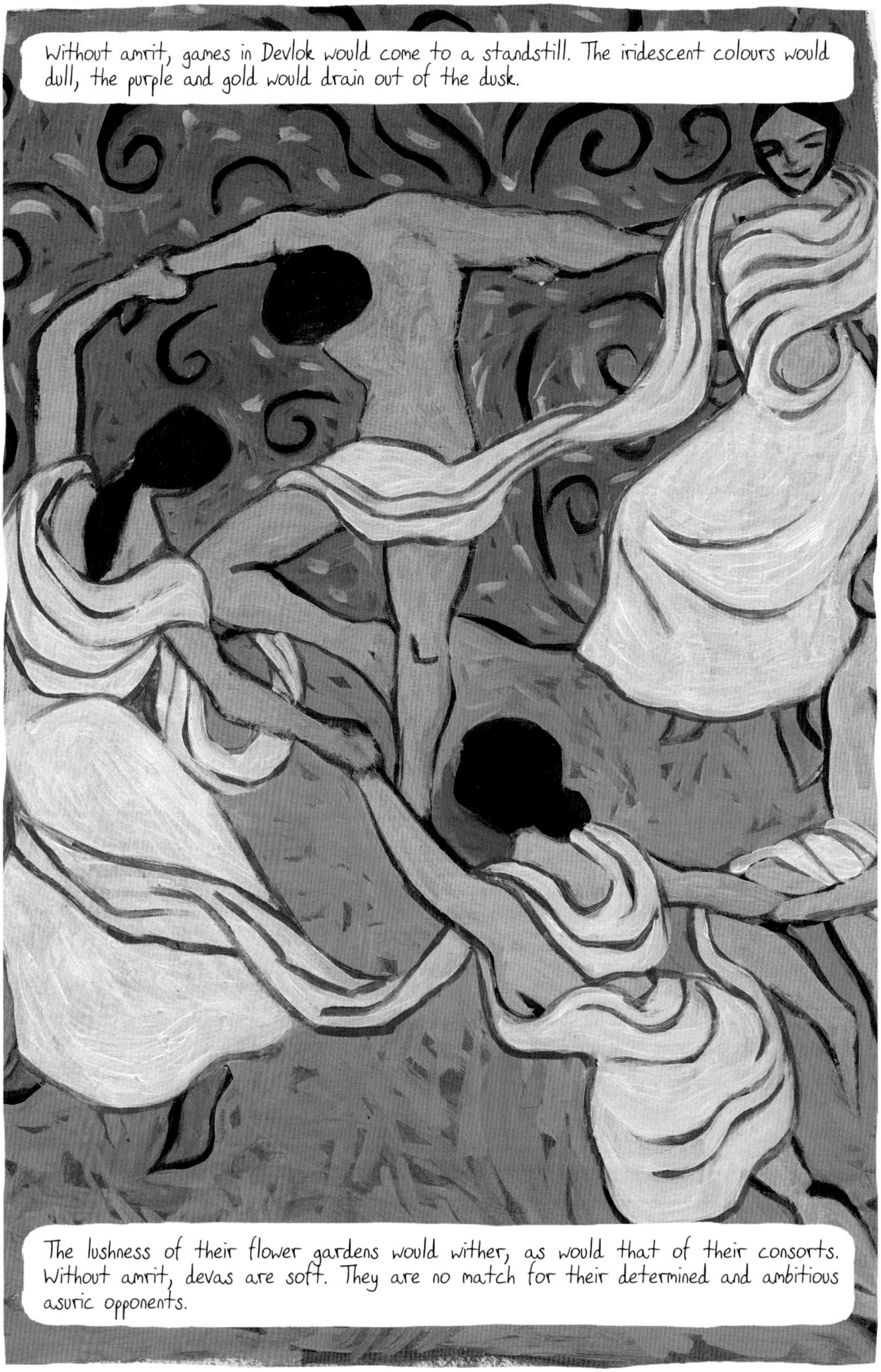
Without amrit, games in Devlok would come to a standstill. The iridescent colours would dull, the purple and gold would drain out of the dusk.
The lushness of their flower gardens would wither, as would that of their consorts. Without amrit, devas are soft. They are no match for their determined and ambitious asuric opponents.

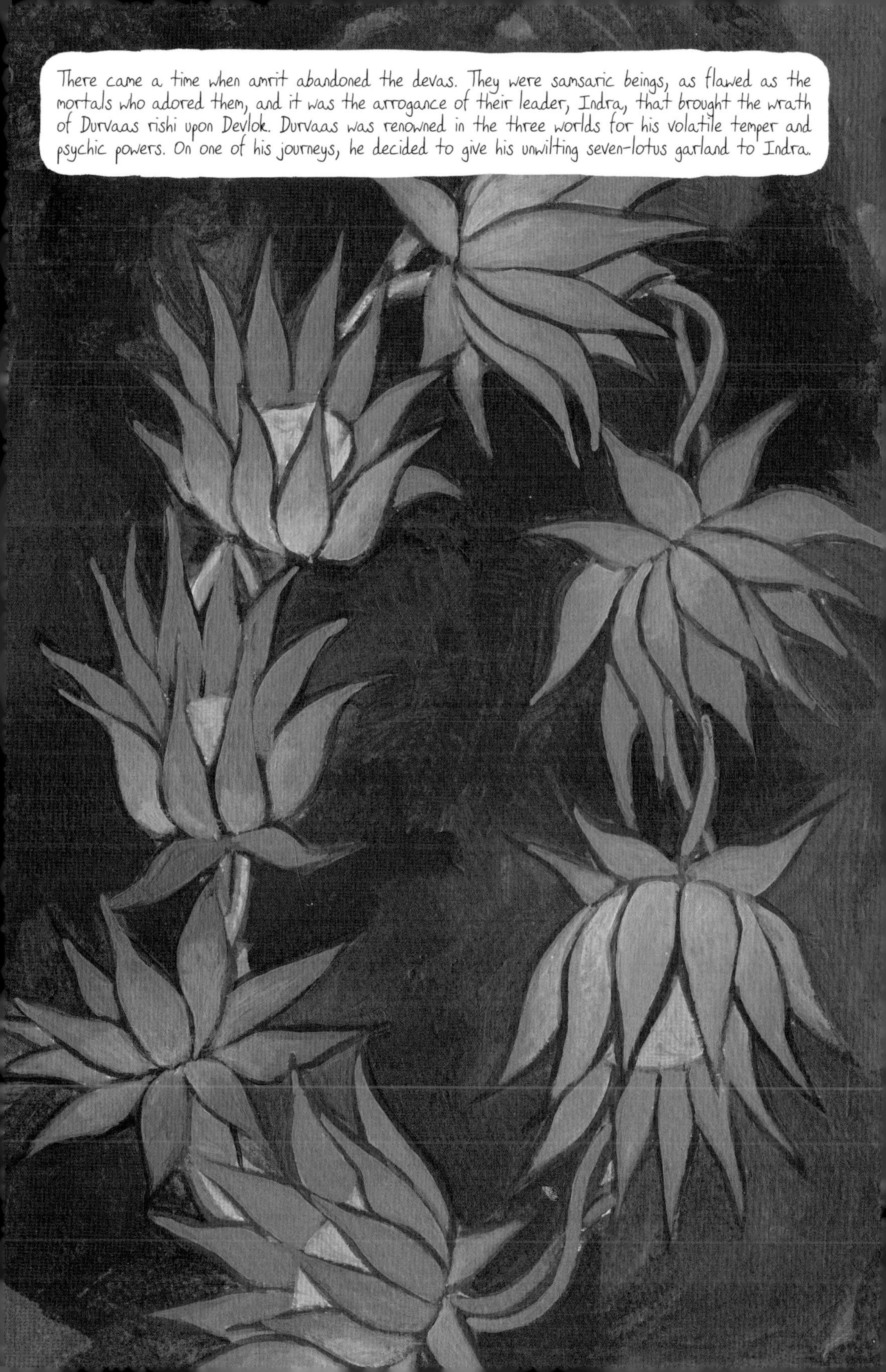
There came a time when amrit abandoned the devas. They were samsaric beings, as flawed as the mortals who adored them, and it was the arrogance of their leader, Indra, that brought the wrath of Durvaas rishi upon Devlok. Durvaas was renowned in the three worlds for his volatile temper and psychic powers. On one of his journeys, he decided to give his unwilting seven-lotus garland to Indra.

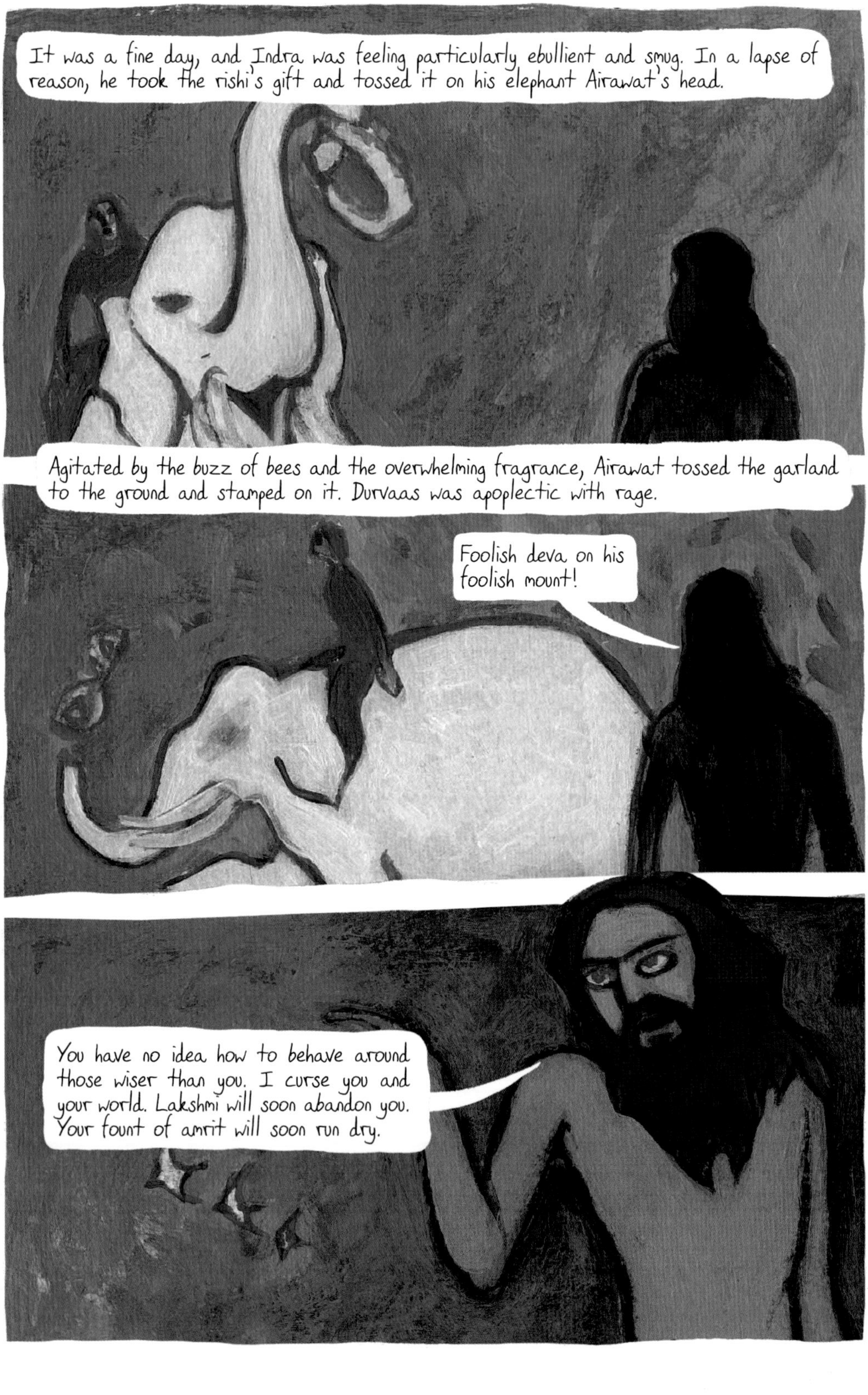
It was a fine day, and Indra was feeling particularly ebullient and smug. In a lapse of reason, he took the rishi's gift and tossed it on his elephant Airawat's head.
Agitated by the buzz of bees and the overwhelming fragrance, Airawat tossed the garland to the ground and stamped on it. Durvaas was apoplectic with rage.
Foolish deva on his foolish mount!
You have no idea how to behave around those wiser than you. I curse you and your world. Lakshmi will soon abandon you. Your fount of amrit will soon run dry.

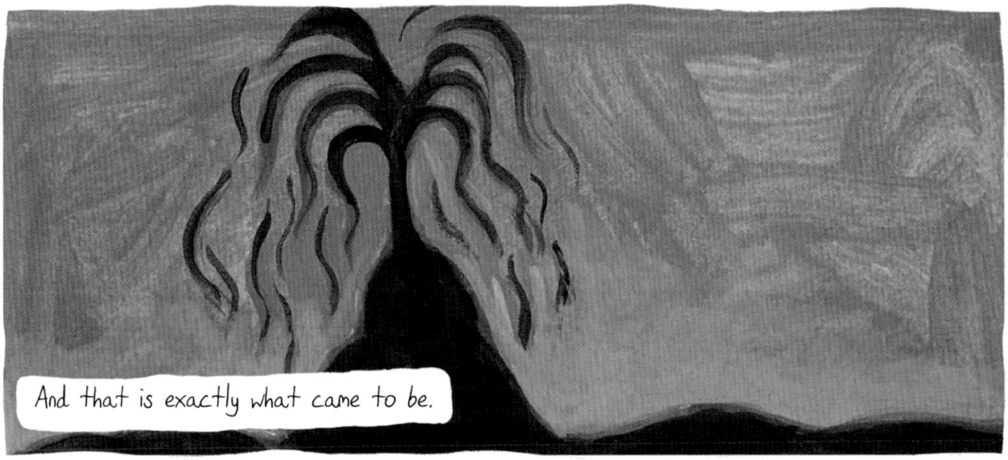
And that is exactly what came to be.

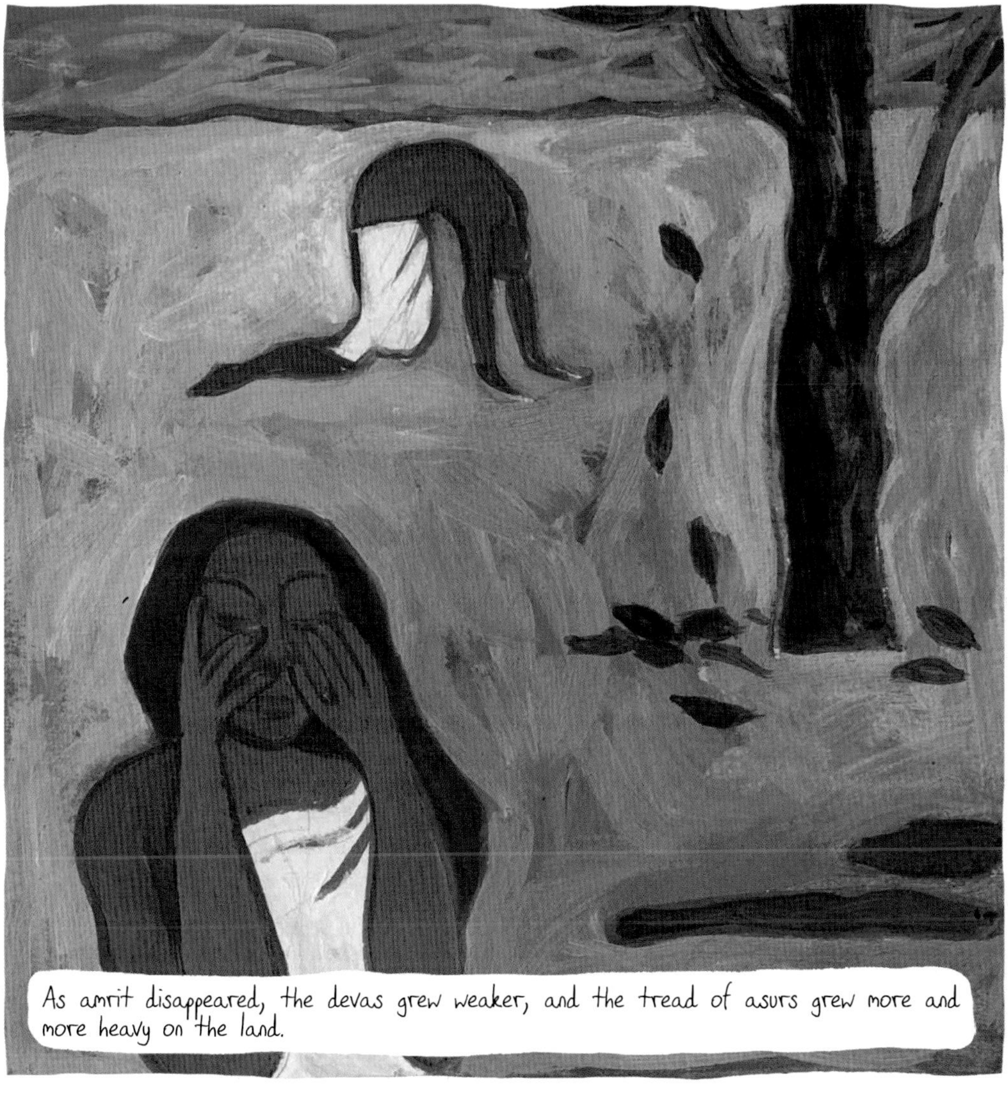
As amrit disappeared, the devas grew weaker, and the tread of asurs grew more and more heavy on the land.

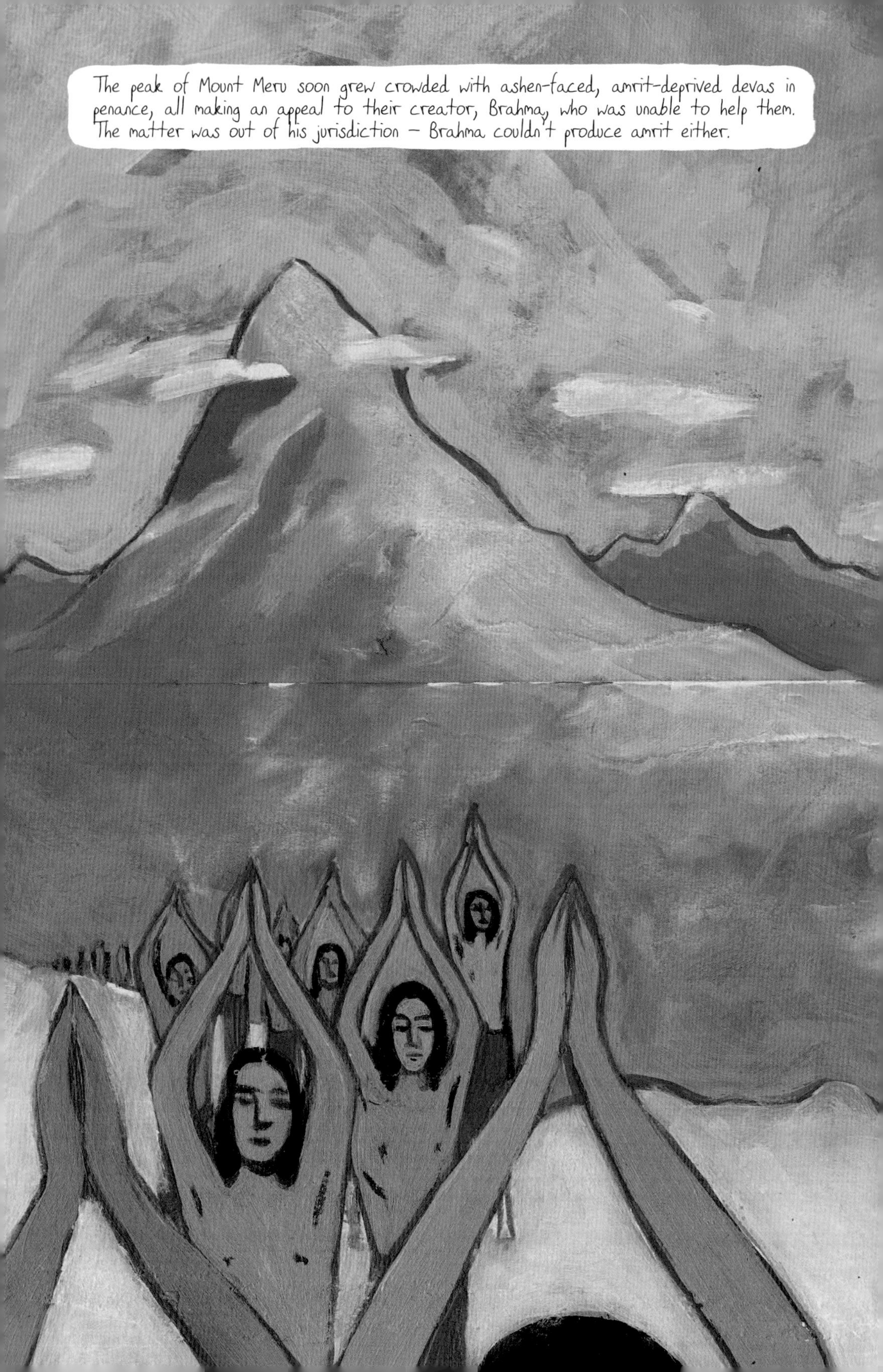
The peak of Mount Meru soon grew crowded with ashen-faced, amrit-deprived devas in penance, all making an appeal to their creator, Brahma, who was unable to help them. The matter was out of his jurisdiction – Brahma couldn't produce amrit either.

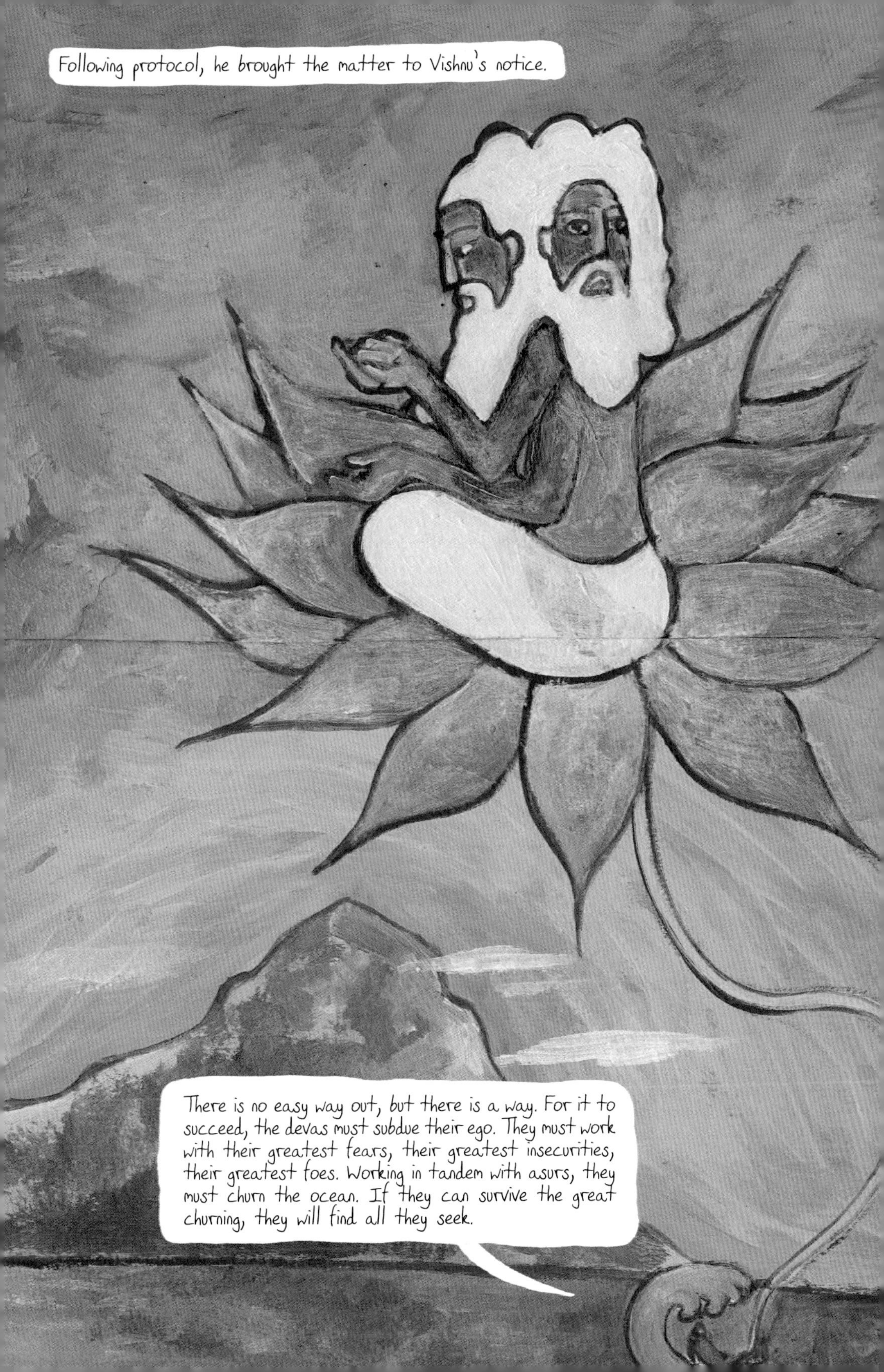
Following protocol, he brought the matter to Vishnu's notice.
There is no easy way out, but there is a way. For it to succeed, the devas must subdue their ego. They must work with their greatest fears, their greatest insecurities, their greatest foes. Working in tandem with asurs, they must churn the ocean. If they can survive the great churning, they will find all they seek.

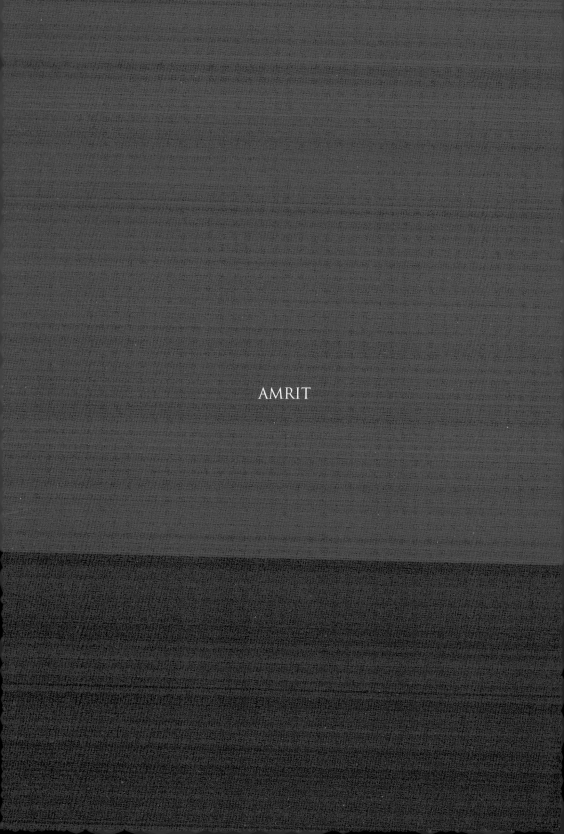

AMRIT

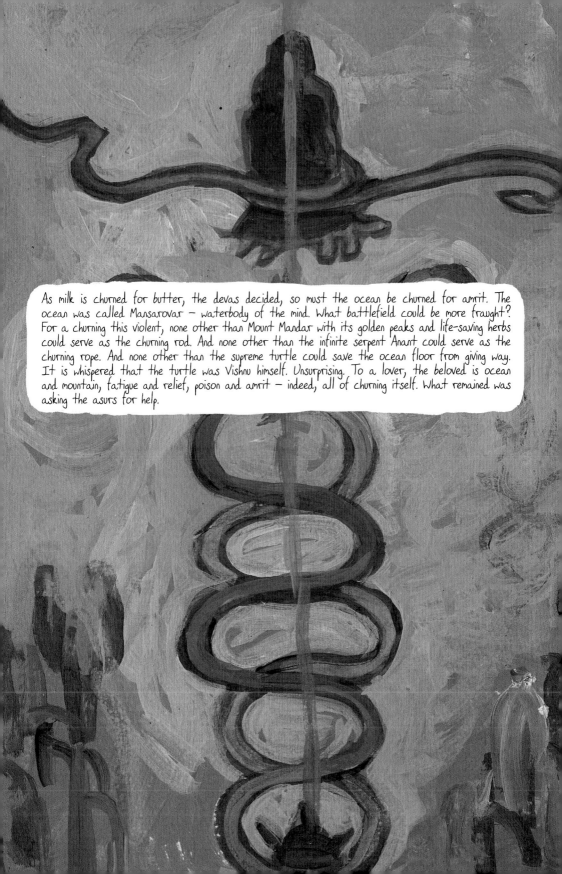

As milk is churned for butter, the devas decided, so must the ocean be churned for amrit. The ocean was called Mansarovar — waterbody of the mind. What battlefield could be more fraught? For a churning this violent, none other than Mount Mandar with its golden peaks and life-saving herbs could serve as the churning rod. And none other than the infinite serpent Anant could serve as the churning rope. And none other than the supreme turtle could save the ocean floor from giving way. It is whispered that the turtle was Vishnu himself. Unsurprising. To a lover, the beloved is ocean and mountain, fatigue and relief, poison and amrit — indeed, all of churning itself. What remained was asking the asurs for help.

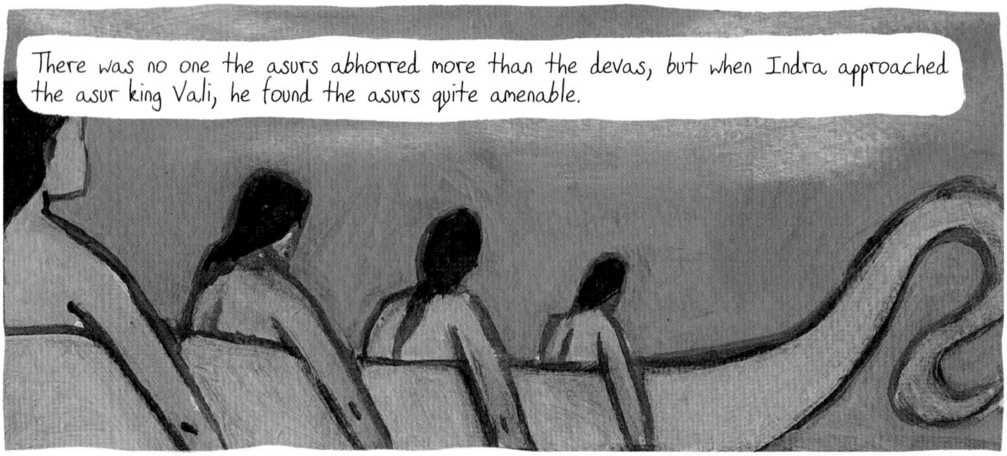
There was no one the asurs abhorred more than the devas, but when Indra approached the asur king Vali, he found the asurs quite amenable.

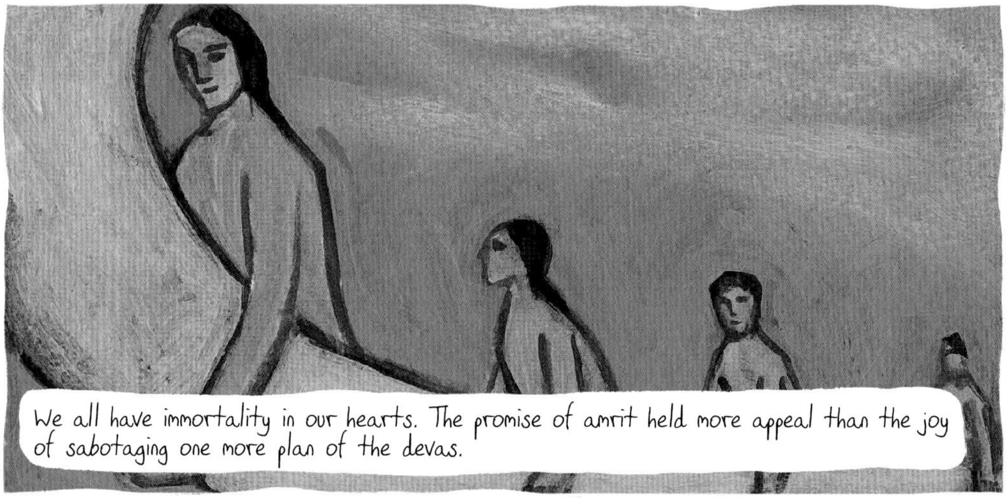
We all have immortality in our hearts. The promise of amrit held more appeal than the joy of sabotaging one more plan of the devas.

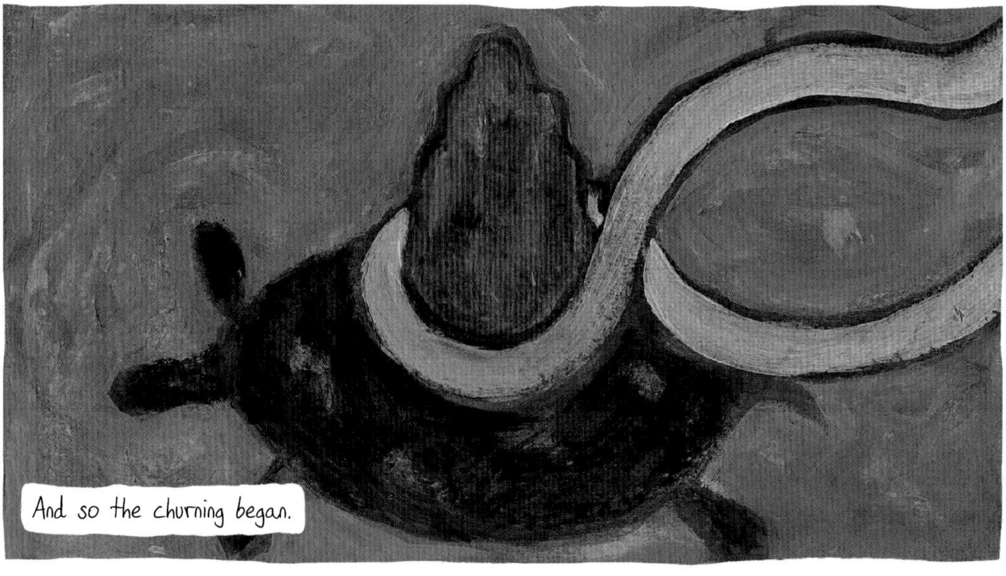
And so the churning began.

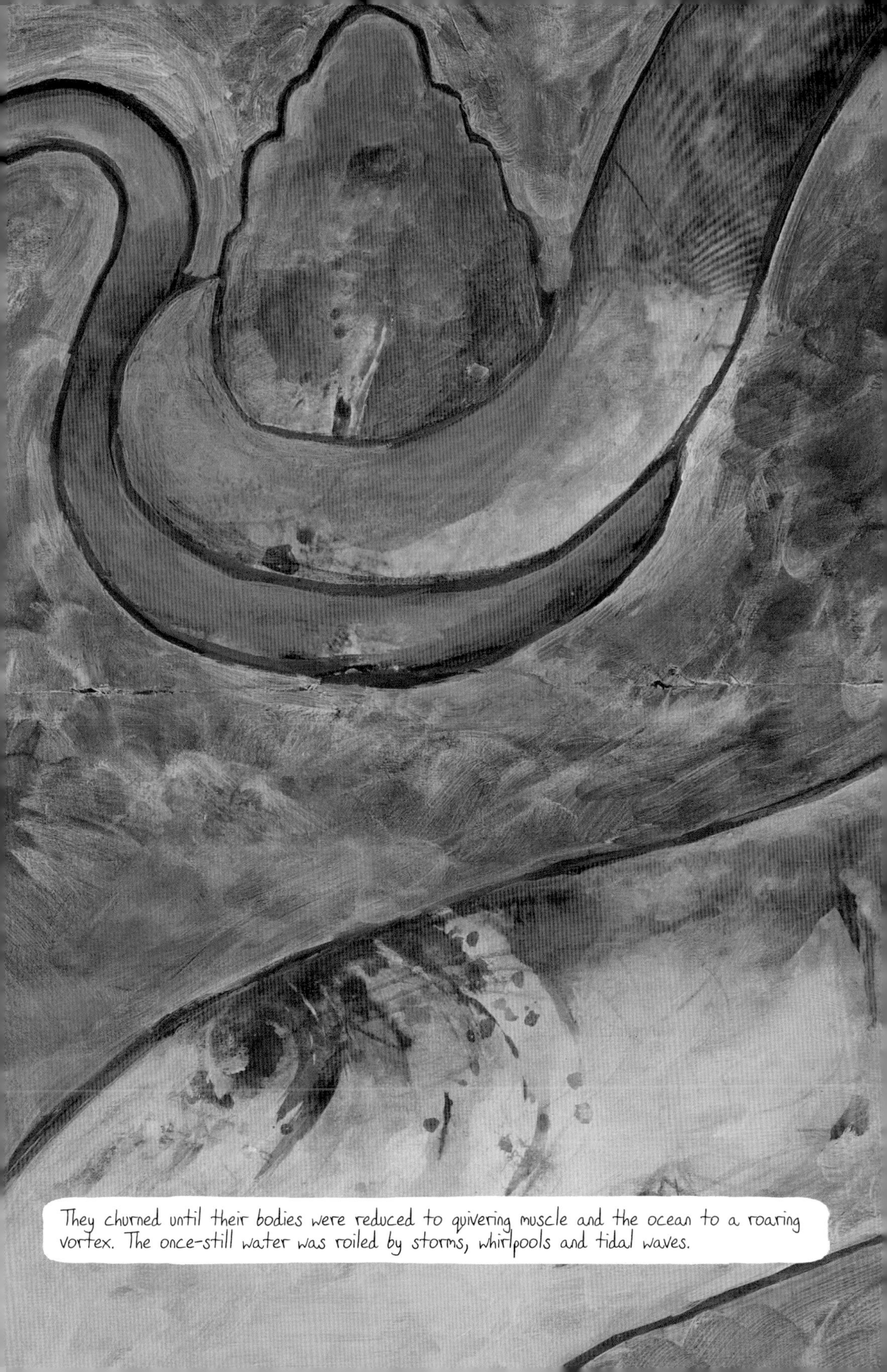
They churned until their bodies were reduced to quivering muscle and the ocean to a roaring vortex. The once-still water was roiled by storms, whirlpools and tidal waves.

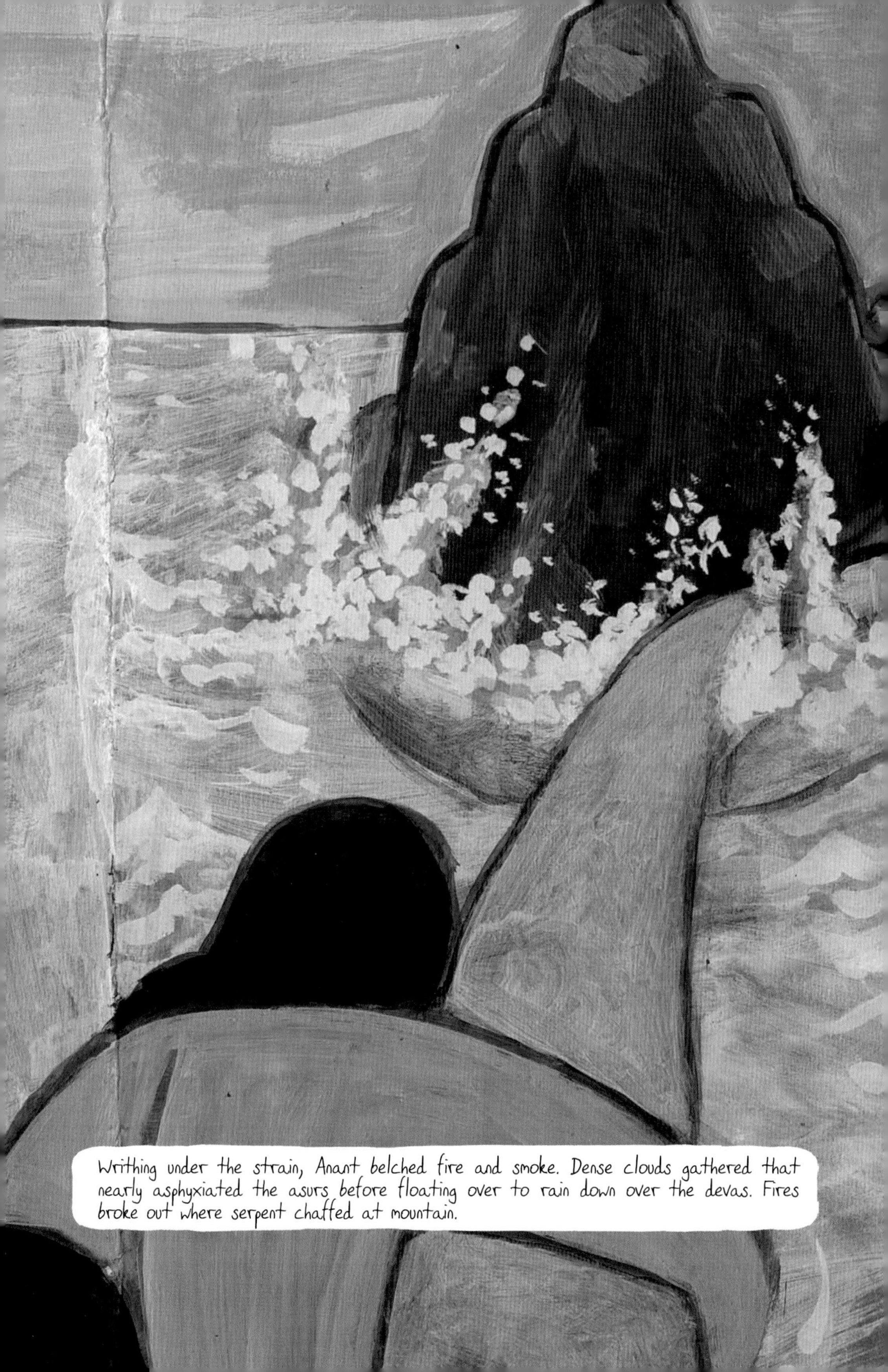
Writhing under the strain, Anant belched fire and smoke. Dense clouds gathered that nearly asphyxiated the asurs before floating over to rain down over the devas. Fires broke out where serpent chaffed at mountain.

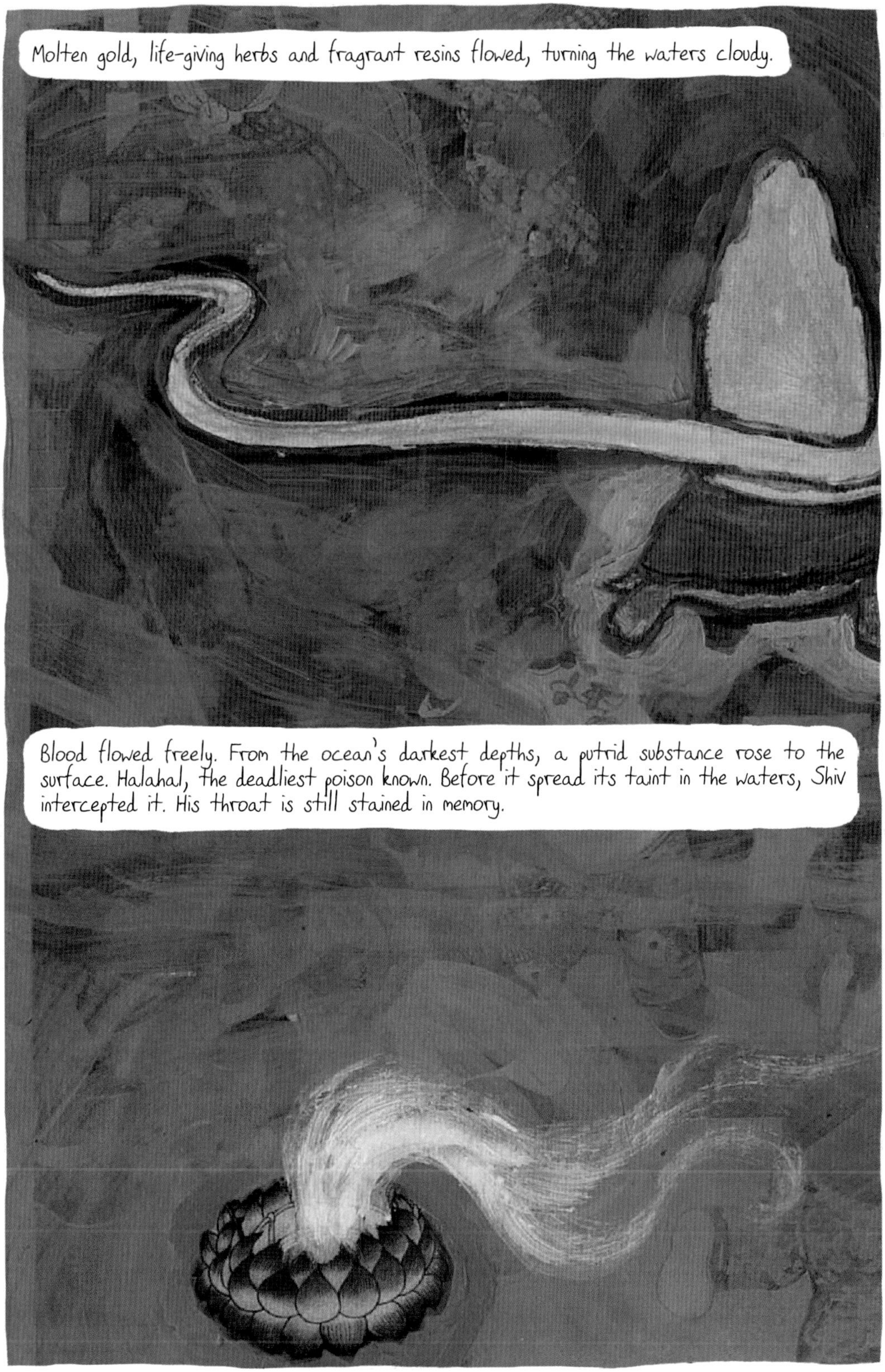
Molten gold, life-giving herbs and fragrant resins flowed, turning the waters cloudy.
Blood flowed freely. From the ocean's darkest depths, a putrid substance rose to the surface. Halahal, the deadliest poison known. Before it spread its taint in the waters, Shiv intercepted it. His throat is still stained in memory.

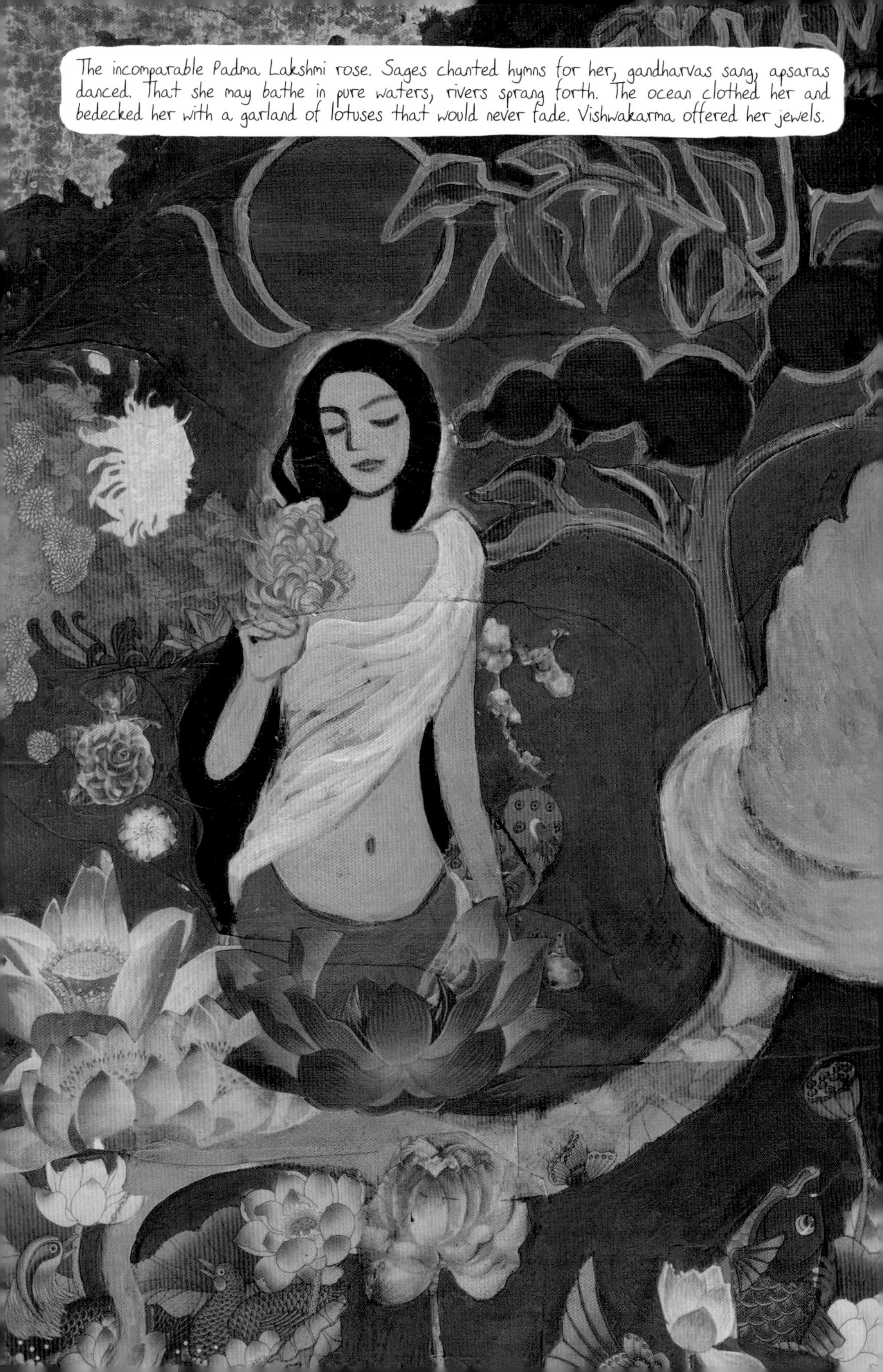
The incomparable Padma Lakshmi rose. Sages chanted hymns for her, gandharvas sang, apsaras danced. That she may bathe in pure waters, rivers sprang forth. The ocean clothed her and bedecked her with a garland of lotuses that would never fade. Vishwakarma offered her jewels.

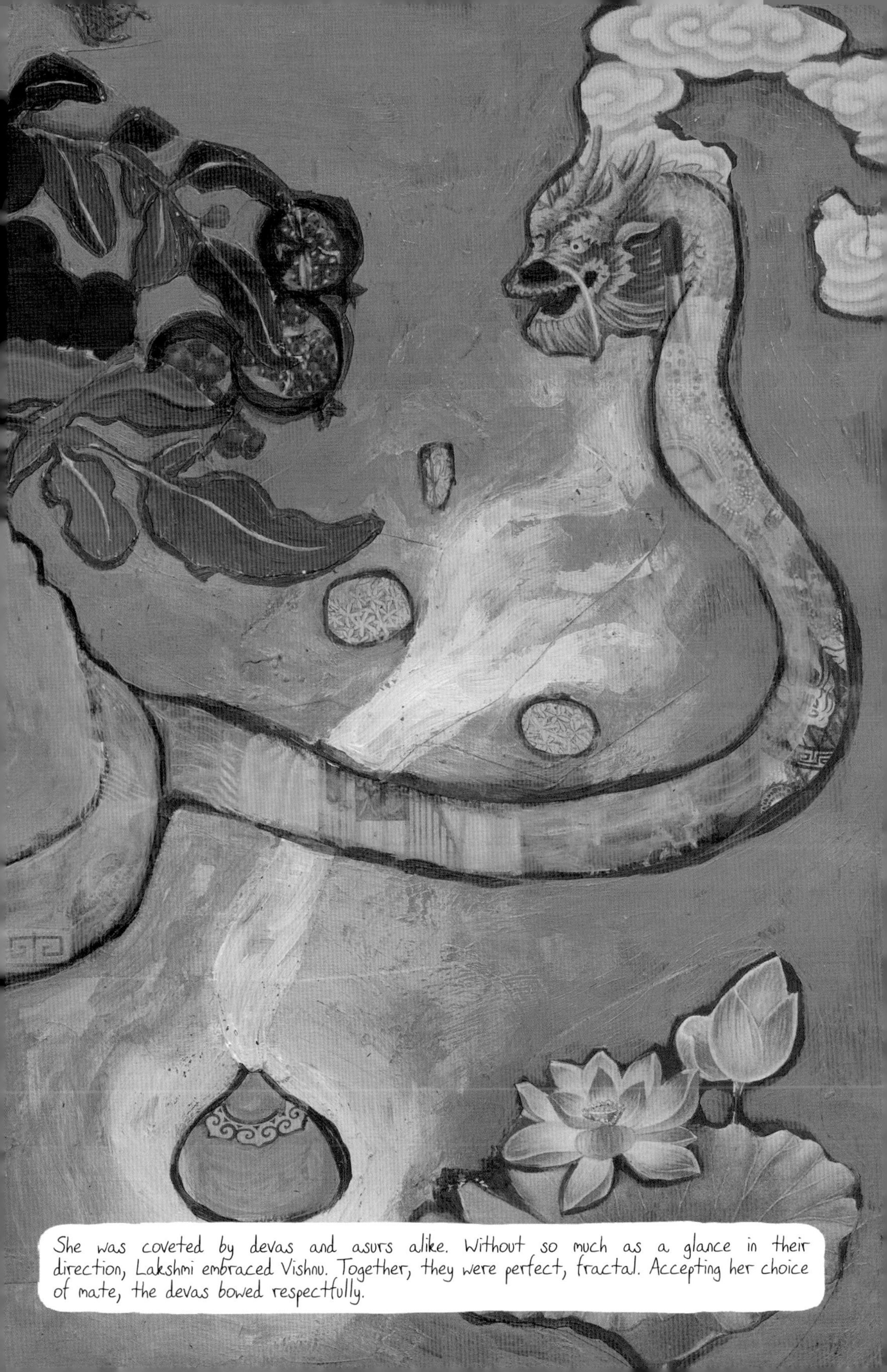
She was coveted by devas and asurs alike. Without so much as a glance in their direction, Lakshmi embraced Vishnu. Together, they were perfect, fractal. Accepting her choice of mate, the devas bowed respectfully.

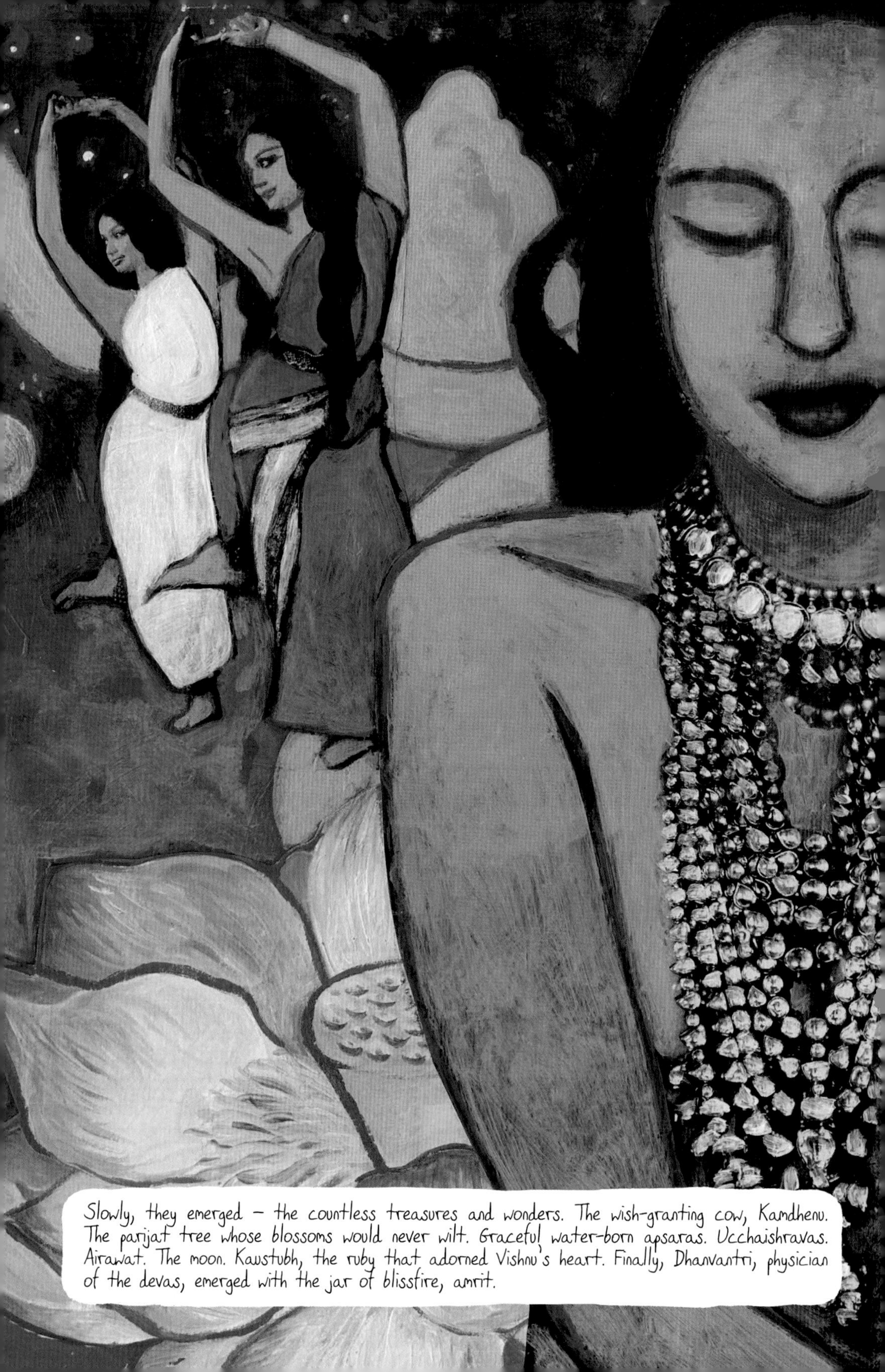
Slowly, they emerged – the countless treasures and wonders. The wish-granting cow, Kamdhenu. The parijat tree whose blossoms would never wilt. Graceful water-born apsaras. Ucchaishravas. Airawat. The moon. Kaustubh, the ruby that adorned Vishnu's heart. Finally, Dhanvantri, physician of the devas, emerged with the jar of blissfire, amrit.

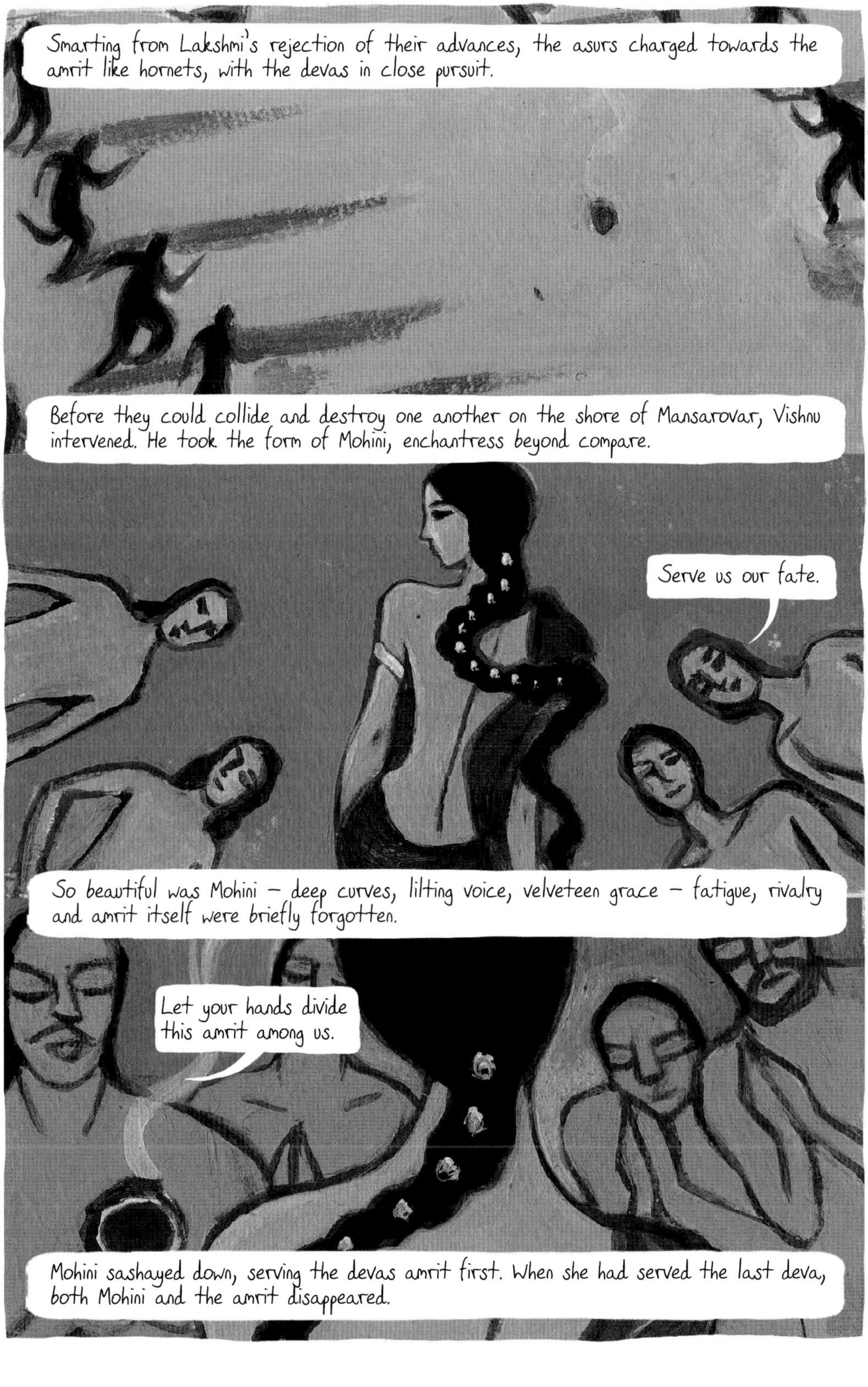
Smarting from Lakshmi's rejection of their advances, the asurs charged towards the amrit like hornets, with the devas in close pursuit.
Before they could collide and destroy one another on the shore of Mansarovar, Vishnu intervened. He took the form of Mohini, enchantress beyond compare.
Serve us our fate.
So beautiful was Mohini – deep curves, lilting voice, velveteen grace – fatigue, rivalry and amrit itself were briefly forgotten.
Let your hands divide this amrit among us.
Mohini sashayed down, serving the devas amrit first. When she had served the last deva, both Mohini and the amrit disappeared.

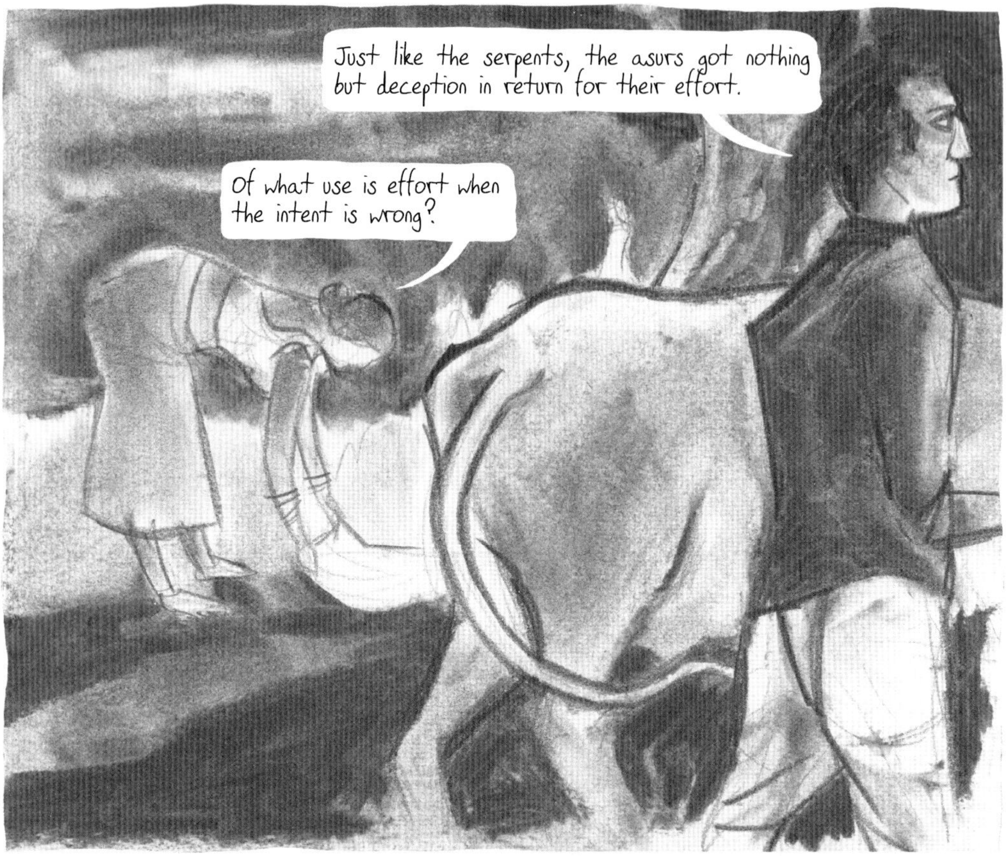
Just like the serpents, the asurs got nothing but deception in return for their effort.
Of what use is effort when the intent is wrong?

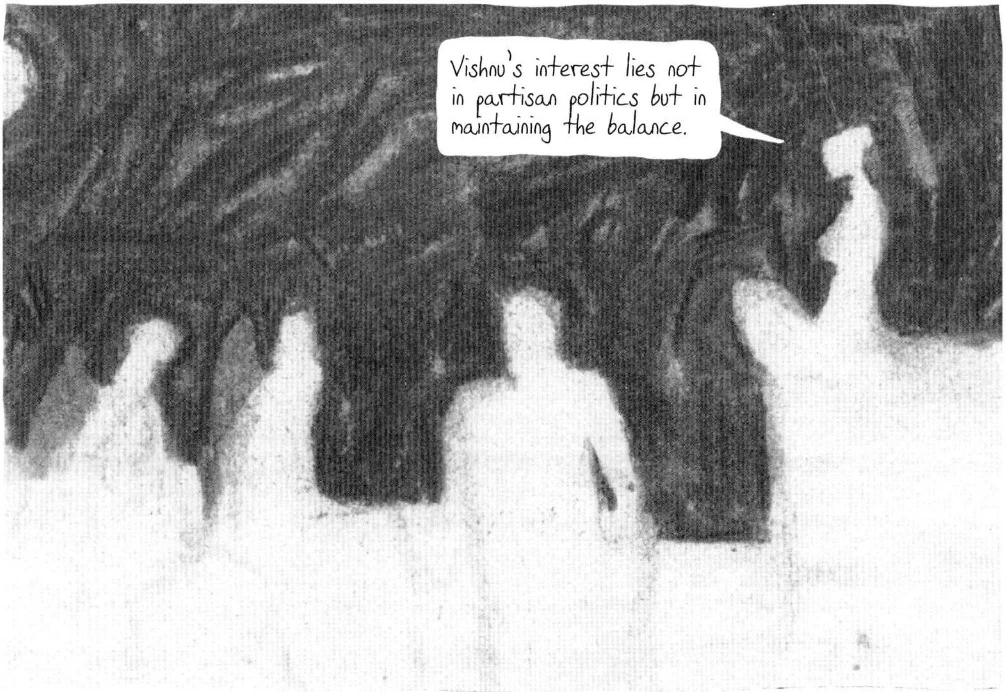
Vishnu's interest lies not in partisan politics but in maintaining the balance.

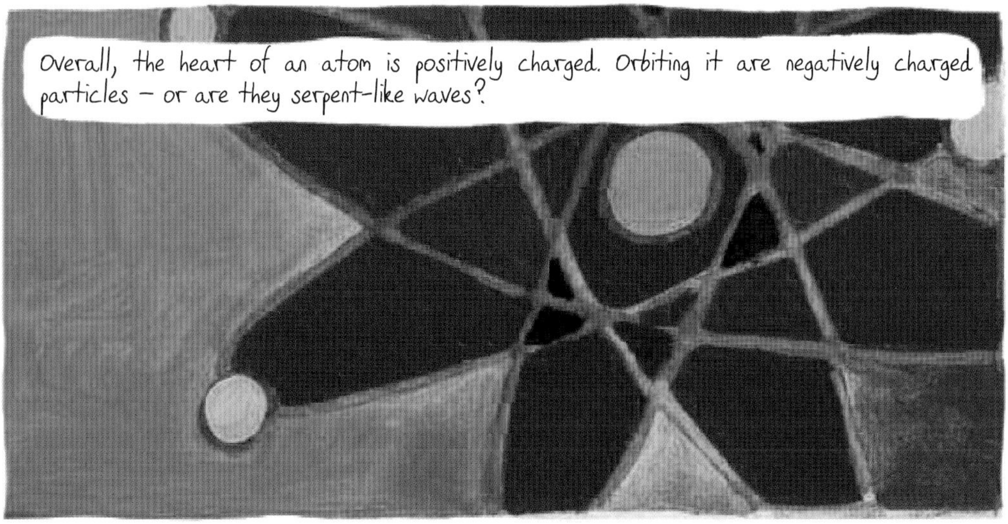
Overall, the heart of an atom is positively charged. Orbiting it are negatively charged particles – or are they serpent-like waves?

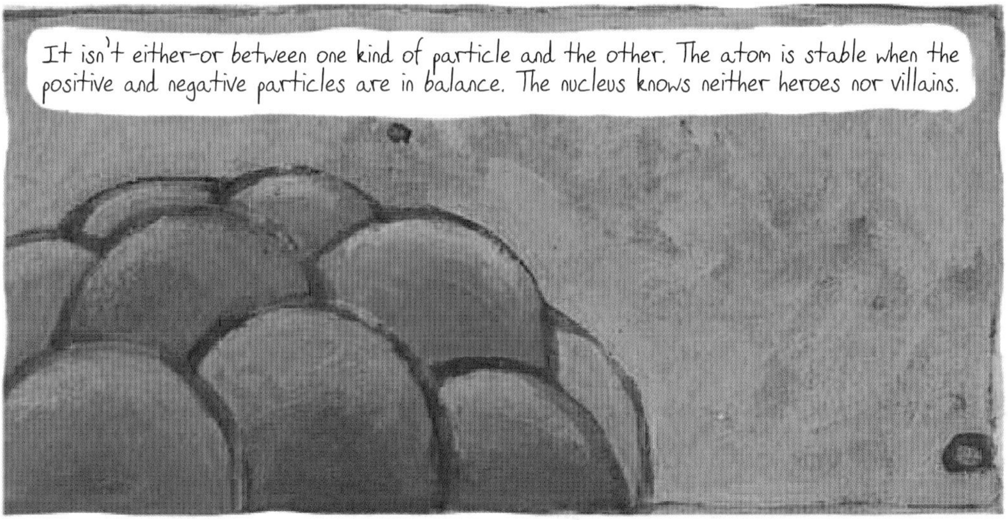
It isn't either-or between one kind of particle and the other. The atom is stable when the positive and negative particles are in balance. The nucleus knows neither heroes nor villains.

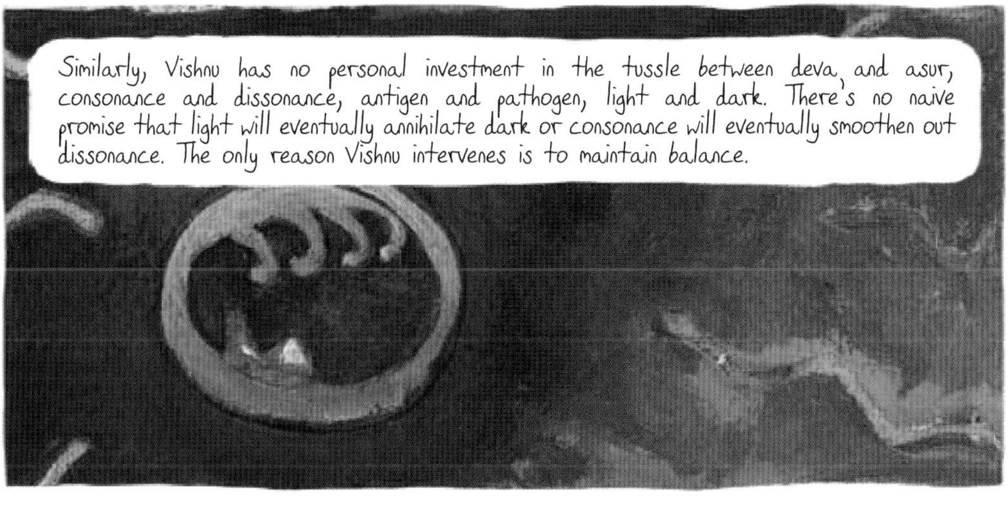
Similarly, Vishnu has no personal investment in the tussle between deva and asur, consonance and dissonance, antigen and pathogen, light and dark. There's no naive promise that light will eventually annihilate dark or consonance will eventually smoothen out dissonance. The only reason Vishnu intervenes is to maintain balance.

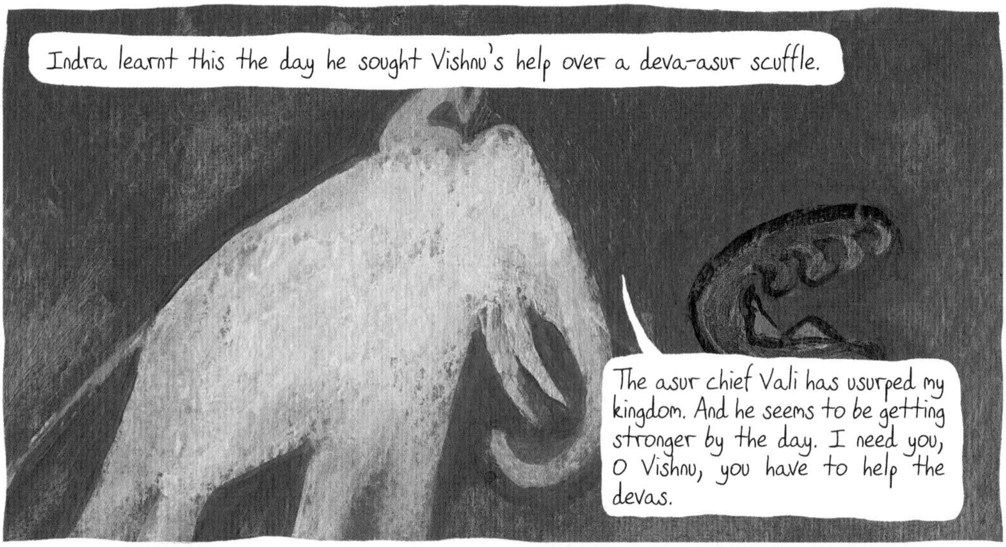
Indra learnt this the day he sought Vishnu's help over a deva-asur scuffle.
The asur chief Vali has usurped my kingdom. And he seems to be getting stronger by the day. I need you, O Vishnu, you have to help the devas.

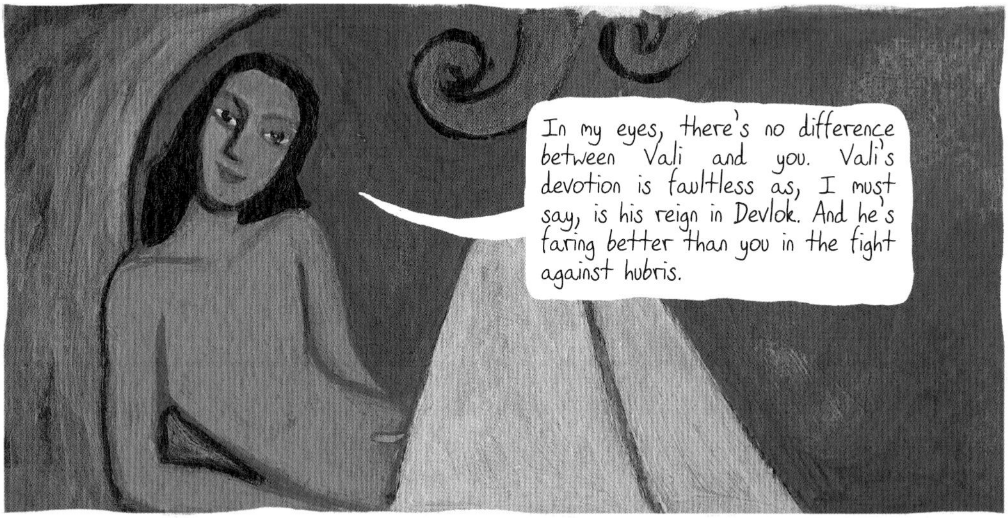
In my eyes, there's no difference between Vali and you. Vali's devotion is faultless as, I must say, is his reign in Devlok. And he's faring better than you in the fight against hubris.

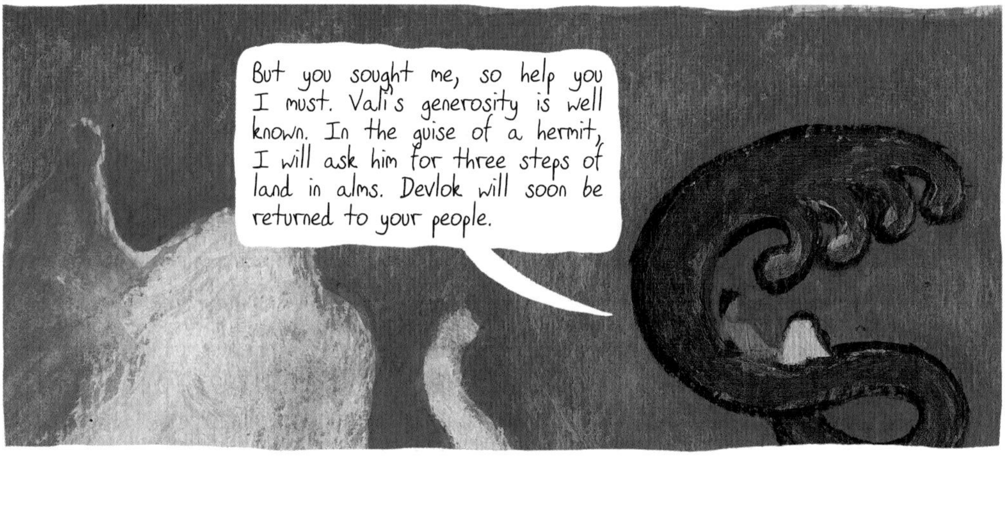
But you sought me, so help you I must. Vali's generosity is well known. In the guise of a hermit, I will ask him for three steps of land in alms. Devlok will soon be returned to your people.

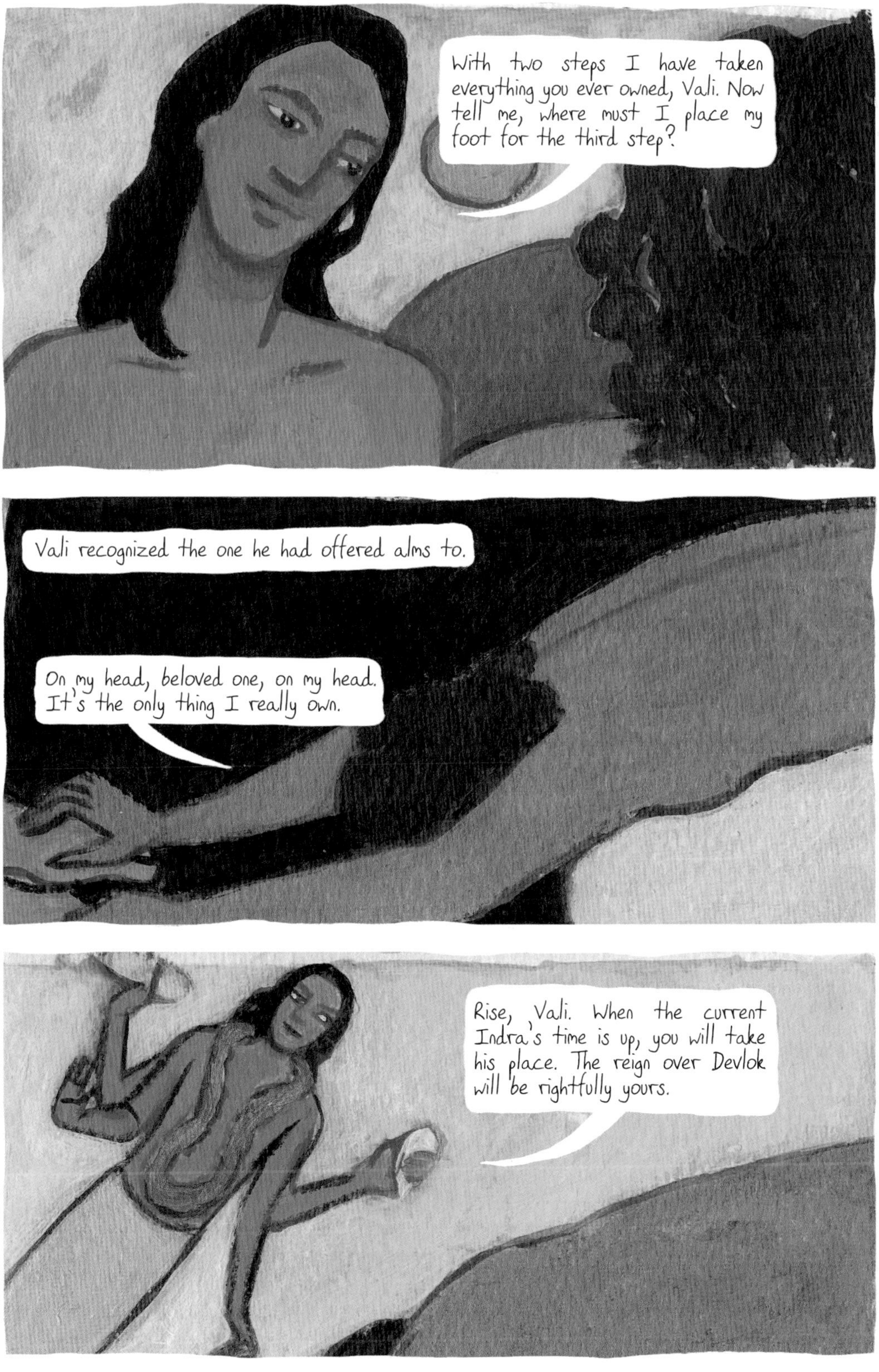
With two steps I have taken everything you ever owned, Vali. Now tell me, where must I place my foot for the third step?
Vali recognized the one he had offered alms to.
On my head, beloved one, on my head. It's the only thing I really own.
Rise, Vali. When the current Indra's time is up, you will take his place. The reign over Devlok will be rightfully yours.

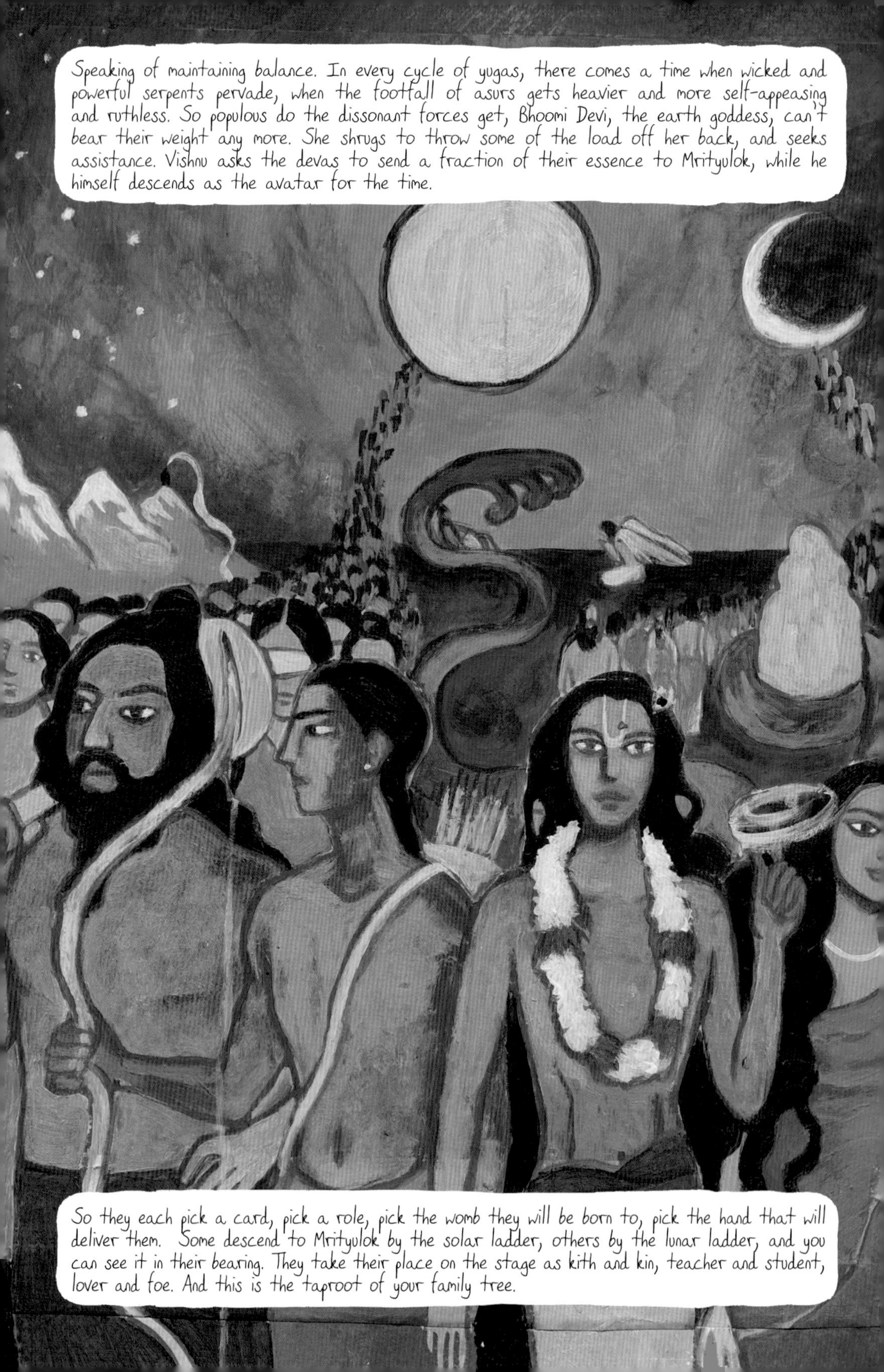
Speaking of maintaining balance. In every cycle of yugas, there comes a time when wicked and powerful serpents pervade, when the footfall of asurs gets heavier and more self-appeasing and ruthless. So populous do the dissonant forces get, Bhoomi Devi, the earth goddess, can't bear their weight any more. She shrugs to throw some of the load off her back, and seeks assistance. Vishnu asks the devas to send a fraction of their essence to Mrityulok, while he himself descends as the avatar for the time.
So they each pick a card, pick a role, pick the womb they will be born to, pick the hand that will deliver them. Some descend to Mrityulok by the solar ladder, others by the lunar ladder, and you can see it in their bearing. They take their place on the stage as kith and kin, teacher and student, lover and foe. And this is the taproot of your family tree.

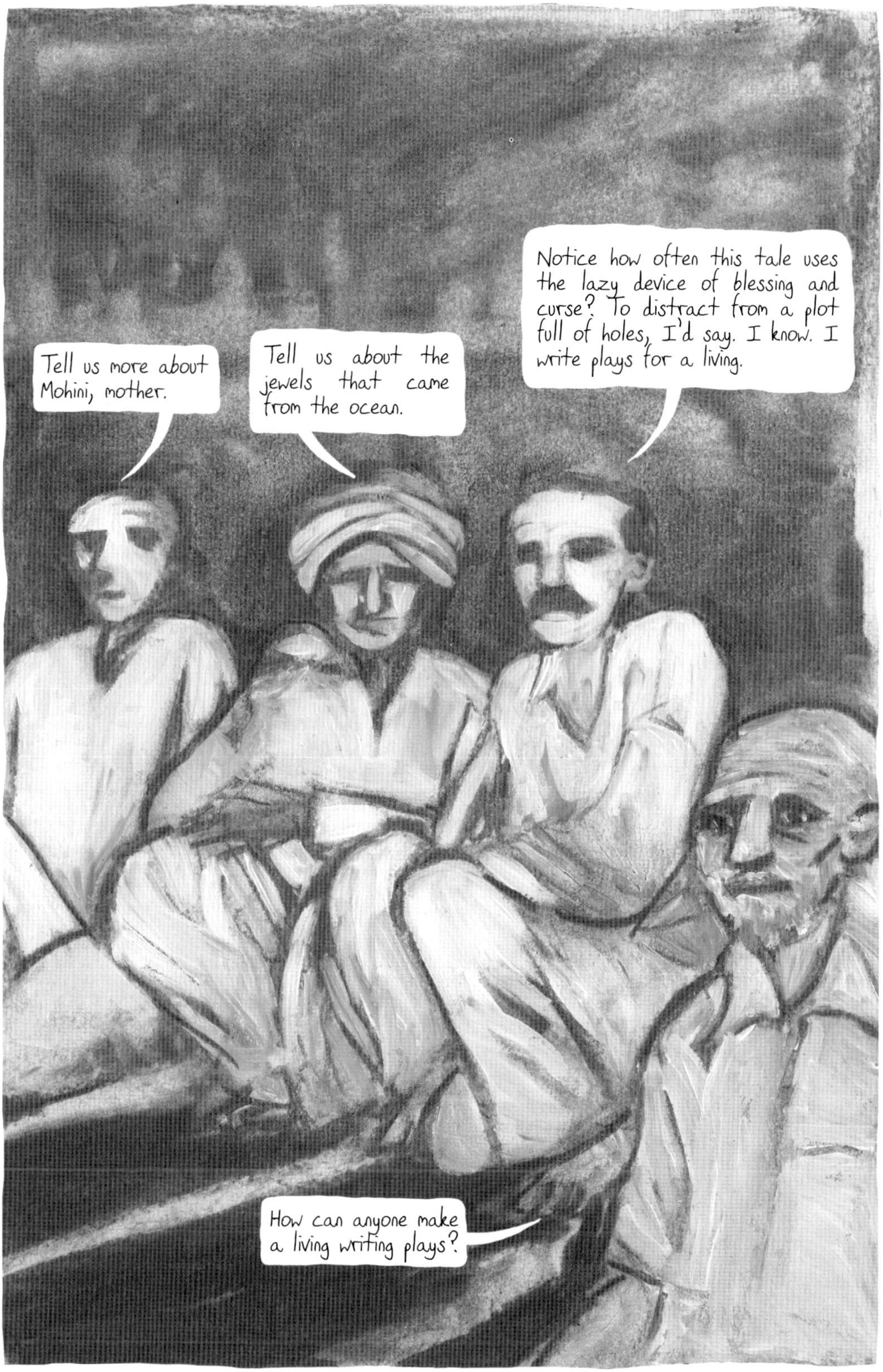
Tell us more about Mohini, mother.
Tell us about the jewels that came from the ocean.
Notice how often this tale uses the lazy device of blessing and curse? To distract from a plot full of holes, I'd say. I know. I write plays for a living.
How can anyone make a living writing plays?

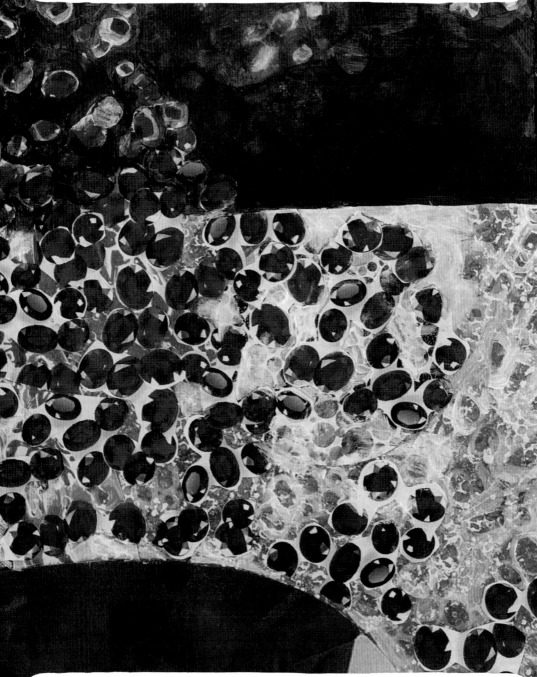

I will tell you about Indra's net, the most spectacular Indrajaal. Created by a clever illusionist in such a manner that it stretches out in all directions. A single, perfect ruby hangs in each eye of the net.

Since the net extends infinitely, an infinite number of fiery rubies glitter. It is a breathtaking sight, but that isn't where the wonder ends.

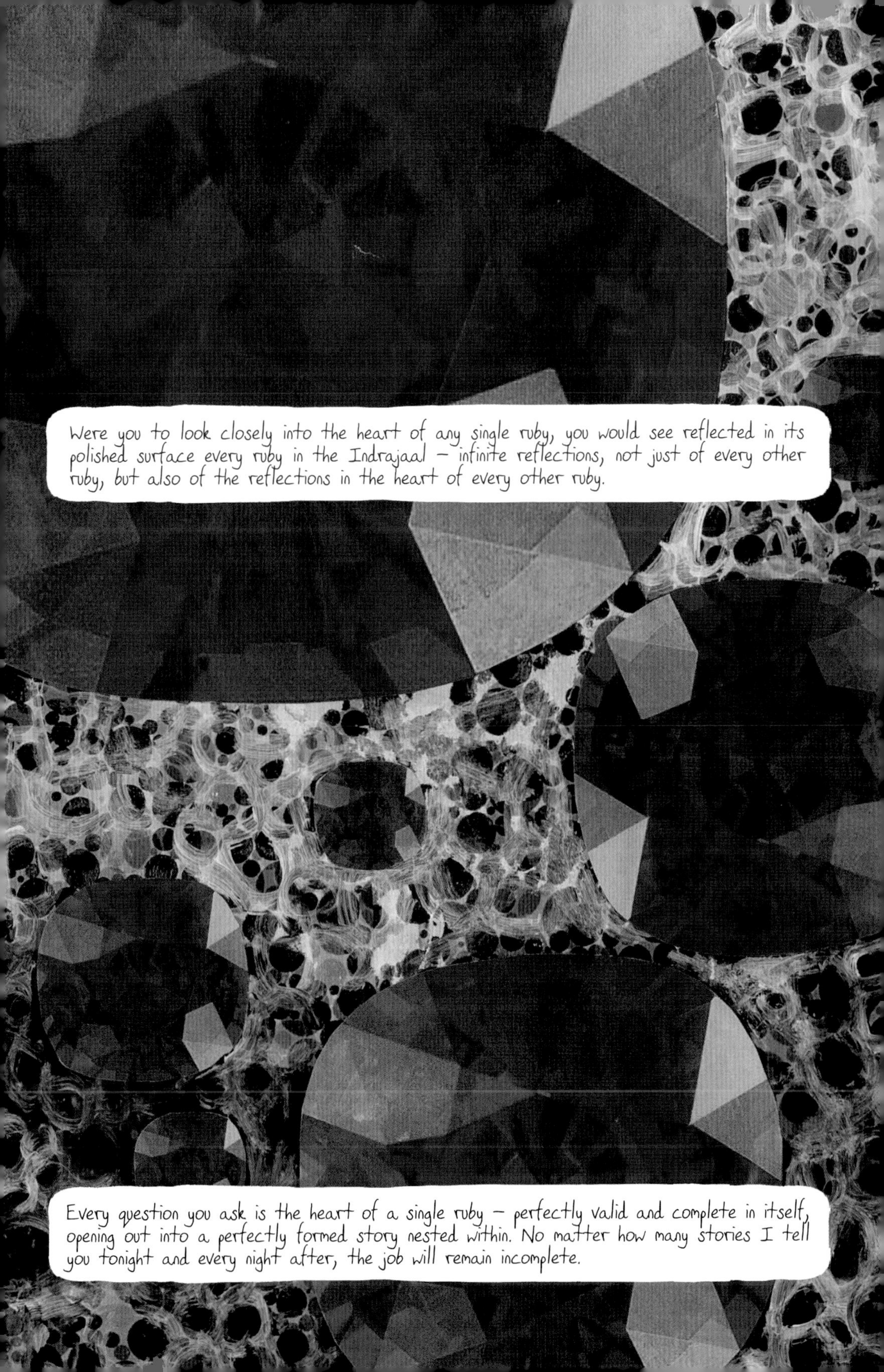
Were you to look closely into the heart of any single ruby, you would see reflected in its polished surface every ruby in the Indrajaal – infinite reflections, not just of every other ruby, but also of the reflections in the heart of every other ruby.
Every question you ask is the heart of a single ruby – perfectly valid and complete in itself, opening out into a perfectly formed story nested within. No matter how many stories I tell you tonight and every night after, the job will remain incomplete.

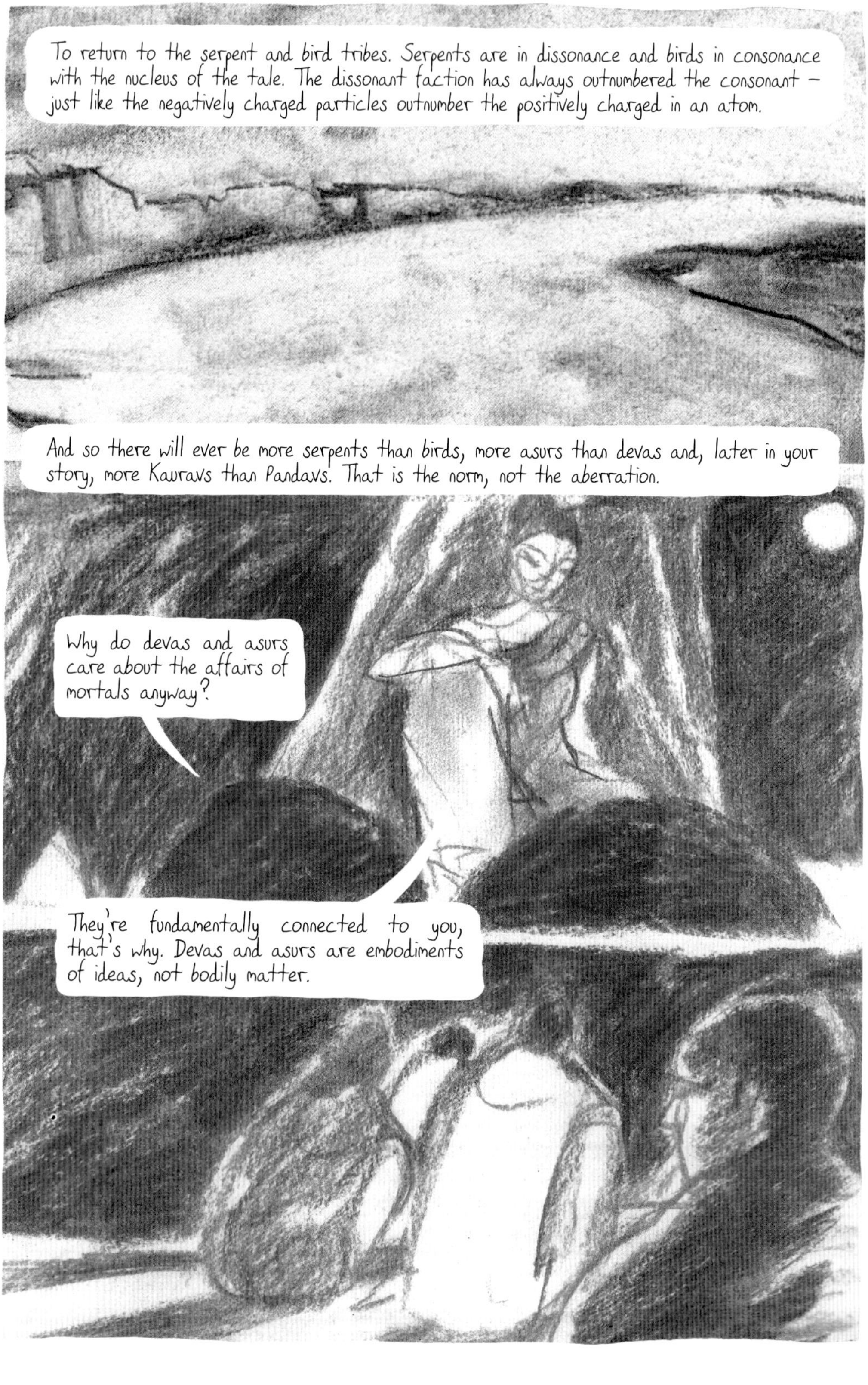
To return to the serpent and bird tribes. Serpents are in dissonance and birds in consonance with the nucleus of the tale. The dissonant faction has always outnumbered the consonant – just like the negatively charged particles outnumber the positively charged in an atom.
And so there will ever be more serpents than birds, more asurs than devas and, later in your story, more Kauravs than Pandavs. That is the norm, not the aberration.
Why do devas and asurs care about the affairs of mortals anyway?
They're fundamentally connected to you, that's why. Devas and asurs are embodiments of ideas, not bodily matter.

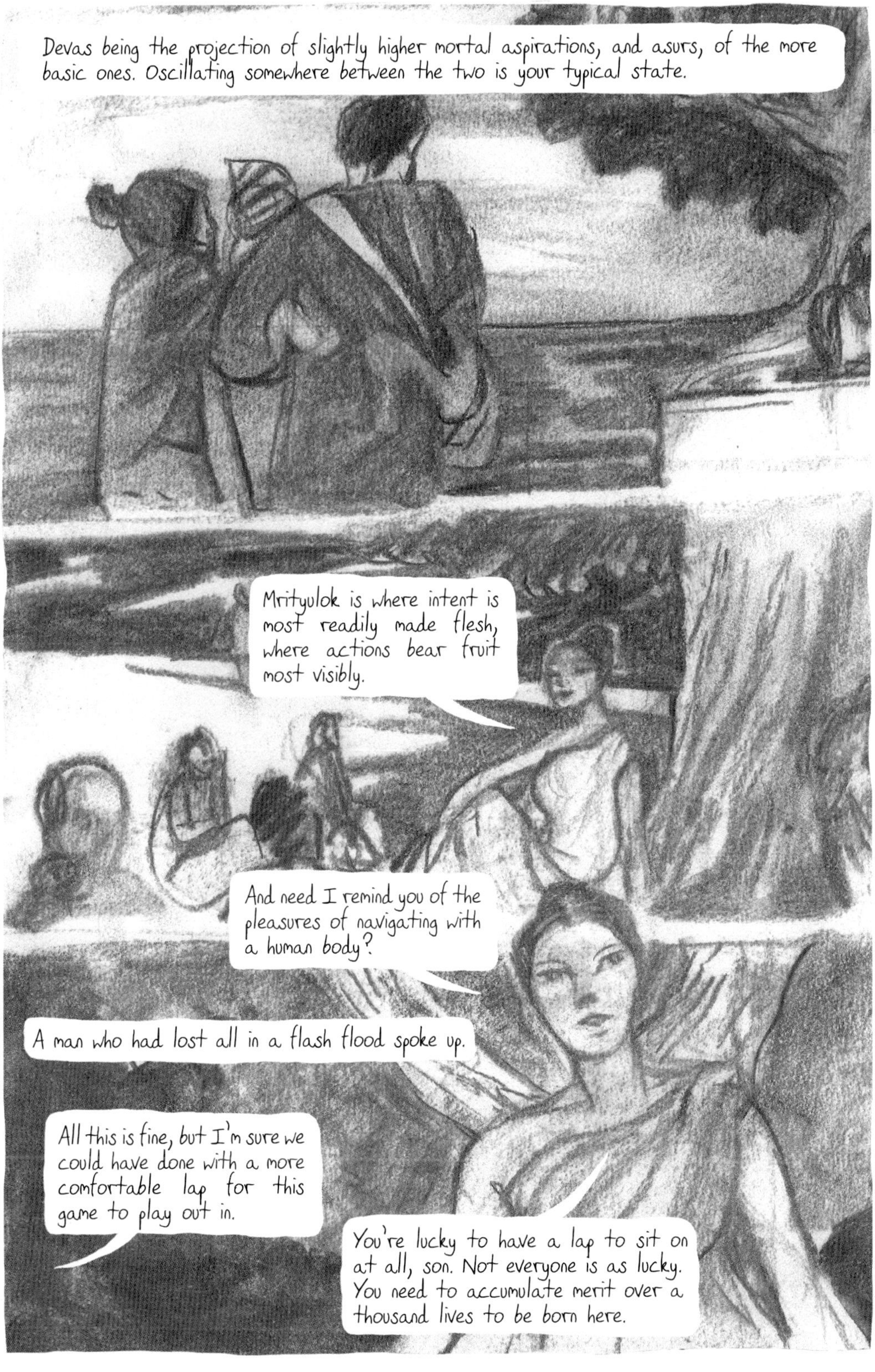
Devas being the projection of slightly higher mortal aspirations, and asurs, of the more basic ones. Oscillating somewhere between the two is your typical state.
Mrityulok is where intent is most readily made flesh, where actions bear fruit most visibly.
And need I remind you of the pleasures of navigating with a human body?
A man who had lost all in a flash flood spoke up.
All this is fine, but I'm sure we could have done with a more comfortable lap for this game to play out in.
You're lucky to have a lap to sit on at all, son. Not everyone is as lucky. You need to accumulate merit over a thousand lives to be born here.

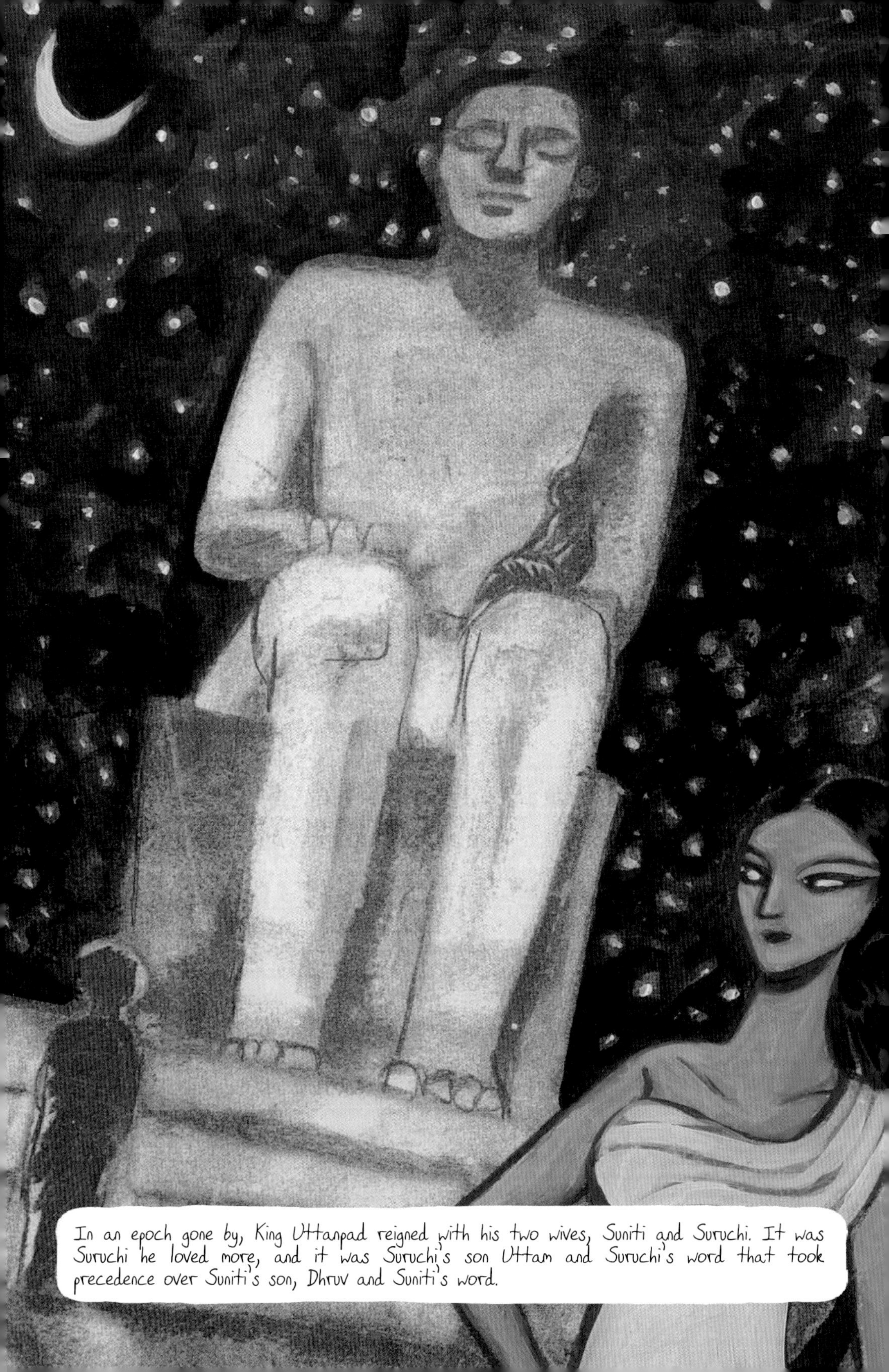
In an epoch gone by, King Uttanpad reigned with his two wives, Suniti and Suruchi. It was Suruchi he loved more, and it was Suruchi's son Uttam and Suruchi's word that took precedence over Suniti's son, Dhruv and Suniti's word.

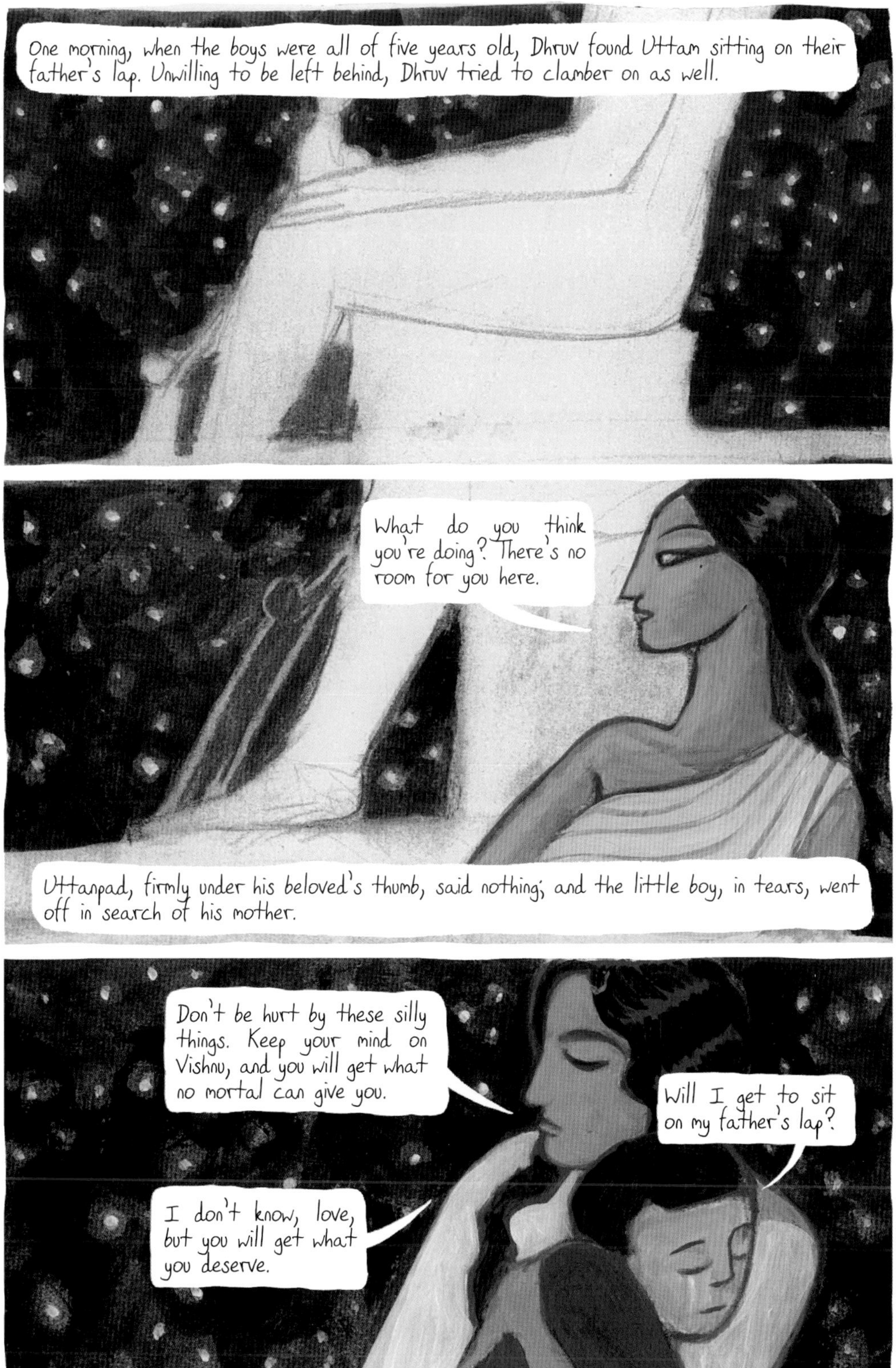
One morning, when the boys were all of five years old, Dhruv found Uttam sitting on their father's lap. Unwilling to be left behind, Dhruv tried to clamber on as well.
What do you think you're doing? There's no room for you here.
Uttanpad, firmly under his beloved's thumb, said nothing; and the little boy, in tears, went off in search of his mother.
Don't be hurt by these silly things. Keep your mind on Vishnu, and you will get what no mortal can give you.
Will I get to sit on my father's lap?
I don't know, love, but you will get what you deserve.

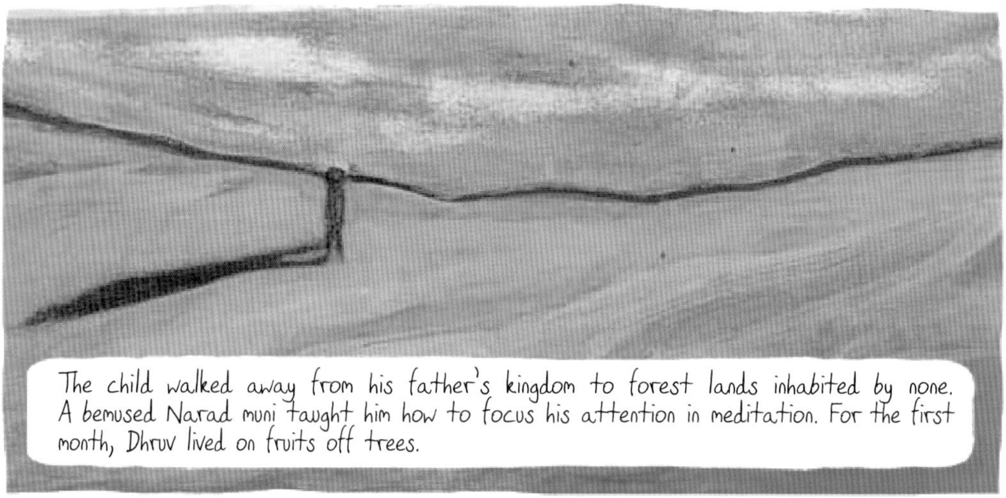
The child walked away from his father's kingdom to forest lands inhabited by none. A bemused Narad muni taught him how to focus his attention in meditation. For the first month, Dhruv lived on fruits off trees.

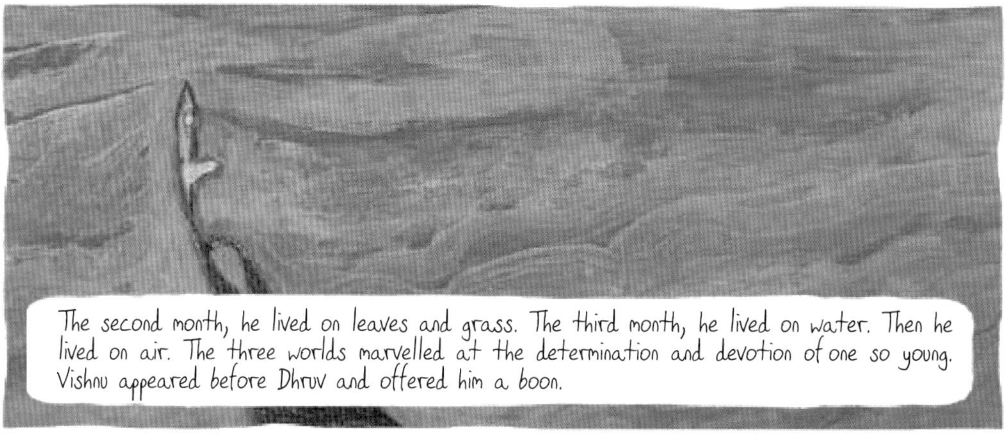
The second month, he lived on leaves and grass. The third month, he lived on water. Then he lived on air. The three worlds marvelled at the determination and devotion of one so young. Vishnu appeared before Dhruv and offered him a boon.

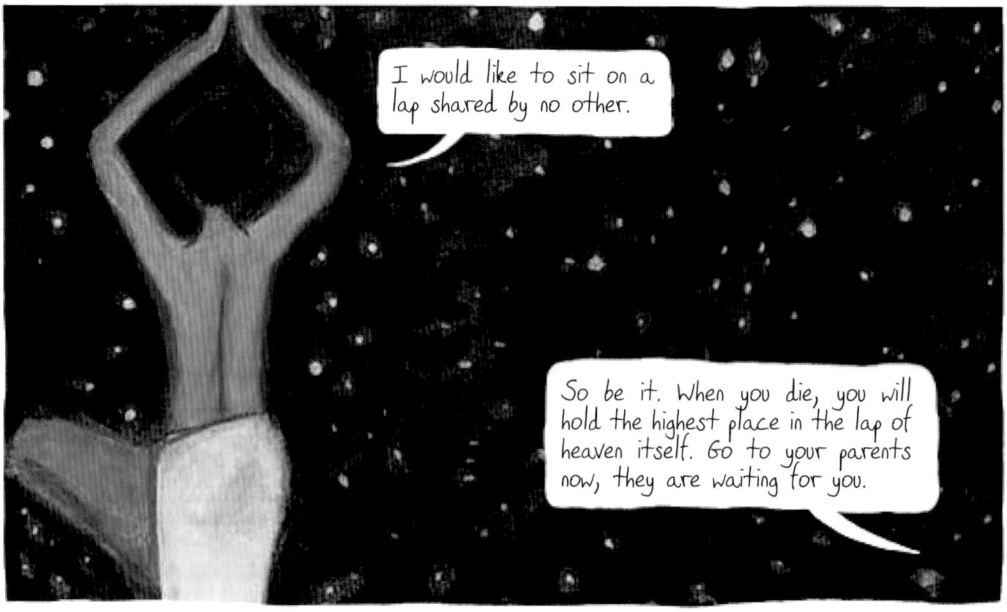
I would like to sit on a lap shared by no other.
So be it. When you die, you will hold the highest place in the lap of heaven itself. Go to your parents now, they are waiting for you.

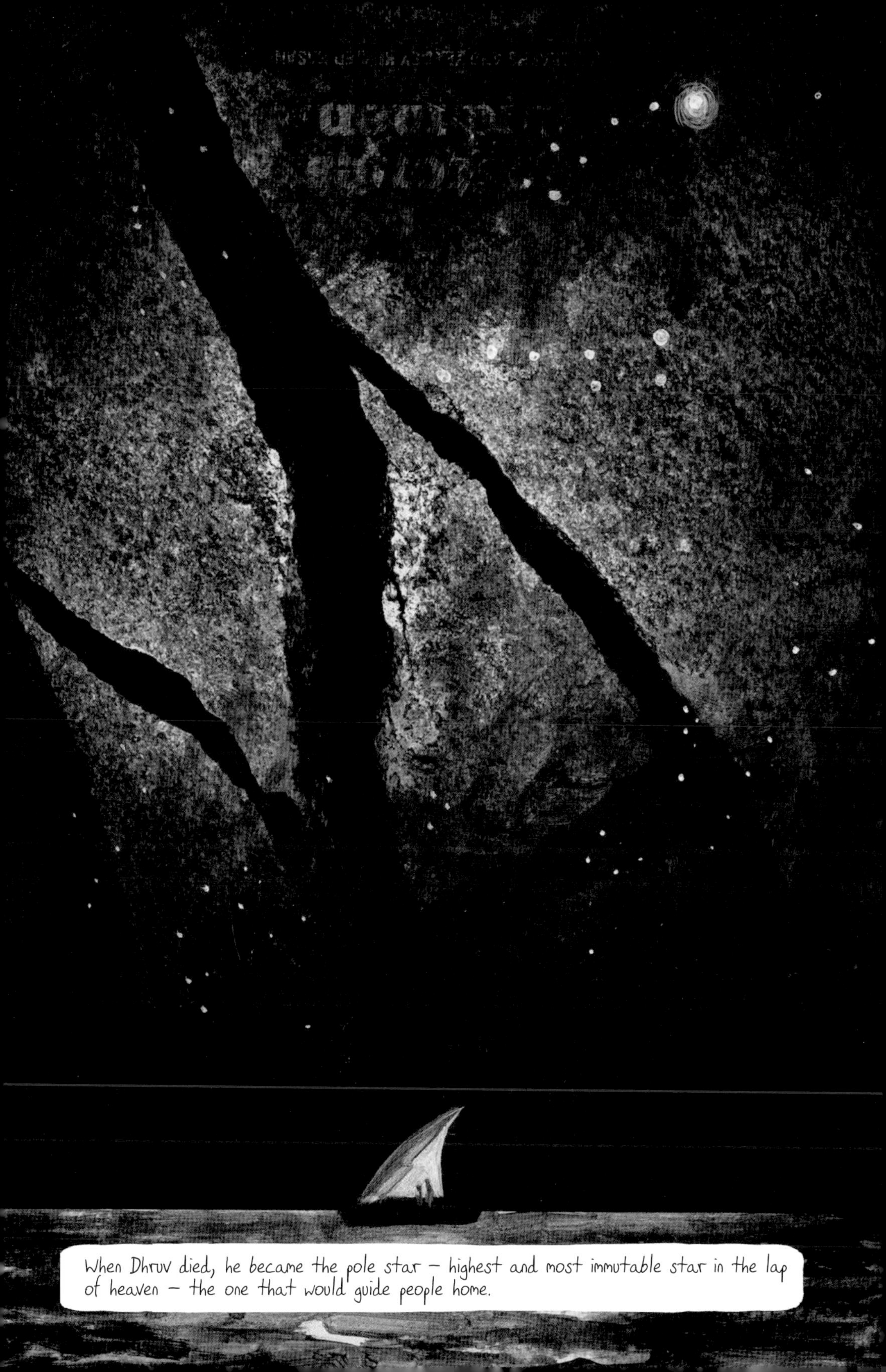
When Dhruv died, he became the pole star – highest and most immutable star in the lap of heaven – the one that would guide people home.

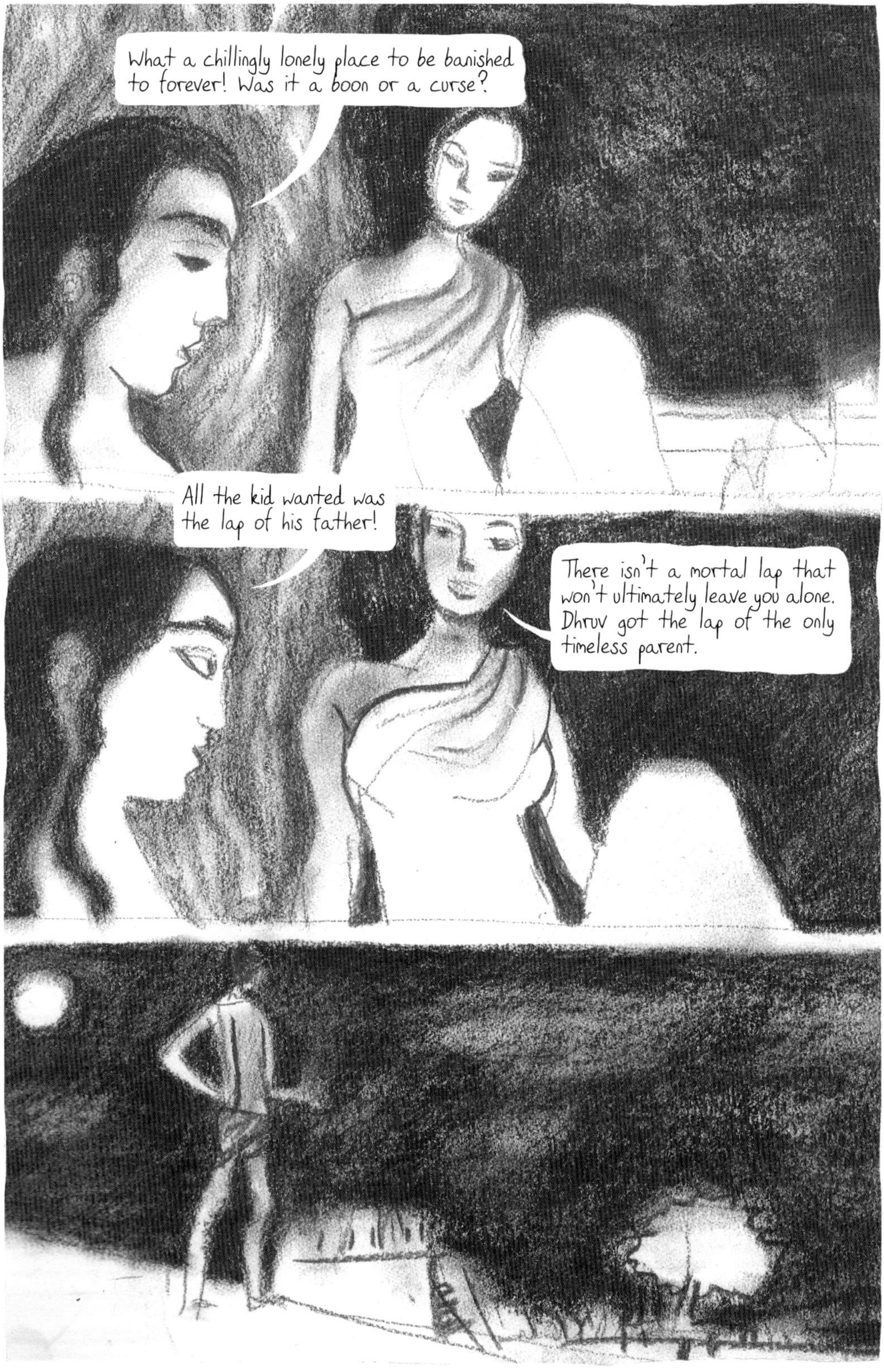
What a chillingly lonely place to be banished to forever! Was it a boon or a curse?
All the kid wanted was the lap of his father!
There isn't a mortal lap that won't ultimately leave you alone. Dhruv got the lap of the only timeless parent.

JANMEJAYA'S FIRE

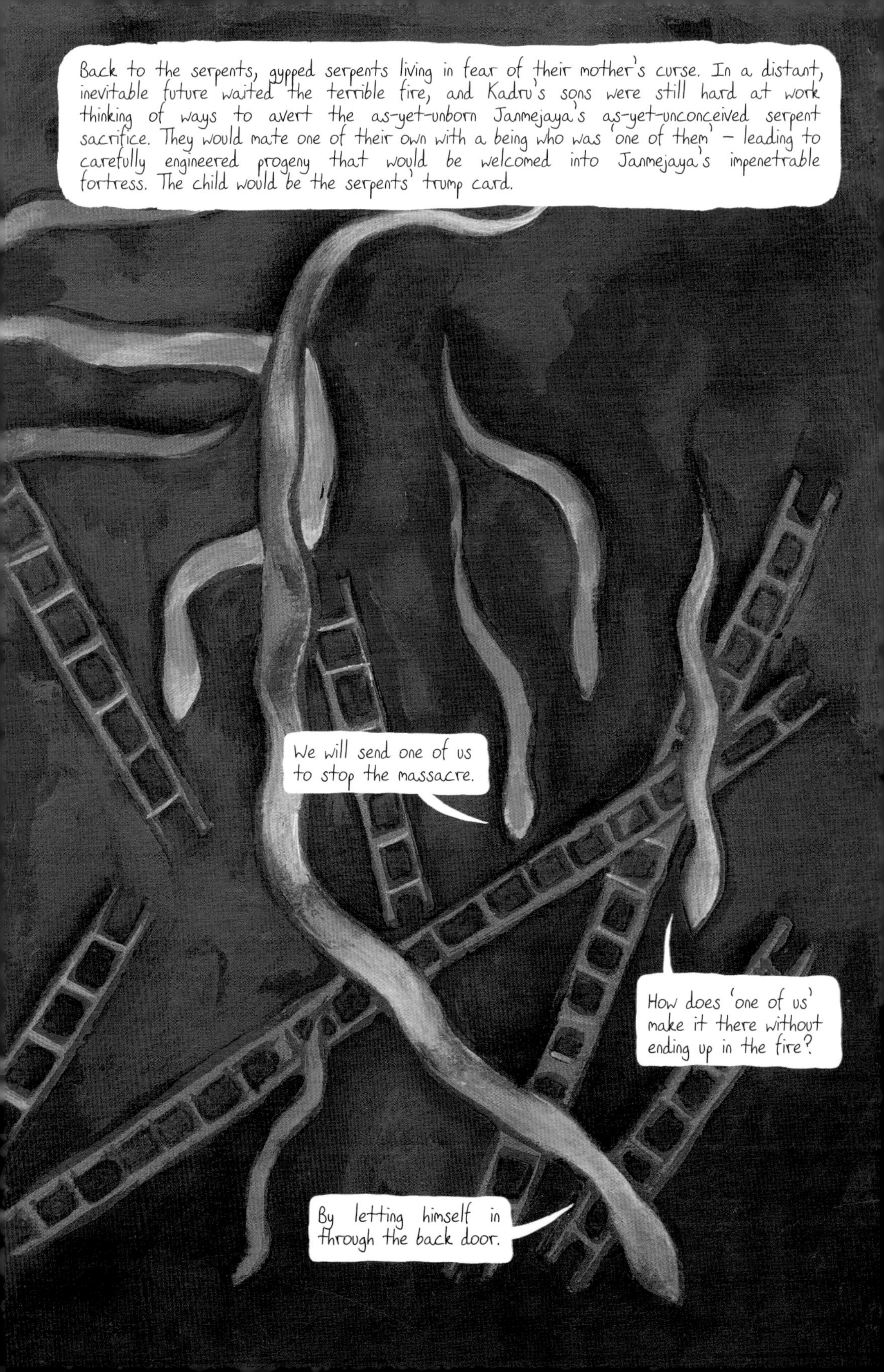
Back to the serpents, gypped serpents living in fear of their mother's curse. In a distant, inevitable future waited the terrible fire, and Kadru's sons were still hard at work thinking of ways to avert the as-yet-unborn Janmejaya's as-yet-unconceived serpent sacrifice. They would mate one of their own with a being who was 'one of them' – leading to carefully engineered progeny that would be welcomed into Janmejaya's impenetrable fortress. The child would be the serpents' trump card.
We will send one of us to stop the massacre.
How does 'one of us' make it there without ending up in the fire?
By letting himself in through the back door.

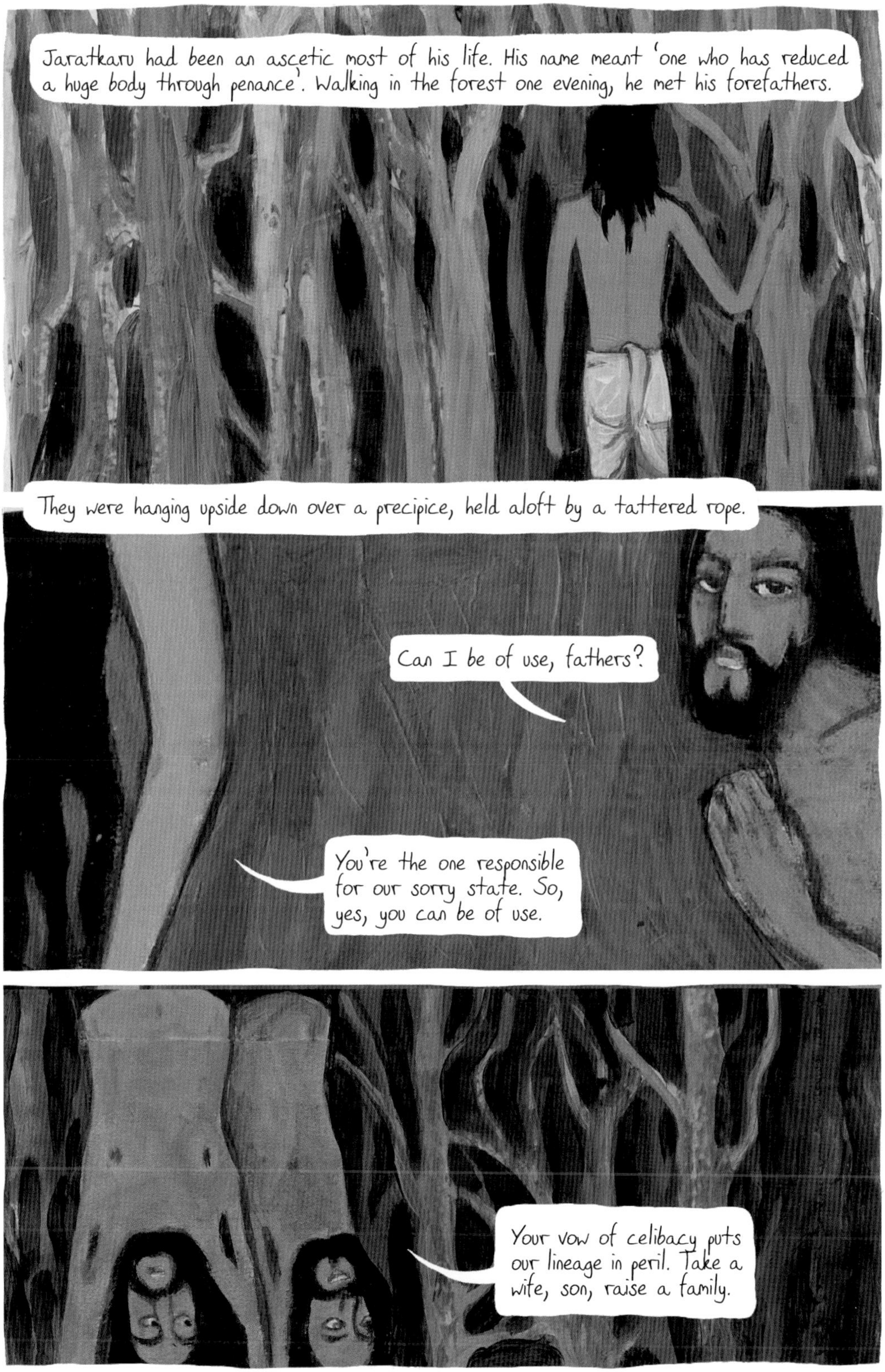
Jaratkaru had been an ascetic most of his life. His name meant 'one who has reduced a huge body through penance'. Walking in the forest one evening, he met his forefathers.
They were hanging upside down over a precipice, held aloft by a tattered rope.
Can I be of use, fathers?
You're the one responsible for our sorry state. So, yes, you can be of use.
Your vow of celibacy puts our lineage in peril. Take a wife, son, raise a family.

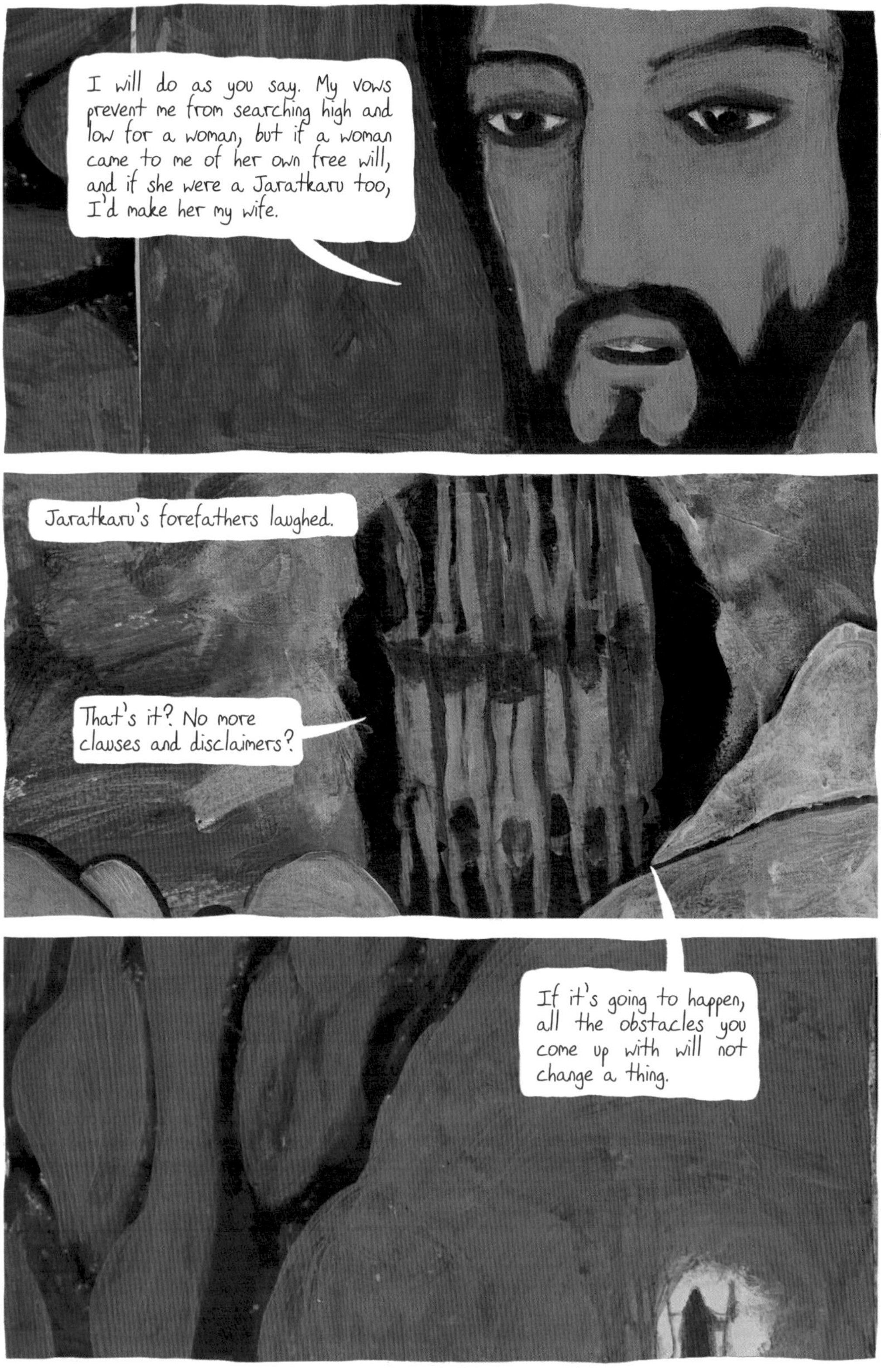
I will do as you say. My vows prevent me from searching high and low for a woman, but if a woman came to me of her own free will, and if she were a Jaratkaru too, I'd make her my wife.
Jaratkaru's forefathers laughed.
That's it? No more clauses and disclaimers?
If it's going to happen, all the obstacles you come up with will not change a thing.

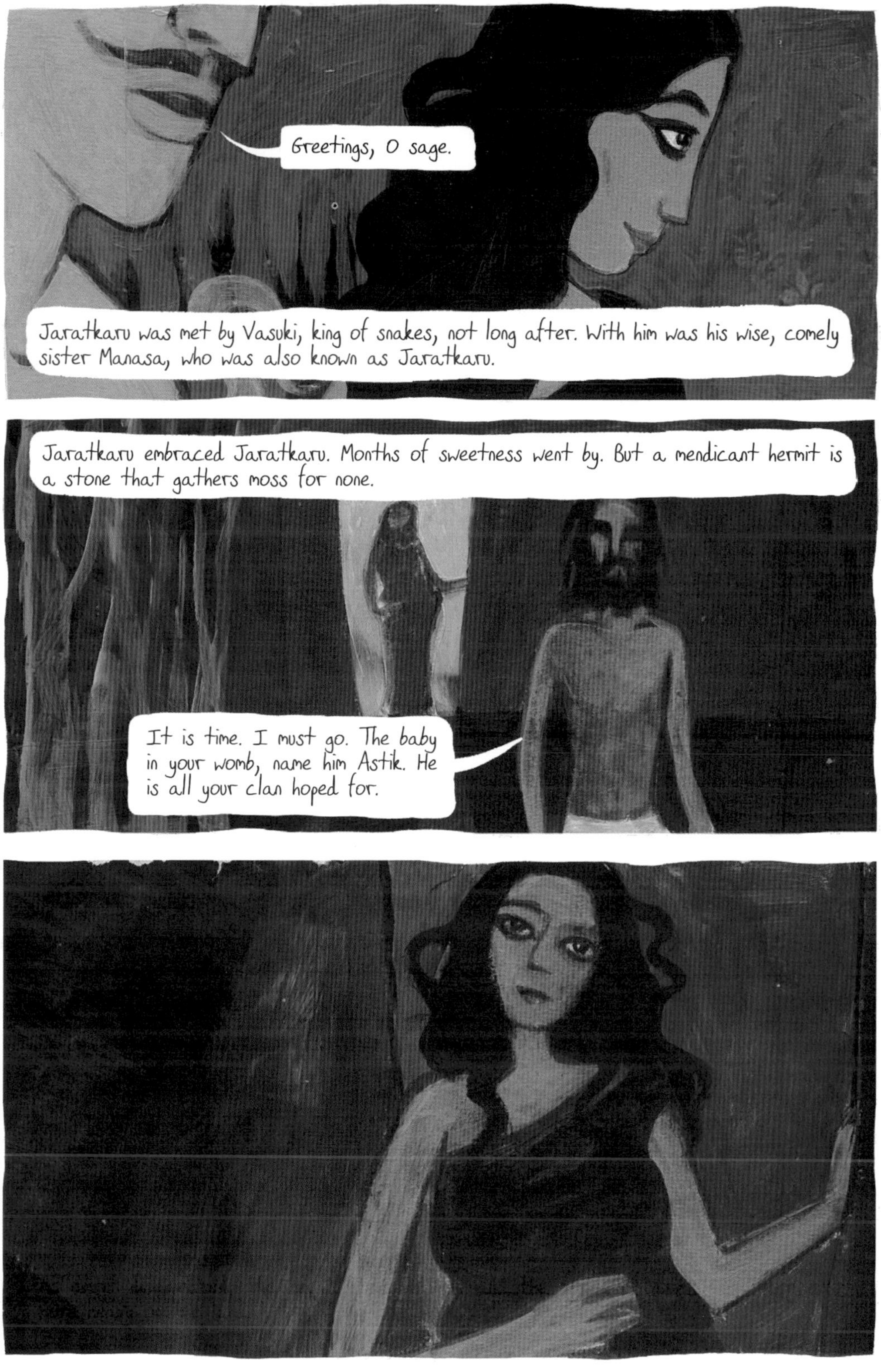
Greetings, O sage.
Jaratkaru was met by Vasuki, king of snakes, not long after. With him was his wise, comely sister Manasa, who was also known as Jaratkaru.
Jaratkaru embraced Jaratkaru. Months of sweetness went by. But a mendicant hermit is a stone that gathers moss for none.
It is time. I must go. The baby in your womb, name him Astik. He is all your clan hoped for.

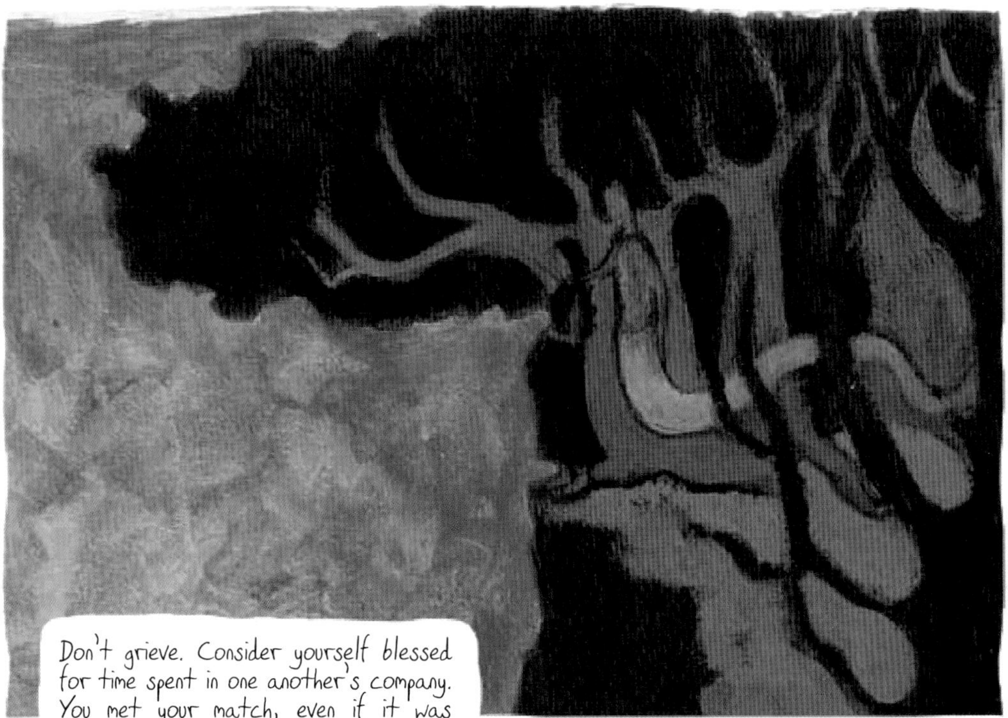

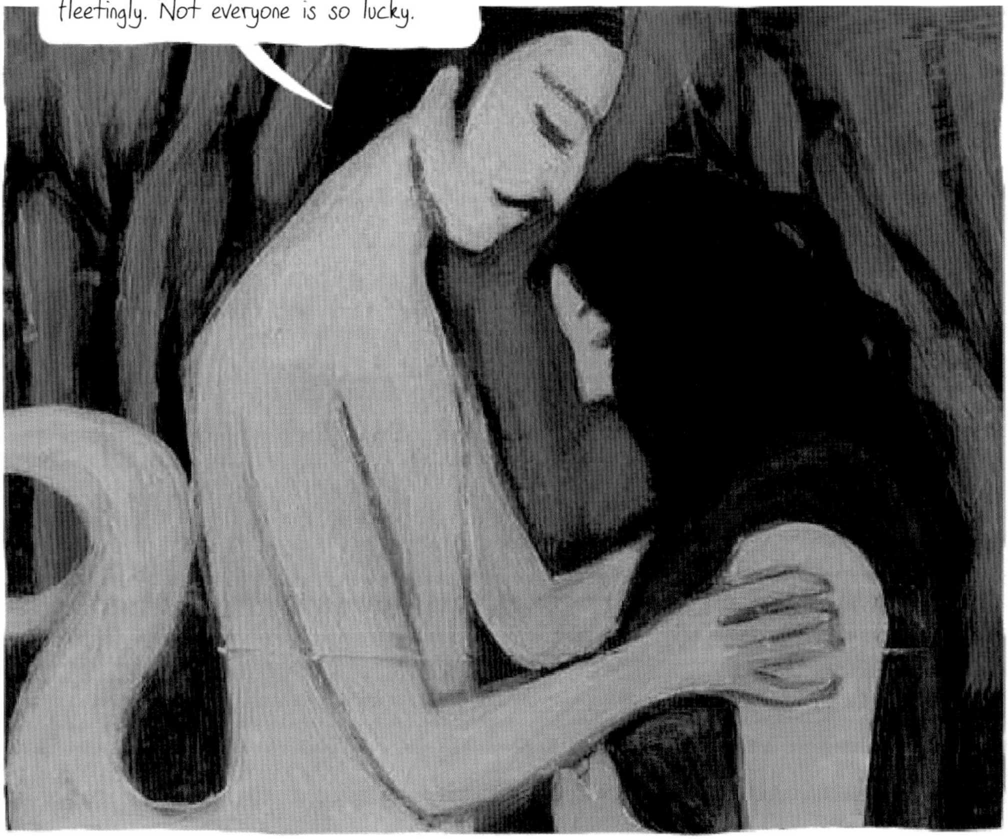
Don't grieve. Consider yourself blessed for time spent in one another's company. You met your match, even if it was fleetingly. Not everyone is so lucky.

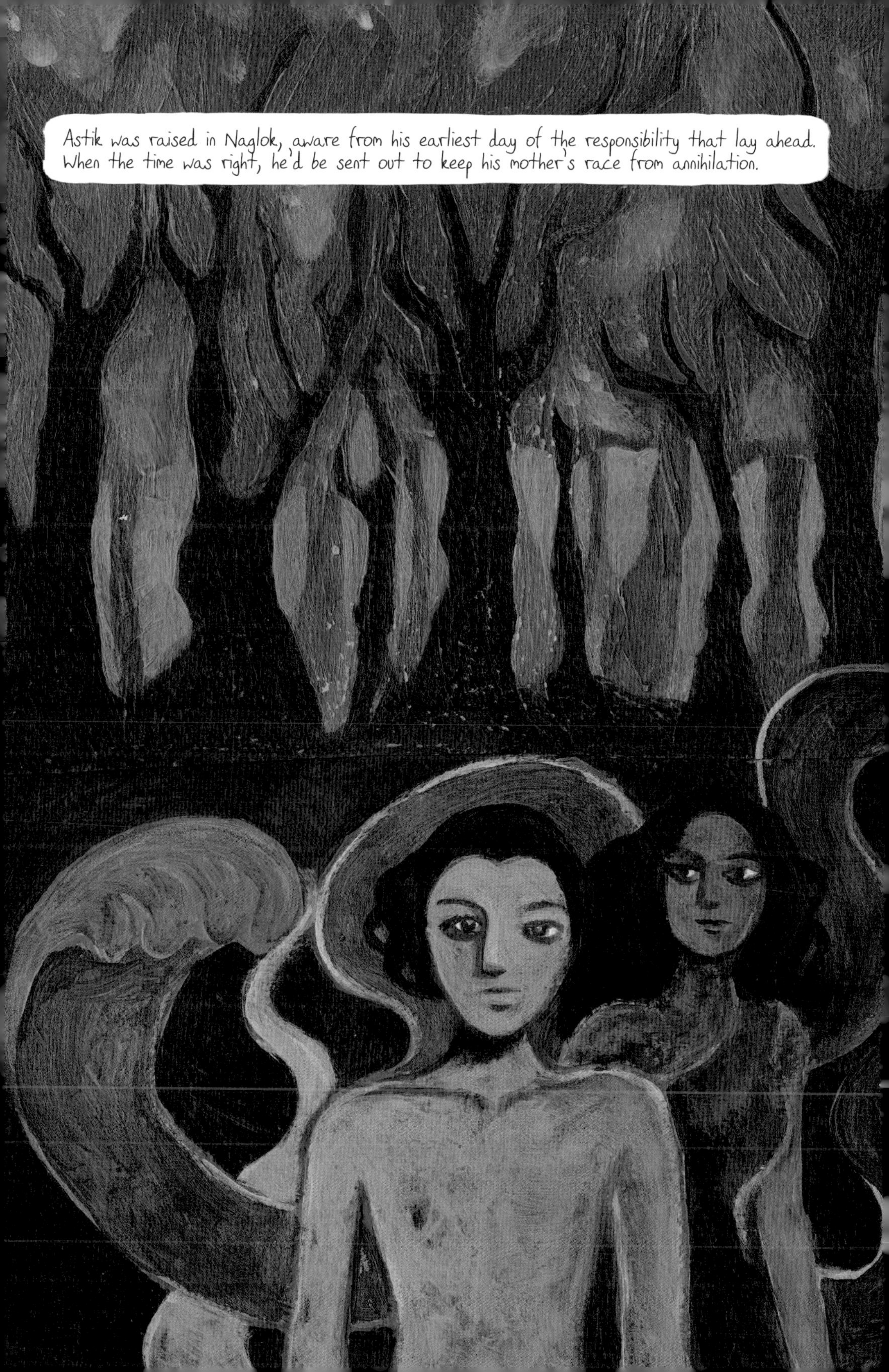
Astik was raised in Naglok, aware from his earliest day of the responsibility that lay ahead. When the time was right, he'd be sent out to keep his mother's race from annihilation.

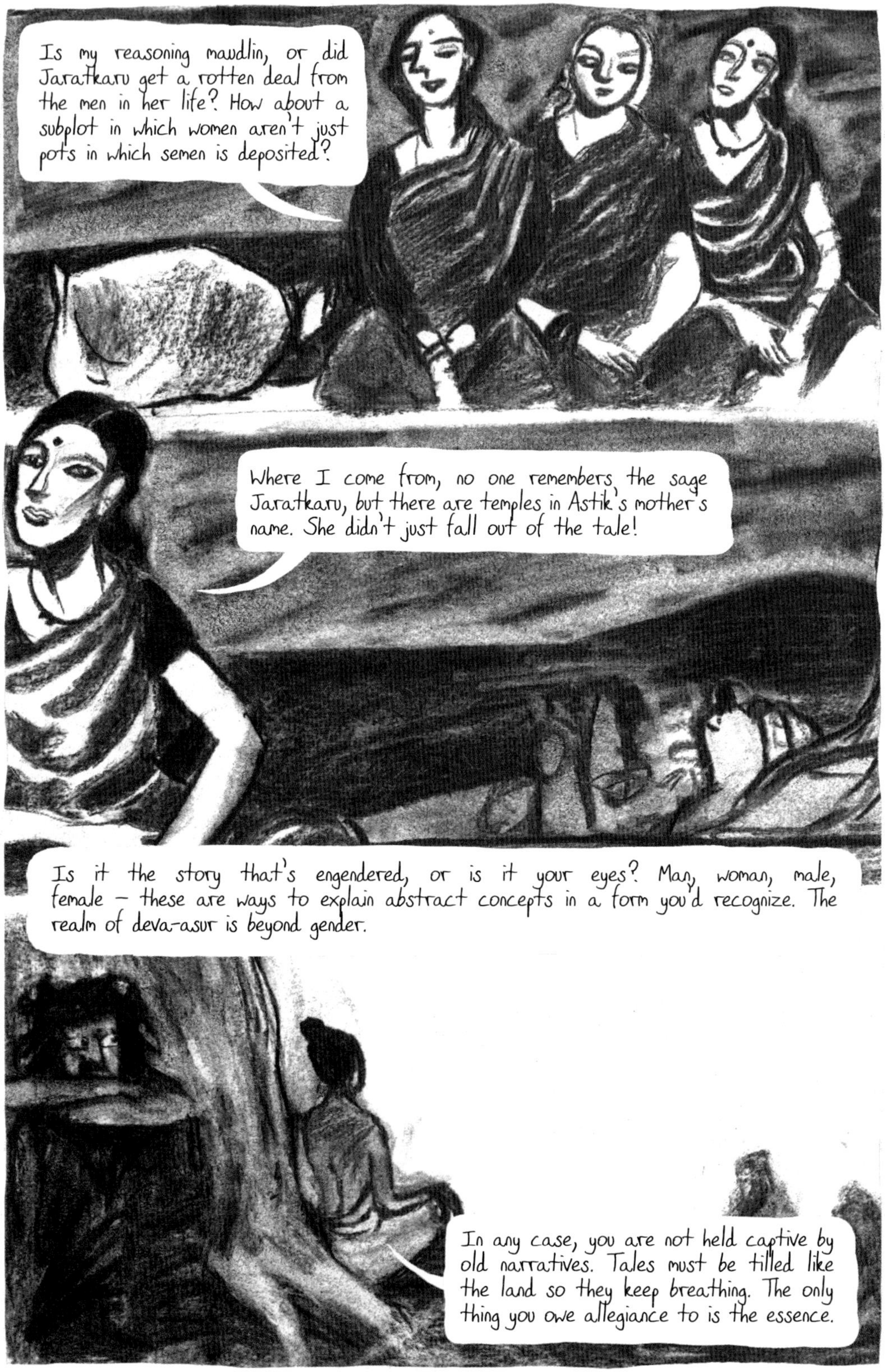
Is my reasoning maudlin, or did Jaratkaru get a rotten deal from the men in her life? How about a subplot in which women aren't just pots in which semen is deposited?
Where I come from, no one remembers the sage Jaratkaru, but there are temples in Astik's mother's name. She didn't just fall out of the tale!
Is it the story that's engendered, or is it your eyes? Man, woman, male, female – these are ways to explain abstract concepts in a form you'd recognize. The realm of deva-asur is beyond gender.
In any case, you are not held captive by old narratives. Tales must be tilled like the land so they keep breathing. The only thing you owe allegiance to is the essence.

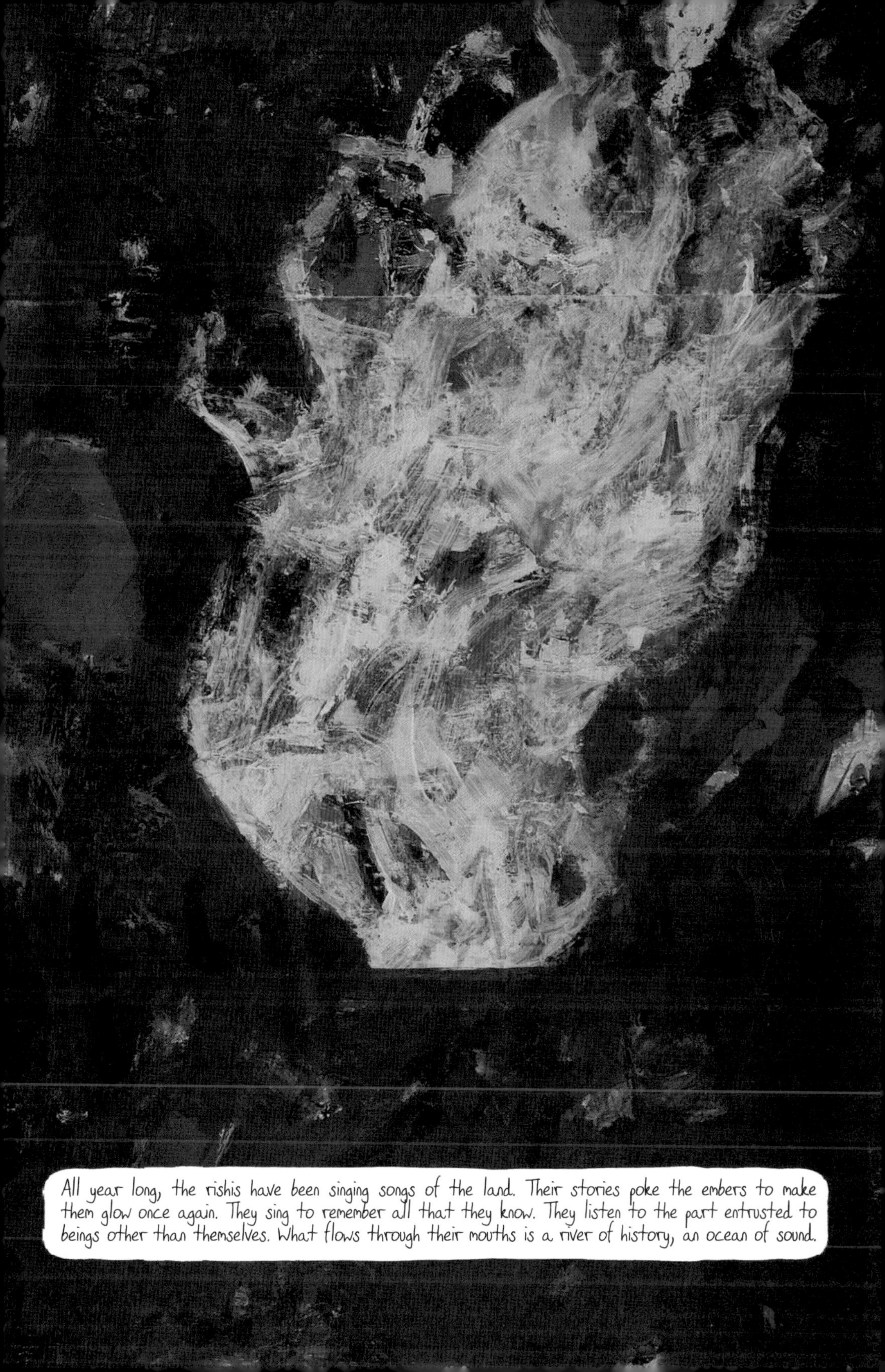
All year long, the rishis have been singing songs of the land. Their stories poke the embers to make them glow once again. They sing to remember all that they know. They listen to the part entrusted to beings other than themselves. What flows through their mouths is a river of history, an ocean of sound.

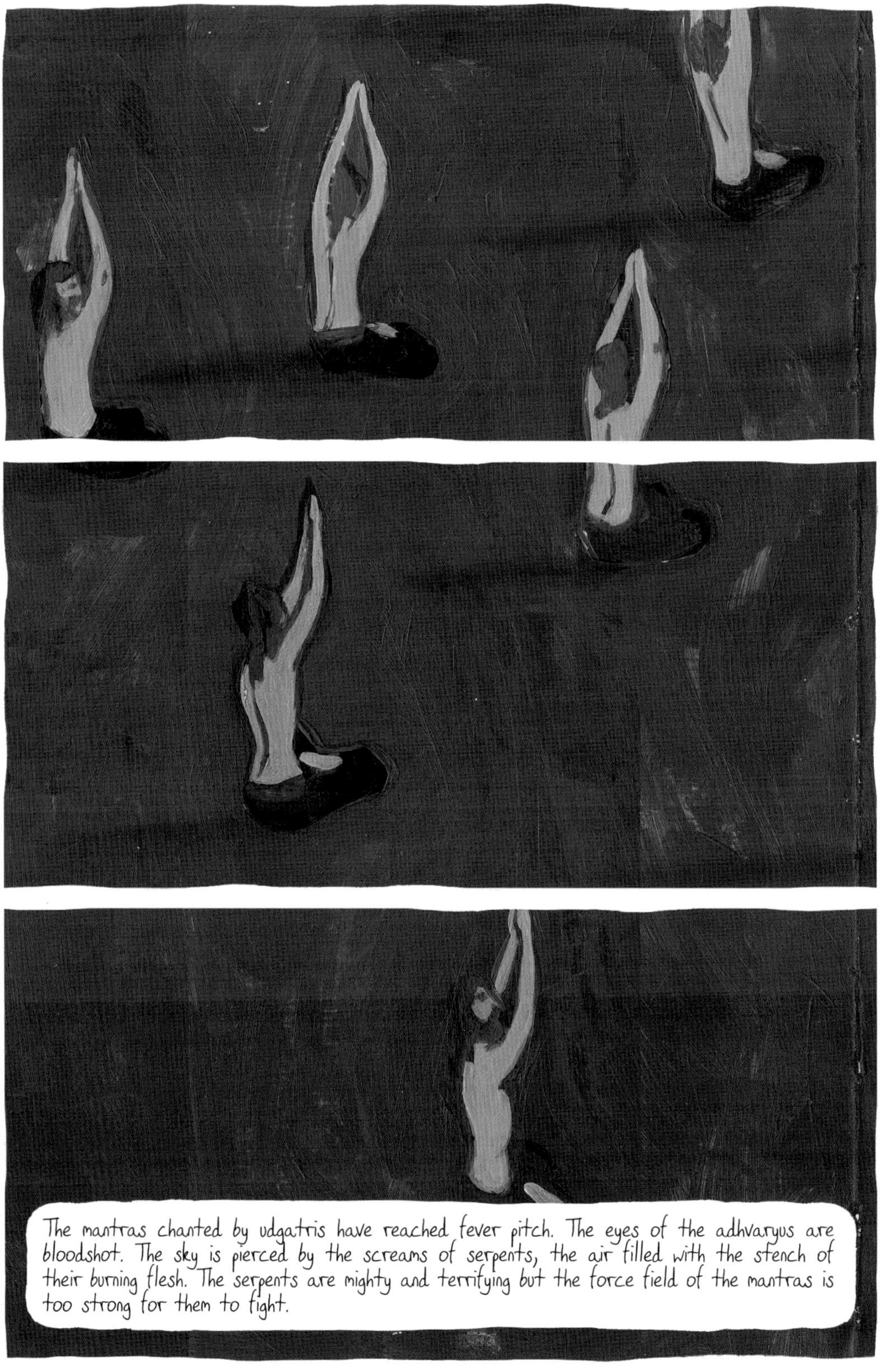
The mantras chanted by udgatris have reached fever pitch. The eyes of the adhvaryus are bloodshot. The sky is pierced by the screams of serpents, the air filled with the stench of their burning flesh. The serpents are mighty and terrifying but the force field of the mantras is too strong for them to fight.

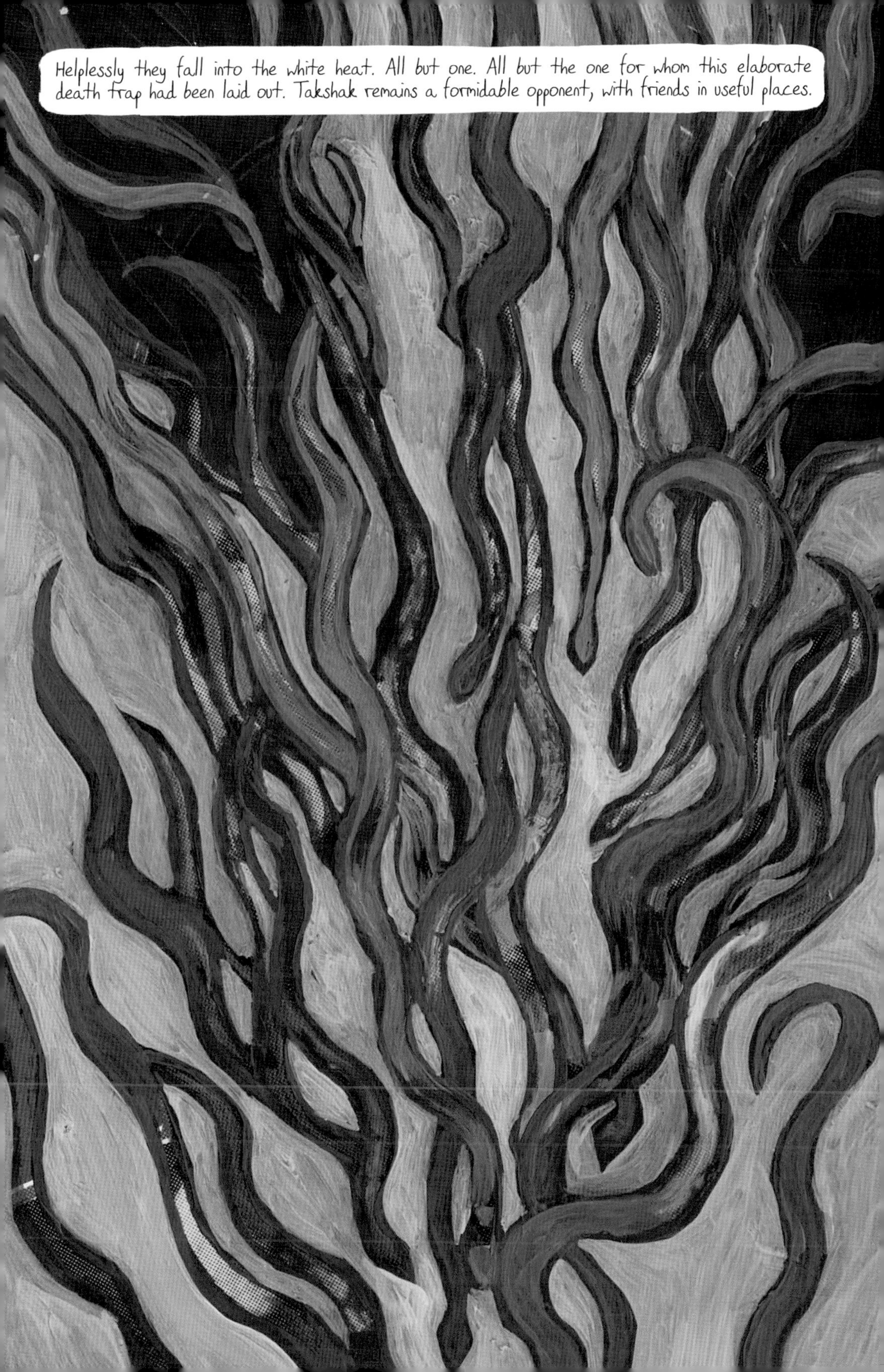
Helplessly they fall into the white heat. All but one. All but the one for whom this elaborate death trap had been laid out. Takshak remains a formidable opponent, with friends in useful places.

He is hidden deep in the bosom of Devlok. His protector is none other than Indra.

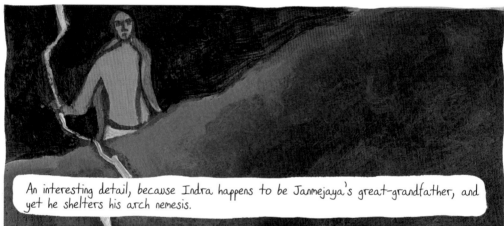

An interesting detail, because Indra happens to be Janmejaya's great-grandfather, and yet he shelters his arch nemesis.

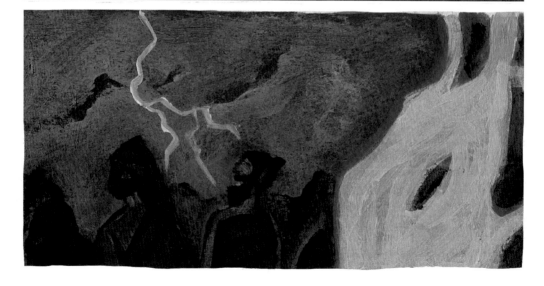

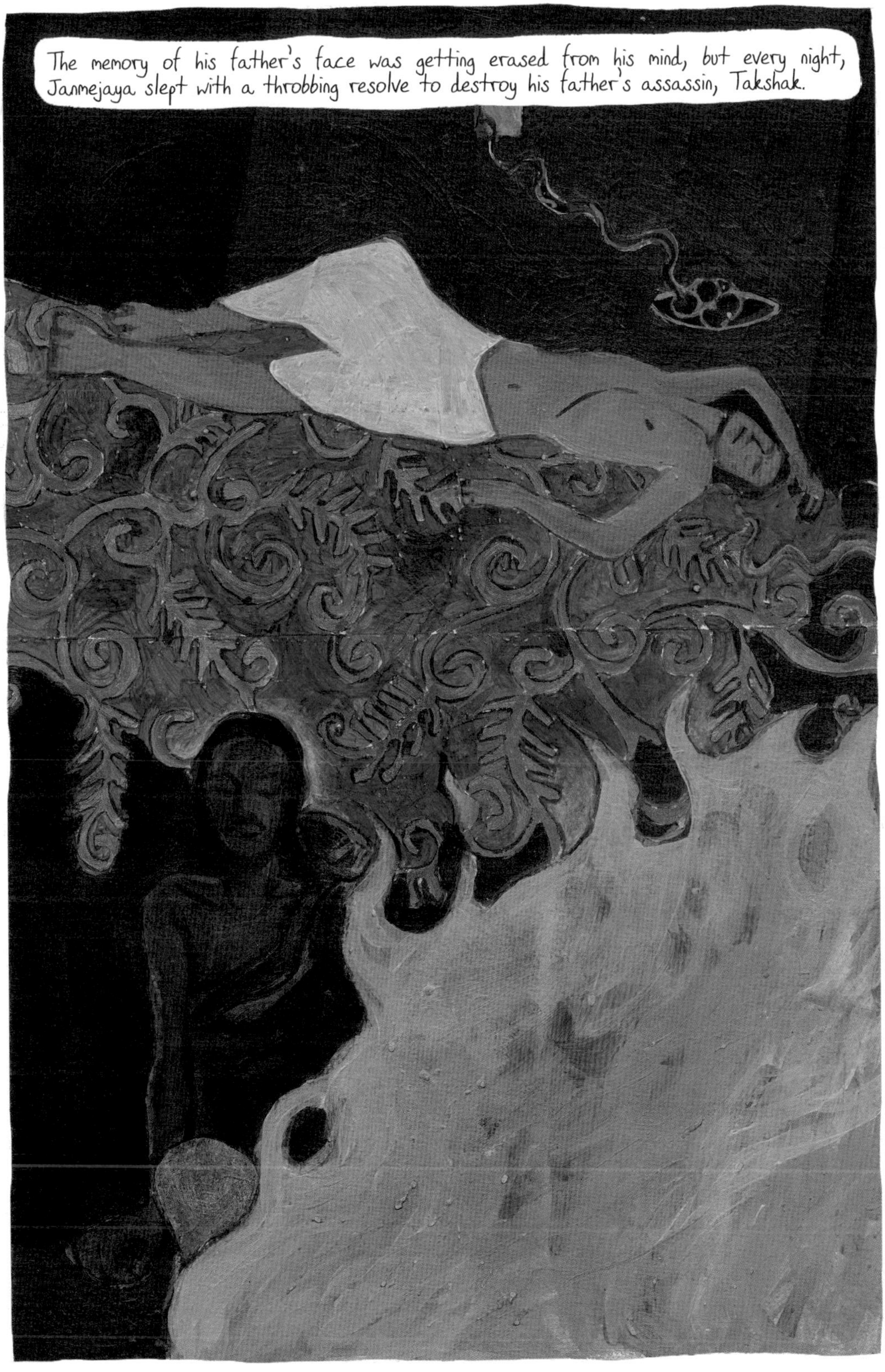
The memory of his father's face was getting erased from his mind, but every night, Janmejaya slept with a throbbing resolve to destroy his father's assassin, Takshak.

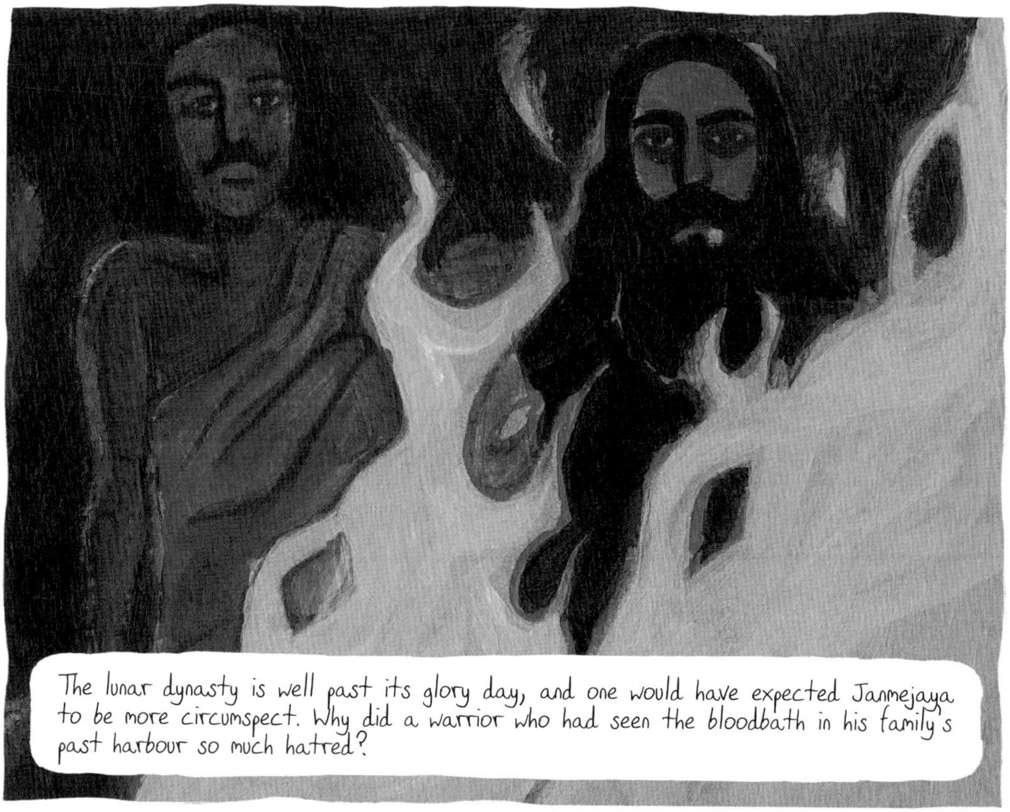
The lunar dynasty is well past its glory day, and one would have expected Janmejaya to be more circumspect. Why did a warrior who had seen the bloodbath in his family's past harbour so much hatred?

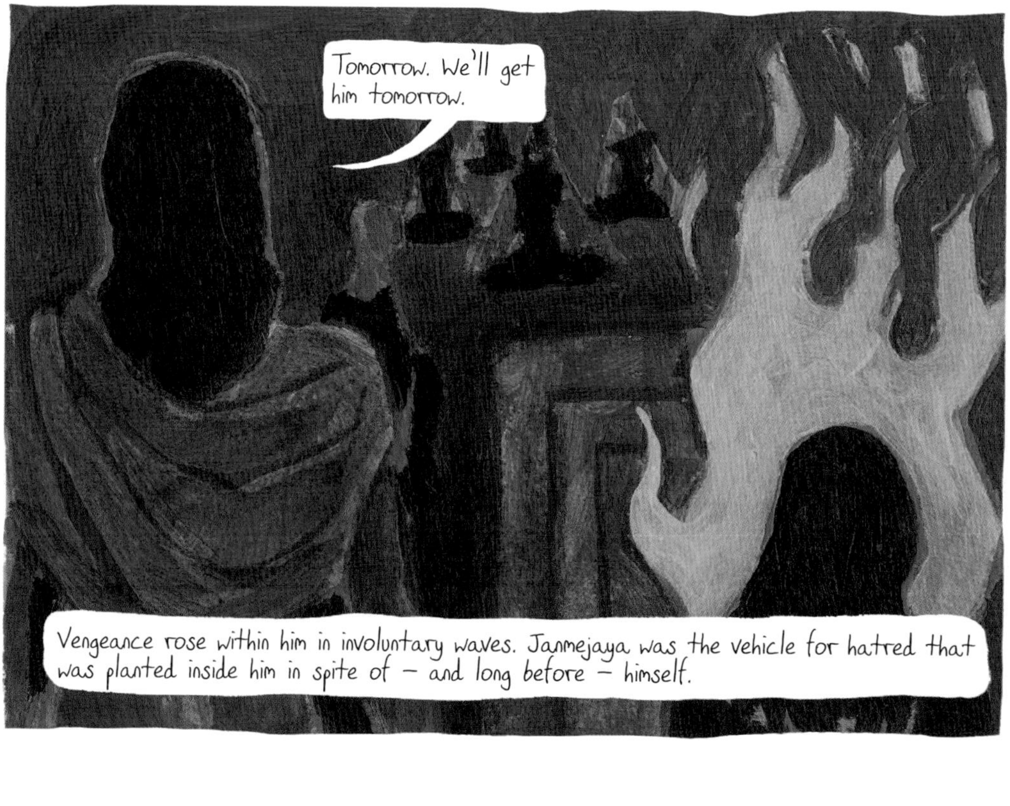
Tomorrow. We'll get him tomorrow.
Vengeance rose within him in involuntary waves. Janmejaya was the vehicle for hatred that was planted inside him in spite of – and long before – himself.

SUPPORTING CAST

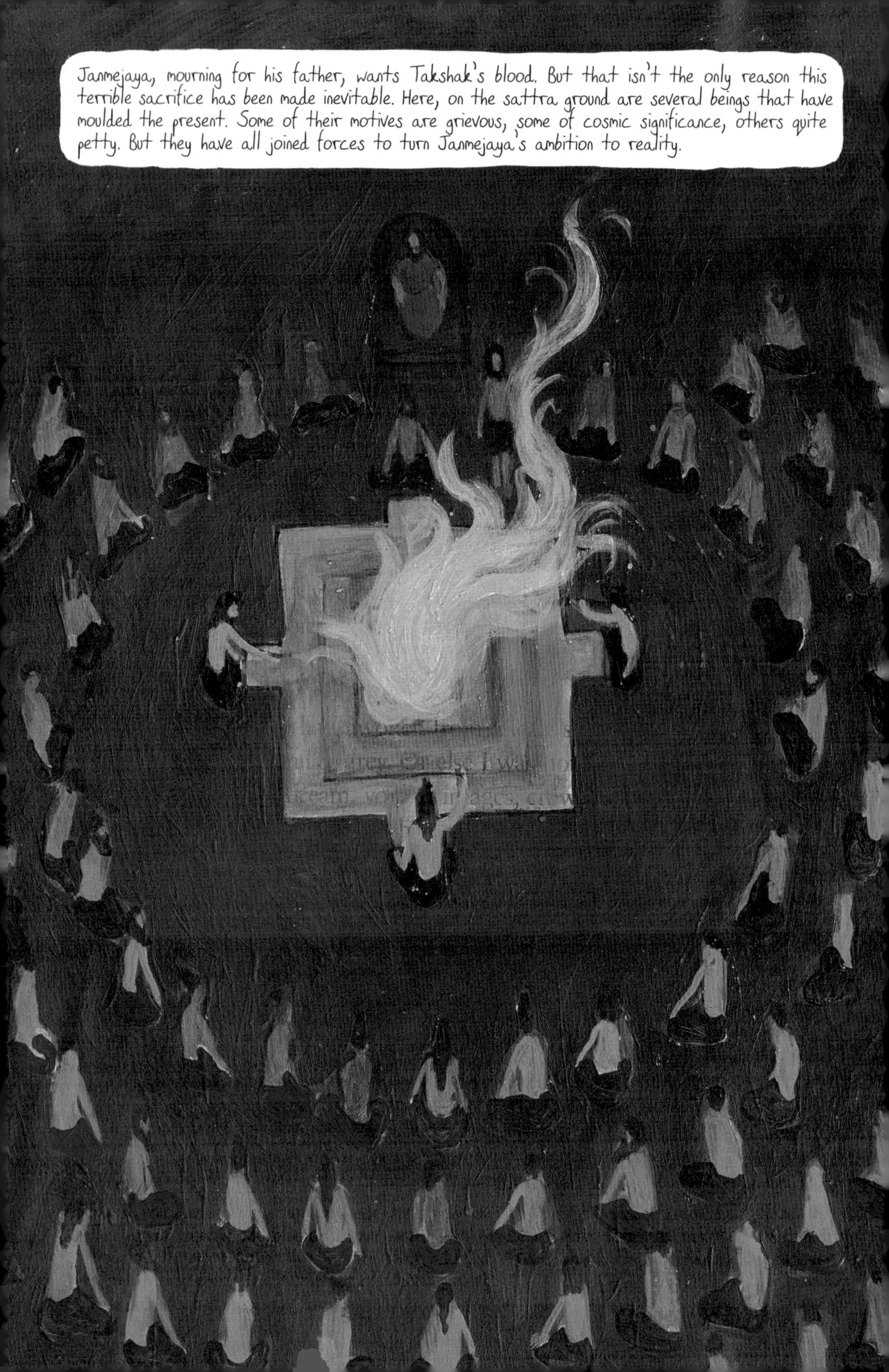
Janmejaya, mourning for his father, wants Takshak's blood. But that isn't the only reason this terrible sacrifice has been made inevitable. Here, on the sattra ground are several beings that have moulded the present. Some of their motives are grievous, some of cosmic significance, others quite petty. But they have all joined forces to turn Janmejaya's ambition to reality.

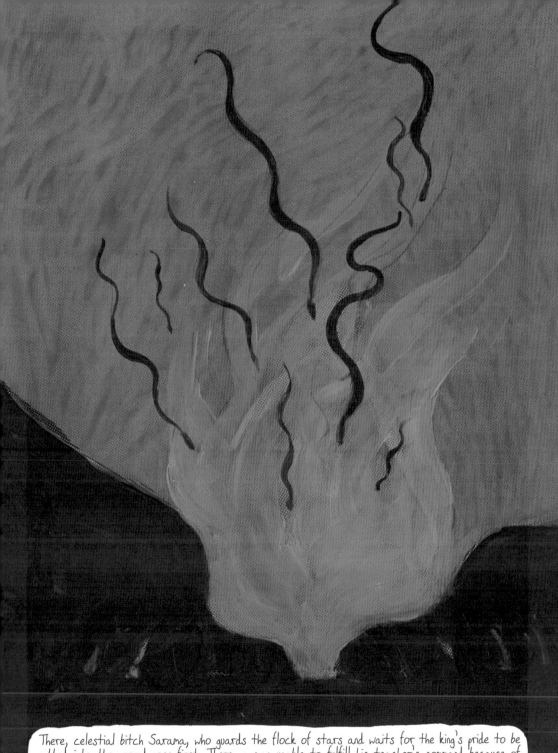

There, celestial bitch Sarama, who guards the flock of stars and waits for the king's pride to be rubbed into the ground nose-first. There, a man unable to fulfill his teacher's command because of Takshak. There, Vyas, grandsire of the clan, who has intervened in the fate of Hastinapur countless times, but who sits in silence now. There, an unknown priest who has predicted that a yagna on this ground will be fruitless. There, Indra protecting Takshak because of old debts. And, biding his time, the young lad Astik, who will bring an end to this madness.

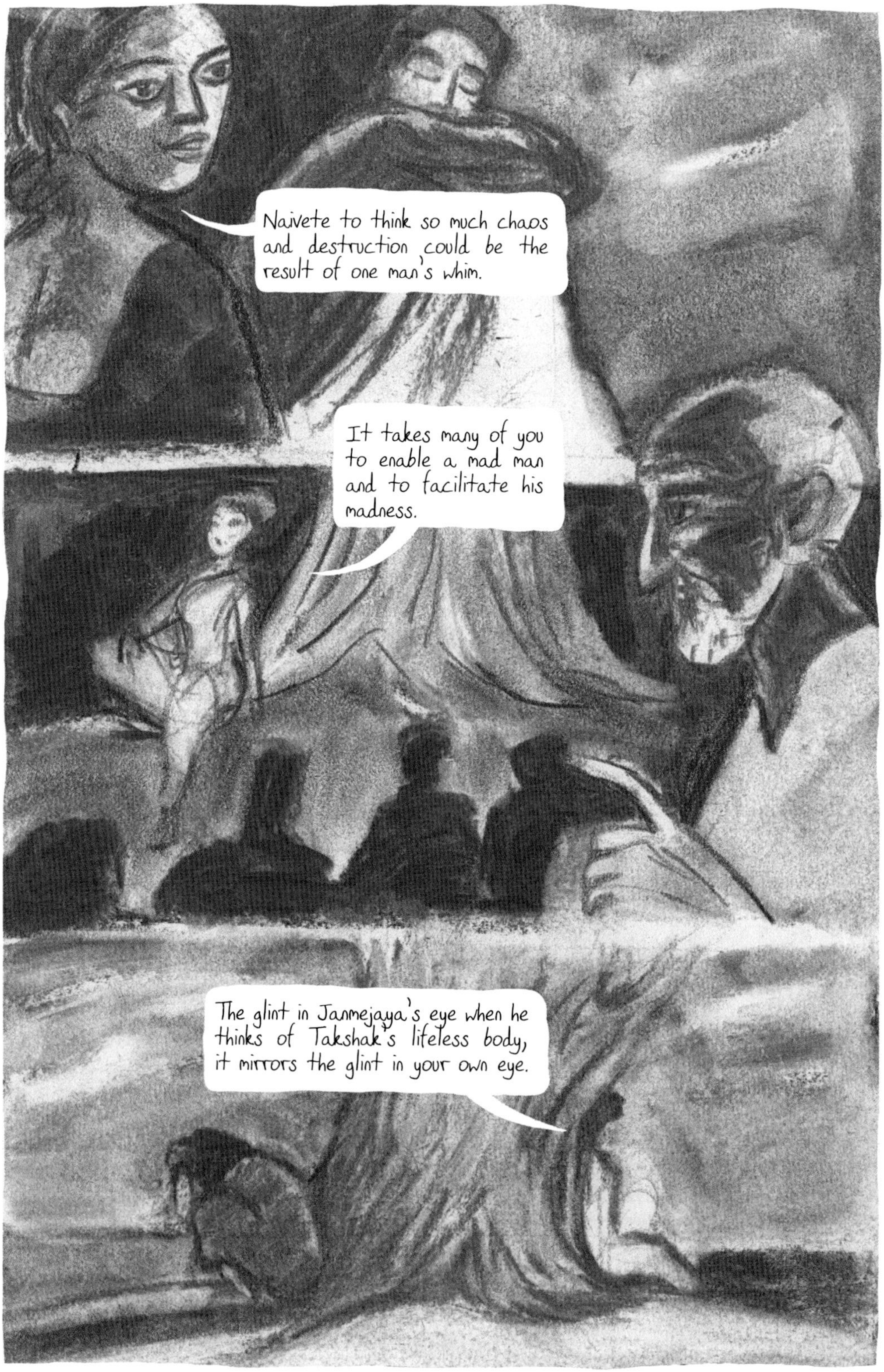
Naivete to think so much chaos and destruction could be the result of one man's whim.
It takes many of you to enable a mad man and to facilitate his madness.
The glint in Janmejaya's eye when he thinks of Takshak's lifeless body, it mirrors the glint in your own eye.

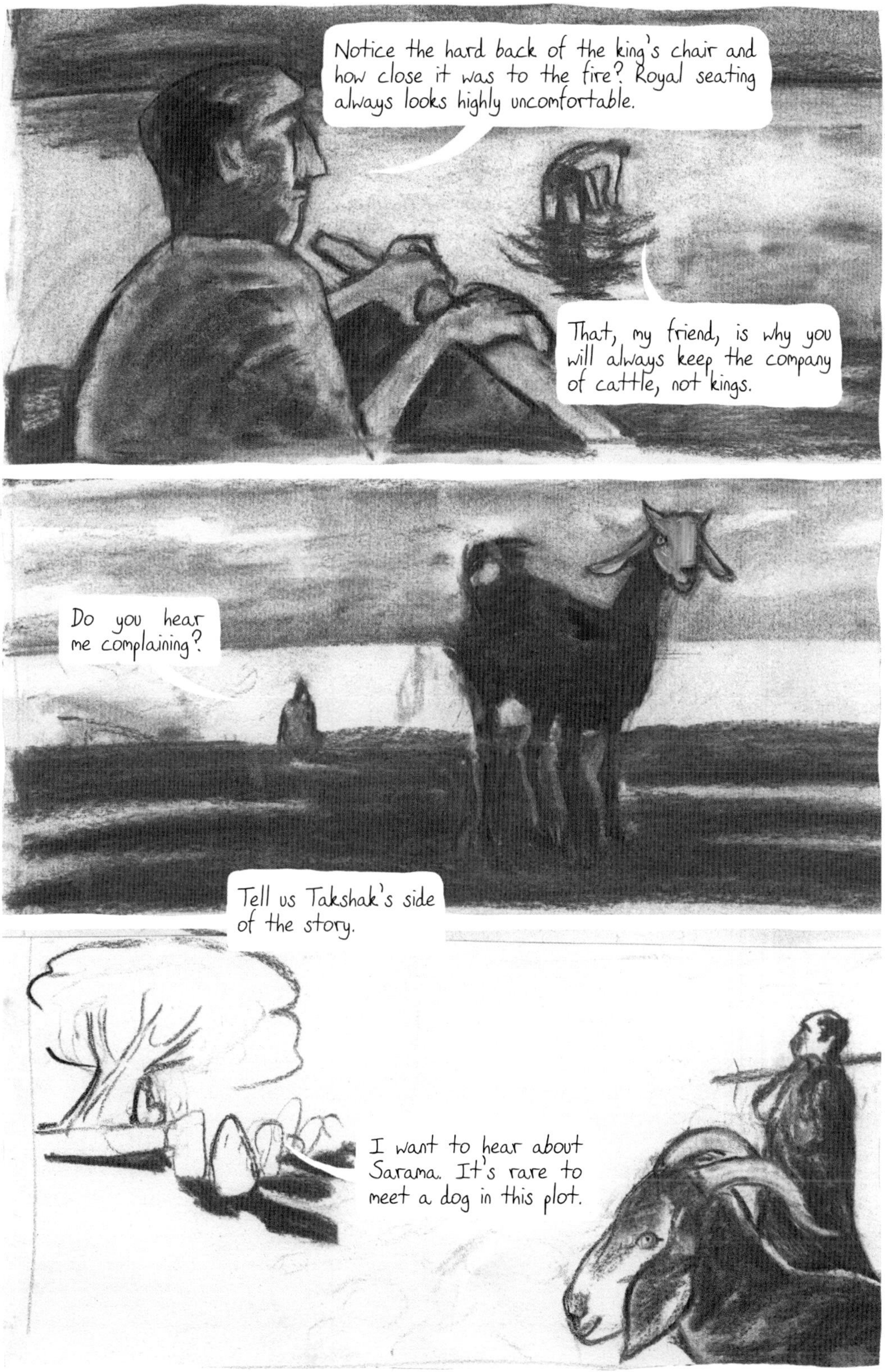
Notice the hard back of the king's chair and how close it was to the fire? Royal seating always looks highly uncomfortable.
That, my friend, is why you will always keep the company of cattle, not kings.
Do you hear me complaining?
Tell us Takshak's side of the story.
I want to hear about Sarama. It's rare to meet a dog in this plot.

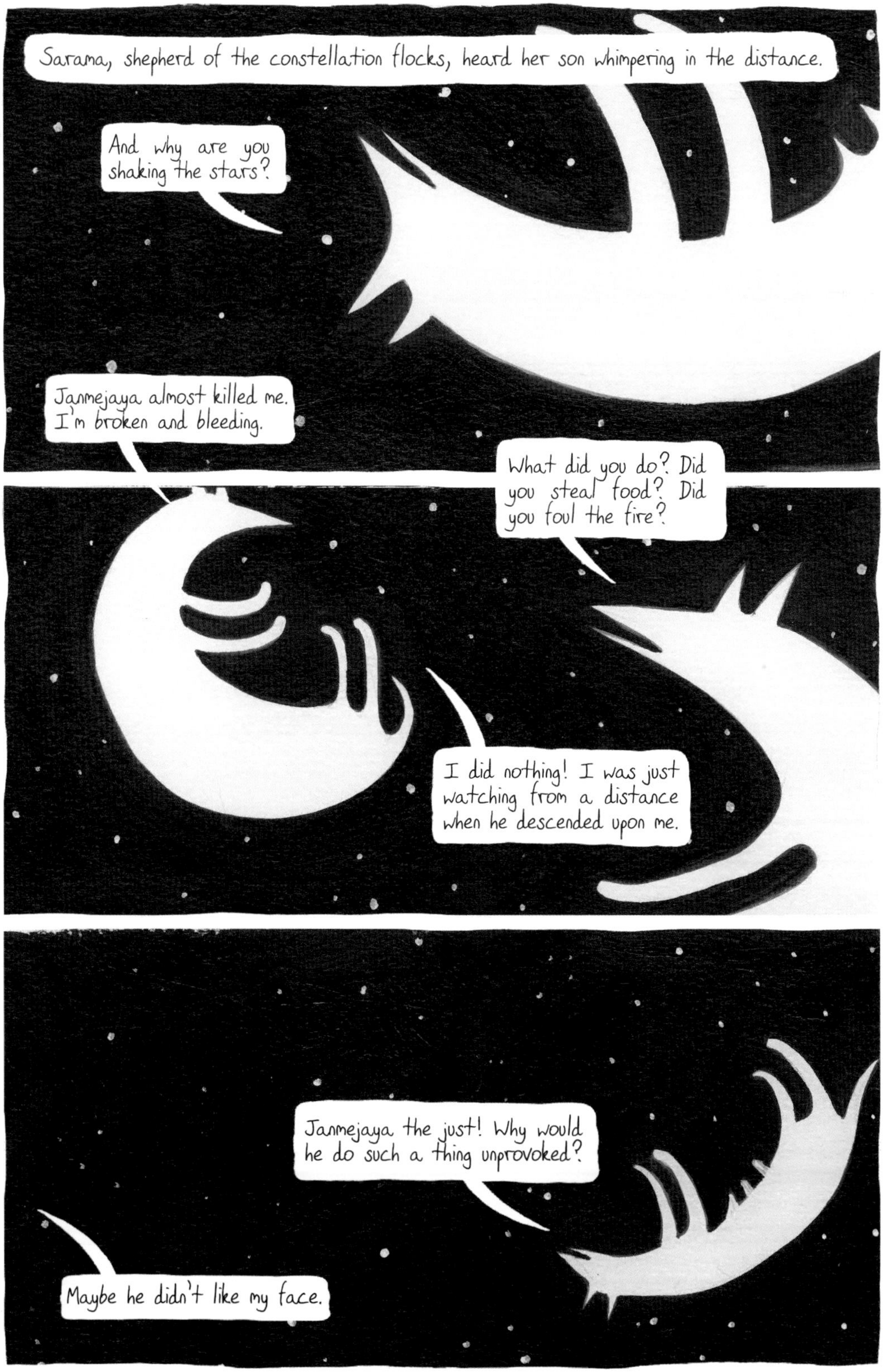
Sarama, shepherd of the constellation flocks, heard her son whimpering in the distance.
And why are you shaking the stars?
Janmejaya almost killed me. I'm broken and bleeding.
What did you do? Did you steal food? Did you foul the fire?
I did nothing! I was just watching from a distance when he descended upon me.
Janmejaya the just! Why would he do such a thing unprovoked?
Maybe he didn't like my face.

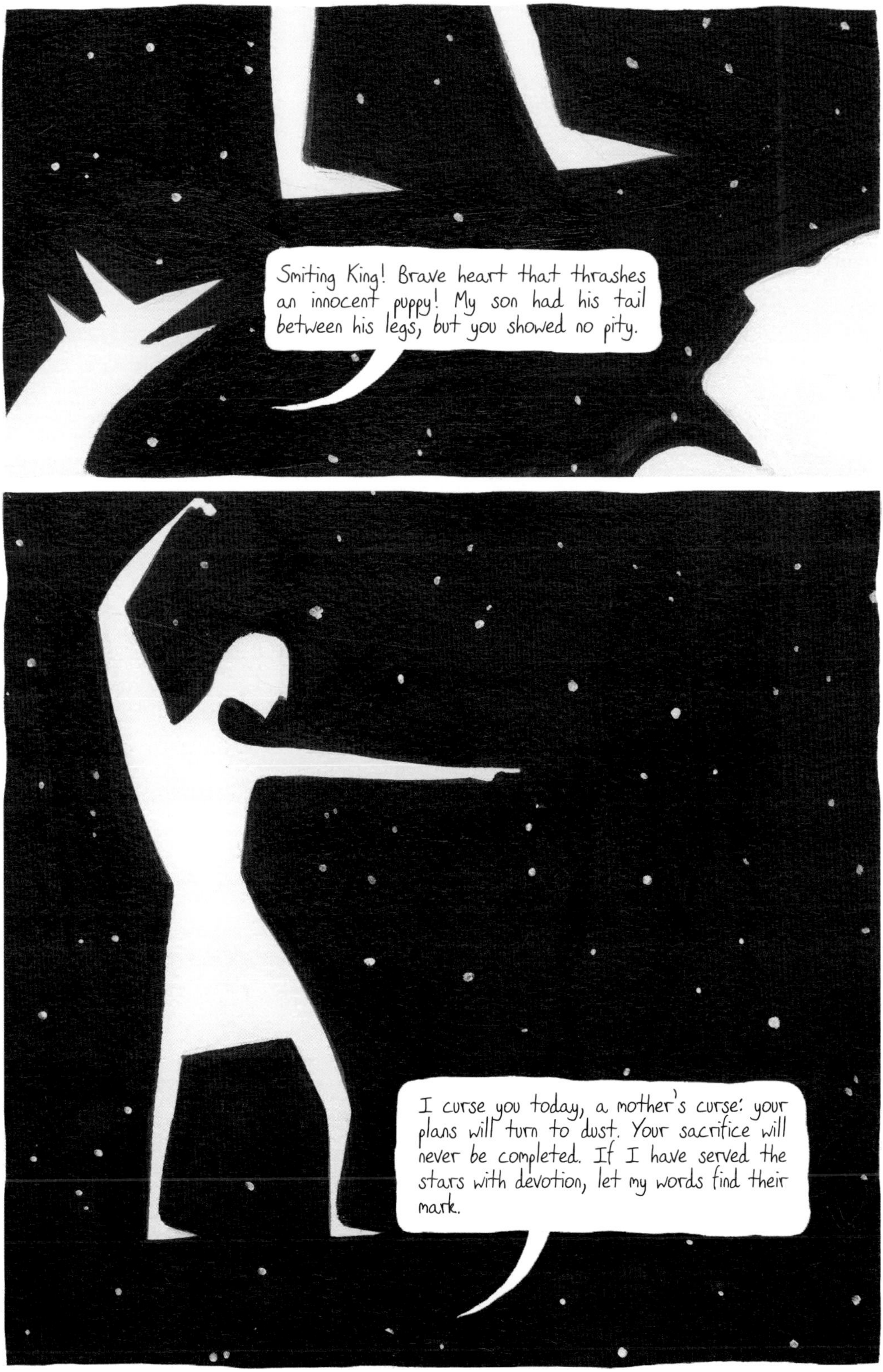
Smiting King! Brave heart that thrashes an innocent puppy! My son had his tail between his legs, but you showed no pity.
I curse you today, a mother's curse: your plans will turn to dust. Your sacrifice will never be completed. If I have served the stars with devotion, let my words find their mark.

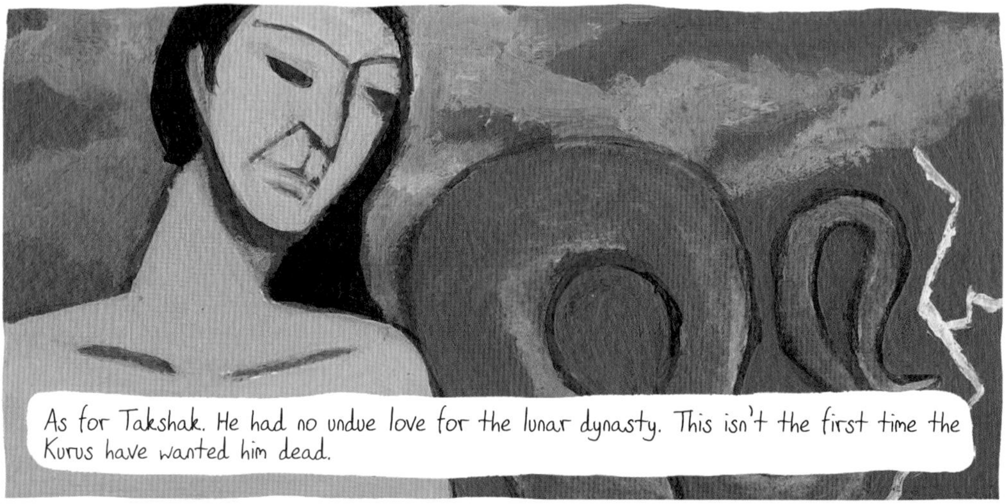
As for Takshak. He had no undue love for the lunar dynasty. This isn't the first time the Kurus have wanted him dead.

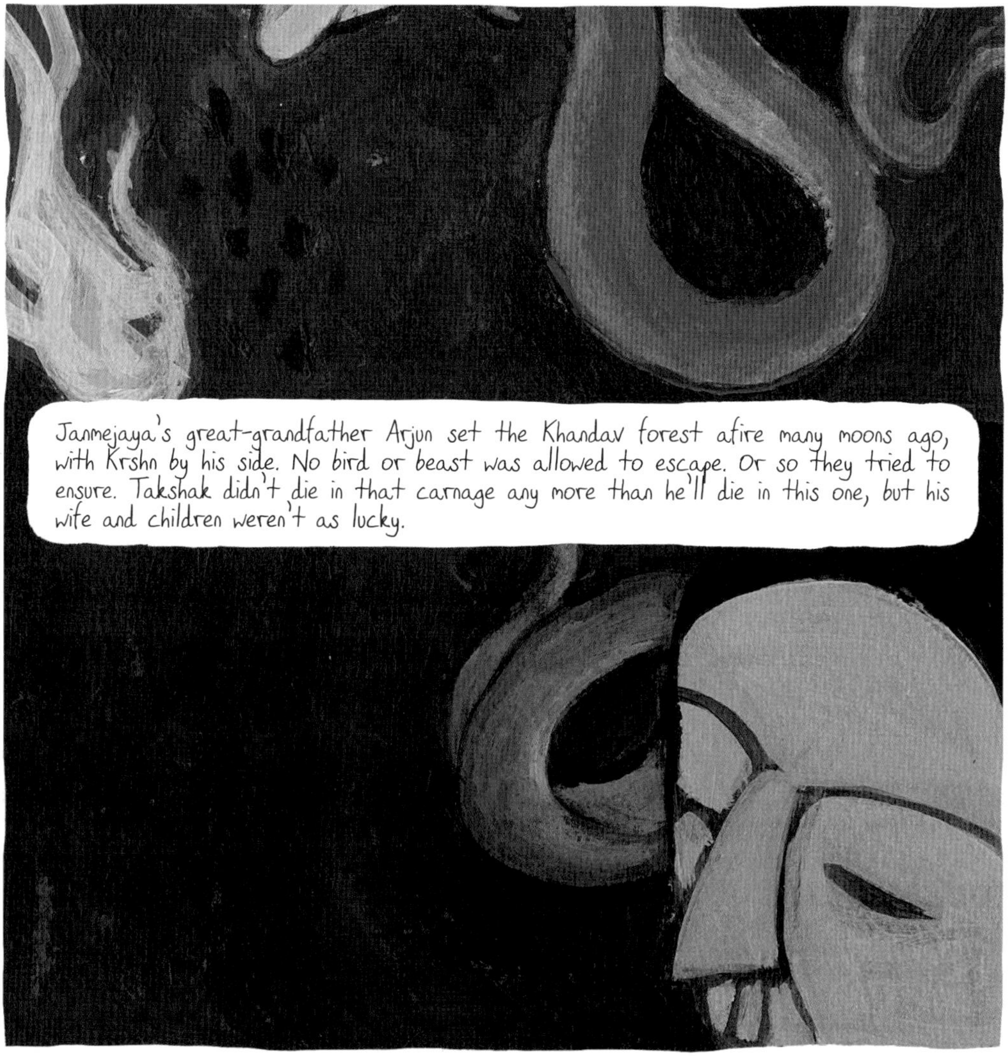
Janmejaya's great-grandfather Arjun set the Khandav forest afire many moons ago, with Krshn by his side. No bird or beast was allowed to escape. Or so they tried to ensure. Takshak didn't die in that carnage any more than he'll die in this one, but his wife and children weren't as lucky.

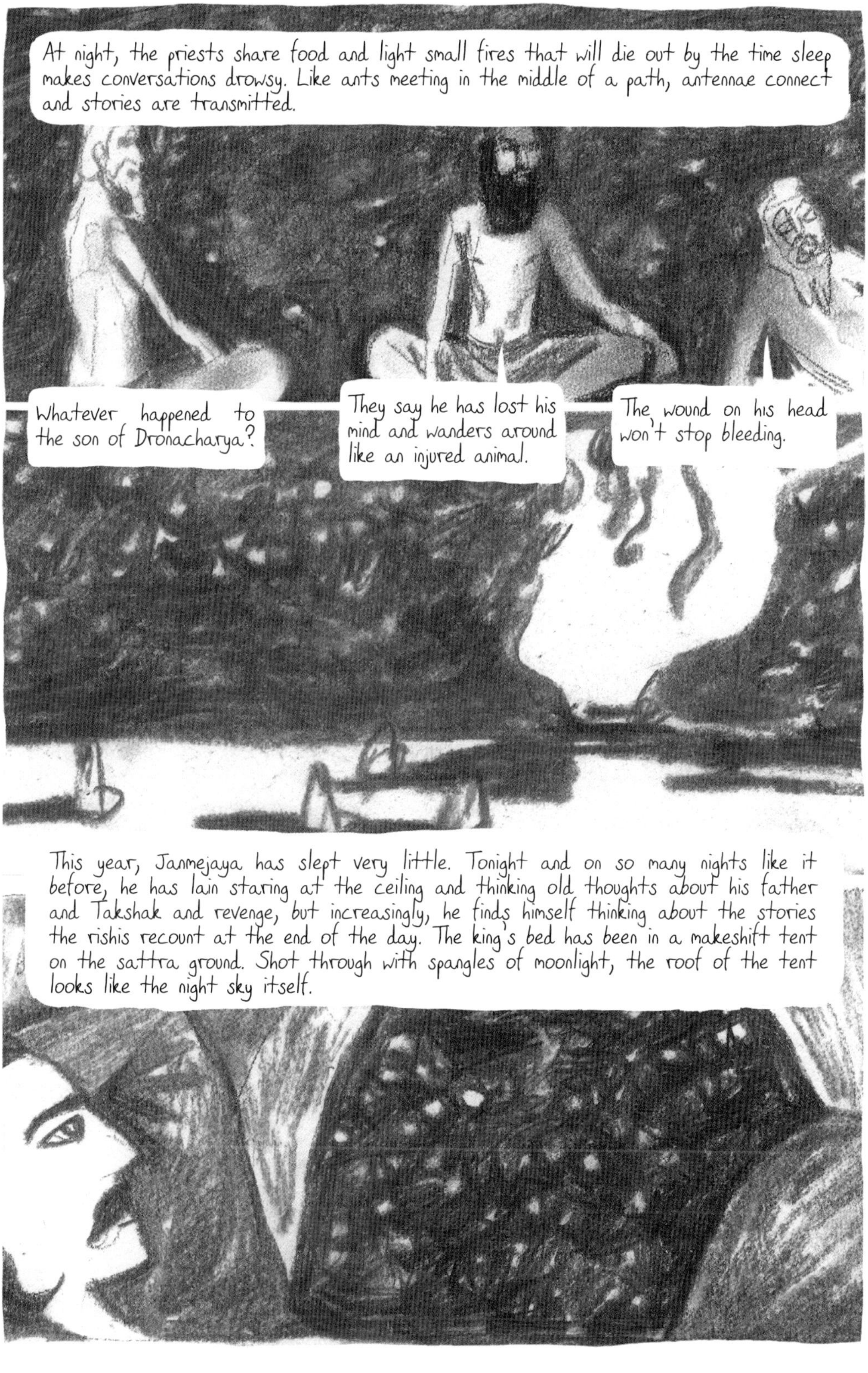
At night, the priests share food and light small fires that will die out by the time sleep makes conversations drowsy. Like ants meeting in the middle of a path, antennae connect and stories are transmitted.
Whatever happened to the son of Dronacharya?
They say he has lost his mind and wanders around like an injured animal.
The wound on his head won't stop bleeding.
This year, Janmejaya has slept very little. Tonight and on so many nights like it before, he has lain staring at the ceiling and thinking old thoughts about his father and Takshak and revenge, but increasingly, he finds himself thinking about the stories the rishis recount at the end of the day. The king's bed has been in a makeshift tent on the sattra ground. Shot through with spangles of moonlight, the roof of the tent looks like the night sky itself.

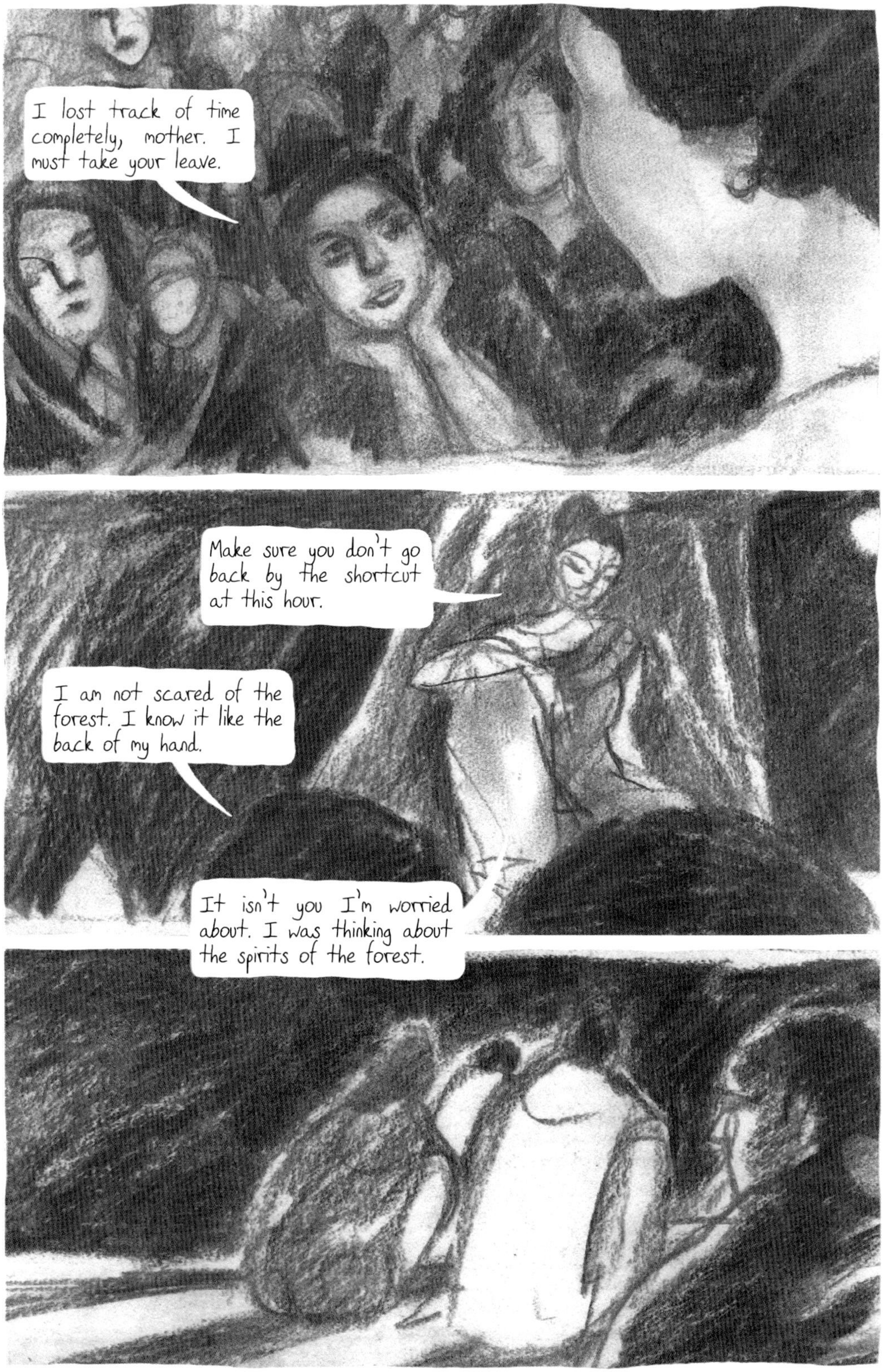
I lost track of time completely, mother. I must take your leave.
Make sure you don't go back by the shortcut at this hour.
I am not scared of the forest. I know it like the back of my hand.
It isn't you I'm worried about. I was thinking about the spirits of the forest.

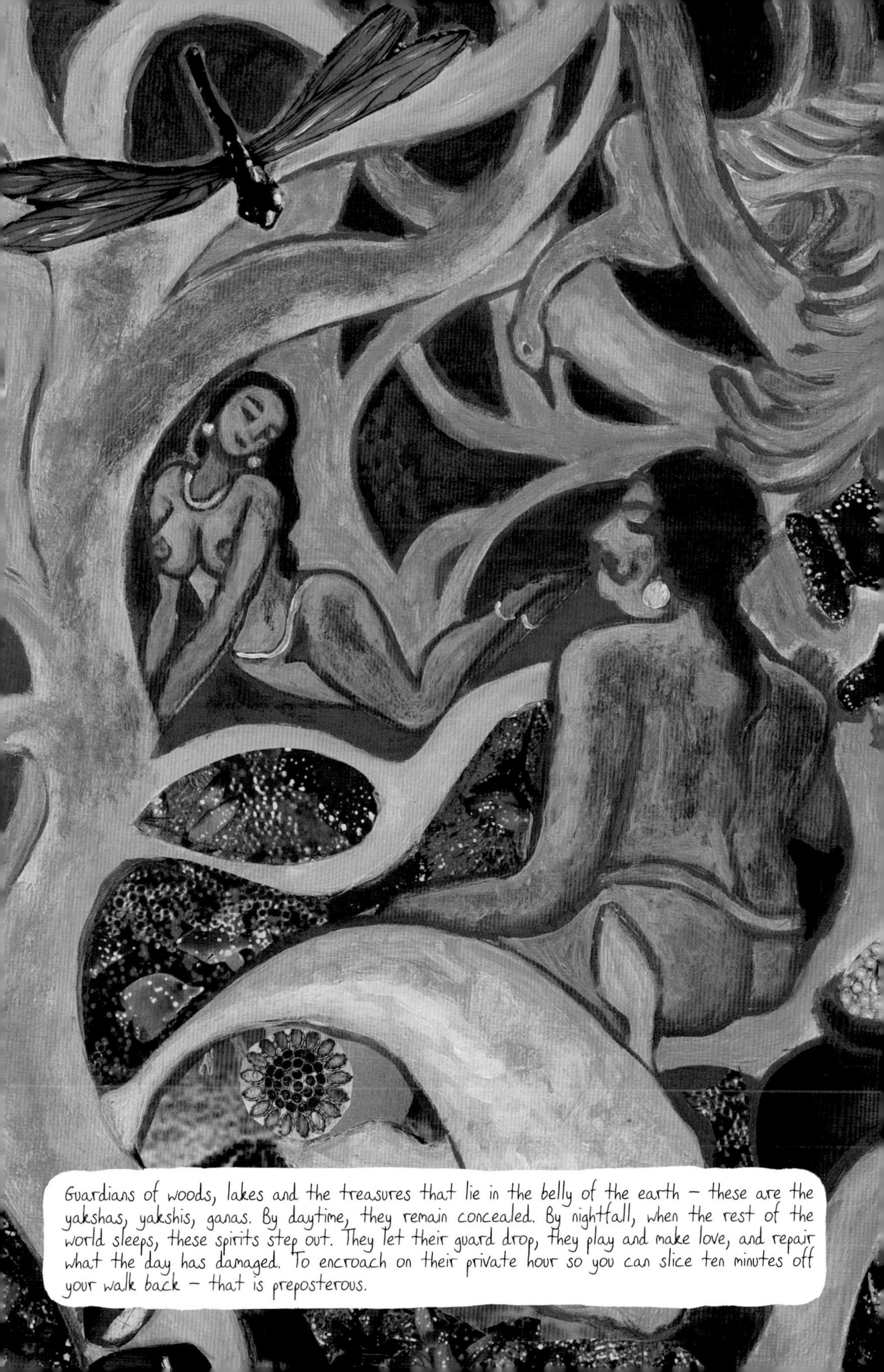
Guardians of woods, lakes and the treasures that lie in the belly of the earth – these are the yakshas, yakshis, ganas. By daytime, they remain concealed. By nightfall, when the rest of the world sleeps, these spirits step out. They let their guard drop, they play and make love, and repair what the day has damaged. To encroach on their private hour so you can slice ten minutes off your walk back – that is preposterous.

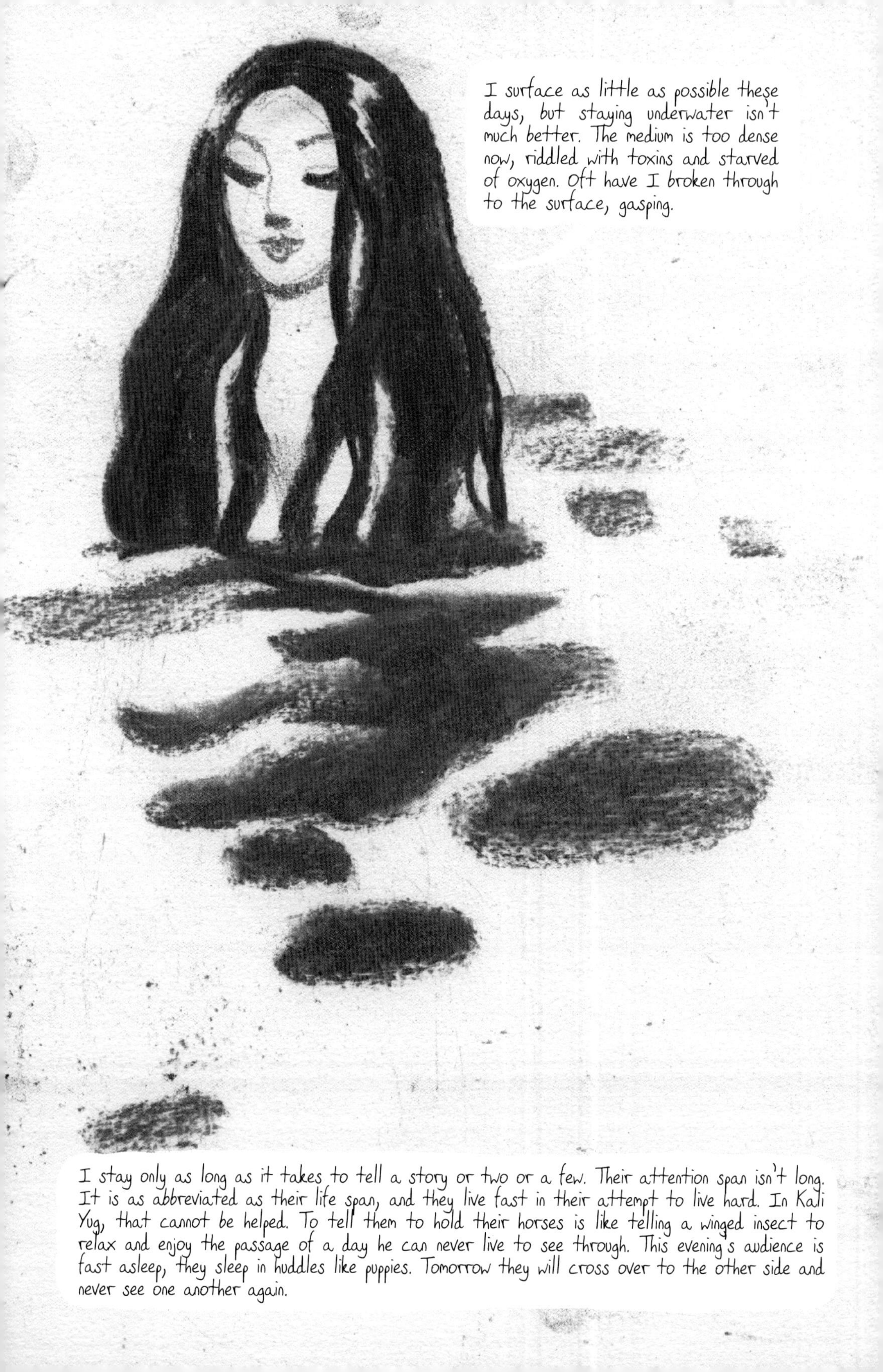
I surface as little as possible these days, but staying underwater isn't much better. The medium is too dense now, riddled with toxins and starved of oxygen. Oft have I broken through to the surface, gasping.
I stay only as long as it takes to tell a story or two or a few. Their attention span isn't long. It is as abbreviated as their life span, and they live fast in their attempt to live hard. In Kali Yug, that cannot be helped. To tell them to hold their horses is like telling a winged insect to relax and enjoy the passage of a day he can never live to see through. This evening's audience is fast asleep, they sleep in huddles like puppies. Tomorrow they will cross over to the other side and never see one another again.

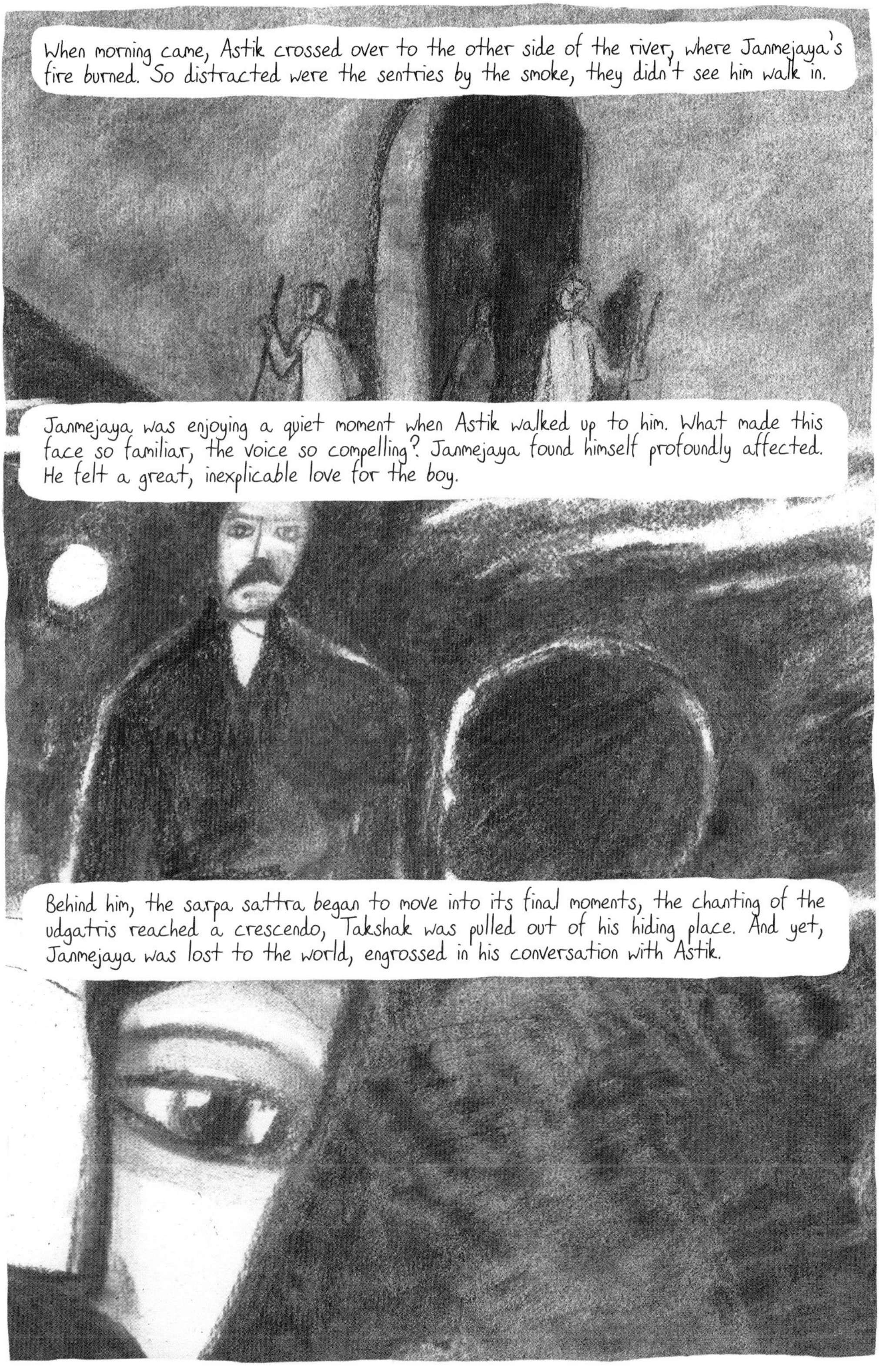
When morning came, Astik crossed over to the other side of the river, where Janmejaya's fire burned. So distracted were the sentries by the smoke, they didn't see him walk in.
Janmejaya was enjoying a quiet moment when Astik walked up to him. What made this face so familiar, the voice so compelling? Janmejaya found himself profoundly affected. He felt a great, inexplicable love for the boy.
Behind him, the sarpa sattra began to move into its final moments, the chanting of the udgatris reached a crescendo, Takshak was pulled out of his hiding place. And yet, Janmejaya was lost to the world, engrossed in his conversation with Astik.

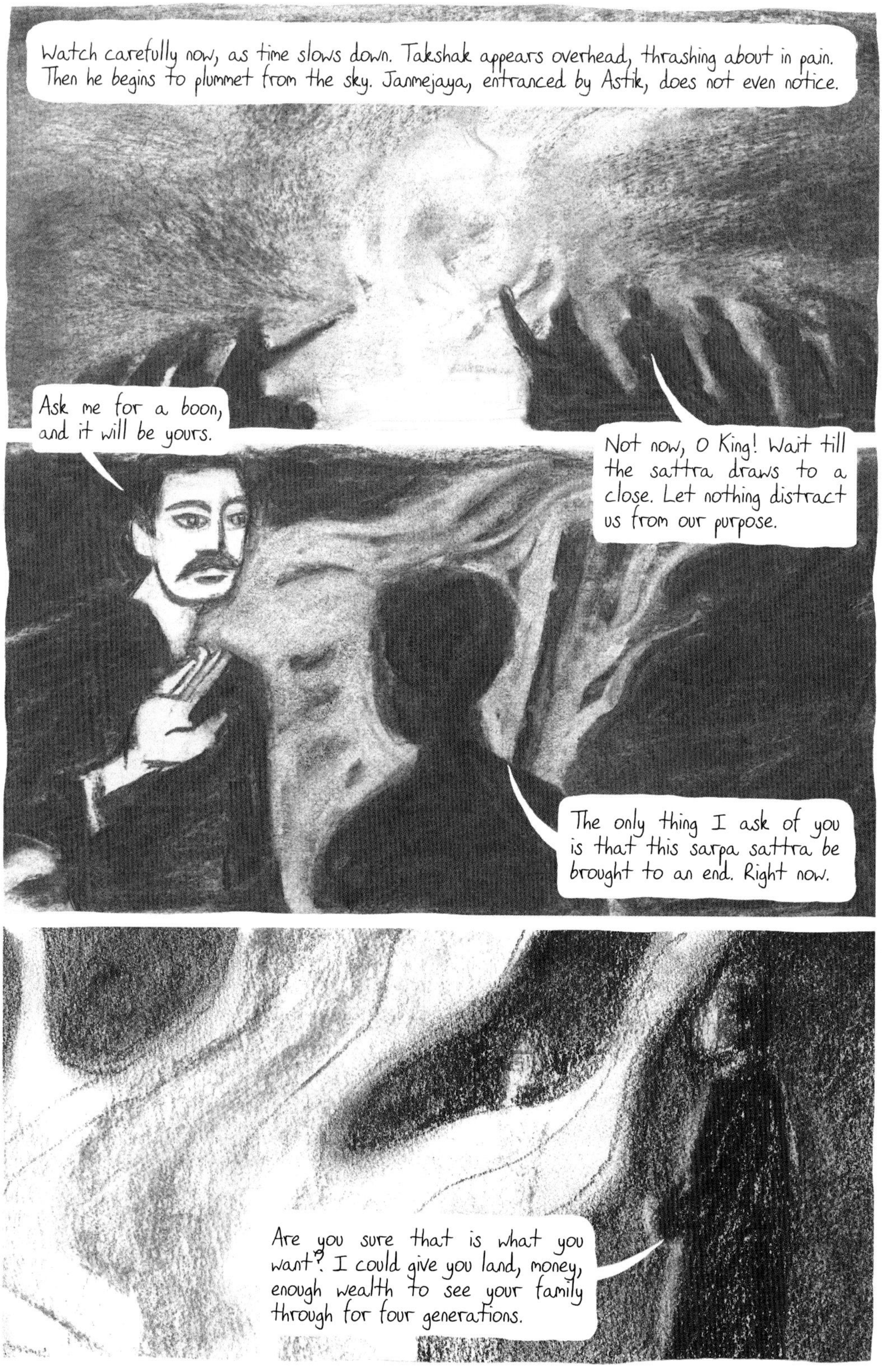
Watch carefully now, as time slows down. Takshak appears overhead, thrashing about in pain. Then he begins to plummet from the sky. Janmejaya, entranced by Astik, does not even notice.
Ask me for a boon, and it will be yours.
Not now, O King! Wait till the sattra draws to a close. Let nothing distract us from our purpose.
The only thing I ask of you is that this sarpa sattra be brought to an end. Right now.
Are you sure that is what you want? I could give you land, money, enough wealth to see your family through for four generations.

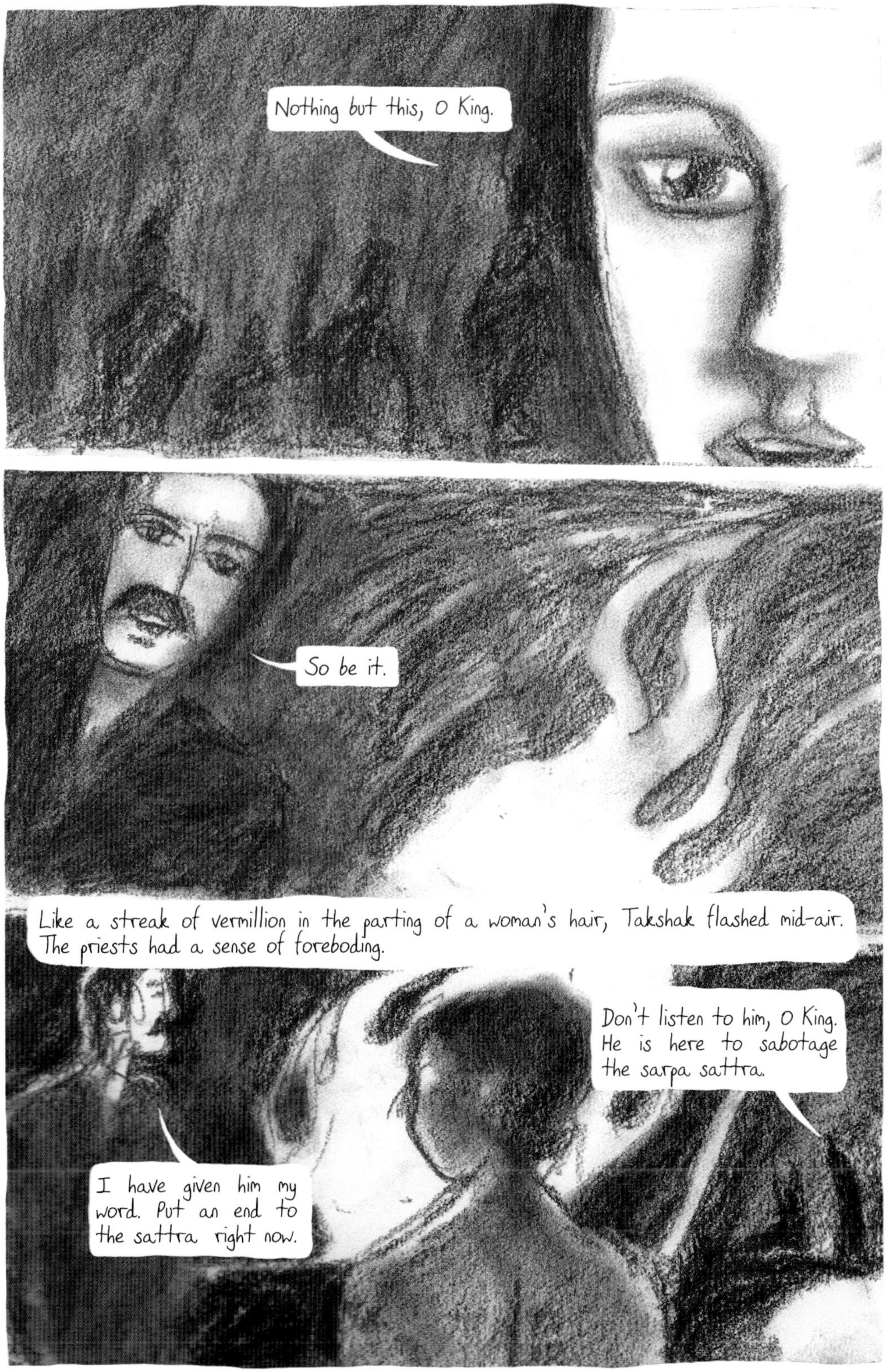
Nothing but this, O King.
So be it.
Like a streak of vermillion in the parting of a woman's hair, Takshak flashed mid-air. The priests had a sense of foreboding.
Don't listen to him, O King. He is here to sabotage the sarpa sattra.
I have given him my word. Put an end to the sattra right now.

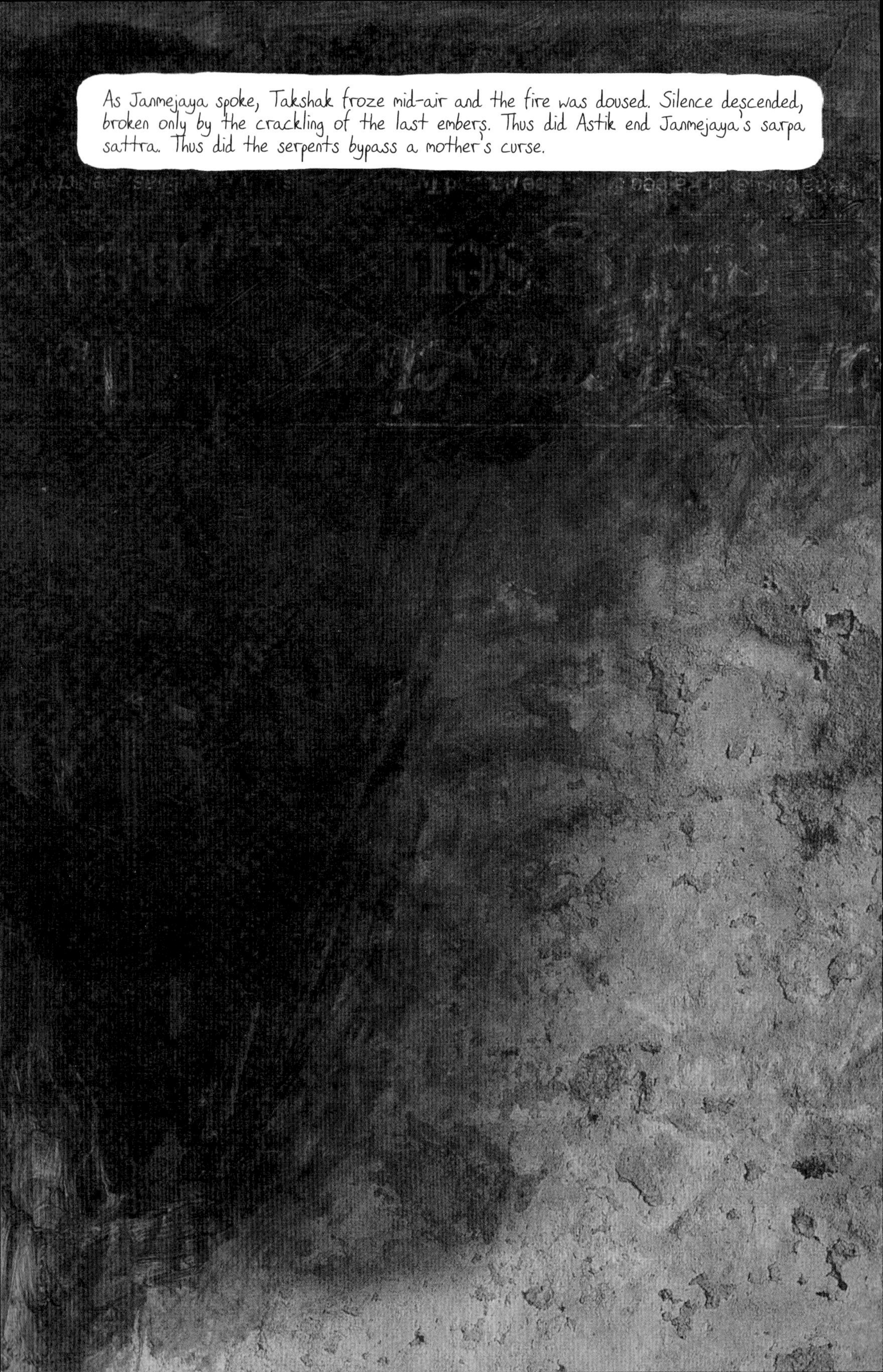
As Janmejaya spoke, Takshak froze mid-air and the fire was doused. Silence descended, broken only by the crackling of the last embers. Thus did Astik end Janmejaya's sarpa sattra. Thus did the serpents bypass a mother's curse.

RIVERBANK UNIONS

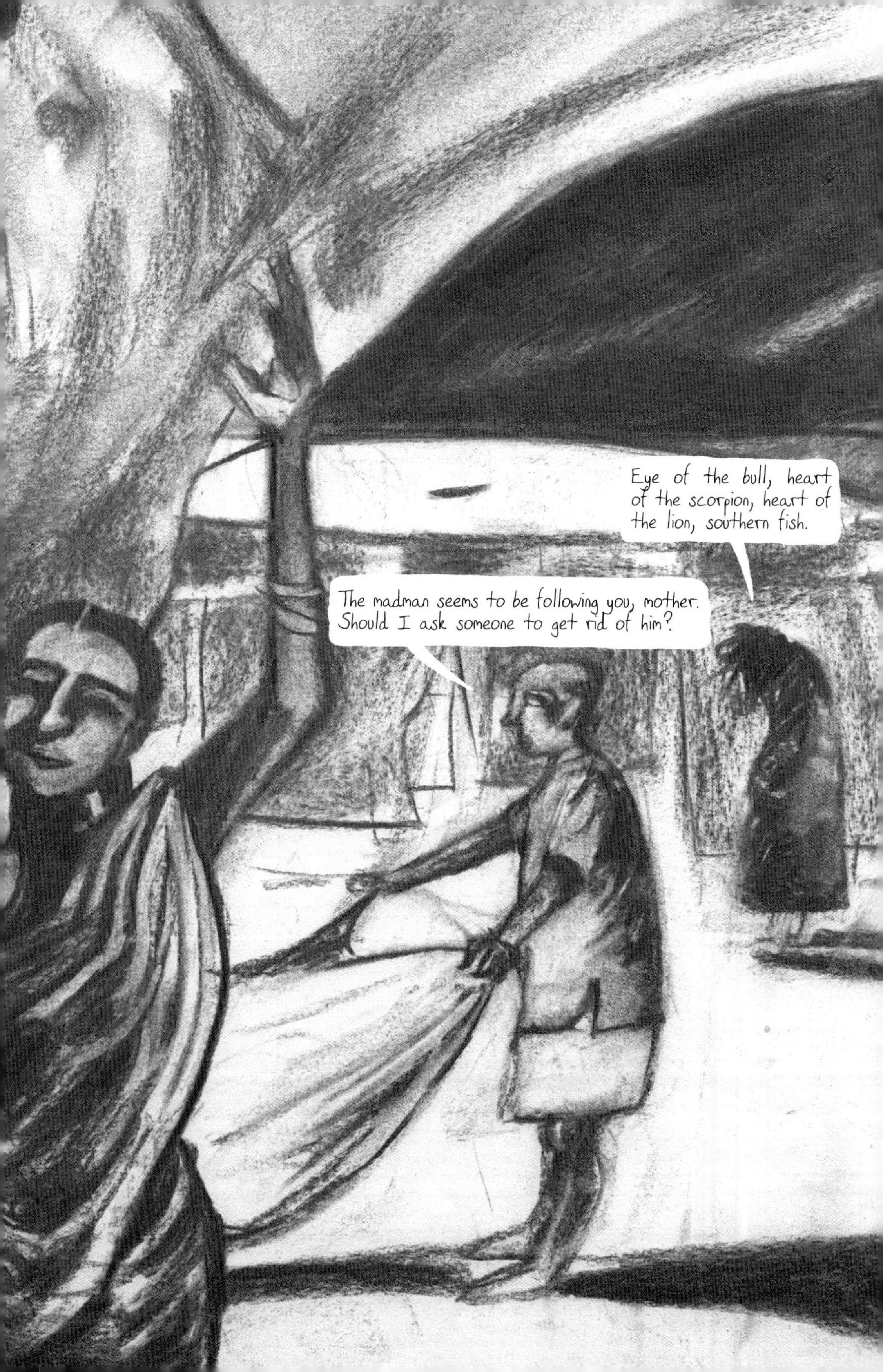
Eye of the bull, heart of the scorpion, heart of the lion, southern fish.
The madman seems to be following you, mother. Should I ask someone to get rid of him?

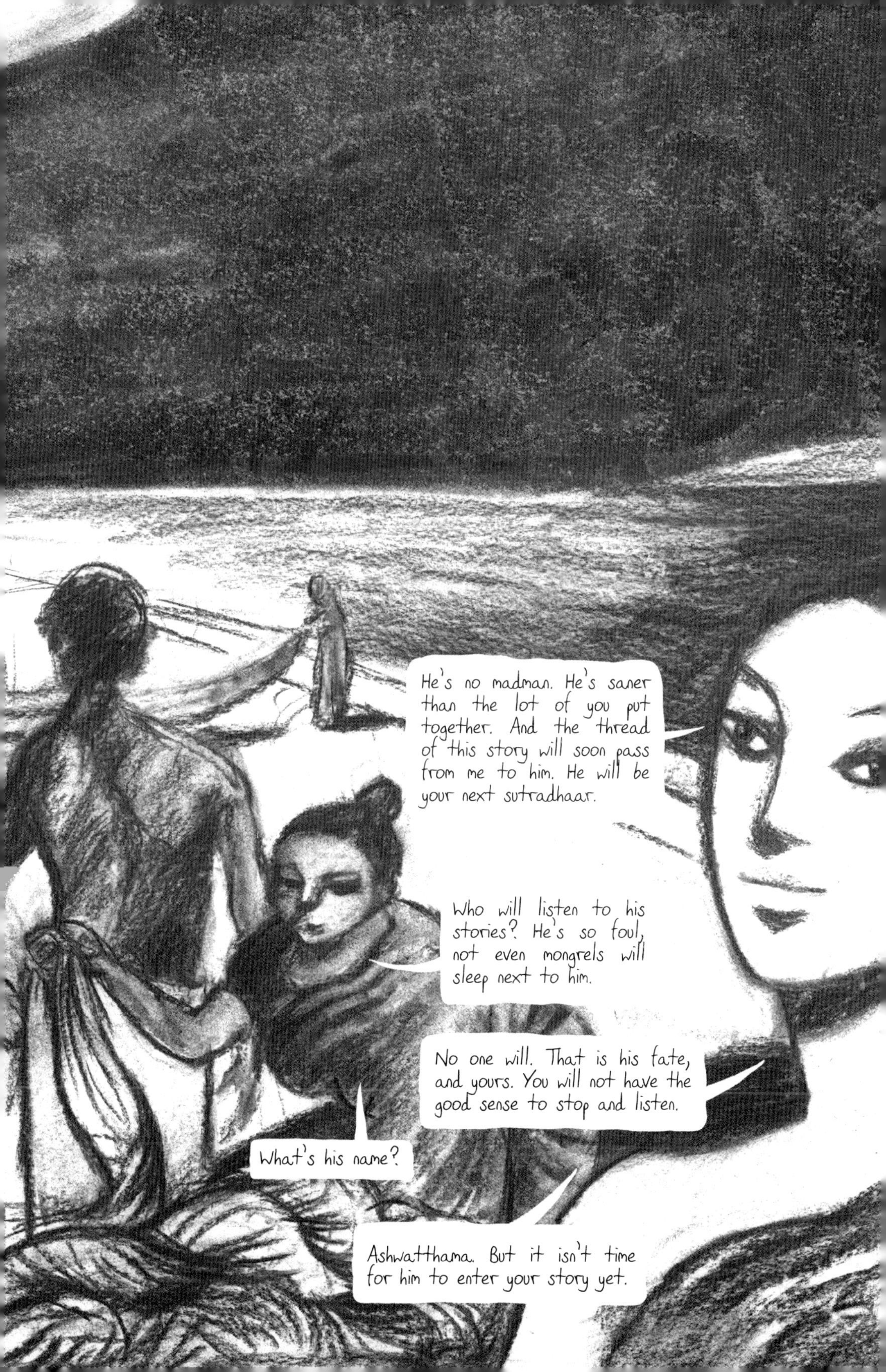
He's no madman. He's saner than the lot of you put together. And the thread of this story will soon pass from me to him. He will be your next sutradhaar.
Who will listen to his stories? He's so foul, not even mongrels will sleep next to him.
No one will. That is his fate, and yours. You will not have the good sense to stop and listen.
What's his name?
Ashwatthama. But it isn't time for him to enter your story yet.

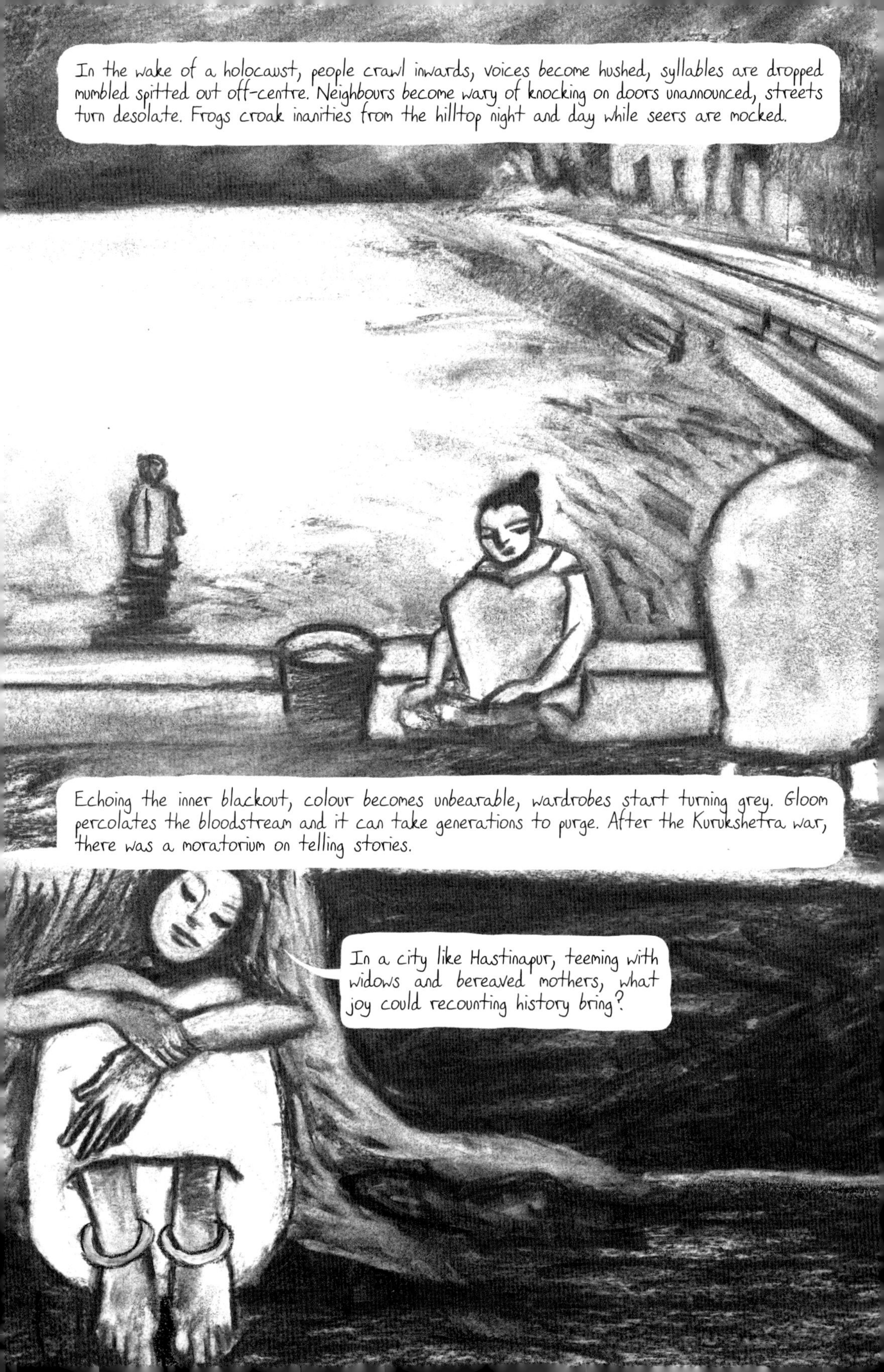
In the wake of a holocaust, people crawl inwards, voices become hushed, syllables are dropped mumbled spitted out off-centre. Neighbours become wary of knocking on doors unannounced, streets turn desolate. Frogs croak inanities from the hilltop night and day while seers are mocked.
Echoing the inner blackout, colour becomes unbearable, wardrobes start turning grey. Gloom percolates the bloodstream and it can take generations to purge. After the Kurukshetra war, there was a moratorium on telling stories.
In a city like Hastinapur, teeming with widows and bereaved mothers, what joy could recounting history bring?

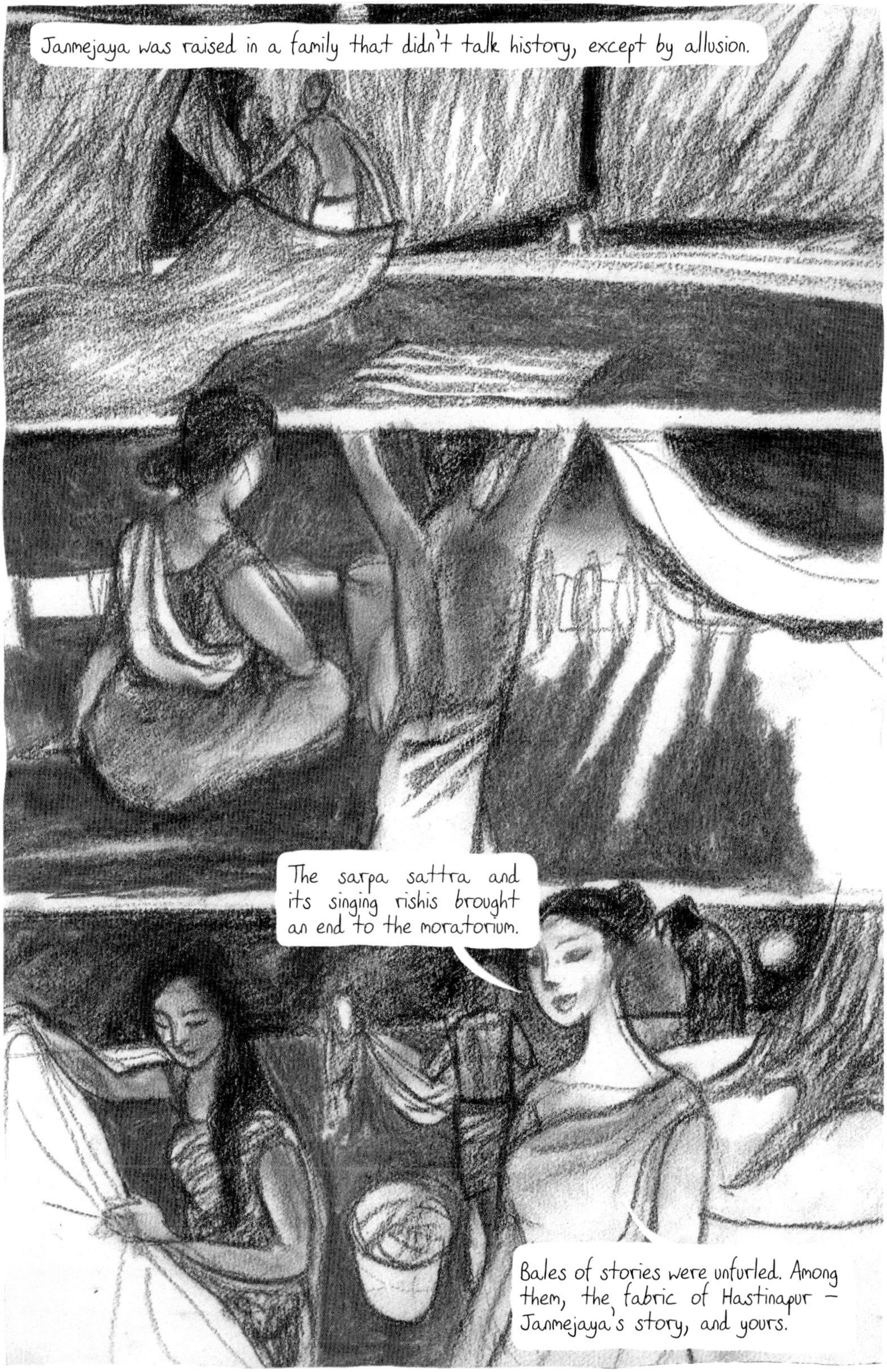
Janmejaya was raised in a family that didn't talk history, except by allusion.
The sarpa sattra and its singing rishis brought an end to the moratorium.
Bales of stories were unfurled. Among them, the fabric of Hastinapur – Janmejaya's story, and yours.

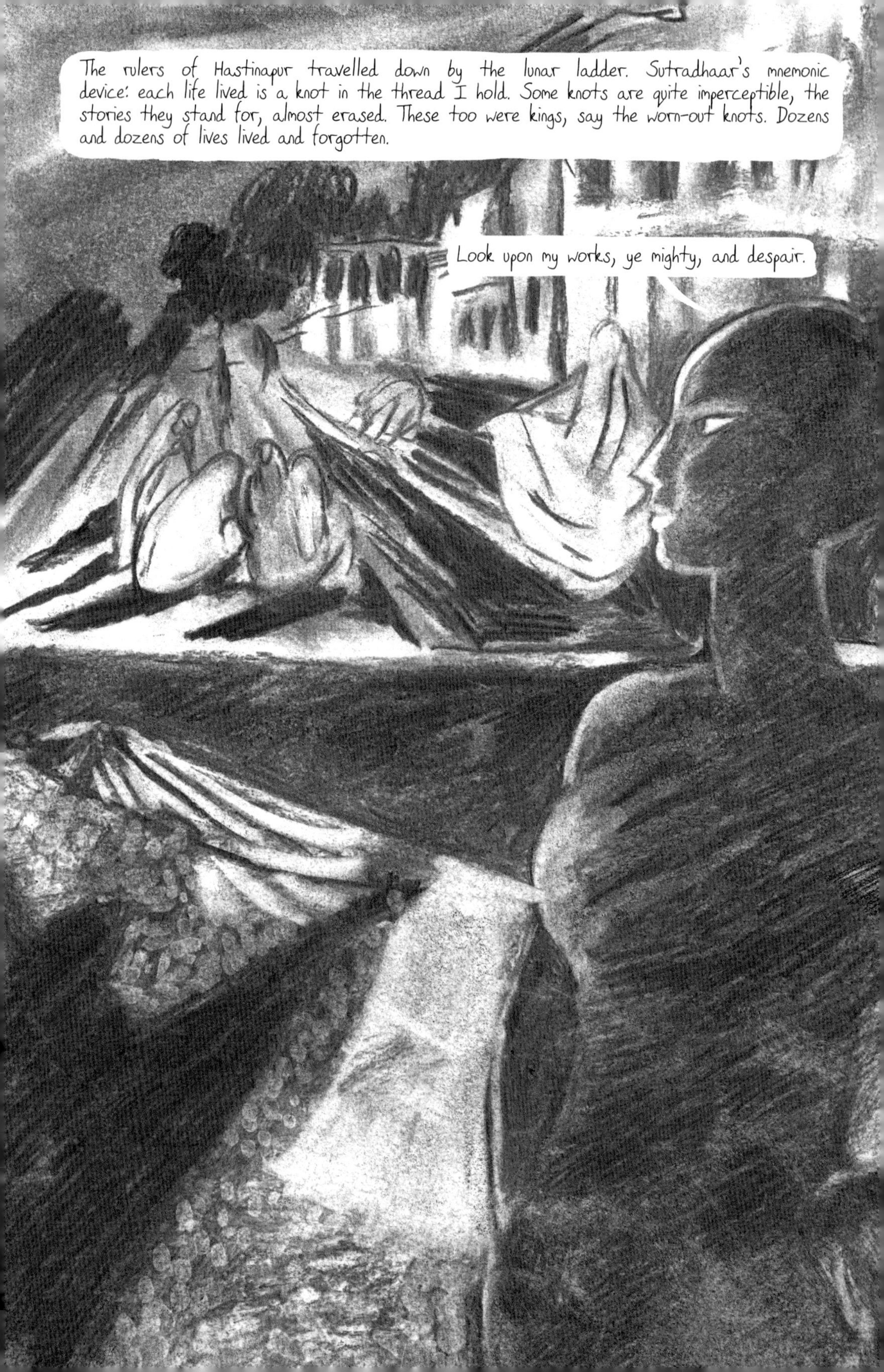
The rulers of Hastinapur travelled down by the lunar ladder. Sutradhaar's mnemonic device: each life lived is a knot in the thread I hold. Some knots are quite imperceptible, the stories they stand for, almost erased. These too were kings, say the worn-out knots. Dozens and dozens of lives lived and forgotten.
Look upon my works, ye mighty, and despair.

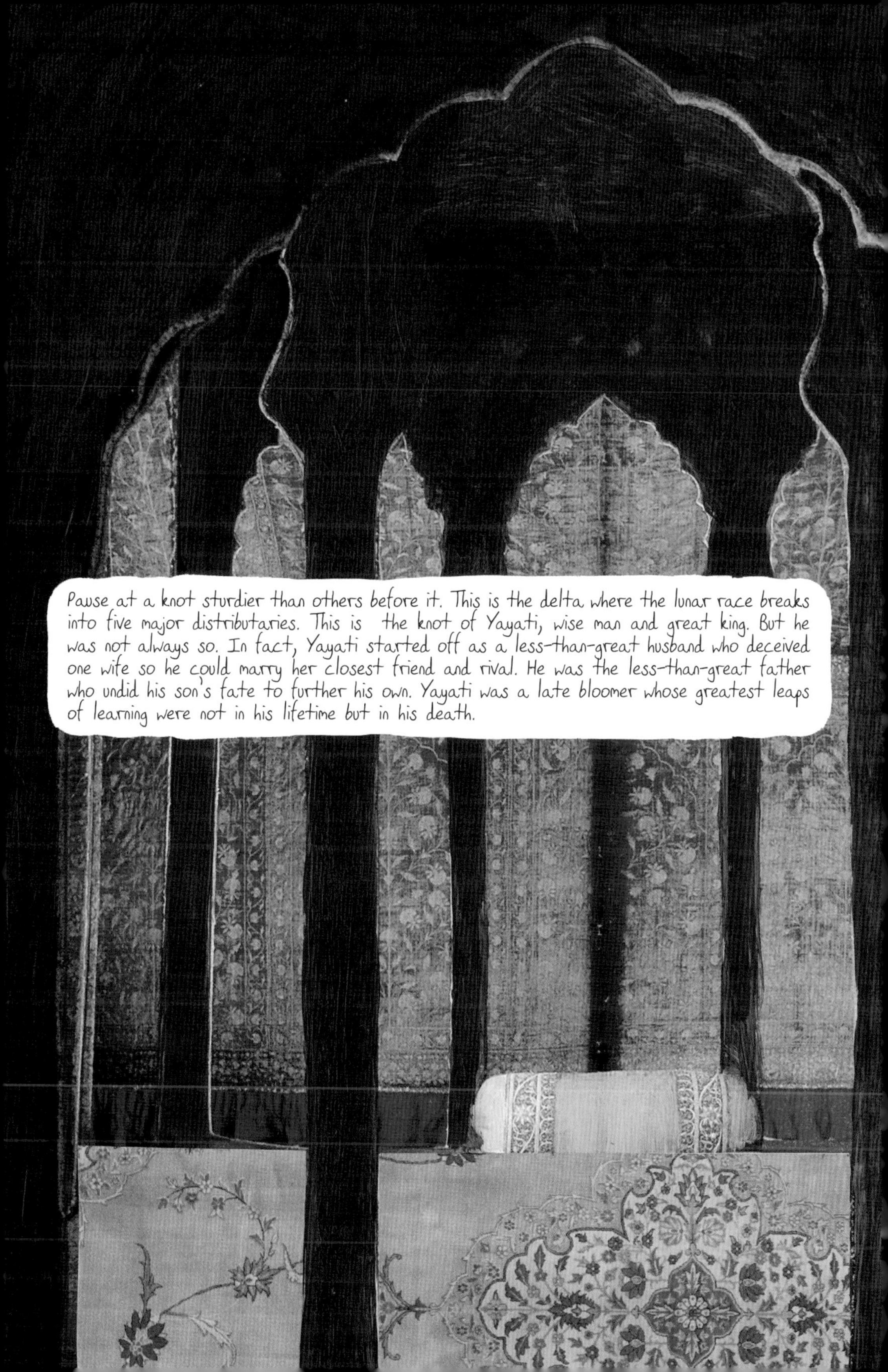
Pause at a knot sturdier than others before it. This is the delta where the lunar race breaks into five major distributaries. This is the knot of Yayati, wise man and great king. But he was not always so. In fact, Yayati started off as a less-than-great husband who deceived one wife so he could marry her closest friend and rival. He was the less-than-great father who undid his son's fate to further his own. Yayati was a late bloomer whose greatest leaps of learning were not in his lifetime but in his death.

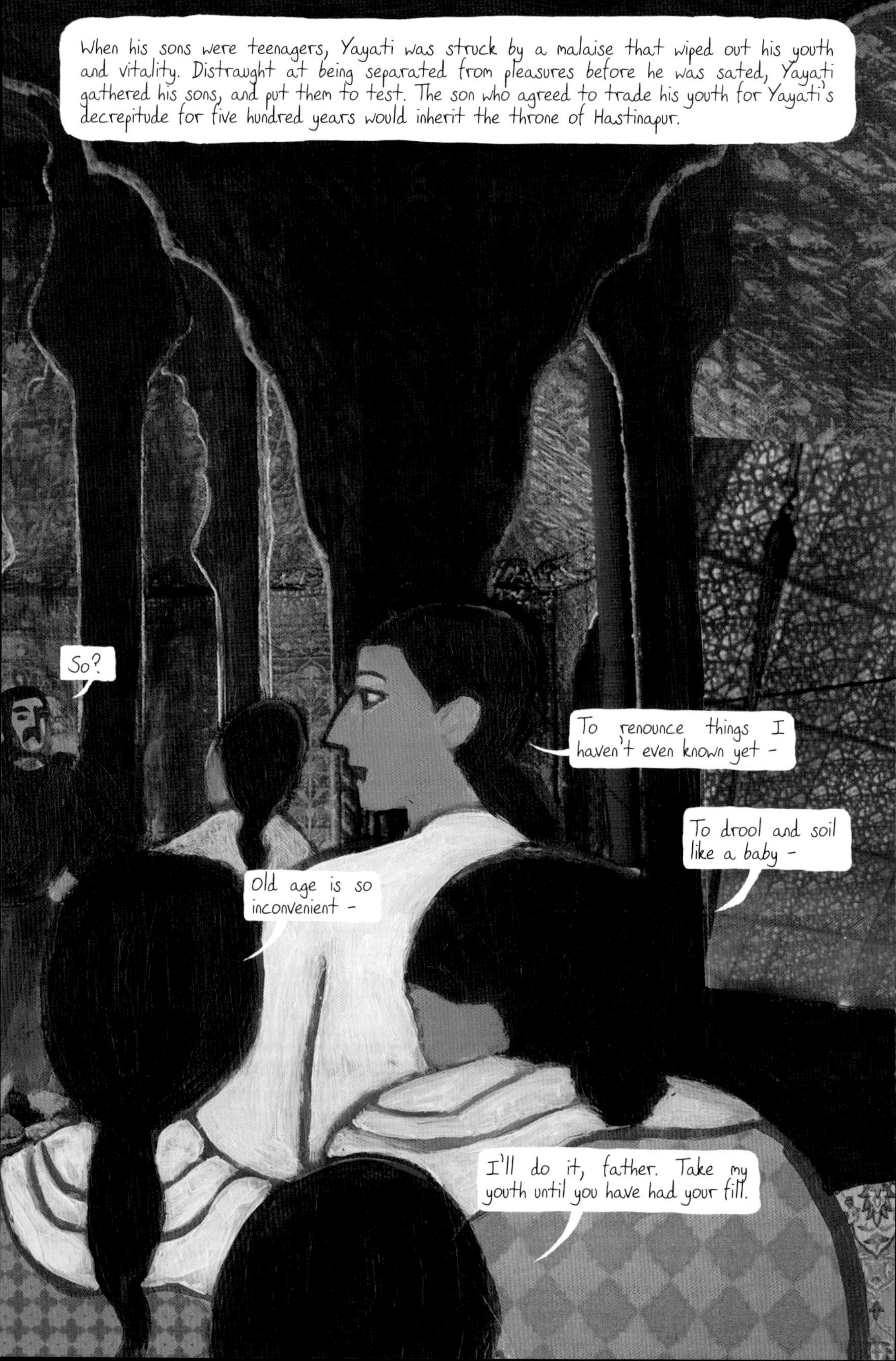
When his sons were teenagers, Yayati was struck by a malaise that wiped out his youth and vitality. Distraught at being separated from pleasures before he was sated, Yayati gathered his sons, and put them to test. The son who agreed to trade his youth for Yayati's decrepitude for five hundred years would inherit the throne of Hastinapur.
So?
To renounce things I haven't even known yet -
To drool and soil like a baby -
Old age is so inconvenient -
I'll do it, father. Take my youth until you have had your fill.

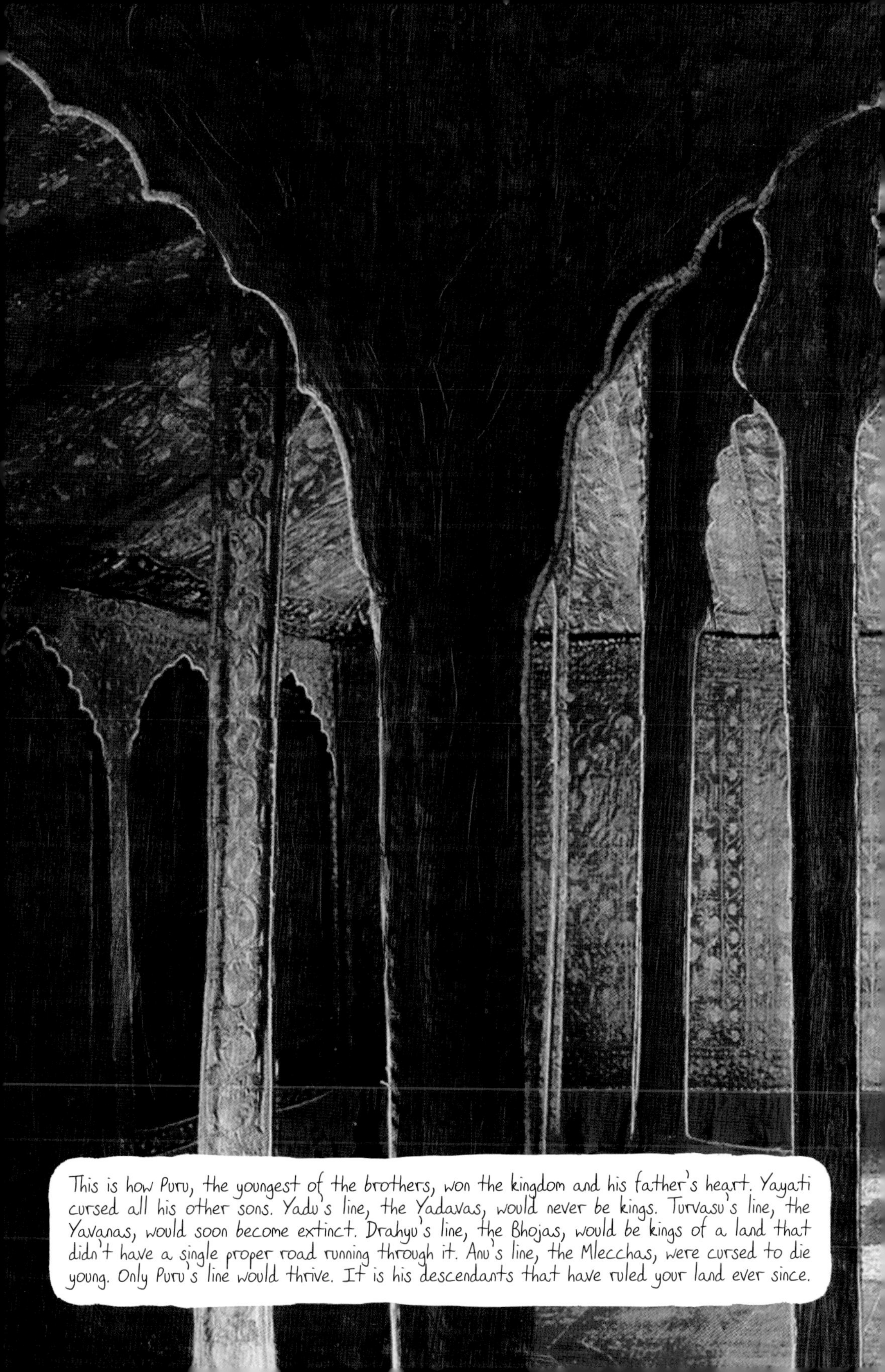
This is how Puru, the youngest of the brothers, won the kingdom and his father's heart. Yayati cursed all his other sons. Yadu's line, the Yadavas, would never be kings. Turvasu's line, the Yavanas, would soon become extinct. Drahyu's line, the Bhojas, would be kings of a land that didn't have a single proper road running through it. Anu's line, the Mlecchas, were cursed to die young. Only Puru's line would thrive. It is his descendants that have ruled your land ever since.

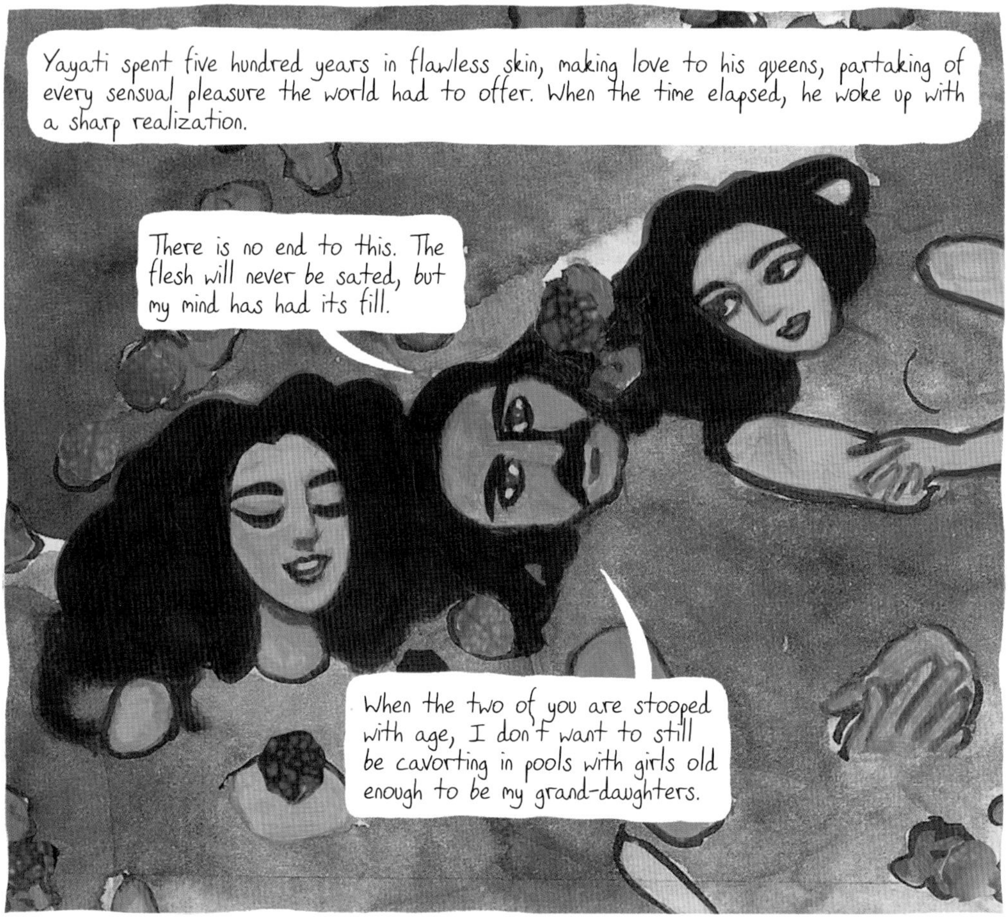
Yayati spent five hundred years in flawless skin, making love to his queens, partaking of every sensual pleasure the world had to offer. When the time elapsed, he woke up with a sharp realization.
There is no end to this. The flesh will never be sated, but my mind has had its fill.
When the two of you are stooped with age, I don't want to still be cavorting in pools with girls old enough to be my grand-daughters.

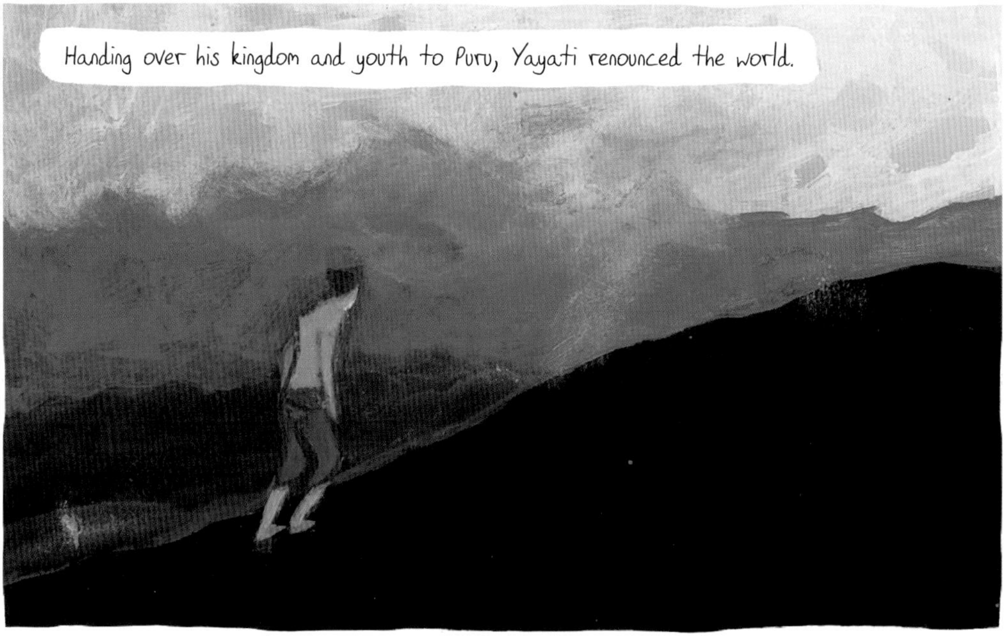
Handing over his kingdom and youth to Puru, Yayati renounced the world.

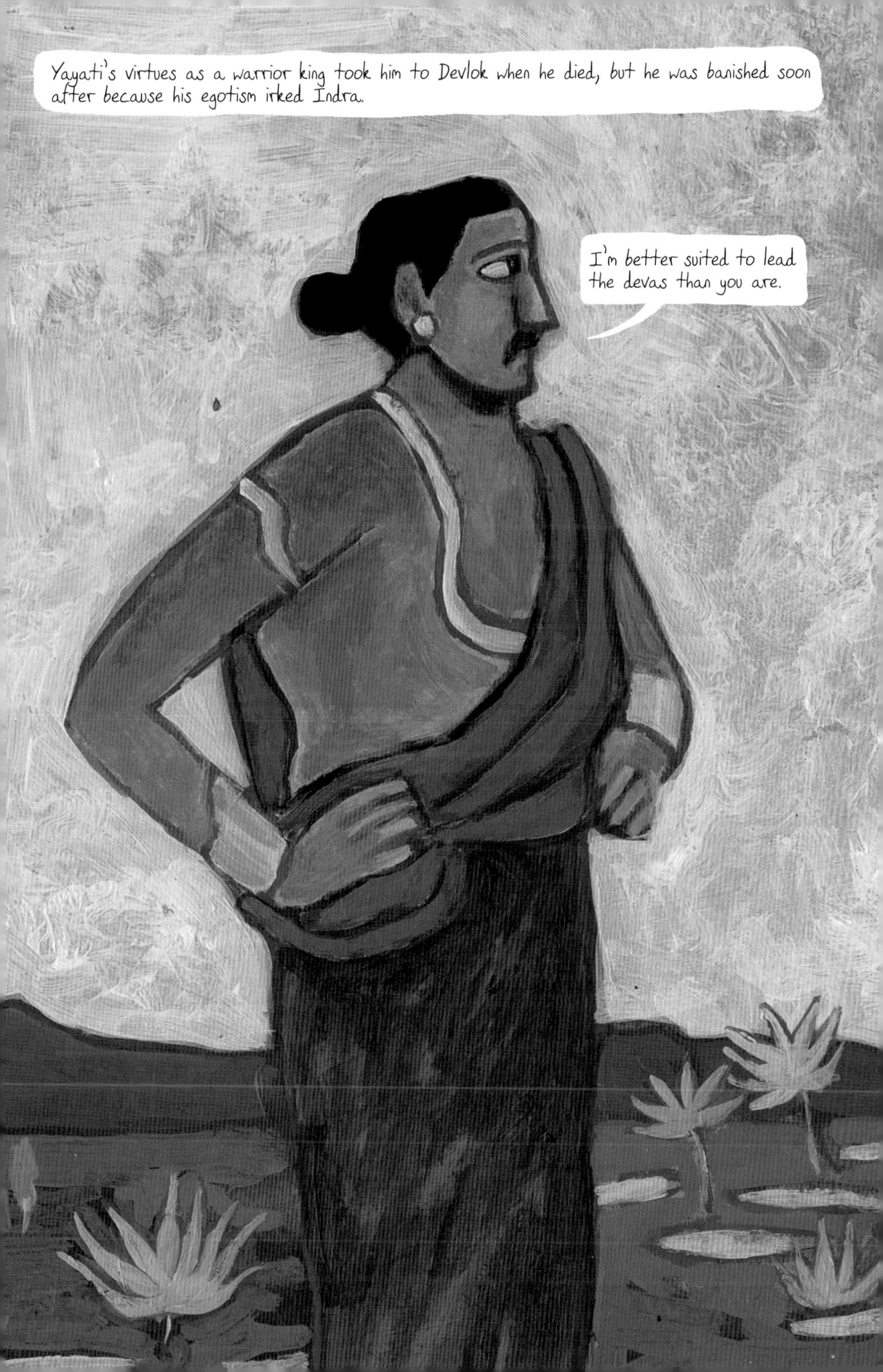
Yayati's virtues as a warrior king took him to Devlok when he died, but he was banished soon after because his egotism irked Indra.
I'm better suited to lead the devas than you are.

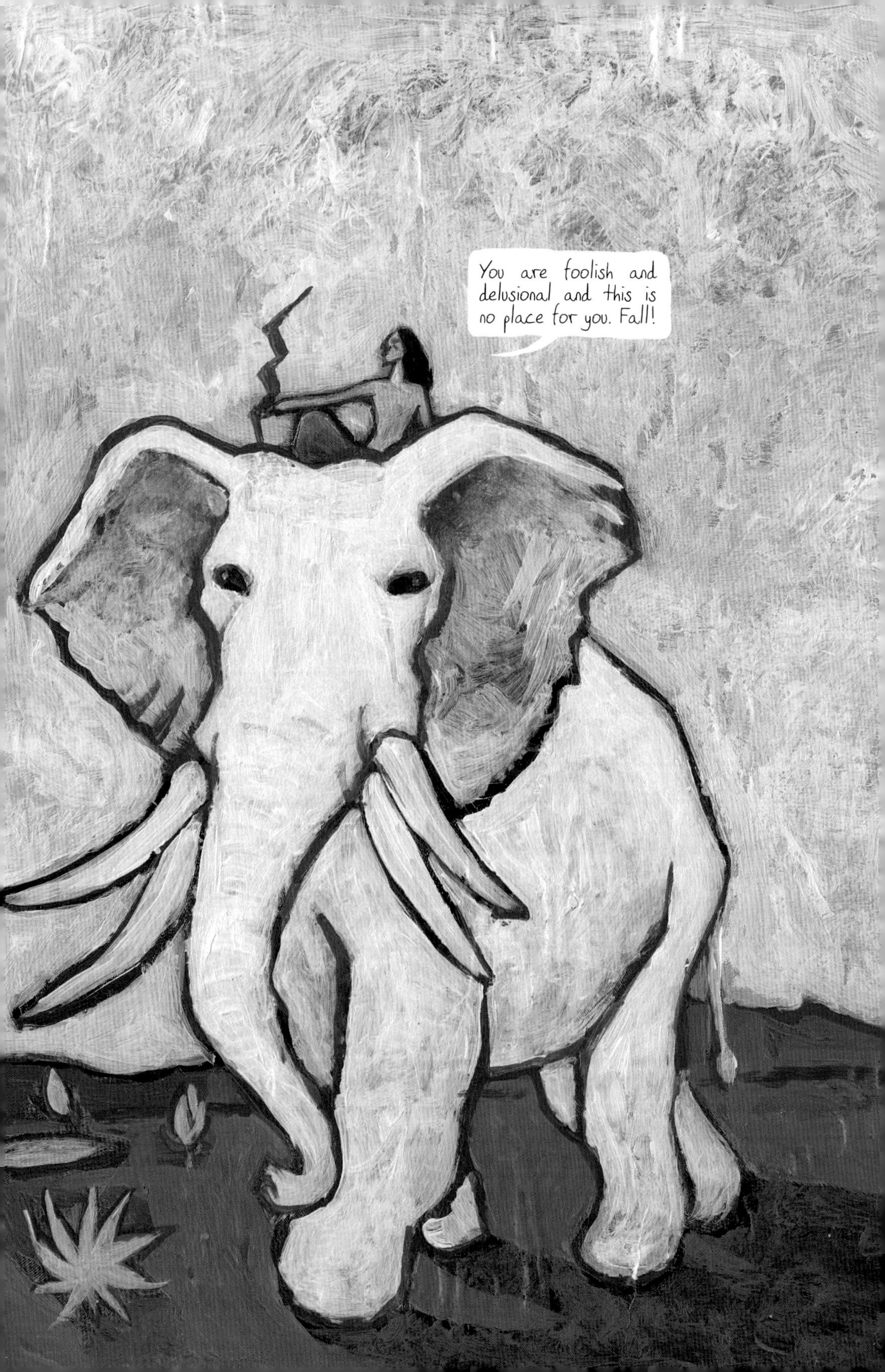
You are foolish and delusional and this is no place for you. Fall!

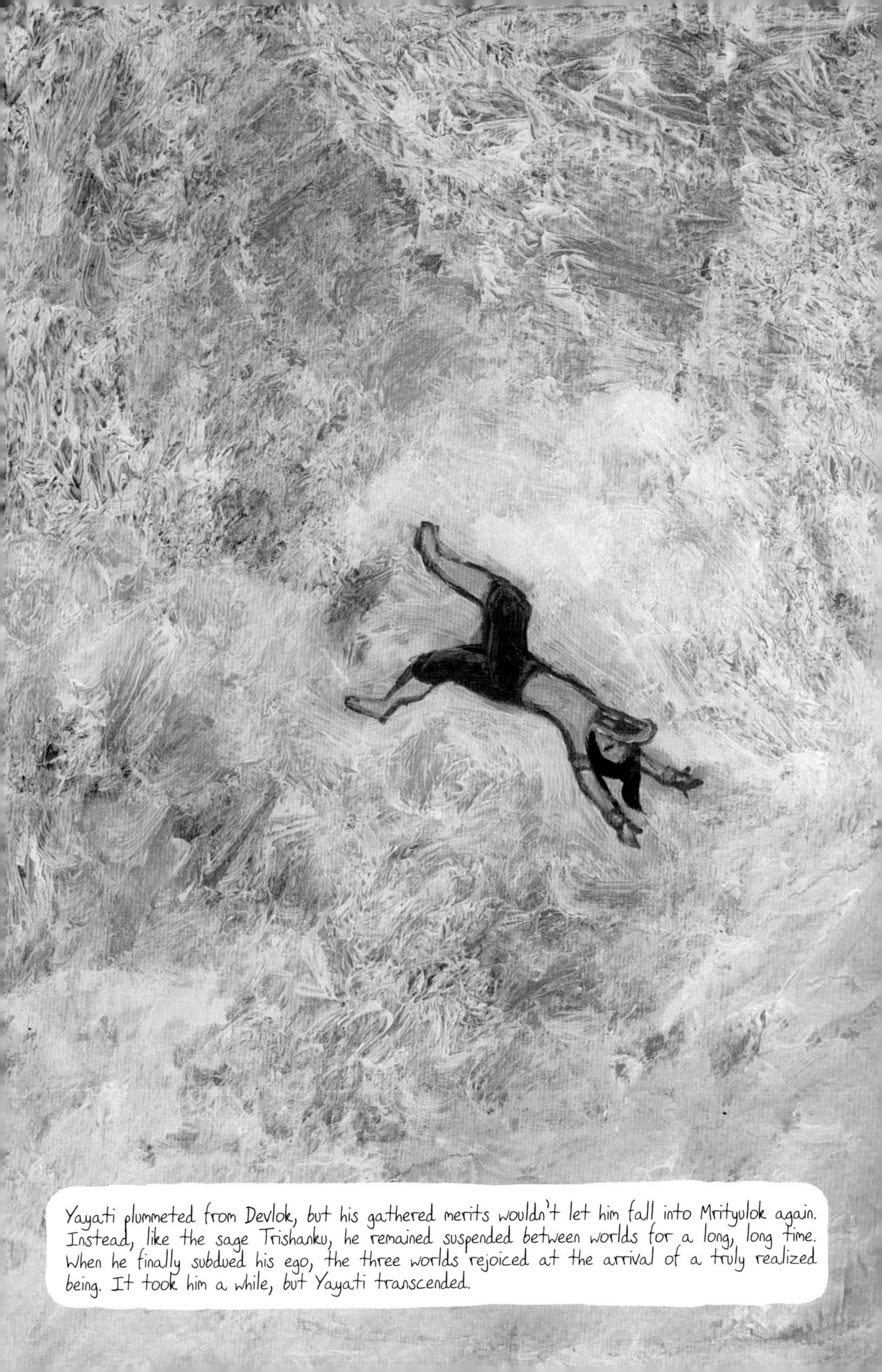
Yayati plummeted from Devlok, but his gathered merits wouldn't let him fall into Mrityulok again. Instead, like the sage Trishanku, he remained suspended between worlds for a long, long time. When he finally subdued his ego, the three worlds rejoiced at the arrival of a truly realized being. It took him a while, but Yayati transcended.

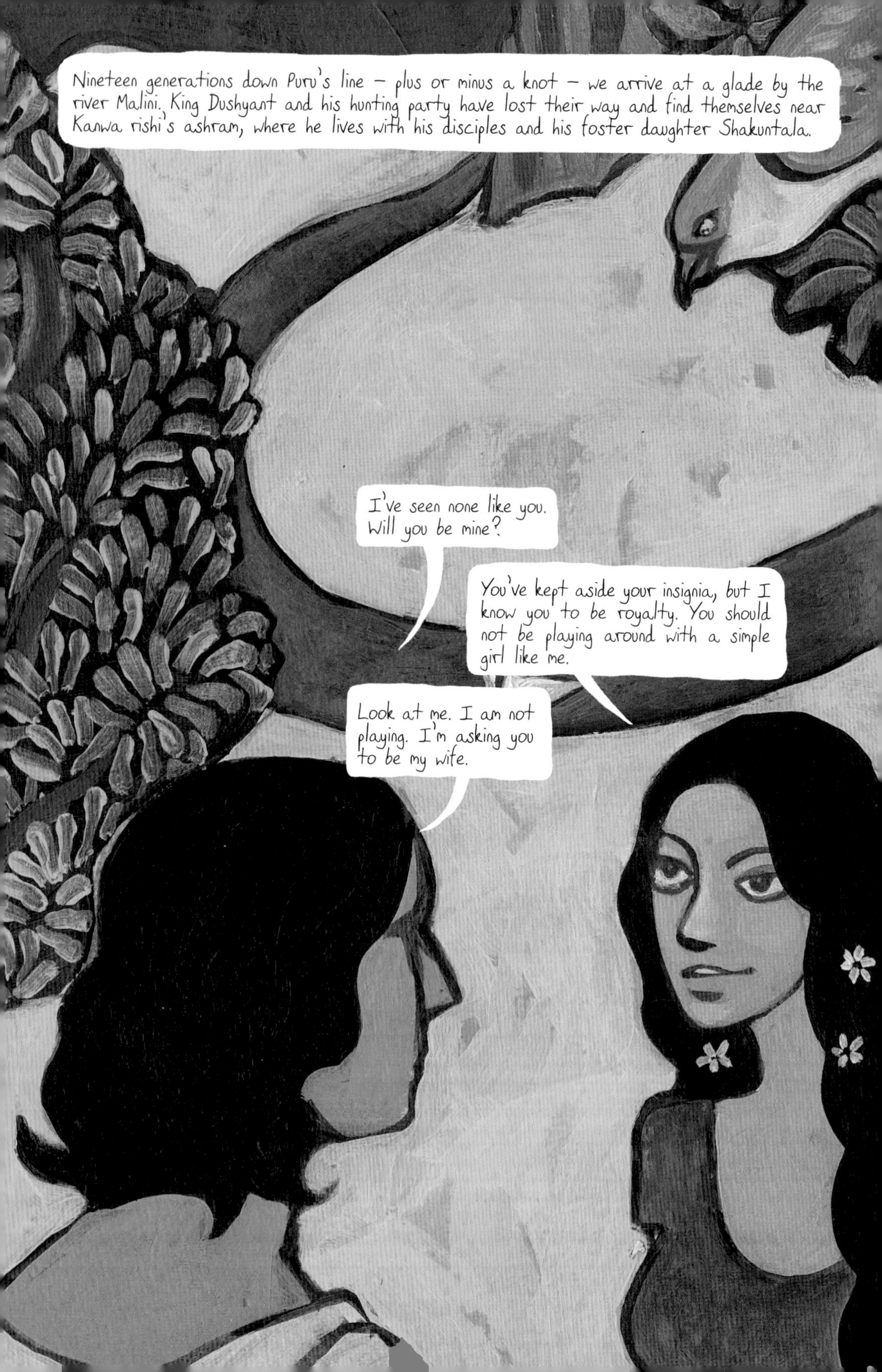
Nineteen generations down Puru's line – plus or minus a knot – we arrive at a glade by the river Malini. King Dushyant and his hunting party have lost their way and find themselves near Kanwa rishi's ashram, where he lives with his disciples and his foster daughter Shakuntala.
I've seen none like you. Will you be mine?
You've kept aside your insignia, but I know you to be royalty. You should not be playing around with a simple girl like me.
Look at me. I am not playing. I'm asking you to be my wife.

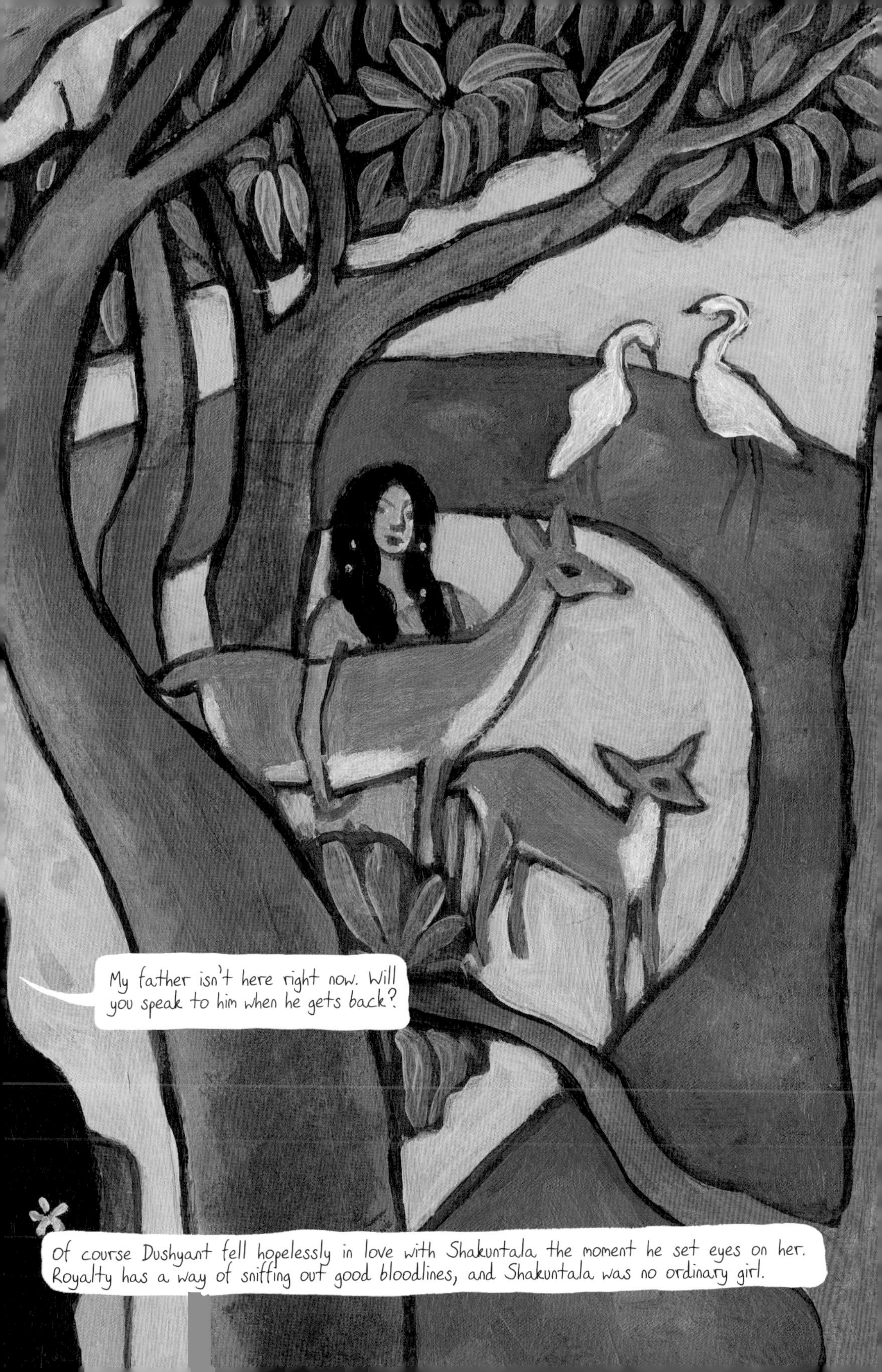
My father isn't here right now. Will you speak to him when he gets back?
Of course Dushyant fell hopelessly in love with Shakuntala the moment he set eyes on her. Royalty has a way of sniffing out good bloodlines, and Shakuntala was no ordinary girl.

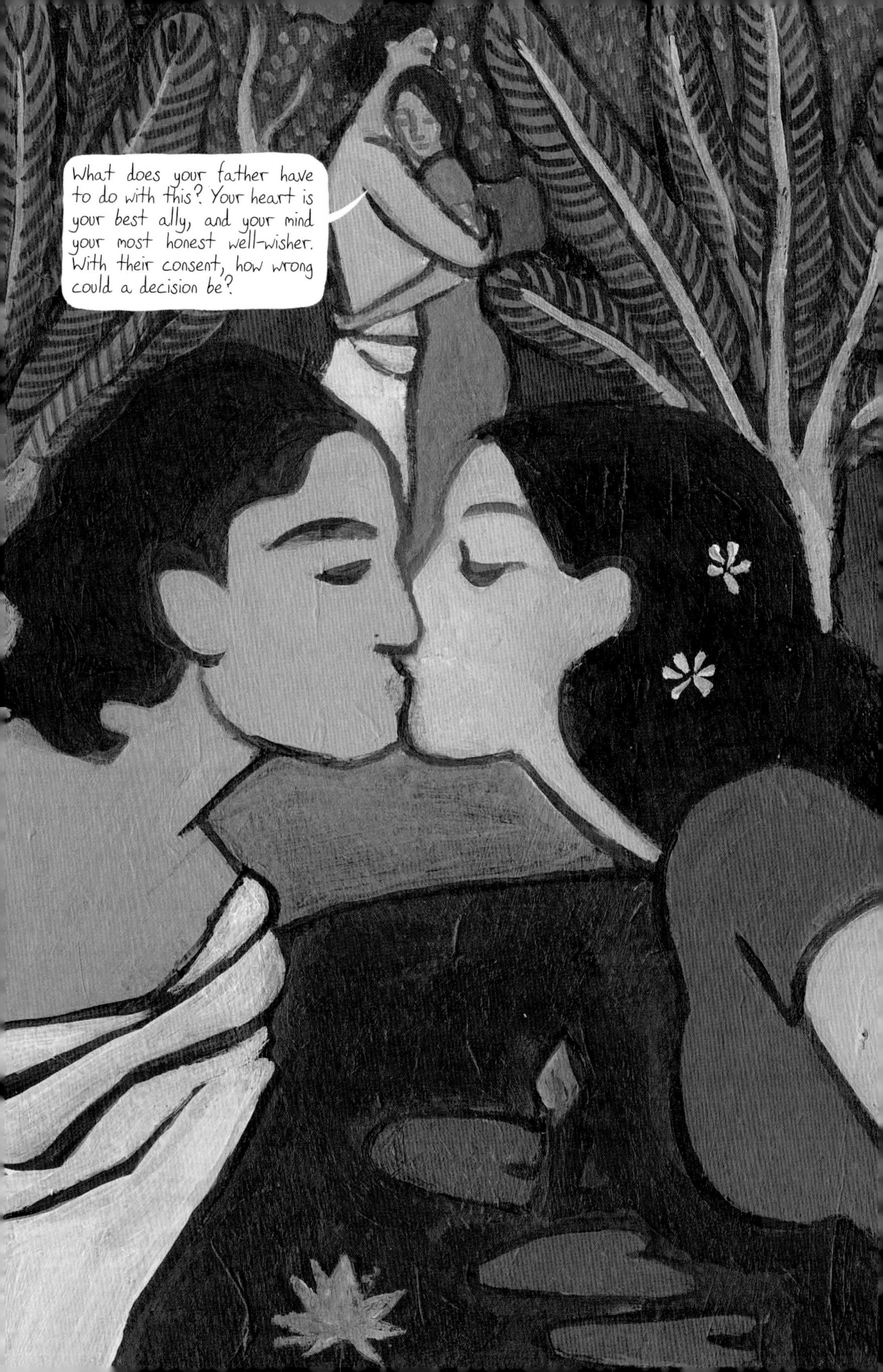
What does your father have to do with this? Your heart is your best ally, and your mind your most honest well-wisher. With their consent, how wrong could a decision be?

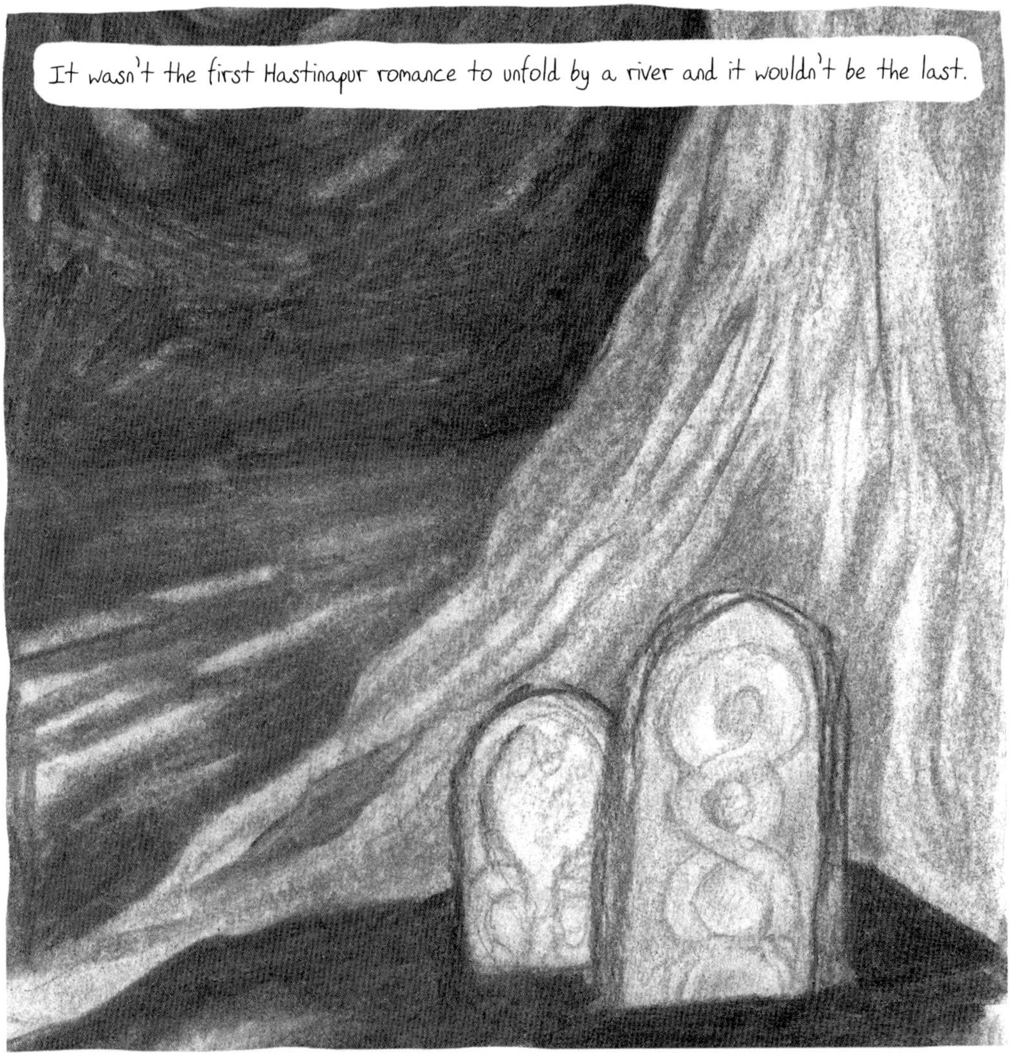
It wasn't the first Hastinapur romance to unfold by a river and it wouldn't be the last.

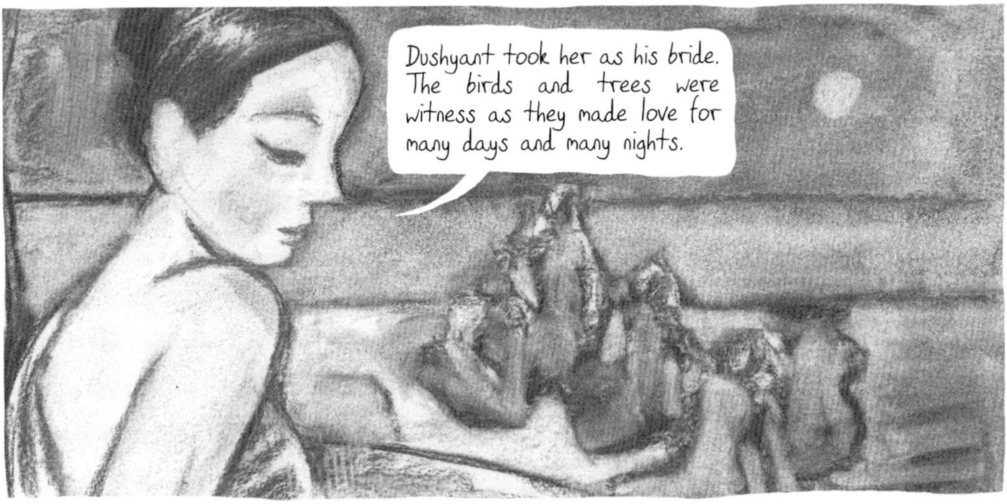
Dushyant took her as his bride. The birds and trees were witness as they made love for many days and many nights.

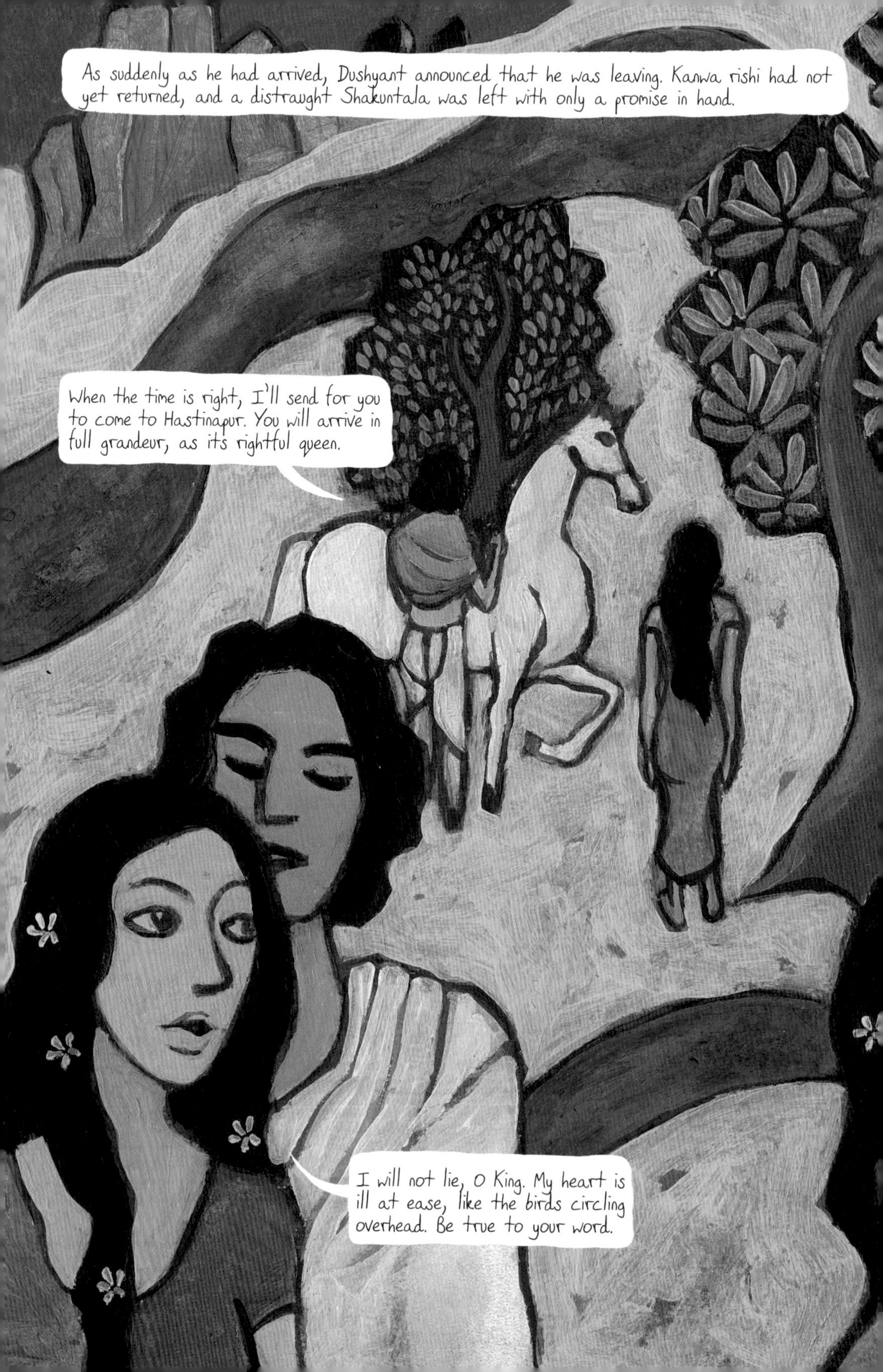
As suddenly as he had arrived, Dushyant announced that he was leaving. Kanwa rishi had not yet returned, and a distraught Shakuntala was left with only a promise in hand.
When the time is right, I'll send for you to come to Hastinapur. You will arrive in full grandeur, as its rightful queen.
I will not lie, O King. My heart is ill at ease, like the birds circling overhead. Be true to your word.

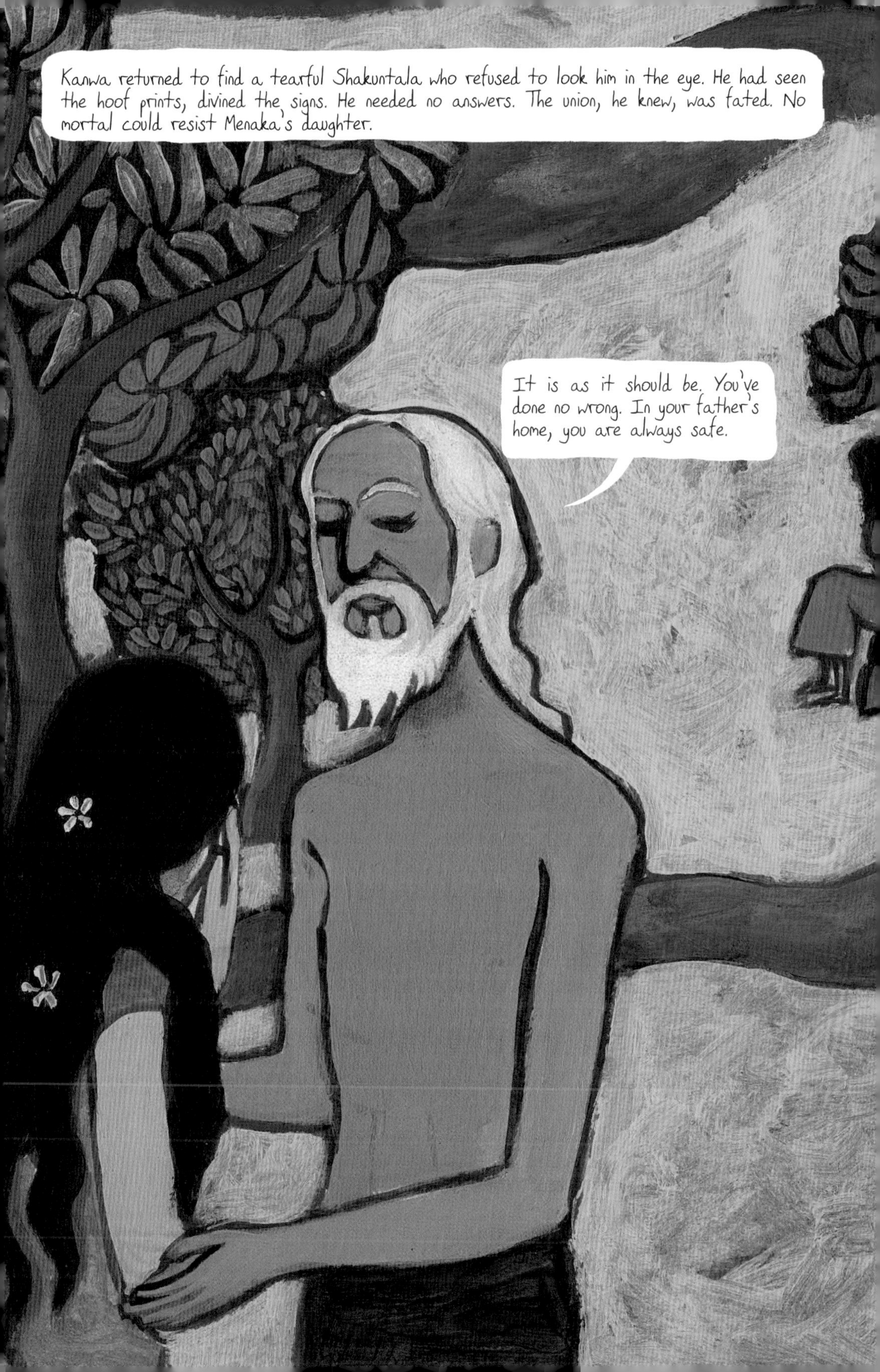
Kanwa returned to find a tearful Shakuntala who refused to look him in the eye. He had seen the hoof prints, divined the signs. He needed no answers. The union, he knew, was fated. No mortal could resist Menaka's daughter.
It is as it should be. You've done no wrong. In your father's home, you are always safe.

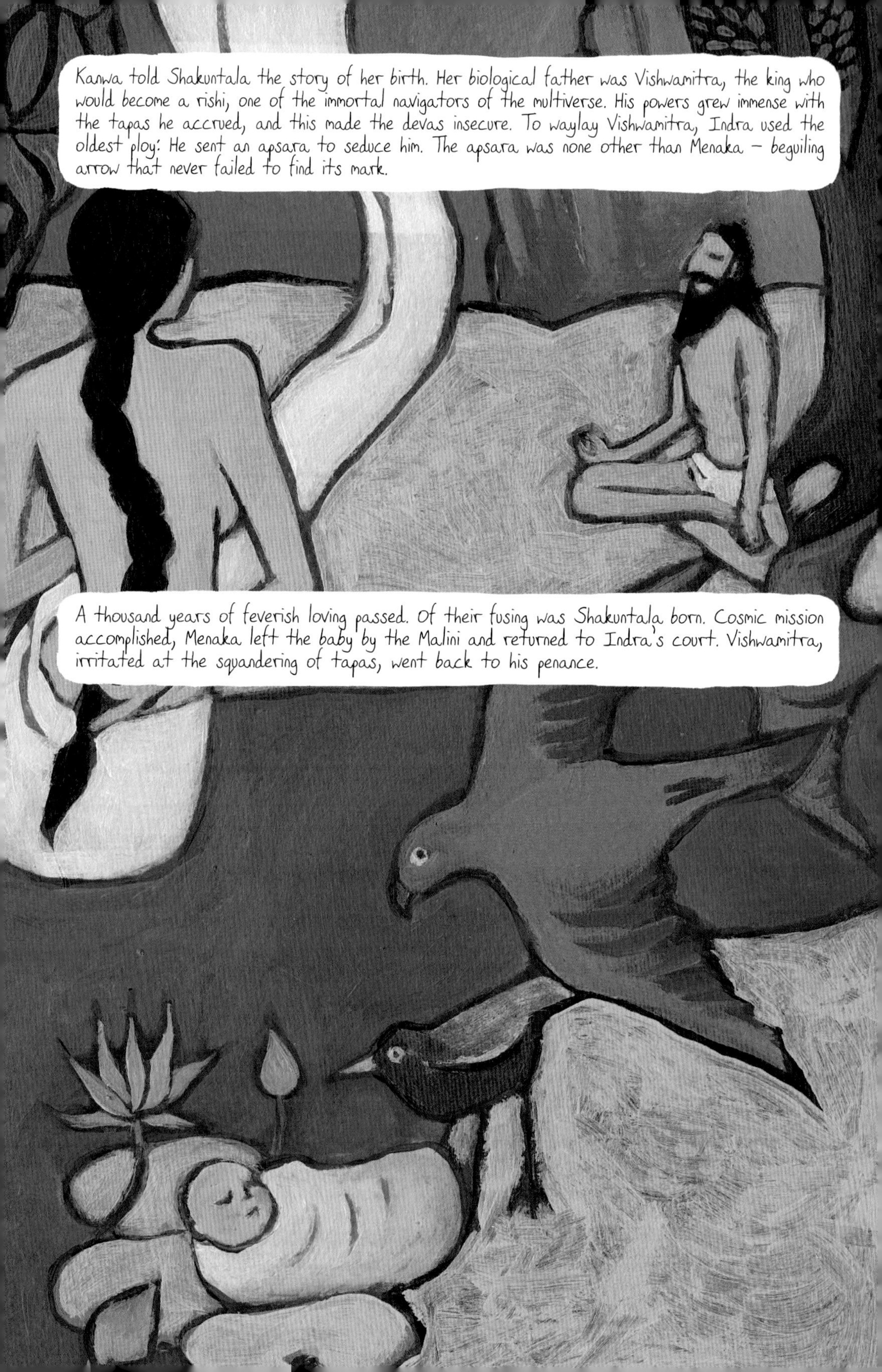
Kanwa told Shakuntala the story of her birth. Her biological father was Vishwamitra, the king who would become a rishi, one of the immortal navigators of the multiverse. His powers grew immense with the tapas he accrued, and this made the devas insecure. To waylay Vishwamitra, Indra used the oldest ploy: He sent an apsara to seduce him. The apsara was none other than Menaka – beguiling arrow that never failed to find its mark.
A thousand years of feverish loving passed. Of their fusing was Shakuntala born. Cosmic mission accomplished, Menaka left the baby by the Malini and returned to Indra's court. Vishwamitra, irritated at the squandering of tapas, went back to his penance.

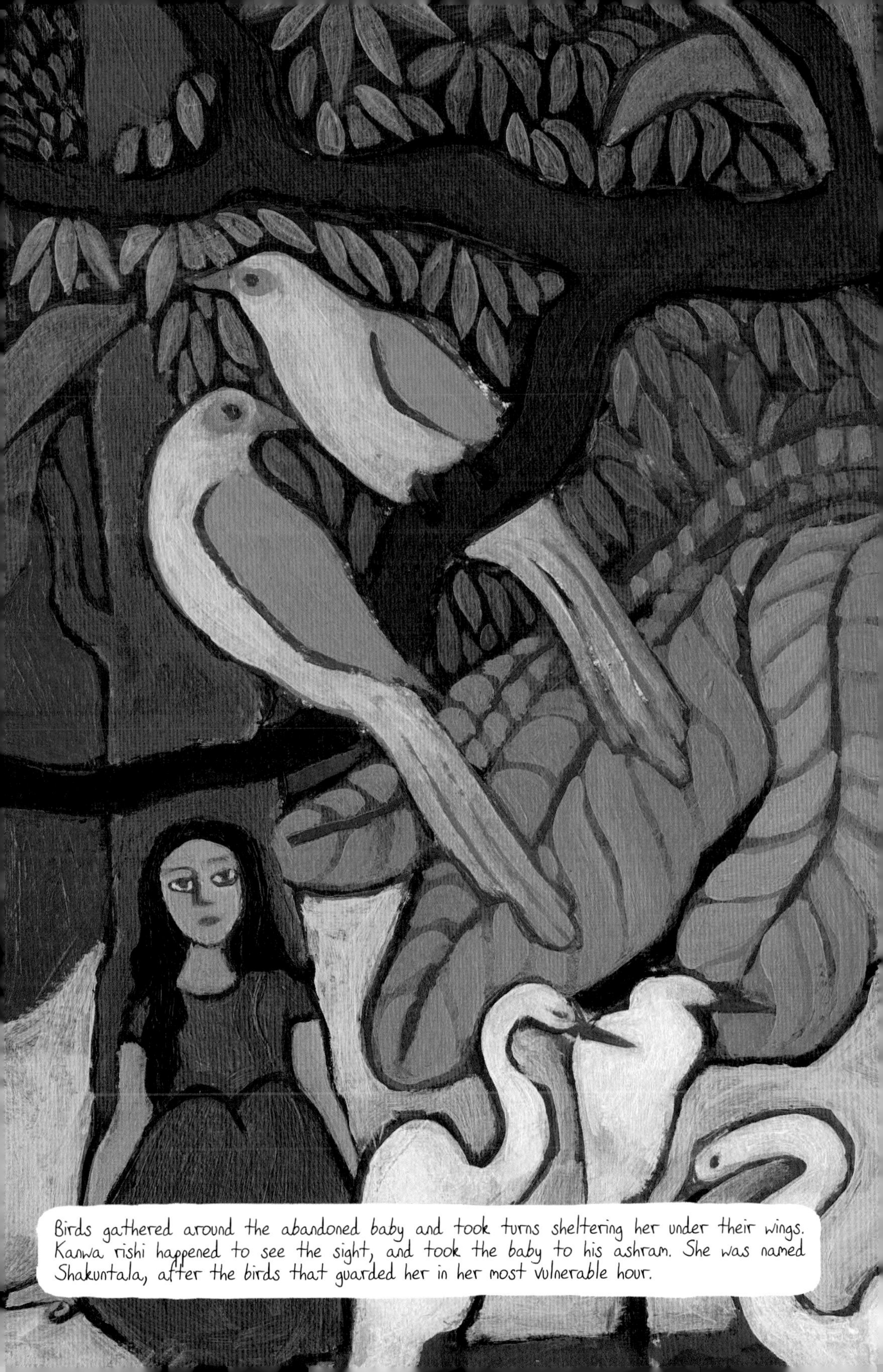
Birds gathered around the abandoned baby and took turns sheltering her under their wings. Kanwa rishi happened to see the sight, and took the baby to his ashram. She was named Shakuntala, after the birds that guarded her in her most vulnerable hour.

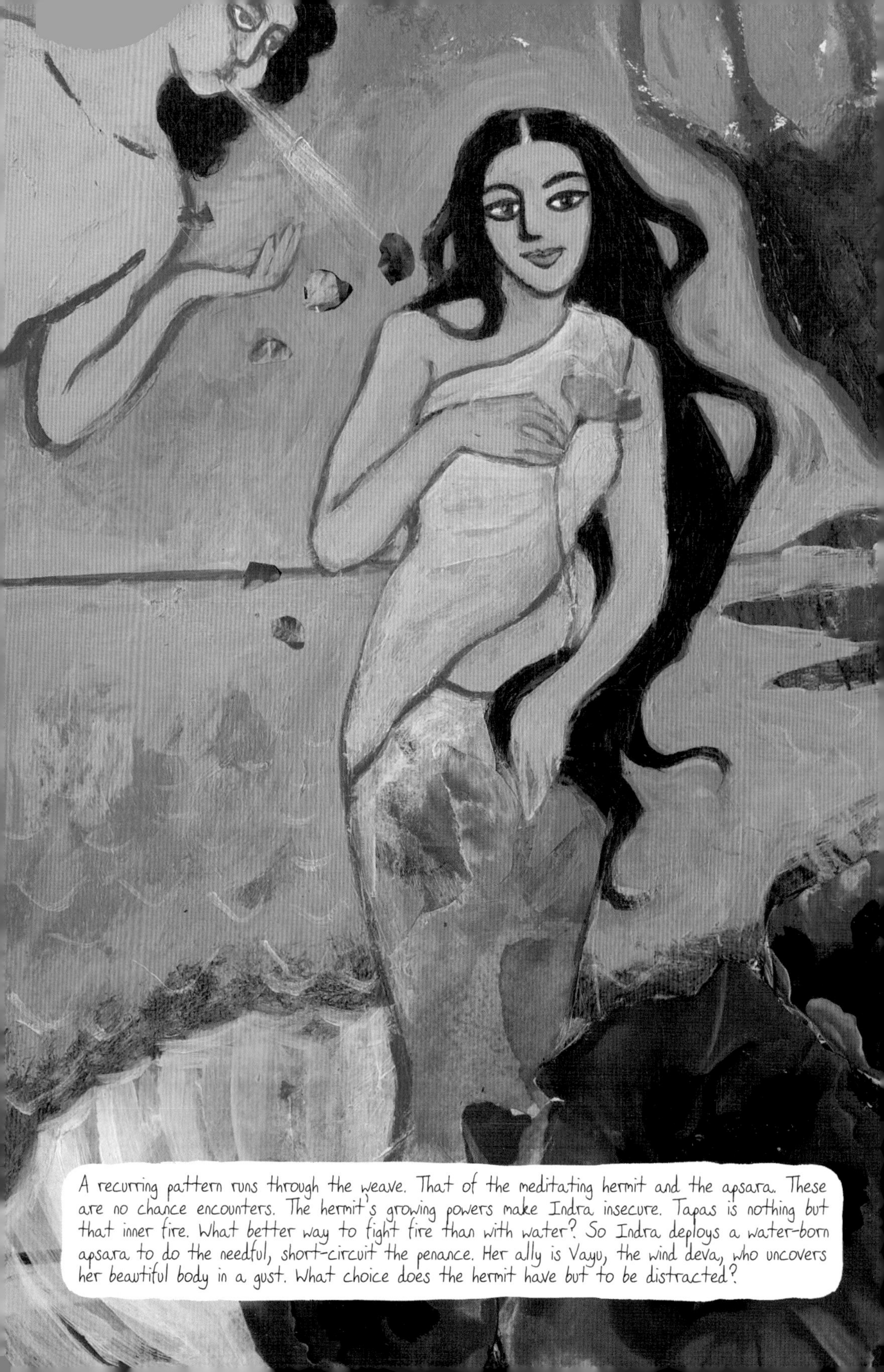
A recurring pattern runs through the weave. That of the meditating hermit and the apsara. These are no chance encounters. The hermit's growing powers make Indra insecure. Tapas is nothing but that inner fire. What better way to fight fire than with water? So Indra deploys a water-born apsara to do the needful, short-circuit the penance. Her ally is Vayu, the wind deva, who uncovers her beautiful body in a gust. What choice does the hermit have but to be distracted?

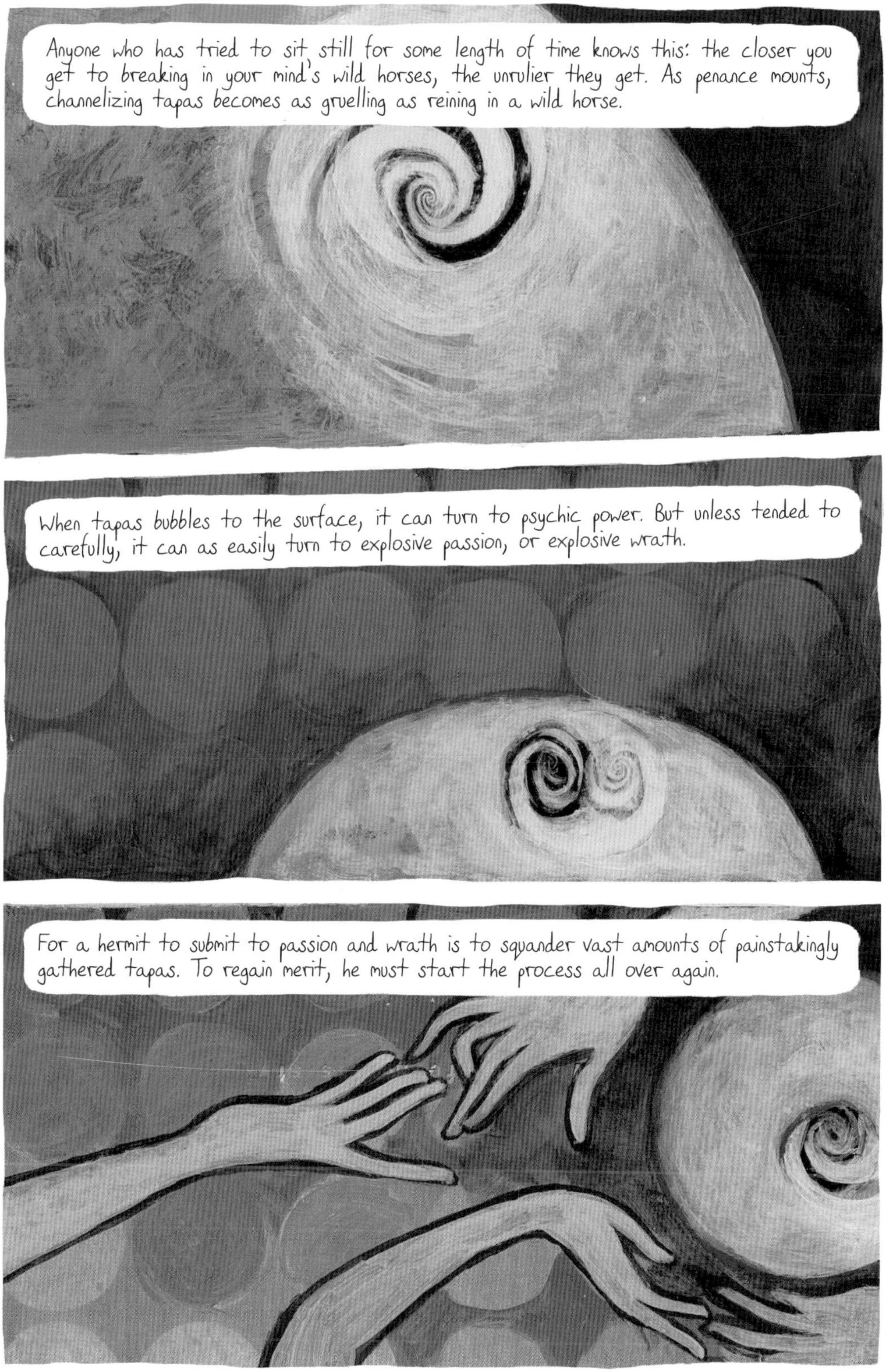
Anyone who has tried to sit still for some length of time knows this: the closer you get to breaking in your mind's wild horses, the unrulier they get. As penance mounts, channelizing tapas becomes as gruelling as reining in a wild horse.
When tapas bubbles to the surface, it can turn to psychic power. But unless tended to carefully, it can as easily turn to explosive passion, or explosive wrath.
For a hermit to submit to passion and wrath is to squander vast amounts of painstakingly gathered tapas. To regain merit, he must start the process all over again.

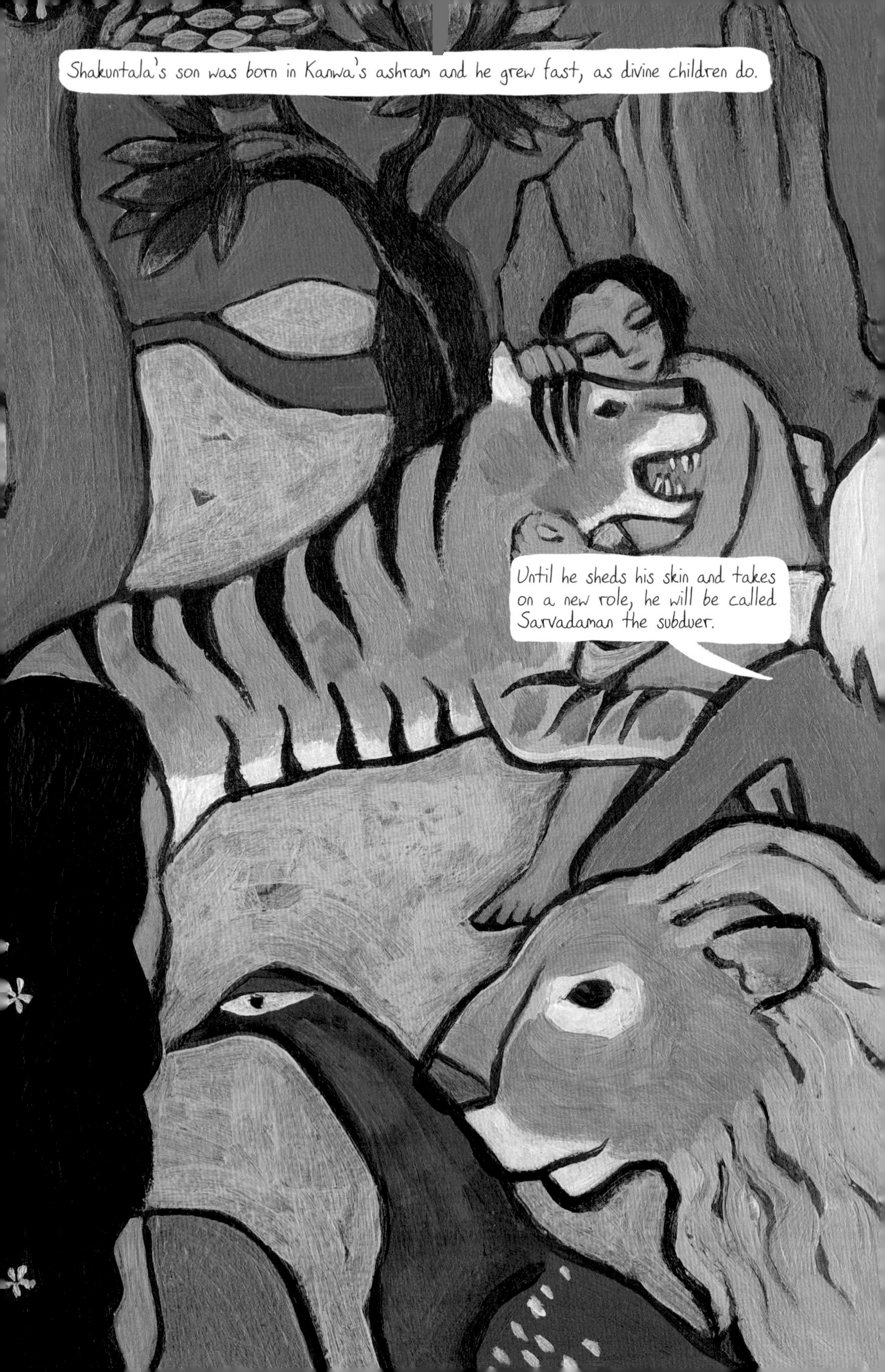
Shakuntala's son was born in Kanwa's ashram and he grew fast, as divine children do.
Until he sheds his skin and takes on a new role, he will be called Sarvadaman the subduer.

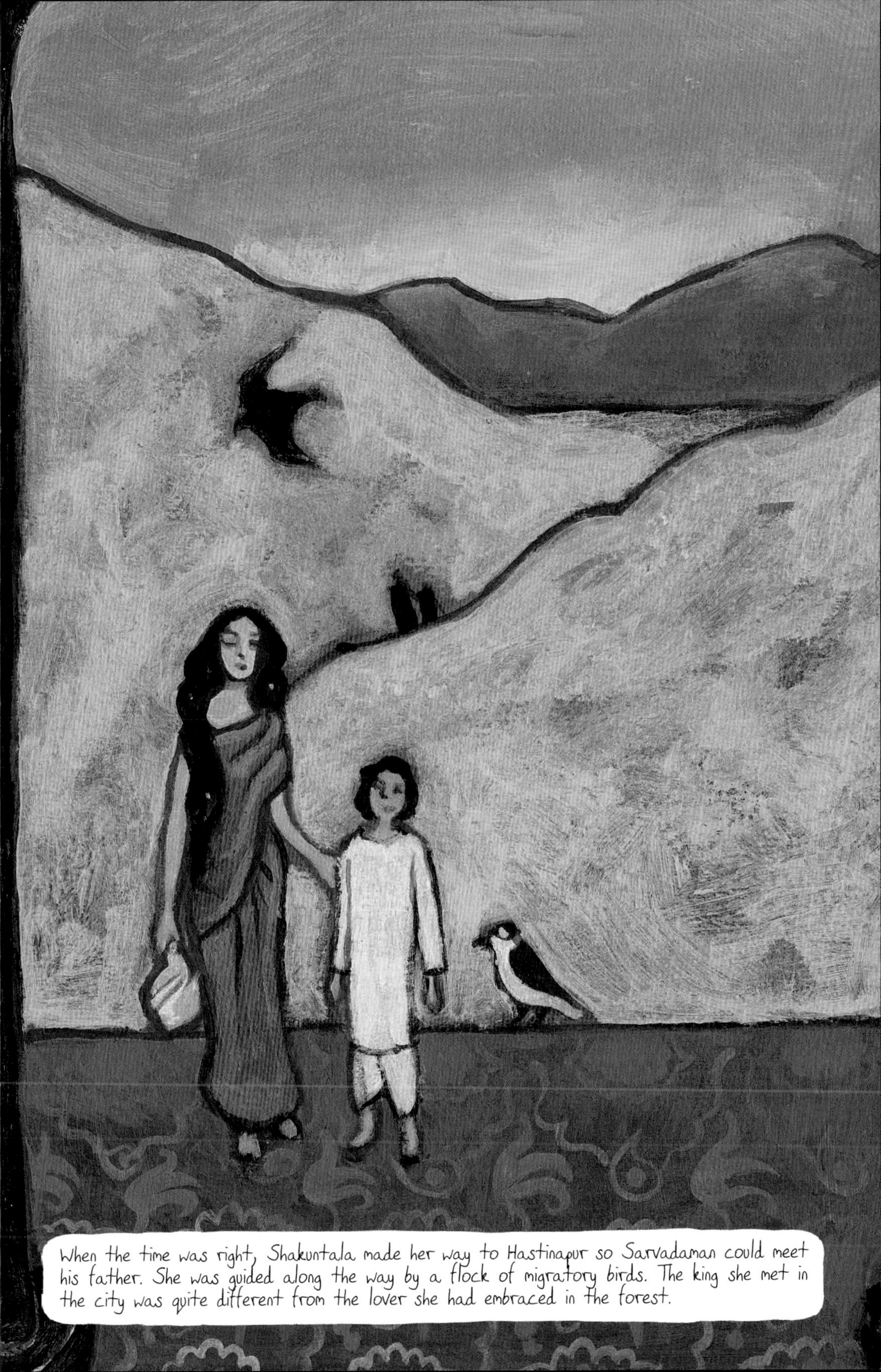
When the time was right, Shakuntala made her way to Hastinapur so Sarvadaman could meet his father. She was guided along the way by a flock of migratory birds. The king she met in the city was quite different from the lover she had embraced in the forest.

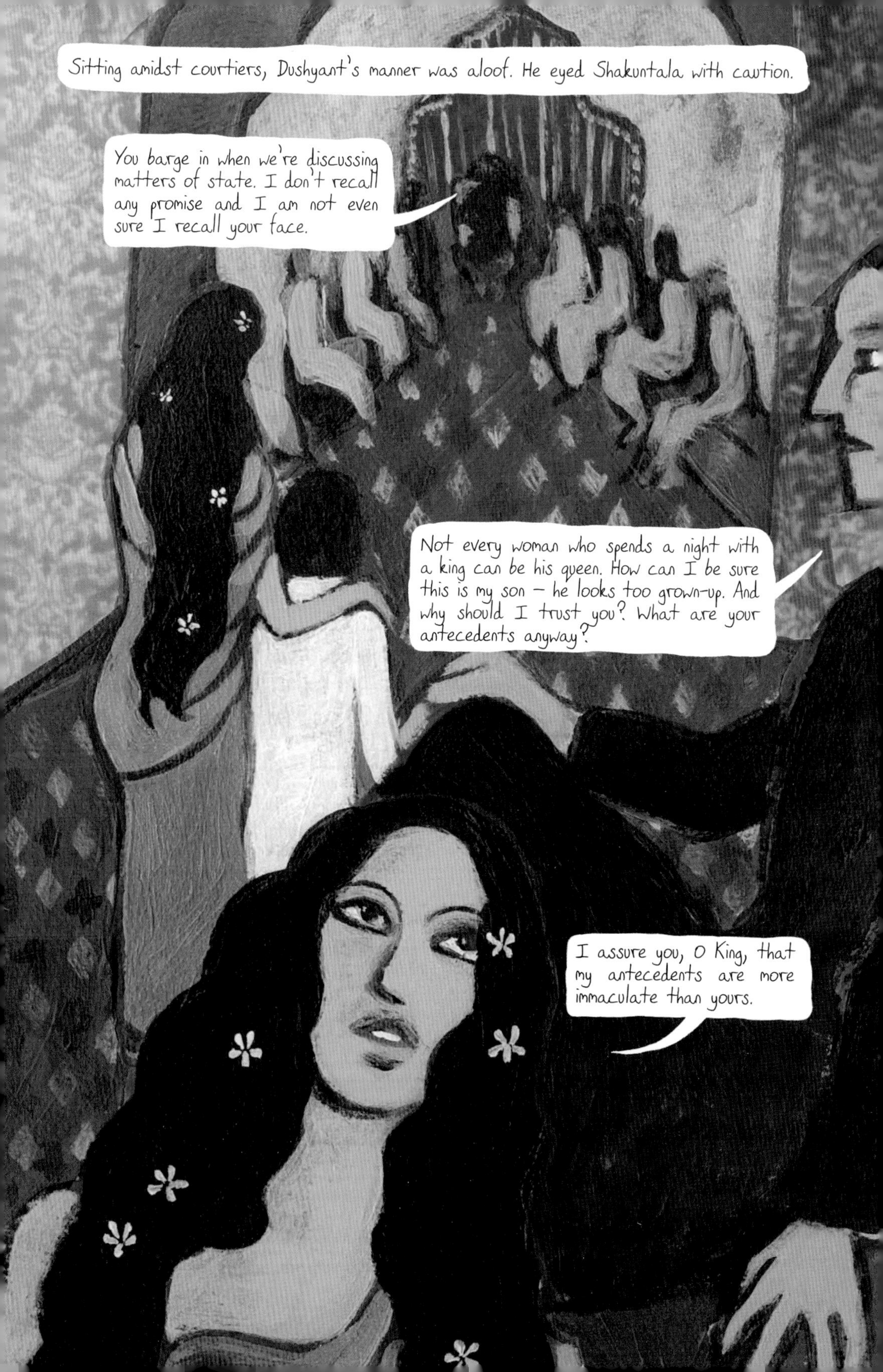
Sitting amidst courtiers, Dushyant's manner was aloof. He eyed Shakuntala with caution.
You barge in when we're discussing matters of state. I don't recall any promise and I am not even sure I recall your face.
Not every woman who spends a night with a king can be his queen. How can I be sure this is my son – he looks too grown-up. And why should I trust you? What are your antecedents anyway?
I assure you, O King, that my antecedents are more immaculate than yours.

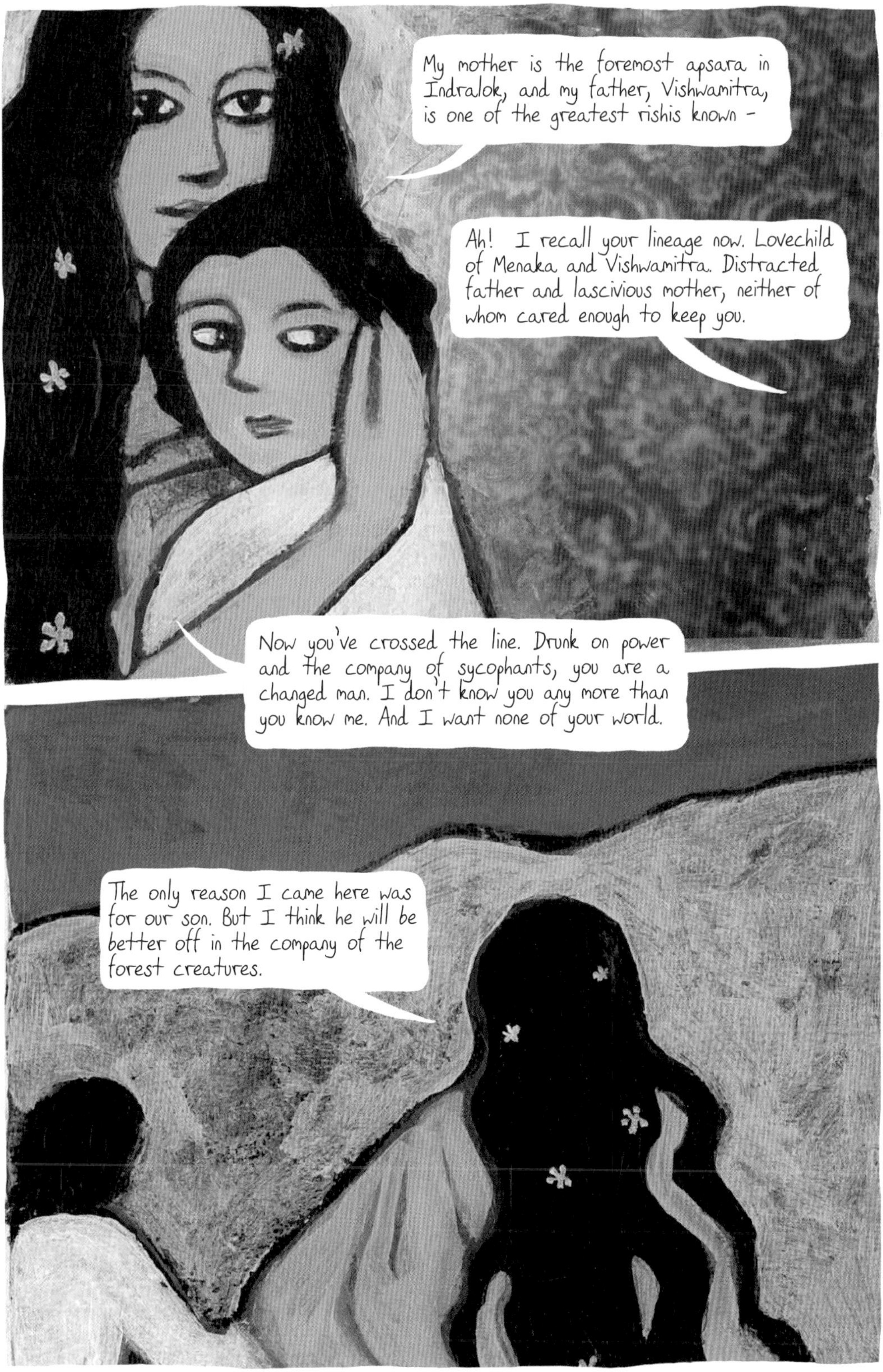
My mother is the foremost apsara in Indralok, and my father, Vishwamitra, is one of the greatest rishis known -
Ah! I recall your lineage now. Lovechild of Menaka and Vishwamitra. Distracted father and lascivious mother, neither of whom cared enough to keep you.
Now you've crossed the line. Drunk on power and the company of sycophants, you are a changed man. I don't know you any more than you know me. And I want none of your world.
The only reason I came here was for our son. But I think he will be better off in the company of the forest creatures.

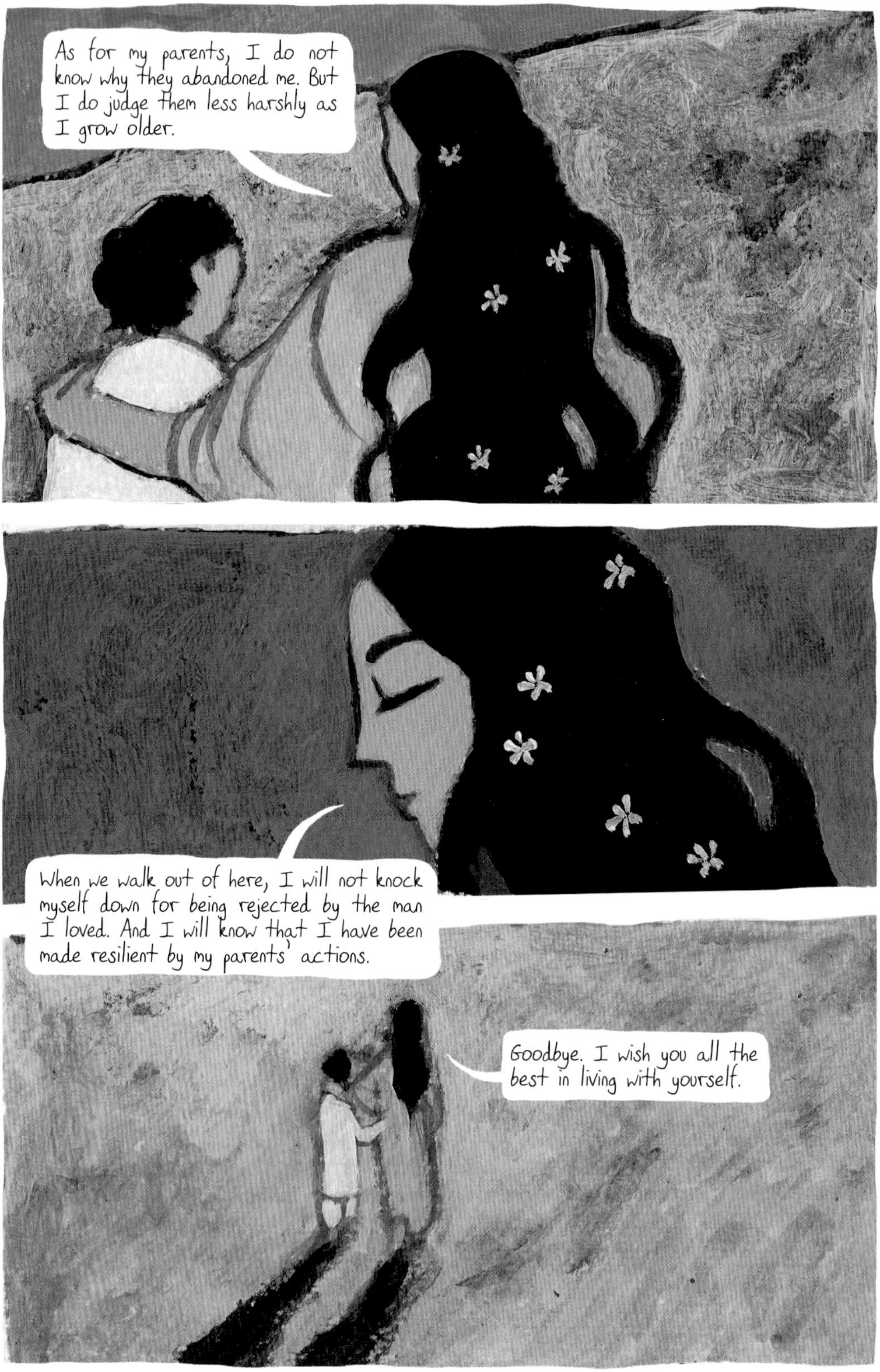
As for my parents, I do not know why they abandoned me. But I do judge them less harshly as I grow older.
When we walk out of here, I will not knock myself down for being rejected by the man I loved. And I will know that I have been made resilient by my parents' actions.
Goodbye. I wish you all the best in living with yourself.

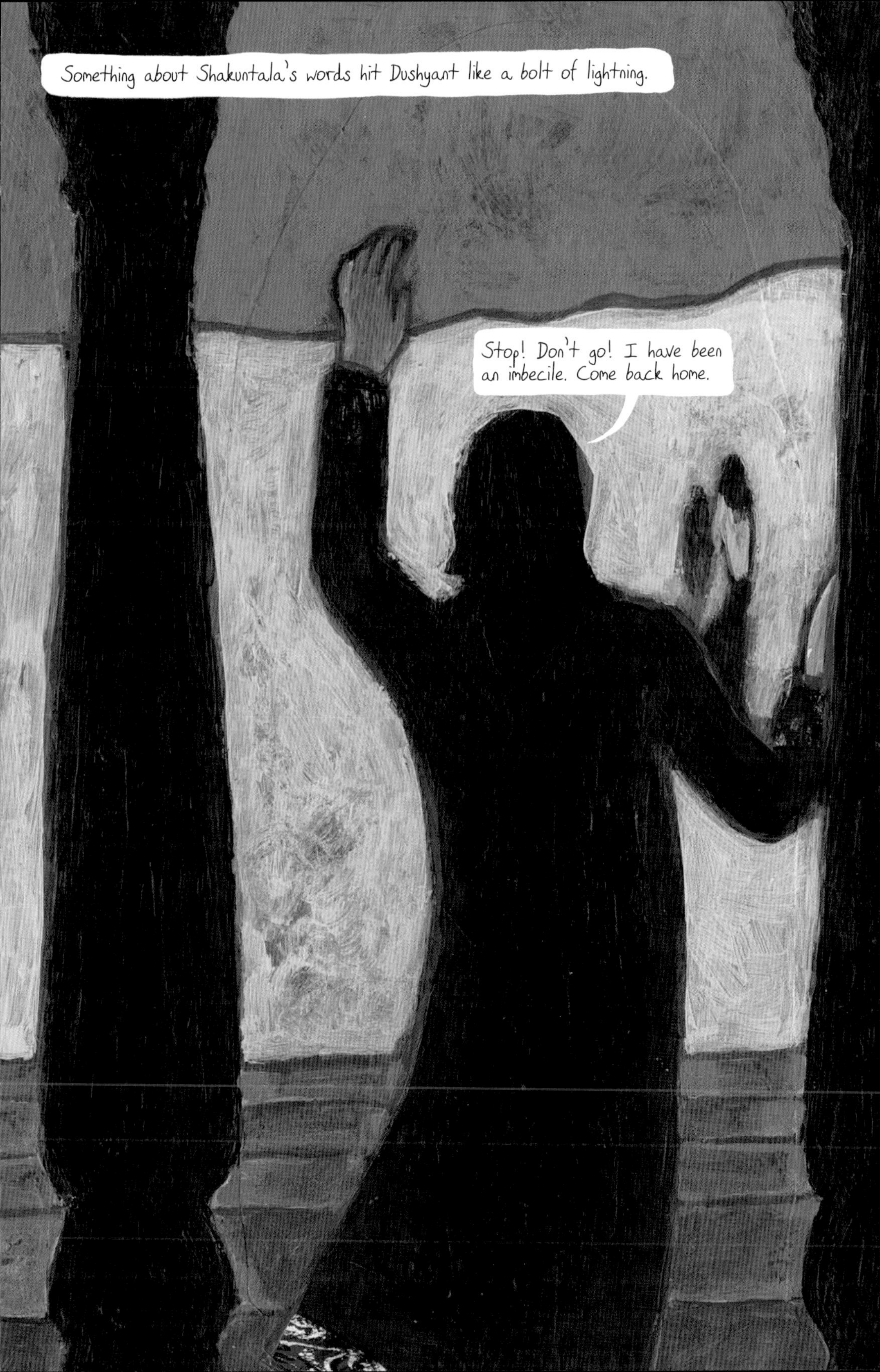
Something about Shakuntala's words hit Dushyant like a bolt of lightning.
Stop! Don't go! I have been an imbecile. Come back home.

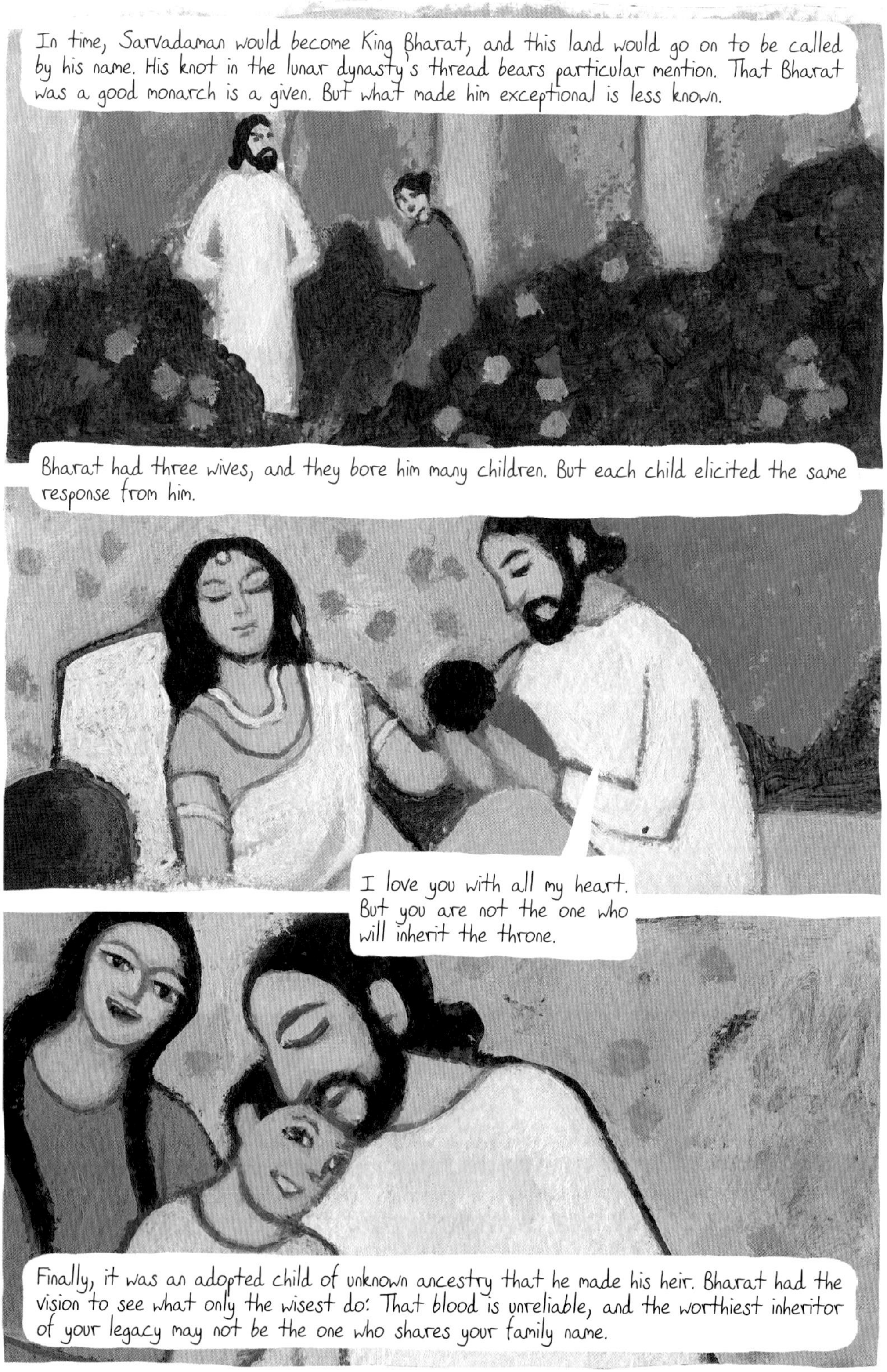
In time, Sarvadaman would become King Bharat, and this land would go on to be called by his name. His knot in the lunar dynasty's thread bears particular mention. That Bharat was a good monarch is a given. But what made him exceptional is less known.
Bharat had three wives, and they bore him many children. But each child elicited the same response from him.
I love you with all my heart. But you are not the one who will inherit the throne.
Finally, it was an adopted child of unknown ancestry that he made his heir. Bharat had the vision to see what only the wisest do: That blood is unreliable, and the worthiest inheritor of your legacy may not be the one who shares your family name.

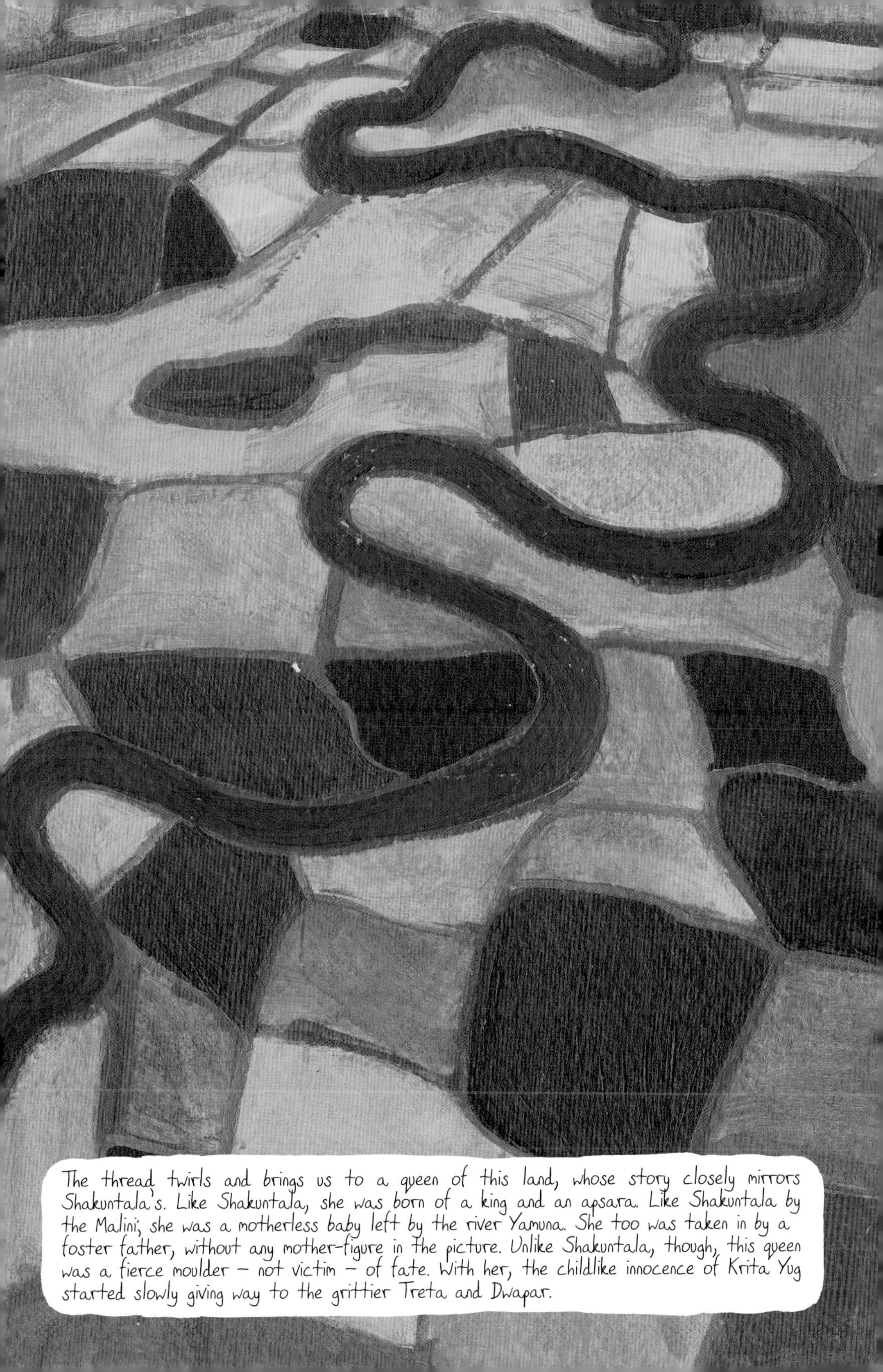
The thread twirls and brings us to a queen of this land, whose story closely mirrors Shakuntala's. Like Shakuntala, she was born of a king and an apsara. Like Shakuntala by the Malini, she was a motherless baby left by the river Yamuna. She too was taken in by a foster father, without any mother-figure in the picture. Unlike Shakuntala, though, this queen was a fierce moulder – not victim – of fate. With her, the childlike innocence of Krita Yug started slowly giving way to the grittier Treta and Dwapar.

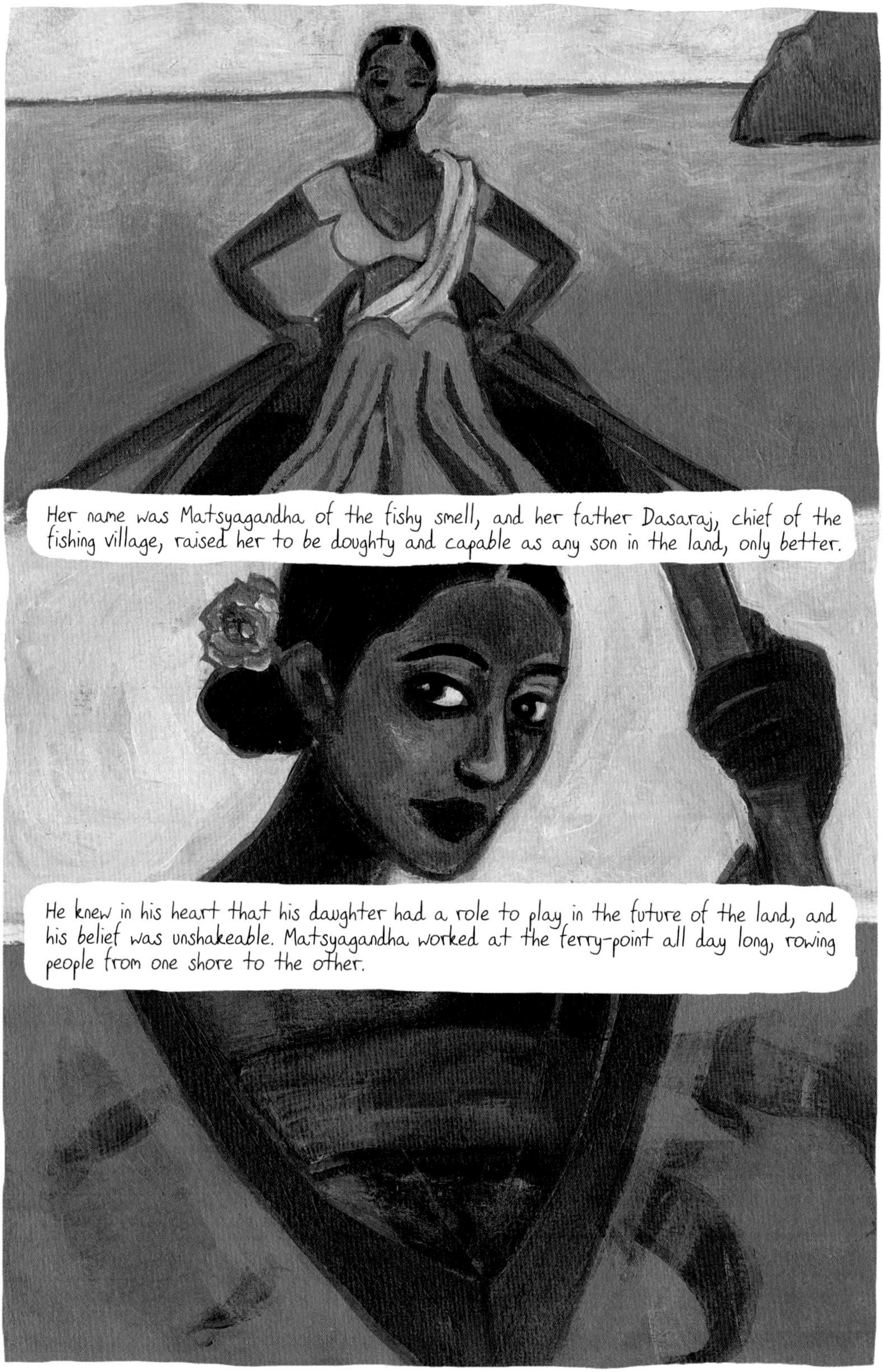
Her name was Matsyagandha of the fishy smell, and her father Dasaraj, chief of the fishing village, raised her to be doughty and capable as any son in the land, only better.
He knew in his heart that his daughter had a role to play in the future of the land, and his belief was unshakeable. Matsyagandha worked at the ferry-point all day long, rowing people from one shore to the other.

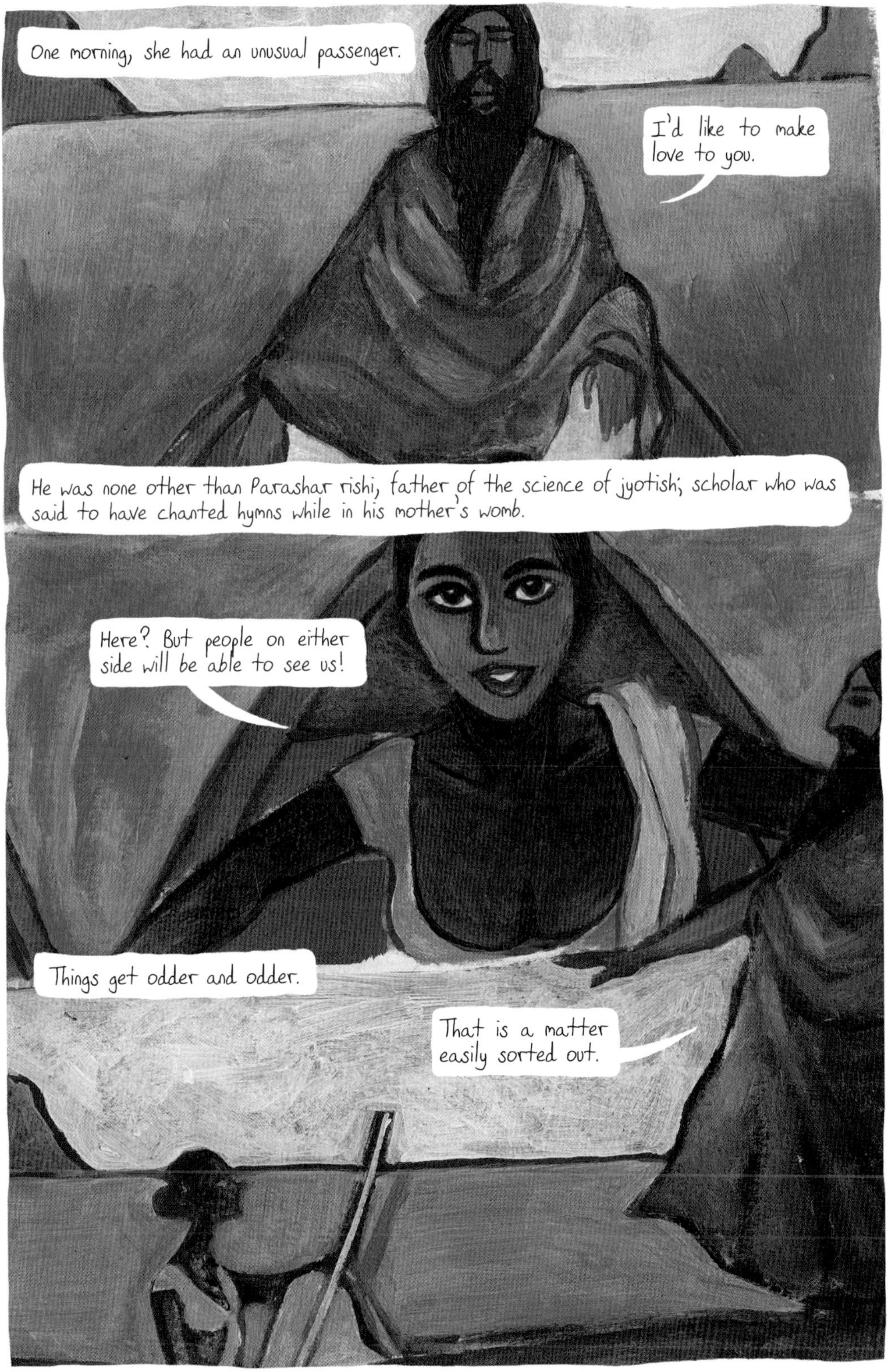
One morning, she had an unusual passenger.
I'd like to make love to you.
He was none other than Parashar rishi, father of the science of jyotish; scholar who was said to have chanted hymns while in his mother's womb.
Here? But people on either side will be able to see us!
Things get odder and odder.
That is a matter easily sorted out.

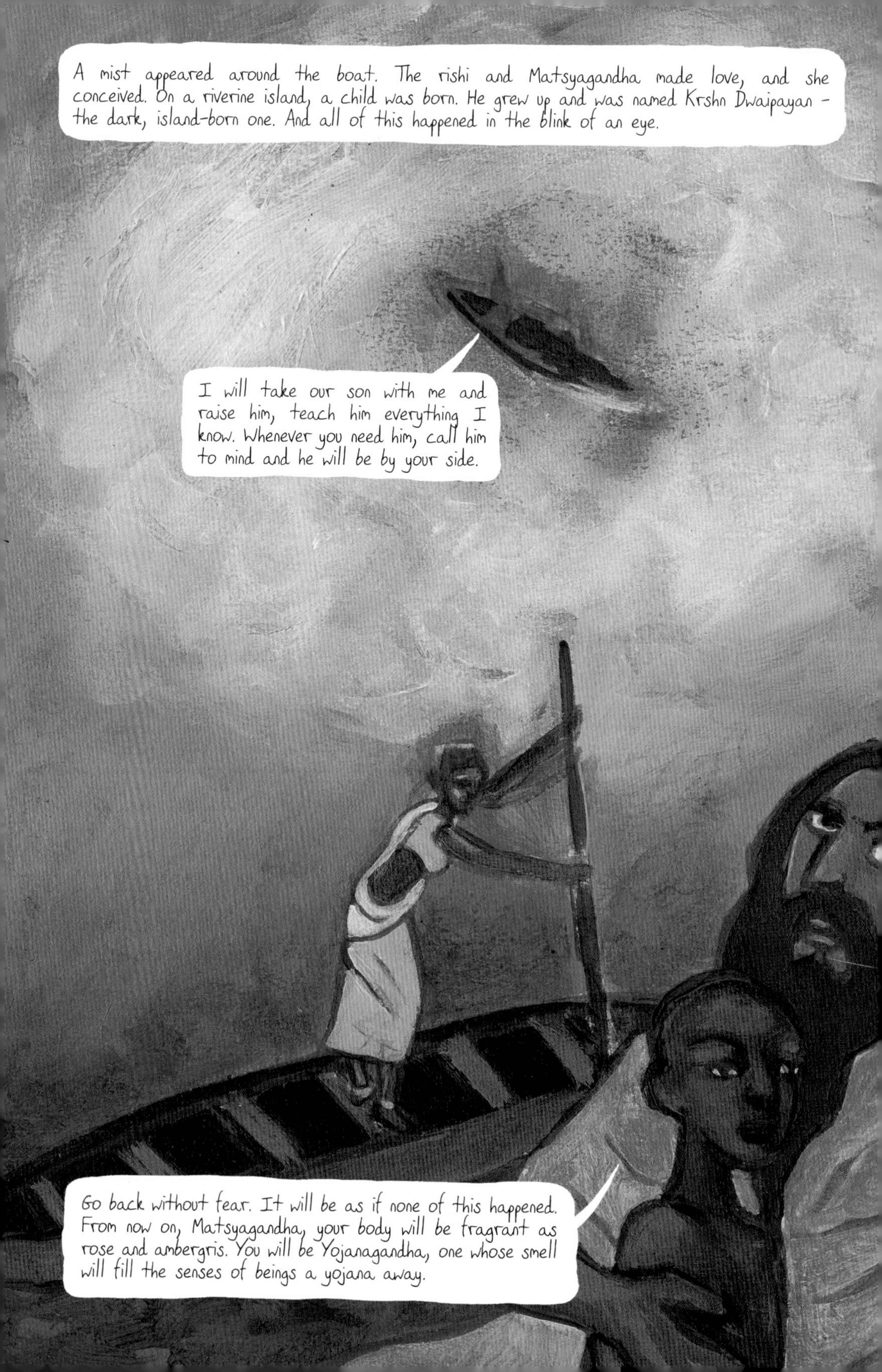
A mist appeared around the boat. The rishi and Matsyagandha made love, and she conceived. On a riverine island, a child was born. He grew up and was named Krshn Dwaipayan - the dark, island-born one. And all of this happened in the blink of an eye.
I will take our son with me and raise him, teach him everything I know. Whenever you need him, call him to mind and he will be by your side.
Go back without fear. It will be as if none of this happened. From now on, Matsyagandha, your body will be fragrant as rose and ambergris. You will be Yojanagandha, one whose smell will fill the senses of beings a yojana away.

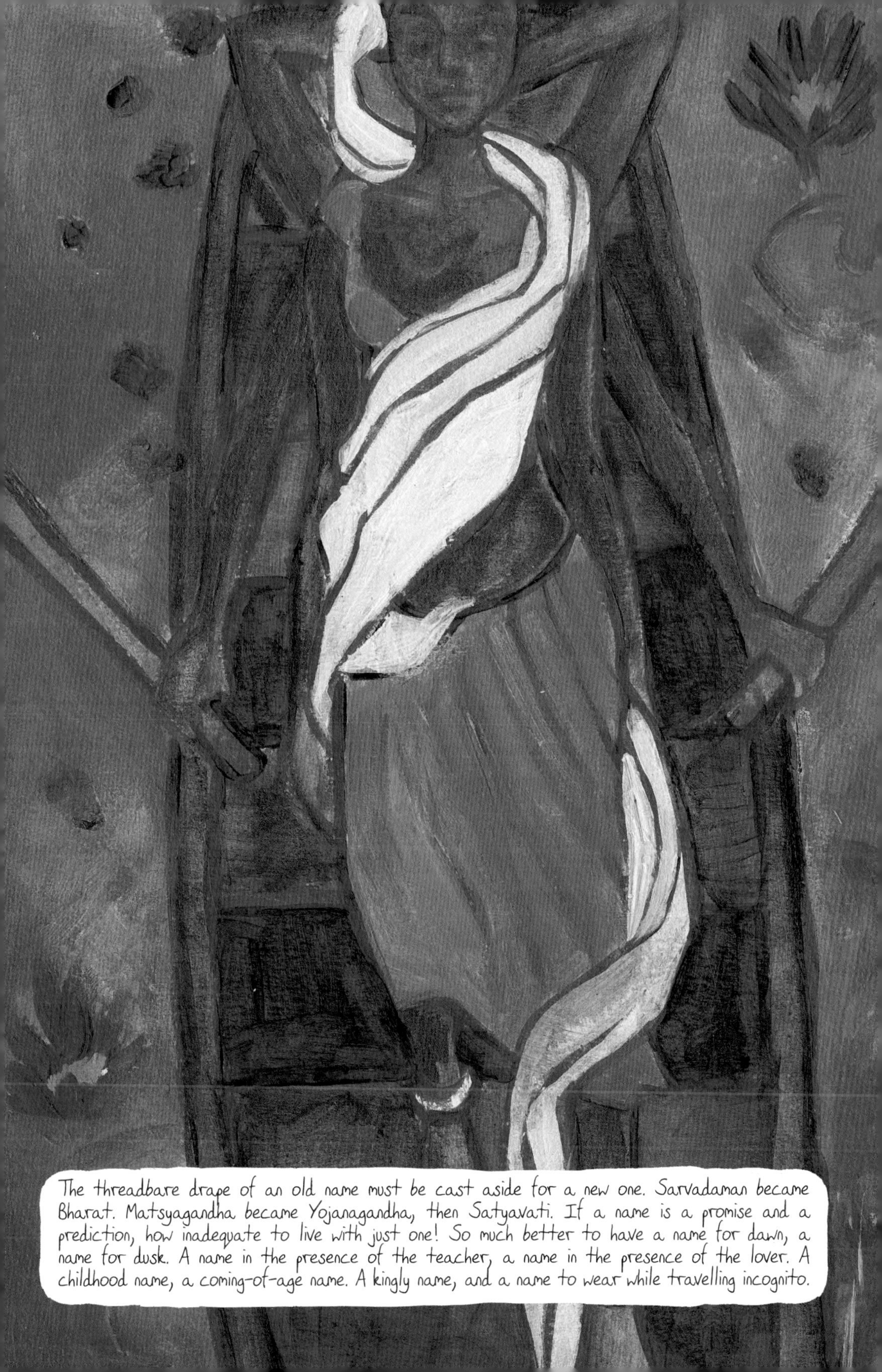
The threadbare drape of an old name must be cast aside for a new one. Sarvadaman became Bharat. Matsyagandha became Yojanagandha, then Satyavati. If a name is a promise and a prediction, how inadequate to live with just one! So much better to have a name for dawn, a name for dusk. A name in the presence of the teacher, a name in the presence of the lover. A childhood name, a coming-of-age name. A kingly name, and a name to wear while travelling incognito.

GANGA

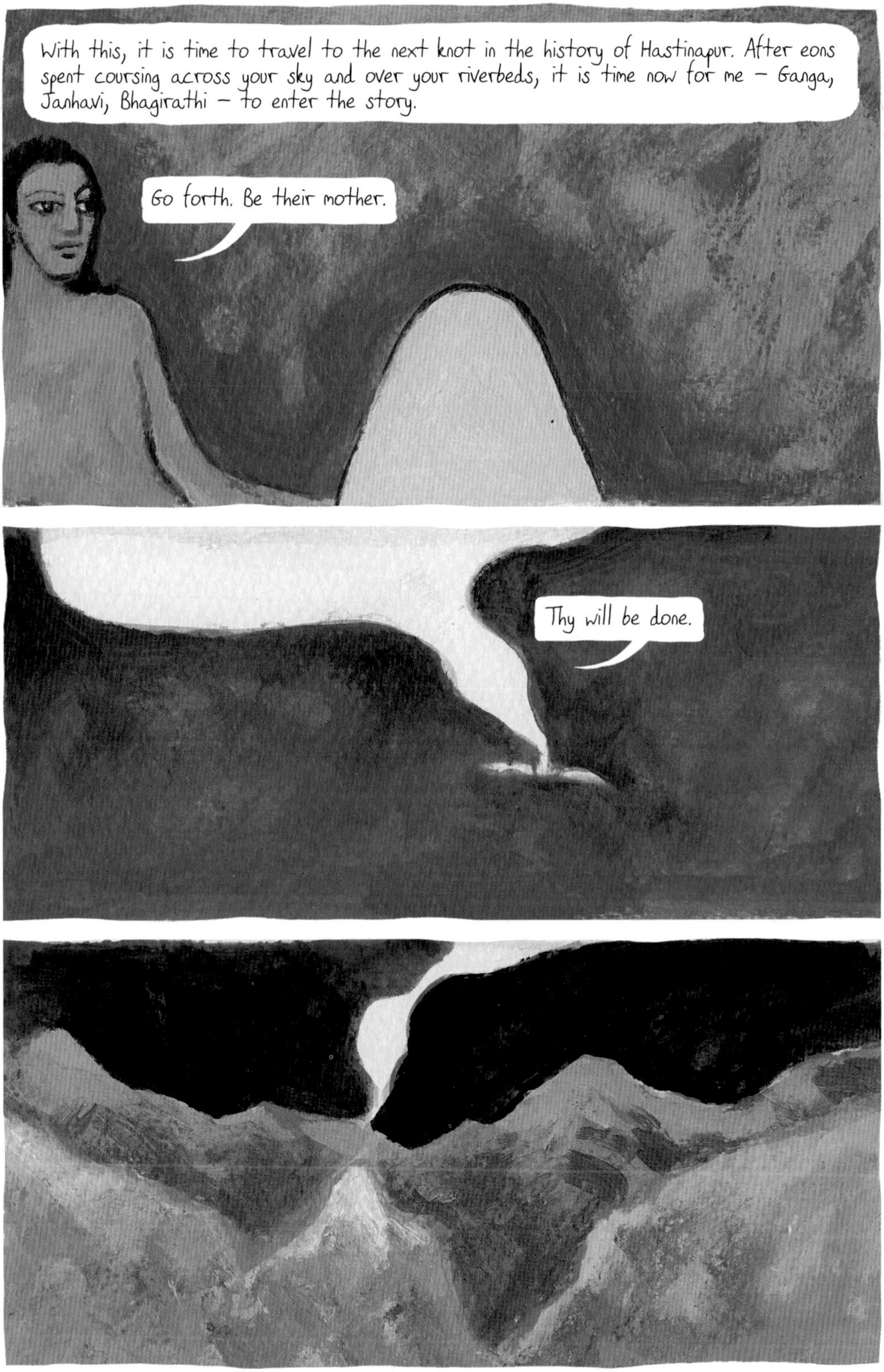
With this, it is time to travel to the next knot in the history of Hastinapur. After eons spent coursing across your sky and over your riverbeds, it is time now for me – Ganga, Janhavi, Bhagirathi – to enter the story.
Go forth. Be their mother.
Thy will be done.

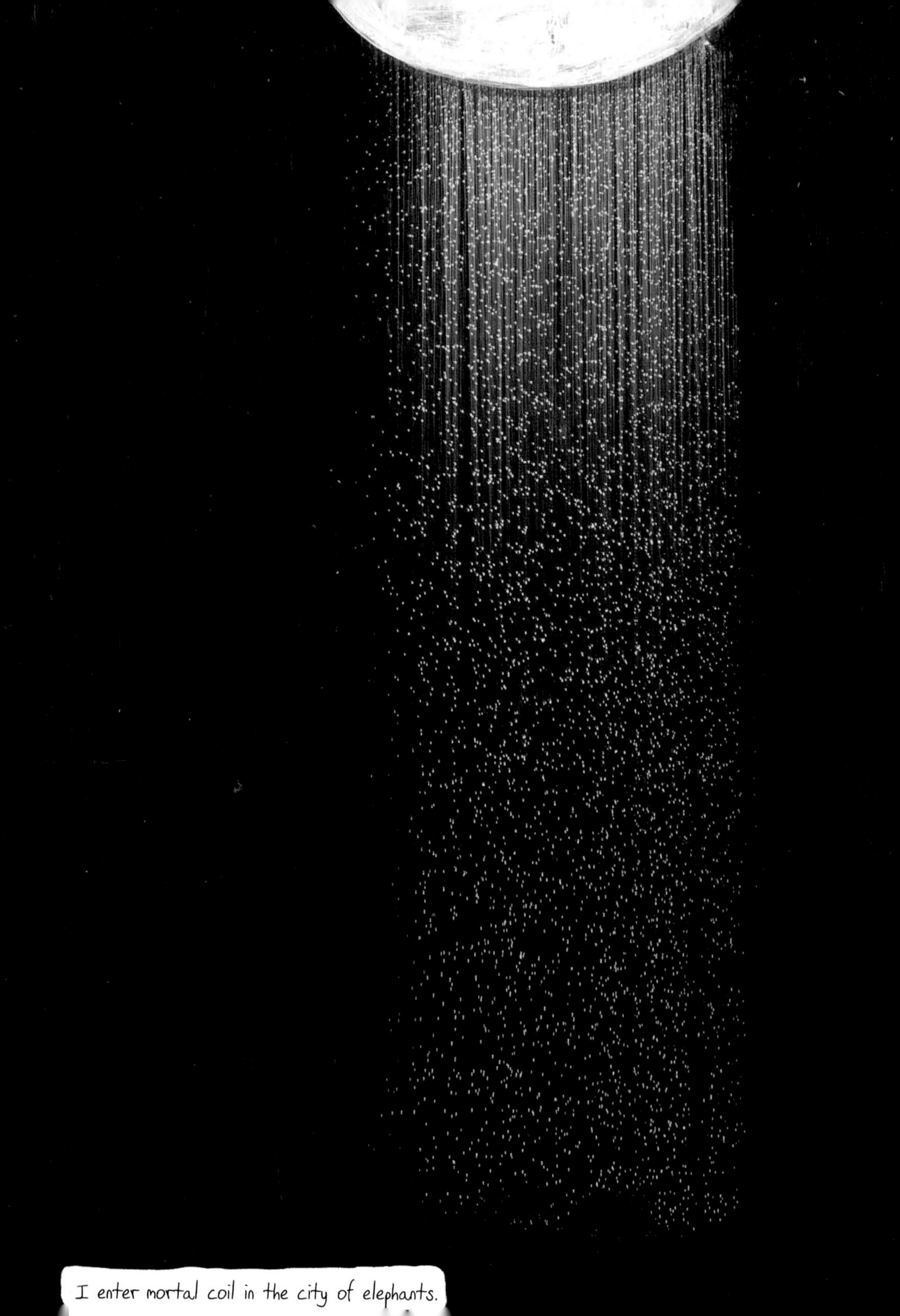
I enter mortal coil in the city of elephants.

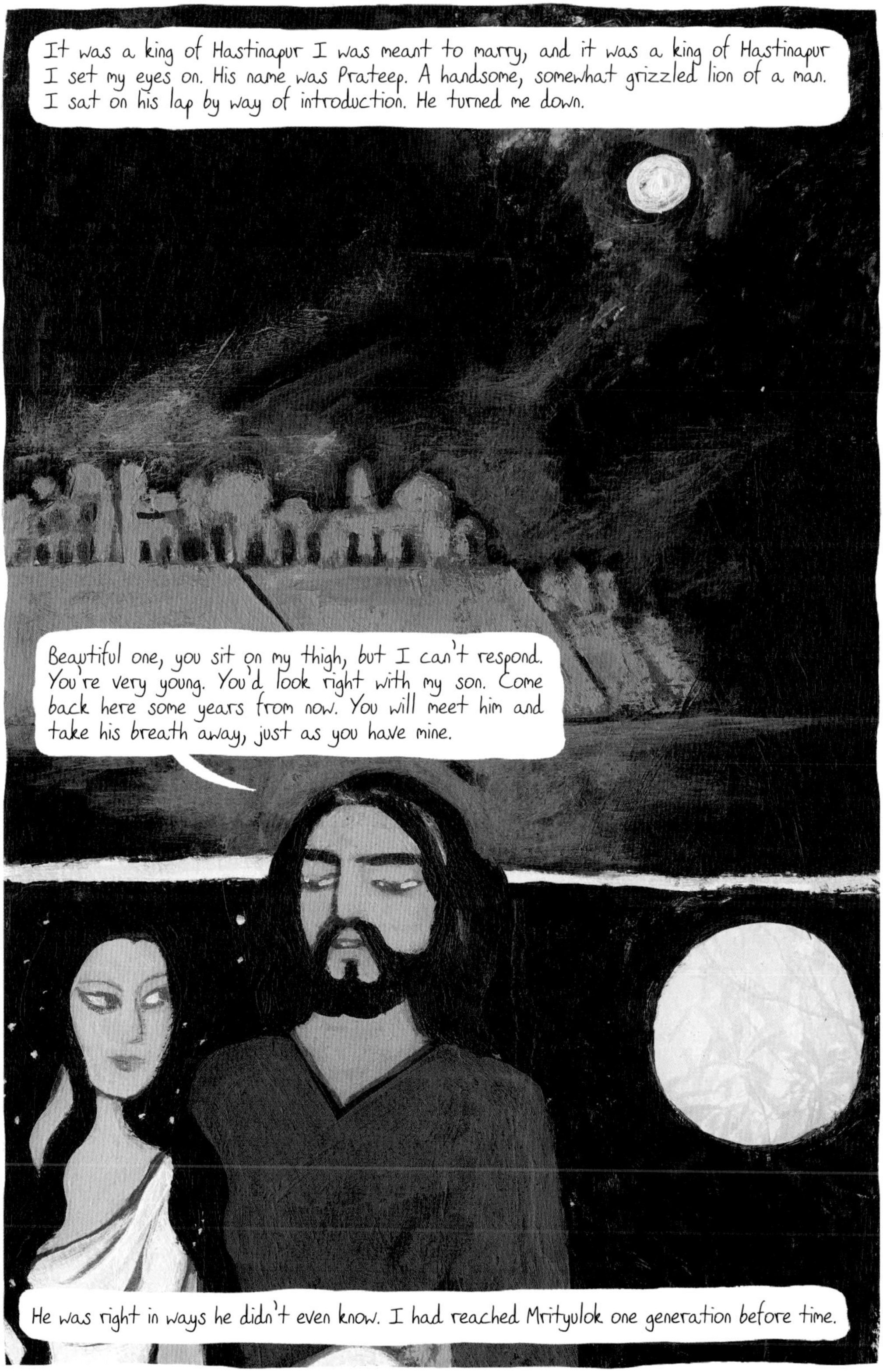
It was a king of Hastinapur I was meant to marry, and it was a king of Hastinapur I set my eyes on. His name was Prateep. A handsome, somewhat grizzled lion of a man. I sat on his lap by way of introduction. He turned me down.
Beautiful one, you sit on my thigh, but I can't respond. You're very young. You'd look right with my son. Come back here some years from now. You will meet him and take his breath away, just as you have mine.
He was right in ways he didn't even know. I had reached Mrityulok one generation before time.

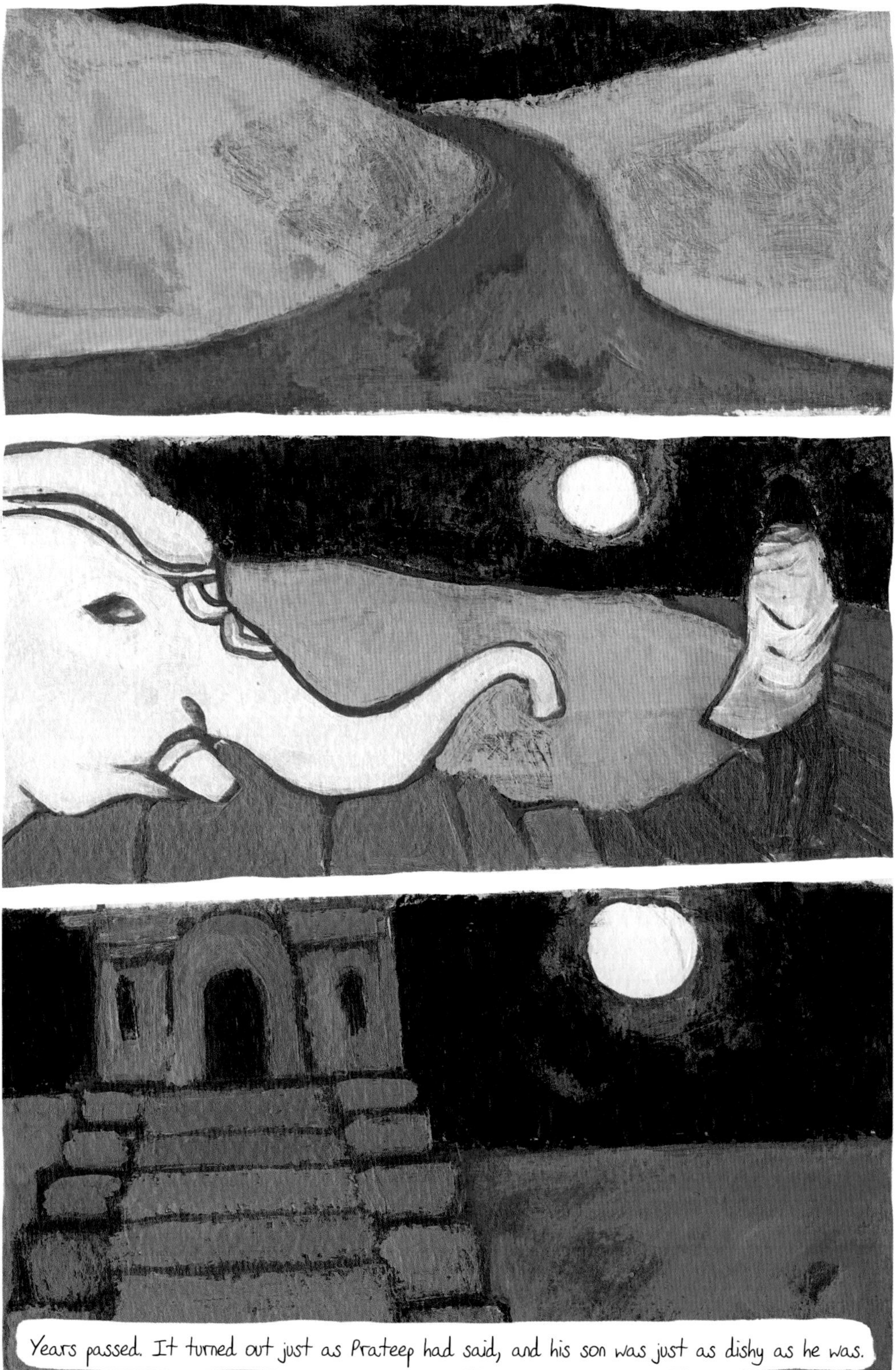
Years passed. It turned out just as Prateep had said, and his son was just as dishy as he was.

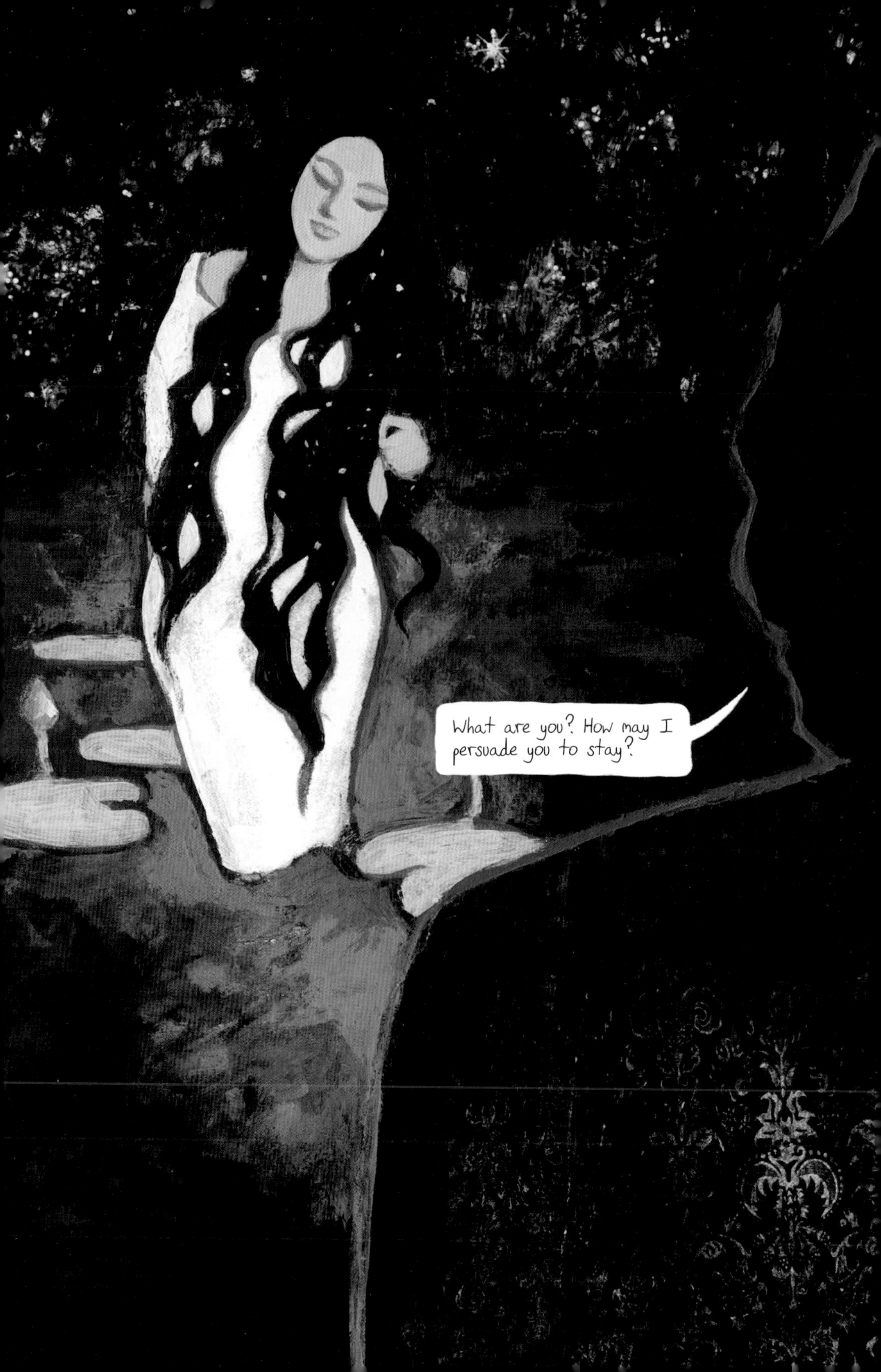
What are you? How may I persuade you to stay?

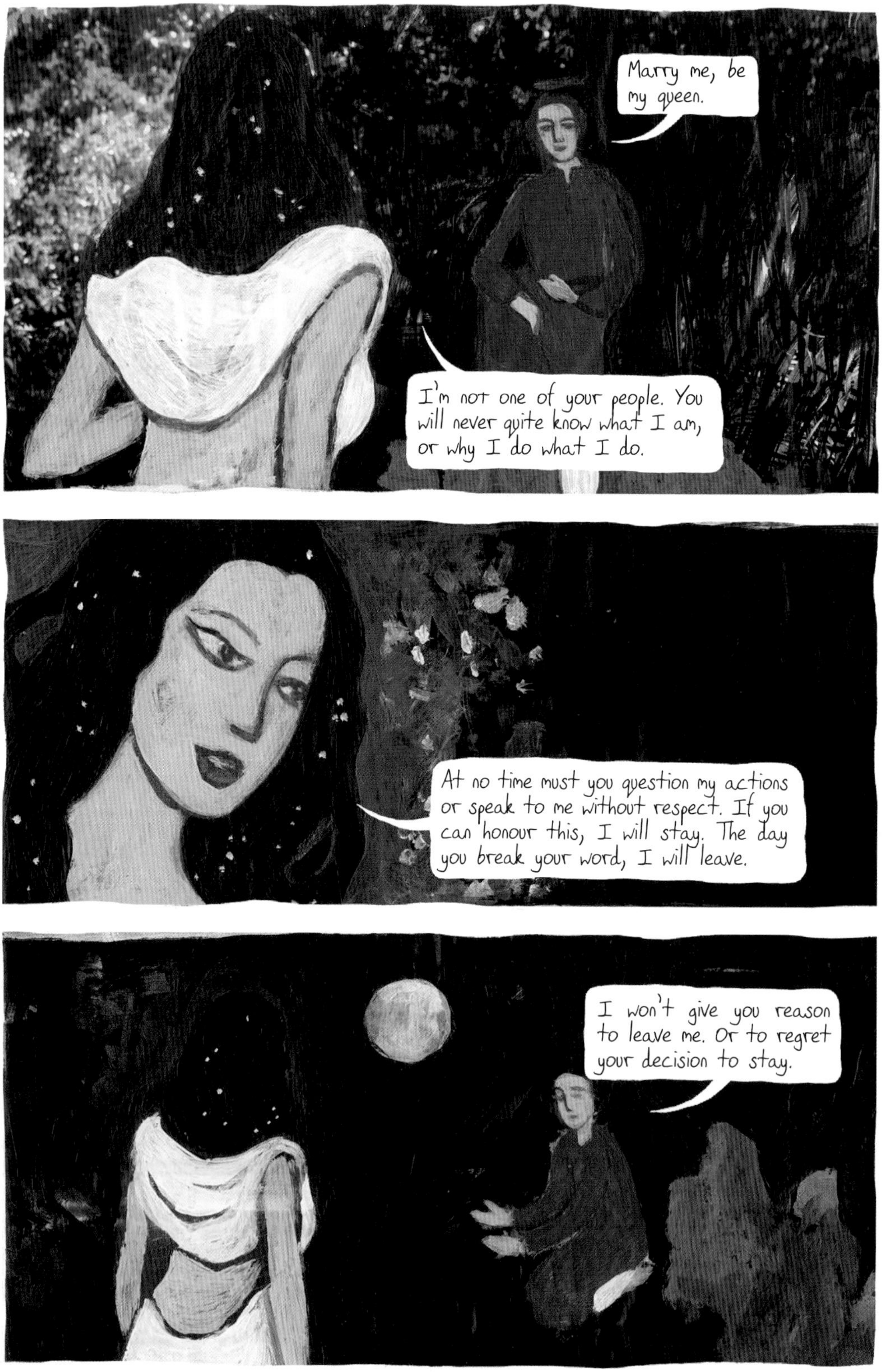
Marry me, be my queen.
I'm not one of your people. You will never quite know what I am, or why I do what I do.
At no time must you question my actions or speak to me without respect. If you can honour this, I will stay. The day you break your word, I will leave.
I won't give you reason to leave me. Or to regret your decision to stay.

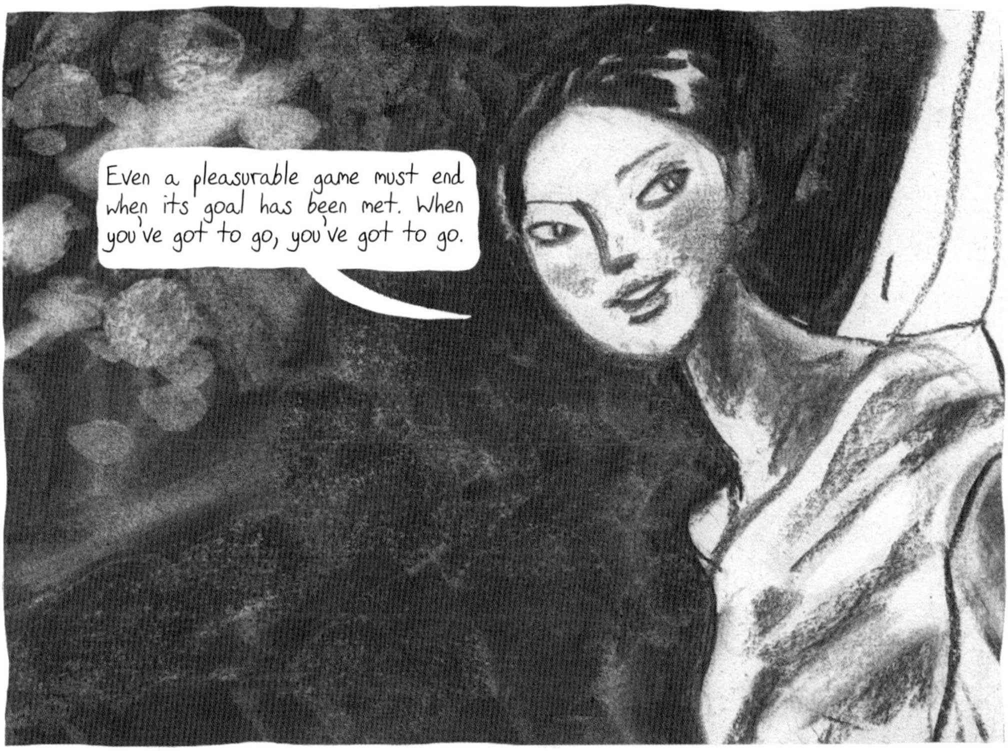
Even a pleasurable game must end when its goal has been met. When you've got to go, you've got to go.

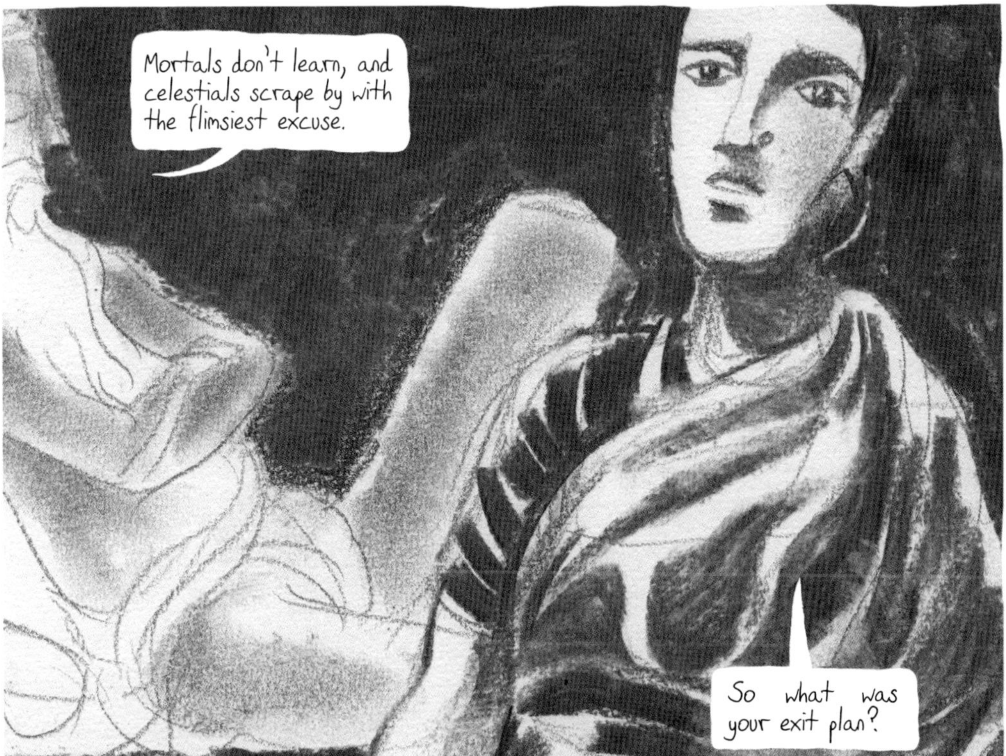
Mortals don't learn, and celestials scrape by with the flimsiest excuse.
So what was your exit plan?

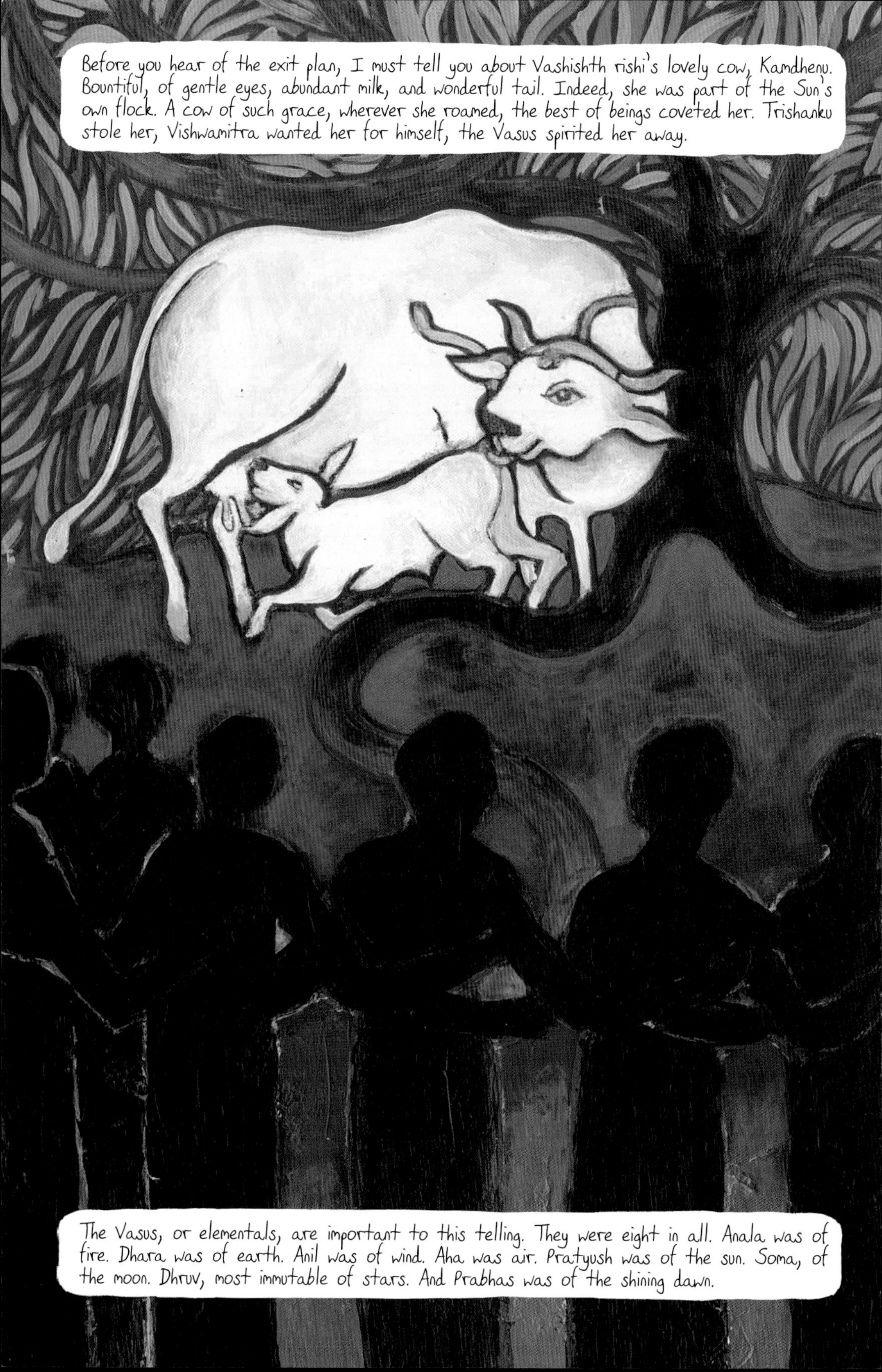
Before you hear of the exit plan, I must tell you about Vashishth rishi's lovely cow, Kamdhenu. Bountiful, of gentle eyes, abundant milk, and wonderful tail. Indeed, she was part of the Sun's own flock. A cow of such grace, wherever she roamed, the best of beings coveted her. Trishanku stole her, Vishwamitra wanted her for himself, the Vasus spirited her away.
The Vasus, or elementals, are important to this telling. They were eight in all. Anala was of fire. Dhara was of earth. Anil was of wind. Aha was air. Pratyush was of the sun. Soma, of the moon. Dhruv, most immutable of stars. And Prabhas was of the shining dawn.

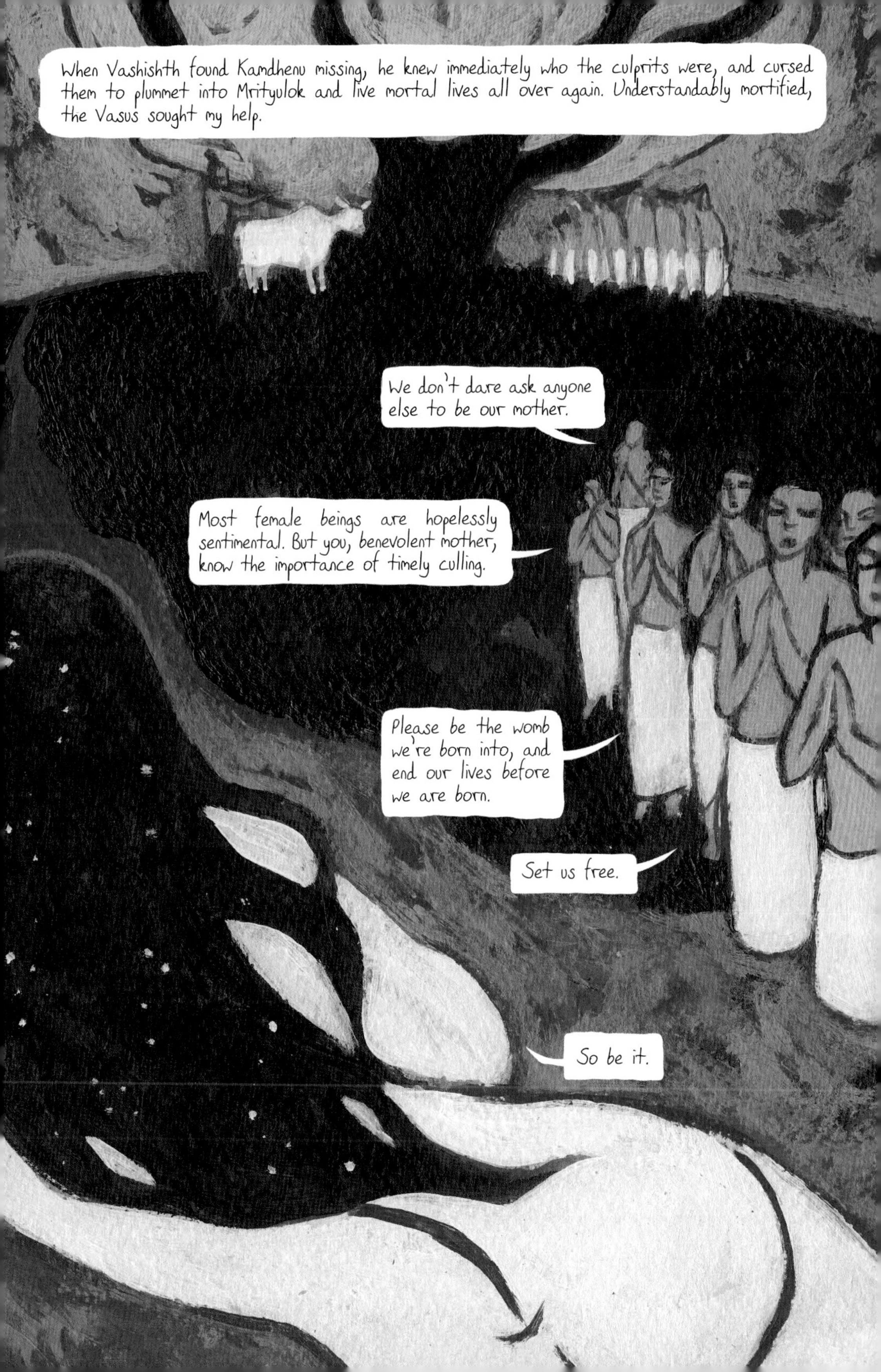
When Vashishth found Kamdhenu missing, he knew immediately who the culprits were, and cursed them to plummet into Mrityulok and live mortal lives all over again. Understandably mortified, the Vasus sought my help.
We don't dare ask anyone else to be our mother.
Most female beings are hopelessly sentimental. But you, benevolent mother, know the importance of timely culling.
Please be the womb we're born into, and end our lives before we are born.
Set us free.
So be it.

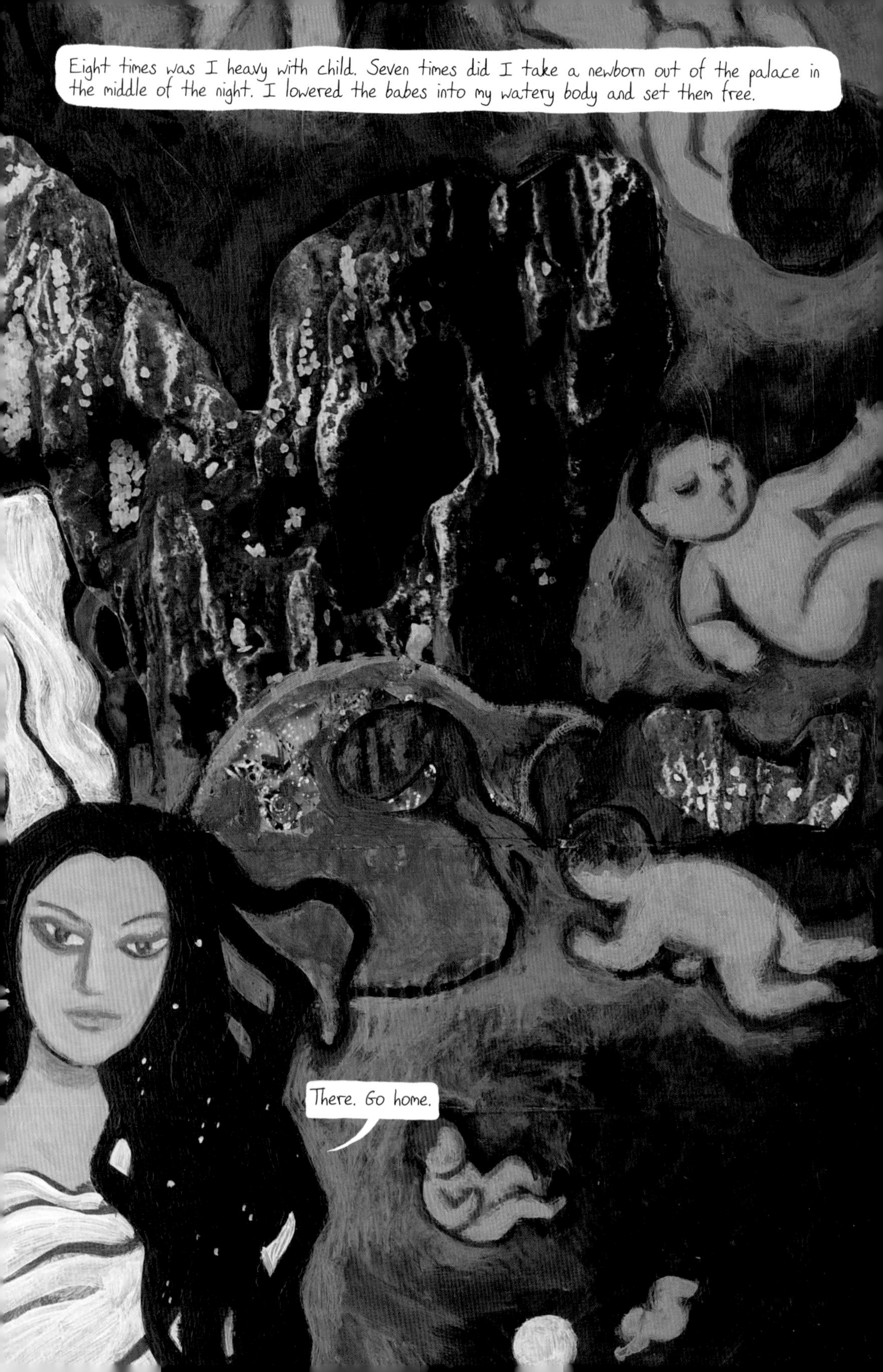
Eight times was I heavy with child. Seven times did I take a newborn out of the palace in the middle of the night. I lowered the babes into my watery body and set them free.
There. Go home.

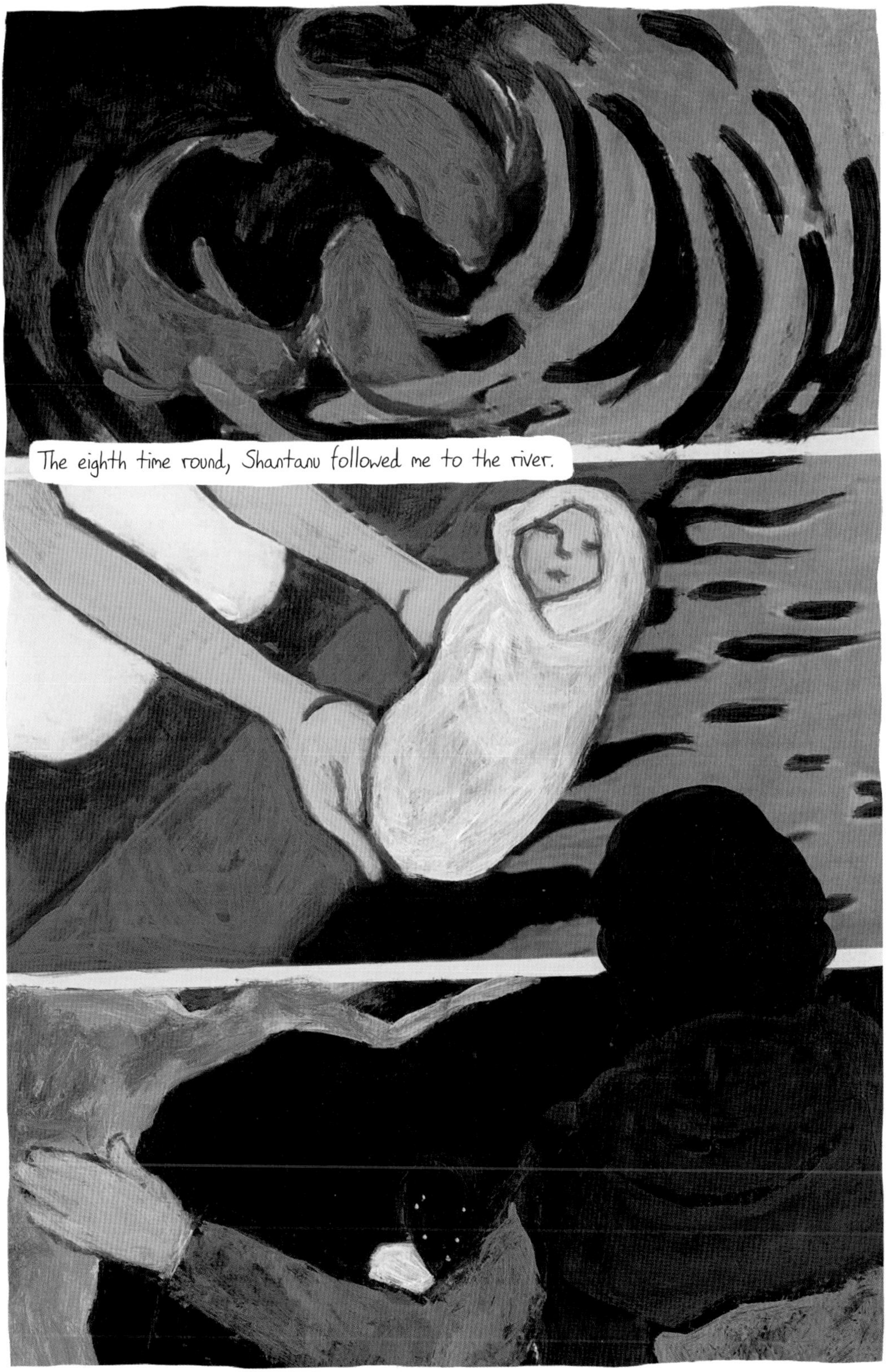
The eighth time round, Shantanu followed me to the river.

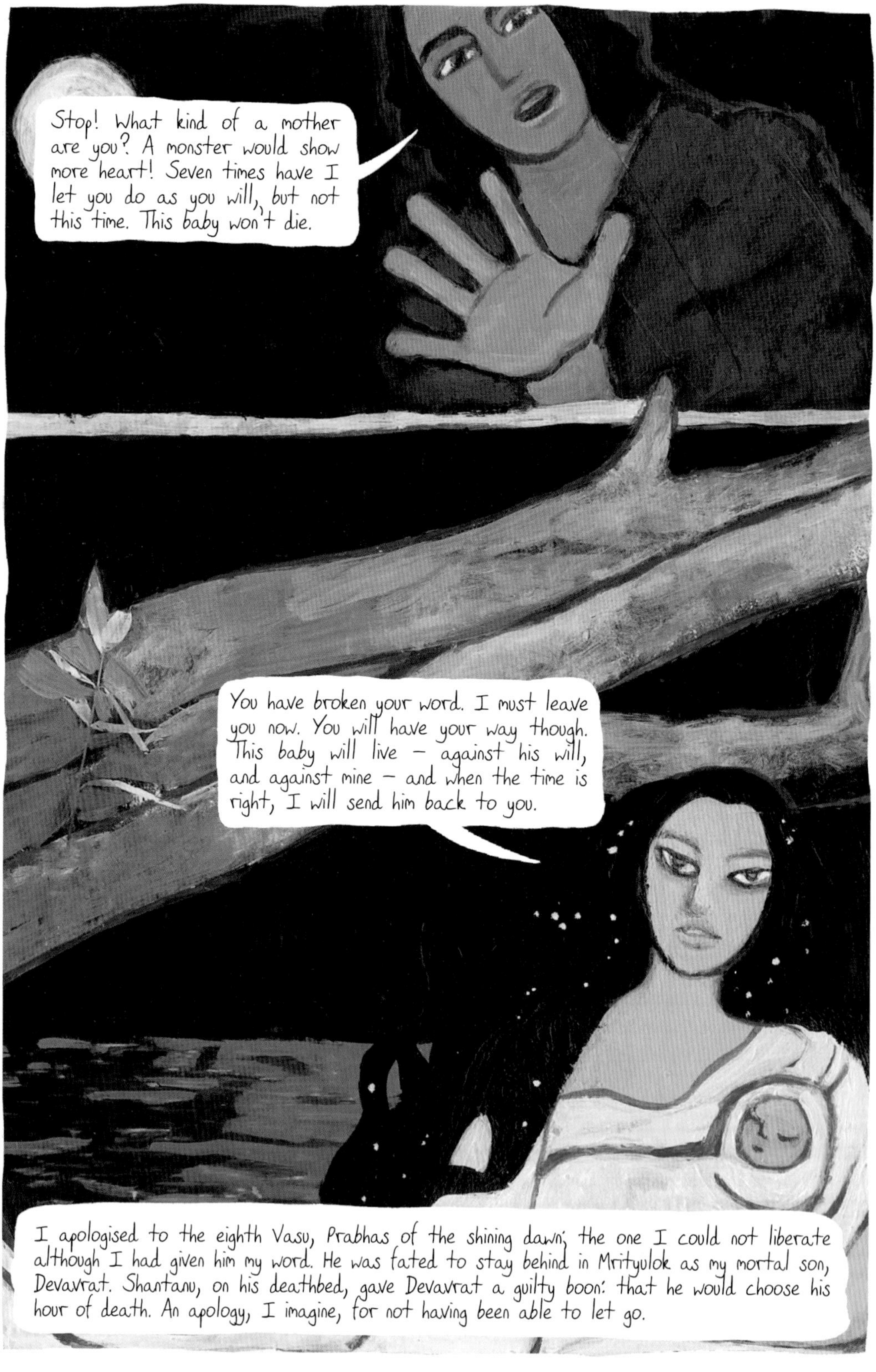
Stop! What kind of a mother are you? A monster would show more heart! Seven times have I let you do as you will, but not this time. This baby won't die.
You have broken your word. I must leave you now. You will have your way though. This baby will live – against his will, and against mine – and when the time is right, I will send him back to you.
I apologised to the eighth Vasu, Prabhas of the shining dawn; the one I could not liberate although I had given him my word. He was fated to stay behind in Mrityulok as my mortal son, Devavrat. Shantanu, on his deathbed, gave Devavrat a guilty boon: that he would choose his hour of death. An apology, I imagine, for not having been able to let go.

BHEESHM, AMBA

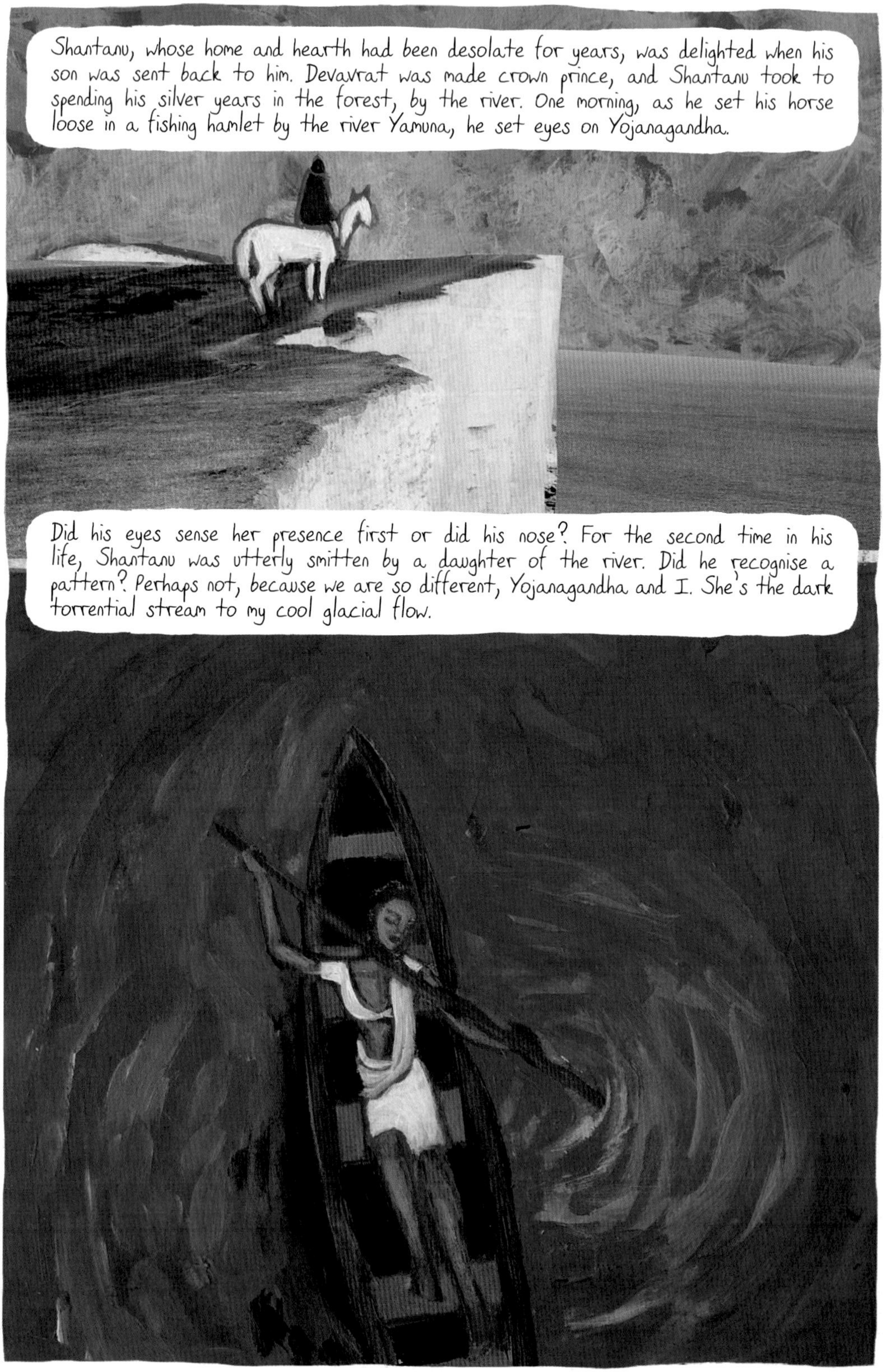
Shantanu, whose home and hearth had been desolate for years, was delighted when his son was sent back to him. Devavrat was made crown prince, and Shantanu took to spending his silver years in the forest, by the river. One morning, as he set his horse loose in a fishing hamlet by the river Yamuna, he set eyes on Yojanagandha.
Did his eyes sense her presence first or did his nose? For the second time in his life, Shantanu was utterly smitten by a daughter of the river. Did he recognise a pattern? Perhaps not, because we are so different, Yojanagandha and I. She's the dark torrential stream to my cool glacial flow.

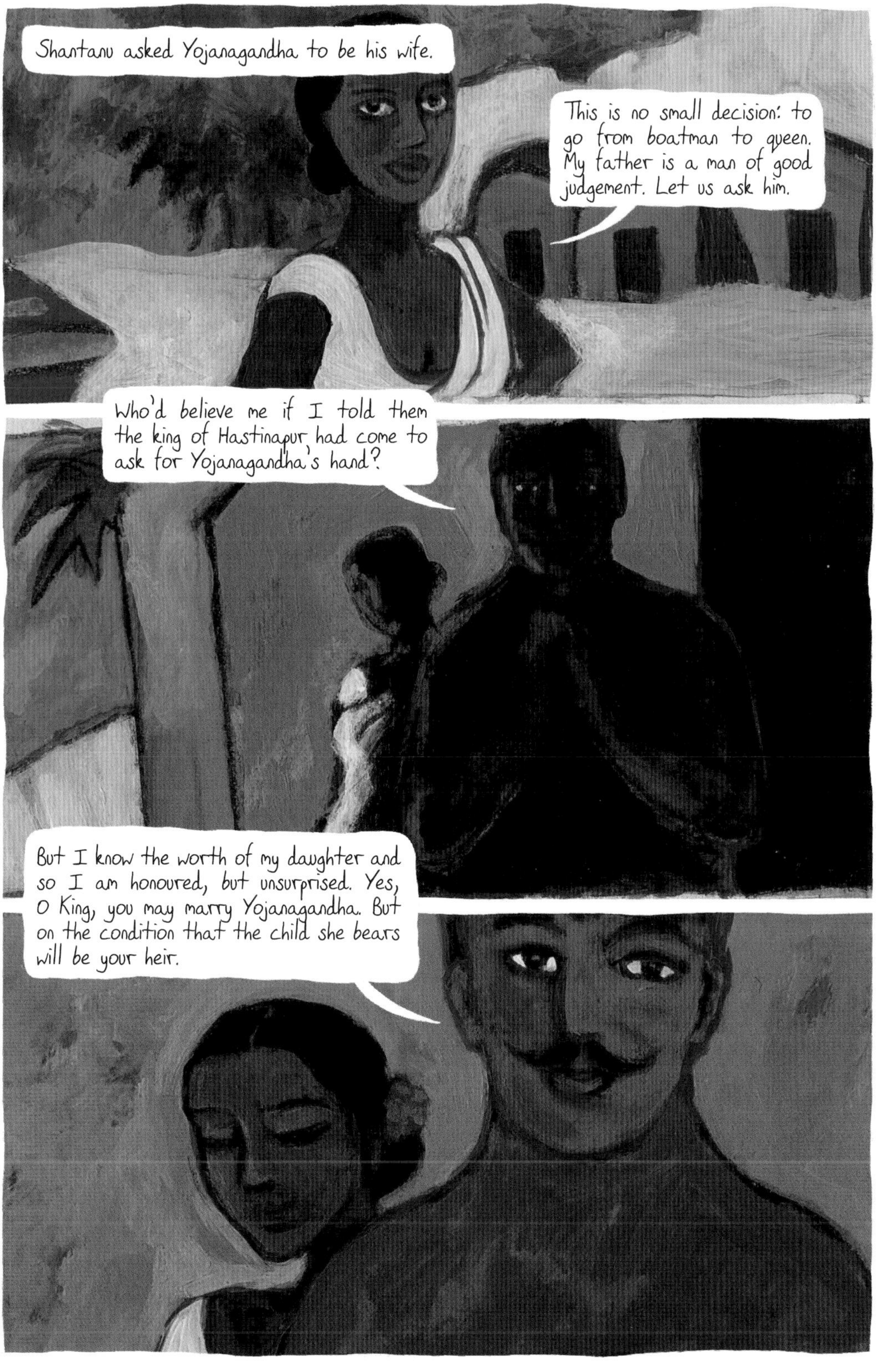
Shantanu asked Yojanagandha to be his wife.
This is no small decision: to go from boatman to queen. My father is a man of good judgement. Let us ask him.
Who'd believe me if I told them the king of Hastinapur had come to ask for Yojanagandha's hand?
But I know the worth of my daughter and so I am honoured, but unsurprised. Yes, O King, you may marry Yojanagandha. But on the condition that the child she bears will be your heir.

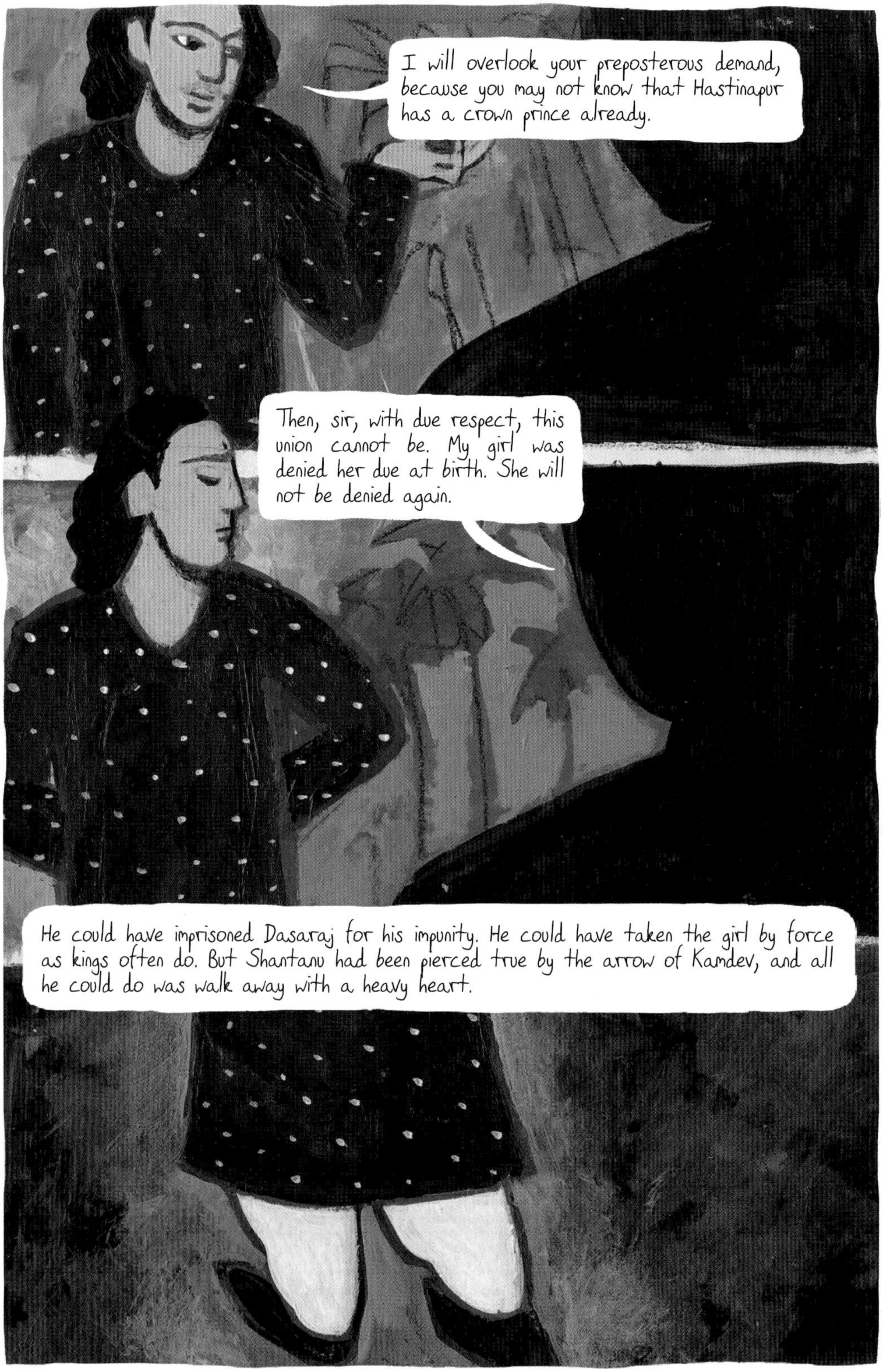
I will overlook your preposterous demand, because you may not know that Hastinapur has a crown prince already.
Then, sir, with due respect, this union cannot be. My girl was denied her due at birth. She will not be denied again.
He could have imprisoned Dasaraj for his impunity. He could have taken the girl by force as kings often do. But Shantanu had been pierced true by the arrow of Kamdev, and all he could do was walk away with a heavy heart.

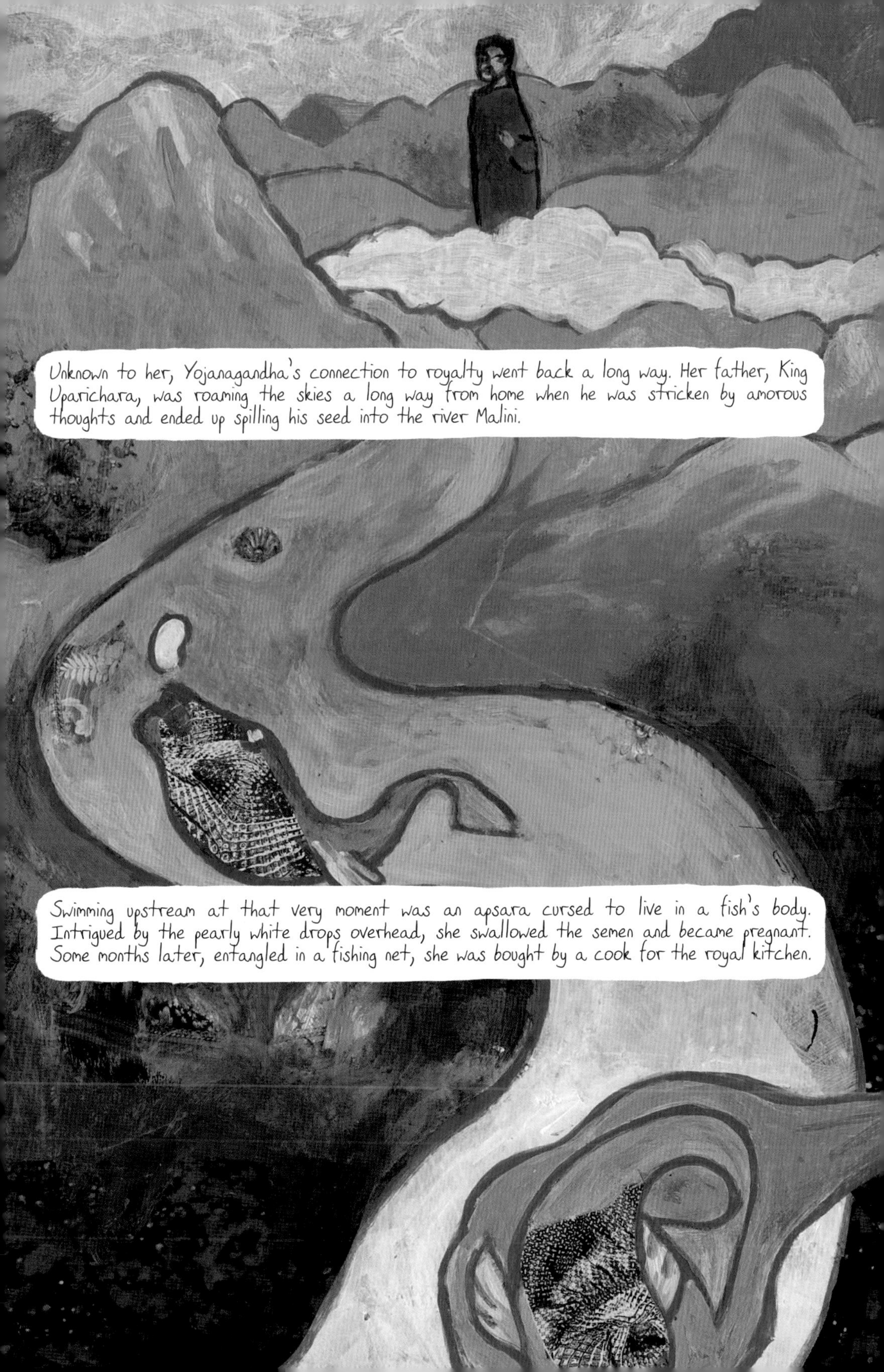
Unknown to her, Yojanagandha's connection to royalty went back a long way. Her father, King Uparichara, was roaming the skies a long way from home when he was stricken by amorous thoughts and ended up spilling his seed into the river Malini.
Swimming upstream at that very moment was an apsara cursed to live in a fish's body. Intrigued by the pearly white drops overhead, she swallowed the semen and became pregnant. Some months later, entangled in a fishing net, she was bought by a cook for the royal kitchen.

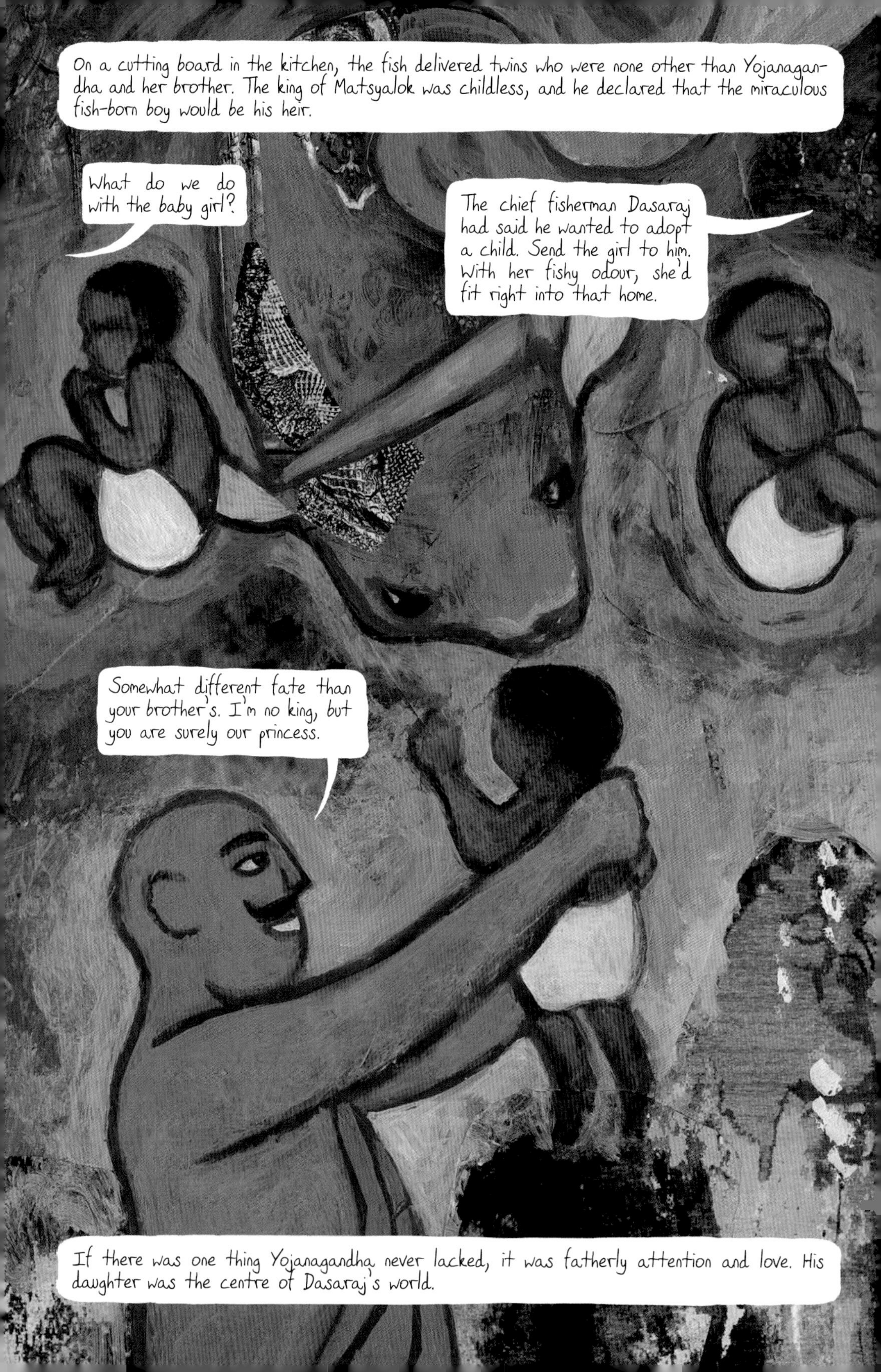
On a cutting board in the kitchen, the fish delivered twins who were none other than Yojanagandha and her brother. The king of Matsyalok was childless, and he declared that the miraculous fish-born boy would be his heir.
What do we do with the baby girl?
The chief fisherman Dasaraj had said he wanted to adopt a child. Send the girl to him. With her fishy odour, she'd fit right into that home.
Somewhat different fate than your brother's. I'm no king, but you are surely our princess.
If there was one thing Yojanagandha never lacked, it was fatherly attention and love. His daughter was the centre of Dasaraj's world.

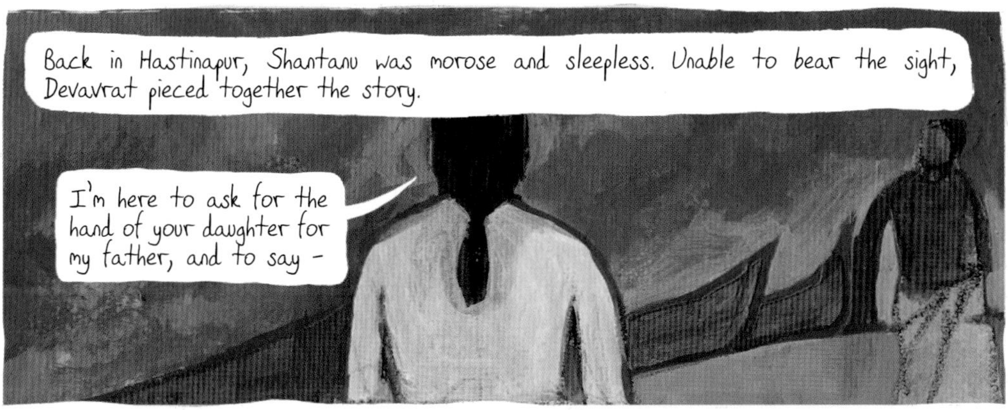
Back in Hastinapur, Shantanu was morose and sleepless. Unable to bear the sight, Devavrat pieced together the story.
I'm here to ask for the hand of your daughter for my father, and to say -

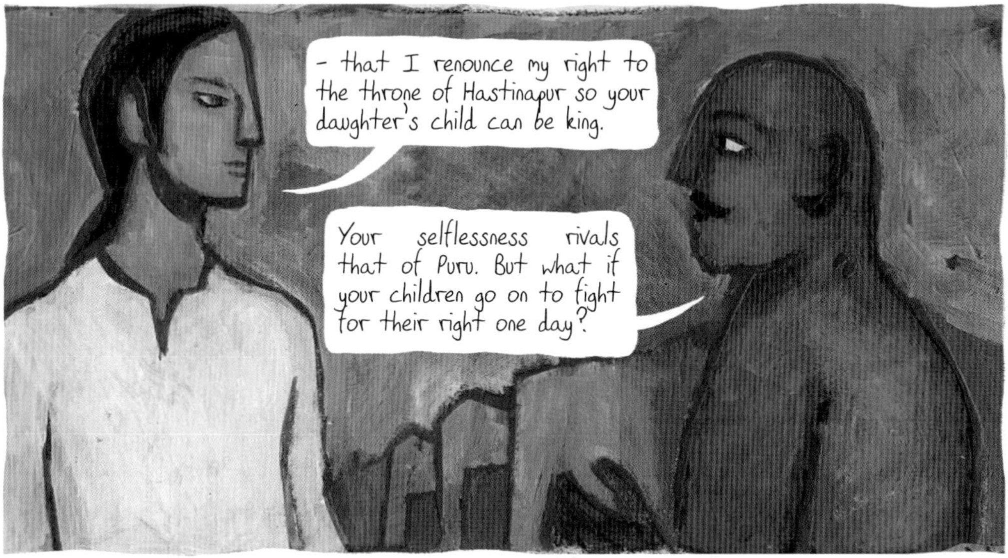
- that I renounce my right to the throne of Hastinapur so your daughter's child can be king.
Your selflessness rivals that of Puru. But what if your children go on to fight for their right one day?

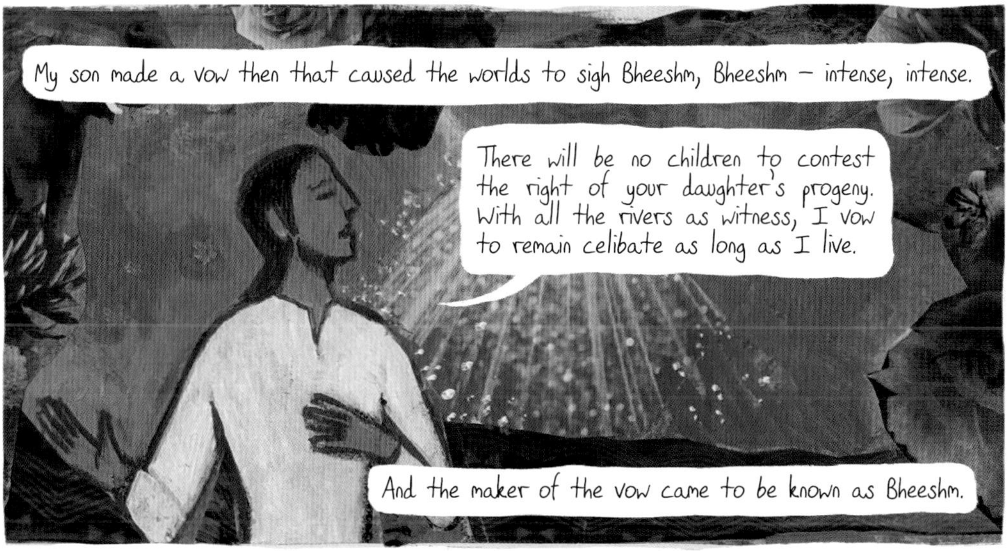
My son made a vow then that caused the worlds to sigh Bheeshm, Bheeshm – intense, intense.
There will be no children to contest the right of your daughter's progeny. With all the rivers as witness, I vow to remain celibate as long as I live.
And the maker of the vow came to be known as Bheeshm.

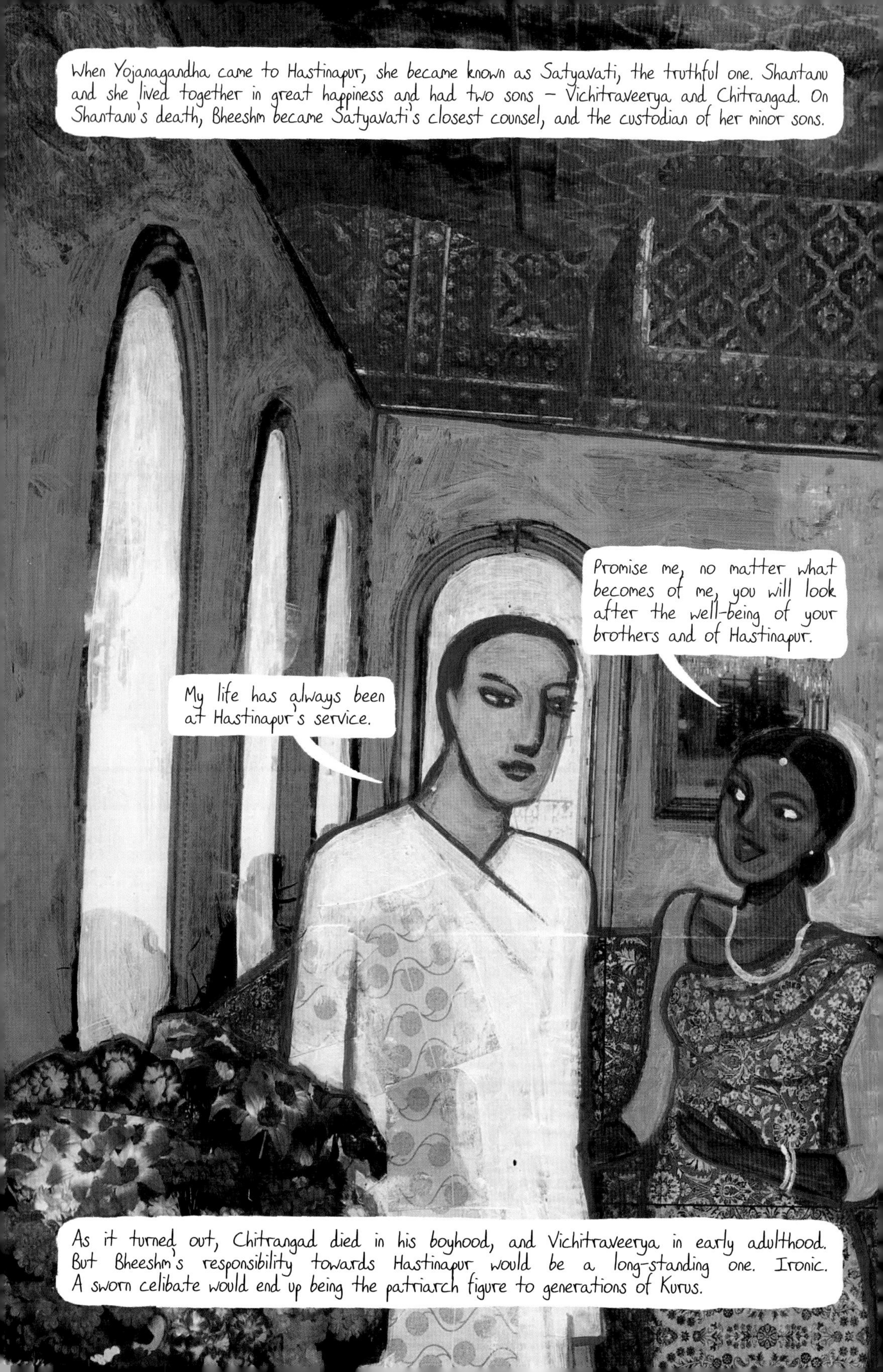
When Yojanagandha came to Hastinapur, she became known as Satyavati, the truthful one. Shantanu and she lived together in great happiness and had two sons – Vichitraveerya and Chitrangad. On Shantanu's death, Bheeshm became Satyavati's closest counsel, and the custodian of her minor sons.
Promise me, no matter what becomes of me, you will look after the well-being of your brothers and of Hastinapur.
My life has always been at Hastinapur's service.
As it turned out, Chitrangad died in his boyhood, and Vichitraveerya in early adulthood. But Bheeshm's responsibility towards Hastinapur would be a long-standing one. Ironic. A sworn celibate would end up being the patriarch figure to generations of Kurus.

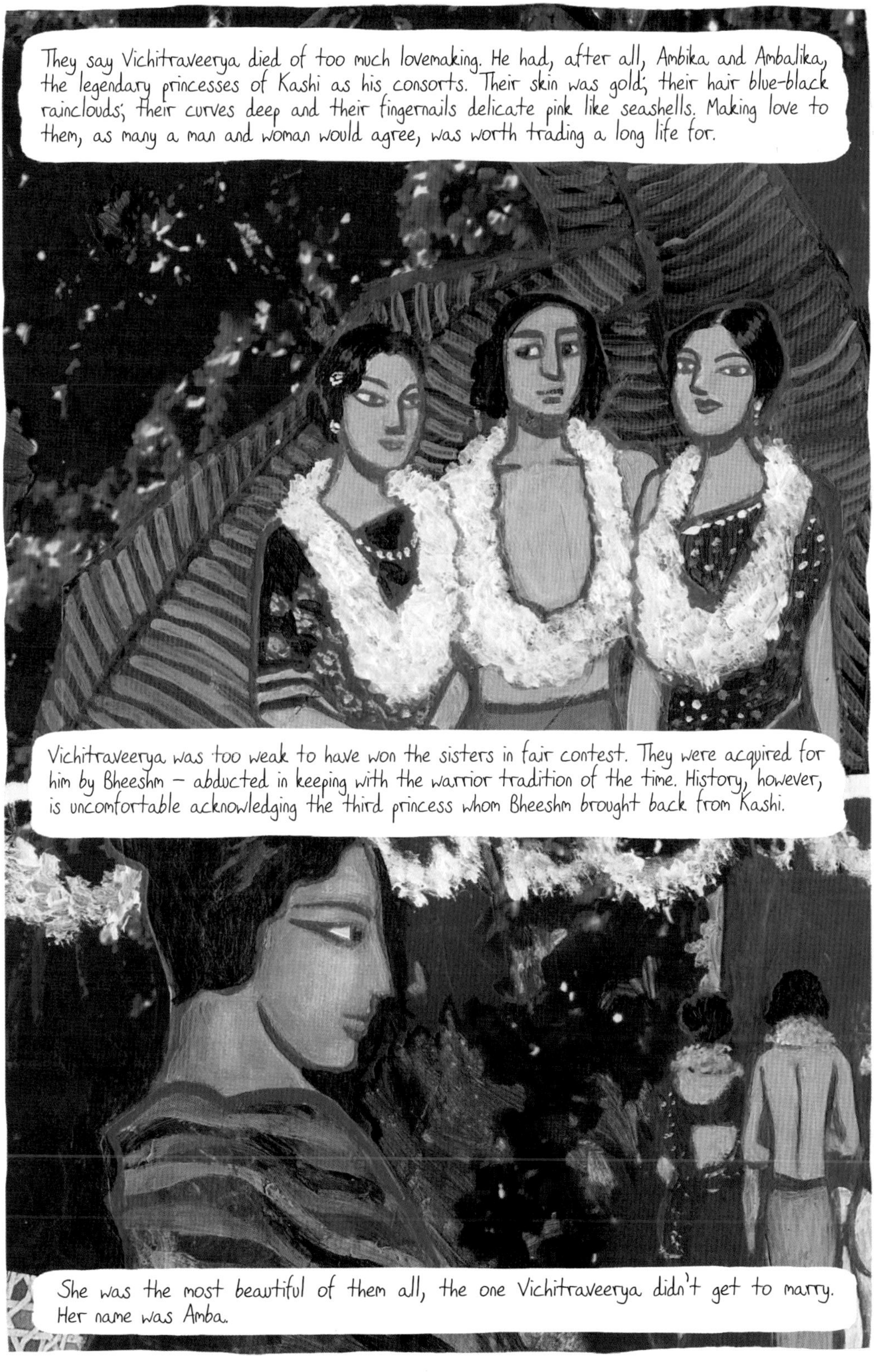
They say Vichitraveerya died of too much lovemaking. He had, after all, Ambika and Ambalika, the legendary princesses of Kashi as his consorts. Their skin was gold; their hair blue-black rainclouds; their curves deep and their fingernails delicate pink like seashells. Making love to them, as many a man and woman would agree, was worth trading a long life for.
Vichitraveerya was too weak to have won the sisters in fair contest. They were acquired for him by Bheeshm – abducted in keeping with the warrior tradition of the time. History, however, is uncomfortable acknowledging the third princess whom Bheeshm brought back from Kashi.
She was the most beautiful of them all, the one Vichitraveerya didn't get to marry. Her name was Amba.

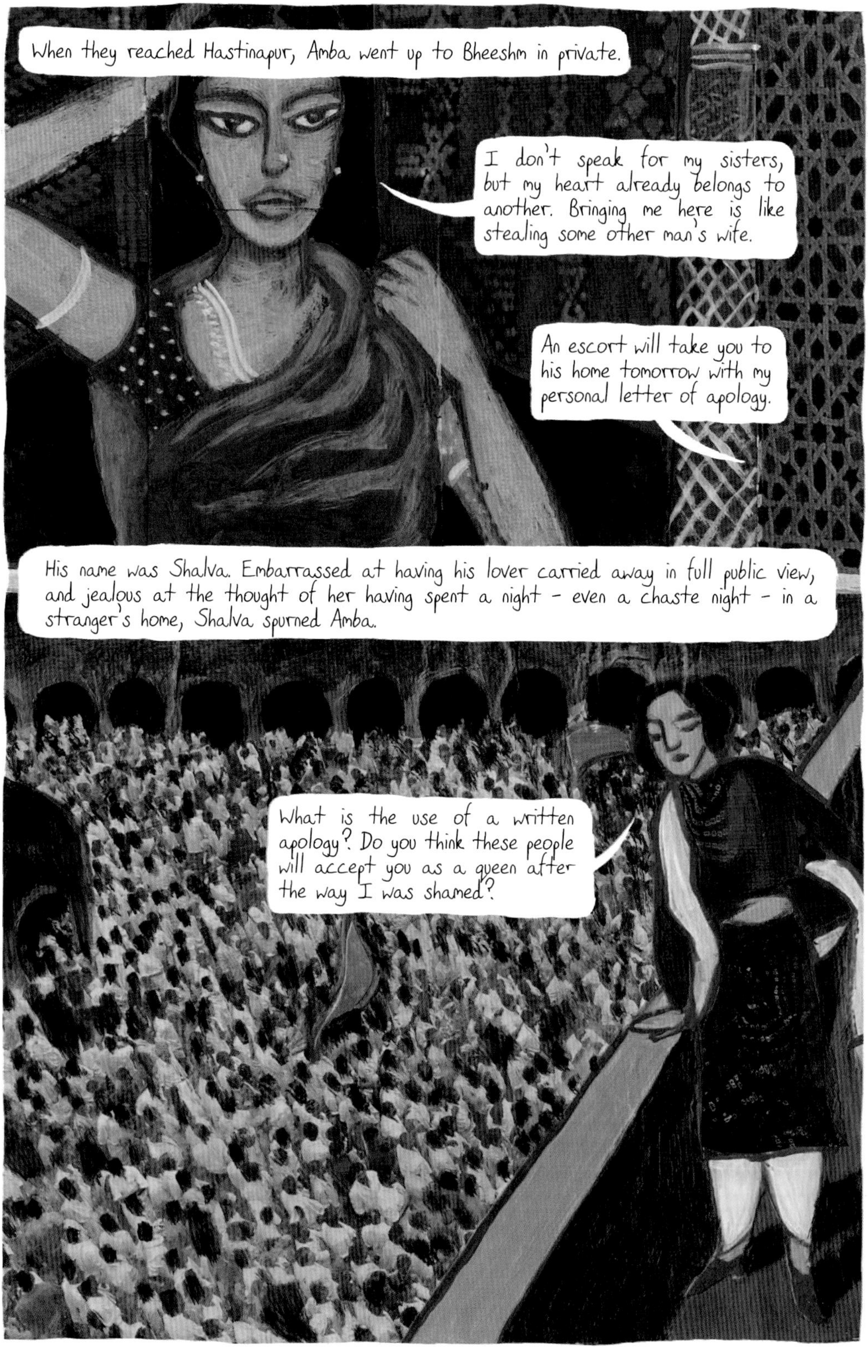
When they reached Hastinapur, Amba went up to Bheeshm in private.
I don't speak for my sisters, but my heart already belongs to another. Bringing me here is like stealing some other man's wife.
An escort will take you to his home tomorrow with my personal letter of apology.
His name was Shalva. Embarrassed at having his lover carried away in full public view, and jealous at the thought of her having spent a night - even a chaste night - in a stranger's home, Shalva spurned Amba.
What is the use of a written apology? Do you think these people will accept you as a queen after the way I was shamed?

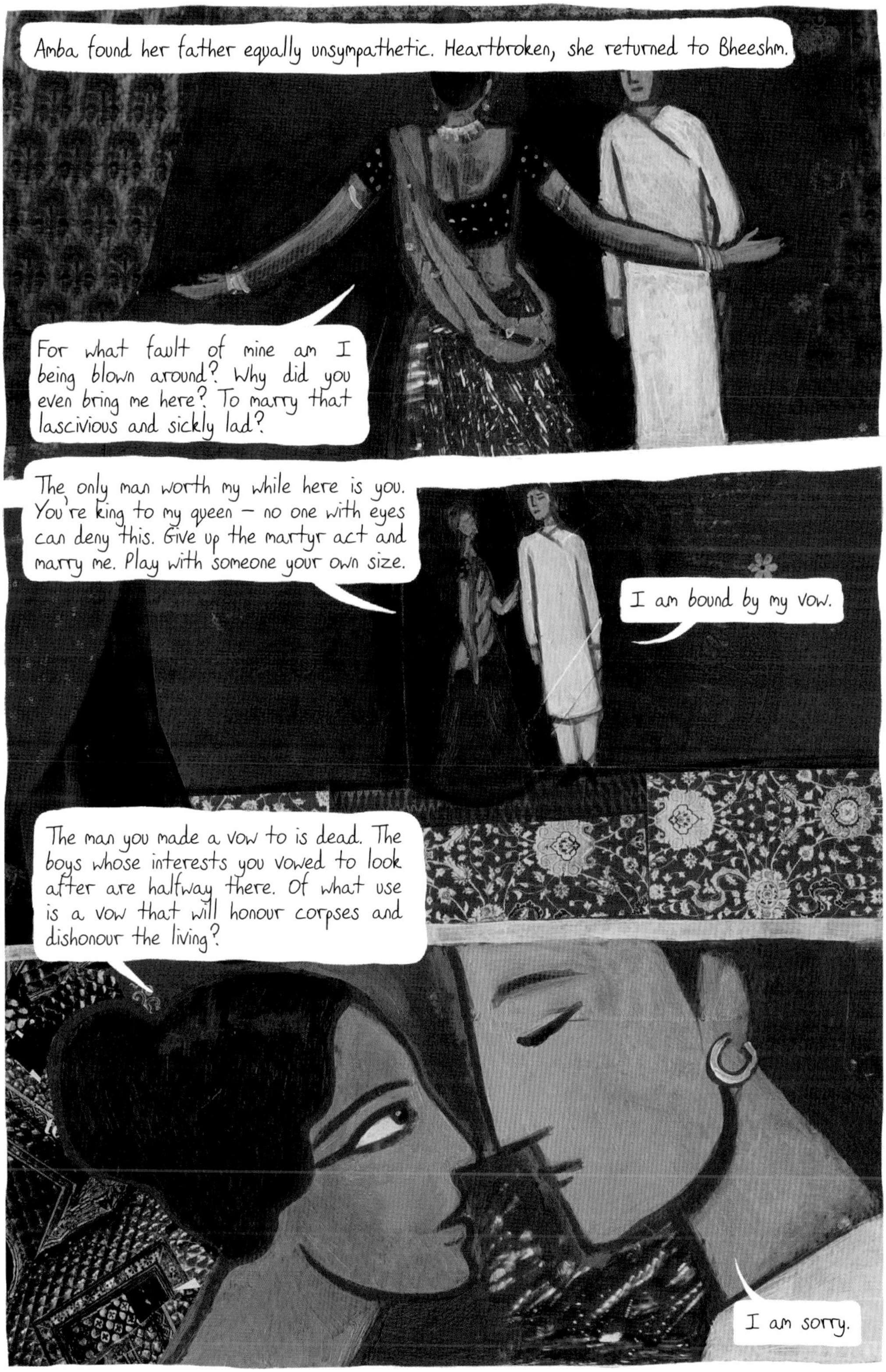
Amba found her father equally unsympathetic. Heartbroken, she returned to Bheeshm.
For what fault of mine am I being blown around? Why did you even bring me here? To marry that lascivious and sickly lad?
The only man worth my while here is you. You're king to my queen — no one with eyes can deny this. Give up the martyr act and marry me. Play with someone your own size.
I am bound by my vow.
The man you made a vow to is dead. The boys whose interests you vowed to look after are halfway there. Of what use is a vow that will honour corpses and dishonour the living?
I am sorry.

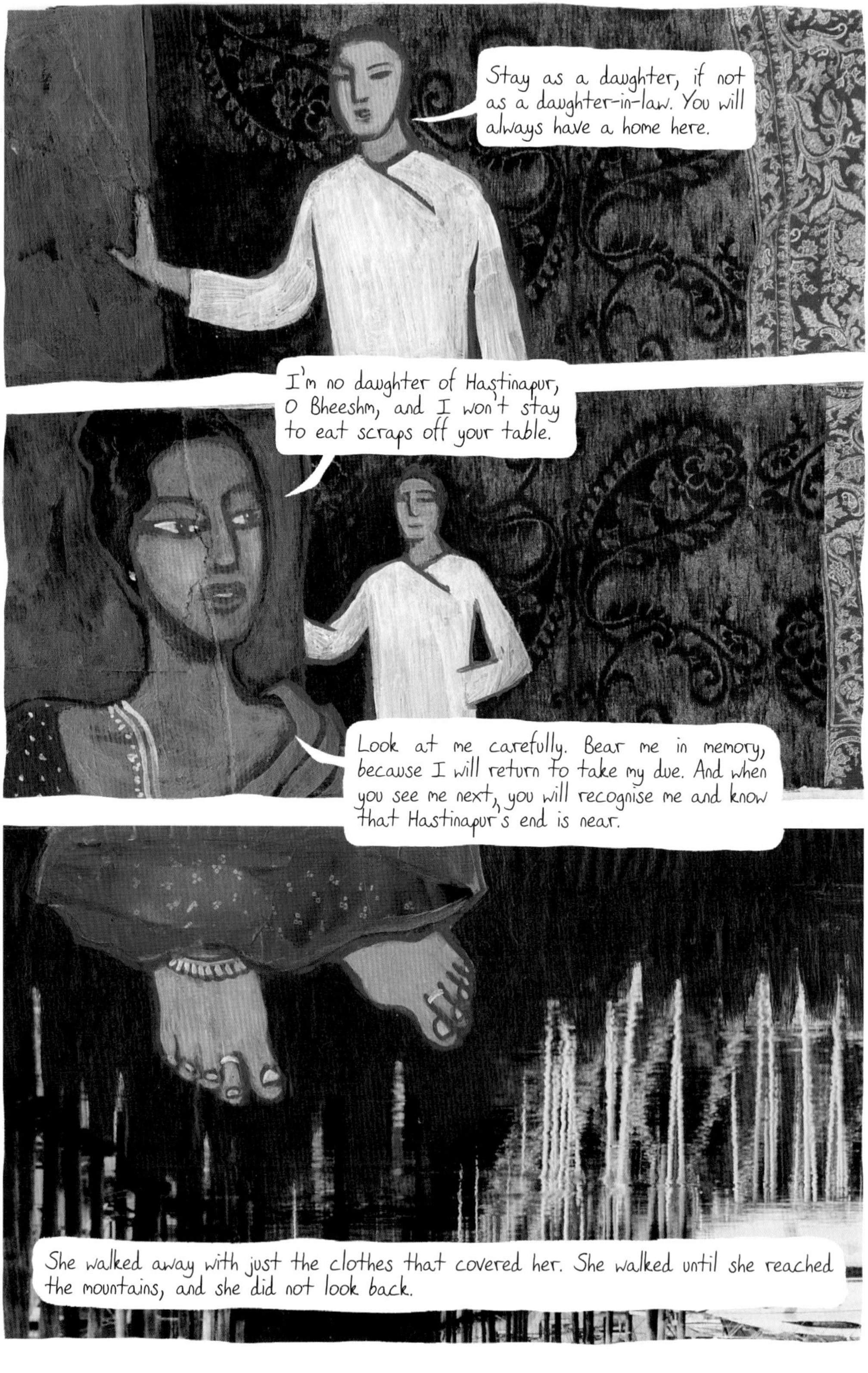
Stay as a daughter, if not as a daughter-in-law. You will always have a home here.
I'm no daughter of Hastinapur, O Bheeshm, and I won't stay to eat scraps off your table.
Look at me carefully. Bear me in memory, because I will return to take my due. And when you see me next, you will recognise me and know that Hastinapur's end is near.
She walked away with just the clothes that covered her. She walked until she reached the mountains, and she did not look back.

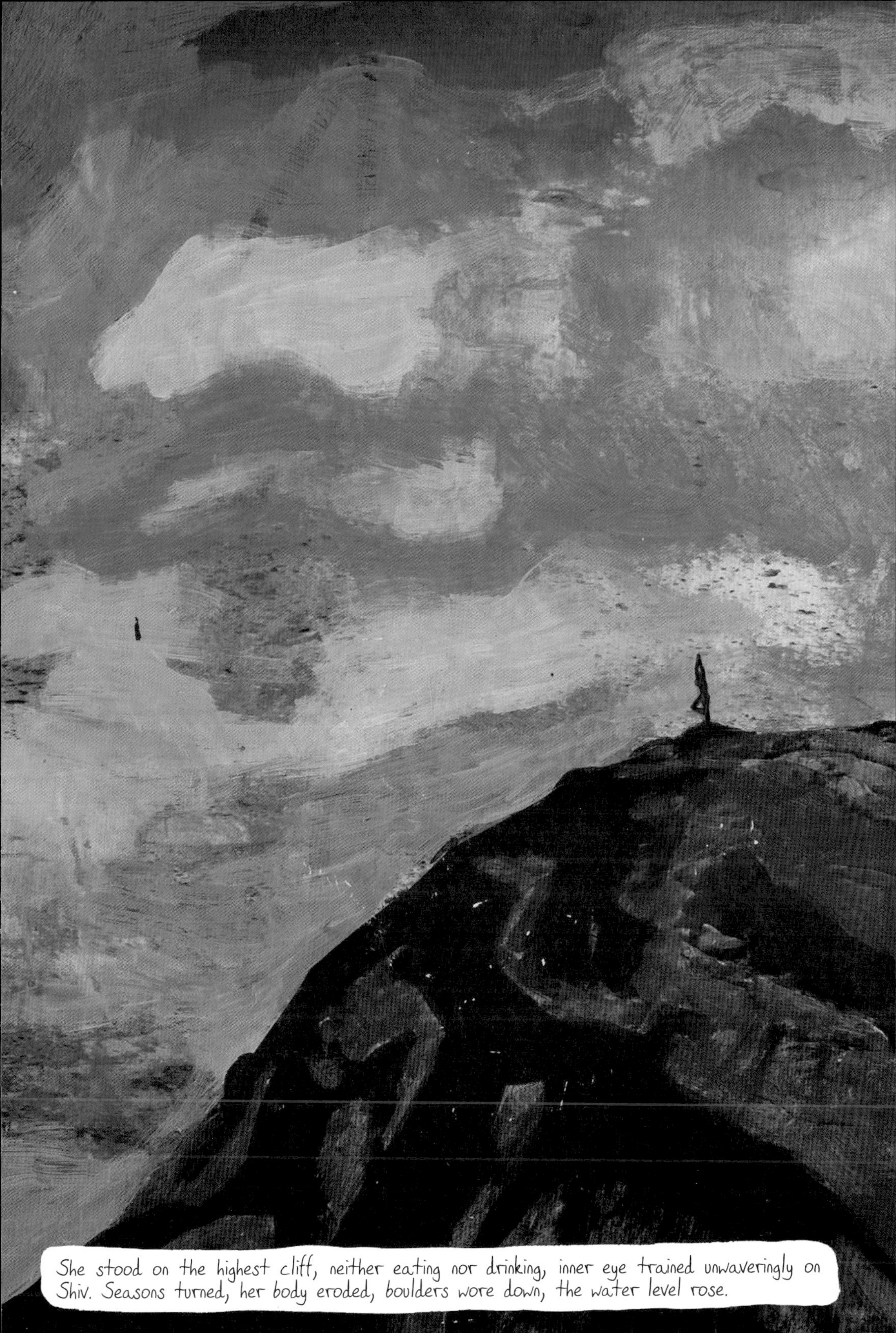
She stood on the highest cliff, neither eating nor drinking, inner eye trained unwaveringly on Shiv. Seasons turned, her body eroded, boulders wore down, the water level rose.

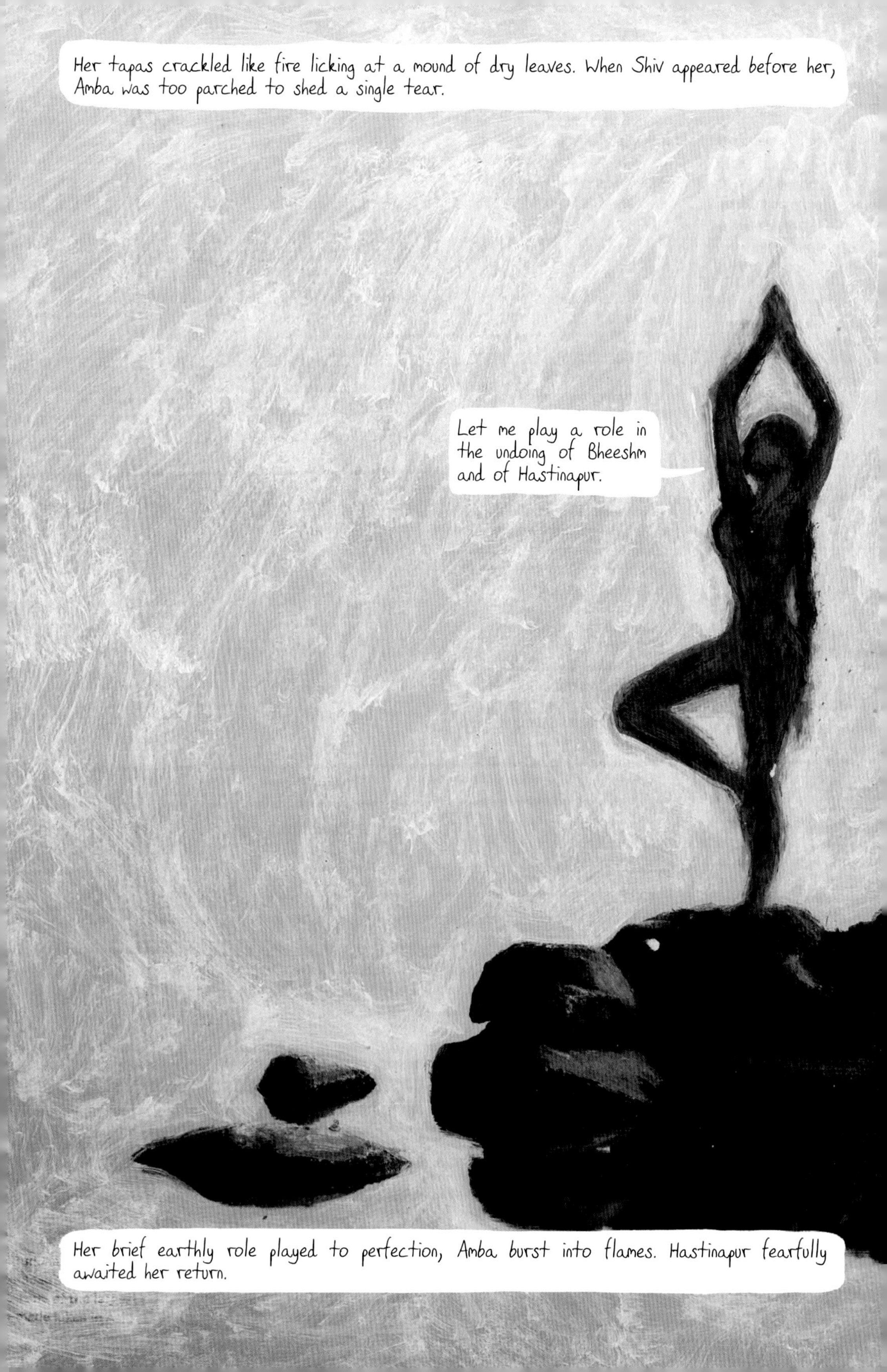
Her tapas crackled like fire licking at a mound of dry leaves. When Shiv appeared before her, Amba was too parched to shed a single tear.
Let me play a role in the undoing of Bheeshm and of Hastinapur.
Her brief earthly role played to perfection, Amba burst into flames. Hastinapur fearfully awaited her return.

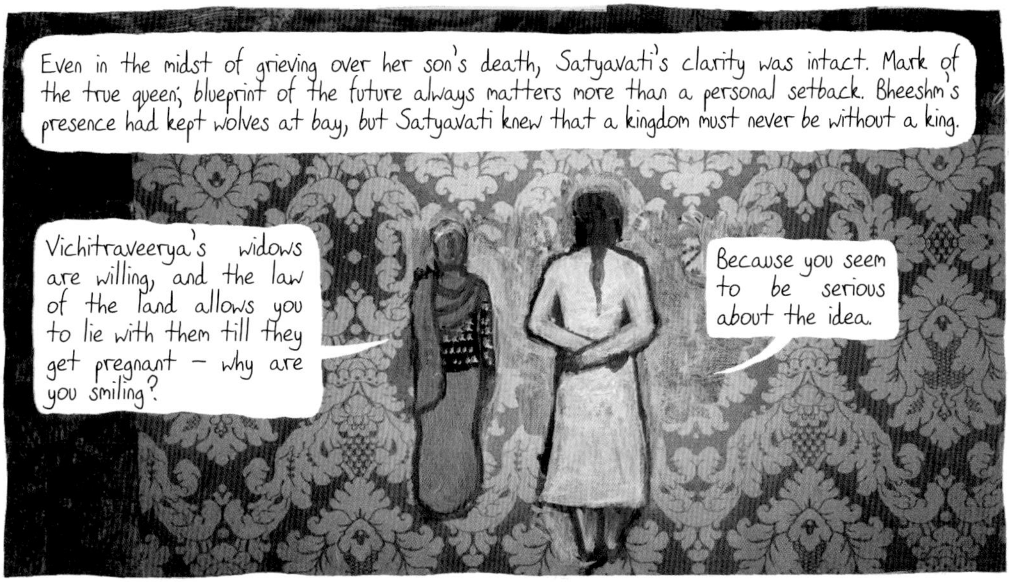
Even in the midst of grieving over her son's death, Satyavati's clarity was intact. Mark of the true queen; blueprint of the future always matters more than a personal setback. Bheeshm's presence had kept wolves at bay, but Satyavati knew that a kingdom must never be without a king.
Vichitraveerya's widows are willing, and the law of the land allows you to lie with them till they get pregnant – why are you smiling?
Because you seem to be serious about the idea.

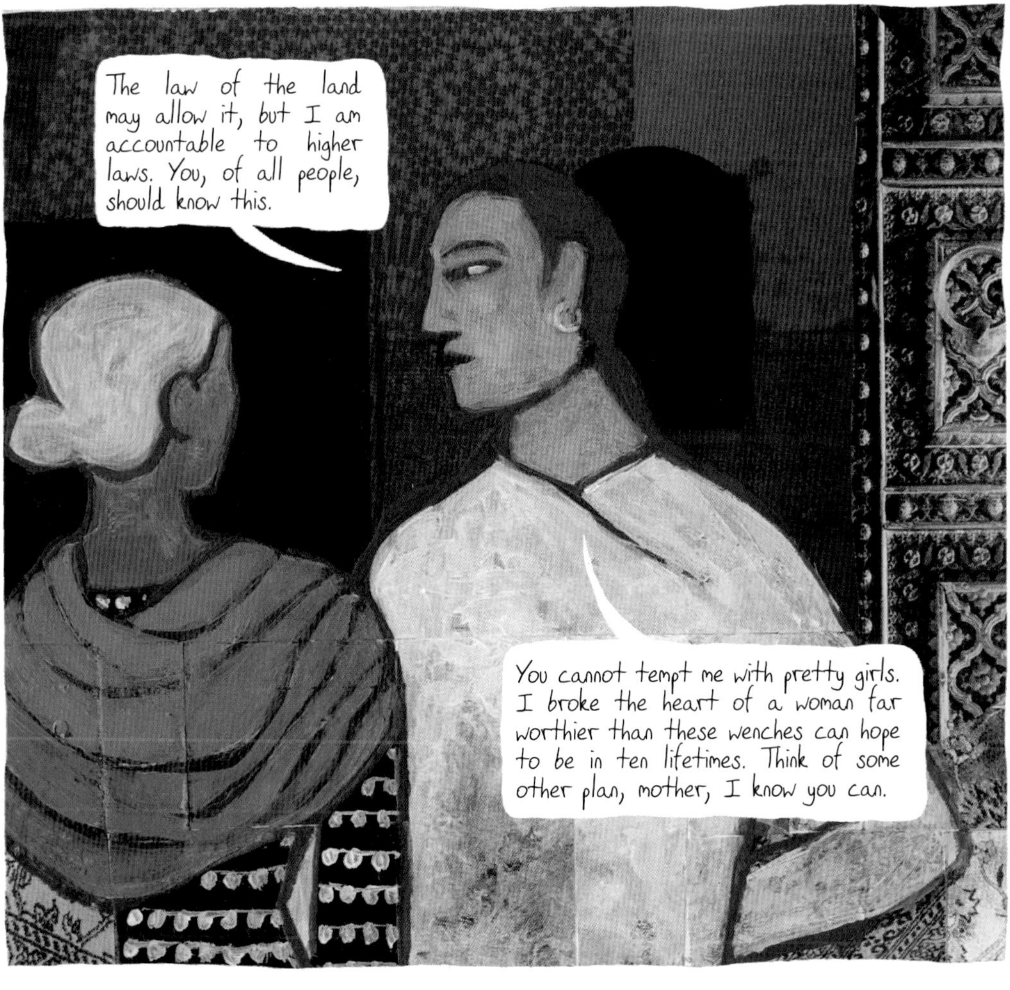
The law of the land may allow it, but I am accountable to higher laws. You, of all people, should know this.
You cannot tempt me with pretty girls. I broke the heart of a woman far worthier than these wenches can hope to be in ten lifetimes. Think of some other plan, mother, I know you can.

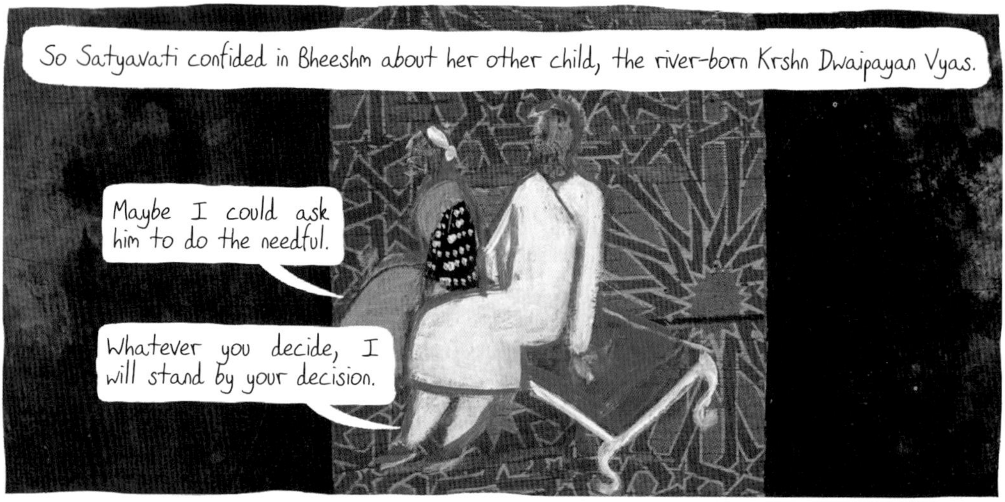
So Satyavati confided in Bheeshm about her other child, the river-born Krshn Dwaipayan Vyas.
Maybe I could ask him to do the needful.
Whatever you decide, I will stand by your decision.

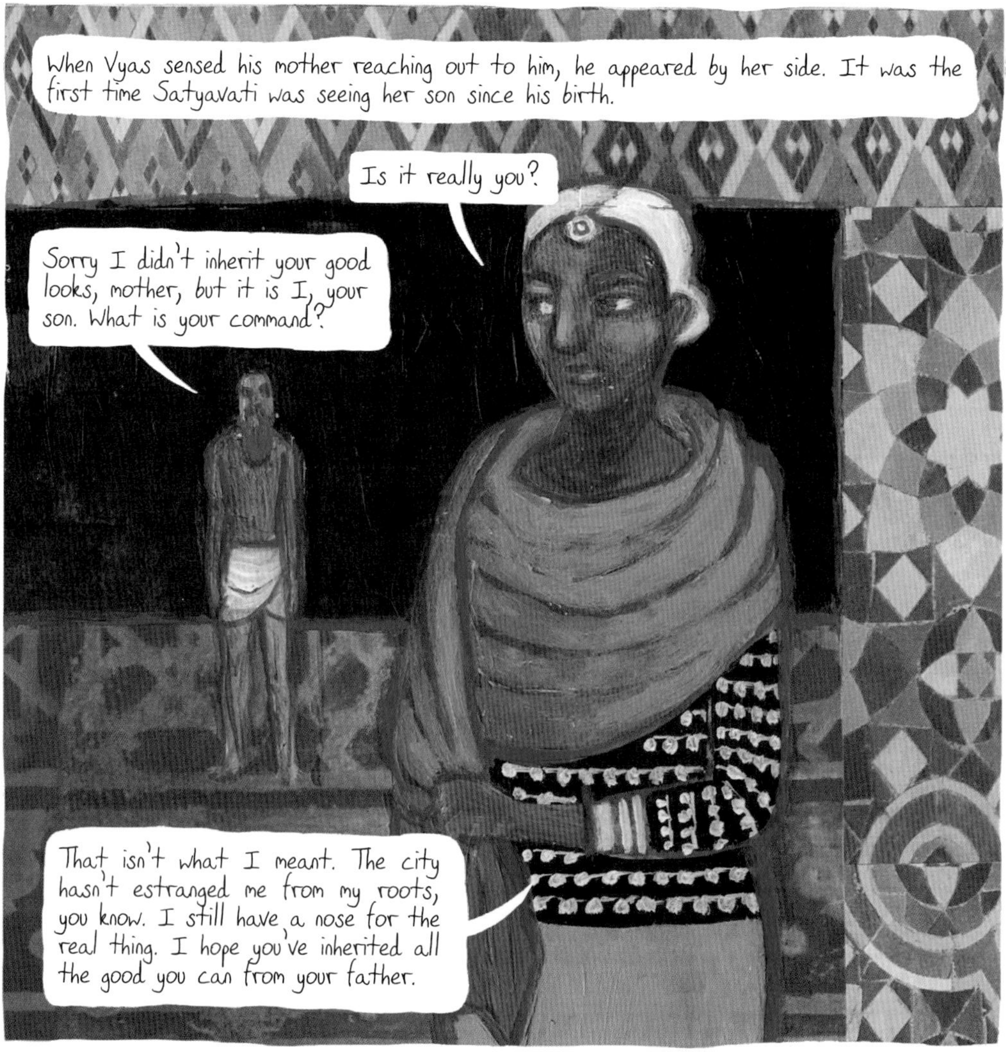
When Vyas sensed his mother reaching out to him, he appeared by her side. It was the first time Satyavati was seeing her son since his birth.
Is it really you?
Sorry I didn't inherit your good looks, mother, but it is I, your son. What is your command?
That isn't what I meant. The city hasn't estranged me from my roots, you know. I still have a nose for the real thing. I hope you've inherited all the good you can from your father.

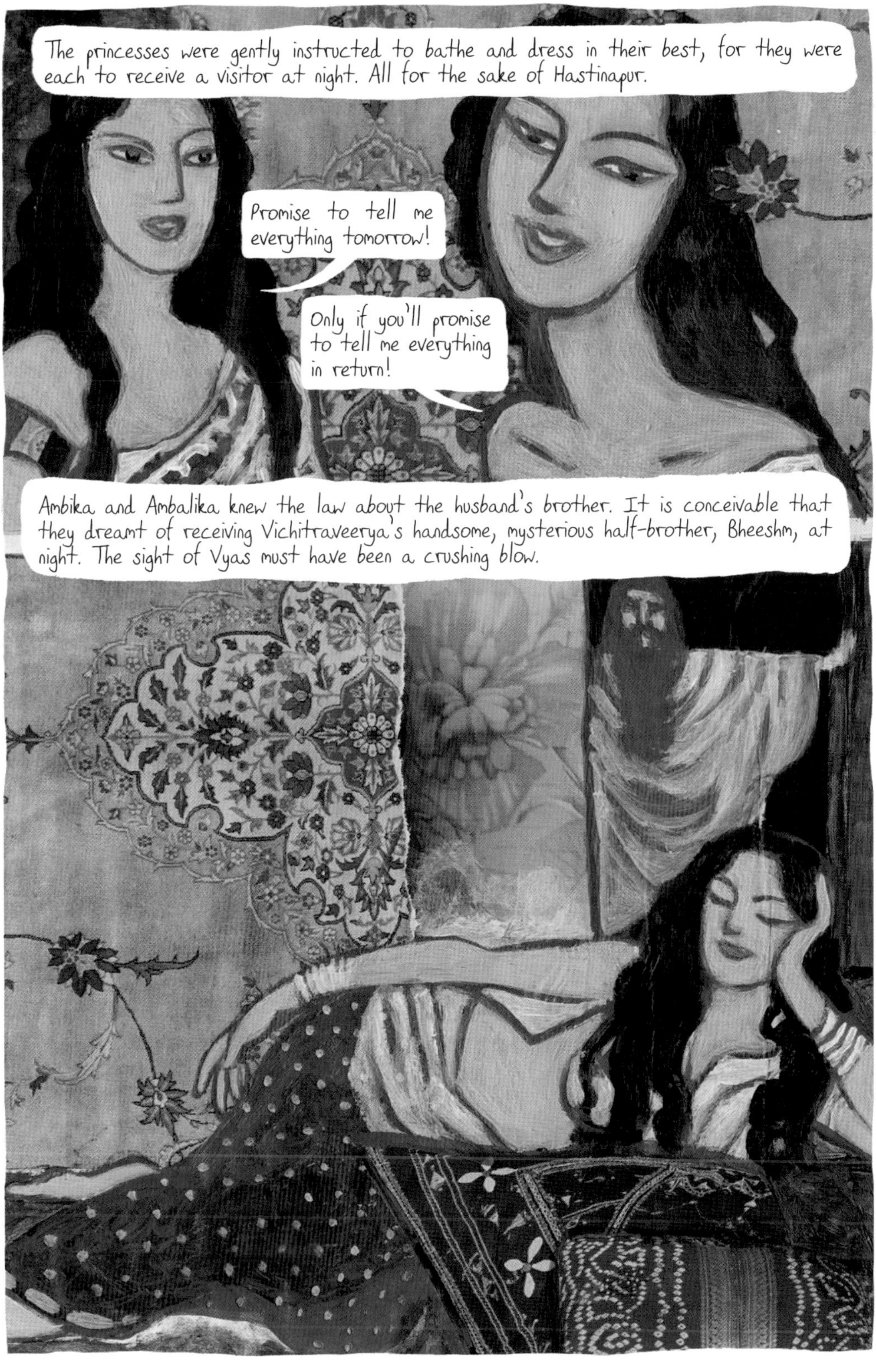
The princesses were gently instructed to bathe and dress in their best, for they were each to receive a visitor at night. All for the sake of Hastinapur.
Promise to tell me everything tomorrow!
Only if you'll promise to tell me everything in return!
Ambika and Ambalika knew the law about the husband's brother. It is conceivable that they dreamt of receiving Vichitraveerya's handsome, mysterious half-brother, Bheeshm, at night. The sight of Vyas must have been a crushing blow.

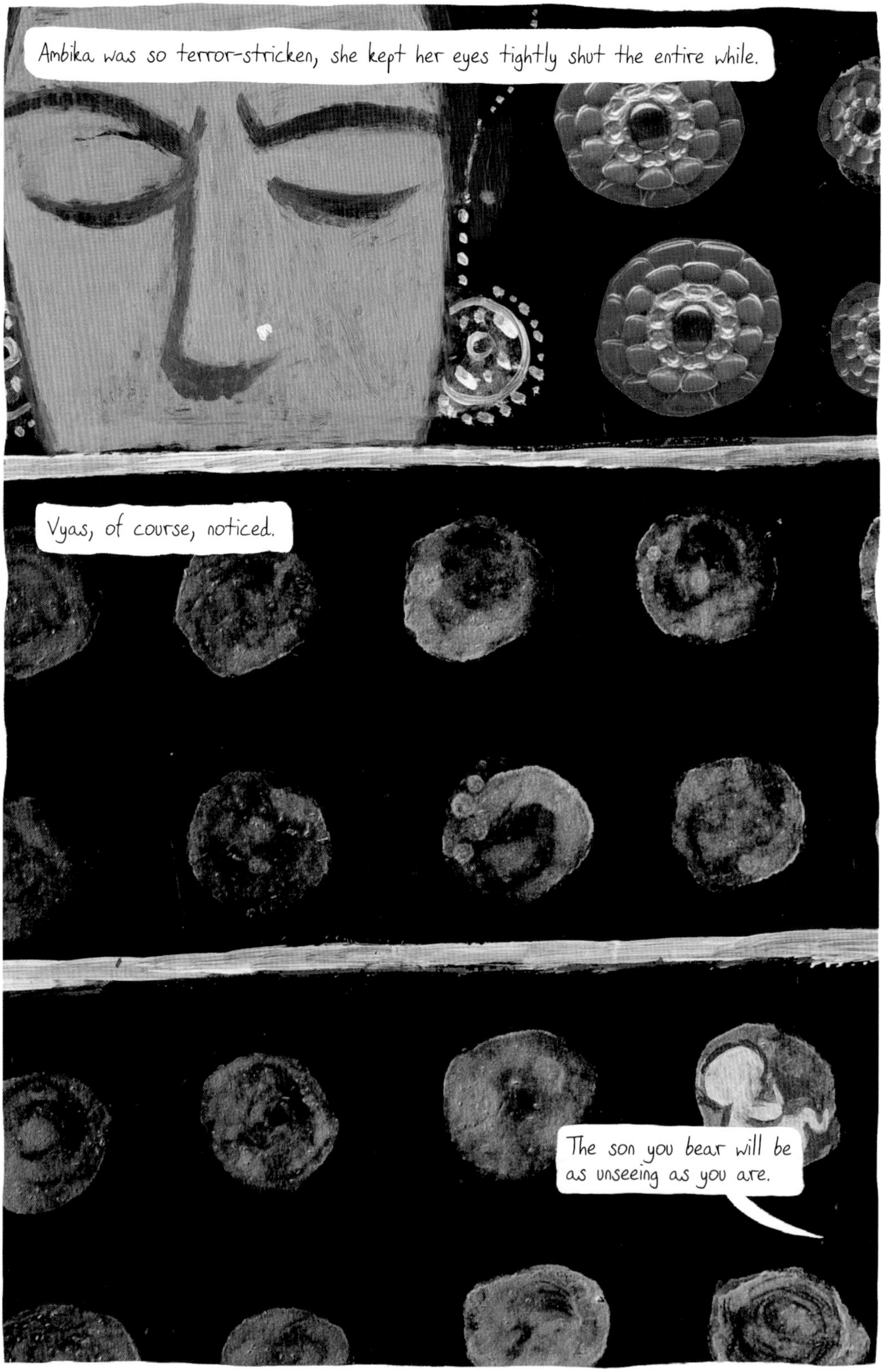
Ambika was so terror-stricken, she kept her eyes tightly shut the entire while.
Vyas, of course, noticed.
The son you bear will be as unseeing as you are.

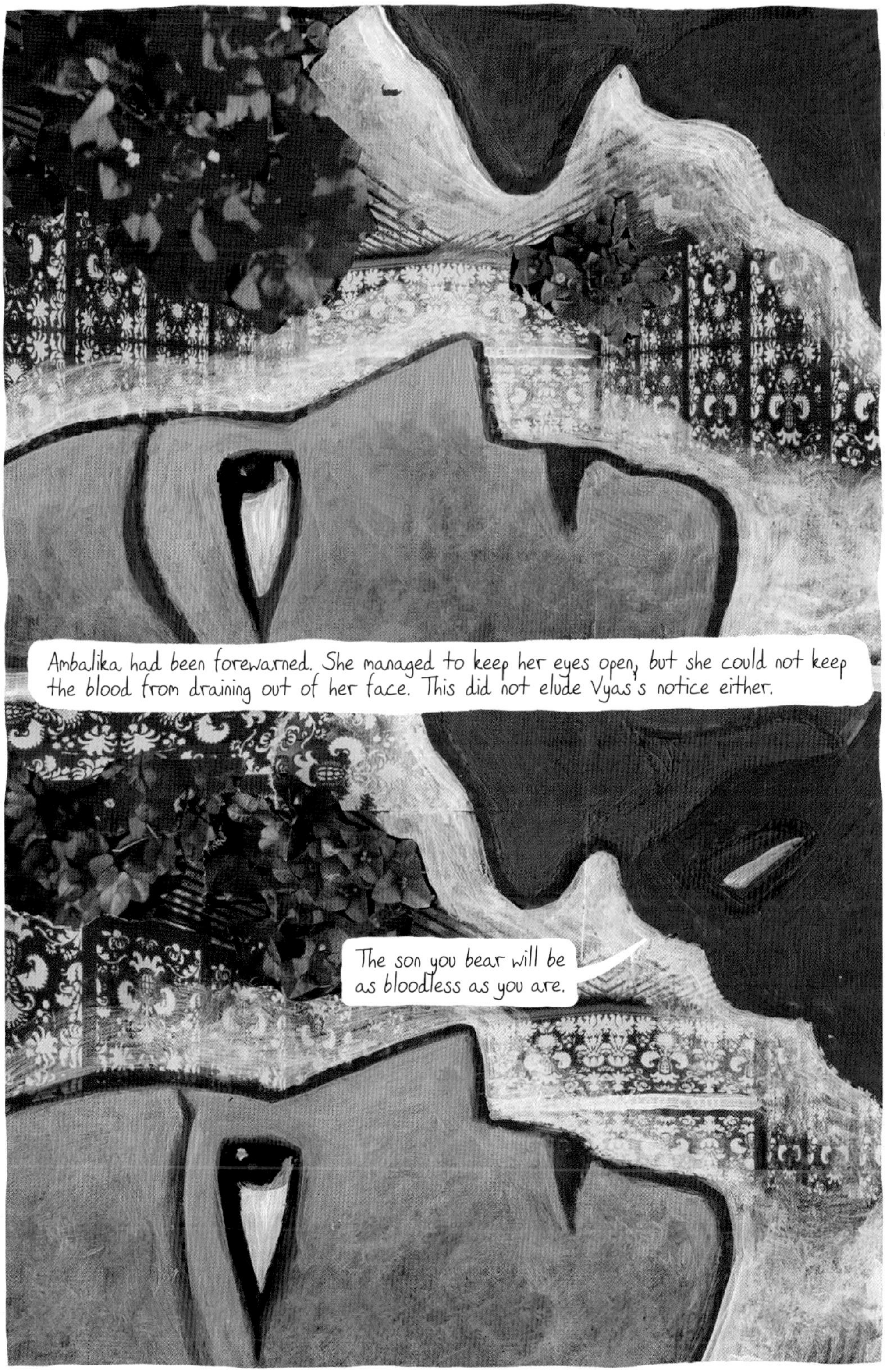
Ambalika had been forewarned. She managed to keep her eyes open, but she could not keep the blood from draining out of her face. This did not elude Vyas's notice either.
The son you bear will be as bloodless as you are.

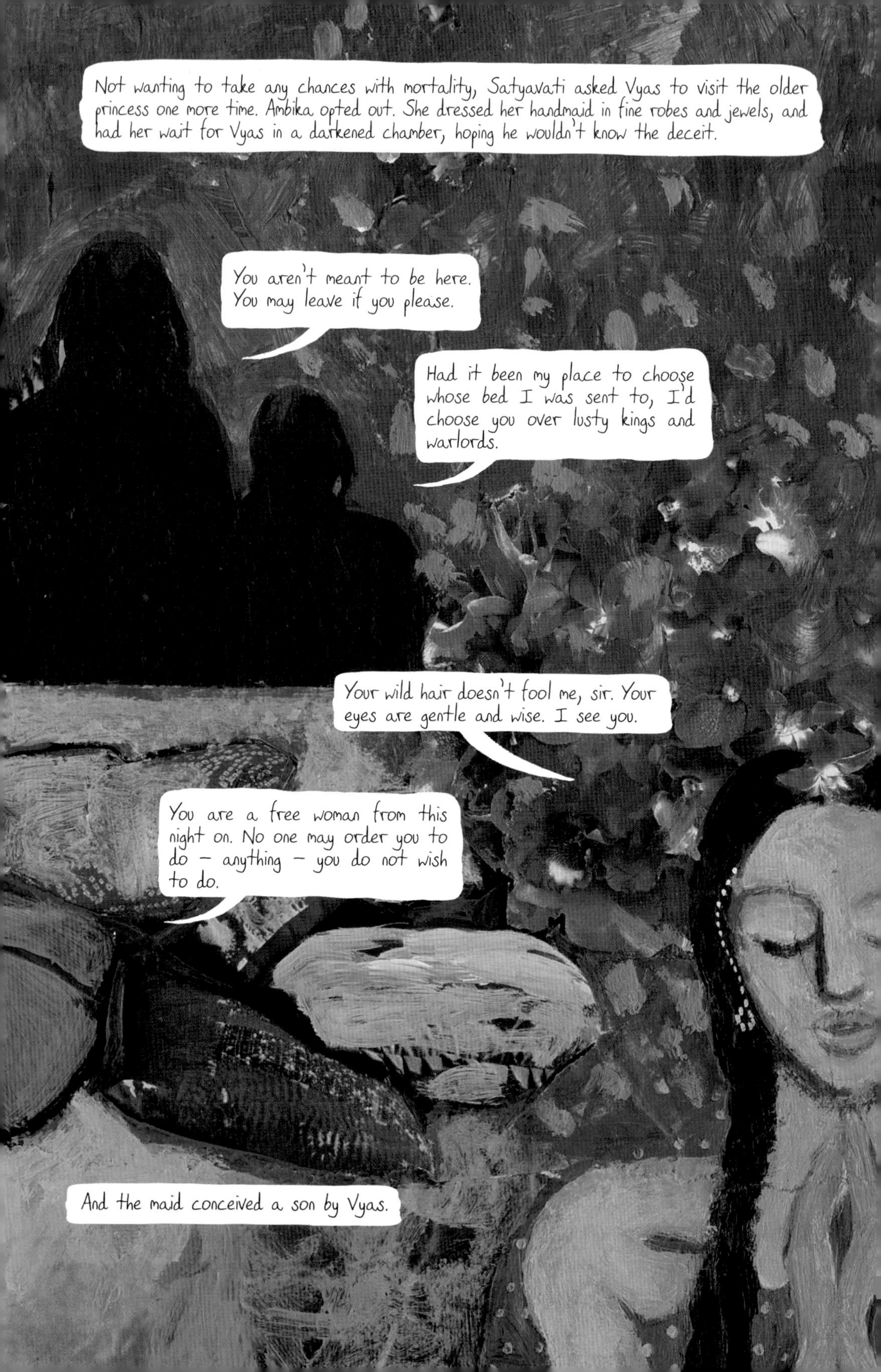
Not wanting to take any chances with mortality, Satyavati asked Vyas to visit the older princess one more time. Ambika opted out. She dressed her handmaid in fine robes and jewels, and had her wait for Vyas in a darkened chamber, hoping he wouldn't know the deceit.
You aren't meant to be here. You may leave if you please.
Had it been my place to choose whose bed I was sent to, I'd choose you over lusty kings and warlords.
Your wild hair doesn't fool me, sir. Your eyes are gentle and wise. I see you.
You are a free woman from this night on. No one may order you to do – anything – you do not wish to do.
And the maid conceived a son by Vyas.

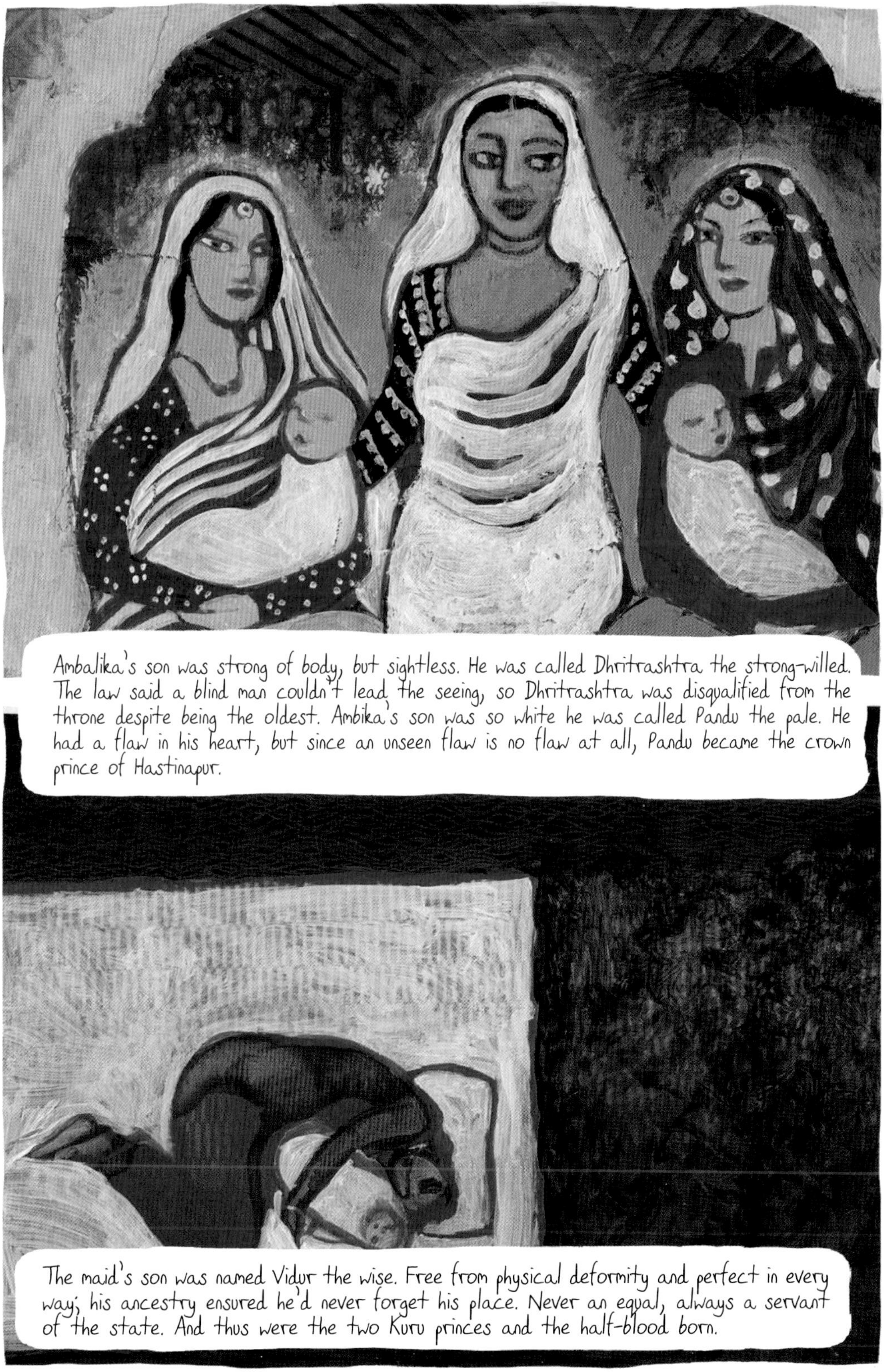
Ambalika's son was strong of body, but sightless. He was called Dhritrashtra the strong-willed. The law said a blind man couldn't lead the seeing, so Dhritrashtra was disqualified from the throne despite being the oldest. Ambika's son was so white he was called Pandu the pale. He had a flaw in his heart, but since an unseen flaw is no flaw at all, Pandu became the crown prince of Hastinapur.
The maid's son was named Vidur the wise. Free from physical deformity and perfect in every way; his ancestry ensured he'd never forget his place. Never an equal, always a servant of the state. And thus were the two Kuru princes and the half-blood born.

EARTH, WIND, FIRE, WATER

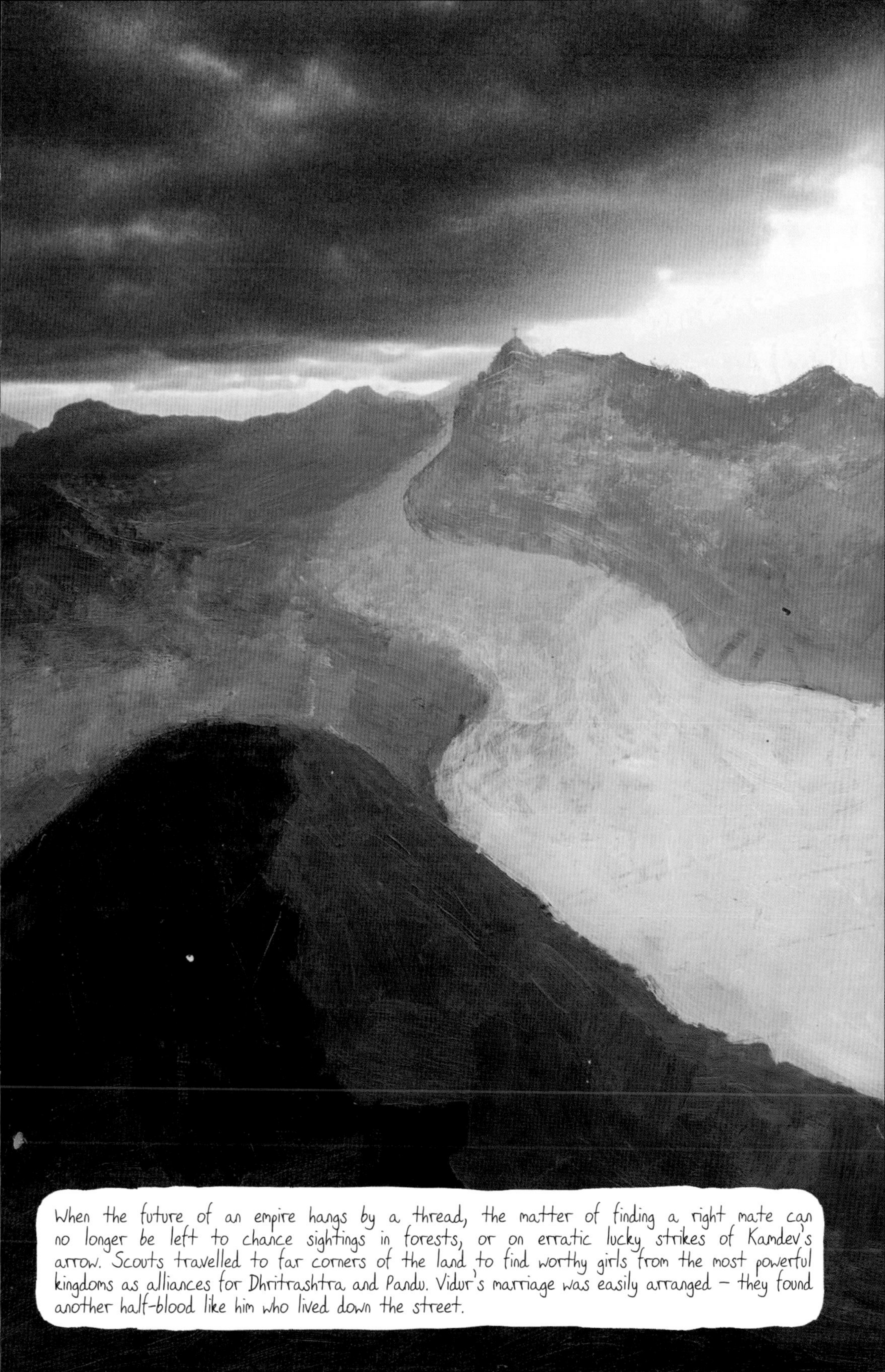
When the future of an empire hangs by a thread, the matter of finding a right mate can no longer be left to chance sightings in forests, or on erratic lucky strikes of Kamdev's arrow. Scouts travelled to far corners of the land to find worthy girls from the most powerful kingdoms as alliances for Dhritrashtra and Pandu. Vidur's marriage was easily arranged – they found another half-blood like him who lived down the street.

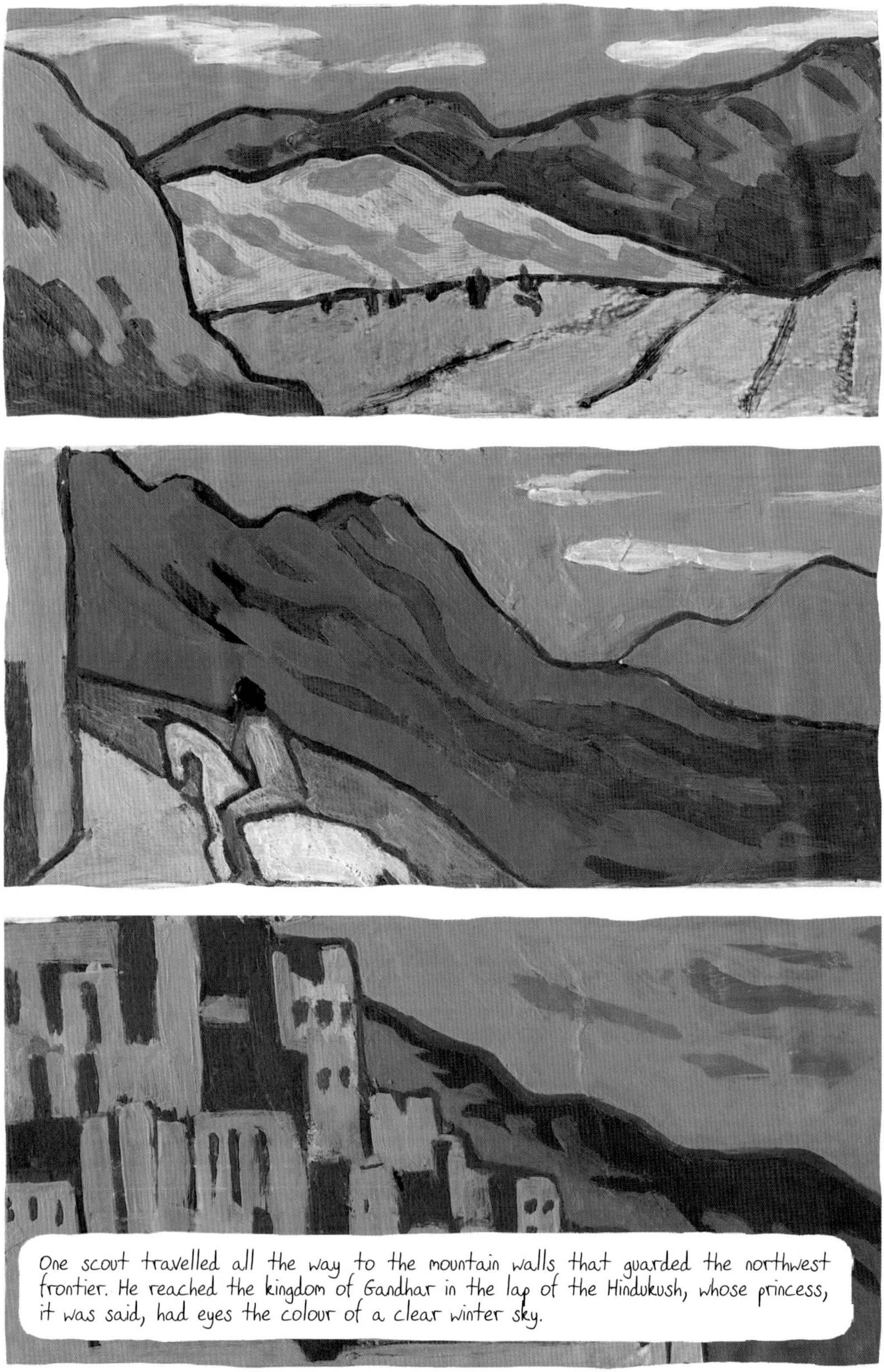
One scout travelled all the way to the mountain walls that guarded the northwest frontier. He reached the kingdom of Gandhar in the lap of the Hindukush, whose princess, it was said, had eyes the colour of a clear winter sky.

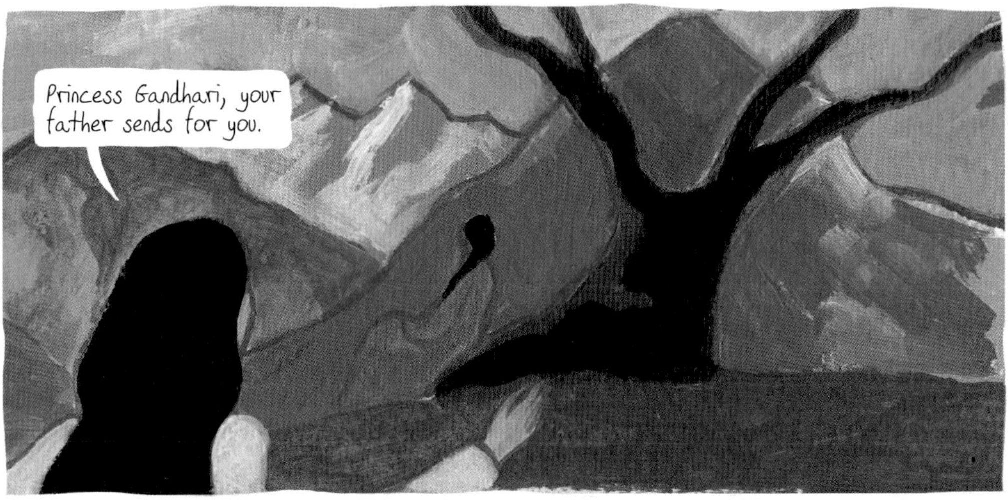
Princess Gandhari, your father sends for you.

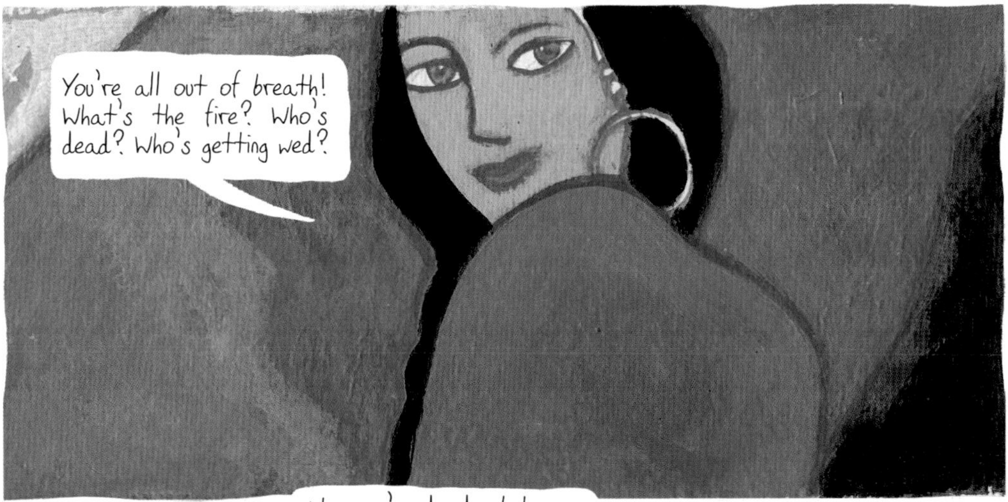
You're all out of breath! What's the fire? Who's dead? Who's getting wed?

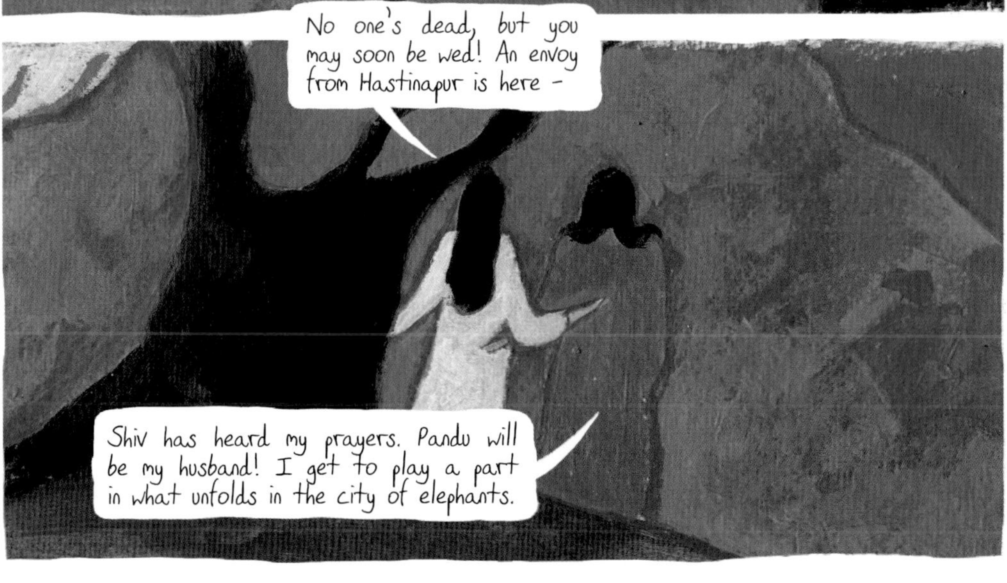
No one's dead, but you may soon be wed! An envoy from Hastinapur is here -
Shiv has heard my prayers. Pandu will be my husband! I get to play a part in what unfolds in the city of elephants.

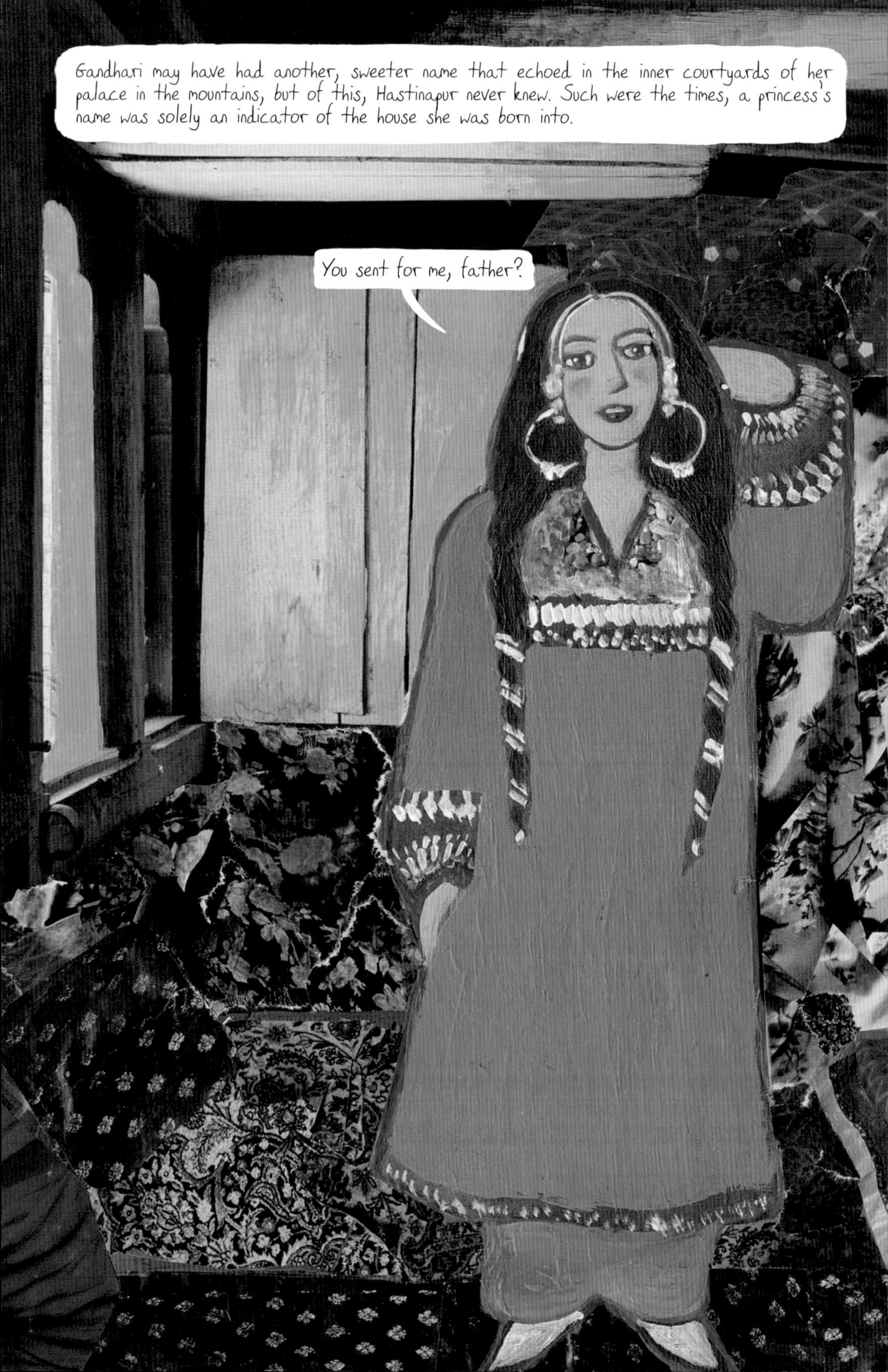
Gandhari may have had another, sweeter name that echoed in the inner courtyards of her palace in the mountains, but of this, Hastinapur never knew. Such were the times, a princess's name was solely an indicator of the house she was born into.
You sent for me, father?

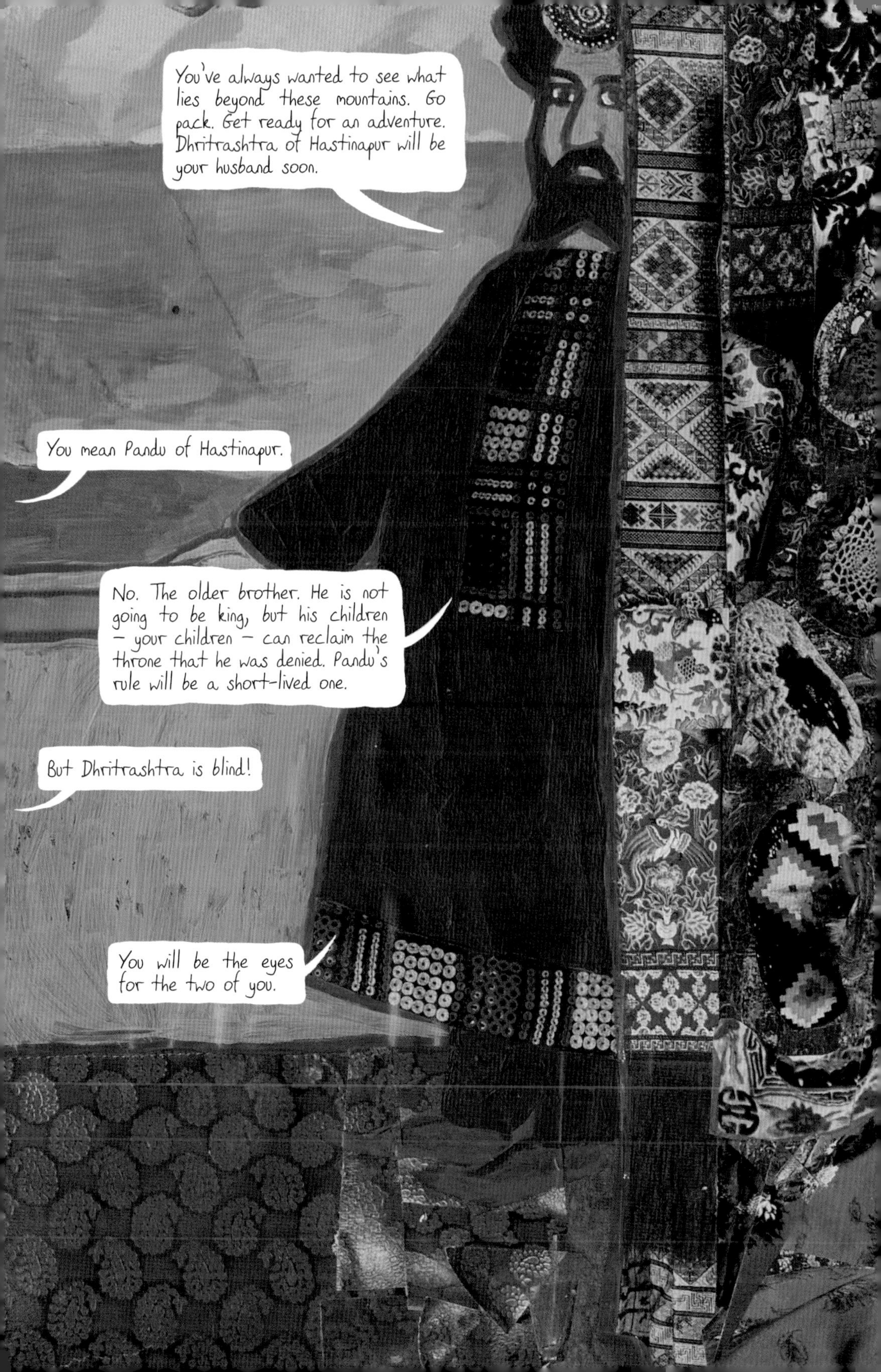

You've always wanted to see what lies beyond these mountains. Go pack. Get ready for an adventure. Dhritrashtra of Hastinapur will be your husband soon.
You mean Pandu of Hastinapur.
No. The older brother. He is not going to be king, but his children – your children – can reclaim the throne that he was denied. Pandu's rule will be a short-lived one.
But Dhritrashtra is blind!
You will be the eyes for the two of you.

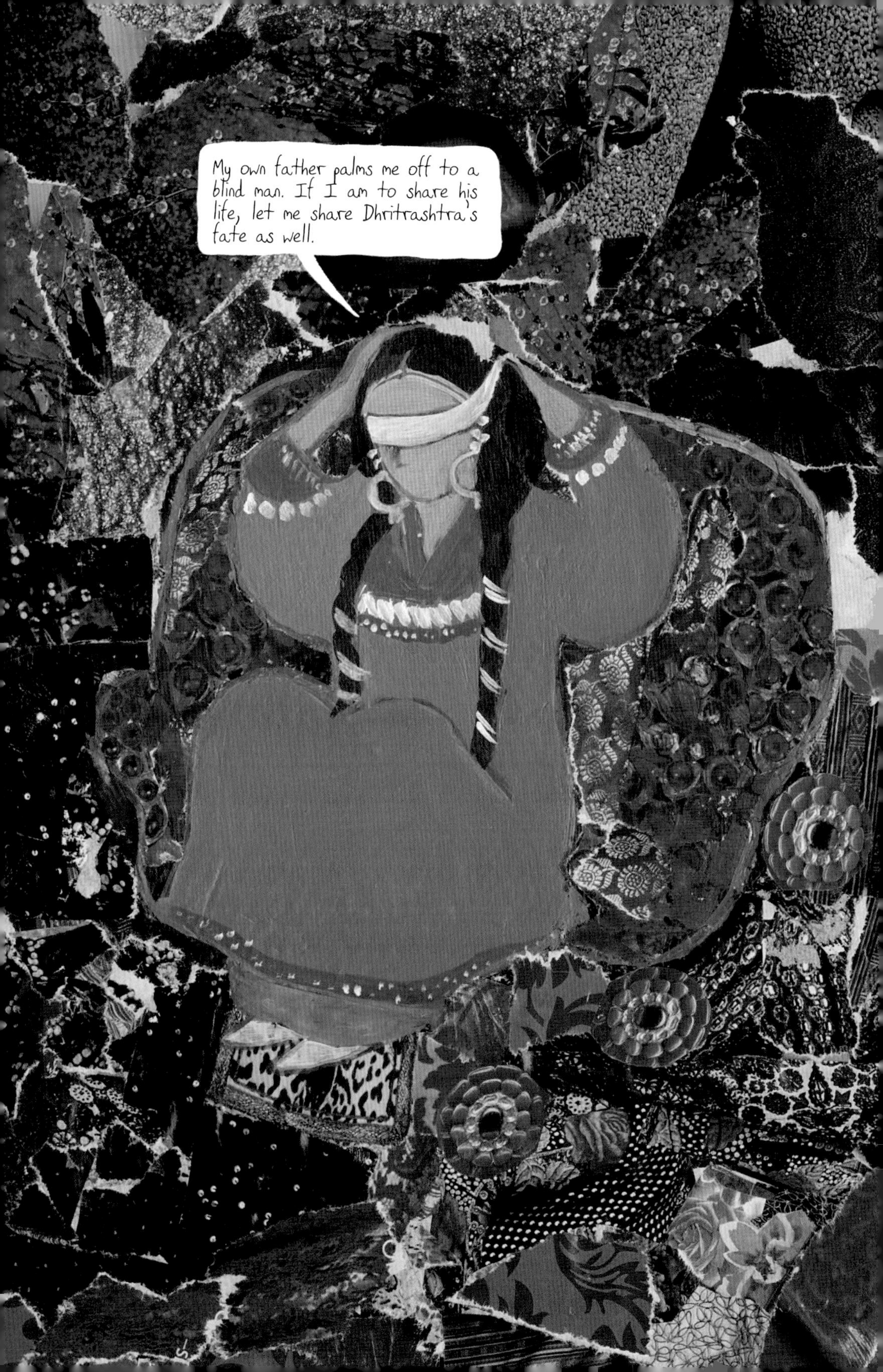
My own father palms me off to a blind man. If I am to share his life, let me share Dhritrashtra's fate as well.

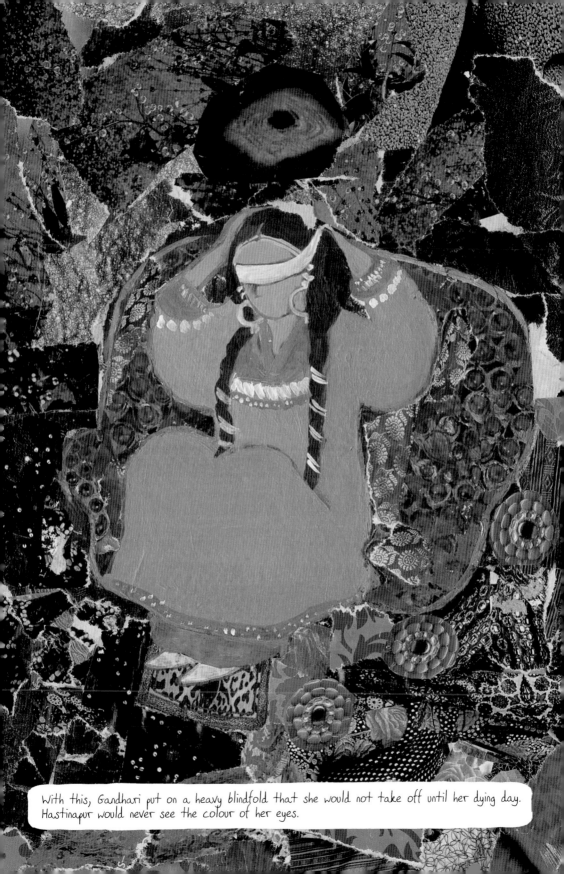

With this, Gandhari put on a heavy blindfold that she would not take off until her dying day. Hastinapur would never see the colour of her eyes.

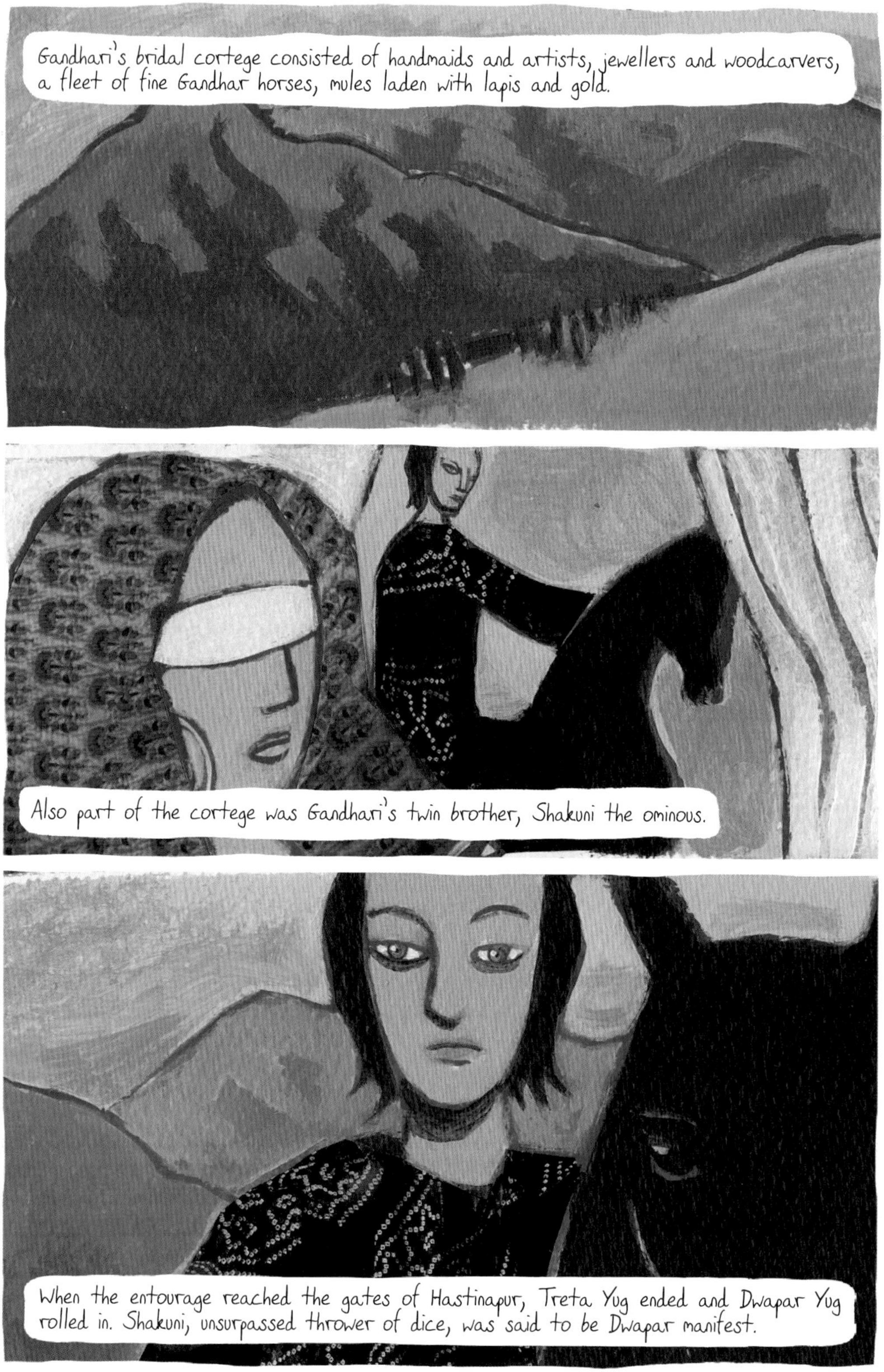
Gandhari's bridal cortege consisted of handmaids and artists, jewellers and woodcarvers, a fleet of fine Gandhar horses, mules laden with lapis and gold.
Also part of the cortege was Gandhari's twin brother, Shakuni the ominous.
When the entourage reached the gates of Hastinapur, Treta Yug ended and Dwapar Yug rolled in. Shakuni, unsurpassed thrower of dice, was said to be Dwapar manifest.

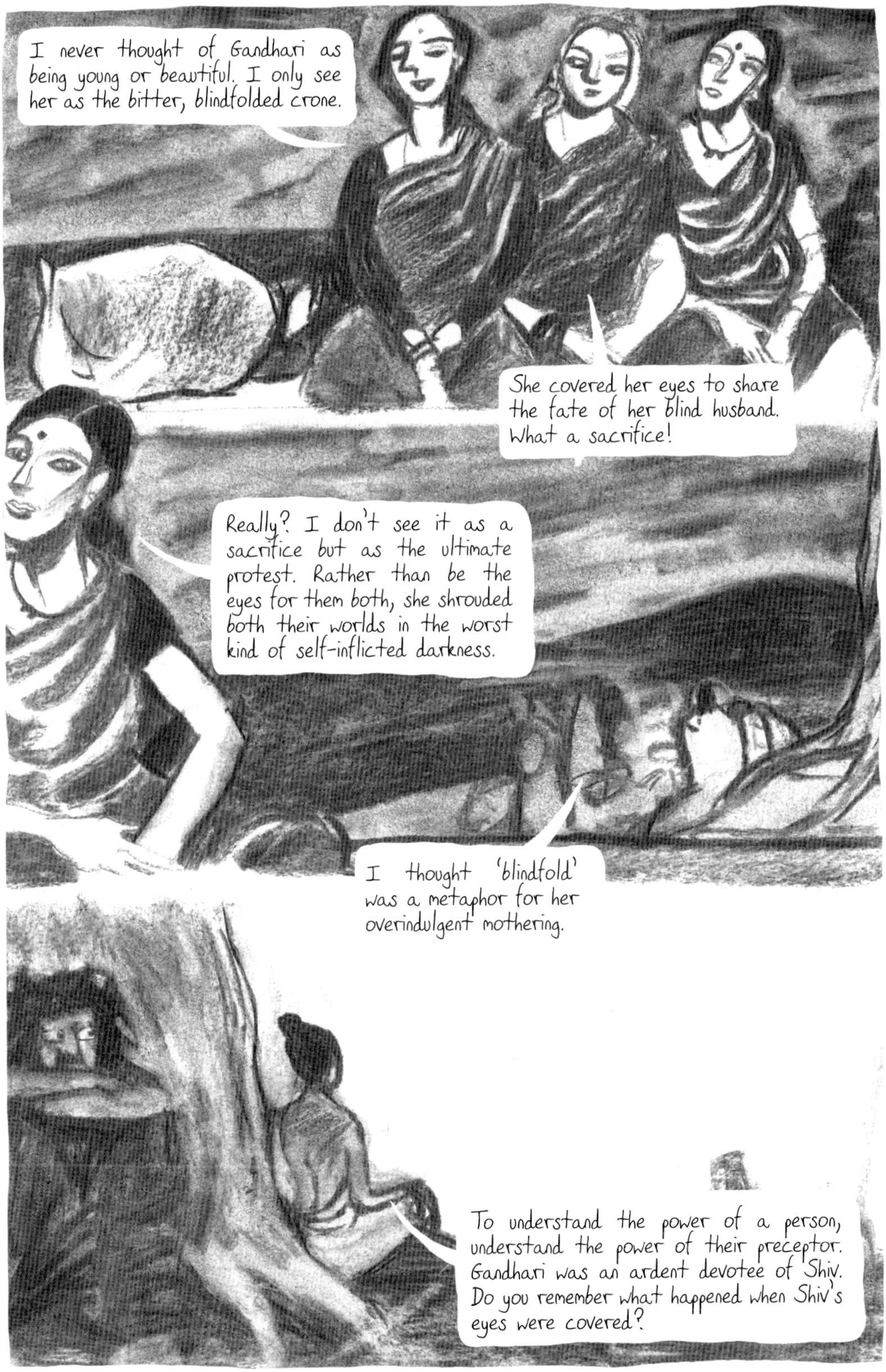
I never thought of Gandhari as being young or beautiful. I only see her as the bitter, blindfolded crone.
She covered her eyes to share the fate of her blind husband. What a sacrifice!
Really? I don't see it as a sacrifice but as the ultimate protest. Rather than be the eyes for them both, she shrouded both their worlds in the worst kind of self-inflicted darkness.
I thought 'blindfold' was a metaphor for her overindulgent mothering.
To understand the power of a person, understand the power of their preceptor. Gandhari was an ardent devotee of Shiv. Do you remember what happened when Shiv's eyes were covered?

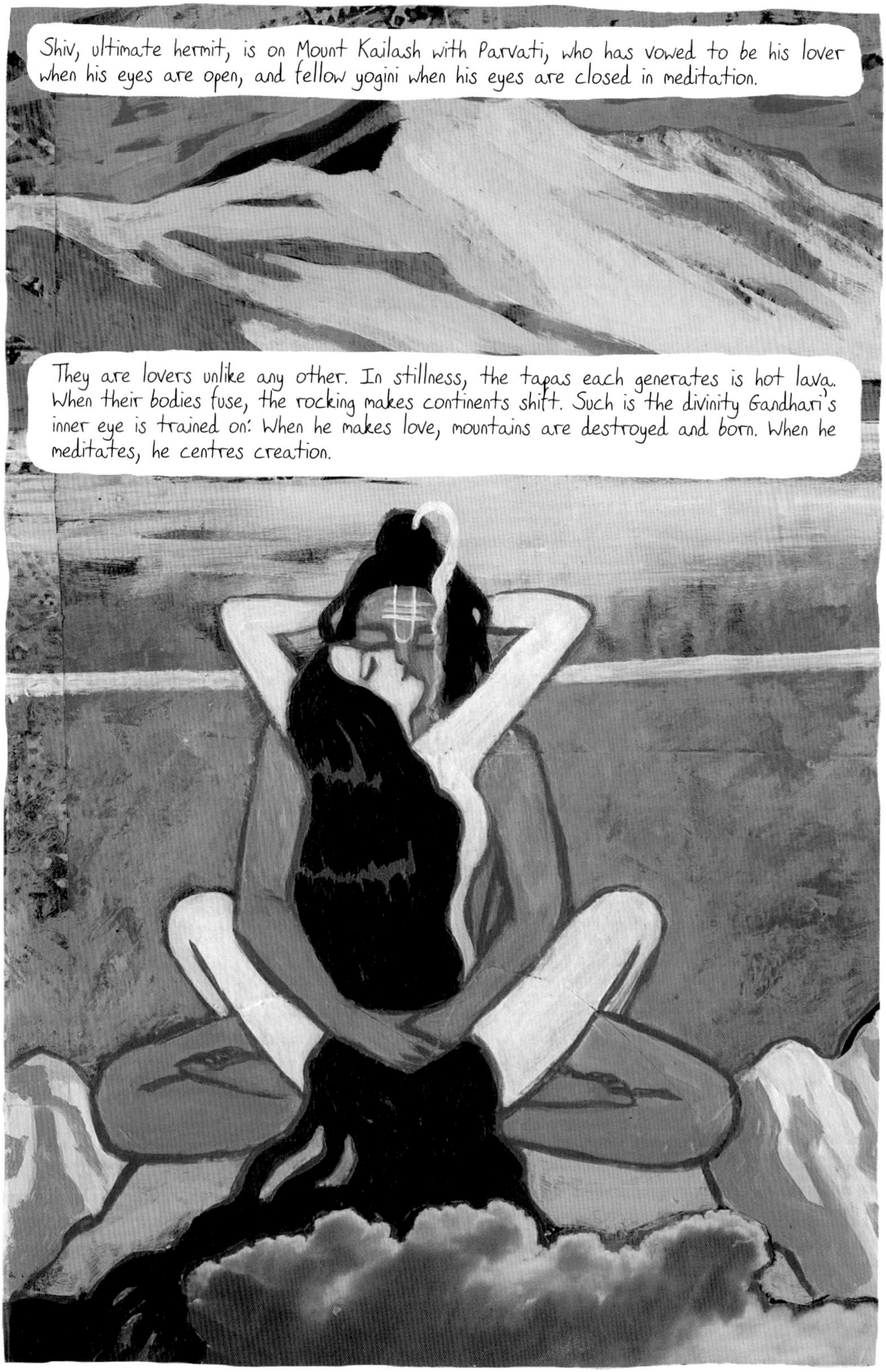
Shiv, ultimate hermit, is on Mount Kailash with Parvati, who has vowed to be his lover when his eyes are open, and fellow yogini when his eyes are closed in meditation.
They are lovers unlike any other. In stillness, the tapas each generates is hot lava. When their bodies fuse, the rocking makes continents shift. Such is the divinity Gandhari's inner eye is trained on: When he makes love, mountains are destroyed and born. When he meditates, he centres creation.

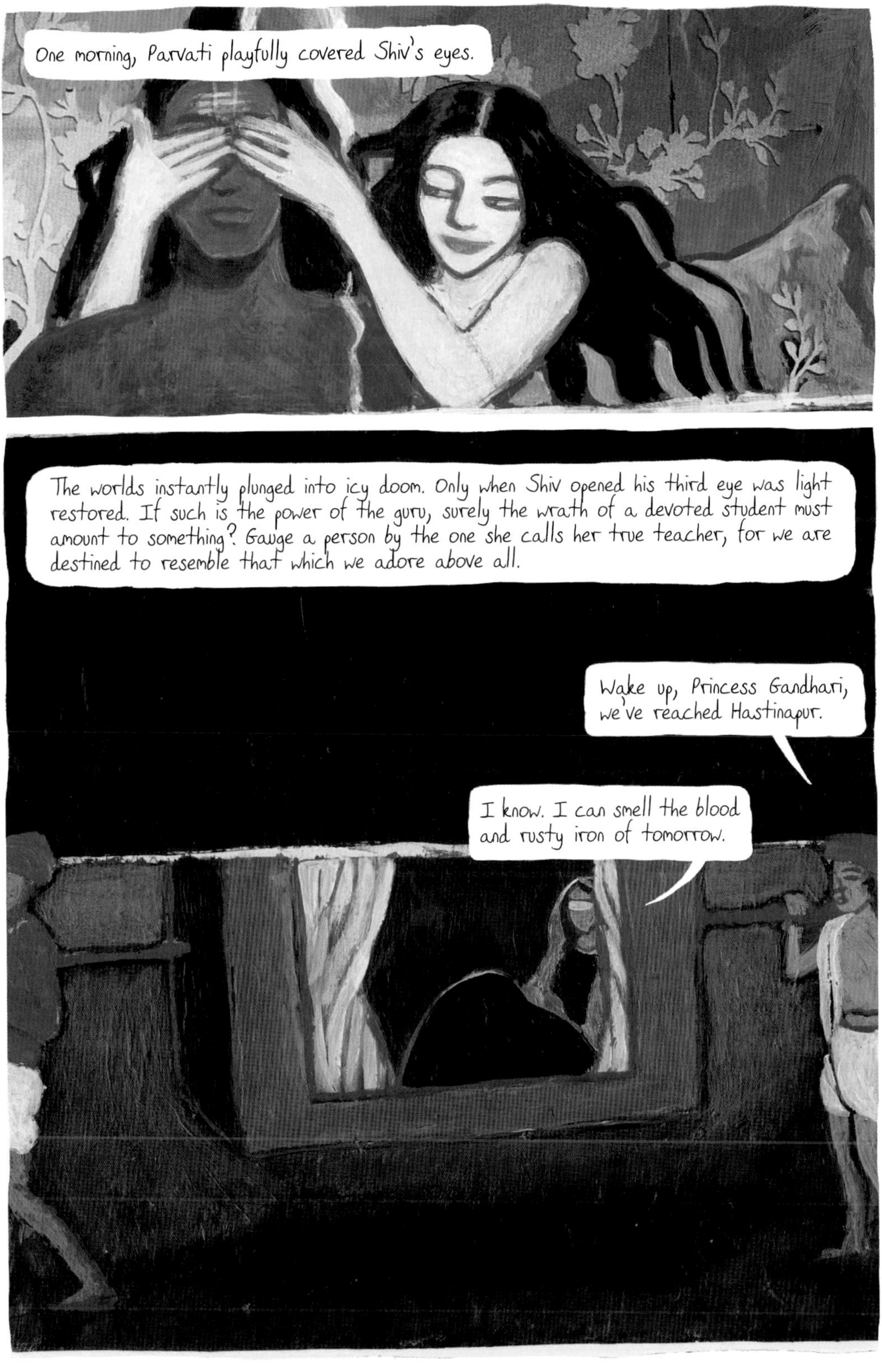
One morning, Parvati playfully covered Shiv's eyes.
The worlds instantly plunged into icy doom. Only when Shiv opened his third eye was light restored. If such is the power of the guru, surely the wrath of a devoted student must amount to something? Gauge a person by the one she calls her true teacher, for we are destined to resemble that which we adore above all.
Wake up, Princess Gandhari, we've reached Hastinapur.
I know. I can smell the blood and rusty iron of tomorrow.

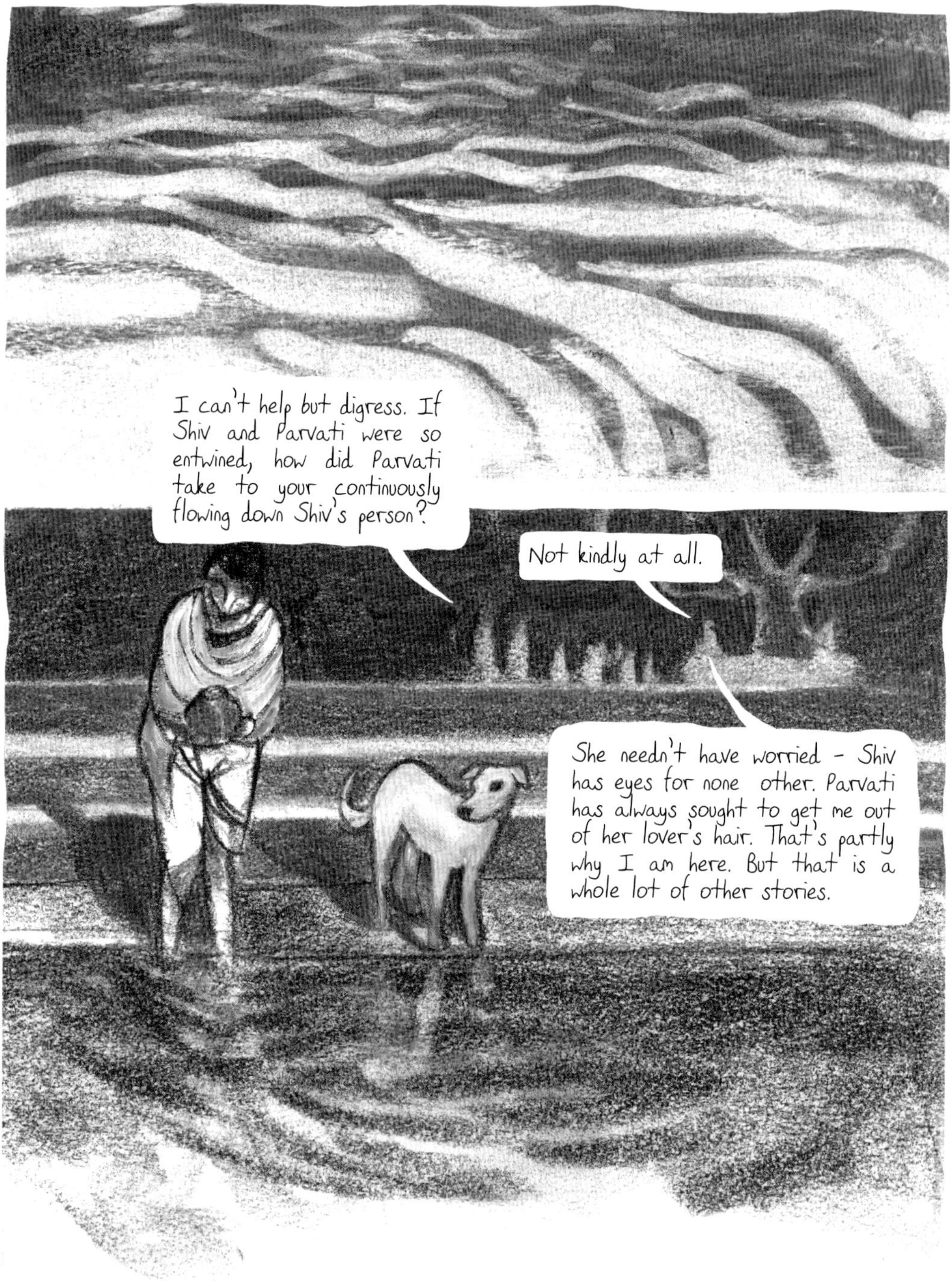
I can't help but digress. If Shiv and Parvati were so entwined, how did Parvati take to your continuously flowing down Shiv's person?
Not kindly at all.
She needn't have worried - Shiv has eyes for none other. Parvati has always sought to get me out of her lover's hair. That's partly why I am here. But that is a whole lot of other stories.

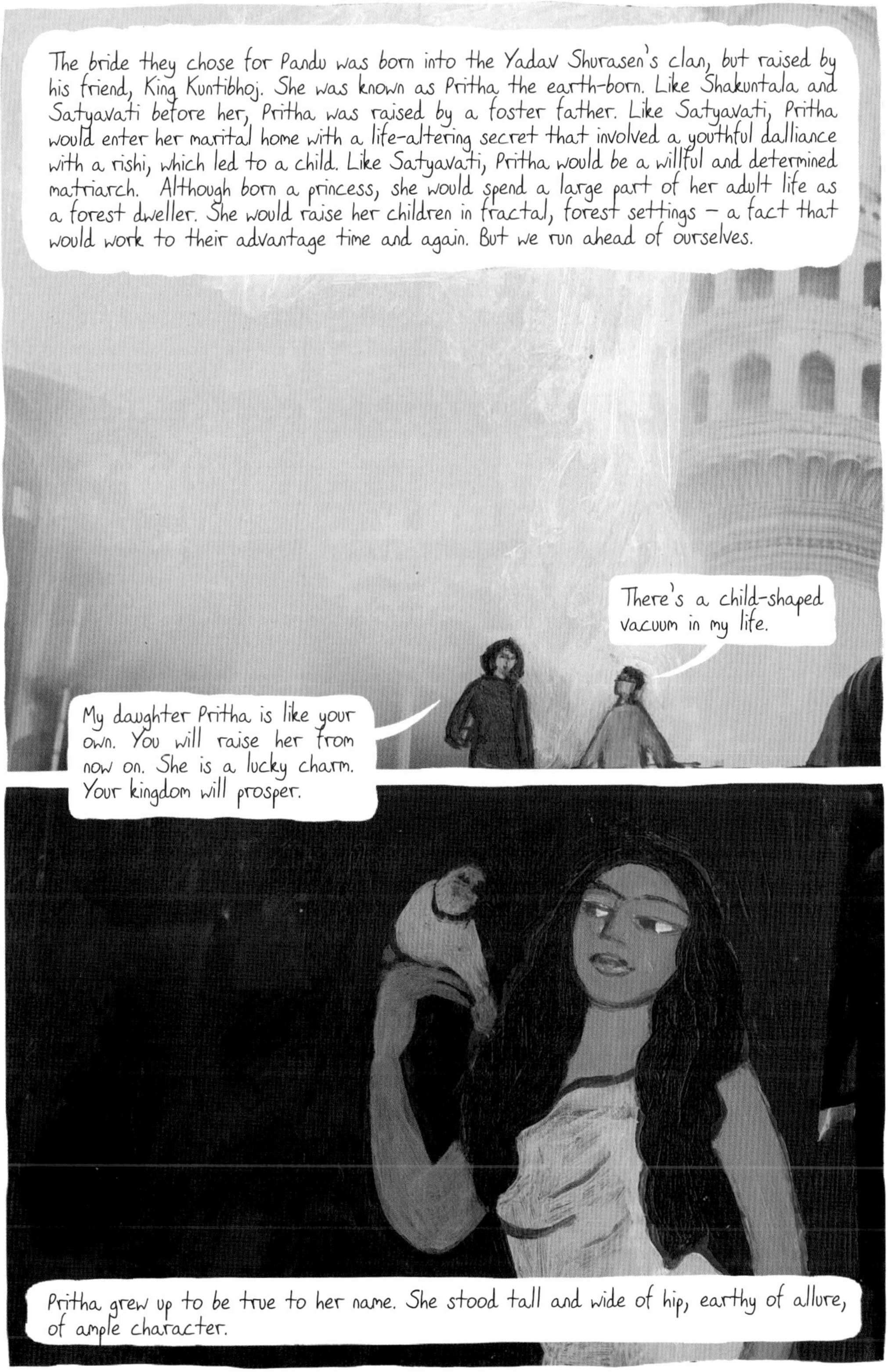
The bride they chose for Pandu was born into the Yadav Shurasen's clan, but raised by his friend, King Kuntibhoj. She was known as Pritha the earth-born. Like Shakuntala and Satyavati before her, Pritha was raised by a foster father. Like Satyavati, Pritha would enter her marital home with a life-altering secret that involved a youthful dalliance with a rishi, which led to a child. Like Satyavati, Pritha would be a willful and determined matriarch. Although born a princess, she would spend a large part of her adult life as a forest dweller. She would raise her children in fractal, forest settings – a fact that would work to their advantage time and again. But we run ahead of ourselves.
My daughter Pritha is like your own. You will raise her from now on. She is a lucky charm. Your kingdom will prosper.
There's a child-shaped vacuum in my life.
Pritha grew up to be true to her name. She stood tall and wide of hip, earthy of allure, of ample character.

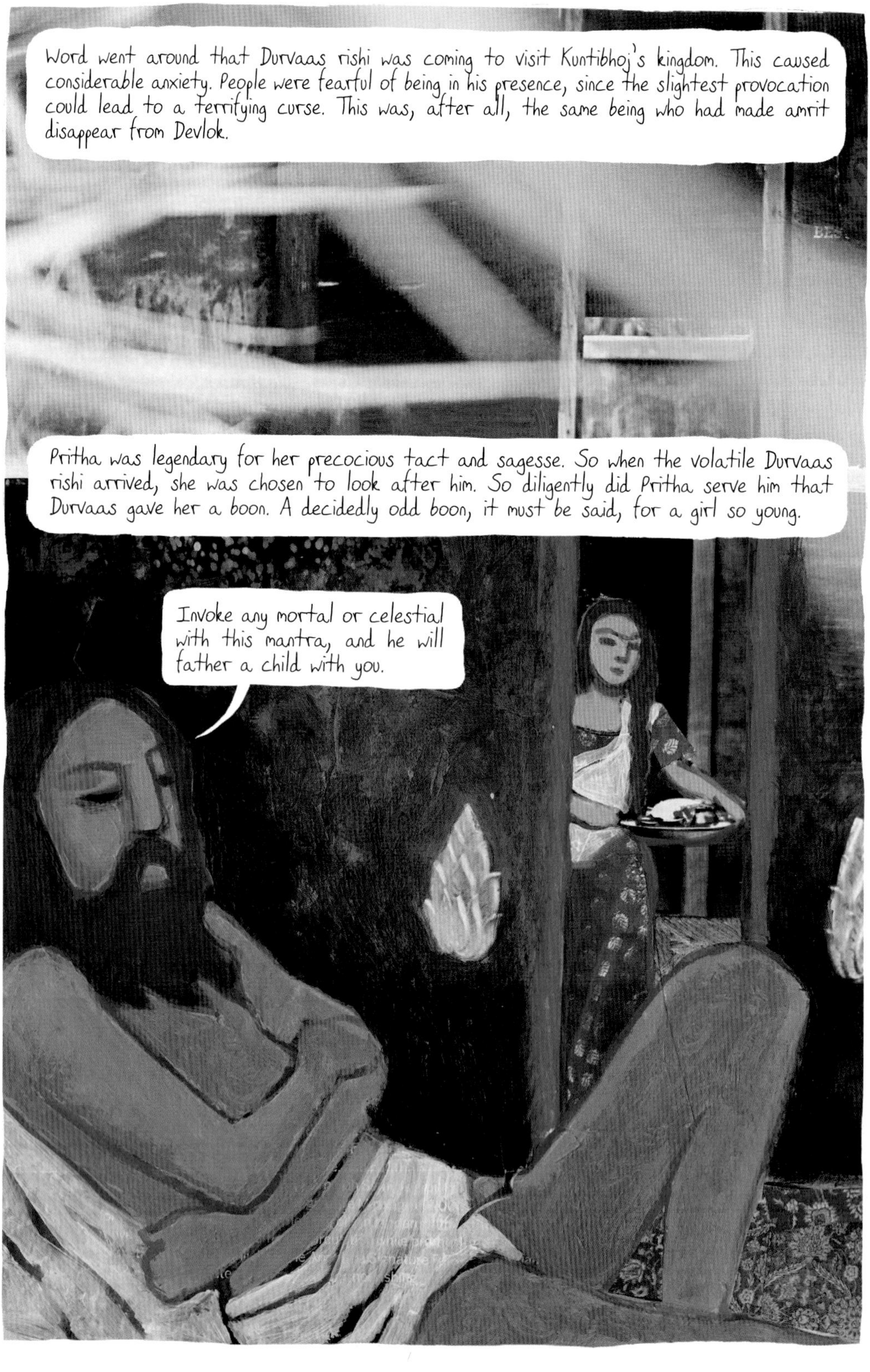
Word went around that Durvaas rishi was coming to visit Kuntibhoj's kingdom. This caused considerable anxiety. People were fearful of being in his presence, since the slightest provocation could lead to a terrifying curse. This was, after all, the same being who had made amrit disappear from Devlok.
Pritha was legendary for her precocious tact and sagesse. So when the volatile Durvaas rishi arrived, she was chosen to look after him. So diligently did Pritha serve him that Durvaas gave her a boon. A decidedly odd boon, it must be said, for a girl so young.
Invoke any mortal or celestial with this mantra, and he will father a child with you.

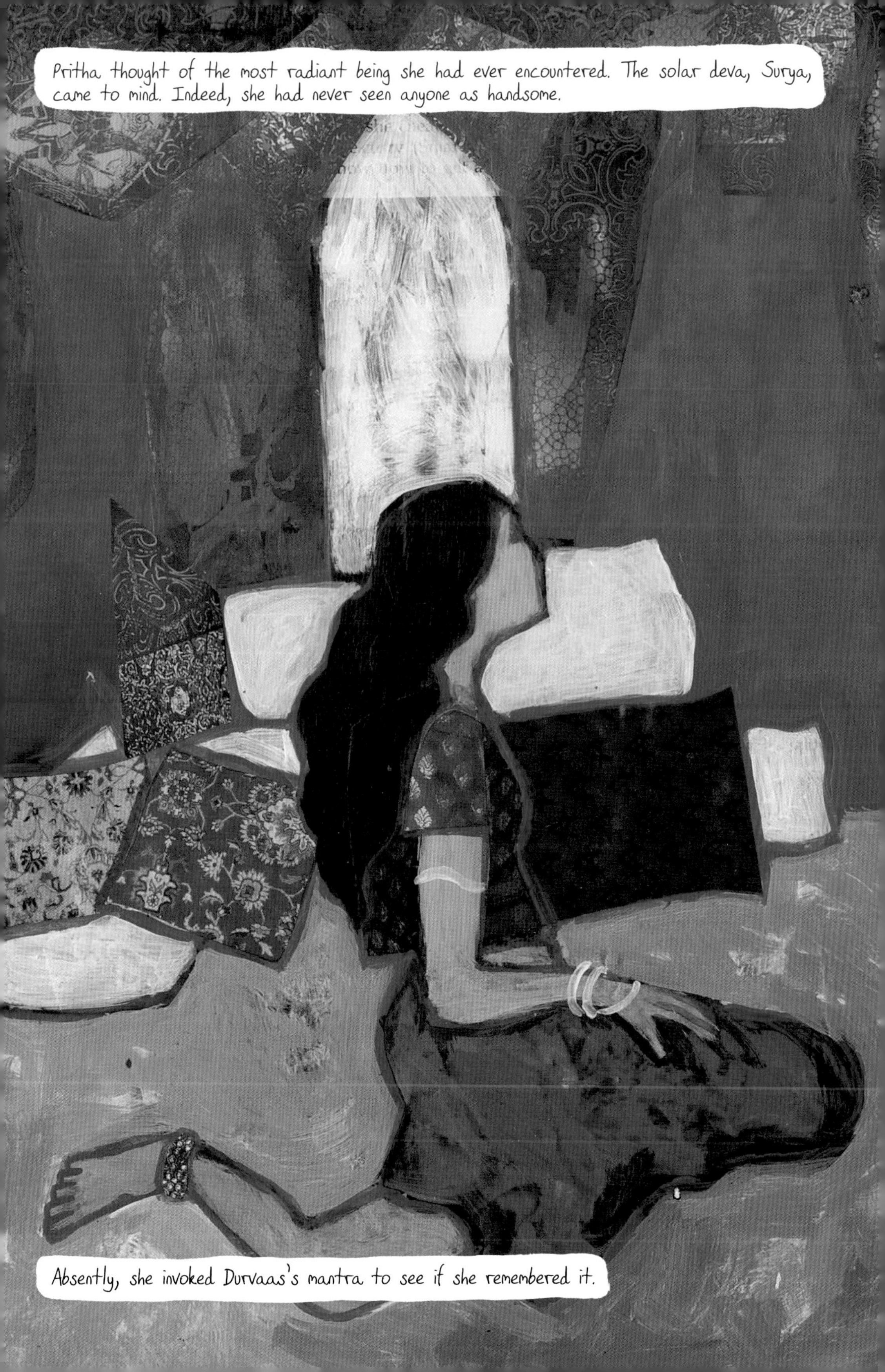
Pritha thought of the most radiant being she had ever encountered. The solar deva, Surya, came to mind. Indeed, she had never seen anyone as handsome.
Absently, she invoked Durvaas's mantra to see if she remembered it.

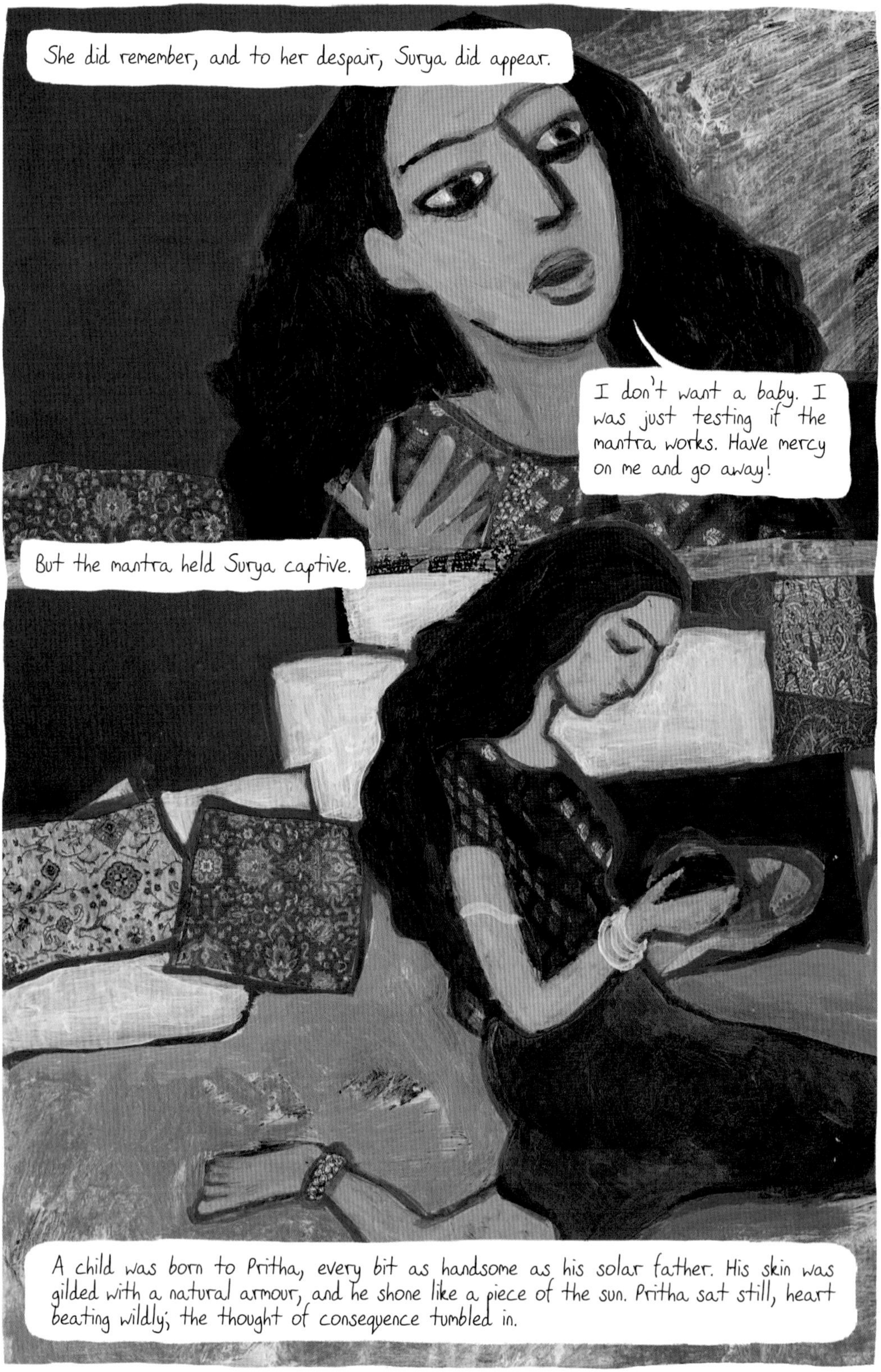
She did remember, and to her despair, Surya did appear.
I don't want a baby. I was just testing if the mantra works. Have mercy on me and go away!
But the mantra held Surya captive.
A child was born to Pritha, every bit as handsome as his solar father. His skin was gilded with a natural armour, and he shone like a piece of the sun. Pritha sat still, heart beating wildly; the thought of consequence tumbled in.

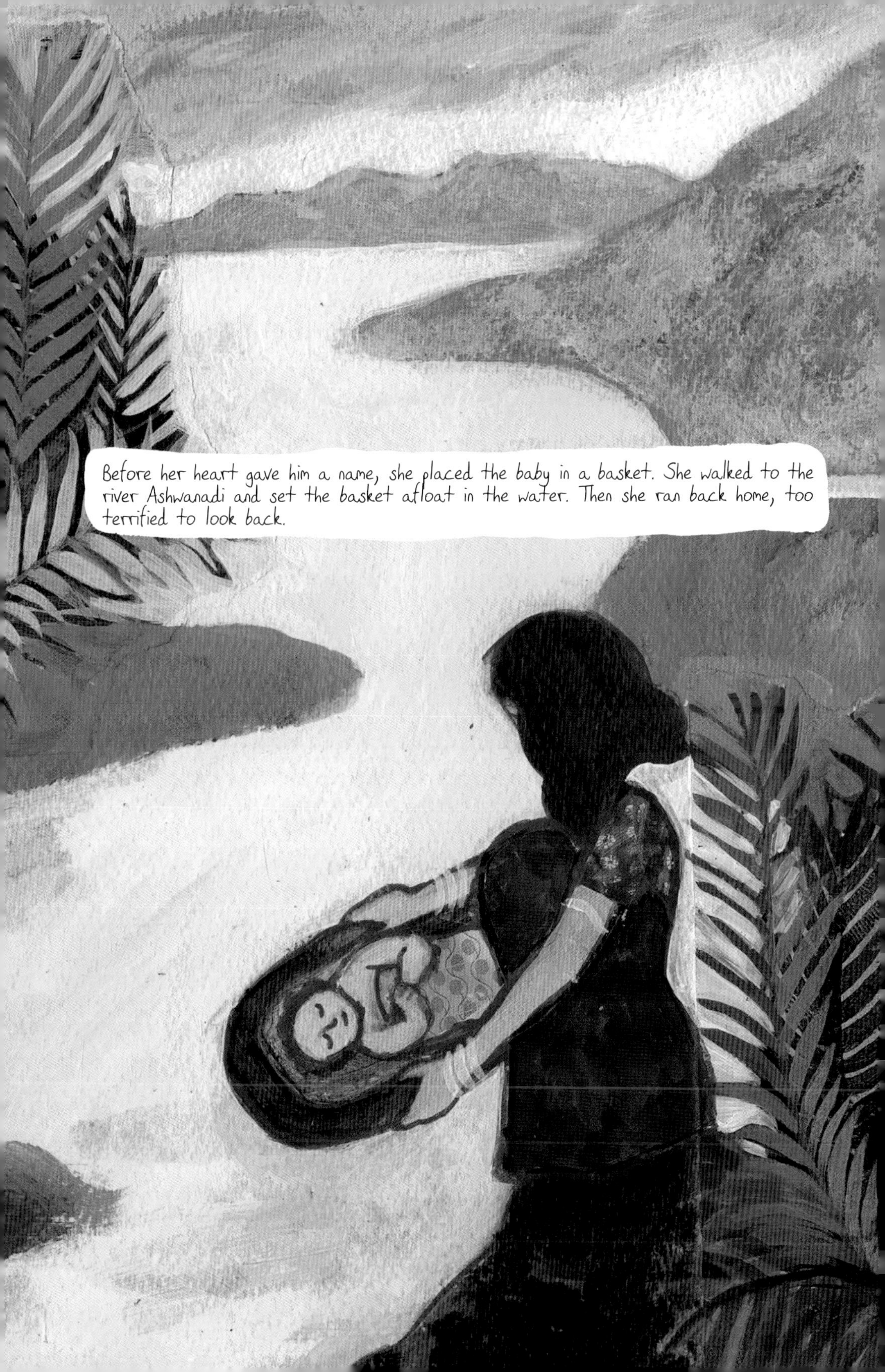
Before her heart gave him a name, she placed the baby in a basket. She walked to the river Ashwanadi and set the basket afloat in the water. Then she ran back home, too terrified to look back.

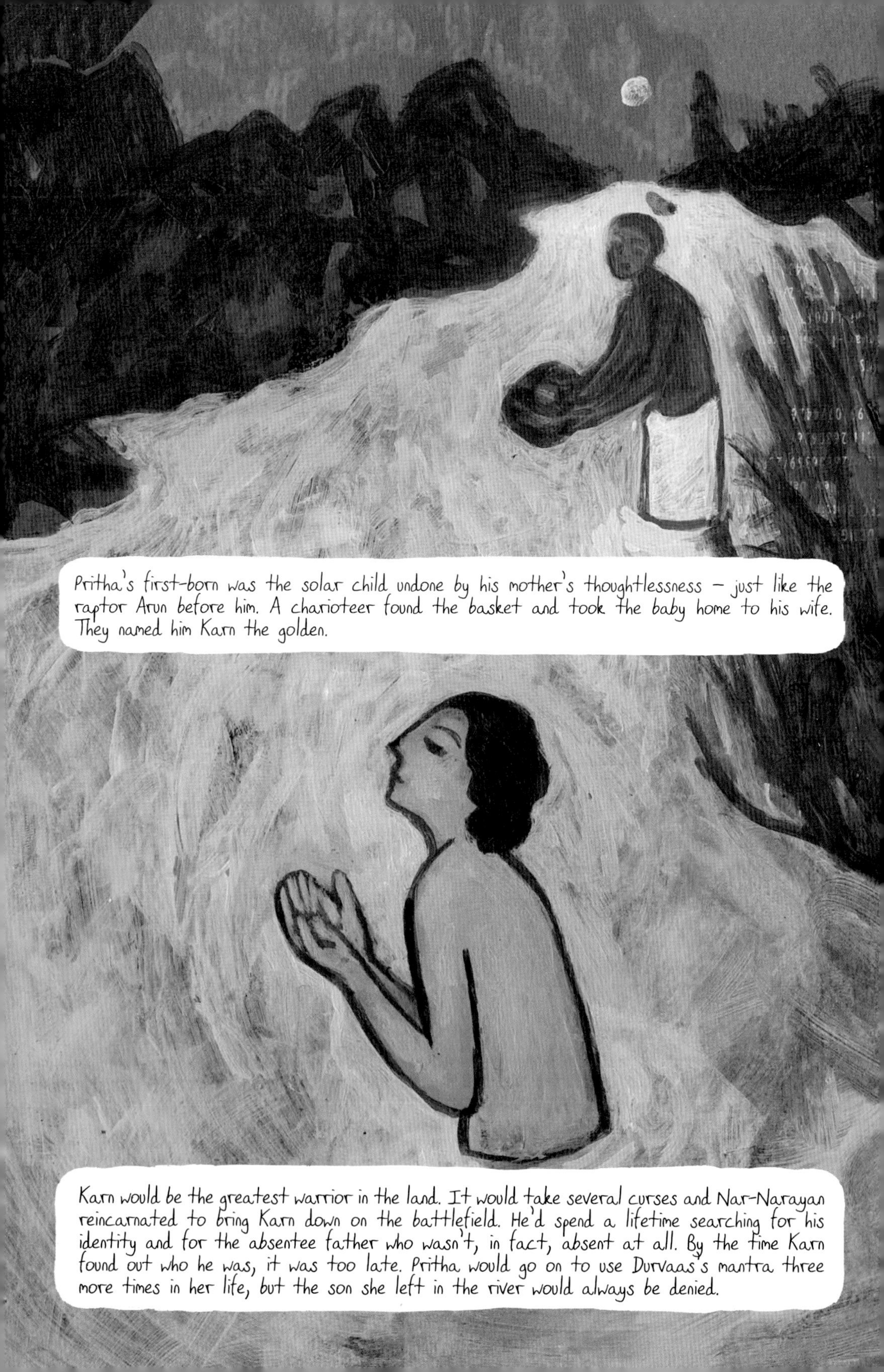
Pritha's first-born was the solar child undone by his mother's thoughtlessness – just like the raptor Arun before him. A charioteer found the basket and took the baby home to his wife. They named him Karn the golden.
Karn would be the greatest warrior in the land. It would take several curses and Nar-Narayan reincarnated to bring Karn down on the battlefield. He'd spend a lifetime searching for his identity and for the absentee father who wasn't, in fact, absent at all. By the time Karn found out who he was, it was too late. Pritha would go on to use Durvaas's mantra three more times in her life, but the son she left in the river would always be denied.

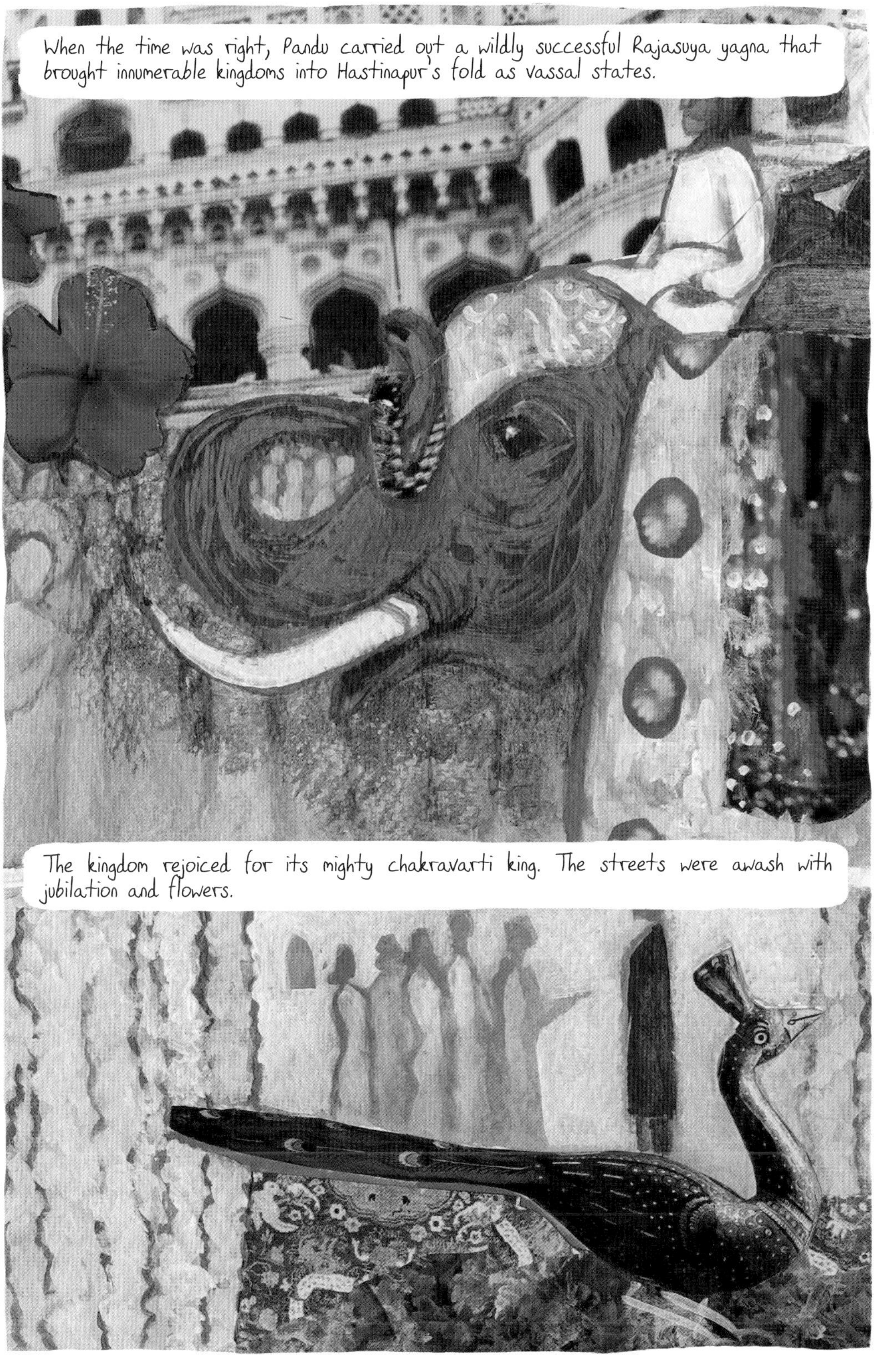
When the time was right, Pandu carried out a wildly successful Rajasuya yagna that brought innumerable kingdoms into Hastinapur's fold as vassal states.
The kingdom rejoiced for its mighty chakravarti king. The streets were awash with jubilation and flowers.

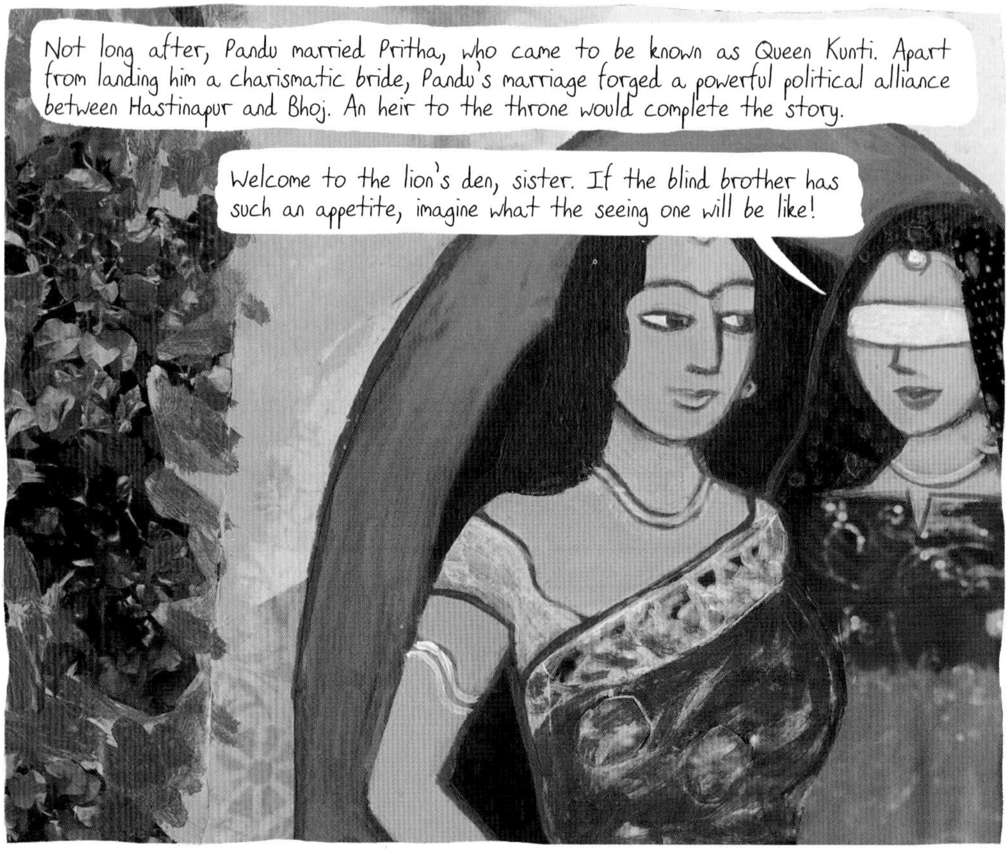
Not long after, Pandu married Pritha, who came to be known as Queen Kunti. Apart from landing him a charismatic bride, Pandu's marriage forged a powerful political alliance between Hastinapur and Bhoj. An heir to the throne would complete the story.
Welcome to the lion's den, sister. If the blind brother has such an appetite, imagine what the seeing one will be like!

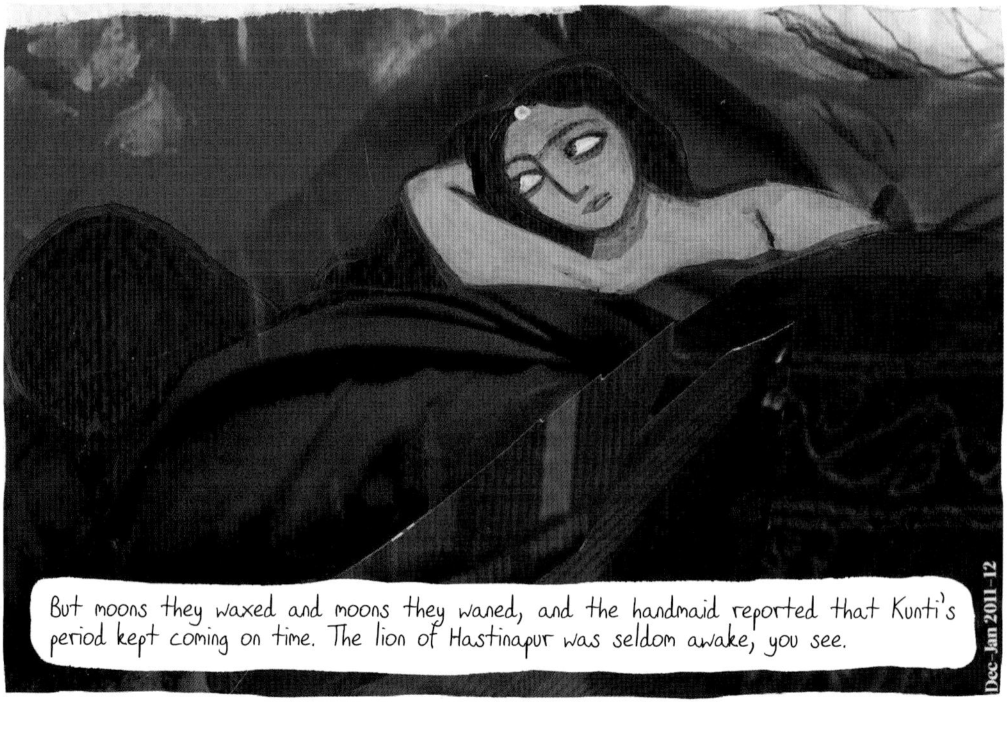
But moons they waxed and moons they waned, and the handmaid reported that Kunti's period kept coming on time. The lion of Hastinapur was seldom awake, you see.
Dec–Jan 2011-12

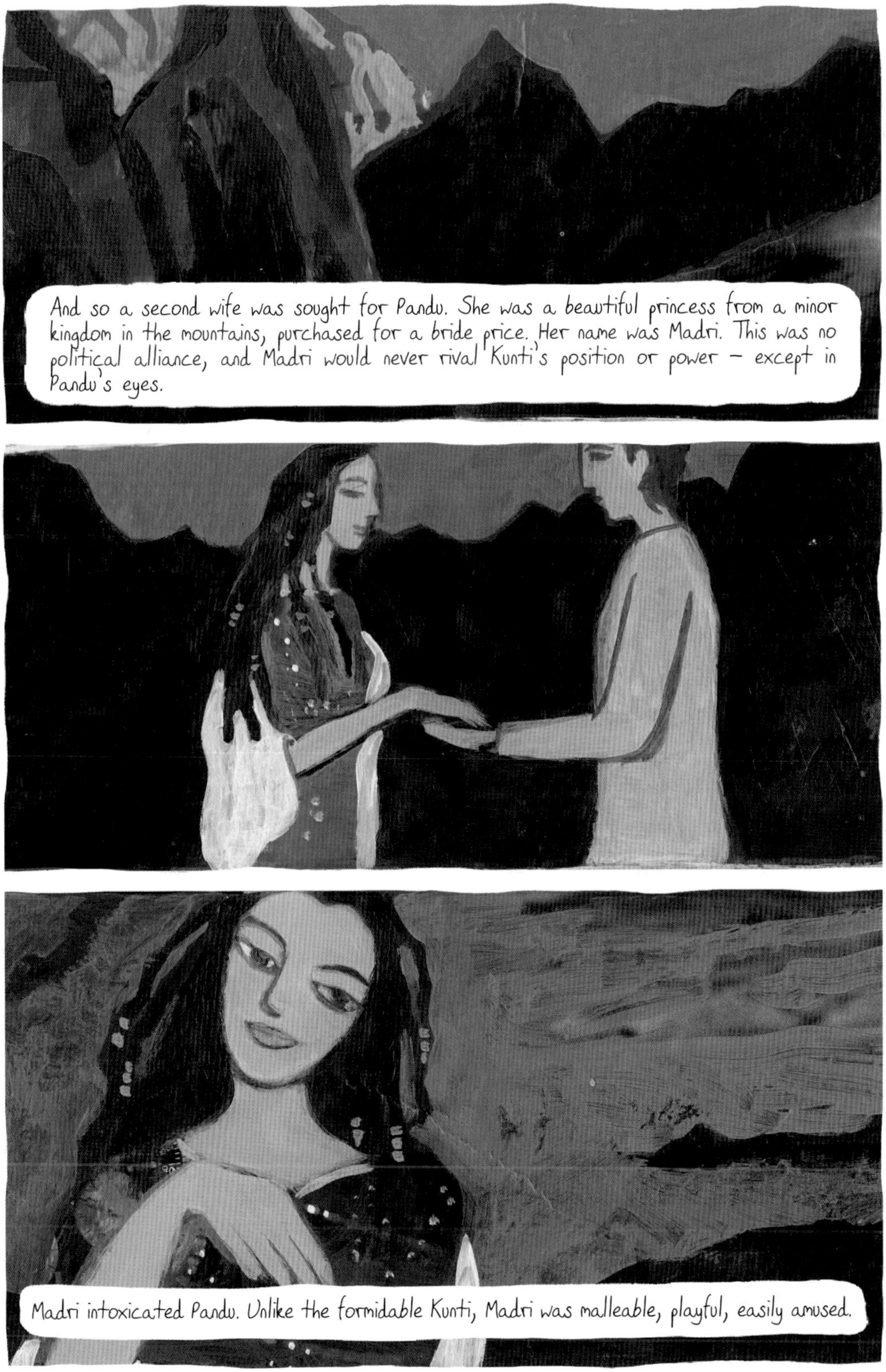
And so a second wife was sought for Pandu. She was a beautiful princess from a minor kingdom in the mountains, purchased for a bride price. Her name was Madri. This was no political alliance, and Madri would never rival Kunti's position or power – except in Pandu's eyes.
Madri intoxicated Pandu. Unlike the formidable Kunti, Madri was malleable, playful, easily amused.

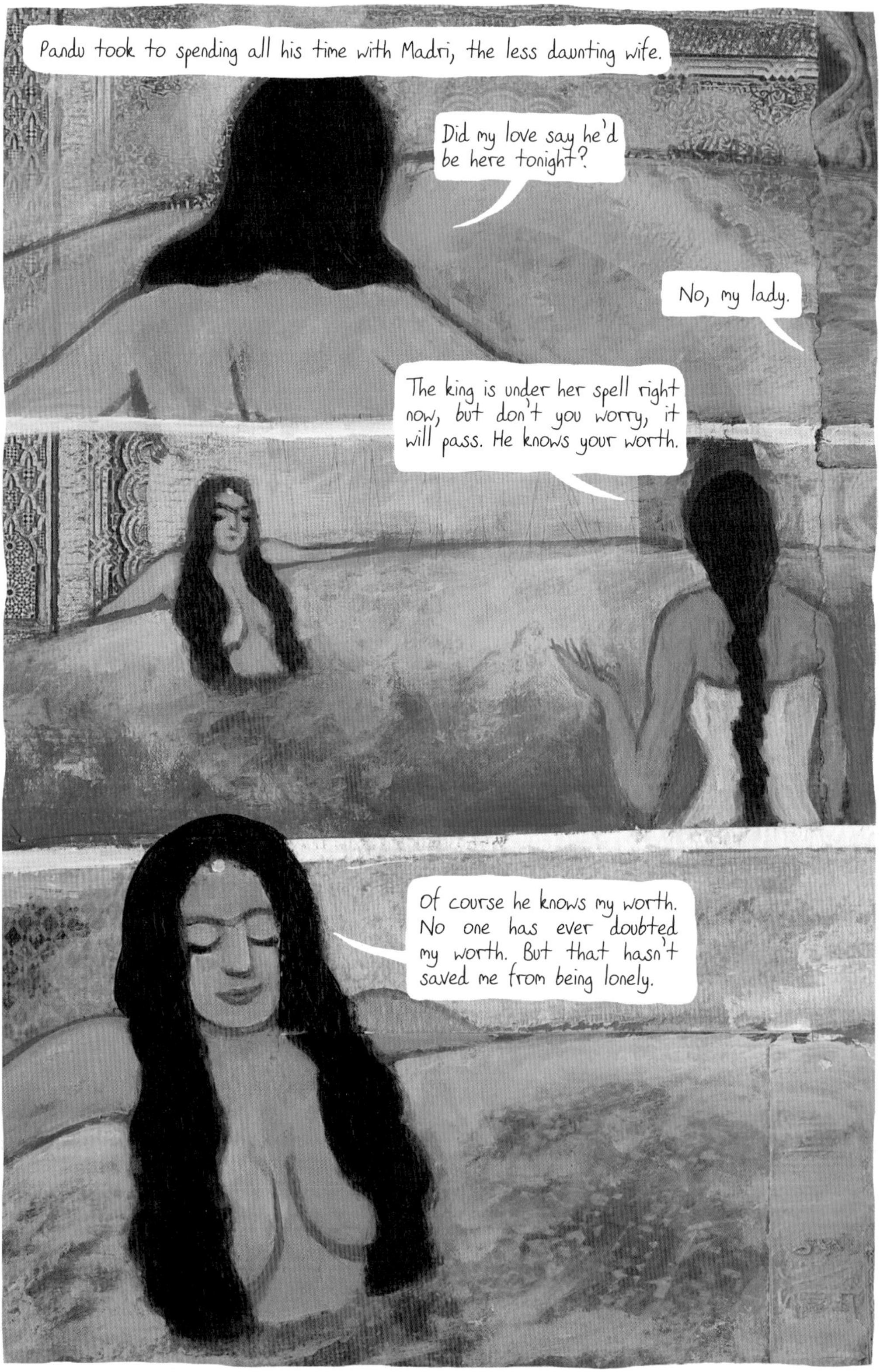
Pandu took to spending all his time with Madri, the less daunting wife.
Did my love say he'd be here tonight?
No, my lady.
The king is under her spell right now, but don't you worry, it will pass. He knows your worth.
Of course he knows my worth. No one has ever doubted my worth. But that hasn't saved me from being lonely.

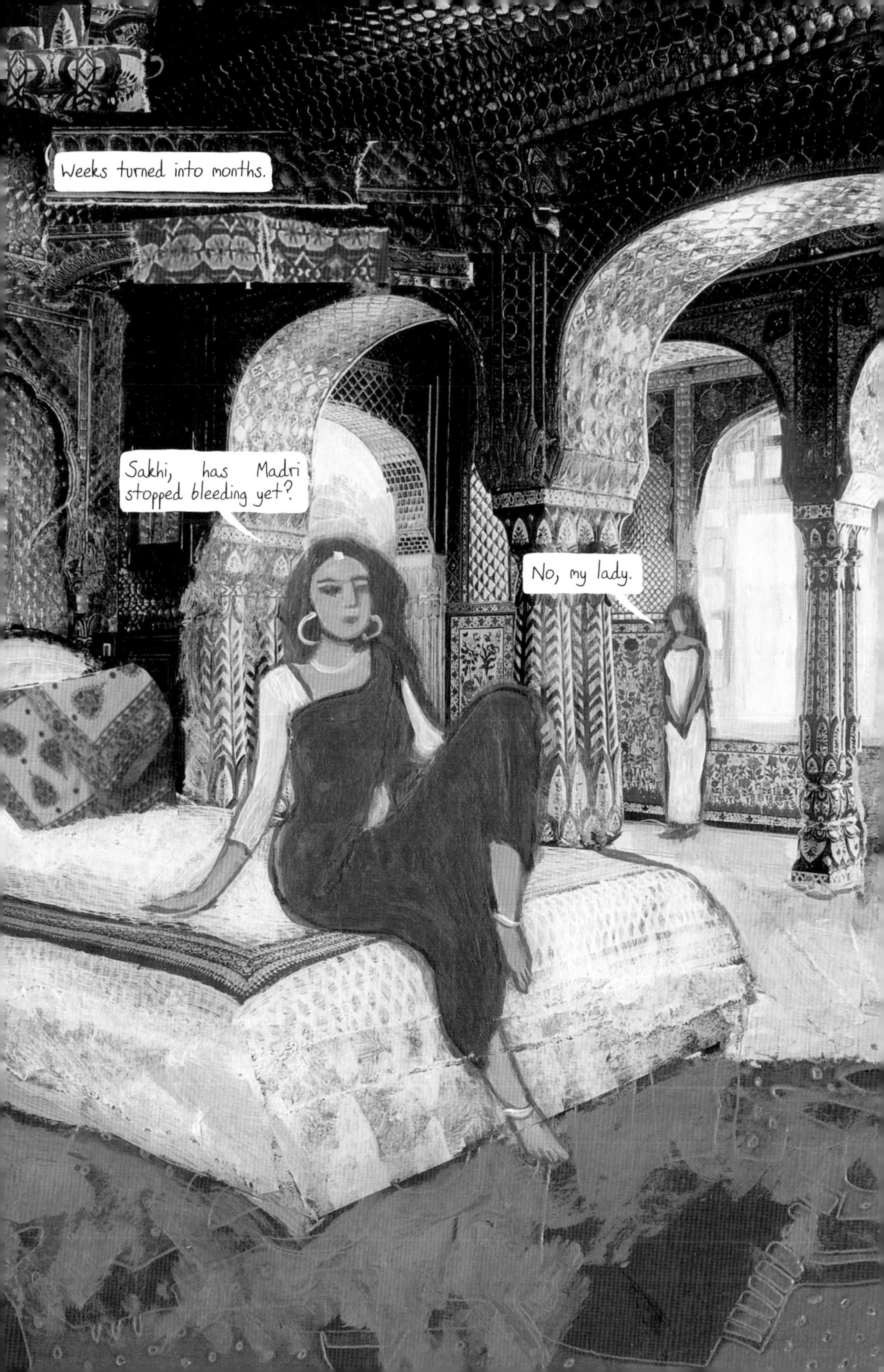
Weeks turned into months.
Sakhi, has Madri stopped bleeding yet?
No, my lady.

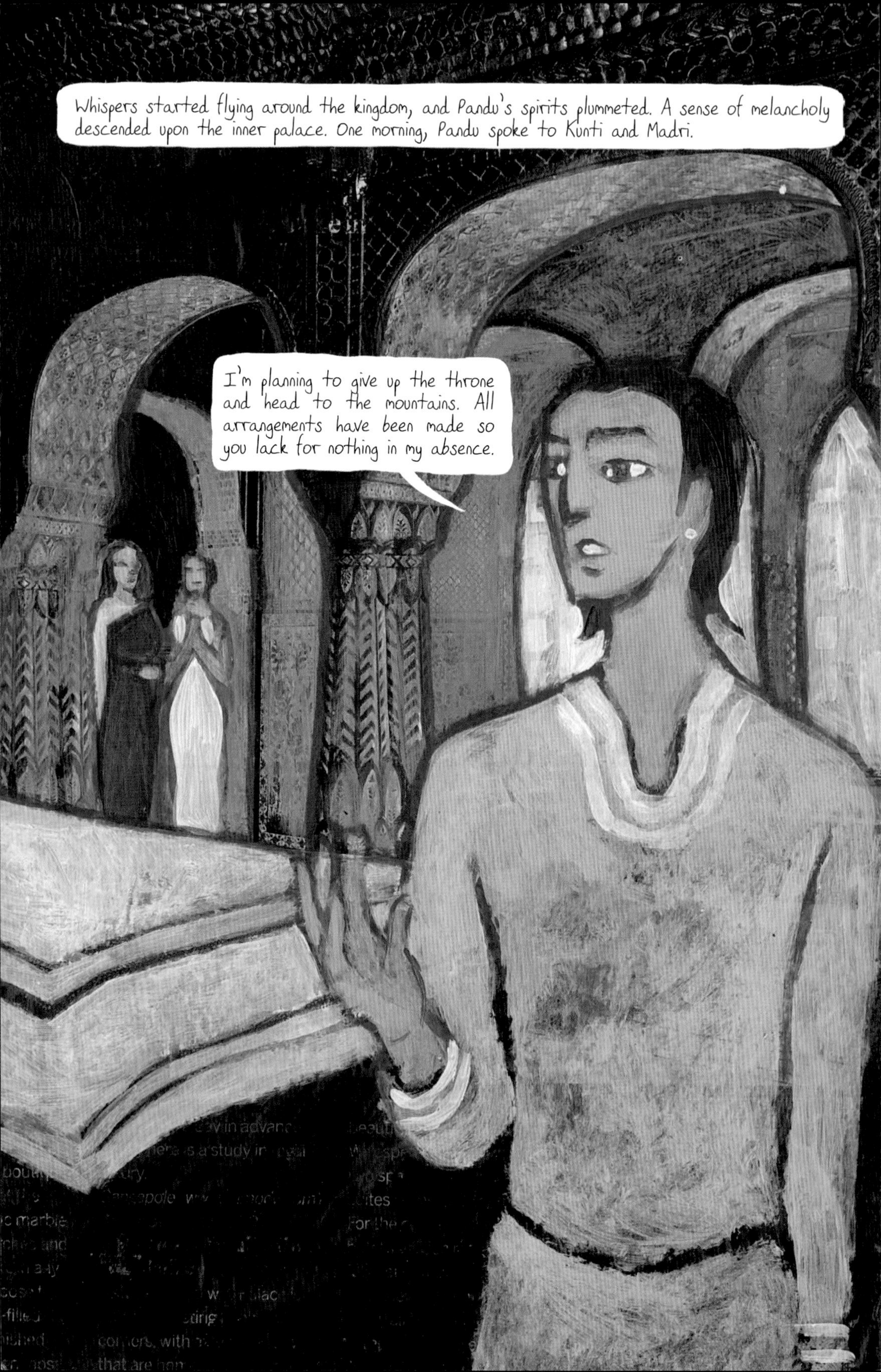
Whispers started flying around the kingdom, and Pandu's spirits plummeted. A sense of melancholy descended upon the inner palace. One morning, Pandu spoke to Kunti and Madri.
I'm planning to give up the throne and head to the mountains. All arrangements have been made so you lack for nothing in my absence.

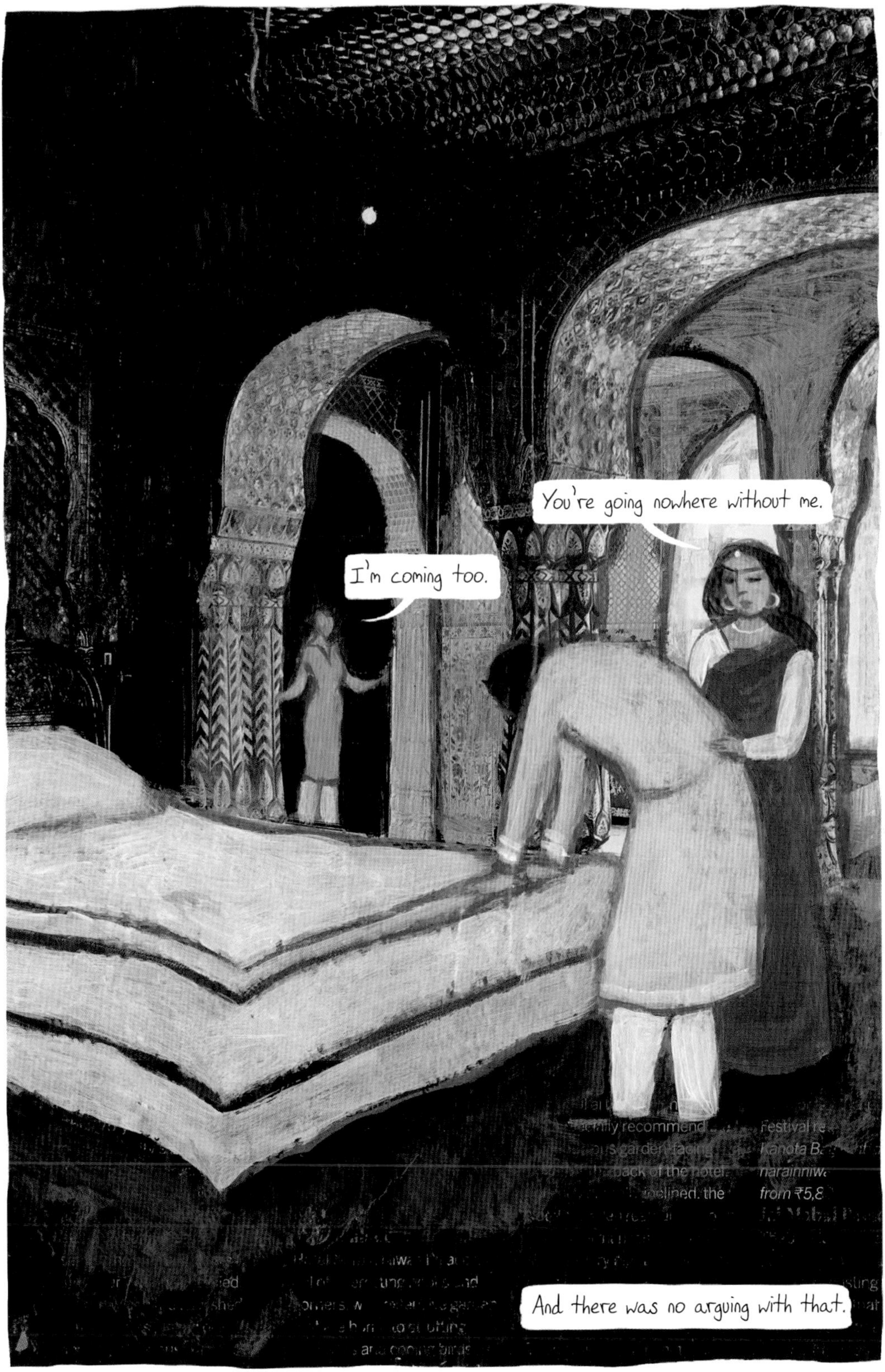
I'm coming too.
You're going nowhere without me.
And there was no arguing with that.

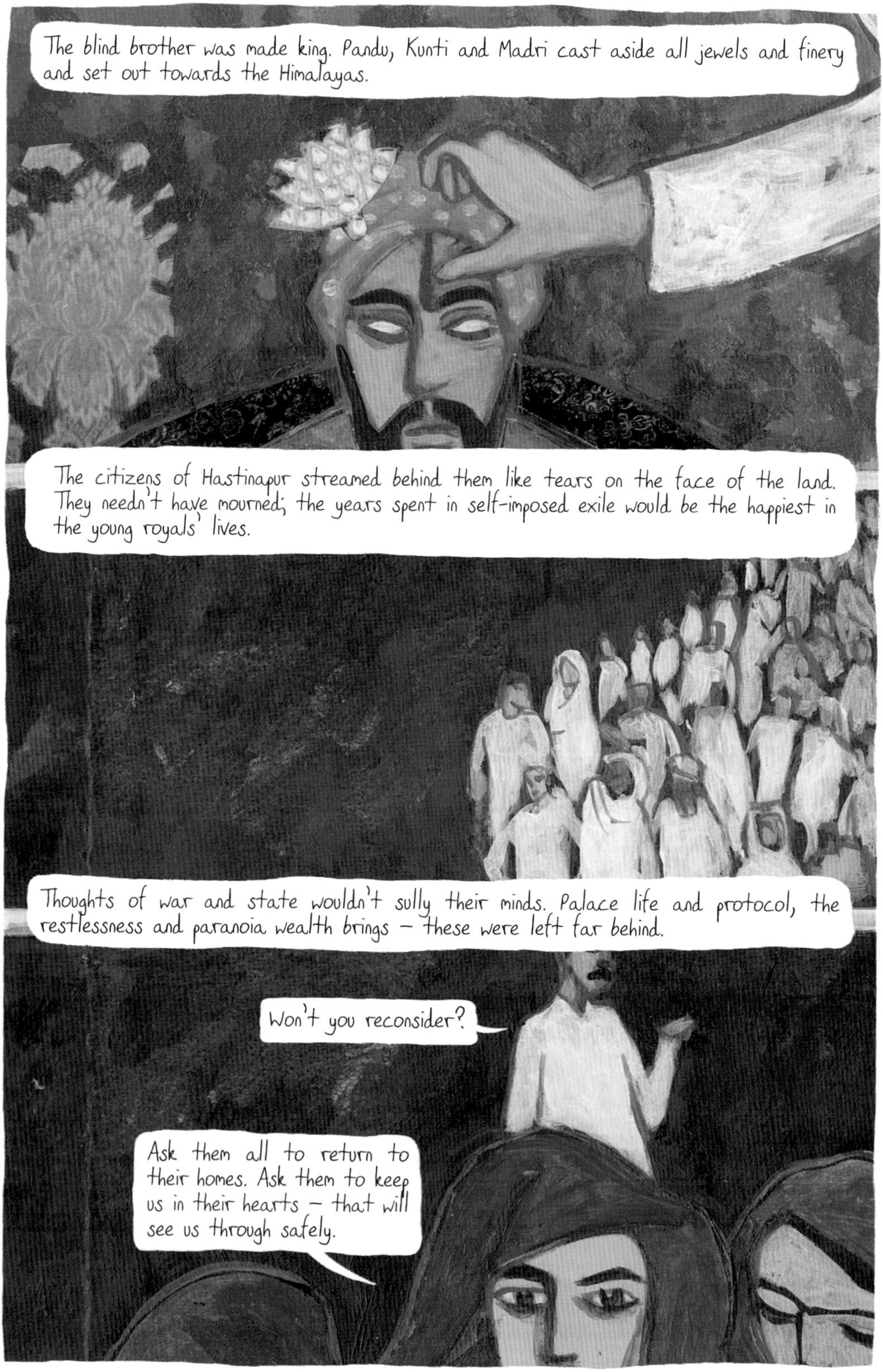
The blind brother was made king. Pandu, Kunti and Madri cast aside all jewels and finery and set out towards the Himalayas.
The citizens of Hastinapur streamed behind them like tears on the face of the land. They needn't have mourned; the years spent in self-imposed exile would be the happiest in the young royals' lives.
Thoughts of war and state wouldn't sully their minds. Palace life and protocol, the restlessness and paranoia wealth brings – these were left far behind.
Won't you reconsider?
Ask them all to return to their homes. Ask them to keep us in their hearts – that will see us through safely.

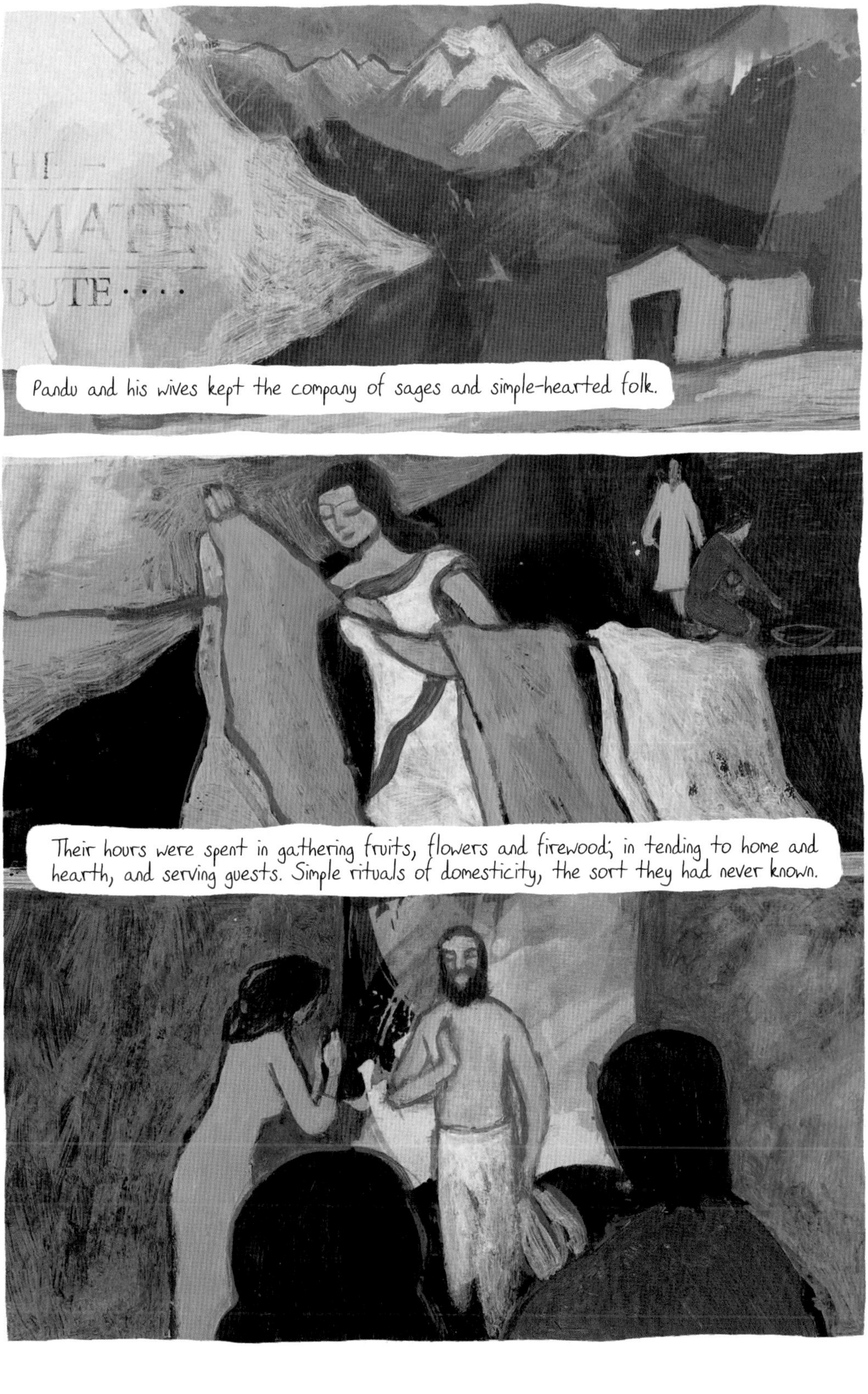
Pandu and his wives kept the company of sages and simple-hearted folk.
Their hours were spent in gathering fruits, flowers and firewood; in tending to home and hearth, and serving guests. Simple rituals of domesticity, the sort they had never known.

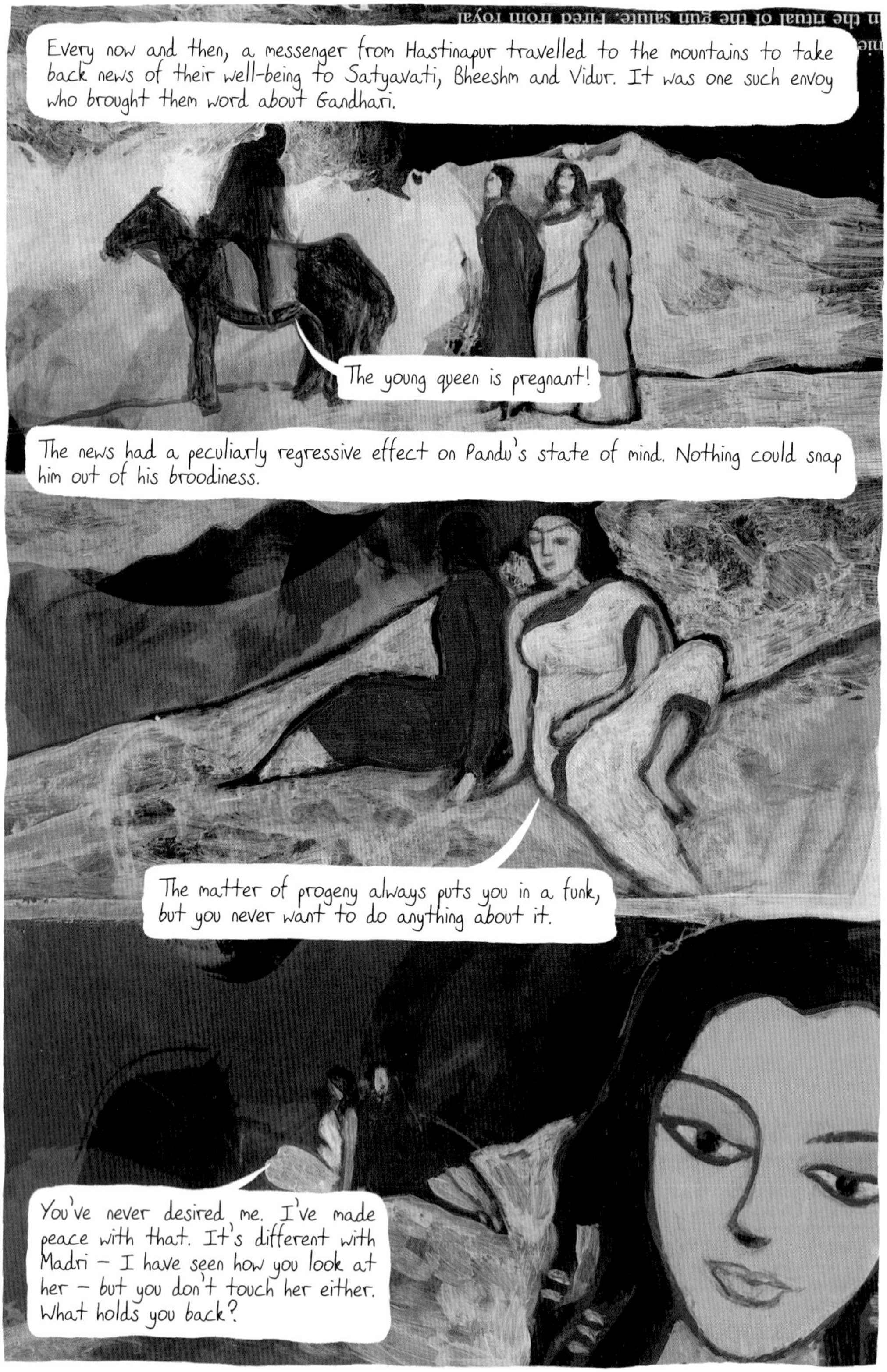
Every now and then, a messenger from Hastinapur travelled to the mountains to take back news of their well-being to Satyavati, Bheeshm and Vidur. It was one such envoy who brought them word about Gandhari.
The young queen is pregnant!
The news had a peculiarly regressive effect on Pandu's state of mind. Nothing could snap him out of his broodiness.
The matter of progeny always puts you in a funk, but you never want to do anything about it.
You've never desired me. I've made peace with that. It's different with Madri – I have seen how you look at her – but you don't touch her either. What holds you back?

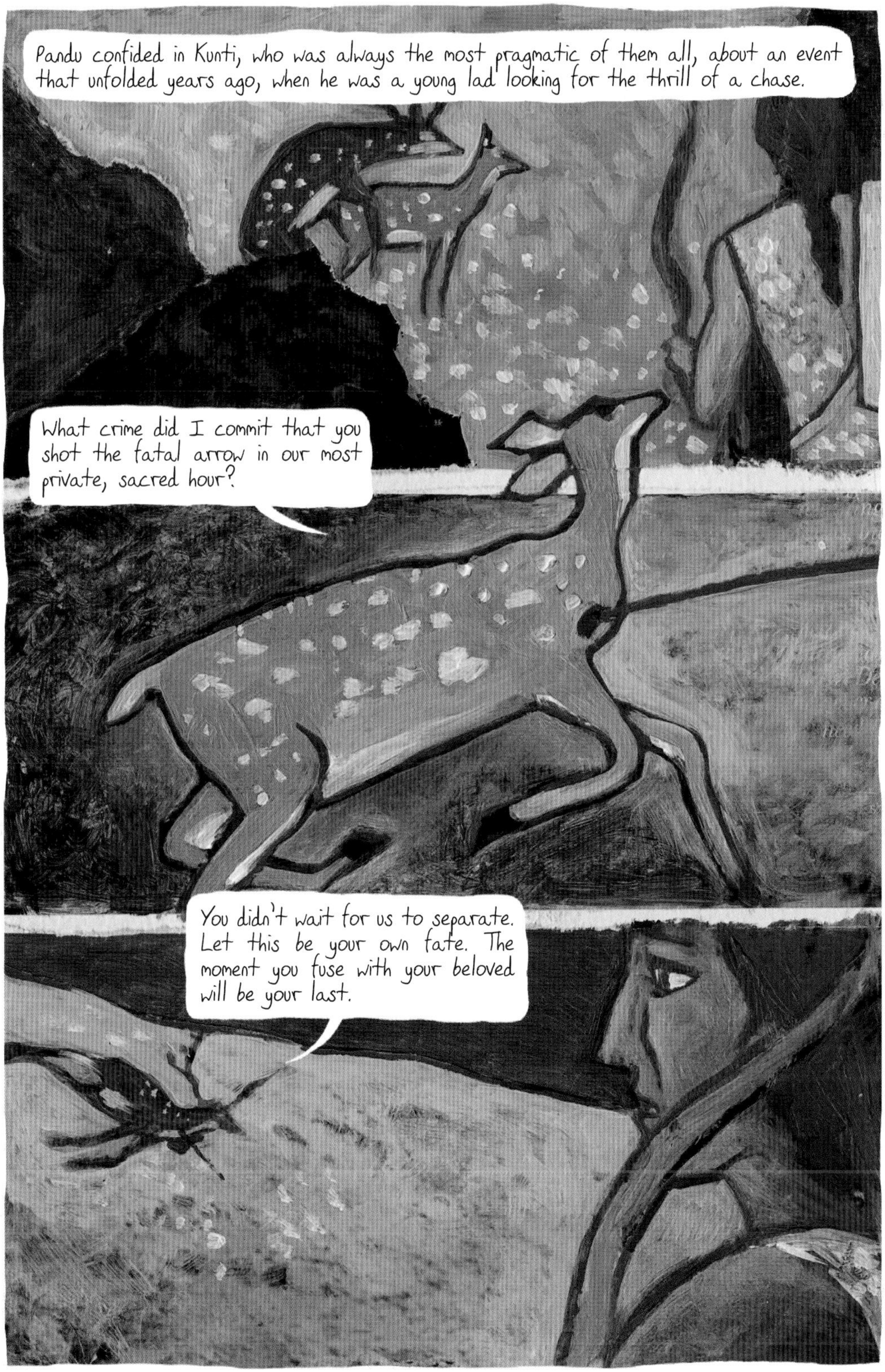
Pandu confided in Kunti, who was always the most pragmatic of them all, about an event that unfolded years ago, when he was a young lad looking for the thrill of a chase.
What crime did I commit that you shot the fatal arrow in our most private, sacred hour?
You didn't wait for us to separate. Let this be your own fate. The moment you fuse with your beloved will be your last.

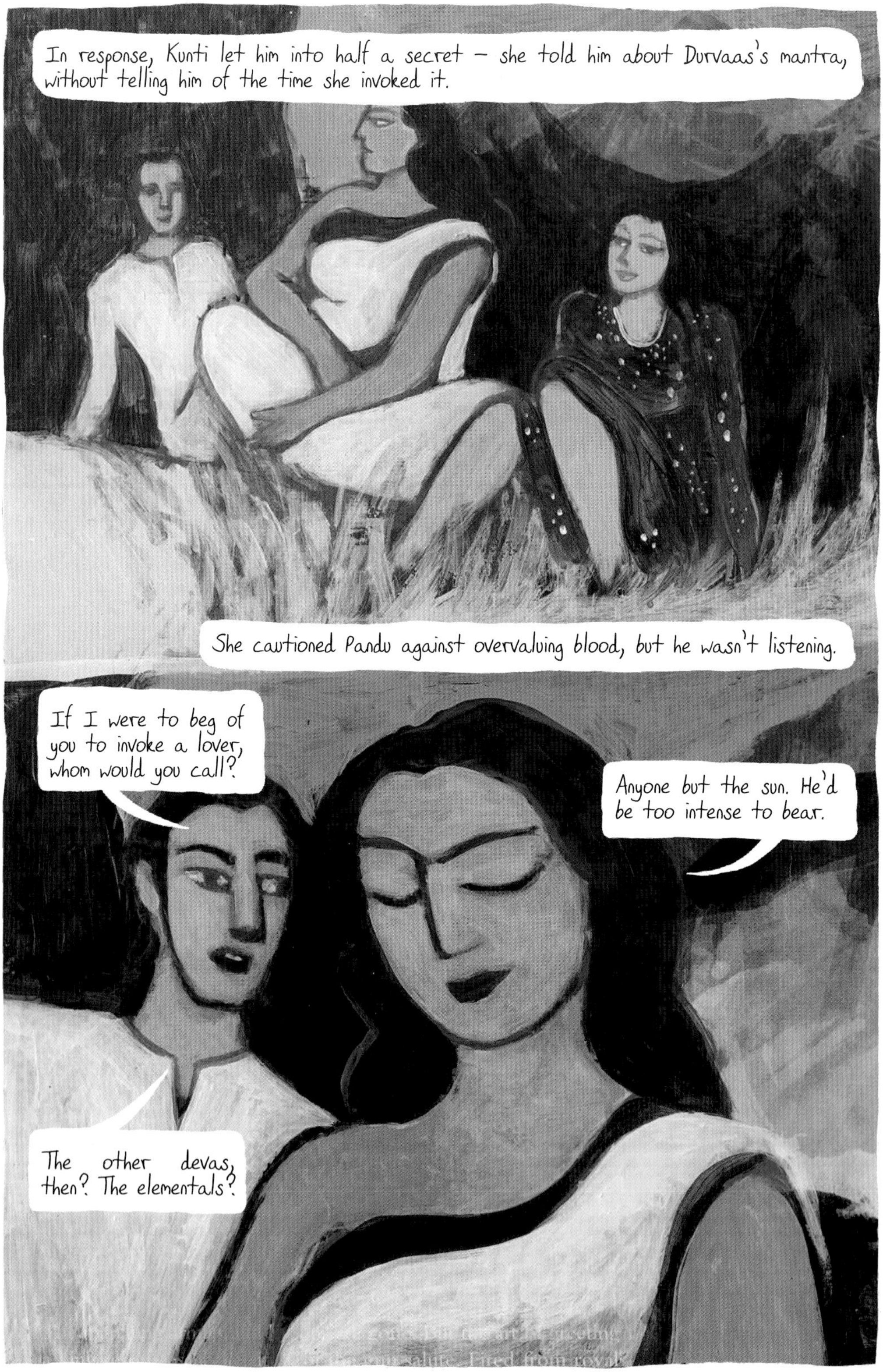
In response, Kunti let him into half a secret – she told him about Durvaas's mantra, without telling him of the time she invoked it.
She cautioned Pandu against overvaluing blood, but he wasn't listening.
If I were to beg of you to invoke a lover, whom would you call?
Anyone but the sun. He'd be too intense to bear.
The other devas, then? The elementals?

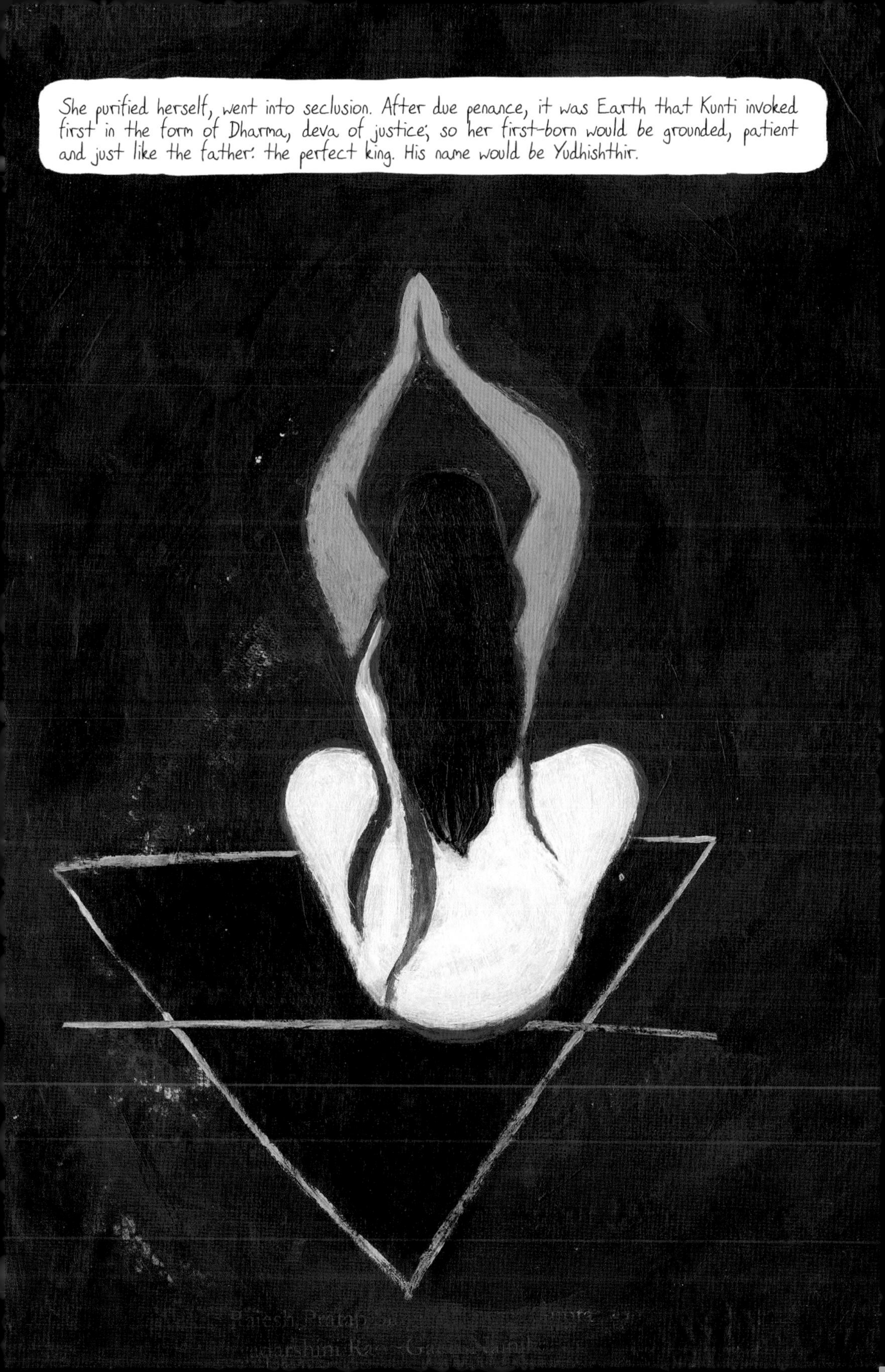
She purified herself, went into seclusion. After due penance, it was Earth that Kunti invoked first in the form of Dharma, deva of justice; so her first-born would be grounded, patient and just like the father: the perfect king. His name would be Yudhishthir.

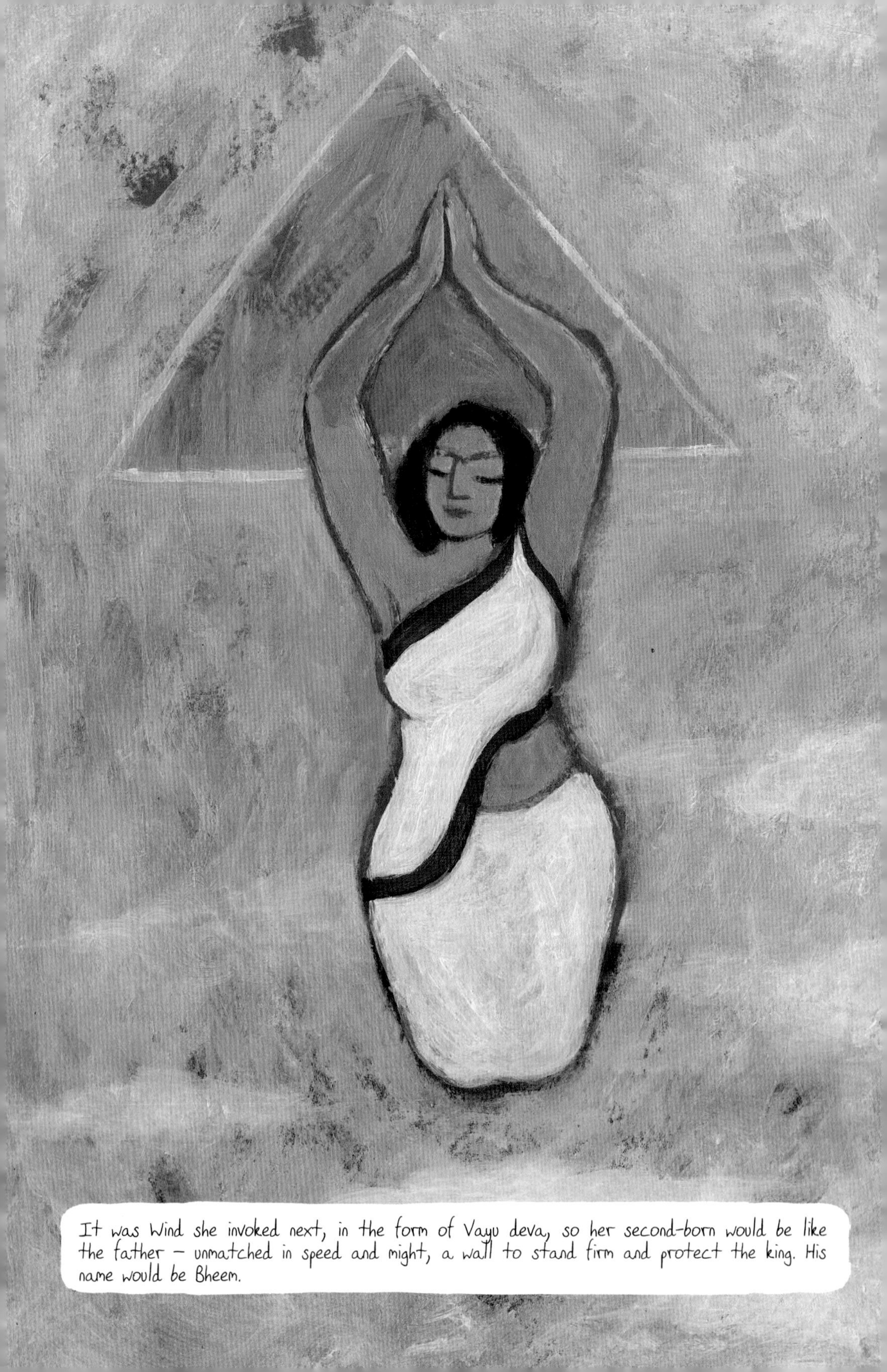
It was Wind she invoked next, in the form of Vayu deva, so her second-born would be like the father – unmatched in speed and might, a wall to stand firm and protect the king. His name would be Bheem.

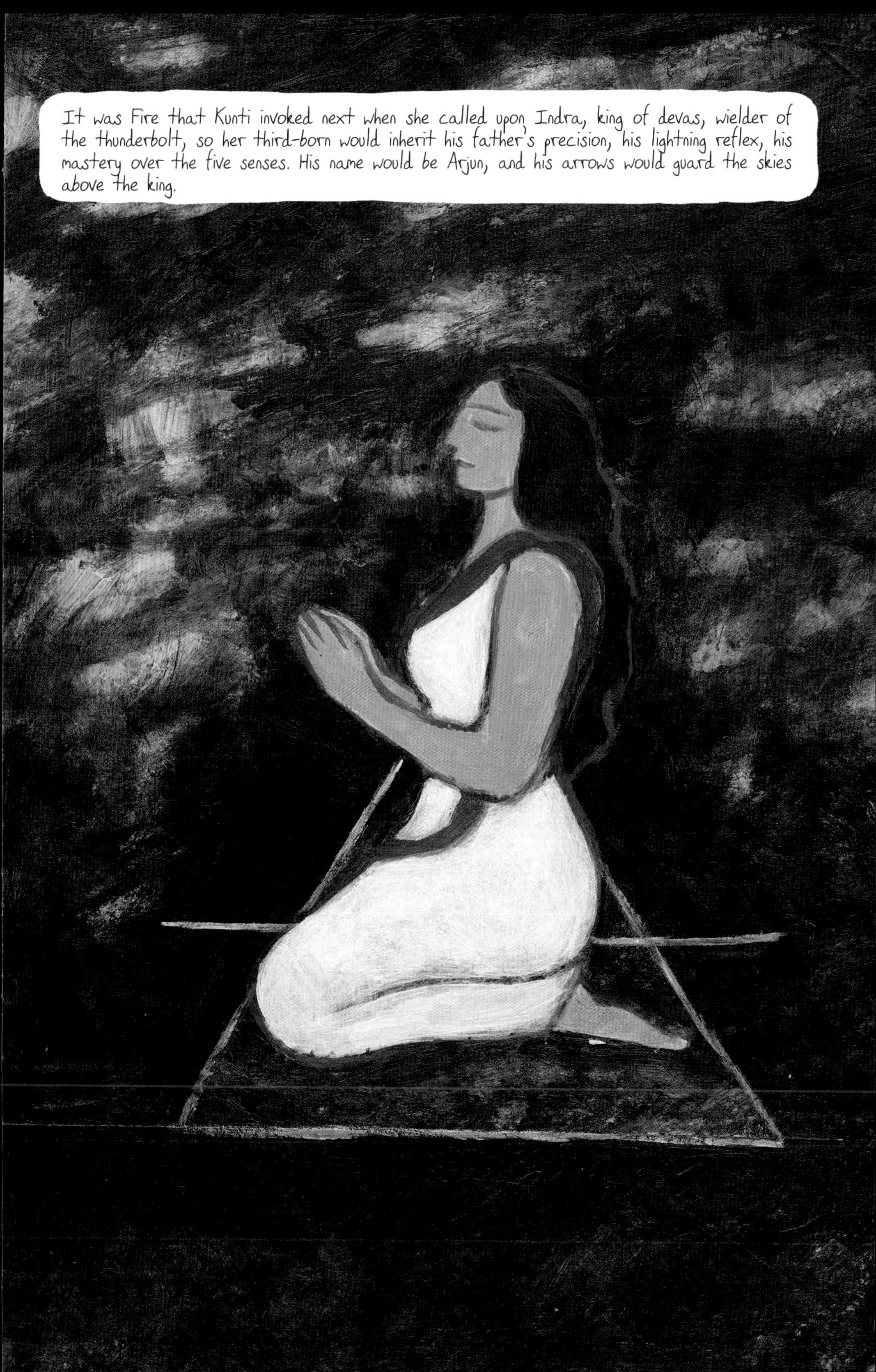
It was Fire that Kunti invoked next when she called upon Indra, king of devas, wielder of the thunderbolt, so her third-born would inherit his father's precision, his lightning reflex, his mastery over the five senses. His name would be Arjun, and his arrows would guard the skies above the king.

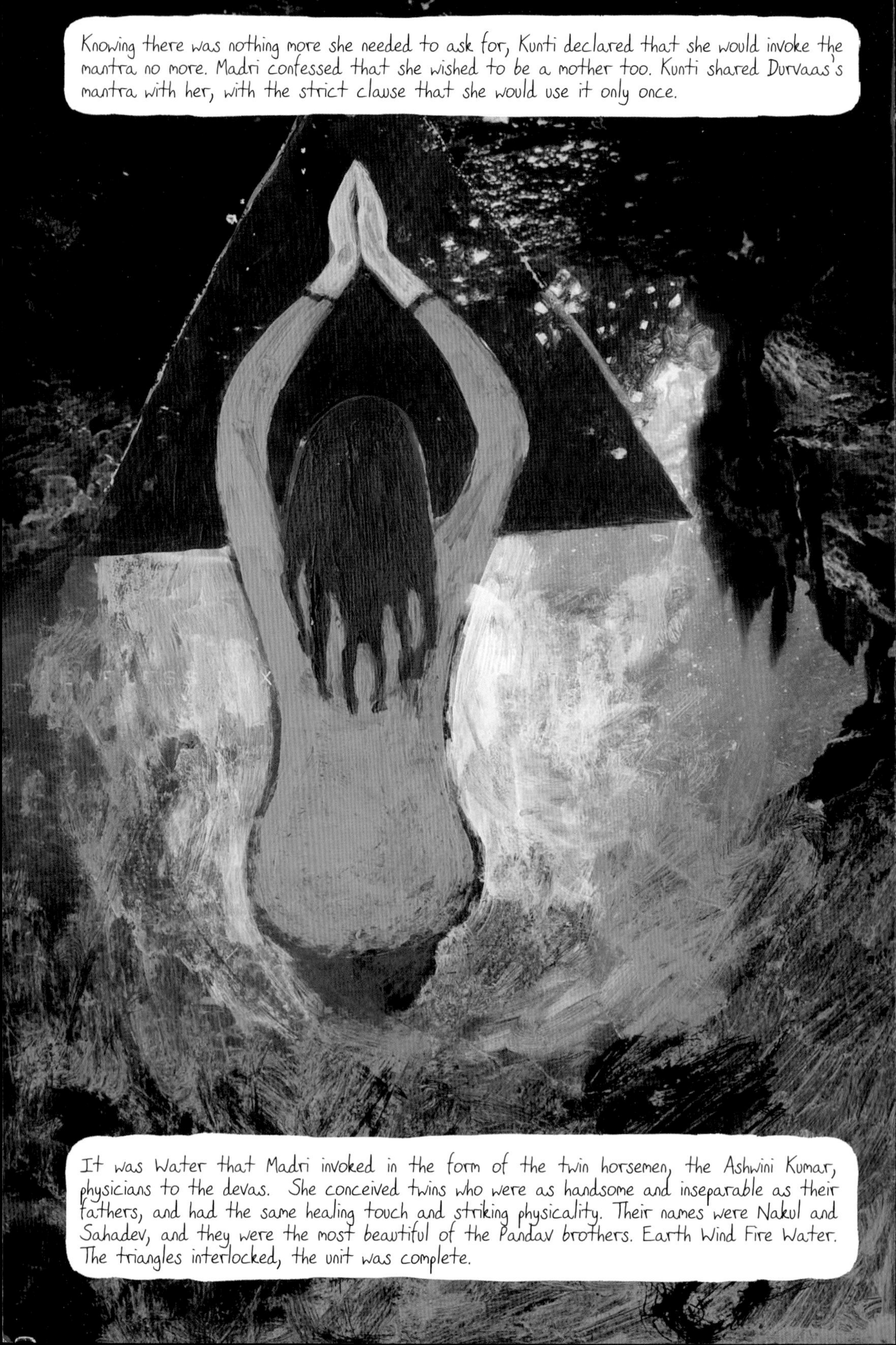
Knowing there was nothing more she needed to ask for, Kunti declared that she would invoke the mantra no more. Madri confessed that she wished to be a mother too. Kunti shared Durvaas's mantra with her, with the strict clause that she would use it only once.
It was Water that Madri invoked in the form of the twin horsemen, the Ashwini Kumar, physicians to the devas. She conceived twins who were as handsome and inseparable as their fathers, and had the same healing touch and striking physicality. Their names were Nakul and Sahadev, and they were the most beautiful of the Pandav brothers. Earth Wind Fire Water. The triangles interlocked, the unit was complete.

REPTILIAN MOTHER
AVIAN MOTHER

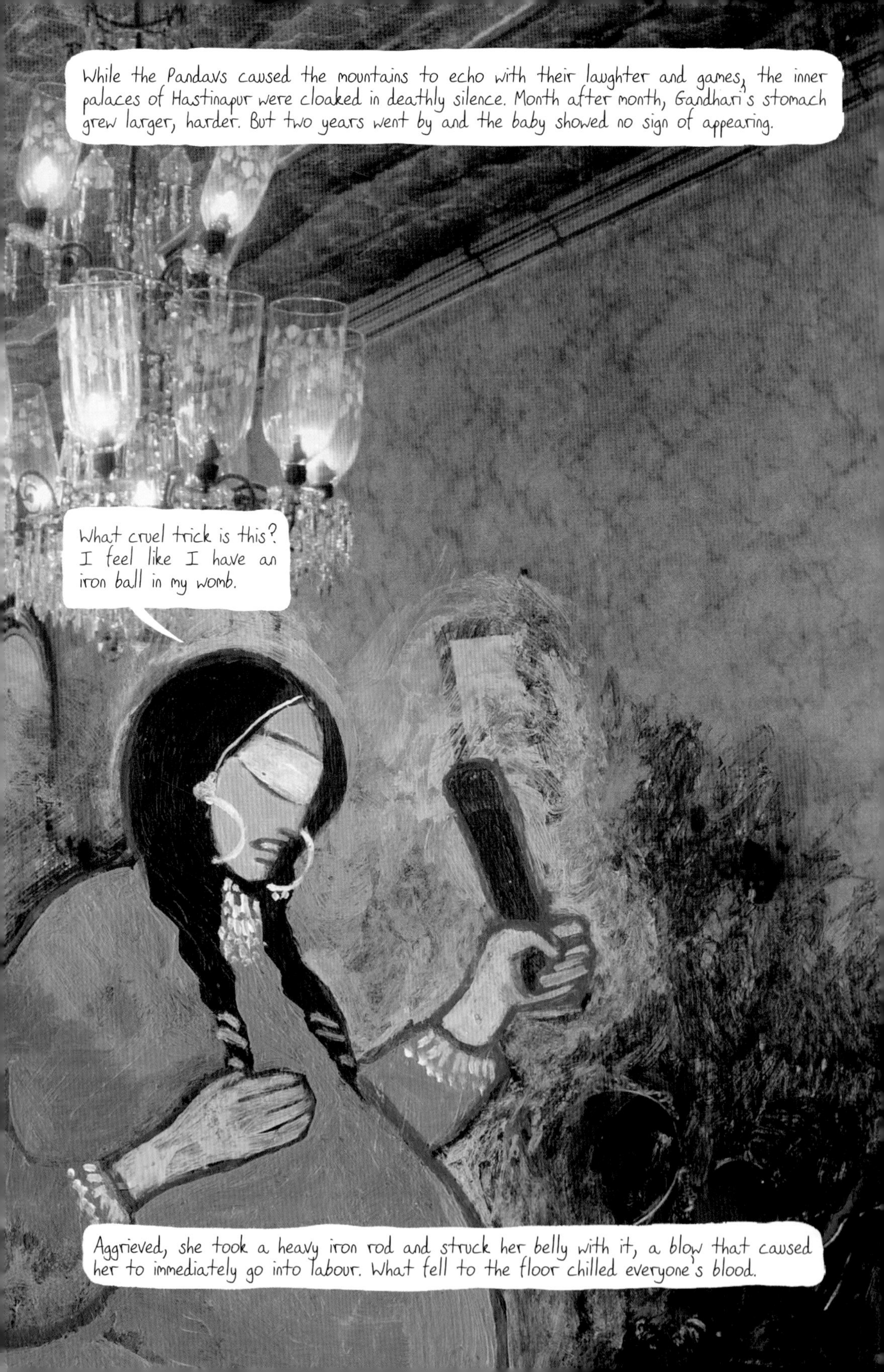
While the Pandavs caused the mountains to echo with their laughter and games, the inner palaces of Hastinapur were cloaked in deathly silence. Month after month, Gandhari's stomach grew larger, harder. But two years went by and the baby showed no sign of appearing.
What cruel trick is this? I feel like I have an iron ball in my womb.
Aggrieved, she took a heavy iron rod and struck her belly with it, a blow that caused her to immediately go into labour. What fell to the floor chilled everyone's blood.

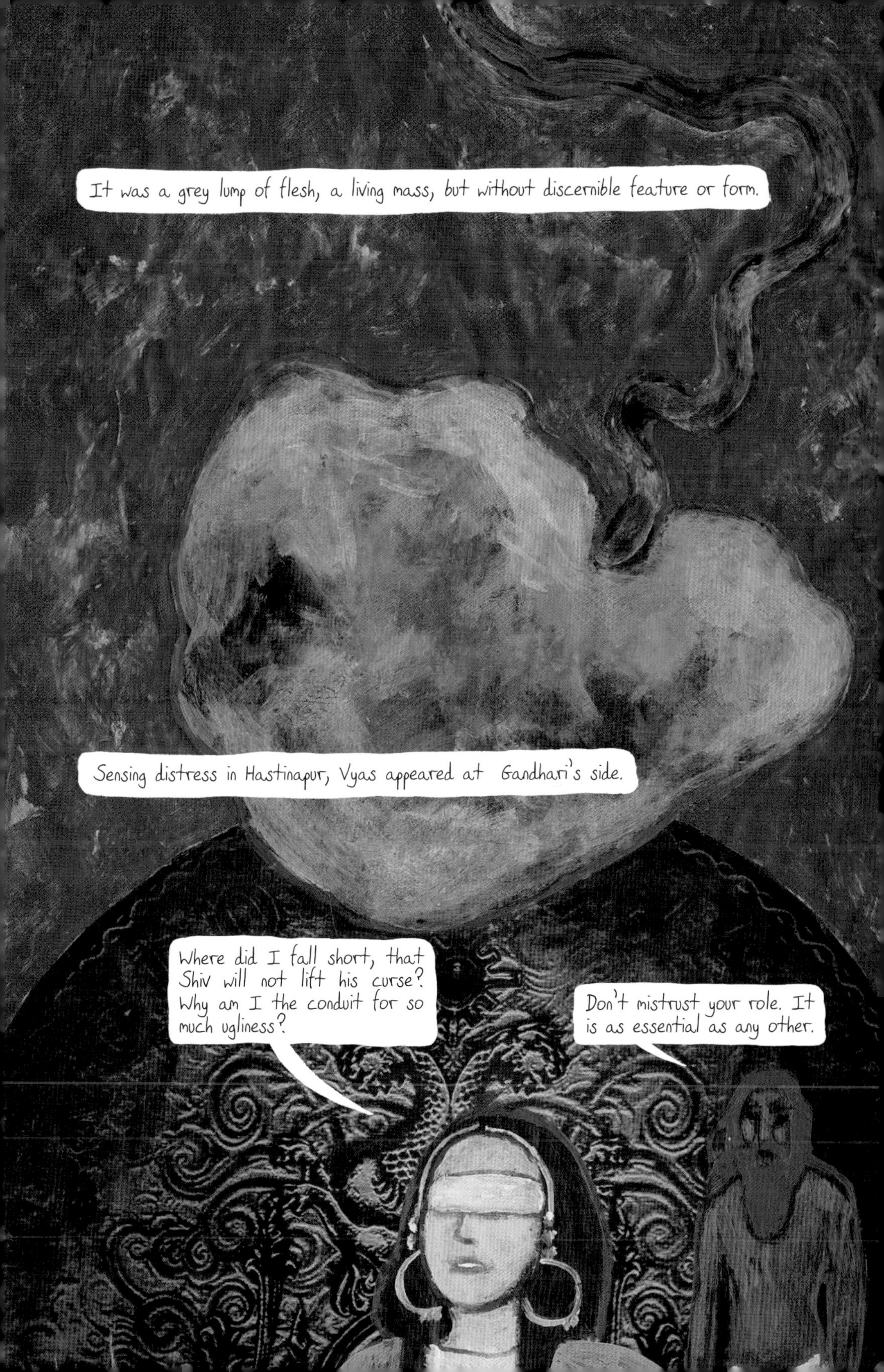
It was a grey lump of flesh, a living mass, but without discernible feature or form.
Sensing distress in Hastinapur, Vyas appeared at Gandhari's side.
Where did I fall short, that Shiv will not lift his curse? Why am I the conduit for so much ugliness?
Don't mistrust your role. It is as essential as any other.

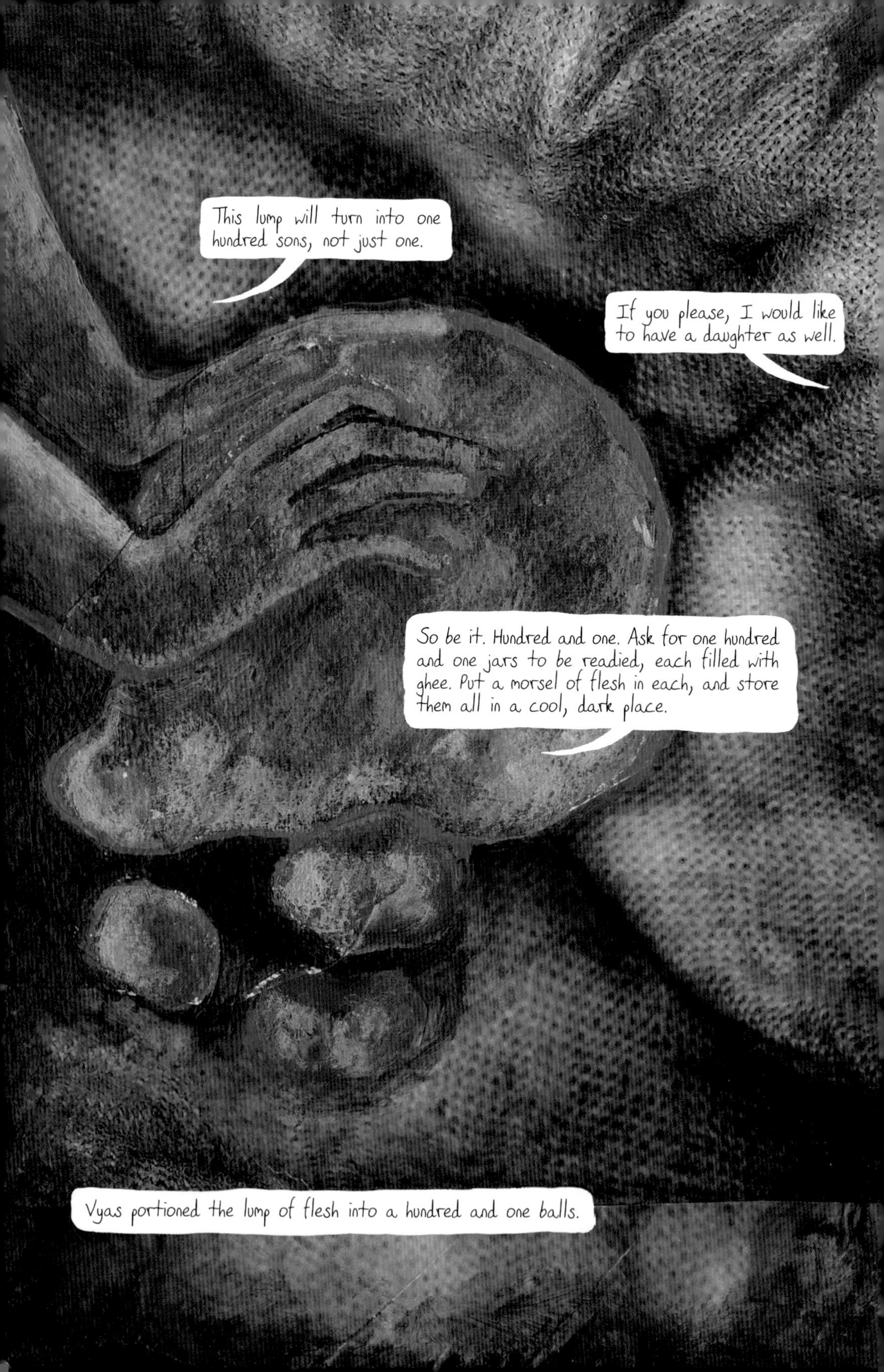
This lump will turn into one hundred sons, not just one.
If you please, I would like to have a daughter as well.
So be it. Hundred and one. Ask for one hundred and one jars to be readied, each filled with ghee. Put a morsel of flesh in each, and store them all in a cool, dark place.
Vyas portioned the lump of flesh into a hundred and one balls.

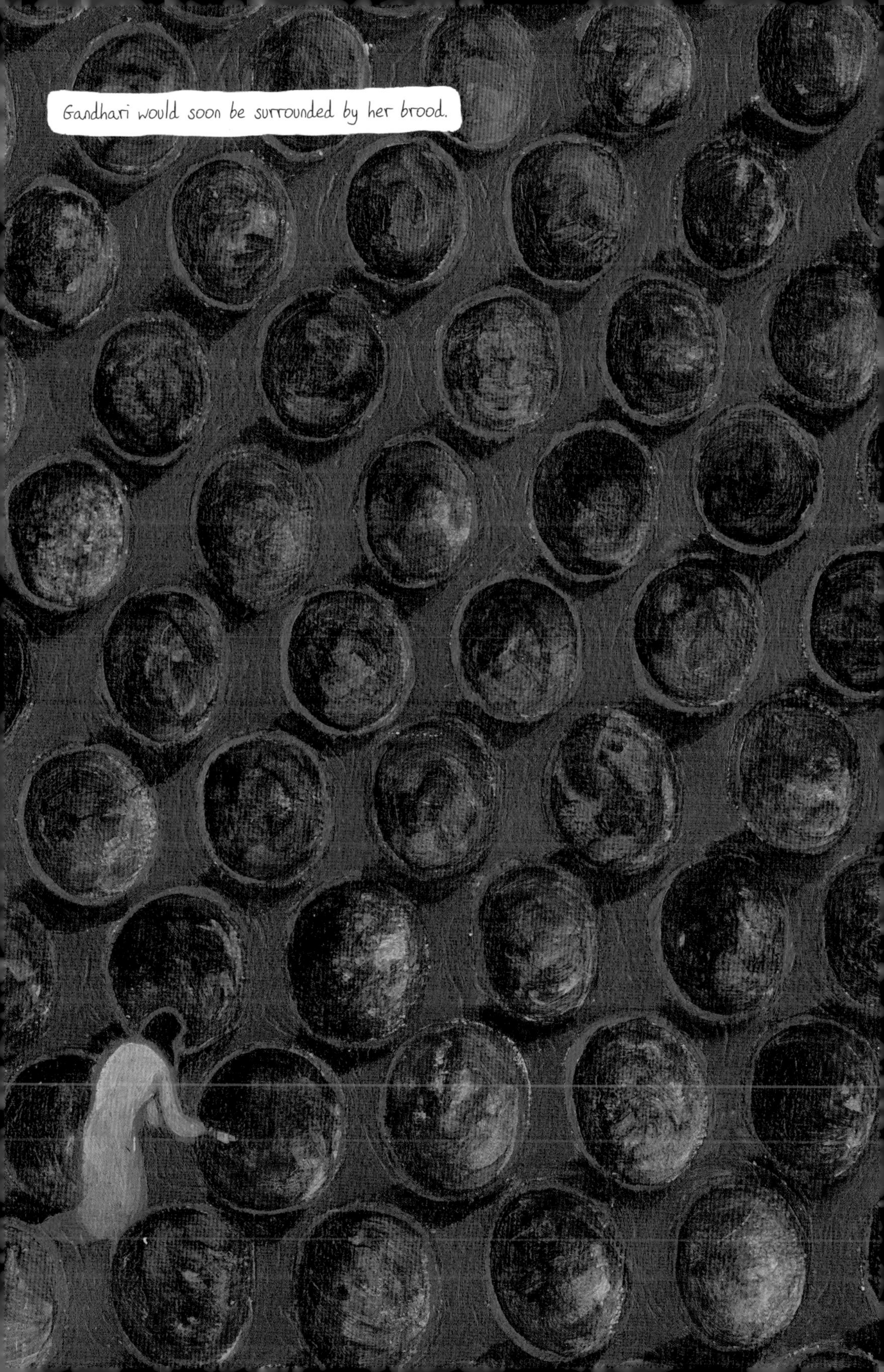
Gandhari would soon be surrounded by her brood.

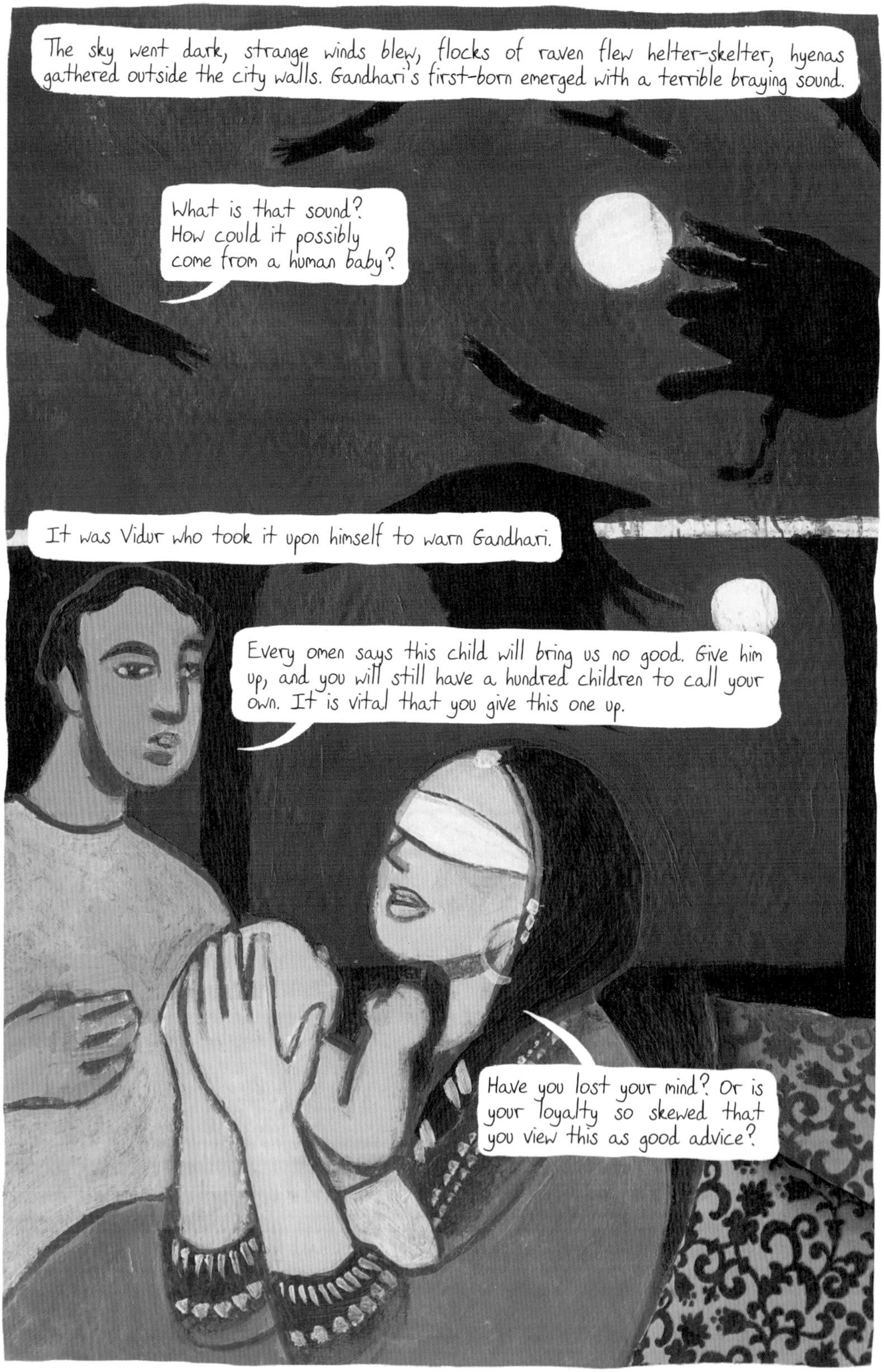
The sky went dark, strange winds blew, flocks of raven flew helter-skelter, hyenas gathered outside the city walls. Gandhari's first-born emerged with a terrible braying sound.
What is that sound? How could it possibly come from a human baby?
It was Vidur who took it upon himself to warn Gandhari.
Every omen says this child will bring us no good. Give him up, and you will still have a hundred children to call your own. It is vital that you give this one up.
Have you lost your mind? Or is your loyalty so skewed that you view this as good advice?

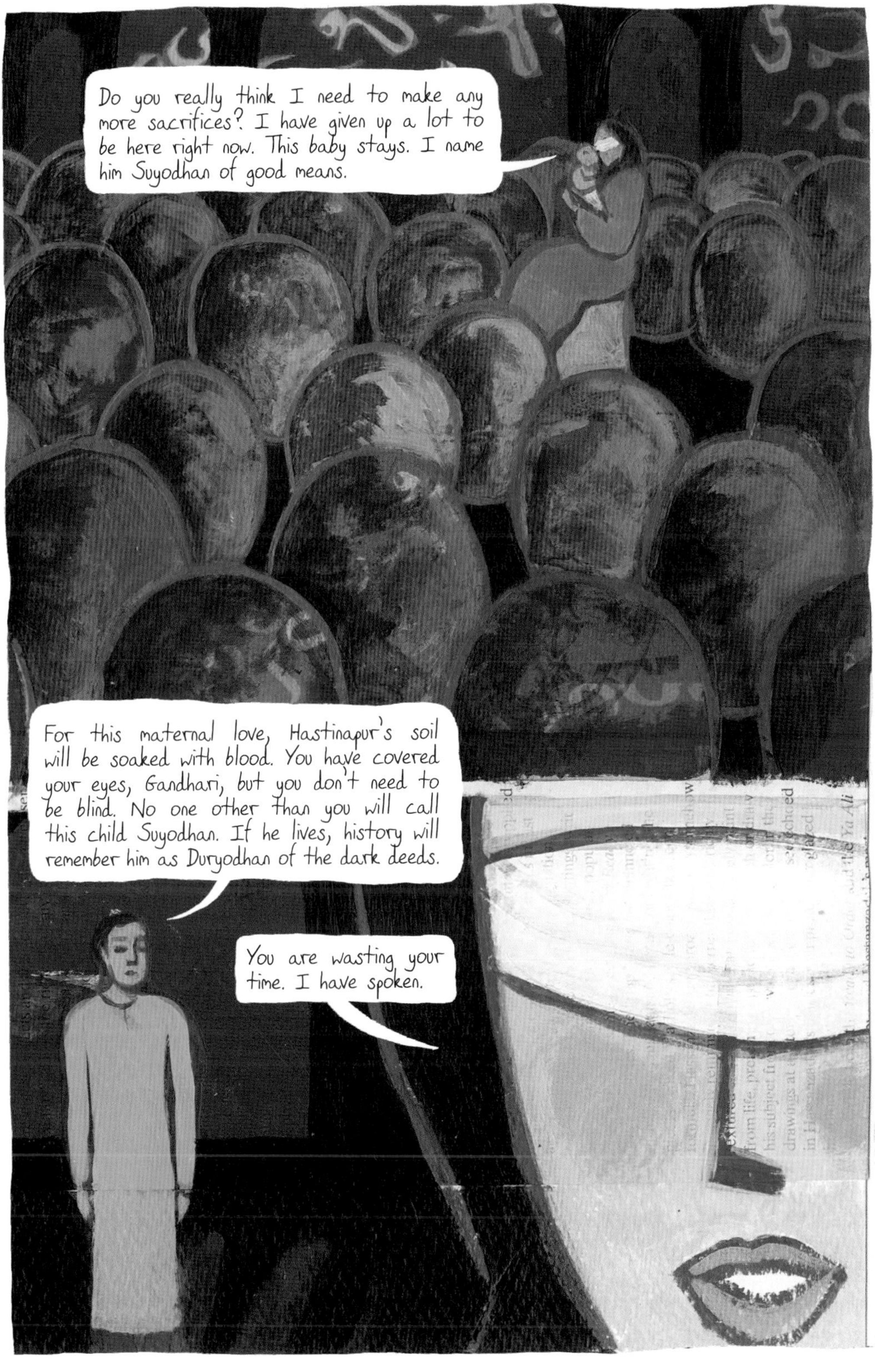
Do you really think I need to make any more sacrifices? I have given up a lot to be here right now. This baby stays. I name him Suyodhan of good means.
For this maternal love, Hastinapur's soil will be soaked with blood. You have covered your eyes, Gandhari, but you don't need to be blind. No one other than you will call this child Suyodhan. If he lives, history will remember him as Duryodhan of the dark deeds.
You are wasting your time. I have spoken.

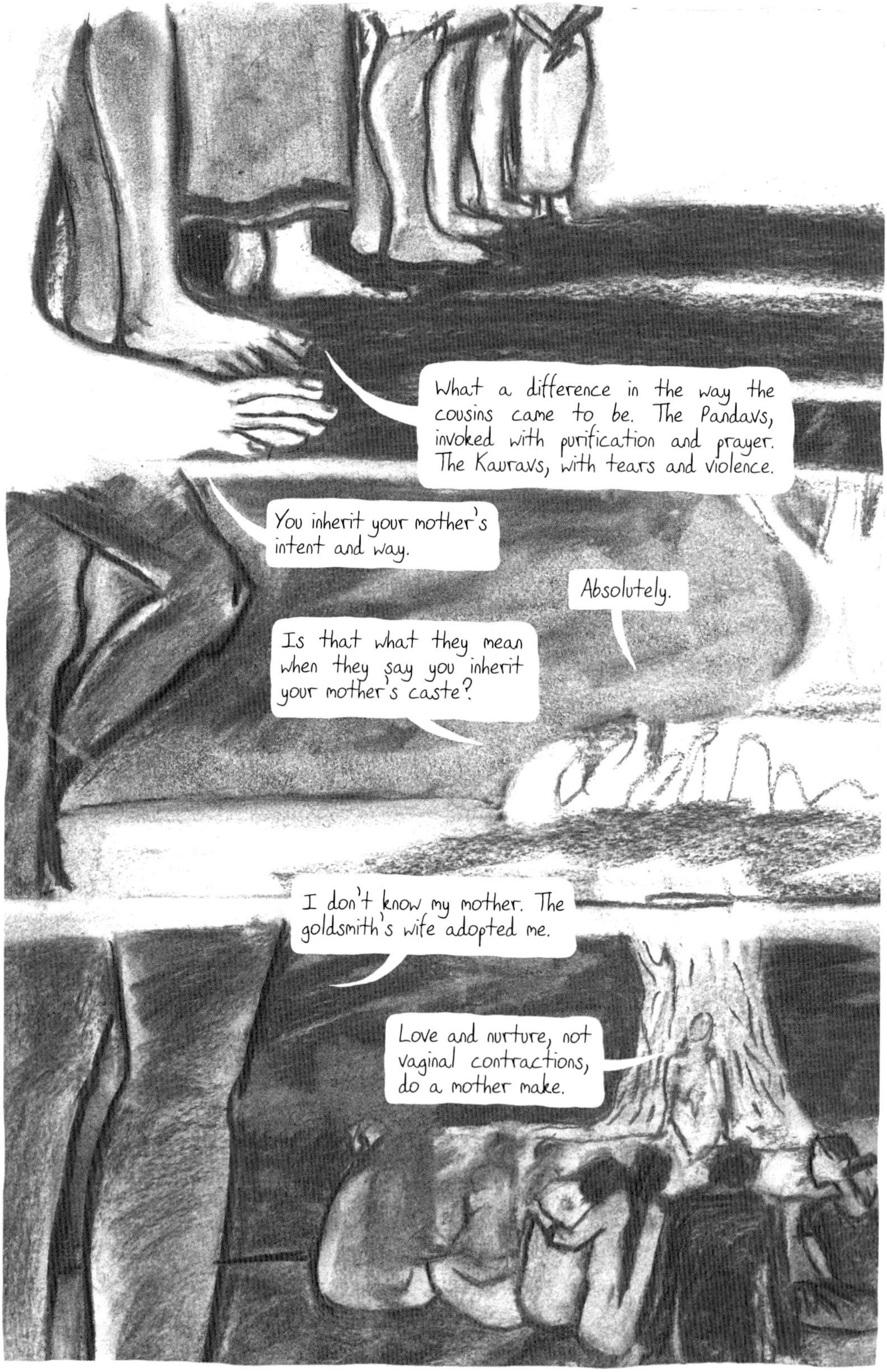
What a difference in the way the cousins came to be. The Pandavs, invoked with purification and prayer. The Kauravs, with tears and violence.
You inherit your mother's intent and way.
Absolutely.
Is that what they mean when they say you inherit your mother's caste?
I don't know my mother. The goldsmith's wife adopted me.
Love and nurture, not vaginal contractions, do a mother make.

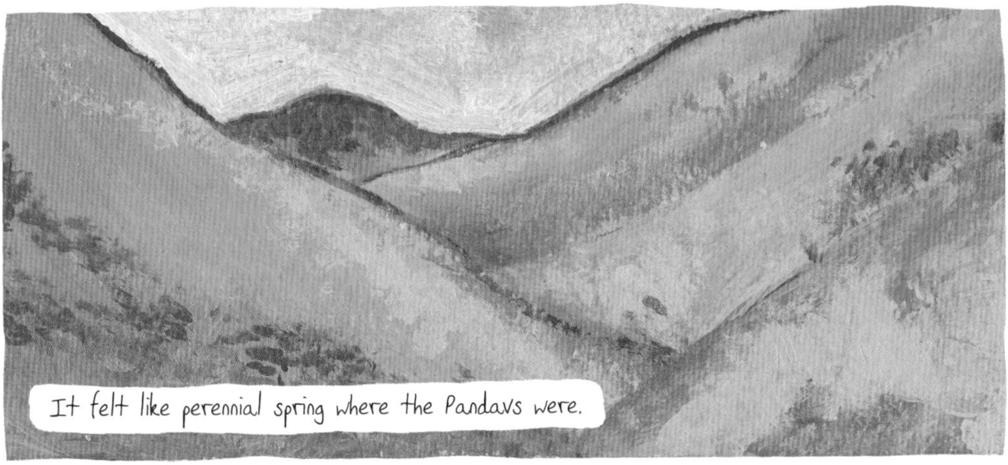
It felt like perennial spring where the Pandavs were.

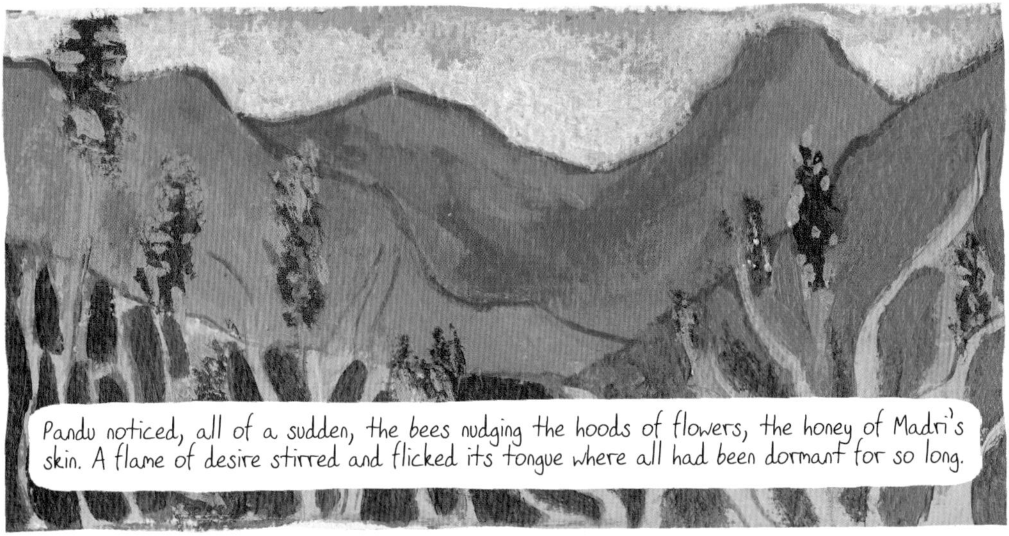
Pandu noticed, all of a sudden, the bees nudging the hoods of flowers, the honey of Madri's skin. A flame of desire stirred and flicked its tongue where all had been dormant for so long.

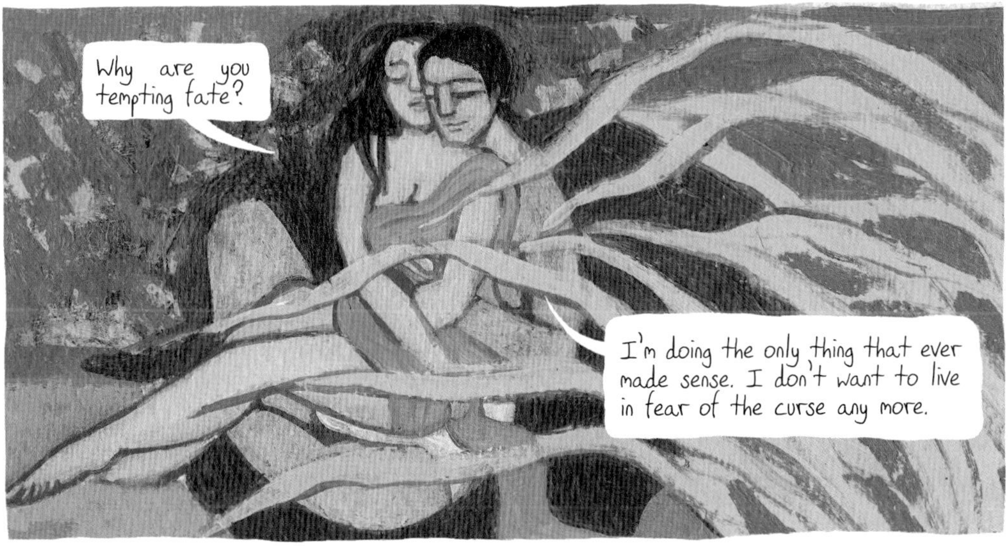
Why are you tempting fate?
I'm doing the only thing that ever made sense. I don't want to live in fear of the curse any more.

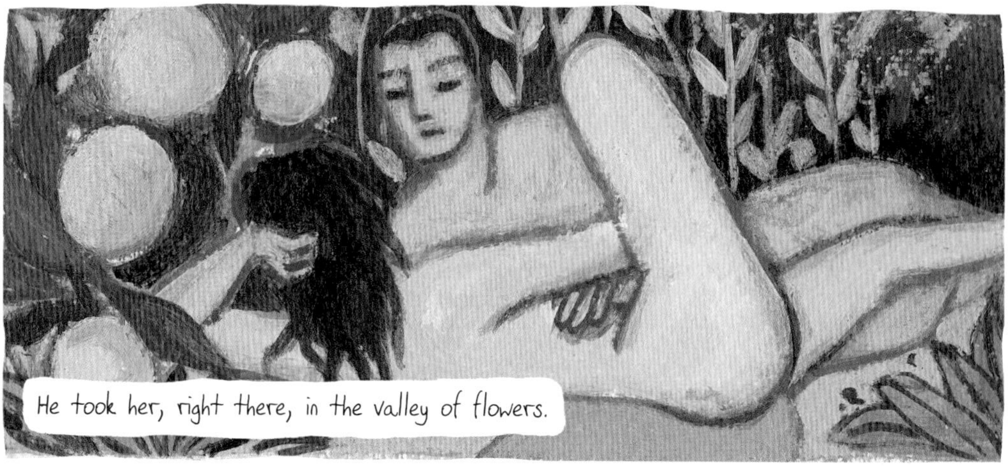
He took her, right there, in the valley of flowers.

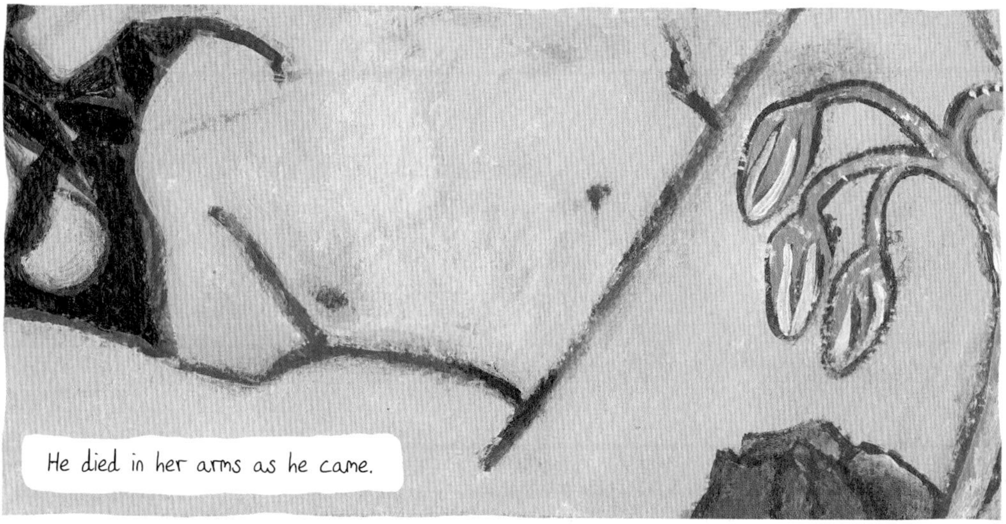
He died in her arms as he came.

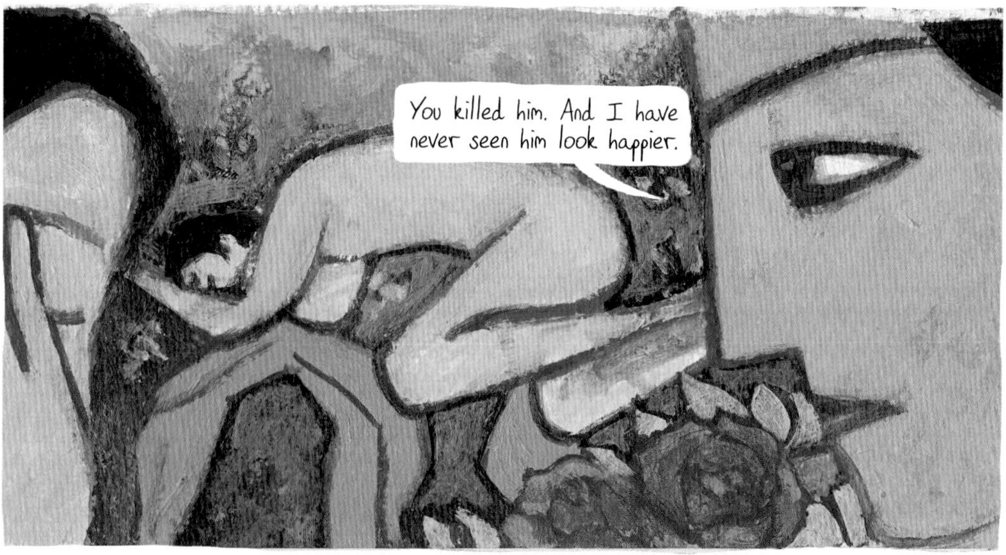
You killed him. And I have never seen him look happier.

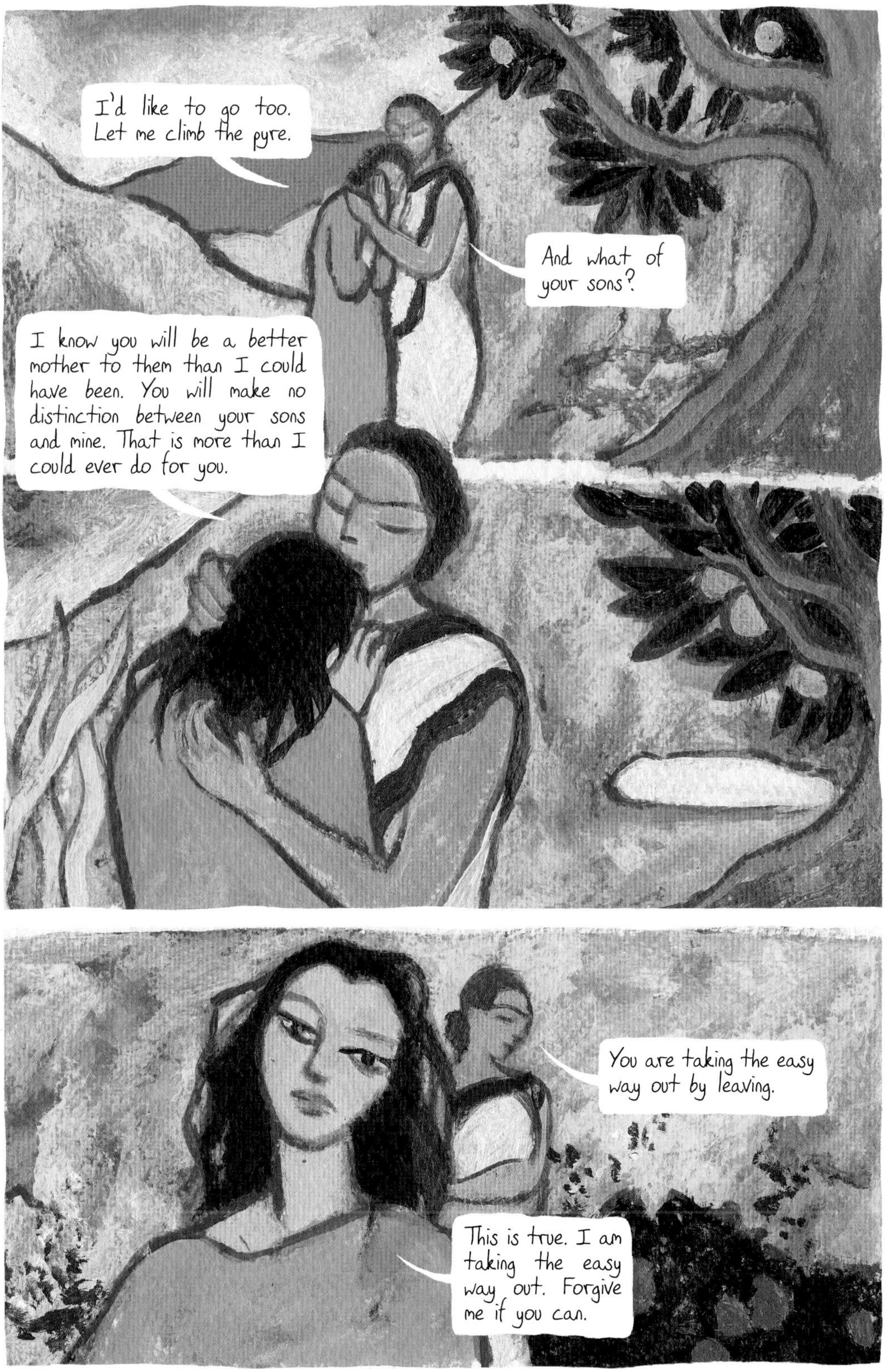
I'd like to go too. Let me climb the pyre.
And what of your sons?
I know you will be a better mother to them than I could have been. You will make no distinction between your sons and mine. That is more than I could ever do for you.
You are taking the easy way out by leaving.
This is true. I am taking the easy way out. Forgive me if you can.

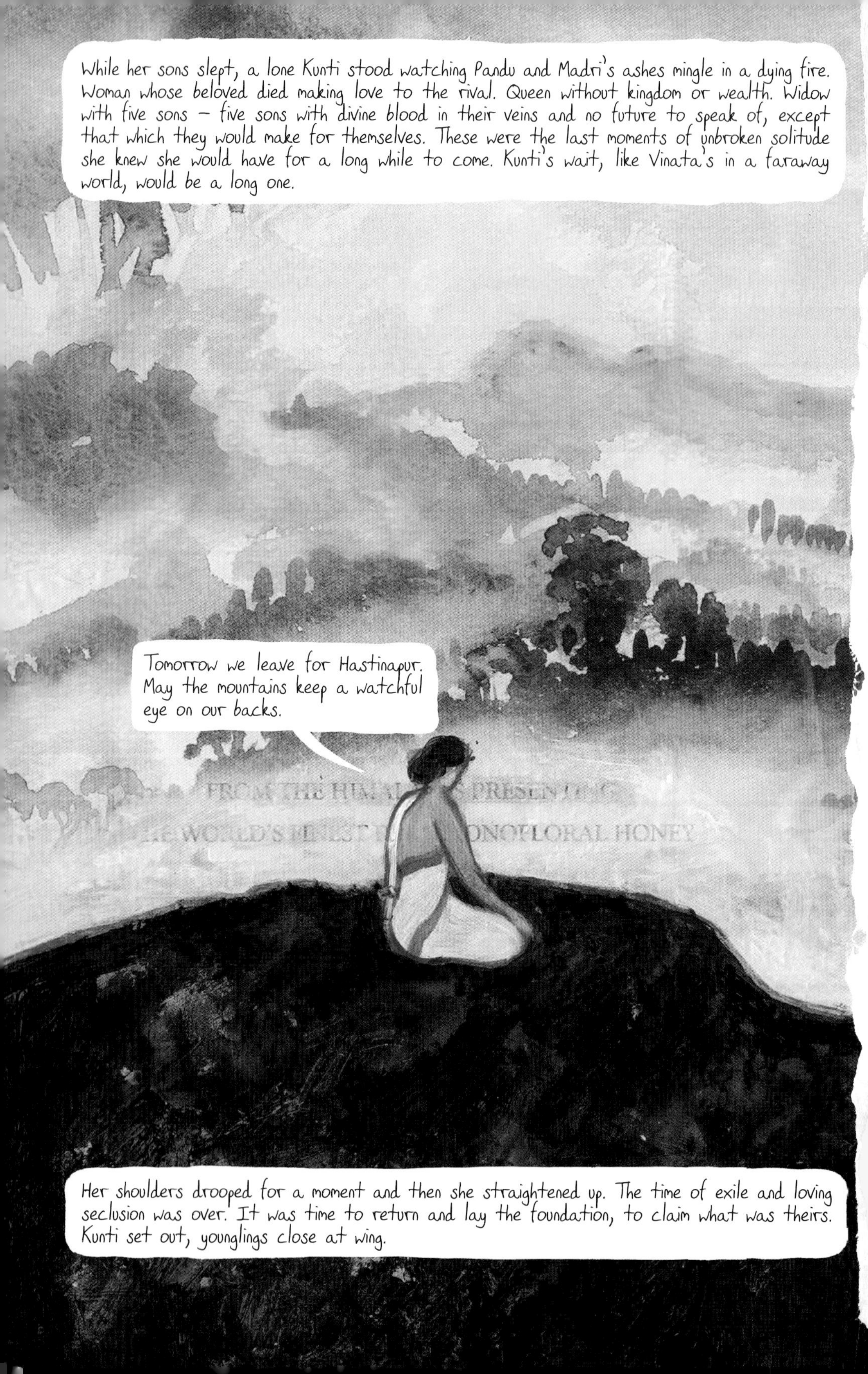
While her sons slept, a lone Kunti stood watching Pandu and Madri's ashes mingle in a dying fire. Woman whose beloved died making love to the rival. Queen without kingdom or wealth. Widow with five sons – five sons with divine blood in their veins and no future to speak of, except that which they would make for themselves. These were the last moments of unbroken solitude she knew she would have for a long while to come. Kunti's wait, like Vinata's in a faraway world, would be a long one.
Tomorrow we leave for Hastinapur. May the mountains keep a watchful eye on our backs.
Her shoulders drooped for a moment and then she straightened up. The time of exile and loving seclusion was over. It was time to return and lay the foundation, to claim what was theirs. Kunti set out, younglings close at wing.

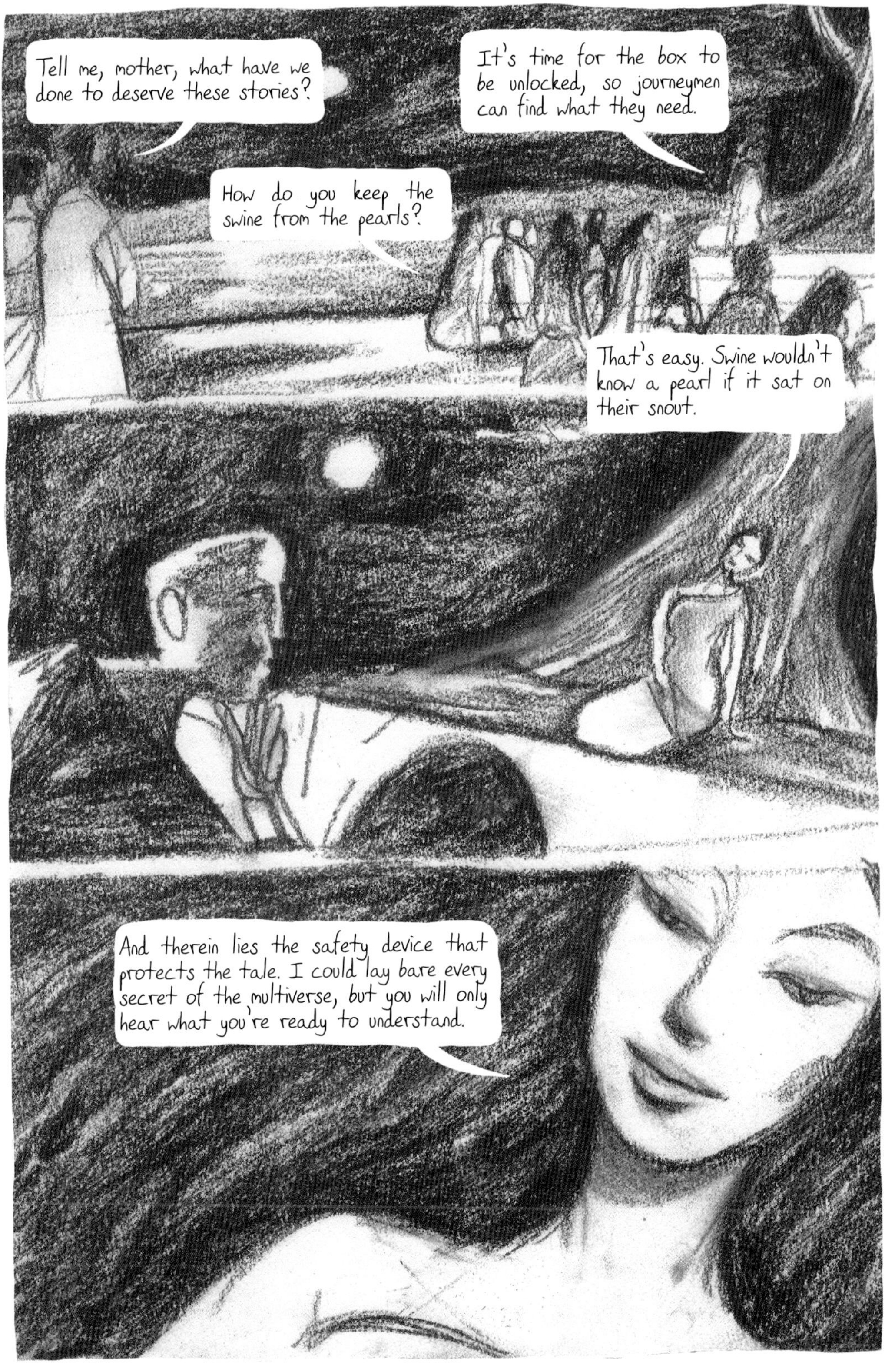
Tell me, mother, what have we done to deserve these stories?
It's time for the box to be unlocked, so journeymen can find what they need.
How do you keep the swine from the pearls?
That's easy. Swine wouldn't know a pearl if it sat on their snout.
And therein lies the safety device that protects the tale. I could lay bare every secret of the multiverse, but you will only hear what you're ready to understand.

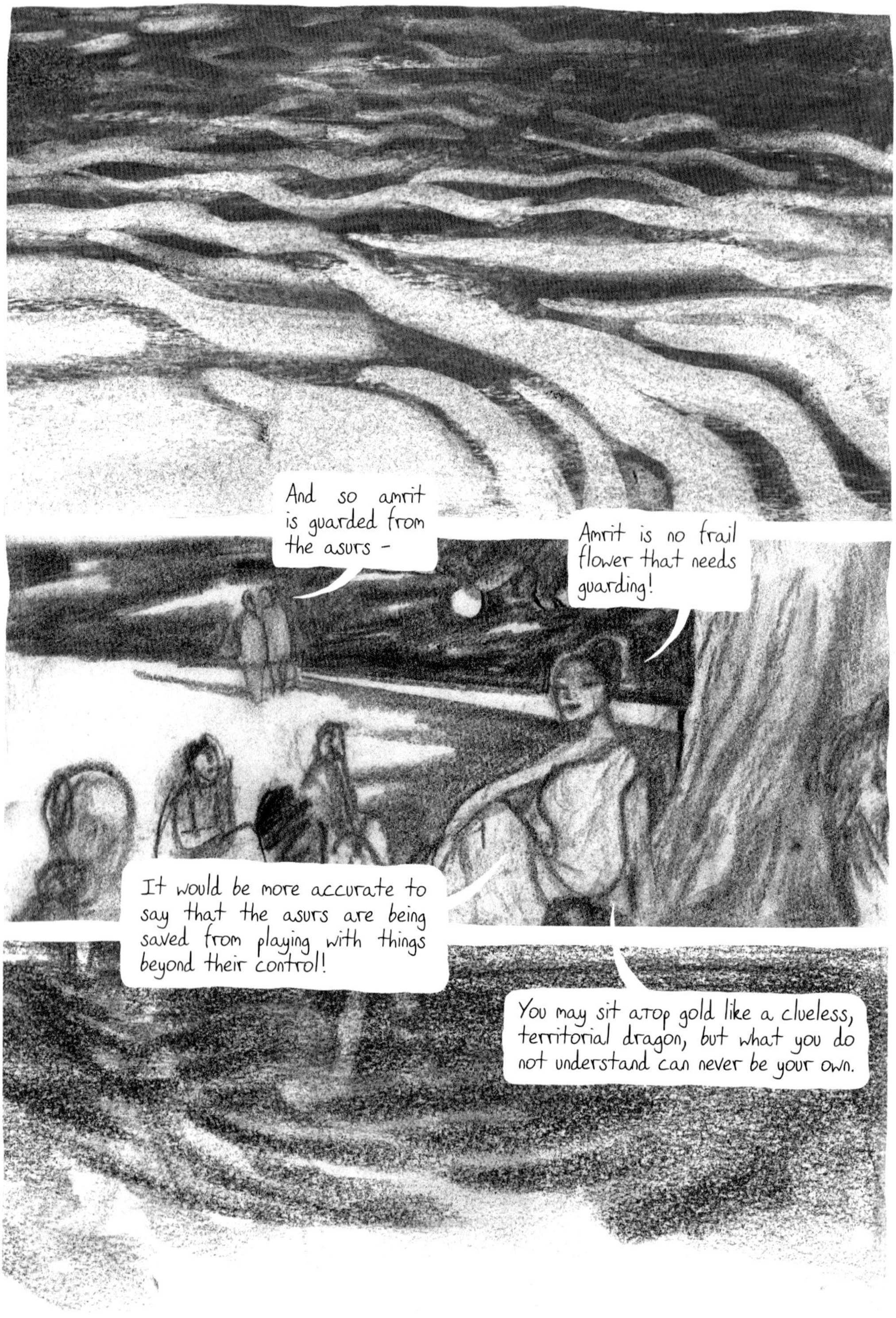
And so amrit is guarded from the asurs -
Amrit is no frail flower that needs guarding!
It would be more accurate to say that the asurs are being saved from playing with things beyond their control!
You may sit atop gold like a clueless, territorial dragon, but what you do not understand can never be your own.

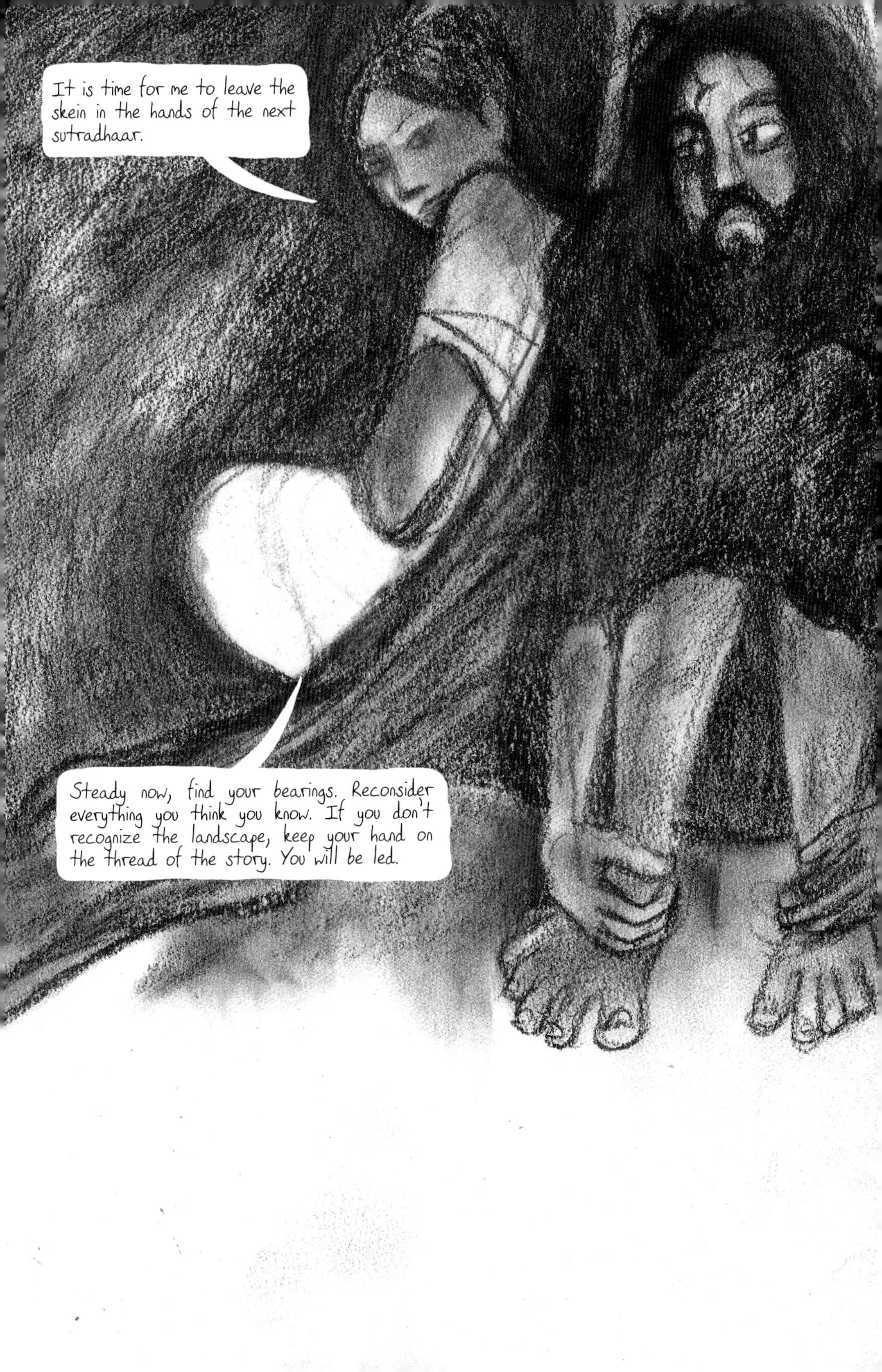
It is time for me to leave the skein in the hands of the next sutradhaar.
Steady now, find your bearings. Reconsider everything you think you know. If you don't recognize the landscape, keep your hand on the thread of the story. You will be led.

AUTHOR's NOTE

The Need for Retelling Stories

Cosmic tales are like fish tanks in their need for continuous aeration. Without the air of time and context continually bubbling through them, they are dead habitat, a crypt of code and guesswork, an oppressively 'heavy' environment accessible only to academics and people with cumbersome diving equipment and breathing apparatus. The copper of an age-old story is polished with each good retelling – it glows warm and beautiful.

A story passed down through the ages via oral storytellers cannot help but alter. A good storyteller, like a good teacher, speaks in the language of the hour. Her only allegiance is to the essence of the tale; the essence safeguarded, she is free to improvise the narrative to reflect the time. There are very many stories, and each is an individual thread. The storyteller who wields and unfurls these myriad threads is traditionally known as the sutradhaar, threadbearer.

In the sutradhaar tradition, there are many worlds and they exist cyclically and simultaneously. The exact geographical location of all these worlds is within you. Diana Eck describes this phenomenon as 'organic ontology': human body as primary schema for understanding the wider cosmos. In such a setting, history-centric questions like 'when exactly' and 'where exactly' are rendered irrelevant. History is just one of these many stories, and it is recounted not to reminisce about a musty old past, but to prepare the ground for a future that hasn't come about yet.

Asking Questions

The sutradhaar's audience would typically consist of pilgrims and householders, vagrants and nomads, believers and sceptics, mad men and passersby – people who gather of their own free will, and leave when they must. They all ask questions. Not all questions are diamonds of insight. Some are simple – Why them? Who is she? What happens next? – but they are asked nonetheless. Almost all questions get a story in response. There are times when the question is left unanswered – sometimes because the questioner isn't ready for an answer yet, sometimes because the answer is waiting to unfold a little later, sometimes because a readymade answer would make things too easy.

There is a growing fear of having our palms skinned for making ignorant queries. The only time we feel safe enough to ask a question is when we know half the answer. Else we sit still in a crowded room, hoping some extroverted other will speak what's on our mind. Contemporary forums for question-asking are almost always crowded rooms that seem better suited for derisive conversation and the show-off questioner than for one asking a sincere question. When you question the origins of the universe, it isn't the universe you're testing; you're testing the depth, sturdiness and mettle of your own self.

Opening a Sealed Vault

The abundance of our epoch keeps us from noticing an extraordinary truth: Access to information, something we assume is rightfully ours, was never intended to be this easy. And it was certainly not meant to be open-source. For the greatest part of our collective history, esoteric knowledge was the exclusive preserve of the elite – royalty, noblesse, priests – and its transfer from person to person was highly selective and ritualized. The fortress of sacred texts and the written word was even more impregnable. What sages and priests were privy to, not even the king of the land could access. This was how things remained until as recently as two hundred years ago.

And then something happened that was unprecedented. Across lands, cultures, races, belief systems – almost in unison – custodians of secret knowledge threw open the sealed vaults. The internet, that Aquarian Age crystal ball, only turned this sharing into a forest fire. The reservoirs of knowledge are now for our asking; all we need is our attention, and our question.

Looping Stories

All too often, the Mahabharat is reduced to the sum total of two things – the fratricidal battle between the Kuru princes and the battlefield dialogue between the avatar, Krshn, and his protégé Arjun. (The latter is often, erroneously, served up as a standalone.) The real scope of the Mahabharat, however, extends a good distance on either side of these events. It sprawls from fantastic creation myths to gritty battlefields; from bodily preoccupations to the material and spiritual; from grooming kings to encouraging renunciates. An ambitious arena, and yet, at its core, the Mahabharat is a treatise on something as elementary as right conduct and excellent form. It concerns itself with the hows of being the good student, good teacher, good lover, good leader, good householder, good king.

At the end of every story is the nub of a new beginning. The snakes versus birds rivalry in the Adi Parva is no careless latter-day addition to Mahabharatan lore; it is a fitting abstract metaphor for the mortal rivalries that will come to pass later in the tale. The story of the Kuru princes is but an echo of much older conflicts in subtler realms and surreal landscapes. Like the multiverse it encodes, the nature of the Mahabharat is fractal recursive.

Amruta Patil
August 2012

Note about spellings: The reader may encounter unfamiliarly rendered proper noun spellings in this book. This has been done in an attempt to revert to the phonetically correct version of the name rather than perpetuate colonial-era distortions.

GLOSSARY

Acharya: Suffix that means 'teacher' or 'scholar'.

Adhvaryu: Priests who chanted hymns from the Yajur Veda during a yagna.

Adi: Primordial

Airawat: Many-tusked white elephant. Indra's mount.

Amba: Eldest Kashi princess who refuses to marry prince Vichitraveerya of Hasti-napur and vows vengeance against Hastinapur and Bheeshm.

Ambika: Middle princess of Kashi. Wife of Vichitraveerya. Mother of Dhritrashtra (through Krshn Dwaipayan Vyas).

Ambalika: Youngest princess of Kashi. Wife of Vichitraveerya. Mother of Pandu (through Krshn Dwaipayan).

Amrit: Blissfire, spice, nectar of immortality. Devas have the privilege of consuming it, asurs and other beings do not (leading to a continual tussle between the two). A select few – like Vishnu, Garud, Lakshmi, Shiv, Brahma, the rishis – don't need amrit for immortality or divine vision.

Anant: Also known as Shesh Nag. Magical serpent son of Kashyap and Kadru; oldest among their thousand children. Anant renounces the ambitions of the serpent tribe to serve Vishnu. His tail is the axis that centres the world.

Anshavtar: Partial manifestation of divinity on earth. (Also see 'Avatar')

Apsara: Water-born celestial of incomparable physical beauty and grace, born during the churning of the ocean. Closely associated with music and dance. Part of devlok, apsaras assist Indra in maintaining status quo by distracting hermits who are becoming powerful enough to pose a threat to the devas. Masculine counterpart of an apsara is the Gandharva.

Arjun: Third-born Pandava. Born of Indra and Kunti. (Also see 'Nar-Narayan')

Arun: Older son of Vinata and Kashyap. Brother of Garud who went on to become Surya's charioteer. (Also see 'Birds')

Ashwatthama: Son of Dronacharya (preceptor of the Kaurav and Pandav princes) and Kripi. Childhood friend of the Pandavs, he later became the assassin of their sons. He was cursed to immortality (and to a perpetually bleeding wound) by Krshn.

Ashwini Kumar: Twin horsemen devas. Fathers of the Pandavs, Nakul and Sahadev (through Madri). Legendary for their skills of healing and divination, and their way with animals.

Astik: Son of Jaratkaru and Jaratkaru. Bred from mortal and serpent blood, with the express purpose of putting an end to Janmejaya's serpent sacrifice.

Asur: Dissonant forces, akin to anti-gods (the word 'asur' cannot be equated with demons). Sons of Kashyap and his wives Danu and Diti. Danu's sons are the Danavs, and Diti's are the Daityas, They are strong, resourceful, capricious, and their aim is to attain amrit and devlok. To be an asur is not a permanent fate. On subduing personal ambition and the instinct to dominate, they have been known to transcend their asuric state.

Avatar: Complete manifestation of Vishnu on earth during a given epoch. There can only be one avatar in any given epoch. The roles essayed by other devas on earth are known as 'anshavtar' or 'partial manifestation'.

Bheem: Second-born Pandav. Son of Vayu, the wind deva, and Kunti.

Bheeshm: Also known as Devvrat. Son of Ganga and Shantanu of Hastinapur. A self-avowed celibate, he is the grandfather-figure and guardian to the princes of Hastinapur.

Birds: In this story, 'birds' refers to the bird tribe led by solar raptors Garud and Arun, sons of Kashyap and Vinata. The overarching aim of the bird tribe is to evolve, raise the self and subdue the ego. Neither Arun nor Garud reproduced, so there are no 'direct descendants' of the bird tribe. The only way to be part of the bird tribe is by aligning oneself to the Truth Sun via right aspiration and service.

Bharat: Also known as Sarvadaman. King of Hastinapur. Son of Dushyant and Shakuntala.

Brahma: One of the divine triad, associated with creating worlds. Depicted rising from Vishnu's navel. He has various sons born of different parts of his body – a kind of philosophical mitosis. His feminine counterpart is Saraswati, goddess of wisdom, music, and learning.

Brihaspati: Preceptor of the devas. Associated with the planet Jupiter.

Chakravarti: 'One whose wheels are turning'. An epithet used for a powerful, conquering king.

Churning of the Ocean: Event in which the devas and asurs churn the Mansarovar in unison, in a quest for amrit and other bounties.

Cow: Referred to in the Vedas as being part of 'the Sun's own flock', the cow is a metaphor for the gentle, devoted conduit of the truth; rays of the Truth Sun. To steal or harm a cow is, therefore, to harm a conduit of truth. The cow also represents autonomy: a creature who provides food (in the form of milk and ghee) and fuel (in the form of dung) – and is thus seen as the perfect gift for a hermit. (Also see 'Sun')

Daksha: One of Brahma's sons. A regal, virile, masculine entity (like Kashyap), Daksha has several wives and innumerable progeny. Aditi, Danu and Diti are among his daughters.

Dasaraj: Chief of a fishing village by the Yamuna. Foster father of Matsyagandha.

Devas: Consonant forces, akin to the Western notion of gods (but without the capital 'G'). Sons of Kashyap and his wife Aditi. Devas are aligned with Vishnu, and made immortal with the gift of amrit. Their continual personal battle is against insecurity, and getting caught up in sensual pleasures. The leader of the devas is given the title 'Indra'.

Devlok: Also known as Indralok, Swargalok, Swarlok. Realm of Gods. A harmonious place, endowed with all pleasures and comforts. Attaining Devlok is a transient state and beings lulled into complacence are often thrown back to serve their time in mrityulok.

Dhanvantri: Physician of the devas, who brings forth amrit during the churning of the ocean.

Dharma: Also known as Yama or Yama Dharma. Deva associated with justice and death. Father of the oldest Pandava, Yudhishthir (through Kunti).

Dhritrashtra: Son of Ambika by Krshn Dwaipayan Vyas. Born sightless. Married to Gandhari. Father of hundred sons and one daughter.

Dhruv: Son of King Uttanpaad and Suniti who attains the position of Dhruv Tara (Pole star) as a reward for his immutable devotion to Vishnu.

Durvaas: Hot-headed rishi. Son of Atri rishi and Anasuya. (Also see 'Navigators of the Multiverse')

Duryodhan: First-born Kaurav prince. Son of Dhritrashtra and Gandhari.

Dushyant: King of Hastinapur. Married to Shakuntala, father of Bharat.

Ganga: Celestial and earthly river. In her earthly form, she is Queen Ganga, wife of Shantanu of Hastinapur. Mother of Bheeshm. In her celestial form she is known as Akashganga ('Ganga of the Sky', Sanskrit term for the Milky Way).

Gandhari: Princess of Gandhar, daughter of Subal, sister of Shakuni. Wife of King Dhritrashtra of Hastinapur. Mother of the 101 Kauravs.

Garud: Also known as 'Suparna' – one with beautiful feathers. Younger son of Vinata and Kashyap. Brother of Arun. Vishnu's mount. Foremost among the bird tribe.

Hastinapur: Capital of the lunar dynasty, on the banks of the Yamuna.

Hotri: Priests who chanted hymns from the Rig Veda during a yagna.

Indra: Leader of the devas. 'Indra' is a title, and different world cycles have different beings as Indra. No matter who the Indra of the given era is, his wife is Shachi and his mount, the white elephant Airawat. Indra is the bearer of the thunderbolt, and this refers to his perfect control over his 'indriya' – five senses. Father of the Pandav Arjun (through Kunti).

Indrajaal: Bejewelled, illusory, infinite net in Indra's abode in which every jewel reflects every other jewel in its polished heart.

Jaratkaru: One who has reduced a large body through terrible penance. The name of both Astik's mother and father.

Janmejaya: Descendent of the lunar race of Hastinapur. He is the great-grandson of the Pandav warrior Arjun, and the son of Parikshit. Janmejaya is the one who aspires to annihilate all serpents via the sarpa sattra.

Jyotish: Vedic system of astrology which is Sidereal (as opposed to the Tropical system followed by Western astrology), and uses the locations of 27 nakshatras (constellations) in its calculations. Believed to have been originated by Parashar rishi.

Kamdhenu: Wish-granting cow who belonged to Vashishth rishi.

Kalkoot: Also known as 'Halaahal'. The virulent poison that emerges from the Mansarovar when the churning first begins. Shiv saves the living world from sure death by drinking it all – his throat is stained purple in memory. Kalkoot is a metaphor for the seemingly unbearable bitterness, hardship and physical pain that are guaranteed to raise their head when internal 'churning' begins.

Karn: Child born to Kunti before her marriage with Pandu. Fathered by Surya, Karn is born with a golden armour and earrings. Abandoned at birth by Kunti, he is raised by the charioteer Adhirath and his wife Radha.

Kanwa: Rishi who lives by the river Malini. Foster father of Shakuntala.

Kauravs: Hundred sons and one daughter of King Dhritrashtra of Hastinapur, and Gandhari. The fratricidal battle between the Kauravas and their cousins, the Pandavs on the field of Kurukshetra, is the popular locus of the Mahabharat.

Kashyap: One of the mind-born sons of Brahma, father of most of life as we know it. Husband of Vinata and Kadru, Daksha's daughters.

Krshn: The avatar of Vishnu during the Treta/Dwapar Yug. Born into the lunar Yadav race. Cousin and spiritual guide to the Pandavs.

Kunti: Also known as Pritha. Daughter of the Yadav chief Shursen, foster child of King Kuntibhoj, aunt of Krshn, wife of Pandu. Biological mother of three of the five Pandavs, she also fosters the two sons of Madri.

Leela: Divine play that leads to the continuous formation and dissolution of worlds.

Lunar dynasty: Lineage from which Krshn and the rulers of Hastinapur descend.

Madri: Princess of Madralok. Second wife of Pandu of Hastinapur. Mother of the Pandav fraternal twins, Nakul and Sahadev.

Mandar: Pine-cone-shaped mountain used as a churning rod during the churning of the ocean.

Mantra: Sacred syllable or phrase repeated in invocation or incantation.

Marichi: One of Brahma's mind-born sons.

Malini: One of Ganga's riverine sisters.

Mansarovar: Ocean of the Mind. Also known as Ocean of Milk, which must be churned in tandem by the arch rivals, devas and asurs, before it yields treasures and amrit.

Matsyagandha: Also known as Yojanagandha and Satyavati. Mother of Krshn Dwaipayan Vyas (through Parashar rishi). Wife of Shantanu and the mother of his sons Chitrangad and Vichitraveerya.

Menaka: One of the foremost apsaras in Indra's court. Mother of Shakuntala (through Vishwamitra rishi).

Meru: Mountain in Devlok.

Mohini: Vishnu's incarnation as the supreme enchantress, whose role is to distract serpents and asurs and prevent them from partaking of any amrit.

Mrityulok: Realm of mortals, the earth.

Naglok: Abode of the magical serpents (nagas).

Nakul: Fraternal twin to Sahadev, the youngest of the Pandavs. Born of the Ashwini twins (and Madri). Married to Draupadi. Renowned for his physical beauty.

Nar-Narayan: Binary pairing of Narayan (Vishnu) as eternal companion to the human-souled Nar. Arjun and Krshn are seen as Nar-Narayan reincarnated.

Narad muni: One of Brahma's mind-born sons. Narad is the singing, Vishnu-loving rishi who travels between the three worlds sharing gossip and cautionary notes and lessons in devotion. He is celibate and causes much consternation among the fecund like Daksha and Kashyap by his encouragement of renunciation.

Navigators of the multiverse: Associated with the constellation Saptarishi (Ursa Major), these are the seven rishis who oversee the workings of the multiverse in a given epoch. By some accounts, the sapta rishi include Vashishth, Atri, Kashyap, Bharadwaj, Jamdagni, Gautam and Vishwamitra.

Padma Lakshmi: Lotus-born Lakshmi, Vishnu's consort.

Pandu: Son of Ambalika by Vyas. Younger brother of Dhritrashtra. He was married to the princesses Kunti and Madri.

Pandavs: Five non-biological sons of Pandu of Hastinapur (through his wives Kunti and Madri). The Pandavs share a common wife, Draupadi.

Parashar rishi: Son of Vashishth rishi and Arundhati. Father of Krshn Dwaipayan Vyas (through Satyavati, while she was known as Matsyagandha).

Parva: Epoch. Also means 'knot in the thread'.

Pitri: Deceased ancestors who need their descendants to keep reproducing so the lineage continues. Thus the renunciate hermit is the biggest threat to the pitris.

Rishis: Realized beings who live like itinerant hermits. The true seers and 'navigators of the multiverse', they are not caught up in sensory traps like the devas and asurs and mortals. They travel through time and worlds, making subtle alterations to force field and circumstance that lead to cataclysmic (positively transforming) results in the future.

Sahadev: Fraternal twin to Nakul, the youngest of the Pandavs. Born of the Ashwini Kumar (and Madri). Renowned for his physical beauty.

Sarama: The celestial guard dog who looks after flocks of stars along with her son, Sarameya.

Sarpa Sattra: Serpent sacrifice.

Satyavati: Queen of Hastinapur, foster child of the fishing village chieftain, Dasaraj. Mother of Krshn Dwaipayan Vyas (by Parashar rishi), Vichitraveerya and Chitrangad (by King Shantanu). (Also see 'Vyas' and 'Matsyagandha')

Serpents: Magical, powerful, disciplined but self-serving progeny of Kashyap and his wife Kadru. The serpent tribe refers to mythical creatures, not to be confused with snakes. The overarching aims of the serpent tribe are self-preservation and world domination. Their princes are Anant, Vasuki and Takshak.

Seven-lotus garland: Unfading, unwilting garland belonging to Durvaas.

Shakuntala: Daughter of the apsara Menaka and Vishwamitra. Wife of King Dushyant of Hastinapur. Mother of Bharat. Her name comes from the Shakunta, raptors who looked after her when she was abandoned at birth.

Shakuni: Twin brother of Gandhari, princess of Gandhar. An expert gambler.

Shantanu: King of Hastinapur. Married to Ganga (with whom he fathered Bheeshm) and then to Satyavati (with whom he fathered Chitrangad and Vichitraveerya).

Shiv: One of the divine triad, associated with the necessary dissolution of worlds. His consort is Sati (later reborn as Parvati).

Shukra: Preceptor of the asurs. Associated with the planet Venus, but not viewed in the feminine aspect.

Sun: Metaphor for universal truth. Not to be confused with the solar deva.

Suparna: One of beautiful feathers. (Also see 'Garud')

Surya: Deva associated with the sun. Married to Sanjana and Chhaya.

Sutradhaar: One who carries the thread. The traditional term for a storyteller.

Takshak: Prince of the serpent tribe.

Tapas: Inner heat, essential energy that comes from focused effort towards bodily purification and spiritual enlightenment. While a yagna represents the 'outer fire' of sacrifice, tapas represents the inner fire.

Trishanku: A king of the solar dynasty, Trishanku was too flawed and doubt-riddled to remain in devlok, and too accomplished to be allowed to fall back into mrityulok. So he remained suspended in a state of limbo between the two. The term 'Trishanku's heaven' refers to a confused middle ground between one's aspirations and one's current situation.

Ucchaishravas: Winged white steed who emerges during the churning of the ocean.

Udgatris: Priests who chanted hymns of the Sama Veda during a yagna.

Uparichara: Biological father of Matsyagandha.

Vaikunth: Also known as Vishnulok. Abode of Vishnu, Lakshmi, Anant, Garud.

Vali: Leader of the asurs, Indra's foe. Vishnu promises Vali that he will be the Indra after Indra Purandar's reign is over. Ironically, when Vali becomes the Indra, yet another asur takes his place as the anti-Indra.

Valkhilyas: A clan of diminutive rishis, each the size of a human thumb.

Vasus: The eight elementals forced to manifest as Ganga's mortal sons as a punishment for stealing Vashishth's cow, Kamdhenu. Seven of them were drowned at birth by Ganga (and, thus, liberated); the eighth lived on as Bheeshm.

Vasuki: Leader of the serpent tribe.

Vayu: Also known as Marut. Deva associated with wind and speed. Father of Bheem (through Kunti) and Hanuman (through Anjana).

Vidur: Younger brother to the Hastinapur princes Dhritrashtra and Pandu. Born of Krshn Dwaipayan Vyas and a servant girl.

Vishnu: One of the divine triad, associated with the preservation of worlds.

Vishnulok: Also known as Vaikunth. Realm of Vishnu, Brahma, Anant Sheshnag, Garud and Padma Lakshmi.

Vishwakarma: Presiding deity of all craftsmen and architects.

Vishwamitra: King who became one of the sapta rishis. He had a long-standing rivalry with Vashishth rishi – a rivalry often played out through their disciples.

Vyas: Credited to be the author of the Mahabharat epic, Krshn Dwaipayan Vyas divided the Vedas to make them accessible to the world age. 'Krshn Dwaipayan' means 'dark-skinned, island-born one'. Son of Satyavati and Parashar rishi and the biological father of Dhritrashtra, Pandu and Vidur.

Yagna: Sacrifice which revolves around a sacred fire presided over by the yajmaan (the king) and tended to by priests performing different roles. (Also see 'Hotri', 'Udgatri', 'Adhvaryu')

Yaksha: Nocturnal spirit connected with forests and water bodies. Female counterpart is the Yakshi.

Yamuna: One of Ganga's sister rivers, on whose bank Hastinapur is located.

Yayati: King of Hastinapur. Married to Sharmishtha and Devayani (daughters of the Asur chief Vali and the Asur preceptor Shukra, respectively).

Yogini: Female master practitioner of yoga. Masculine counterpart is Yogi.

Yugas: The four stages of the cycle of time – Krita, Treta, Dwapar and Kali. The names of the four Yugas correspond with those of dice throws.

Yudhishthir: Oldest Pandav. Born of Kunti and Dharma.

SUGGESTED READING

Aurobindo, *Hymns to the Mystic Fire*, Sri Aurobindo Ashram Trust, 1996

Bibek Debroy (trans.), *The Holy Vedas*, BR Publishing Corporation, 1999

Bibek Debroy (trans.), *The Mahabharata* (Volume 1), Penguin Books India, 2010

Bibek Debroy and Dipavali Debroy (trans.), *The Holy Puranas* in 3 volumes, BR Publishing Corporation, 2002

Chaturvedi Badrinath, *The Mahabharata: An Inquiry in the Human Condition*, Orient Longman, 2006

Chogyam Trungpa, *Shambhala: The Scared of the Warrior*, Shambhala, 2007

Coleman Barks (trans.), *The Essential Rumi*, HarperOne, 1995

Devdutt Pattanaik, *Jaya: An Illustrated Retelling of the Mahabharata*, Penguin Books India, 2011

Devdutt Pattanaik, *Myth = Mithya: A Handbook of Indian Mythology*, Penguin Books India, 2008

Diana L. Eck, *Darsan: Seeing the Divine Image in India*, Motilal Banarasidass Publishers, 1998

Diana L. Eck, *India: A Sacred Geography*, Harmony Books, 2012

Durga Bhagwat, *Vyas Parva*, Mauja Prakāśana Gṛha, 1962

Iravati Karve, *Yuganta: The End of an Epoch*, Disha Books, 2006

Jean-Claude Carriere, *In Search of the Mahabharat*, Macmillan, 2001

Joseph Campbell, *The Inner Reached of the Outer Space*, New World Library, 2002

Joseph Campbell, *The Power of Myth*, Anchor Books, 1991

Karen Armstrong, *A Short History of Myth*, Penguin Books India, 2005

Kisari Mohan Ganguli (trans.), *The Mahabharata in 4 volumes*, Munshiram Manoharlal Publishers, 2004

Rajiv Malhotra, *Being Different: An Indian Challenge to Western Universalism*, HarperCollins *Publishers* India, 2011

Roberto Calasso, *Ka*, Vintage Books, 1998

S.L. Bhairappa, *Parva*, Sahitya Akademi, 2009

Vettam Mani, *Puranic Enclycopedia*, Motilal Banarasidass Publishers, 2010

Wendy Doniger O'Flaherty (trans.), *Rig Veda*, Penguin Books India, 2005

A.K. Ramanujan, 'Repetition in the Mahabharata', *Essays on the Mahabharata*, edited by Arvind Sharma, Motilal Banarasidass Publishers, 1991

Christopher Minkowski, 'Snakes, Sattras and the Mahabharata', *Essays on the Mahabharata*, edited by Arvind Sharma, Motilal Banarasidass Publishers, 1991

Wendy Doniger, 'Violence in the Mahabharata' and 'Dharma in the Mahabharata', *The Hindus: An Alternative History*, Penguin Books India, 2007

ACKNOWLEDGEMENTS

To the ... eye of the Seer and prophet of every race, Ariadne's thread stretches beyond that 'historic period' without break or flaw, surely and steadily, into the very night of time; and the hand which holds it is too mighty to drop it or even let it break.
~ H.P. Blavatsky in *The Secret Doctrine*.

I give thanks to the kalyanmitras. To the teachers, I bow.

Prashant Trivedi, who first ignited the spark, taught me about right attitude, occupation and speech. The towering shadows of Jalaluddin Rumi and Chogyam Trungpa Rinpoche: the former, for lessons in loving the Shams-Sun with gentleness and abandon; the latter, for lessons in queenly posture and the warrior's path.

This is nothing if not a collaborative project. In spirit as in form, *Adi Parva* owes gratitude to the multitudes. To oral storytellers who have carried the tale down with as much meticulousness as our DNA does genetic information. To the ones who transcribed, translated and housed the tales in text so they would still remain accessible in changing times. The work of countless wise men and women – seers, seekers, philosophers, writers, historians, painters, photographers – has instructed and inspired these pages, as well as the person I've become in the making of this work. Death wasn't a deterrent either. Dead men taught me to paint (in as much as my limitations allowed me to learn) – Odilon Redon, Paul Gauguin, Paul Cezanne, those anonymous hands at work in Rajasthani miniature painting workshops. Dead women flow in my veins as creative mothers: Helena Petrovna Blavatsky, Frida Kahlo, Amrita Sher-Gil.

Thank you, Carl Sagan, for changing the way I look up at the nightsky; Bibek Debroy whose clear, accessible translations of the Mahabharat and the Puranas give this work a sturdy foundation. For inspiring, tireless conversations about human life, beliefs and mythologies: my elder brother Devdutt Pattanaik, Kabir Saxena, and Stefano Noia.

Thank you, Pilar Munoz and Brigitte Macias of La Maison des Auteurs. V.K. Karthika of HarperCollins India and Marion Mazauric of Au Diable Vauvert: they trusted the work first, and put their money where their mouth was. Marielle Morin, thank you for cleaning up ambiguities in the English manuscript with grace and flair and ferrying the tale to French shores. La Maison des Auteurs's Artist in Residence programme in Angouleme, France, enabled me to heed the call and work on *Adi*

Parva full-time. A financial grant from the French Embassy, New Delhi, allowed plans to materialize into reality. Deep gratitude to Luke Haokip – longtime collaborator, meticulous co-worker, and friend indeed.

For keeping things real at home, thank you, Alka and Arun Patil, Ajey Patil and Ashwini Joglekar. Anaël Seghezzi, with whom I learnt to paint, thank you for life lessons in beauty, gentleness and tact. For offering wide-open heart, home and kitchen in challenging times: Iggy Ahluwalia, Arnaz Daruwalla, Meena Nathan, Duraisamy Balaguru, Sonia Lazanska Robinson, Anuradha Bhasin, S.K. Saxena, Sridhar Rajan, Menaka Guruswamy. And for Adaleta Maslo-Krkovic, Raashmi Chakravarti, Brinda Datta and the rest of the scattered sisterhood that did not, and will not, let me fall: I offer my love.

First published in hardback in India in 2012 by
HarperCollins *Publishers* India

P-ISBN: 978-93-5029-416-1

4 6 8 10 9 7 5 3

HarperCollins *Publishers*
A-75, Sector 57, Noida, Uttar Pradesh 201301, India
harpercollins.co.in

Typeset in FGAmura

This project was supported by the Cité Internationale de la Bande
Dessinée et de l'Image and its artist residency programme at
La Maison des Auteurs (Angoulême, France).

Printed and bound at
Thomson Press (India) Ltd

Books by Amruta Patil

kari
amruta patil
'A thing of radiant beauty:
witty, smart and swaggering.'
– Neel Mukherjee

ADI PARVA
CHURNING OF THE OCEAN
via AMRUTA PATIL

SAUPTIK
BLOOD AND FLOWERS
via AMRUTA PATIL

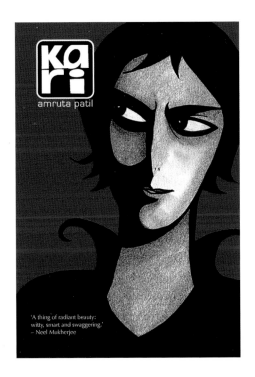

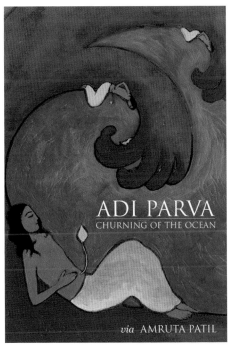

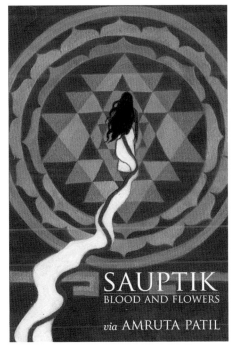

PHOTO: TASHI TOBGYAL

Writer–painter Amruta Patil is the author of
Kari (2008), *Adi Parva: Churning of the Ocean* (2012)
and *Sauptik: Blood and Flowers* (2016).
http://amrutapatil.blogspot.com